Java 9: Building Robust Modular Applications

Master advanced Java features and implement them to build amazing projects

A learning path in two sections

Packt>

BIRMINGHAM - MUMBAI

Java 9: Building Robust Modular Applications

Authors: Dr. Edward Lavieri, Peter Verhas, Jason Lee
Reviewer: Mandar Jog, Dionisios Petrakopoulos
Content Development Editor: Rohit Kumar Singh
Graphics: Jason Monteiro
Production Coordinator: ArvindKumar Gupta

Published on: April 2018

Production reference: 1020418

Published by Packt Publishing Ltd.
Livery Place
35 Livery Street
Birmingham
B3 2PB, UK.

ISBN 978-1-78883-282-3

www.packtpub.com

Mapt

Mapt is an online digital library that gives you full access to over 5,000 books and videos, as well as industry leading tools to help you plan your personal development and advance your career. For more information, please visit our website.

Why subscribe?

- Spend less time learning and more time coding with practical eBooks and Videos from over 4,000 industry professionals

- Improve your learning with Skill Plans built especially for you

- Get a free eBook or video every month

- Mapt is fully searchable

- Copy and paste, print, and bookmark content

PacktPub.com

Did you know that Packt offers eBook versions of every book published, with PDF and ePub files available? You can upgrade to the eBook version at www.PacktPub.com and as a print book customer, you are entitled to a discount on the eBook copy. Get in touch with us at service@packtpub.com for more details.

At www.PacktPub.com, you can also read a collection of free technical articles, sign up for a range of free newsletters, and receive exclusive discounts and offers on Packt books and eBooks.

Table of Contents

Preface   1

Section 1: Mastering Java 9

Chapter 1: The Java 9 Landscape   7
    Java 9 at 20,000 feet   7
    Breaking the monolith   9
    Playing around with the Java Shell   10
    Taking control of external processes   11
    Boosting performance with G1   11
    Measuring performance with JMH   11
    Getting started with HTTP 2.0   12
    Encompassing reactive programming   12
    Expanding the wish list   12
    Summary   13

Chapter 2: Discovering Java 9   15
    Improved Contended Locking [JEP 143]   16
        Improvement goals   17
    Segmented code cache [JEP 197]   17
        Memory allocation   18
    Smart Java compilation, phase two [JEP 199]   19
    Resolving Lint and Doclint warnings [JEP 212]   19
    Tiered attribution for javac [JEP 215]   20
    Annotations pipeline 2.0 [JEP 217]   21
    New version-string scheme [JEP 223]   23
    Generating run-time compiler tests automatically [JEP 233]   23
    Testing class-file attributes generated by Javac [JEP 235]   24
    Storing interned strings in CDS archives [JEP 250]   26
        The problem   26
        The solution   27
    Preparing JavaFX UI controls and CSS APIs for modularization [JEP 253]   27
        JavaFX overview   27
        Implications for Java 9   29
    Compact strings [JEP 254]   30
        Pre-Java 9 status   31
        New with Java 9   31

Merging selected Xerces 2.11.0 updates into JAXP [JEP 255] 31
Updating JavaFX/Media to newer version of GStreamer [JEP 257] 32
HarfBuzz Font-Layout Engine [JEP 258] 33
HiDPI graphics on Windows and Linux [JEP 263] 34
Marlin graphics renderer [JEP 265] 35
Unicode 8.0.0 [JEP 267] 35
  New in Unicode 8.0.0 35
  Updated Classes in Java 9 36
Reserved stack areas for critical sections [JEP 270] 36
  The pre-Java 9 situation 36
  New in Java 9 37
Dynamic linking of language-defined object models [JEP 276] 38
  Proof of concept 39
Additional tests for humongous objects in G1 [JEP 278] 39
Improving test-failure troubleshooting [JEP 279] 41
  Environmental information 41
  Java process information 42
Optimizing string concatenation [JEP 280] 42
HotSpot C++ unit-test framework [JEP 281] 43
Enabling GTK 3 on Linux [JEP 283] 43
New HotSpot build system [JEP 284] 45
Summary 45

Chapter 3: Java 9 Language Enhancements 47
Working with variable handlers [JEP 193] 48
  Working with the AtoMiC Toolkit 49
  Using the sun.misc.Unsafe class 51
Eliding depreciation warnings on import statements [JEP 211] 52
Milling Project Coin [JEP 213] 53
  Using the @SafeVarargs annotation 53
  The try-with-resource statement 54
  Using the diamond operator 56
  Discontinuing use of the underscore 57
  Making use of private interface methods 58
Processing import statements correctly [JEP 216] 60
Summary 62

Chapter 4: Building Modular Applications with Java 9 63
A modular primer 64
Reviewing Java's platform module system [JEP-200] 66
Modularizing JDK source code [JEP-201] 70
  Pre-Java 9 JDK source code organization 71
    Development tools 72
      Deployment 72

Internationalization	72
Monitoring	73
RMI	73
Security	73
Troubleshooting	73
Web services	74
JavaFX tools	74
Java runtime environment	74
Source code	74
Libraries	75
C header files	76
Database	77
JDK source code reorganized	77
Understanding modular run-time images [JEP-220]	**77**
Runtime format adoption	78
Runtime image restructure	78
Supporting common operations	80
De-privileging JDK classes	80
Preserving existing behaviors	80
Getting to know the module system [JEP-261]	**80**
Module paths	81
Access-control boundary violations	82
Runtime	82
Modular Java application packaging [JEP-275]	**84**
Advanced look at the Java Linker	85
Java Packager options	85
JLink - The Java Linker [JEP-282]	**89**
Encapsulating most internal APIs [JEP-260]	**91**
Summary	**92**
Chapter 5: Migrating Applications to Java 9	**93**
Quick review of Project Jigsaw	**94**
Classpath	94
The monolithic nature of the JDK	95
How modules fit into the Java landscape	**96**
Base module	97
Reliable configuration	98
Strong encapsulation	99
Migration planning	**100**
Testing a simple Java application	100
Potential migration issues	103
The JRE	104
Access to internal APIs	104
Accessing internal JARs	105
JAR URL depreciation	105
Extension mechanism	107
The JDK's modularization	108

Advice from Oracle   109
  Preparatory steps   110
    Getting the JDK 9 early access build   110
    Running your program before recompiling 110
    Updating third-party libraries and tools 110
    Compiling your application   111
      Pre-Java 9 -source and -target options 113
      Java 9 -source and -target options   114
    Running jdeps on your code   114
  Breaking encapsulation   117
    The --add-opens option   118
    The --add-exports option   118
    The --permit-illegal-access option   119
  Runtime image changes   119
    Java version schema   119
    JDK and JRE layout   120
  What has been removed   122
  Updated garbage collection   123
  Deployment   124
    JRE version selection   124
    Serialized applets   124
    JNLP update   125
      Nested resources   125
      FX XML extension   125
      JNLP file syntax   127
      Numeric version comparison 128
Useful tools   128
  Java environment - jEnv   129
  Maven   130
    Obtaining the M2Eclipse IDE   131
Summary   134
Chapter 6: Experimenting with the Java Shell   135
What is JShell?   136
Getting Started with JShell   136
Practical uses of JShell   142
  Feedback modes   143
    Creating a custom feedback mode   148
  Listing your assets   150
  Editing in the JShell   151
    Modifying text   151
    Basic navigation   152
    Historical navigation   152
    Advanced editing commands   153
Working with scripts   153
  Start up scripts   153
  Loading scripts   154
  Saving scripts   154

Advanced scripting with JShell	155
Summary	156
Chapter 7: Leveraging the New Default G1 Garbage Collector	157
Overview of garbage collection	158
Object life cycle	158
Object creation	158
Object mid-life	159
Object destruction	159
Garbage collection algorithms	160
Mark and sweep	160
Concurrent mark sweep (CMS) garbage collection	160
Serial garbage collection	161
Parallel garbage collection	161
G1 garbage collection	161
Garbage collection options	162
Java methods relevant to garbage collection	167
The System.gc() method	168
The finalize() method	170
Pre-Java 9 garbage collection	171
Visualizing garbage collection	172
Garbage collection upgrades in Java 8	173
Case study - Games written with Java	174
Collecting garbage with the new Java platform	175
Default garbage collection	175
Depreciated garbage collection combinations	177
Unified garbage collection logging	178
Unified JVM logging (JEP-158)	179
Tags	179
Levels	180
Decorations	180
Output	181
Command-line options	181
Unified GC logging (JEP-271)	181
Garbage collection logging options	182
The gc tag	184
Macros	184
Additional considerations	185
Persistent issues	186
Making objects eligible for garbage collection	186
Summary	189
Chapter 8: Microbenchmarking Applications with JMH	191
Microbenchmarking overview	192
Approach to using JMH	193
Installing Java 9 and Eclipse with Java 9 support	193
Hands-on experiment	196
Microbenchmarking with Maven	198

Benchmarking options   205
  Modes   206
  Time units   207
Techniques for avoiding microbenchmarking pitfalls   207
  Power management   208
  OS schedulers   208
  Time sharing   208
  Eliminating dead-code and constant folding   209
  Run-to-run variance   210
  Cache capacity   210
Summary   211

Chapter 9: Making Use of the ProcessHandle API   213
What are processes?   214
The new ProcessHandle interface   215
Getting the PID of the current process   215
Getting information about a process   216
Listing processes   218
  Listing children   218
  Listing descendants   219
  Listing all processes   220
Waiting for processes   221
Terminating processes   222
A small process controller application   224
  Main class   225
  Parameters class   226
  The ParamsAndHandle class   227
  The ControlDaemon class   228
Summary   231

Chapter 10: Fine-Grained Stack Tracing   233
Overview of the Java Stack   233
The importance of stack information   234
  Example - Restricting callers   236
  Example - Getting logger for caller   239
Working with StackWalker   240
  Getting an instance of StackWalker   240
    RETAIN_CLASS_REFERENCE   240
    SHOW_REFLECT_FRAMES   241
    SHOW_HIDDEN_FRAMES   241
    Final thoughts on enum constants   244
  Accessing classes   244
  Walking methods   245
StackFrame   247
Performance   248

Summary 248

Chapter 11: New Tools and Tool Enhancements 249
The new HTTP client [JEP-110] 250
  The HTTP client before Java 9 250
  Java 9's new HTTP client 253
  New API limitations 254
Simplified Doclet API [JEP-221] 256
  The pre-Java 9 Doclet API 256
    API enums 258
    API classes 258
    API interfaces 259
    Problems with the pre-existing Doclet API 260
  Java 9's Doclet API 260
    Compiler tree API 260
    Language model API 264
      The AnnotatedConstruct interface 265
      The SourceVersion enum 265
      The UnknownEntityException exception 267
HTML5 Javadoc [JEP-224] 268
Javadoc search [JEP-225] 273
  Introducing camel case search 274
Remove launch-time JRE version selection [JEP-231] 274
Parser API for Nashorn [JEP-236] 275
  Nashorn 275
    Using Nashorn as a command-line tool 276
    Using Nashorn as an embedded interpreter 279
  EMCAScript 280
  Parser API 281
Multi-release JAR files [JEP-238] 283
  Identifying multi-release JAR files 283
  Related JDK changes 285
Java-level JVM compiler interface [JEP-243] 286
BeanInfo annotations [JEP-256] 287
  JavaBean 287
  BeanProperty 288
  SwingContainer 289
  BeanInfo classes 289
TIFF image input/output [JEP-262] 290
Platform logging API and service [JEP-264] 292
  The java.util.logging package 293
  Logging in Java 9 295
XML Catalogs [JEP-268] 296
  The OASIS XML Catalog standard 296
  JAXP processors 297
  XML Catalogs prior to Java 9 297

Java 9 platform changes 297
Convenience factory methods for collections [JEP-269] 297
Using collections before Java 9 298
Using new collection literals 301
Platform-specific desktop features [JEP-272] 301
Enhanced method handles [JEP-274] 302
Reason for the enhancement 303
Lookup functions 303
Argument handling 304
Additional combinations 304
Enhanced deprecation [JEP-277] 305
What the @Deprecated annotation really means 306
Summary 307

Chapter 12: Concurrency and Reactive Programming 309
Reactive Programming 310
Reactive programming standardization 311
The New Flow API 313
The Flow.Publisher interface 314
The Flow.Subscriber interface 314
The Flow.Subscription interface 314
The Flow.Processor interface 315
Sample implementation 315
Additional Concurrency Updates 317
Java concurrency 317
Concurrency explained 317
System configurations 318
Java threads 319
Concurrency improvements 322
CompletableFuture API enhancements 323
Class details 324
Enhancements 328
Spin-Wait Hints 329
Summary 330

Chapter 13: Security Enhancements 331
Datagram Transport Layer Security 332
DTLS protocol version 1.0 332
DTLS protocol version 1.2 334
DTLS support in Java 9 337
Creating PKCS12 keystores 338
Keystore primer 338
Java Keystore (JKS) 338
Builder 339
The CallbackHandlerProtection class 340
The PasswordProtection class 340

The PrivateKeyEntry class   341
The SecretKeyEntry class   341
The TrustedCertificateEntry class   342
PKCS12 default in Java 9   343
Improving security application performance   343
Security policy enforcement   344
Permission evaluation   345
The java.Security.CodeSource package   345
Package checking algorithm   346
TLS application-layer protocol negotiation extension   347
TLS ALPN extension   348
The javax.net.ssl package   348
The java.net.ssl package extension   350
Leveraging CPU instructions for GHASH and RSA   351
Hashing   352
OCSP stapling for TLS   353
OCSP stapling primer   354
Changes for the Java 9 platform   355
DRBG-based SecureRandom implementations   356
Summary   357

Chapter 14: Command Line Flags   359
Unified JVM Logging [JEP 158]   359
Command-line options   360
Decorations   363
Levels   364
Output   364
Tags   365
Compiler control [JEP 165]   365
Compilation modes   365
C1 compilation mode   366
C2 compilation mode   366
Tiered compilation   366
Compiler control in Java 9   367
Diagnostic commands [JEP 228]   368
Heap profiling agent [JEP 240]   370
Removing your JHAT [JEP 241]   371
JVM command-line flag argument validation [JEP 245]   372
Compile for older platform versions [JEP 247]   373
Summary   376

Chapter 15: Best Practices In Java 9   377
Support for UTF-8   377
The ResourceBundle class   378
The nested class   379

Fields and constructors	383
Methods	384
Changes in Java 9	390
Unicode 7.0.0	390
The java.lang package	391
The java.text package	392
Additional significance	392
The Linux/AArch64 port	393
Multi-resolution Images	394
Common Locale Data Repository (CLDR)	396
Summary	397
Chapter 16: Future Directions	399
Future Changes to the JDK	400
JDK changes targeted for Java 10	400
Repository consolidation	400
Native-header tool removal	401
JDK-related submitted proposals	402
Parallelize the Full GC Phase in CMS	402
REST APIs for JMX	402
Support heap allocation	404
JDK-related drafted proposals	404
Finalization promptness	404
Java memory model	405
Foreign Function Interfaces	406
Isolated methods	406
Reducing metaspace waste	406
Improving IPv6 support	407
Unboxed argument lists for method handles	408
Enhanced MandelblotSet demo using value types	409
Efficient array comparison intrinsics	410
Future changes to the Java Compiler	410
Policy for retiring javac -source and -target options	410
Pluggable static analyzers	411
Future Changes to the Java Virtual Machine	411
JVM-related submitted proposals	411
Container aware Java	412
Enable execution of Java methods on GPU	413
Epsilon GC - The arbitrarily low overhead garbage (non-) collector	413
JVM-related drafted proposals	414
Provide stable USDT probe points on JVM compiled methods	414
Concurrent monitor deflation	415
Provide a low-overhead way of sampling Java heap allocations	416
Diagnostic Command Framework	416
Enhanced Class Redefinition	417
Enable NUMA mode by default when appropriate	417
Value objects	418

         Align JVM Access Checks   419
    Future Changes to JavaX   419
         JMX specific annotations for registration of managed resources 419
         Modernize the GTK3 Look and Feel Implementation   420
    Ongoing Special Projects   420
         Annotations pipeline 2.0   422
         Audio Synthesis Engine   422
         Caciocavallo   422
         Common VM Interface   422
         Compiler Grammar   423
         Da Vinci Machine   423
         Device I/O   423
         Graal   423
         HarfBuzz Integration   424
         Kona   424
         OpenJFX   424
         Panama   424
         Shenandoah   425
    Summary   425

Section 2: Java 9 Programming Blueprints

Chapter 17: Introduction   429
    New features in Java 8   430
         Lambdas   430
              Streams   433
         The new java.time package   434
         Default methods   434
    New features in Java 9   436
         Java Platform Module System/Project Jigsaw   436
         Process handling API   437
         Concurrency changes   438
         REPL   438
    Projects   439
         Process Viewer/Manager   439
         Duplicate File Finder   439
         Date Calculator   440
         Social Media Aggregator   440
         Email filter   441
         JavaFX photo management   442
         A client/server note application   442
         Serverless Java   443
         Android desktop synchronization client   443
    Getting started   444
    Summary   450

Chapter 18: Managing Processes in Java   451
  Creating a project   452
  Bootstrapping the application   455
  Defining the user interface   456
  Initializing the user interface   459
  Adding menus   467
  Updating the process list   471
  Summary   473

Chapter 19: Duplicate File Finder   475
  Getting started   476
  Building the library   477
    Concurrent Java with a Future interface   479
    Modern database access with JPA   486
  Building the command-line interface   493
  Building the graphical user interface   504
  Summary   517

Chapter 20: Date Calculator   519
  Getting started   520
  Building the library   520
    A timely interlude   522
      Duration   522
      Period   523
      Clock   524
        Instant   524
        LocalDate   525
        LocalTime   525
        LocalDateTime   525
        ZonedDateTime   525
      Back to our code   526
      A brief interlude on testing   537
  Building the command-line interface   540
  Summary   542

Chapter 21: Sunago - A Social Media Aggregator   543
  Getting started   544
    Setting up the user interface   549
    Setting up the controller   551
    Writing the model class   551
    Finishing up the controller   553
    Adding an image for the item   555
    Building the preferences user interface   556
    Saving user preferences   560
    Plugins and extensions with the Service Provider Interface   562
    Resource handling with try-with-resources   563

Adding a network - Twitter 567
Registering as a Twitter developer 568
Adding Twitter preferences to Sunago 571
OAuth and logging on to Twitter 574
Adding a model for Twitter 579
Implementing a Twitter client 581
A brief look at internationalization and localization 582
Making our JAR file fat 584
Adding a refresh button 587
Adding another network - Instagram 589
Registering as an Instagram developer 590
Implementing the Instagram client 591
Loading our plugins in Sunago 594
Summary 598

Chapter 22: Sunago - An Android Port 599
Getting started 600
Building the user interface 611
Android data access 619
Android services 627
Android tabs and fragments 633
Summary 642

Chapter 23: Email and Spam Management with MailFilter 643
Getting started 644
A brief look at the history of email protocols 644
JavaMail, the Standard Java API for Email 648
Building the CLI 652
Building the GUI 670
Building the service 677
Summary 681

Chapter 24: Photo Management with PhotoBeans 683
Getting started 684
Bootstrapping the project 684
Branding your application 687
NetBeans modules 690
TopComponent - the class for tabs and windows 692
Nodes, a NetBeans presentation object 700
Lookup, a NetBeans fundamental 701
Writing our own nodes 702
Performing Actions 706
Services - exposing decoupled functionality 707
PhotoViewerTopComponent 711
Integrating JavaFX with the NetBeans RCP 714

NetBeans preferences and the Options panel	716
Adding a primary panel	718
Adding a secondary panel	720
Loading and saving preferences	724
Reacting to changes in preferences	725
Summary	726
Chapter 25: Taking Notes with Monumentum	729
Getting started	730
Microservice frameworks on the JVM	731
Creating the application	733
Creating REST Services	739
Adding MongoDB	741
Dependency injection with CDI	746
Finish the notes resource	748
Adding authentication	751
Building the user interface	762
Summary	772
Chapter 26: Serverless Java	773
Getting started	774
Planning the application	776
Building your first function	776
DynamoDB	780
Simple Email Service	785
Simple Notification Service	787
Deploying the function	788
Creating a role	789
Creating a topic	790
Deploying the function	791
Testing the function	793
Configuring your AWS credentials	798
Summary	801
Chapter 27: DeskDroid - A Desktop Client for Your Android Phone	803
Getting started	804
Creating the Android project	804
Requesting permissions	807
Creating the service	809
Server-sent events	811
Controlling the service state	812
Adding endpoints to the server	813
Getting conversations	814
Sending an SMS message	818
Creating the desktop application	821
Defining the user interface	822
Defining user interface behavior	825

Sending messages 836
Getting updates 840
Security 845
Securing the endpoints 845
Handling authorization requests 848
Authorizing the client 851
Summary 853
Chapter 28: What is Next? 855
Looking back 855
Looking forward 857
Project Valhalla 857
Value types 857
Generic specialization 859
Reified generics 859
Project Panama 859
Project Amber 860
Local-Variable Type Inference 860
Enhanced enums 861
Lambda leftovers 862
Looking around 863
Ceylon 863
Kotlin 866
Summary 869
Bibliography 871
Index 873

Preface

Java 9 and its new features add to the richness of the language--one of the most-used languages to build robust software applications. Java 9 comes with a special emphasis on modularity. Some of the new features of Java 9 are groundbreaking, and if you are an experienced programmer, you will be able to make your enterprise application leaner by implementing these new features. You will be provided with practical guidance in applying the newly acquired knowledge in regards to Java 9 and further information on future developments of the Java platform. You will also work through projects from which you can draw usable examples as you work to solve your own unique challenges.

Who this learning path is for

This learning path is for Java developers who are looking to move a level up and learn how to build robust applications in the latest version of Java.

What this learning path covers

Section 1, Mastering Java 9, gives an overview and explanation of the new features introduced in Java 9 and the importance of the new APIs and enhancements. This module will improve your productivity, making your applications faster. By learning the best practices in Java, you will become the go-to person in your organization for Java 9.

Section 2, Java 9 Programming Blueprints, takes you through 10 comprehensive projects in the book that will showcase the various features of Java 9. It covers various libraries and frameworks in these projects, and also introduces a few more frameworks that complement and extend the Java SDK.

To get the most out of this learning path

1. Some basic knowledge of Java would help.
2. Familiarity with more advanced topics, such as network programming and threads, would be helpful, but is not assumed.

Download the example code files

You can download the example code files for this learning path from your account at `www.packtpub.com`. If you purchased this learning path elsewhere, you can visit `www.packtpub.com/support` and register to have the files emailed directly to you.

You can download the code files by following these steps:

1. Log in or register at `www.packtpub.com`.
2. Select the **SUPPORT** tab.
3. Click on **Code Downloads & Errata**.
4. Enter the name of the learning path in the **Search** box and follow the onscreen instructions.

Once the file is downloaded, please make sure that you unzip or extract the folder using the latest version of:

- WinRAR/7-Zip for Windows
- Zipeg/iZip/UnRarX for Mac
- 7-Zip/PeaZip for Linux

The code bundle for the book is also hosted on GitHub at `https://github.com/PacktPublishing/Java-9-Building-Robust-Modular-Applications/`. We also have other code bundles from our rich catalog of books and videos available at `https://github.com/PacktPublishing/`. Check them out!

Conventions used

There are a number of text conventions used throughout this book.

`CodeInText`: Indicates code words in text, database table names, folder names, filenames, file extensions, pathnames, dummy URLs, user input, and Twitter handles. Here is an example: "Mount the downloaded `WebStorm-10*.dmg` disk image file as another disk in your system."

A block of code is set as follows:

```
module com.three19.irisScan
    {
      // modules that com.three19.irisScan depends upon
      requires com.three19.irisCore;
      requires com.three19.irisData;
    }
```

When we wish to draw your attention to a particular part of a code block, the relevant lines or items are set in bold:

```
[default]
exten => s,1,Dial(Zap/1|30)
exten => s,2,Voicemail(u100)
exten => s,102,Voicemail(b100)
exten => i,1,Voicemail(s0)
```

Any command-line input or output is written as follows:

```
$ mkdir css
$ cd css
```

Bold: Indicates a new term, an important word, or words that you see onscreen. For example, words in menus or dialog boxes appear in the text like this. Here is an example: "Select **System info** from the **Administration** panel."

Warnings or important notes appear like this.

Tips and tricks appear like this.

Get in touch

Feedback from our readers is always welcome.

General feedback: Email `feedback@packtpub.com` and mention the learning path title in the subject of your message. If you have questions about any aspect of this learning path, please email us at `questions@packtpub.com`.

Errata: Although we have taken every care to ensure the accuracy of our content, mistakes do happen. If you have found a mistake in this learning path, we would be grateful if you would report this to us. Please visit `www.packtpub.com/submit-errata`, selecting your learning path, clicking on the Errata Submission Form link, and entering the details.

Piracy: If you come across any illegal copies of our works in any form on the Internet, we would be grateful if you would provide us with the location address or website name. Please contact us at `copyright@packtpub.com` with a link to the material.

If you are interested in becoming an author: If there is a topic that you have expertise in and you are interested in either writing or contributing to a book, please visit `authors.packtpub.com`.

Reviews

Please leave a review. Once you have read and used this learning path, why not leave a review on the site that you purchased it from? Potential readers can then see and use your unbiased opinion to make purchase decisions, we at Packt can understand what you think about our products, and our authors can see your feedback on their book. Thank you!

For more information about Packt, please visit `packtpub.com`.

Mastering Java 9

1

Write reactive, modular, concurrent, and secure code

The Java 9 Landscape

1

Java is already a fully-grown adult in its own right more than two decades since its first release. With a stunning community of developers and wide adoption in a number of industries, the platform continues to evolve and keep up with the rest of the world in terms of performance, security, and scalability. We will begin our journey by exploring the most significant features introduced in Java 9, what are the biggest drivers behind them, and what more we can expect in subsequent developments of the platform, along with some of the things that did not make it in this release.

In this chapter, we will cover the following topics:

- Java 9 at 20,000 feet
- Breaking the monolith
- Playing around with the Java Shell
- Taking control of external processes
- Boosting performance with G1
- Measuring performance with JMH
- Getting ready for HTTP 2.0
- Encompassing reactive programming
- Expanding the wish list

Java 9 at 20,000 feet

You might be asking yourself--isn't Java 9 just a maintenance release with a set of features that did not make it into Java 8? There is plenty of new stuff in Java 9 that makes it a distinct version in its own right.

Inarguably, the modularization of the Java platform (developed as part of project Jigsaw) is the biggest piece of work that makes it successfully in Java 9. Initially planned for Java 8, but postponed, project Jigsaw is also one of the main reasons why the final release of Java 9 was further postponed. Jigsaw also introduces a few notable changes to the Java platform and is one of the reasons Java 9 is considered a major release. We will explore these features in detail in the subsequent chapters.

The **JCP (Java Community Process)** provides the mechanisms to turn a set of feature proposals (also known as **Java Enhancement Proposals** or **JEPs**) into formal specifications that provide the basis to extend the platform with new functionality. Java 9 is no different in that regard. Apart from the Jigsaw-related Java enhancement proposals, there is a long list of other enhancements that made it in Java 9. Throughout this book, we will discuss the various features in terms of logical groups based on the corresponding enhancement proposals, including the following:

- The **Java Shell** (also called **JShell**)--an interactive shell for the Java platform
- New APIs to work with operating system processes in a portable manner
- The **Garbage-first** (**G1**) garbage collector introduced in Java 7 is made the default garbage collector in Java 9
- Adding the **Java Microbenchmark Harness** (**JMH**) tool that can be used to run performance benchmarks against Java applications is included as part of the Java distribution
- Support for the HTTP 2.0 and WebSocket standards by means of a new client API
- Concurrency enhancements among which is the definition of the `Flow` class, which describes an interface for the reactive streams specification in the Java platform

Some of the initial proposals that were accepted for release 9 did not make it there and were postponed for a later release, along with other interesting things that developers may expect in the future.

You can download the JDK 9 distribution for your system from `http://www.oracle.com/technetwork/java/javase/downloads/index.html`, if you are eager to get your hands dirty before trying to move through the other chapters and experimenting with the newly introduced samples and concepts.

Breaking the monolith

Over the years, the utilities of the Java platform have continued to evolve and increase, making it one big monolith. In order to make the platform more suitable for embedded and mobile devices, the publication of stripped down editions such as Java CDC and Java ME was necessary. These, however, did not prove to be flexible enough for modern applications with varying requirements in terms of functionality provided by the JDK. In that regard, the need for a modular system came in as a viral requirement, not only to address modularization of the Java utilities (overall, more than 5000 Java classes and 1500 C++ source files with more than 25,0000 lines of code for the Hotspot runtime), but also to provide a mechanism for developers to create and manage modular applications using the same module system used in the JDK. Java 8 provided an intermediate mechanism to enable applications to use only a subset of the APIs provided by the entire JDK, and that mechanism was named compact profiles. In fact, compact profiles also provided the basis for further work that had to be done in order to break dependencies between the various distinct components of the JDK required to enable implementation of a module system in Java.

The module system itself has been developed under the name of project Jigsaw on the basis of which several Java enhancement proposals and a target JSR (376) were formed. Much was put in place to address the requirements of project Jigsaw--there was evidence of concept implementation with more features proposed than the ones that successfully made it into Java 9. Apart from that, a complete restructuring of the JDK code base has been made along with a complete reorganization of the JDK distributable images.

There was considerable controversy in the community as to whether an existing and mature Java module system such as OSGi should be adopted as part of the JDK instead of providing a completely new module system. However, OSGI targets runtime behavior such as the resolution of module dependencies, installation, uninstallation, starting and stopping of modules (also named bundles in terms of OSGI), custom module classloaders, and so on. Project Jigsaw however targets a compile-time module system where resolution of dependencies happen when the application is compiled. Moreover, installing and uninstalling a module as part of the JDK eliminates the need to include it as a dependency explicitly during compilation. Furthermore, loading of module classes is made possible through the existing hierarchy of classloaders (the bootstrap and the extension and system classloaders), although, there was a possibility of using custom module classloaders pretty much similar to the module classloaders of OSGI. The latter was, however, abandoned; we will discuss Java module classloading in more detail when we talk about the details of the module system in Java.

Additional benefits from the Java module system include enhanced security and performance. By modularizing the JDK and applications into Jigsaw modules, we are able to create well-defined boundaries between components and their corresponding domains. This separation of concerns aligns with the security architecture of the platform and is an enabler of better resource utilization. We have dedicated two detailed chapters to all of the preceding points, and to the topic of adopting Java 9 as well, which also requires a degree of understanding on the possible approaches to migrating existing projects to Java 9.

Playing around with the Java Shell

For a long time, there has been no standard shell shipped with the Java programming language to experiment with new language features or libraries or for rapid prototyping. If you wanted to do this, you could write a test application with a main method, compile it with `javac`, and run it. This could be done either at the command line or using a Java IDE; however, in both cases, this is not as convenient as having an interactive shell for the purpose.

Starting an interactive shell in JDK 9 is as simple as running the following command (assuming the `bin` directory of your JDK 9 installation is in the current path):

```
jshell
```

You may find it somewhat puzzling that an interactive shell has not been introduced earlier in the Java platform as many programming languages, such as Python, Ruby, and a number of others, already come with an interactive shell in their earliest versions; However, this had still not made it on the priority features list for the earlier Java releases, until now, and it is out there and ready for use. The Java shell makes use of a JShell API that provides capabilities to enable autocompletion or evaluation of expressions and code snippets, among other features. A full chapter is dedicated to discussing the details of the Java shell so that developers can make the best use out of it.

Taking control of external processes

Up to JDK 9, if you wanted to create a Java process and handle process input/output, you had to use either the `Runtime.getRuntime.exec()` method, which allows us to execute a command in a separate OS process and get a `java.lang.Process` instance over which to provide certain operations in order to manage the external process, or use the new `java.lang.ProcessBuilder` class with some more enhancements in regard to interacting with the external process and also create a `java.lang.Process` instance to represent the external process. Both mechanisms were inflexible and also non-portable as the set of commands executed by the external processes were highly dependent on the operating system (additional effort had to be exerted in order to make the particular process operations portable across multiple operating systems). A chapter is dedicated to the new process API, providing developers with the knowledge of creating and managing external processes in a much easier way.

Boosting performance with G1

The G1 garbage collector was already introduced in JDK 7 and is now enabled by default in JDK 9. It is targeted for systems with multiple processing cores and a lot of available memory. What are the benefits of the G1 compared to previous types of garbage collectors? How does it achieve these improvements? Is there a need to manually tune it, and in what scenarios? These, and several more questions regarding G1, will be discussed in a separate chapter.

Measuring performance with JMH

On many occasions, Java applications may suffer from performance degradation. Exacerbating the issue is a lack of performance tests that can provide at least a minimal set of guarantees that performance requirements are met and, moreover, the performance of certain features will not degrade over time. Measuring performance of Java applications is not trivial, especially due to the fact that there is a number of compiler and runtime optimizations that may affect performance statistics. For that reason, additional measures such as warm-up phases and other tricks must be used in order to provide more accurate performance measurements. The Java Microbenchmark Harness is a framework that incorporates a number of techniques along with a convenient API that can be used for this purpose. It is not a new tool, but is included with the distribution of Java 9. If you have not added JMH to your toolbox yet, read the detailed chapter on the usage of JMH in the context of Java 9 application development.

Getting started with HTTP 2.0

HTTP 2.0 is the successor of the HTTP 1.1 protocol, and this new version of the protocol addresses some limitations and drawbacks of the previous one. HTTP 2.0 improves performance in several ways and provides capabilities such as request/response multiplexing in a single TCP connection, sending of responses in a server-push, flow control, and request prioritization, among others.

Java provides the `java.net.HttpURLConnection` utility that can be used to establish a non-secure HTTP 1.1 connection. However, the API was considered difficult to maintain and further extended with the support for HTTP 2.0 and, so, an entirely new client API was introduced in order to establish a connection via the HTTP 2.0 or the web socket protocols. The new HTTP 2.0 client, along with the capabilities it provides, will be covered in a dedicated chapter.

Encompassing reactive programming

Reactive programming is a paradigm used to describe a certain pattern for propagation of changes in a system. Reactiveness is not built in Java itself, but reactive data flows can be established using third-party libraries such as RxJava or project Reactor (part of the Spring Framework). JDK 9 also addresses the need for an API that aids the development of highly-responsive applications built around the idea of reactive streams by providing the `java.util.concurrent.Flow` class for the purpose. The `Flow` class, along with other related changes introduced in JDK 9, will be covered in a separate chapter.

Expanding the wish list

Apart from all of the new stuff in JDK 9, a whole new set of features is expected in future releases of the platform. Among these are the following:

- **Generics over primitive types**: This is one of the features planned for JDK 10 as part of project Valhalla. Other language enhancements, such as value handles, are already part of Java 9 and will be introduced later in this book.

- **Reified generics**: This is another featured part of project Valhalla that aims to provide the ability to preserve generic types at runtime. The related goals are listed as follows:
    - The foreign functional interface aims to introduce a new API to call and manage native functions. The API addresses some of the drawbacks of JNI and especially a lack of simplicity for use by application developers. The foreign functional interface is developed as part of project Panama in the JDK ecosystem.
    - New money and currency API (developed under JSR 354) was initially planned for Java 9, but was postponed.
    - New lightweight JSON API (developed under JSR 353) was also planned for Java 9, but postponed to Java 10.

These are just some of the new things one may expect in subsequent releases of the JDK. Project Penrose aims to bridge the gap between the module system in Java and the OSGi module system, and to provide different methodologies for interoperability between the two systems.

The Graal VM is another interesting research project that is a potential candidate for subsequent releases of the Java platform. It aims to bring the runtime performance of Java to dynamic languages such as JavaScript or Ruby.

A chapter dedicated to the future of JDK discusses all of these points in detail.

Summary

In this brief introductory chapter, we revealed the small universe of capabilities provided by JDK 9. The module system introduced in this release of the platform is indisputably a cornerstone in the development of Java applications. We also discovered that a number of other major features and changes are introduced in JDK 9 that deserve special attention and will be discussed in great detail in subsequent chapters.

In the next chapter, we will take a look at 26 internal changes to the Java platform.

Discovering Java 9 2

Java 9 represents a major release and consists of a large number of internal changes to the Java platform. Collectively, these internal changes represent a tremendous set of new possibilities for Java developers, some stemming from developer requests, others from Oracle-inspired enhancements. In this chapter, we will review 26 of the most important changes. Each change is related to a **JDK Enhancement Proposal** (**JEP**). JEPs are indexed and housed at `openjdk.java.net/jeps/0`. You can visit this site for additional information on each JEP.

> The JEP program is part of Oracle's support for open source, open innovation, and open standards. While other open source Java projects can be found, OpenJDK is the only one supported by Oracle.

In this chapter, we will cover changes to the Java platform. These changes have several impressive implications, including:

- Heap space efficiencies
- Memory allocation
- Compilation process improvements
- Type testing
- Annotations
- Automated runtime compiler tests
- Improved garbage collection

Improved Contended Locking [JEP 143]

The JVM uses Heap space for classes and objects. The JVM allocates memory on the heap whenever we create an object. This helps facilitate Java's garbage collection which releases memory previously used to hold objects that no longer have a reference to it. Java Stack memory is a bit different and is usually much smaller than heap memory.

The JVM does a good job of managing data areas that are shared by multiple threads. It associates a monitor with every object and class; these monitors have locks that are controlled by a single thread at any one time. These locks, controlled by the JVM, are, in essence, giving the controlling thread the object's monitor.

So, what is contended locking? When a thread is in a queue for a currently locked object, it is said to be in contention for that lock. The following diagram shows a high-level view of this contention:

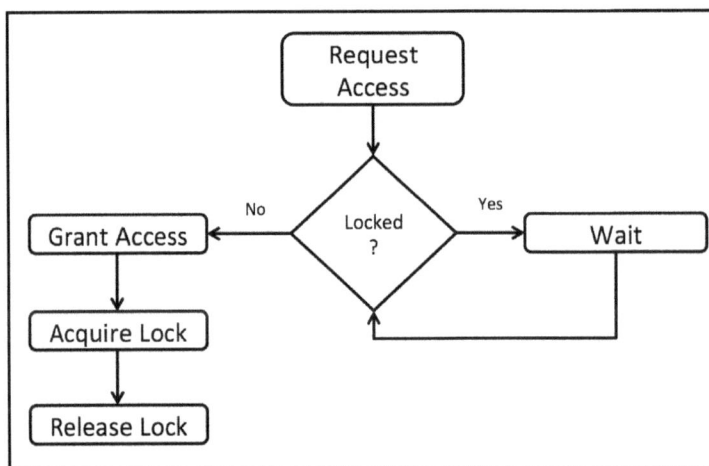

As you can see in the preceding illustration, any threads in waiting cannot use a locked object until it is released.

Improvement goals

The general goal of JEP 143 was to increase the overall performance of how the JVM manages contention over locked Java object monitors. The improvements to contended locking were all internal to the JVM and do not require any developer actions to benefit from them. The overall improvement goals were related to faster operations. These include:

- Faster monitor enter
- Faster monitor exit
- Faster notifications

The notifications are the `notify()` and `notifyAll()` operations that are called when the locked status of an object is changed. Testing this improvement is not something you can easily accomplish. Greater efficiency, at any level, is welcome, so this improvement is one we can be thankful for even without any easily observable testing.

Segmented code cache [JEP 197]

The segmented code cache JEP (197) upgrade was completed and results in faster, more efficient execution time. At the core of this change was the segmentation of the code cache into three distinct segments--non-method, profiled, and non-profiled code.

A code cache is the area of memory where the Java Virtual Machine stores generated native code.

Each of the aforementioned code cache segments will hold a specific type of compiled code. As you can see in the following diagram, the code heap areas are segmented by type of compiled code:

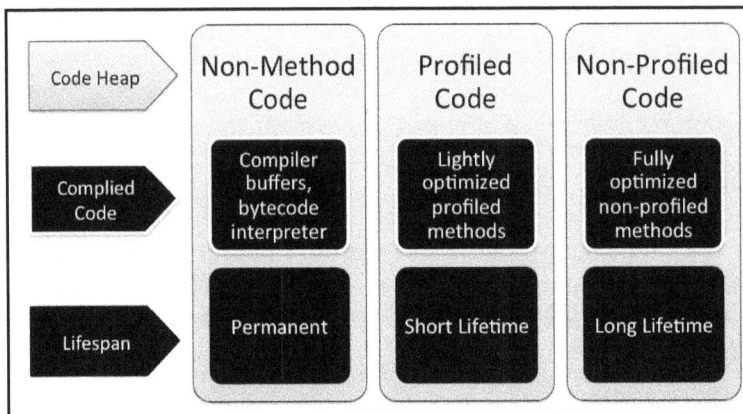

Code Heap	Non-Method Code	Profiled Code	Non-Profiled Code
Complied Code	Compiler buffers, bytecode interpreter	Lightly optimized profiled methods	Fully optimized non-profiled methods
Lifespan	Permanent	Short Lifetime	Long Lifetime

Memory allocation

The code heap containing non-method code is for JVM internal code and consists of a 3 MB fixed memory block. The rest of the code cache memory is equally allocated for the profiled code and non-profiled code segments. You have control of this via command-line commands.

The following command can be used to define the code heap size for the non-method compiled code:

```
-XX:NonMethodCodeCodeHeapSize
```

The following command can be used to define the code heap size for the profiled compiled methods:

```
-XX:ProfiledCodeHeapSize
```

The following command can be used to define the code heap size for the non-profiled compiled methods:

```
-XX:NonProfiledCodeHeapSize
```

This Java 9 feature certainly stands to improve Java application efficiency. It also impacts other processes that employ the code cache.

Smart Java compilation, phase two [JEP 199]

The JDK Enhancement Proposal 199 is aimed at improving the code compilation process. All Java developers will be familiar with the **javac** tool for compiling source code to bytecode, which is used by the JVM to run Java programs. **Smart Java Compilation**, also referred to as Smart Javac and **sjavac**, adds a *smart* wrapper around the javac process. Perhaps the core improvement sjavac adds is that only the necessary code is recompiled. Necessary code, in this context, is code that has changed since the last compile cycle.

This enhancement might not get developers excited if they only work on small projects. Consider, however, the tremendous gains in efficiency when you continuously have to recompile your code for medium and large projects. The time developers stand to save is enough reason to embrace JEP 199.

How will this change how you compile your code? It probably will not, at least not yet. Javac will remain the default compiler. While sjavac offers efficiencies regarding incremental builds, Oracle has deemed it to not have sufficient stability to become part of the standard compilation workflow.

> You can read more information about the smart javac wrapper tool here: `http://cr.openjdk.java.net/~briangoetz/JDK-8030245/webrev/src/share/classes/com/sun/tools/sjavac/Main.java-.html`.

Resolving Lint and Doclint warnings [JEP 212]

Do not worry if you are not familiar with Lint or Doclint in Java. As you can determine from the section title, they are sources that report warnings to javac. Let's take a look at each one:

- **Lint** analyzes byte code and source code for javac. The goal of Lint is to identify security vulnerabilities in the code being analyzed. Lint can also provide insights into scalability and thread locking concerns. There is more to Lint, and the overall purpose is to save developers time.

You can read more about Lint here:
`https://en.wikipedia.org/wiki/Lint_(software)`.

- **Doclint** is similar to Lint and is specific to javadoc. Both Lint and Doclint report errors and warnings during the compile process. Resolution of these warnings was the focus of JEP 212. When using core libraries, there should not be any warnings. This mindset led to JEP 212, which has been resolved and implemented in Java 9.

A comprehensive list of the Lint and Doclint warnings can be reviewed in the `https://bugs.openjdk.java.net` JDK Bug System.

Tiered attribution for javac [JEP 215]

JEP 215 represents an impressive undertaking to streamline javac's type checking schema. Let's first review how type checking works in Java 8; then we will explore the changes in Java 9.

In Java 8, type checking of poly expressions is handled by a **speculative attribution** tool.

Speculative attribution is a method of type checking as part of javac's compilation process. It has a significant processing overhead.

Using the speculative attribution approach to type checking is accurate, but lacks efficiency. These checks include argument position, and are exponentially slower when testing in the midst of recursion, polymorphism, nested loops, and lambda expressions. So the goal with JEP 215 was to change the type checking schema to create faster results. The results themselves were not inaccurate with speculative attribution; they were just not generated rapidly.

Chapter 2

The new approach, released with Java 9, uses a tiered attribution tool. This tool implements a tiered approach for type checking argument expressions for all method calls. Permissions are also made for method overriding. In order for this new schema to work, new structural types are created for each of the following listed types of method arguments:

- Lambda expressions
- Poly expressions
- Regular method calls
- Method references
- Diamond instance creation expressions

The changes to javac from JEP 215 are more complex than what has been highlighted in this section. There is no immediate impact to developers other than a more efficient javac and time saved.

Annotations pipeline 2.0 [JEP 217]

Java annotations refer to a special kind of metadata that resides inside your Java source code files. They are not stripped by javac, so that they can remain available to the JVM at runtime.

Annotations look similar to JavaDocs references because they start with the @ symbol. There are three types of annotations. Let's examine each:

- The most basic form of annotation is a **marker** annotation. These are standalone annotations with the only component being the name of the animation. Here is an example:

```
@thisIsAMarkerAnnotation
public double computeSometing(double x, double y)
{
  // do something and return a double
}
```

[21]

- The second type of annotation is one that contains a *single value*, or piece of data. As you can see in the following code, the annotation, which starts with the @ symbol, is followed by parentheses containing data:

```
@thisIsAMarkerAnnotation (data="compute x and y
  coordinates")
public double computeSometing(double x, double y)
{
  // do something and return a double
}
```

An alternative way of coding the single value annotation type is to omit the data= component, as illustrated in the following code:

```
@thisIsAMarkerAnnotation ("compute x and y coordinates")
public double computeSometing(double x, double y)
{
  // do something and return a double
}
```

- The third type of annotation is when there is *more than one data component*. With this type of annotation, the data= component cannot be omitted. Here is an example:

```
@thisIsAMarkerAnnotation (data="compute x and y
  coordinates", purpose="determine intersecting point")
public double computeSometing(double x, double y)
{
    // do something and return a double
}
```

So, what has changed in Java 9? To answer this question, we need to recall a couple of changes introduced with Java 8 that impacted Java annotations:

- Lambda expressions
- Repeated annotations
- Java type annotations

These Java 8 related changes impacted Java annotations, but did not usher in a change to how javac processed them. There were some hardcoded solutions that allowed javac to handle the new annotations, but they were not efficient. Moreover, this type of coding (hardcoding workarounds) is difficult to maintain.

So, JEP 217 focused on refactoring the javac annotation pipeline. This refactoring was all internal to javac, so it should not be evident to developers.

New version-string scheme [JEP 223]

Prior to Java 9, the release numbers did not follow industry standard versioning--**semantic versioning**. For example, at the time of writing, the last four JDK releases were:

- JDK 8 update 131
- JDK 8 update 121
- JDK 8 update 112

> **Semantic versioning** uses a major, minor, patch (0.0.0) schema:
> **Major** equates to new API changes that are not backwards compatible.
> **Minor** is when functionality is added that is backwards compatible.
> **Patch** refers to bug fixes or minor changes that are backwards compatible.

Oracle has embraced semantic versioning for Java 9 and beyond. For Java, a **major-minor-security** schema will be used for the first three elements of Java version numbers:

- **Major**: A major release consisting of a significant new set of features
- **Minor**: Revisions and bug fixes that are backwards compatible
- **Security**: Fixes deemed critical to improve security

This description of JEP 223 might make the versioning schema seem basic. To the contrary, a very detailed set of rules and practices have been developed to manage the future version numbers. To demonstrate the complexity, see the following example:

```
1.9.0._32.b19
```

Generating run-time compiler tests automatically [JEP 233]

Java is arguably the most used programming language and resides on an increasingly diverse number of platforms. This exacerbates the problem of running targeted compiler tests in an efficient manner. The purpose of JEP 233 was to create a tool that could automate the runtime compiler tests.

The tool that was created starts by generating a random set of Java source code and/or byte code. The generated code will have three key characteristics:

- Be syntactically correct
- Be semantically correct
- Use a random seed that permits reusing the same randomly-generated code

The source code that is randomly generated will be saved in the following directory:

```
hotspot/test/testlibrary/jit-tester
```

These test cases will be stored for later re-use. They can be run from the `j-treg` directory or from the tool's makefile. One of the benefits of re-running saved tests is to test the stability of your system.

Testing class-file attributes generated by Javac [JEP 235]

The lack of, or insufficient, capability to create tests for class-file attributes was the impetus behind JEP 235. The goal is to ensure javac creates a class-file's attributes completely and correctly. This suggests that even if some attributes are not used by the class-file, all class-files should be generated with a complete set of attributes. There also needs to be a way of testing that the class-files were created correctly, in regards to the file's attributes.

Prior to Java 9, there was no method of testing a class-file's attributes. Running a class and testing the code for anticipated or expected results was the most commonly used method of testing javac generated class-files. This technique falls short of testing to validate the file's attributes.

There are three categories of class-file attributes--attributes used by the JVM, optional attributes, and attributes not used by the JVM.

Attributes used by the JVM include:

- `BootstrapMethods`
- `Code`
- `ConstantValue`
- `Exceptions`
- `StackMapTable`

Optional attributes include:

- `Deprecated`
- `LineNumberTable`
- `LocalVariableTable`
- `LocalVariableTypeTable`
- `SourceDebugExtension`
- `SourceFile`

Attributes not used by the JVM include:

- `AnnotationDefault`
- `EnclosingMethod`
- `InnerClasses`
- `MethodParameters`
- `RuntimeInvisibleAnnotations`
- `RuntimeInvisibleParameterAnnotations`
- `RuntimeInvisibleTypeAnnotations`
- `RuntimeVisibleAnnotations`
- `RuntimeVisibleParameterAnnotations`
- `RuntimeVisibleTypeAnnotations`
- `Signature`
- `Synthetic`

Storing interned strings in CDS archives [JEP 250]

The method in which strings are stored and accessed to and from **Class Data Sharing** (**CDS**) archives is inefficient, excessively time consuming, and wastes memory. The following diagram illustrates the method in which Java stores interned strings in a CDS archive:

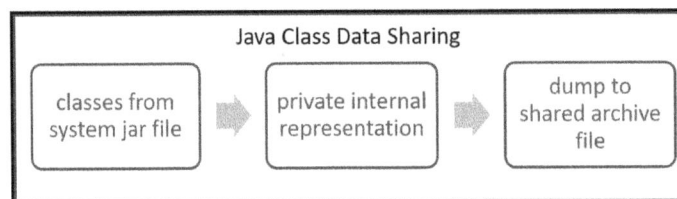

The inefficiency stems from the current storage schema. Especially when the **Class Data Sharing** tool dumps the classes into the shared archive file, the constant pools containing CONSTANT_String items have a UTF-8 string representation.

> UTF-8 is an 8-bit variable-length character encoding standard.

The problem

With the current use of UTF-8, the strings must be converted to string objects, instances of the java.lang.String class. This conversion takes place on-demand which can result in slower systems and unnecessary memory usage. The processing time is extremely short, but the memory usage cannot be overlooked. Every character in an interned string requires at least 3 bytes of memory and potentially more.

A related problem is that the stored strings are not accessible to all JVM processes.

The solution

CDS archives now allocate specific space on the heap for strings:

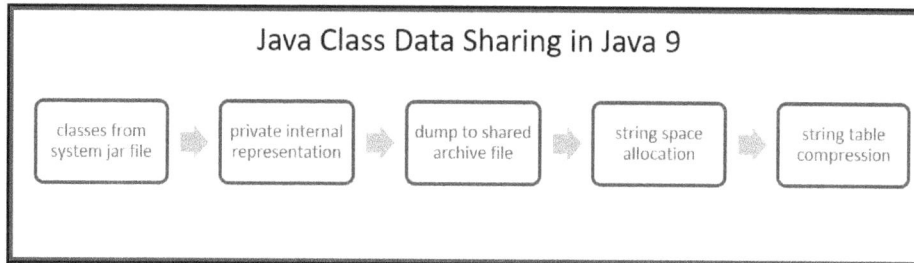

The string space is mapped using a shared-string table, hash tables, and deduplication.

Deduplication is a data compression technique that eliminates duplicative information in an archive.

Preparing JavaFX UI controls and CSS APIs for modularization [JEP 253]

JavaFX is a set of packages that permits the design and development of media-rich graphical user interfaces. JavaFX applications provide developers with a great API for creating a consistent interface for applications. **Cascading Style Sheets** (**CSS**) can be used to customize the interfaces. One of the great things about JavaFX is that the tasks of programming and interface design can easily be separated.

JavaFX overview

There is a wonderful visual scripting tool called Scene Builder that allows you to create graphical user interfaces by using drag and drop and property settings. Scene Builder generates the necessary FXML files that are used by your **Integrated Development Environment** (**IDE**) such as NetBeans.

Here is a sample UI created with Scene Builder:

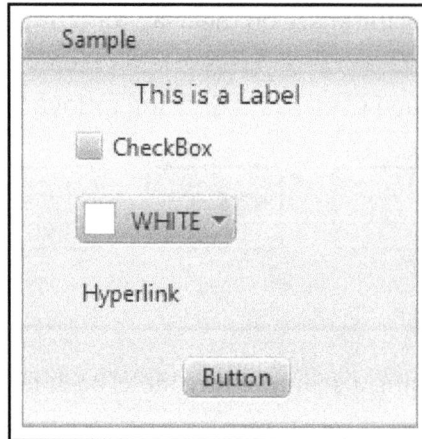

And, here is the FXML file created by Scene Builder:

```
<?xml version="1.0" encoding="UTF-8"?>

<?import java.lang.*?>
<?import java.util.*?>
<?import javafx.scene.control.*?>
<?import javafx.scene.layout.*?>
<?import javafx.scene.paint.*?>
<?import javafx.scene.text.*?>

<AnchorPane id="AnchorPane" maxHeight="-Infinity"
 maxWidth="-Infinity" minHeight="-Infinity"
 minWidth="-Infinity" prefHeight="400.0" prefWidth="600.0"
 xmlns:fx="http://javafx.com/fxml/1"
 xmlns="http://javafx.com/javafx/2.2">
 <children>
   <TitledPane animated="false" collapsible="false"
    layoutX="108.0" layoutY="49.0" text="Sample">
   <content>
     <AnchorPane id="Content" minHeight="0.0" minWidth="0.0"
      prefHeight="180.0" prefWidth="200.0">
     <children>
       <CheckBox layoutX="26.0" layoutY="33.0"
        mnemonicParsing="false" prefWidth="94.0"
        text="CheckBox" />
       <ColorPicker layoutX="26.0" layoutY="65.0" />
       <Hyperlink layoutX="26.0" layoutY="103.0"
        text="Hyperlink" />
```

```
            <Label alignment="CENTER" layoutX="14.0" layoutY="5.0"
             prefWidth="172.0" text="This is a Label"
             textAlignment="CENTER">
             <font>
               <Font size="14.0" />
             </font>
            </Label>
            <Button layoutX="81.0" layoutY="146.0"
             mnemonicParsing="false" text="Button" />
          </children>
        </AnchorPane>
      </content>
    </TitledPane>
  </children>
</AnchorPane>
```

Implications for Java 9

Prior to Java 9, JavaFX controls as well as CSS functionality were only available to developers by interfacing with internal APIs. Java 9's modularization has made the internal APIs inaccessible. Therefore, JEP 253 was created to define public, instead of internal, APIs.

This was a larger undertaking than it might seem. Here are a few actions that were taken as part of this JEP:

- Moving javaFX control skins from the internal to public API (`javafx.scene.skin`)
- Ensuring API consistencies
- Generation of a thorough javadoc

The following classes were moved from internal packages to a public `javafx.scene.control.skin` package:

AccordionSkin	ButtonBarSkin	ButtonSkin	CellSkinBase
CheckBoxSkin	ChoiceBoxSkin	ColorPickerSkin	ComboBoxBaseSkin
ComboBoxListViewSkin	ComboBoxPopupControl	ContextMenuSkin	DateCellSkin
DatePickerSkin	HyperLinkSkin	LabelSkin	LabeledSkinBase
ListCellSkin	ListViewSkin	MenuBarSkin	MenuButtonSkin
MenuButtonSkinbase	NestedTableColumHeader	PaginationSkin	ProgressBarSkin
ProgressIndicatorSkin	RadioButtonSkin	ScrollBarSkin	ScrollPaneSkin
SeparatorSkin	SliderSkin	SpinnerSkin	SplitMenuButtonSkin

SplitPaneSkin	TabPaneSkin	TableCellSkin	TableCellSkinBase
TableColumnHeader	TableHeaderRow	TableHeaderSkin	TableRowSkinBase
TableViewSkin	TableViewSkinBase	TextAreaSkin	TextFieldSkin
TextInputControlSkin	TitledPaneSkin	ToggleButtonSkin	TooBarSkin
TooltipSkin	TreeCellSkin	TreeTableCellSkin	TreeTableRowSkin
TreeTableViewSkin	TreeViewSkin	VirtualContainerBase	VirtualFlow

The public `javafx.css` package now has the additional classes:

- `CascadingStyle.java:public class CascadingStyle implements Comparable<CascadingStyle>`
- `CompoundSelector.java:final public class CompoundSelector extends Selector`
- `CssError.java:public class CssError`
- `Declaration.java:final public class Declaration`
- `Rule.java:final public class Rule`
- `Selector.java:abstract public class Selector`
- `SimpleSelector.java:final public class SimpleSelector extends Selector`
- `Size.java:final public class Size`
- `Style.java:final public class Style`
- `Stylesheet.java:public class Stylesheet`
- `CssParser.java:final public class CssParser`

Compact strings [JEP 254]

The string data type is an important part of nearly every Java app. While JEP 254's aim was to make strings more space-efficient, it was approached with caution so that existing performance and compatibilities would not be negatively impacted.

Pre-Java 9 status

Prior to Java 9, string data was stored as an array of chars. This required 16 bits for each char. It was determined that the majority of String objects could be stored with only 8 bits, or 1 byte of storage. This is due to the fact that most strings consist of Latin-1 characters.

> The ISO Latin-1 Character Set is a single-byte set of character's encodings.

New with Java 9

Starting with Java 9, strings are now internally represented using a byte array along with a flag field for encoding references.

Merging selected Xerces 2.11.0 updates into JAXP [JEP 255]

Xerces is a library used for parsing XML in Java. It was updated to 2.11.0 in late 2010, so JEP 255's aim was to update JAXP to incorporate changes in Xerces 2.11.0.

> JAXP is Java's API for XML processing.

Prior to Java 9, the JDK's latest update regarding XML processing was based on Xerces 2.7.1. There were some additional changes to JDK 7 based on Xerces, 2.10.0. JEP 255 is a further refinement of the JAXP based on Xerces 2.11.0.

Xerces 2.11.0 supports the following standards:

- XML 1.0, Fourth Edition
- Namespaces in XML 1.0, Second Edition
- XML 1.1, Second Edition
- Namespaces in XML 1.1, Second Edition
- XML Inclusions 1.0, Second Edition

- **Document Object Model (DOM)**
  - Level 3
    - Core
    - Load & save
  - Level 2
    - Core
    - Events
- Traversal & Range
- Element Traversal, First Edition
- Simple API for XML 2.0.2
- **Java APIs for XML Processing (JAXP) 1.4**
- Streaming API for XML 1.0
- XML Schema 1.0
- XML Schema 1.1
- XML Schema Definition Language

The JDK was updated to include the following Xerces 2.11.0 categories:

- Catalog resolver
- Datatypes
- Document Object Model Level 3
- XML Schema Validation
- XPointer

The public API for JAXP was not changed in Java 9.

Updating JavaFX/Media to newer version of GStreamer [JEP 257]

JavaFX is used for creating desktop and web applications. JavaFX was created to replace Swing as Java's standard GUI library. The Media class, `javafx.scene.media.Media`, is used to instantiate an object representing a media resource. JavaFX/Media refers to the following class:

```
public final class Media extends java.lang.Object
```

This class provides referential data to a media resource. The `javafx.scene.media` package provides developers with the ability to incorporate media into their JavaFX applications. JavaFX/Media utilizes a GStreamer pipeline.

> GStreamer is a multimedia processing framework that can be used to build systems that take in media from several different formats and, after processing, export them in selected formats.

The purpose of JEP 257 was to ensure JavaFX/Media was updated to include the latest release of GStreamer for stability, performance, and security assurances.

HarfBuzz Font-Layout Engine [JEP 258]

Prior to Java 9, the layout engine used to handle font complexities; specifically fonts that have rendering behaviors beyond what the common Latin fonts have. Java used the uniform client interface, also referred to as ICU, as the defacto text rendering tool. The ICU layout engine has been depreciated and, in Java 9, has been replaced with the HarfBuzz font layout engine.

HarfBuzz is an **OpenType** text rendering engine. This type of layout engine has the characteristic of providing script-aware code to help ensure text is laid out as desired.

> OpenType is an HTML formatted font format specification.

The impetus for the change from the ICU Layout Engine to the HarfBuzz Font Layout Engine was IBM's decision to cease supporting the ICU Layout Engine. Therefore, the JDK was updated to contain the HarfBuzz Font Layout Engine.

HiDPI graphics on Windows and Linux [JEP 263]

JEP 263 was focused on ensuring the crispness of on-screen components, relative to the pixel density of the display. The following terms are relevant to this JEP and are provided along with the below listed descriptive information:

- **DPI-aware application**: An application that is able to detect and scale images for the display's specific pixel density
- **DPI-unaware application**: An application that makes no attempt to detect and scale images for the display's specific pixel density
- **HiDPI graphics**: High dots-per-inch graphics
- **Retina display**: This term was created by Apple to refer to displays with a pixel density of at least 300 pixels per inch

Displaying graphics, both images and graphical user interface components, to the user is typically of paramount performance. Displaying this imagery in high quality can be somewhat problematic. There is large variability in computer monitor DPIs. There are three basic approaches to developing for displays:

- Develop apps without regard for the potential different display dimensions. In other words, create a DPI-unaware application.
- Develop a DPI-aware application that selectively uses pre-rendered image sizes for a given display.
- Develop a DPI-aware application that properly scales images up/down to account for the specific display the application is run on.

Clearly, the first two approaches are problematic, and for different reasons. With the first approach, the user experience is not considered. Of course, if the application was being developed for a very specific display with no expected pixel density variability, then this approach could be viable.

The second approach requires a lot of work on the design and development end to ensure images for each expected display density are created and implemented programmatically. In addition to the tremendous amount of work, the app size will unnecessarily increase, and new and different pixel densities will not have been accounted for.

The third approach is to create a DPI-aware application with efficient and effective scaling capabilities. This approach works well and has been proven with the Mac retina displays.

Prior to Java 9, automatic scaling and sizing was already implemented in Java for the Mac OS X operating system. This capability was added in Java 9 for Windows and Linux operating systems.

Marlin graphics renderer [JEP 265]

JEP 265 replaced the Pisces graphics rasterizer with the Marlin graphics renderer in the Java 2D API. This API is used to draw 2D graphics and animations.

The goal was to replace Pisces with a rasterizer/renderer that was much more efficient and without any quality loss. This goal was realized in Java 9. An intended collateral benefit was to include a developer-accessible API. Previously, the means of interfacing with the AWT and Java 2D was internal.

Unicode 8.0.0 [JEP 267]

Unicode 8.0.0 was released on June 17, 2015. JEP 267 focused on updating the relevant APIs to support Unicode 8.0.0.

New in Unicode 8.0.0

Unicode 8.0.0 added nearly 8,000 characters. Here are the highlights of the release:

- Ahom script for the Tai Ahom language (India)
- Arwi, Tamil language (Arabic)
- Cherokee symbols
- CJK unified ideographs
- Emoji symbols along with flesh-tone symbol modifiers
- Georgian lari currency symbol
- lk language (Uganda)
- Kulango languge (Côte d'Ivoire)

Updated Classes in Java 9

In order to fully comply with the new Unicode standard, several Java classes were updated. The following listed classes were updated for Java 9 to comply with the new Unicode standard:

- `java.awt.font.NumericShaper`
- `java.lang.Character`
- `java.lang.String`
- `java.text.Bidi`
- `java.text.BreakIterator`
- `java.text.Normalizer`

Reserved stack areas for critical sections [JEP 270]

The goal of JEP 270 was to mitigate problems stemming from stack overflows during the execution of critical sections. This mitigation took the form of reserving additional thread stack space.

The pre-Java 9 situation

The JVM throws a `StackOverflowError` when it is asked to perform data computation in a thread that has insufficient stack space and does not have permission to allocate additional space. This is an asynchronous exception. The JVM can also throw the `StackOverflowError` exception synchronously when a method is invoked.

When a method is invoked, an internal process is used to report the Stack Overflow. While the current schema works sufficiently for reporting the error, there is no room for the calling application to easily recover from the error. This can result in being more than a nuisance for developers and users. If the `StackOverflowError` was thrown during a critical computational operation, the data might be corrupted, causing additional problems.

While not the sole cause of these problems, the effected status of locks from the ReentrantLock class were a common cause of undesirable outcomes. This issue was evident in Java 7 because the ConcurrentHasMap code implemented the ReentrantLock class. The ConcurrentHasMap code was modified for Java 8, but problems still persisted for any implementation of the ReentrantLock class. Similar problems existed beyond just ReentrantLock class usage.

The following diagram provides a broad overview of the StackOverflowError problem:

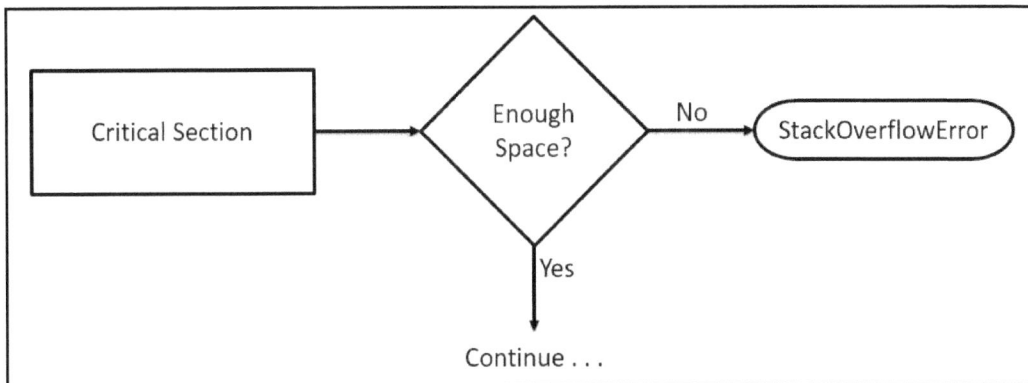

In the next section, we will look at how this issue was resolved for Java 9.

New in Java 9

With the JEP 270 changes for Java 9, a critical section will automatically be given additional space so that it can complete its execution and not suffer from the StackOverflowError. This is predicated on the additional space allocation needs being small. The necessary changes have been made to the JVM to permit this functionality.

The JVM actually delays the StackOverflowError, or at least attempts to, while critical sections are executing. In order to capitalize on this new schema, methods must be annotated with the following:

```
jdk.internal.vm.annotation.ReservedStackAccess
```

When a method has this annotation and a `StackOverflowError` condition exists, temporary access to the reserved memory space is granted. The new process is, at a high level of abstraction, presented as follows:

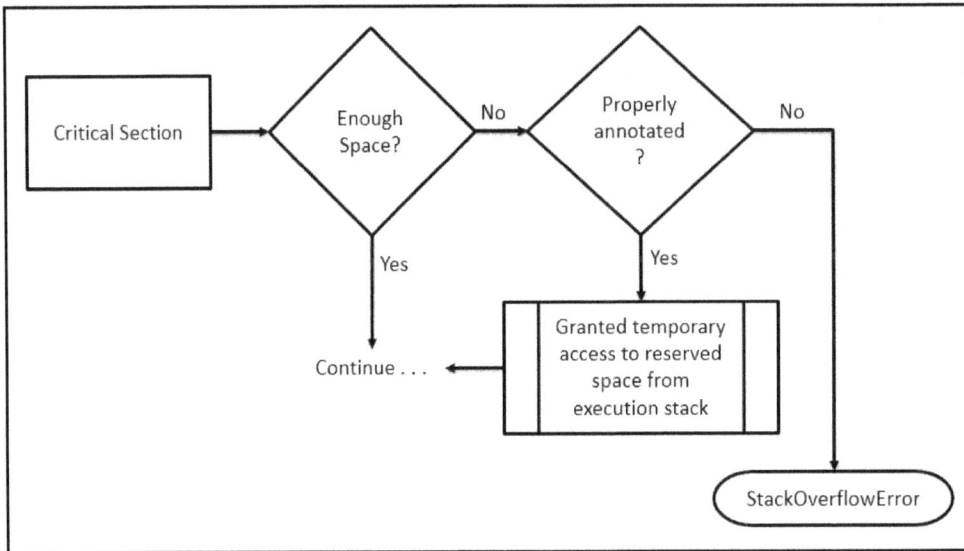

Dynamic linking of language-defined object models [JEP 276]

Java interoperability was enhanced with JEP 276. The necessary JDK changes were made to permit runtime linkers from multiple languages to coexist in a single JVM instance. This change applies to high-level operations, as you would expect. An example of a relevant high-level operation is the reading or writing of a property with elements such as accessors and mutators.

The high-level operations apply to objects of unknown types. They can be invoked with `INVOKEDYNAMIC` instructions. Here is an example of calling an object's property when the object's type is unknown at compile time:

```
INVOKEDYNAMIC "dyn:getProp:age"
```

Proof of concept

Nashorn is a lightweight, high-performance, JavaScript runtime that permits embedding JavaScript in Java applications. This was created for Java 8 and replaced the previous JavaScript scripting engine that was based on Mozilla Rhino. Nashorn already has this functionality. It provides linkage between high-level operations on any object of unknown type, such as `obj.something`, where it produces the following:

```
INVOKEDYNAMIC "dyn.getProp.something"
```

The dynamic linker springs into action and provides, when possible, the appropriate implementation.

Additional tests for humongous objects in G1 [JEP 278]

One of the long-favored features of the Java platform is the behind the scenes garbage collection. JEP 278's focus was to create additional WhiteBox tests for humongous objects as a feature of the G1 garbage collector.

> WhiteBox testing is an API used to query JVM internals. The WhiteBox testing API was introduced in Java 7 and upgraded in Java 8 and Java 9.

The G1 garbage collector works extremely well, but there was room for some improved efficiency. The way the G1 garbage collector worked is based on first dividing the heap into regions of equal size, illustrated as follows:

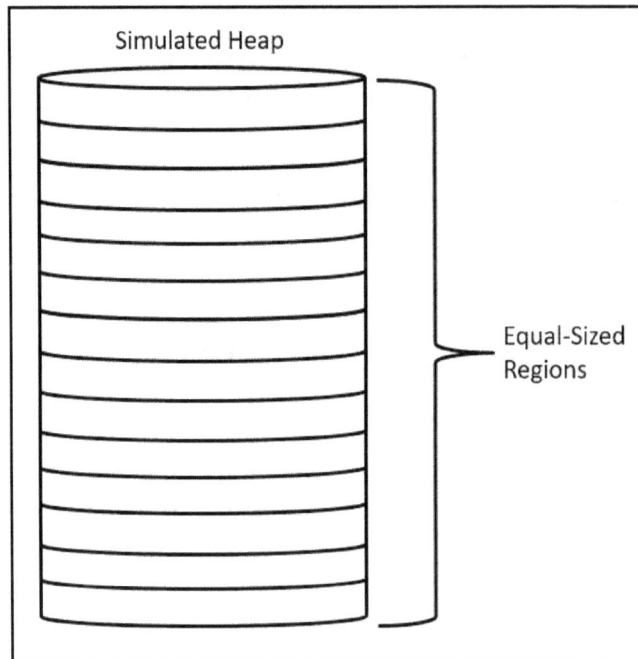

The problem with the G1 garbage collector was how humongous objects were handled.

> A humongous object in the context of garbage collection, is any object that takes up more than one region on the heap.

The problem with humongous objects was that if they took up any part of a region on the heap, the remaining space was not able to be allocated for other objects. In Java 9, the WhiteBox API was extended with four types of new methods:

- Methods with the purpose of blocking full garbage collection and to initiate concurrent marking.
- Methods that can access individual G1 garbage collection heap regions. Access to these regions consist of attribute reading, such as with the current state of the region.

- Methods with direct access to the G1 garbage collection internal variables.
- Methods that can determine if humongous objects reside on the heap and, if so, in what regions.

Improving test-failure troubleshooting [JEP 279]

For developers that do a lot of testing, JEP 279 is worth reading about. Additional functionality has been added in Java 9 to automatically collect information to support troubleshooting test failures as well as timeouts. Collecting readily available diagnostic information during tests stands to provide developers and engineers with greater fidelity in their logs and other output.

There are two basic types of information in the context of testing--environmental and process.

Environmental information

When running tests, the testing environment information can be important for troubleshooting efforts. This information includes the following:

- CPU loads
- Disk space
- I/O loads
- Memory space
- Open files
- Open sockets
- Processes running
- System events
- System messages

Java process information

There is also information available during the testing process directly related to Java processes. These include:

- C stacks
- Core dumps
- Mini dumps
- Heap statistics
- Java stacks

> For additional information on this concept, read about the JDK's regression test harness (jtreg).

Optimizing string concatenation [JEP 280]

JEP 280 is an interesting enhancement for the Java platform. Prior to Java 9, string concatenation was translated by javac into `StringBuilder : : append` chains. This was a sub-optimal translation methodology often requiring `StringBuilder` presizing.

The enhancement changed the string concatenation bytecode sequence, generated by javac, so that it uses `INVOKEDYNAMIC` calls. The purpose of the enhancement was to increase optimization and to support future optimizations without the need to reformat the javac's bytecode.

> See JEP 276 for more information on `INVOKEDYNAMIC`.

The use of `INVOKEDYAMIC` calls to `java.lang.invoke.StringConcatFactory` allows us to use a methodology similar to lambda expressions instead of using StringBuilder's step-wise process. This results in more efficient processing of string concatenation.

HotSpot C++ unit-test framework [JEP 281]

HotSpot is the name of the JVM. This Java enhancement was intended to support the development of C++ unit tests for the JVM. Here is a partial, non-prioritized, list of goals for this enhancement:

- Command-line testing
- Create appropriate documentation
- Debug compile targets
- Framework elasticity
- IDE support
- Individual and isolated unit testing
- Individualized test results
- Integrate with existing infrastructure
- Internal test support
- Positive and negative testing
- Short execution time testing
- Support all JDK 9 build platforms
- Test compile targets
- Test exclusion
- Test grouping
- Testing that requires the JVM to be initialized
- Tests co-located with source code
- Tests for platform-dependent code
- Write and execute unit testing (for classes and methods)

This enhancement is evidence of the increasing extensibility.

Enabling GTK 3 on Linux [JEP 283]

GTK+, formally known as the GIMP toolbox, is a cross-platform tool used for creating **Graphical User Interfaces** (**GUI**). The tool consists of widgets accessible through its API. JEP 283's focus was to ensure GTK 2 and GTK 3 were supported on Linux when developing Java applications with graphical components. The implementation supports Java apps that employ JavaFX, AWT, and Swing.

We can create Java graphical applications with JavaFX, AWT, and Swing. Here is a table to summarize those three approaches as they relate to GTK, prior to Java 9:

Approach	Remarks
JavaFX	• Uses a dynamic GTK function lookup • Interacts with AWT and Swing via JFXPanel • Uses AWT printing functionality
AWT	• Uses a dynamic GTK function lookup
Swing	• Uses a dynamic GTK function lookup

So, what changes were necessary to implement this JEP? For JavaFX, three specific things were changed:

- Automated testing was added for both GTK 2 and GTK 3
- Functionality was added to dynamically load GTK 2
- Support was added for GTK 3

For AWT and Swing, the following changes were implemented:

- Automated testing was added for both GTK 2 and GTK 3
- `AwtRobot` was migrated to GTK 3
- `FileChooserDilaog` was updated for GTK 3
- Functionality was added to dynamically load GTK 3
- The Swing GTK LnF was modified to support GTK 3

Swing GTK LnF is short for Swing GTK look and feel.

New HotSpot build system [JEP 284]

The Java platform used, prior to Java 9, was a build system riddled with duplicate code, redundancies, and other inefficiencies. The build system has been reworked for Java 9 based on the build-infra framework. In this context, infra is short for infrastructure. The overarching goal for JEP 284 was to upgrade the build system to one that was simplified. Specific goals included:

- Leverage existing build system
- Maintainable code
- Minimize duplicate code
- Simplification
- Support future enhancements

You can learn more about Oracle's infrastructure framework at this site: `http://www.oracle.com/technetwork/oem/frmwrk-infra-496656.html`

Summary

In this chapter, we covered some impressive new features of the Java platform, with specific focus on javac, JDK libraries, and various test suites. Memory management improvements, including heap space efficiencies, memory allocation, and improved garbage collection represent a powerful new set of Java platform enhancements. Changes regarding the compilation process resulting in greater efficiencies were part of our chapter. We also covered important improvements, such as with the compilation process, type testing, annotations, and automated runtime compiler tests.

In the next chapter, we will look at several minor language enhancements introduced in Java 9.

3
Java 9 Language Enhancements

In the previous chapter, we gained insight into some exciting new features contained in Java 9. Our focus was on javac, the JDK libraries, and test suites. We learned about memory management improvements including memory allocation, heap optimizations, and enhanced garbage collection. We also covered changes to the compilation process, type testing, annotations, and runtime compiler tests.

This chapter covers some changes in Java 9 that impact variable handlers, depreciation warnings, improvements on Project Coin changes implemented in Java 7, and import statement processing. These represent changes to the Java language itself.

The topics we will cover here are:

- Variable handlers
- Import statement depreciation warnings
- Project Coin
- Import statement processing

Working with variable handlers [JEP 193]

Variable handlers are typed references to variables and are governed by the `java.lang.invoke.VarHandle` abstract class. The `VarHandle` method's signature is polymorphic. This provides for great variability in both method signatures and return types. Here is a code sample demonstrating how a `VarHandle` might be used:

```
    .  .  .

class Example
{
  int myInt;
    .  .  .
}
    .  .  .
class Sample
{
  static final VarHandle VH_MYINT;

  static
  {
    try
    {
      VH_MYINT =
        MethodHandles.lookup().in(Example.class)
        .findVarHandle(Example.class, "myInt", int.class);
    }
    catch (Exception e)
    {
      throw new Error(e);
    }
  }
}

    .  .  .
```

As you can see in the preceding code snippet, the `VarHandle.lookup()` performs the same operation as those that are performed by a `MethodHandle.lookup()` method.

The aim of this JEP was to standardize the way in which methods of the following classes are invoked:

- `java.util.concurrent.atomic`
- `sun.misc.Unsafe</li>`

Specifically, methods that:

- accessed/mutated object fields
- accessed/mutated elements of an array

In addition, this JEP resulted in two fence operations for memory ordering and object reachability. In the spirit of due diligence, special attention was given to ensure the JVM's safety. It was important to ensure that memory errors did not result from these changes. Data integrity, usability, and, of course, performance were key components of the aforementioned due diligence and are explained as follows:

- **Safety**: Corrupt memory states must not be possible.
- **Data integrity**: Ensure access to an object's field uses identical rules used by:
  - `getfield` byte code
  - `putfield` byte code
- **Usability**: The benchmark for usability was the `sun.misc.Unsafe` API. The goal was to make the new API easier to use than the benchmark.
- **Performance**: There could be no degradation of performance compared to the use of the `sun.misc.Unsafe` API. The goal was to outperform that API.

> In Java, a fence operation is what javac does to force a constraint on memory in the form of a barrier instruction. These operations occur before and after the barrier instruction, essentially fencing them in.

Working with the AtoMiC Toolkit

The `java.util.concurrent.atomic` package is a collection of 12 sub-classes that support operations on single variables that are thread-safe and lock-free. In this context, thread-safe refers to code that accesses or mutates a shared single variable without impeding on other threads executing on the variable at the same time. This superclass was introduced in Java 7.

Here is a list of the 12 sub-classes in the AtoMiC Toolkit. The class names, as you would expect, are self-descriptive:

Atomic subclass
`java.util.concurrent.atomic.AtomicBoolean`
`java.util.concurrent.atomic.AtomicInteger`
`java.util.concurrent.atomic.AtomicIntegerArray`
`java.util.concurrent.atomic.AtomicIntegerFieldUpdater<T>`
`java.util.concurrent.atomic.AtomicLong`
`java.util.concurrent.atomic.AtomicLongArray`
`java.util.concurrent.atomic.AtomicLongFieldUpdater<T>`
`java.util.concurrent.atomic.AtomicMarkableReference<V>`
`java.util.concurrent.atomic.AtomicReference<V>`
`java.util.concurrent.atomic.AtomicReferenceArray<E>`
`java.util.concurrent.atomic.AtomicReferenceFieldUpdater<T,V>`
`java.util.concurrent.atomic.AtomicStampedReference<V>`

Volatile variables, fields, and array elements can be asynchronously modified by concurrent threads.

> In Java, the `volatile` keyword is used to inform the javac utility to read the value, field, or array element from the main memory and not to cache them.

Here is a code snippet that demonstrates the use of the volatile keyword for an instance variable:

```
public class Sample
{
  private static volatile Sample myVolatileVariable; // a
   volatile instance variable

  public static Sample getVariable() // getter method
  {
    if (myVolatileVariable != null)
    {
```

```
      return myVolatileVariable;
  }
  // this section executes if myVolatileVariable == null
  synchronized(Sample.class)
  {
    if (myVolatileVariable == null)
    {
      myVolatileVariable =  new Sample();
    }
  }
}
```

Using the sun.misc.Unsafe class

The `sun.misc.Unsafe` class, like other `sun` classes, is not officially documented or supported. It has been used to circumvent some of Java's built-in memory management safety features. While this can be viewed as a window to greater control and flexibility in our code, it is a terrible programming practice.

The class had a single private constructor, so an instance of the class could not easily be instantiated. So, if we tried to instantiate an instance with `myUnsafe = new Unsafe()`, a `SecurityException` would be thrown in most circumstances. This somewhat unreachable class has over 100 methods that permitted operations on arrays, classes, and objects. Here is a brief sampling of those methods:

Arrays	Classes	Objects
arrayBaseOffset	defineAnonymousClass	allocateInstance
arrayIndexScale	defineClass	objectFieldOffset
	ensureClassInitialized	
	staticFieldOffset	

Here is a secondary grouping of the `sun.misc.Unsafe` class method for information, memory, and synchronization:

Information	Memory	Synchronization
addressSize	allocateMemory	compareAndSwapInt
pageSize	copyMemory	monitorEnter
	freeMemory	monitorExit
	getAddress	putOrderedEdit
	getInt	tryMonitorEnter
	putInt	

The `sun.misc.Unsafe` class was earmarked for removal in Java 9. There was actually some opposition to this decision in the programming industry. To put their concerns to rest, the class has been depreciated, but will not be completely removed. A special flag can be sent to the JVM to utilize the original API.

Eliding depreciation warnings on import statements [JEP 211]

This is one of the more simplistic JEPs for Java 9. Quite often, when we compile our programs, we receive many warnings and errors. The compiler errors must be fixed as they are typically syntactical in nature. The warnings, on the other hand, should be reviewed and appropriately addressed. Some of the warning messages are ignored by developers.

This JEP provides slight relief in the number of warnings we receive. Specifically, depreciation warnings caused by import statements are no longer generated. Prior to Java 9, we could suppress deprecated warning messages with the following annotation:

```
@SupressWarnings
```

Now, with Java 9, the compiler will suppress depreciated warnings if one or more of the following cases is true:

- If the `@Deprecated` annotation is used
- If the `@SuppressWarnings` annotation is used
- If the use of the warning-generating code and the declaration are within the ancestor class
- If the use of the warning-generating code is within an import statement

The fourth condition listed was an addition in Java 9.

Milling Project Coin [JEP 213]

Project Coin was a feature set of minor changes introduced in Java 7. These changes are listed as follows:

- Strings in `switch` statements
- Binary integral literals
- Using underscores in numeric literals
- Implementing multi-catch
- Allowing for more precise re-throwing of exceptions
- Generic instance creation improvements
- Addition of the `try-with-resources` statement
- Improvements to invoking `varargs` methods

Detailed information can be found in the following Oracle presentation: `http://www.oracle.com/us/technologies/java/project-coin-428201.pdf`.

JEP 213 focused on improvements to Project Coin's enhancements. There were five such enhancements, each detailed as follows.

Using the @SafeVarargs annotation

In Java 9, we can use the `@SafeVarargs` annotation with private instance methods. When we use this annotation, we are asserting that the method does not contain any harmful operations on the `varargs` passed as parameters to the method.

The syntax for usage is:

```
@SafeVarargs // this is the annotation
static void methodName(...)
{

    /*
    The contents of the method or constructor must not
    perform any unsafe or potentially unsafe operations
    on the varargs parameter or parameters.
    */

}
```

Use of the `@SafeVarargs` annotation is restricted to:

- Static methods
- Final instance methods
- Private instance methods

The try-with-resource statement

The `try-with-resource` statement previously required a new variable to be declared for each resource in the statement when a final variable was used. Here is the syntax for the `try-with-resource` statement prior to Java 9 (in Java 7 or 8):

```
try ( // open resources )
{
  // use resources
} catch (// error)
{  // handle exceptions
}
// automatically close resources
```

Here is a code snippet using the preceding syntax:

```
try ( Scanner xmlScanner = new Scanner(new File(xmlFile));
{
   while (xmlScanner.hasNext())
   {
      // read the xml document and perform needed operations
   }
   xmlScanner.close();
} catch (FileNotFoundException fnfe)
   {
      System.out.println("Your XML file was not found.");
   }
```

Now, with Java 9, the `try-with-resource` statement can manage final variables without requiring a new variable declaration. So, we can now rewrite the earlier code, as shown here in Java 9:

```
Scanner xmlScanner = new Scanner(newFile(xmlFile));
try ( while (xmlScanner.hasNext())
{
   {
      // read the xml document and perform needed operations
   }
    xmlScanner.close();
} catch (FileNotFoundException fnfe)
   {
      System.out.println("Your XML file was not found.");
   }
```

As you can see, the `xmlScanner` object reference is contained inside the `try-with-resource` statement block, which provides for automatic resource management. The resource will automatically be closed as soon as the `try-with-resource` statement block is exited.

> You can also use a `finally` block as part of the `try-with-resource` statement.

Using the diamond operator

Introduced in Java 9, the diamond operator can be used with anonymous classes if the inferred data type is denotable. When a data type is inferred, it suggests that the Java Compiler can determine the data types in a method's invocation. This includes the declaration and any included arguments.

> The diamond operator is the less-than and greater-than symbol pair (<>). It is not new to Java 9; rather, the specific use with anonymous classes is.

The diamond operator was introduced in Java 7 and made instantiating generic classes simpler. Here is a pre-Java 7 example:

```
ArrayList<Student> roster = new ArrayList<Student>();
```

Then, in Java 7, we could rewrite it:

```
ArrayList<Student> roster = new ArrayList<>();
```

The problem was that this method could not be used for anonymous classes. Here is an example in Java 8 that works fine:

```
public interface Example<T>
{
  void aMethod()
  {
    // interface code goes here
  }
}

Example example = new Example<Integer>()
{
  @Override
  public void aMethod()
  {
    // code
  }
};
```

While the preceding code works fine, when we change it to use the diamond operator, as shown here, a compiler error will occur:

```
public interface Example<T>
{
```

```
    void aMethod()
    {
      // interface code goes here
    }
  }

  Example example = new Example<>()
  {
    @Override
    public void aMethod()
    {
      // code
    }
  };
```

The error results from using the diamond operator with anonymous inner classes. Java 9 to the rescue. While the preceding code results in a compile time error in Java 8, it works fine in Java 9.

Discontinuing use of the underscore

The underscore character (_) can no longer be used as a legal identifier name. Earlier attempts to remove the underscore in an identifier name were incomplete. The use of such would generate a combination of errors and warnings. With Java 9, the warnings are now errors. Consider the following sample code:

```
public class Java9Tests
{
  public static void main(String[] args)
  {
    int _ = 319;
    if ( _ > 300 )
    {
      System.out.println("Your value us greater than 300.");
    }
    else
    {
      System.out.println("Your value is not greater than 300.");
    }
  }
}
```

The preceding code, in Java 8, will result in compiler warnings for `int _ = 319;` and `if ( _ > 300 )` statements. The warning is *as of release 9, '_' is a keyword, and may not be used as an identifier*. So, in Java 9, you will not be able to use the underscore by itself as a legal identifier.

> **TIP**
>
> It is considered bad programming practice to use identifier names that are not self-descriptive. So, the use of the underscore character by itself as an identifier name should not be a problematic change.

Making use of private interface methods

Lambda expressions were a big part of the Java 8 release. As a follow-up to that improvement, private methods in interfaces are now feasible. Previously, we could not share data between non-abstract methods of an interface. With Java 9, this data sharing is possible. Interface methods can now be private. Let's look at some sample code.

This first code snippet is how we might code an interface in Java 8:

```
. . .
public interface characterTravel
{
  pubic default void walk()
  {
    Scanner scanner = new Scanner(System.in);
    System.out.println("Enter desired pacing: ");
    int p = scanner.nextInt();
    p = p +1;
  }
  public default void run()
  {
    Scanner scanner = new Scanner(System.in);
    System.out.println("Enter desired pacing: ");
    int p = scanner.nextInt();
    p = p +4;
  }
  public default void fastWalk()
  {
    Scanner scanner = new Scanner(System.in);
    System.out.println("Enter desired pacing: ");
    int p = scanner.nextInt();
    p = p +2;
  }
  public default void retreat()
```

```
  {
    Scanner scanner = new Scanner(System.in);
    System.out.println("Enter desired pacing: ");
    int p = scanner.nextInt();
    p = p - 1;
  }
  public default void fastRetreat()
  {
    Scanner scanner = new Scanner(System.in);
    System.out.println("Enter desired pacing: ");
    int p = scanner.nextInt();
    p = p - 4;
  }
}
```

Now, in Java 9, we can rewrite this code. As you can see next, the redundant code has been moved into a single private method called `characterTravel`:

```
. . .
public interface characterTravel
{
  pubic default void walk()
  {
    characterTravel("walk");
  }
  public default void run()
  {
    characterTravel("run");
  }
  public default void fastWalk()
  {
    characterTravel("fastWalk");
  }
  public default void retreat()
  {
    characterTravel("retreat");
  }
  public default void fastRetreat()
  {
    characterTravel("fastRetreat");
  }
  private default void characterTravel(String pace)
  {
    Scanner scanner = new Scanner(System.in);
    System.out.println("Enter desired pacing: ");
    int p = scanner.nextInt();
    if (pace.equals("walk"))
```

```
{
  p = p +1;
}
else if (pace.equals("run"))
{
  p = p + 4;
}
else if (pace.equals("fastWalk"))
{
  p = p + 2;
}
else if (pace.equals("retreat"))
{
  p = p - 1;
}
else if (pace.equals("fastRetreat"))
{
  p = p - 4;
}
else
{
  //
}
```

Processing import statements correctly [JEP 216]

JEP 216 was issued as a fix to javac in regards to how import statements are processed. Prior to Java 9, there were instances where the order of import statements would impact if the source code was accepted or not.

When we develop applications in Java, we typically add import statements as we need them, resulting in an unordered list of import statements. IDEs do a great job of color-coding import statements that are not used, as well as informing us of import statements we need but that have not been included. It should not matter what order the import statements are in; there is no applicable hierarchy.

javac compiles classes in two primary steps. Specific to handling import statements, these steps are type resolution and member resolution. The type resolution consists of a review of the abstract syntax tree to identify declarations of classes and interfaces. The member resolution includes determining the class hierarchy and individual class variables and members.

With Java 9, the order we list import statements in our classes and files will no longer impact the compilation process. Let's look at an example:

```
package samplePackage;

import static SamplePackage.OuterPackage.Nested.*;
import SamplePackage.Thing.*;

public class OuterPackage
{
  public static class Nested implements Inner
  {
    // code
  }
}

package SamplePackage.Thing;

public interface Inner
{
  // code
}
```

In the preceding example, type resolution occurs and results in the following realizations:

- `SamplePackage.OuterPackage` exists
- `SamplePackage.OuterPackage.Nested` exists
- `SamplePackage.Thing.Innner` exists

The next step is member resolution, and this is where the problem existed prior to Java 9. Here is an overview of the sequential steps javac would use to conduct the member resolution for our sample code:

1. Resolution of `SamplePackage.OuterPackage` begins.
2. The `SamplePackage.OuterPackage.Nested` import is processed.
3. Resolution of the `SamplePackage.Outer.Nested` class begins.
4. The inner interface is type checked, although, because it is not in scope at this point, inner cannot be resolved.
5. Resolution of `SamplePackage.Thing` begins. This step includes importing all member types of `SamplePackage.Thing` into scope.

So the error occurs, in our example, because `Inner` is out of scope when resolution is attempted. If steps 4 and 5 were swapped, it would not have been a problem.

The solution to the problem, implemented in Java 9, was to break the member resolution steps into additional sub-steps. Here are those steps:

1. Analyze the import statements.
2. Create the hierarchy (class and interfaces).
3. Analyze class headers and type parameters.

Summary

In this chapter, we covered changes in Java 9 with regards to variable handlers and how they relate to the Atomic Toolkit. We also covered depreciation warnings and why they are now suppressed under specific circumstances. Five enhancements to changes introduced with Java 7 as part of Project Coin were also reviewed. Finally, we explored the improvements to import statement processing.

In the next chapter, we will examine the structure of a Java module as specified by Project Jigsaw. We will take a deep dive into how Project Jigsaw is implemented as part of the Java platform. Code snippets from a sample e-commerce application are used throughout the chapter to demonstrate Java 9's modular system. Internal changes to the Java platform, in regards to the modular system, are also discussed.

4
Building Modular Applications with Java 9

In the last chapter, we covered changes in Java 9 with regards to variable handlers and how they related to the AtoMiC Toolkit. We also covered depreciation warnings and why they are now suppressed under specific circumstances. Five enhancements to changes introduced with Java 7 as part of *Project Coin* were also reviewed. Finally, we explored the improvements to import statement processing.

In this chapter, we will examine the structure of a Java module as specified by *Project Jigsaw*. We will take a deep-dive into how *Project Jigsaw* is implemented as part of the Java platform. We will also review key internal changes to the Java platform as they relate to the modular system.

The topics we will cover here are:

- An introduction to Java modularity
- Review of the Java platform's module system
- Modularizing JDK source code
- Modular runtime images
- Getting to know the module system
- Modular Java application packaging
- The Java linker
- Encapsulation of internal APIs

A modular primer

Before we dive into the Java 9 enhancements in this chapter, let's examine what modularity is in the context of Java.

We can define the term **modular** as a type of design or construction, in our context, of computer software. This type of software design involves a set of modules that collectively comprise the whole. A house, for example, can be built as a single structure or in a modular fashion where each room is constructed independently and joined to create a home. With this analogy, you could selectively add or not add modules in the creation of your home. The collection of modules, in our analogy, becomes the design of your home. Your design does not need to use every module, only the ones you want. So, for example, if there are basement and bonus room modules and your design does not include those modular rooms, those modules are not used to build your home. The alternative would be that every home would include every room, not just the ones that are used. This, of course, would be wasteful. Let's see how that correlates to software.

This concept can be applied to computer architecture and software systems. Our systems can be comprised of several components instead of one behemoth system. As you can likely imagine, this provides us with some specific benefits:

- We should be able to scale our Java applications to run on small devices
- Our Java applications will be smaller
- Our modular code can be more targeted
- Increased use of the object-oriented programming model
- Additional opportunities for encapsulation
- Our code will be more efficient
- Java applications will have increased performance
- Overall system complexity is reduced
- Testing and debugging is easier
- Code maintenance is easier

The shift to a modular system for Java was necessary for several reasons. Here are the primary conditions of the Java platform as of Java 9 that led to the creation of the module system for the Java 9 platform:

- The **Java Development Kit (JDK)** was simply too big. This made it difficult to support small devices. Even with the compact profiles discussed in the next section, supporting some small devices was difficult at best and, in some cases, not possible.
- Due to the over-sized JDK, it was difficult to support truly optimized performance with our Java applications. In this case, smaller is better.
- The **Java Runtime Environment (JRE)** was too large to efficiently test and maintain our Java applications. This results in time consuming, inefficient testing, and maintenance operations.
- The **Java Archive (JAR)** files were also too large. This made supporting small devices problematic.
- Because the JDK and JRE were all encompassing, security was of great concern. Internal APIs, for example, that were not used by the Java application, were still available due to the nature of the public access modifier.
- Finally, our Java applications were unnecessarily large.

Modular systems have the following requirements:

- There must be a common interface to permit interoperability among all connected modules
- Isolated and connected testing must be supported
- Compile time operations must be able to identify which modules are in use
- Runtime support for modules

A module is a new concept and component in Java 9; it is a named collection of data and code. Specifically, modules are a collection of:

- Packages
- Classes
- Interfaces
- Code
- Data
- Resources

Key to successful implementation, a module in Java 9 is self-described in its modular declaration. Module names must be unique and typically use the reverse domain name schema. Here is an example declaration:

```
module com.three19.irisScan { }
```

Module declarations are contained in a `module-info.java` file that should be in the module's root folder. As one might expect, this file is compiled into a `module-info.class` file and will be placed in the appropriate output directory. These output directories are established in the module source code.

In the next sections, we will look at specific changes for Java 9 in regards to modularity.

Reviewing Java's platform module system [JEP-200]

The core aim of JEP-200 was to modularize the **Java Development Kit** (**JDK**) using the **Java Platform Module System** (**JPMS**). Prior to Java 9, our familiarity with the JDK includes awareness of its major components:

- Java runtime environment (JRE)
- The interpreter (java)
- Compiler (javac)
- The archiver (jar)
- Document generator (javadoc)

The task of modularizing the JDK was to break it into components that could be combined at compile time or runtime. The modular structure is based on the following modular profiles established as compact profiles in Java 8. Each of the three profiles is detailed in the following tables:

Compact profile 1:

java.io	java.lang.annotation	java.lang.invoke
java.lang.ref	lava.lang.reflect	java.math
java.net	java.nio	java.nio.channels
java.nio.channels.spi	java.nio.charset	java.nio.charset.spi
java.nio.file	java.nio.file.attribute	java.nio.file.spi

java.security	java.security.cert	java.security.interfaces
java.security.spec	java.text	java.text.spi
java.time	java.time.chrono	java.time.format
java.time.temporal	java.time.zone	java.util
java.util.concurrent	java.util.concurrent.atomic	java.util.concurrent.locks
java.util.function	java.util.jar	java.util.logging
java.util.regex	java.util.spi	java.util.stream
java.util.zip	javax.crypto	javax.crypto.interfaces
javax.crypto.spec	javax.net	javax.net.ssl
javax.script	javax.security.auth	javax.security.auth.callback
javax.security.auth.login	javax.security.auth.spi	javax.security.auth.spi
javax.security.auth.x500	javax.security.cert	

Compact profile 2:

java.rmi	java.rmi.activation	java.rmi.dgc
java.rmi.registry	java.rmi.server	java.sql
javax.rmi.ssl	javax.sql	javax.transaction
javax.transaction.xa	javax.xml	javax.xml.database
javax.xml.namespace	javax.xml.parsers	javax.xml.stream
javax.xml.stream.events	javax.xml.stream.util	javax.xml.transform
javax.xml.transform.dom	javax.xml.transform.sax	javax.xml.transform.stax
javax.xml.transform.stream	javax.xml.validation	javax.xml.xpath
org.w3c.dom	org.w3c.dom.bootstrap	org.w3c.dom.events
org.w3c.dom.ls	org.xml.sax	org.xml.sax.ext
org.xml.sax.helpers		

Compact profile 3:

java.lang.instrument	java.lang.management	java.security.acl
java.util.prefs	javax.annotation.processing	javax.lang.model
javax.lang.model.element	javax.lang.model.type	javax.lang.model.util
javax.management	javax.management.loading	javax.management.modelmbean
javax.management.monitor	javax.management.openmbean	javax.management.relation
javax.management.remote	javax.management.remote.rmi	javax.management.timer
javax.naming	javax.naming.directory	javax.naming.event
javax.naming.ldap	javax.naming.spi	javax.security.auth.kerberos
javax.security.sasl	javax.sql.rowset	javax.sql.rowset.serial
javax.sql.rowest.spi	javax.tools	javax.xml.crypto
javax.xml.crypto.dom	javax.xml.crypto.dsig	javax.xml.crypto.dsig.dom
javax.xml.crypto.dsig.keyinfo	javax.xml.crypto.dsig.spec	org.ieft.jgss

The three compact module profiles represent the basis for the standardized modular system in Java 9. The effectiveness of this standardization relies on the following six principles:

- All JCP-governed modules must start with the string `java.`. So, if a module on spatial utilities was being developed it would have a name such as `java.spatial.util`.

> **JCP** refers to the **Java Community Process**. JCP allows developers to create technical specifications for Java. You can learn more about JCP and become a member at the official JCP website--`http://www.jcp.org`.

- Non-JCP modules are considered part of the JDK and their names must start with the string `jdk.`.
- Ensure method invocation chaining works properly. This is best illustrated with the following flowchart:

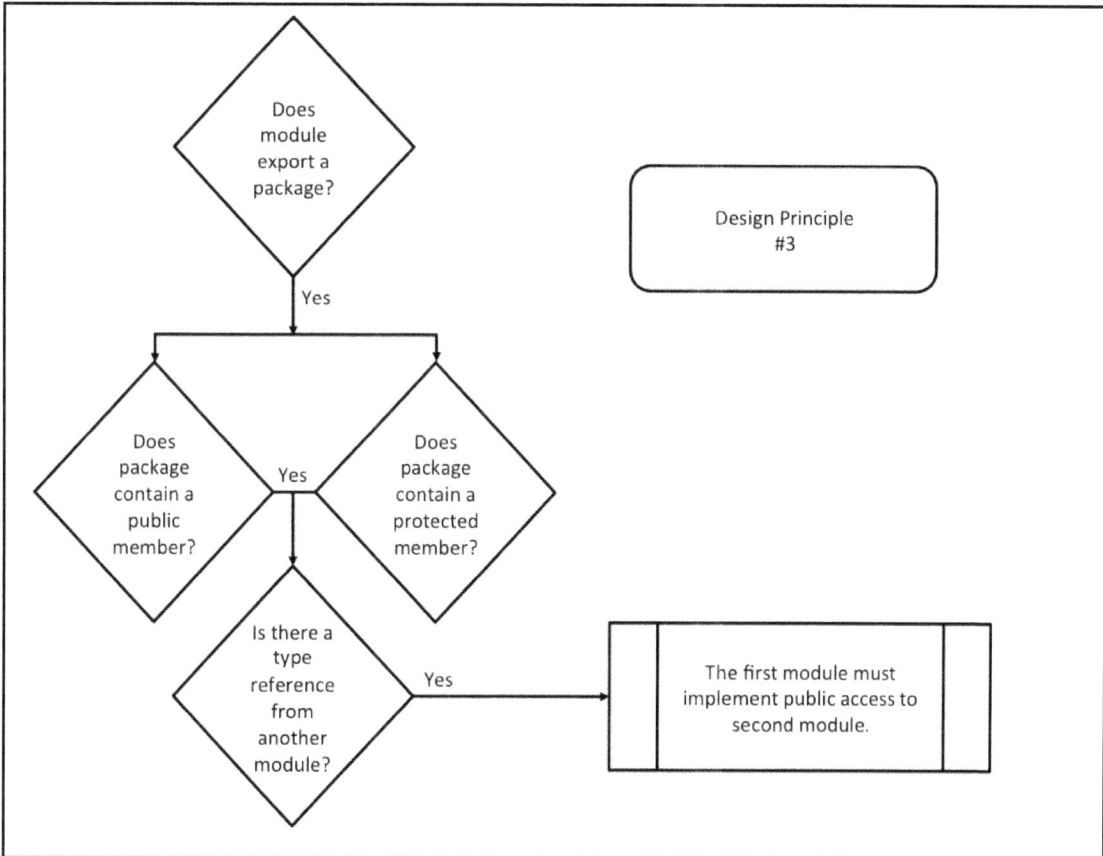

As you can see in the preceding flowchart, it only applies to modules that export a package.

- The fourth principle deals with both standard and non-standard API packages being used in a standard module. The following flowchart illustrates the implementation of this principle's covenants:

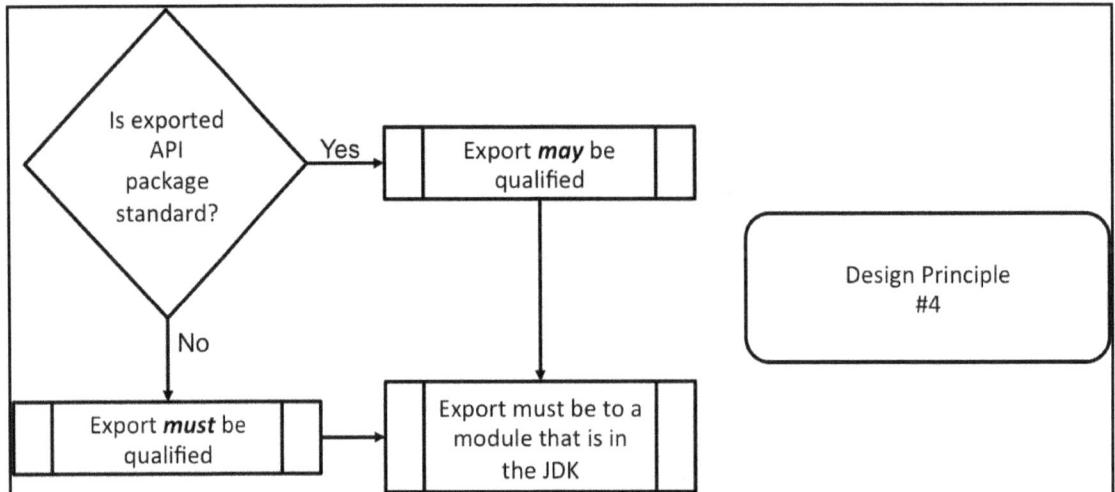

- The fifth design principle is that standard modules can be dependent upon more than one non-standard module. While this dependency is permitted, implied readability access to non-standard modules is not.
- The final design principle ensures non-standard modules do not export standard API packages.

Modularizing JDK source code [JEP-201]

As previously mentioned, Project Jigsaw had the goal of modularization. The envisioned standard modular system would be applied to the Java SE platform and the JDK. In addition to efficiency gains, the modular shift would result in better security and ease maintainability. The enhancement detailed in JEP-201 focused on JDK source code reorganization. Let's take a closer look.

Reorganizing the JDK's source code is a significant task and was accomplished with the following subset of goals:

- Provide JDK developers insights and familiarity with the new Java 9 modular system. So, this goal was aimed at developers of the JDK, not mainstream developers.
- Ensure modular boundaries are established and maintained throughout the JDK build process. This was a necessary precaution so the modular system would be stable throughout Java 9's enhancements and, more specifically, in implementing the modular system.
- The third goal was to ensure future enhancements, specifically with *Project Jigsaw*, could be easily integrated into the new modular system.

The significance of this source code reorganization cannot be overstated. The pre-Java 9 source code organization is 20 years old. This overdue JDK source code reorganization will make the code much easier to maintain. Let's look at the previous organization of the JDK source code and then examine the changes.

Pre-Java 9 JDK source code organization

The JDK is a compilation of code files, tools, libraries, and more. The following illustration provides an overview of the JDK components:

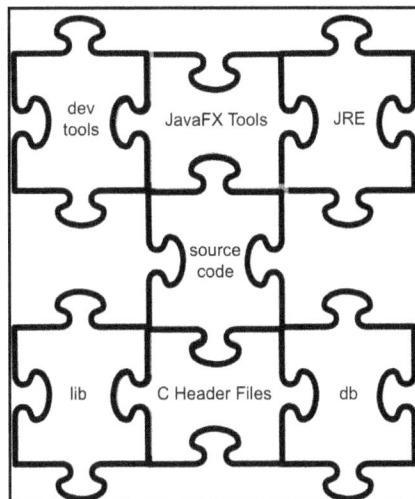

The pre-Java 9 organization of the JDK components in the preceding illustration are detailed in the next seven subsections.

Development tools

The development tools are located in the `bin` directory. These tools include seven broad categorizations, each detailed in the subsequent sections.

Deployment

This is a set of tools intended to help deploy Java applications:

- `appletviewer`: This tool gives you the ability to run and debug Java applets without the need for a web browser.
- `extcheck`: This tool allows you to find conflicts in JAR files.
- `jar`: This tool is used for creating and manipulating JAR files. JAR files are Java Archive files.
- `java`: This is the Java application launcher.
- `javac`: This is the Java Compiler.
- `javadoc`: This tool generates API documentation.
- `javah`: This tool allows you to write native methods; it generates C header files.
- `javap`: This tool disassembles class files.
- `javapackager`: For signing and packaging Java applications, including JavaFX.
- `jdb`: This is the Java debugger.
- `jdeps`: This is an analyzer for Java class dependencies.
- `pack200`: This is a tool that compresses JAR files into `pack200` files. The compression ratio using this tool is impressive.
- `unpack200`: This tool unpacks `pack200` files resulting in JAR files.

Internationalization

If you are interested in creating localizable applications, the following tool might come in handy:

- `native2ascii`: This tool creates Unicode Latin-1 from normal text.

Monitoring

Monitoring tools used for providing JVM performance data include:

- jps: This is the **JVM process status tool** (**jps**). It provides a list of HotSpot JVMs on a specific system.
- jstat: This is the JVM statistics monitoring tool. It collects log data and performance information from a machine with a HotSpot JVM.
- jstatd: This is the **jstat** daemon tool. It runs an RMI server app for monitoring HotSpot JVM operations.

RMI

RMI tools are **Remote Method Invocation** tools. They help developers create applications that operate over a network to include the internet:

- rmic: This tool can generate stubs and skeletons for objects over a network
- rmiregistry: This is a registry service for remote objects
- rmid: This tool is an activation system daemon for RMI
- serialver: This tool returns the class serialVersionUID value

Security

This set of security tools empowers developers to create security policies that can be enforced on the developer's computer system as well as on remote systems:

- keytool: This tool manages security certificates and keystores
- jarsigner: This tool generates and verifies JAR signatures for creating/opening JAR files
- policytool: This tool has a graphical user interface that helps developers manage their security policy files

Troubleshooting

These experimental troubleshooting tools are useful for very specific troubleshooting. They are experimental and, therefore, not officially supported:

- jinfo: This tool provides configuration information for specific processes, files, or servers.

- `jhat`: This is a heap dump tool. It instantiates a web server so that a heap can be viewed with a browser.
- `jmap`: This displays heap and shared object memory maps from a process, file, or server.
- `jsadebugd`: This is Java's Serviceability Agent Debug Daemon. It acts as a debug server for a process or file.
- `jstack`: This is a Java Stack Trace tool that provides a thread stack trace for a process, file, or server.

Web services

This set of tools provides a utility that can be used with **Java Web Start** and other web services:

- `javaws`: This is a command line tool that launches Java Web Start.
- `schemagen`: This tool generates schemas for Java architecture. These schemas are used for XML binding.
- `wsgen`: This tool is used for generating JAX-WS artifacts that are portable.
- `wsimport`: This tool is used for importing portable JAX-WS artifacts.
- `xjc`: This is the binding compiler that is used for XML binding.

JavaFX tools

The JavaFX tools are located in a few different places including `bin`, `man`, and `lib` directories.

Java runtime environment

The **Java runtime environment** (JRE) is located in the `jre` directory. Key contents include the **Java Virtual Machine** (JVM) and class libraries.

Source code

The JDK's source code, pre-Java 9, has the following basic organizational schema:

```
source code / [shared, OS-specific] / [classes / native] / Java API
    package name / [.file extension]
```

Let's look at this a bit closer. After the source code, we have two options. If the code is cross-platform, then it is a shared directory; otherwise, it is operating system specific. For example:

```
src/share/...
src/windows/...
```

Next, we have the classes directory or a native language directory. For example:

```
src/share/classes/...
src/share/classes/java/...
```

Next, we have the name of the Java API package followed by the file extension. The file extensions depend on content such as `.java`, `.c`, and more.

Libraries

The `lib` directory houses class libraries that are needed by one or more of the development tools in the `bin` directory. Here is a list of files in a typical Java 8 `lib` directory:

```
Command Prompt

C:\Program Files\Java\jdk1.8.0_121\lib>dir
 Volume in drive C is OS
 Volume Serial Number is 608F-FF3F

 Directory of C:\Program Files\Java\jdk1.8.0_121\lib

02/06/2017  09:41 AM    <DIR>          .
02/06/2017  09:41 AM    <DIR>          ..
02/06/2017  09:41 AM         1,896,072 ant-javafx.jar
02/06/2017  09:41 AM        17,426,940 ct.sym
02/06/2017  09:41 AM           163,047 dt.jar
02/06/2017  09:41 AM            18,432 ir.idl
02/06/2017  09:41 AM            36,038 javafx-mx.jar
02/06/2017  09:41 AM             1,682 jawt.lib
02/06/2017  09:41 AM           407,728 jconsole.jar
02/06/2017  09:41 AM           741,084 jvm.lib
02/06/2017  09:41 AM    <DIR>          missioncontrol
02/06/2017  09:41 AM               640 orb.idl
02/06/2017  09:41 AM             4,646 packager.jar
02/06/2017  09:41 AM         2,419,817 sa-jdi.jar
02/06/2017  09:41 AM        18,238,573 tools.jar
02/06/2017  09:41 AM    <DIR>          visualvm
              12 File(s)     41,354,699 bytes
               4 Dir(s)  884,427,616,256 bytes free

C:\Program Files\Java\jdk1.8.0_121\lib>
```

Reviewing the directory listing does not provide a great level of granular insight. We can list the classes contained in any of the `.jar` files with the following command--`jar tvf fileName.jar`. As an example, here is the class listing generated from executing `jar tvf javafx-mx.jar` at the command line:

```
Command Prompt

C:\Program Files\Java\jdk1.8.0_121\lib>jar tvf javafx-mx.jar
     0 Mon Dec 12 12:01:10 CST 2016 META-INF/
    25 Mon Dec 12 12:01:10 CST 2016 META-INF/MANIFEST.MF
     0 Mon Dec 12 12:00:54 CST 2016 com/
     0 Mon Dec 12 12:00:54 CST 2016 com/oracle/
     0 Mon Dec 12 12:00:54 CST 2016 com/oracle/javafx/
     0 Mon Dec 12 12:00:56 CST 2016 com/oracle/javafx/jmx/
   963 Mon Dec 12 12:00:54 CST 2016 com/oracle/javafx/jmx/MXExtensionImpl.class
   667 Mon Dec 12 12:00:54 CST 2016 com/oracle/javafx/jmx/SGMXBean.class
   728 Mon Dec 12 12:00:56 CST 2016 com/oracle/javafx/jmx/SGMXBeanImpl$1.class
 12268 Mon Dec 12 12:00:56 CST 2016 com/oracle/javafx/jmx/SGMXBeanImpl.class
     0 Mon Dec 12 12:00:56 CST 2016 com/oracle/javafx/jmx/json/
   744 Mon Dec 12 12:00:56 CST 2016 com/oracle/javafx/jmx/json/ImmutableJSONDocument.class
  1052 Mon Dec 12 12:00:56 CST 2016 com/oracle/javafx/jmx/json/JSONDocument$IteratorWrapper.class
  1068 Mon Dec 12 12:00:56 CST 2016 com/oracle/javafx/jmx/json/JSONDocument$Type.class
 11846 Mon Dec 12 12:00:56 CST 2016 com/oracle/javafx/jmx/json/JSONDocument.class
   893 Mon Dec 12 12:00:56 CST 2016 com/oracle/javafx/jmx/json/JSONException.class
   936 Mon Dec 12 12:00:56 CST 2016 com/oracle/javafx/jmx/json/JSONFactory.class
  1973 Mon Dec 12 12:00:56 CST 2016 com/oracle/javafx/jmx/json/JSONReader$EventType.class
   800 Mon Dec 12 12:00:56 CST 2016 com/oracle/javafx/jmx/json/JSONReader.class
   590 Mon Dec 12 12:00:56 CST 2016 com/oracle/javafx/jmx/json/JSONWriter$Container.class
  1115 Mon Dec 12 12:00:56 CST 2016 com/oracle/javafx/jmx/json/JSONWriter$ContainerType.class
  4781 Mon Dec 12 12:00:56 CST 2016 com/oracle/javafx/jmx/json/JSONWriter.class
     0 Mon Dec 12 12:00:56 CST 2016 com/oracle/javafx/jmx/json/impl/
  1288 Mon Dec 12 12:00:56 CST 2016 com/oracle/javafx/jmx/json/impl/JSONMessages.class
  4966 Mon Dec 12 12:00:56 CST 2016 com/oracle/javafx/jmx/json/impl/JSONScanner.class
  2273 Mon Dec 12 12:00:56 CST 2016 com/oracle/javafx/jmx/json/impl/JSONStreamReaderImpl$1.class
  8241 Mon Dec 12 12:00:56 CST 2016 com/oracle/javafx/jmx/json/impl/JSONStreamReaderImpl.class
  5486 Mon Dec 12 12:00:56 CST 2016 com/oracle/javafx/jmx/json/impl/JSONSymbol.class
   916 Mon Dec 12 12:00:56 CST 2016 com/oracle/javafx/jmx/json/impl/JSONMessagesBundle.properties
  1968 Mon Dec 12 12:00:56 CST 2016 com/oracle/javafx/jmx/json/impl/JSONMessagesBundle_ja.properties
  1284 Mon Dec 12 12:00:56 CST 2016 com/oracle/javafx/jmx/json/impl/JSONMessagesBundle_zh_CN.properties

C:\Program Files\Java\jdk1.8.0_121\lib>
```

C header files

The `/include` directory contains C header files. These files primarily support the following:

- **Java Native Interface (JNI)**: This is used for native-code programming support. The JNI is used to embed Java native methods and the JVM into native apps.
- **JVM Tool Interface (JVM TI)**: This is used by tools for state inspections and execution control for apps running the JVM.

Database

The Apache Derby relational database is stored in the /db directory. You can learn more about Java DB at the following sites:

```
http://docs.oracle.com/javadb/support/overview.html
```

```
http://db.apache.org/derby/manuals/#docs_10.11
```

JDK source code reorganized

In a previous section, you learned that the pre-Java 9 source code organization schema was as follows:

```
source code / [shared, OS-specific] / [classes / native] / Java API
  package name / [.file extension]
```

In Java 9, we have a new modular schema. That schema follows:

```
source code / module / [shared, OS-specific] / [classes / native /
configuration] / [ package / include / library ] /
  [.file extension]
```

There are a few differences in the new schema, most notably the module name. After the shared or OS-specific directory, there is either the classes directory, the native directory for C or C++ source files, or a configuration directory. This seemingly rudimentary organization schema changes results in a much more maintainable code base.

Understanding modular run-time images [JEP-220]

Java 9's modular system required changes to the runtime images for compatibility. Benefits of these changes include enhancements in the following areas:

- Maintainability
- Performance
- Security

Core to these changes was a new URI schema used for resource naming. These resources include modules and classes.

> A **Uniform Resource Identifier** (**URI**) is similar to a **URL** (**Uniform Resource Locator**) in that it identifies the name and location of something. For a URL, that something is a web page; for a URI, it is a resource.

There were five primary goals for JEP-220 and these are detailed in the following sections.

Runtime format adoption

A run-time format was created for Java 9, for adoption by stored classes and other resource files. This format is applicable for stored classes and resources under the following circumstances:

- When the new run-time format has greater efficiencies (time and space) than the pre-Java 9 JAR format.

> A **JAR** file is a **Java ARchieve** file. This is a compressed file format based on the legacy ZIP format.

- When stored classes and other resources can be individually isolated and loaded.
- When JDK and library classes and resources can be stored. This includes app modules as well.
- When they are devised in such a way as to promote future enhancements. This requires them to be extensible, documented, and flexible.

Runtime image restructure

There are two types of runtime images in Java--JDK and JRE. With Java 9, both of these image types were restructured to differentiate between files that can be used and modified by users to internal files that can be used but not modified by developers and their apps.

The JDK build system, prior to Java 9, produces both a JRE and a JDK. The JRE is a complete implementation of the Java platform. The JDK includes the JRE as well as other tools and libraries. A notable change in Java 9 is that the JRE subdirectory is no longer part of the JDK image. This change was made, in part, to ensure both image types (JDK and JRE) have identical image structures. With a common and reorganized structure, future changes will be more efficiently integrated.

> If you created custom plugins prior to Java 9 that address a specific structure, your app might not work in Java 9. This is also true if you are explicitly addressing `tools.jar`.

The following diagram provides a high-level view of the contents of each image before Java 9's release:

JRE Image	JDK Image
• bin • lib	• jre • bin • demo • sample • man • include • lib

The Java 9 runtime images are illustrated in the following diagram. As shown, a full JDK image contains the same directories as a modular runtime image as well as demo, sample, man, and includes directories:

Modular RunTime Image	Full JDK Image
• bin • conf • lib	• bin • conf • lib • demo • sample • man • include

There is no longer a difference between a JRE or JDK image. Now, with Java 9, a JDK image is a JRE image that contains a full set of dev tools.

Supporting common operations

Developers occasionally must write code that performs operations requiring access to the runtime image. Java 9 includes support for these common operations. This is possible due to the restructuring and standardized JDK and JRE runtime image structures.

De-privileging JDK classes

Java 9 allows privilege revocation for individual JDK classes. This change strengthens system security in that it ensures JDK classes only receive the permissions required for system operations.

Preserving existing behaviors

The final goal of the JEP-220 was to ensure currently existing classes are not negatively impacted. This refers to applications that do not have dependencies on internal JDK or JRE runtime images.

Getting to know the module system [JEP-261]

The purpose of this JEP was the implementation of the new module system for the Java platform. You will recall that the modular system was created to provide reliable configuration and strong encapsulation for Java programs. Key to this implementation was the concept of link time. As illustrated here, link time is an optional phase in between compile time and runtime. This phase allows the assembly of the appropriate modules into an optimized runtime image. This is possible, in part, due to the jlink linking tool which you will learn more about later in this chapter:

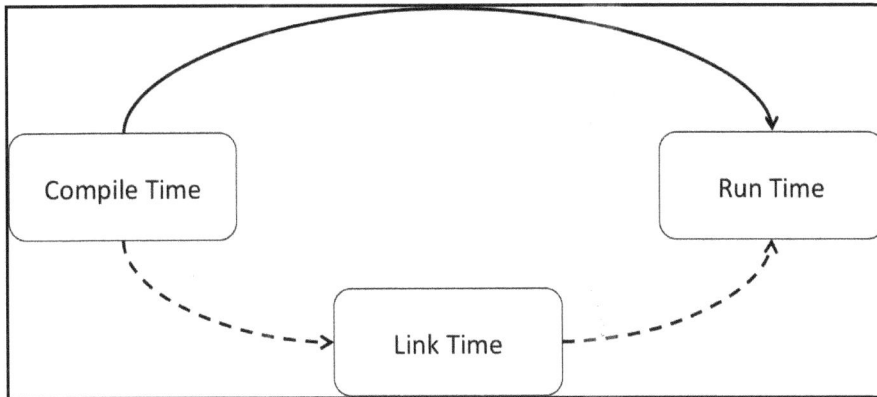

Module paths

It is important to organize modules so that they can be easily located. The module path, a sequence of module components or directories, provides the organizational structure used by searches. These path components are searched for in order, returning the first path component that comprises a module.

Modules and their paths should not be considered to be the same as packages or class paths. They are indeed different and have a greater level of fidelity. The key difference is that, with classpaths, a singular component is searched for. Module path searches return complete modules. This type of search is possible by searching the following paths, in the presented order, until a module is returned:

- Compilation module path
- Upgrade module path
- System modules
- Application module path

Let's briefly review each of these paths. The compilation module path is only applicable at compile time and contains the module definitions. The upgrade module path has the compiled module definitions. The system modules are built-in and include Java SE and JDK modules. The final path, the application module path, has the compiled module definitions from the application modules as well as the library modules.

Access-control boundary violations

As a professional developer, you always want your code to be secure, portable, and bug-free, which requires strict adherence to Java constructs such as encapsulation. There are occasions, such as with white box testing, that you need to break the encapsulation that the JVM mandates. This mandate permits cross-modular access.

To permit breaking the encapsulation, you can add an `add-exports` option in your module declaration. Here is the syntax you will use:

```
module com.three19.irisScan
{
  - - add-exports <source-module>/<package> = <target-module>
  (, <target-module> )*
}
```

Let's take a closer look at the preceding syntax. The `<source-module>` and `<target-module>` are module names and `<package>` is the name of the package. Using the `add-exports` option permits us to violate access-control boundaries.

There are two rules regarding using the add-exports option:

- It can be used multiple times in a module
- Each use must be of a unique pairing of `<source-module>` and `<target-module>`

> It is not recommended that the add-exports option be used unless absolutely necessary. Its use permits dangerous access to a library module's internal API. This type of use makes your code dependent on the internal API not changing, which is beyond your control.

Runtime

The HotSpot virtual machine implements the `<options>` for the `jmod` and `jlink` command-line tools. Here is the list of `<options>` for the `jmod` command-line tool:

```
■■■ Command Prompt                                                    —    □    ×

C:\Program Files\Java\jdk-9\bin>jmod --help
Usage: jmod (create|extract|list|describe|hash) <OPTIONS> <jmod-file>

Main operation modes:
  create    - Creates a new jmod archive
  extract   - Extracts all the files from the archive
  list      - Prints the names of all the entries
  describe  - Prints the module details
  hash      - Records hashes of tied modules.

Option                               Description
------                               -----------
 --class-path <path>                 Application jar files|dir containing
                                       classes
 --cmds <path>                       Location of native commands
 --config <path>                     Location of user-editable config files
 --dir <path>                        Target directory for extract
 --dry-run                           Dry run of hash mode
 --exclude <pattern-list>            Exclude files matching the supplied
                                       comma separated pattern list, each
                                       element using one the following
                                       forms: <glob-pattern>, glob:<glob-
                                       pattern> or regex:<regex-pattern>
 -h, --help                          Print this usage message
 --hash-modules <regex-pattern>      Compute and record hashes to tie a
                                       packaged module with modules
                                       matching the given <regex-pattern>
                                       and depending upon it directly or
                                       indirectly. The hashes are recorded
                                       in the JMOD file being created, or a
                                       JMOD file or modular JAR on the
                                       module path specified the jmod hash
                                       command.
 --header-files <path>               Location of header files
 --help-extra                        Print help on extra options
 --legal-notices <path>              Location of legal notices
 --libs <path>                       Location of native libraries
 --main-class <class-name>           Main class
 --man-pages <path>                  Location of man pages
 --module-version <module-version>   Module version
 -p, --module-path <path>            Module path
 --target-platform <target-platform> Target platform
 --version                           Version information
 @<filename>                         Read options from the specified file

C:\Program Files\Java\jdk-9\bin>_
```

Here is the list of `<options>` for the `jlink` command-line tool:

```
Command Prompt                                                        —    □    ×

C:\Program Files\Java\jdk-9\bin>jlink --help
Usage: jlink <options> --module-path <modulepath> --add-modules <module>[,<module>...]
Possible options include:
        --add-modules <mod>[,<mod>...]   Root modules to resolve
        --bind-services                  Link in service provider modules and
                                         their dependences
    -c, --compress=<0|1|2>               Enable compression of resources:
                                             Level 0: No compression
                                             Level 1: Constant string sharing
                                             Level 2: ZIP
        --disable-plugin <pluginname>    Disable the plugin mentioned
        --endian <little|big>            Byte order of generated jimage
                                         (default:native)
    -h, --help                           Print this help message
        --ignore-signing-information     Suppress a fatal error when signed
                                         modular JARs are linked in the image.
                                         The signature related files of the
                                         signed modular JARs are not copied to
                                         the runtime image.
        --launcher <name>=<module>[/<mainclass>]
                                         Add a launcher command of the given
                                         name for the module and the main class
                                         if specified
        --limit-modules <mod>[,<mod>...] Limit the universe of observable
                                         modules
        --list-plugins                   List available plugins
    -p, --module-path <path>             Module path
        --no-header-files                Exclude include header files
        --no-man-pages                   Exclude man pages
        --output <path>                  Location of output path
        --save-opts <filename>           Save jlink options in the given file
    -G, --strip-debug                    Strip debug information
        --suggest-providers [<name>,...] Suggest providers that implement the
                                         given service types from the module path
    -v, --verbose                        Enable verbose tracing
        --version                        Version information
        @<filename>                      Read options from file

C:\Program Files\Java\jdk-9\bin>
```

Modular Java application packaging [JEP-275]

One of the great improvements in Java 9 is the size of the runtime binaries generated by the **Java Packager**. This is possible in part due to the **Java Linker**, which is covered in the next section. The Java Packager's workflow has essentially remained the same in Java 9 as it was in Java 8. There have been, as you will see later in this section, new tools added to the workflow.

The Java Packager solely creates JDK 9 applications. This change to the Java Packager is intended to streamline and make the process of generating runtime images more efficient. So, the Java Packager will only create runtime images for the SDK version that it is associated with.

Advanced look at the Java Linker

Prior to the Java Linker tool, jlink, introduced in Java 9, runtime image creation included copying the entire JRE. Then, unused components are removed. Simply put, jlink facilitates the creation of runtime images with only the required modules. jlink is used by the Java Packager to generate an embedded runtime image.

Java Packager options

The syntax for the Java Packager is as follows:

```
javapackager -command [-options]
```

There are five different commands (-command) that can be used. They are described as follows:

command	Description
-createbss	This command is used for converting files from CSS to binary
-createjar	This command, used along with additional parameters, creates a JAR archive file
-deploy	This command is used to generate jnlp and HTML files
-makeall	Combines the -createjar, -deploy, and compilation steps
-signJar	This command creates and signs a JAR file

The [-options] for the -createbss command include:

```
-outdir <dir>
        name of the directory to generate output file to.
-srcdir <dir>
        Base dir of the files to pack.
-srcfiles <files>
        List of files in srcdir. If omitted, all files in srcdir (which
        is a mandatory argument in this case) will be used.
```

The [-options] for the -createjar command include:

```
-appclass <application class>
        qualified name of the application class to be executed.
-preloader <preloader class>
        qualified name of the preloader class to be executed.
-paramfile <file>
        properties file with default named application parameters.
-argument arg
        An unnamed argument to be put in <fx:argument> element in the JNLP
        file.
-classpath <files>
        list of dependent jar file names.
-manifestAttrs <manifest attributes>
        List of additional manifest attributes. Syntax: "name1=value1,
        name2=value2,name3=value3.
-noembedlauncher
        If present, the packager will not add the JavaFX launcher classes
        to the jarfile.
-nocss2bin
        The packager won't convert CSS files to binary form before copying
        to jar.
-runtimeversion <version>
        version of the required JavaFX Runtime.
-outdir <dir>
        name of the directory to generate output file to.
-outfile <filename>
        The name (without the extension) of the resulting file.
-srcdir <dir>
        Base dir of the files to pack.
-srcfiles <files>
        List of files in srcdir. If omitted, all files in srcdir (which
        is a mandatory argument in this case) will be packed.
```

The `[-options]` for the `-deploy` command include:

```
-native <type>
        generate self-contained application bundles (if possible).
        If type is specified then only bundle of this type is created.
        List of supported types includes: installer, image, exe, msi, dmg, pkg, rpm, deb.
-name <name>
        name of the application.
-appclass <application class>
        qualified name of the application class to be executed.
-outdir <dir>
        name of the directory to generate output file to.
-outfile <filename>
        The name (without the extension) of the resulting file.
-srcdir <dir>
        Base dir of the files to pack.
-srcfiles <files>
        List of files in srcdir. If omitted, all files in srcdir (which
        is a mandatory argument in this case) will be used.
-m <modulename>[/<mainclass>]
--module <modulename>[/<mainclass>]
        the initial module to resolve, and the name of the main class
        to execute if not specified by the module
-p <module path>
--module-path <module path>...
        A : separated list of directories, each directory
        is a directory of modules.
--add-modules <modulename>[,<modulename>...]
        root modules to resolve in addition to the initial module
--limit-modules <modulename>[,<modulename>...]
        limit the universe of observable modules
--strip-native-commands <true/false>
        include or exclude the native commands
-title <title>
        title of the application.
-vendor <vendor>
        vendor of the application.
-description <description>
        description of the application.
-embedjnlp
        If present, the jnlp file will be embedded in the html document.
-embedCertificates
        If present, the certificates will be embedded in the jnlp file.
-allpermissions
        If present, the application will require all security permissions
        in the jnlp file.
-updatemode <updatemode>
        sets the update mode for the jnlp file.
-isExtension
        if present, the srcfiles are treated as extensions.
```

Here are the remaining [-options] for the -deploy command:

```
-callbacks
        specifies user callback methods in generated HTML. The format is
        "name1:value1,name2:value2,..."
-templateInFilename
        name of the html template file. Placeholders are in form of
        #XXXX.YYYY(APPID)#
-templateOutFilename
        name of the html file to write the filled-in template to.
-templateId
        Application ID of the application for template processing.
-argument arg
        An unnamed argument to be put in <fx:argument> element in the JNLP
        file.
-preloader <preloader class>
        qualified name of the preloader class to be executed.
-paramfile <file>
        properties file with default named application parameters.
-htmlparamfile <file>
        properties file with parameters for the resulting applet.
-width <width>
        width of the application.
-height <height>
        height of the application.
```

The [-options] for the -makeall command include:

```
-appclass <application class>
        qualified name of the application class to be executed.
-preloader <preloader class>
        qualified name of the preloader class to be executed.
-classpath <files>
        list of dependent jar file names.
-name <name>
        name of the application.
-width <width>
        width of the application.
-height <height>
        height of the application.
-v      enable verbose output.
```

The [-options] for the -signJar include:

```
-keyStore <file>
        Keystore filename.
-alias
        Alias for the key.
-storePass
        Password to check integrity of the keystore or unlock the keystore.
-keyPass
        Password for recovering the key.
-storeType
        Keystore type, the default value is "jks".
-outdir <dir>
        name of the directory to generate output file(s) to.
-srcdir <dir>
        Base dir of the files to signed.
-srcfiles <files>
        List of files in srcdir. If omitted, all files in srcdir (which
        is a mandatory argument in this case) will be signed.
```

The Java Packager is divided into two modules:

```
jdk.packager
jdk.packager.services
```

JLink - The Java Linker [JEP-282]

The Java Linker, commonly referred to as JLink, is a tool that was created to create custom runtime images. This tool collects the appropriate modules along with their dependencies, then optimizes them to create the image. This represents a big change for Java, with the release of Java 9. Before the Java Linker tool, jlink, was available, runtime image creation included initially copying the entire JRE. In a subsequent step, the unused components were removed. In Java 9, jlink creates runtime images with only the needed modules. jlink is used by the Java Packager to generate an embedded runtime image.

As illustrated in a previous section, JEP-282 resulted in link time as an optional phase between compile time and runtime. It is in this phase that the appropriate modules are assembled into an optimized runtime image.

JLink is a command-line linking tool that permits the creation of runtime images containing a smaller subset of the JDK modules. This results in smaller runtime images. The following syntax consists of four components--the jlink command, options, the module path, and the output path:

```
$ jlink <options> ---module-path <modulepath> --output <path>
```

Here is a list of the options that can be used with the `jlink` tool along with brief descriptions of each:

```
Command Prompt                                                          —   □   ×
C:\Program Files\Java\jdk-9\bin>jlink --help
Usage: jlink <options> --module-path <modulepath> --add-modules <module>[,<module>...]
Possible options include:
        --add-modules <mod>[,<mod>...]     Root modules to resolve
        --bind-services                    Link in service provider modules and
                                           their dependences
  -c, --compress=<0|1|2>                   Enable compression of resources:
                                              Level 0: No compression
                                              Level 1: Constant string sharing
                                              Level 2: ZIP
        --disable-plugin <pluginname>      Disable the plugin mentioned
        --endian <little|big>              Byte order of generated jimage
                                           (default:native)
  -h, --help                               Print this help message
        --ignore-signing-information       Suppress a fatal error when signed
                                           modular JARs are linked in the image.
                                           The signature related files of the
                                           signed modular JARs are not copied to
                                           the runtime image.
        --launcher <name>=<module>[/<mainclass>]
                                           Add a launcher command of the given
                                           name for the module and the main class
                                           if specified
        --limit-modules <mod>[,<mod>...]   Limit the universe of observable
                                           modules
        --list-plugins                     List available plugins
  -p, --module-path <path>                 Module path
        --no-header-files                  Exclude include header files
        --no-man-pages                     Exclude man pages
        --output <path>                    Location of output path
        --save-opts <filename>             Save jlink options in the given file
  -G, --strip-debug                        Strip debug information
        --suggest-providers [<name>,...]   Suggest providers that implement the
                                           given service types from the module path
  -v, --verbose                            Enable verbose tracing
        --version                          Version information
        @<filename>                        Read options from file

C:\Program Files\Java\jdk-9\bin>
```

The module path tells the linker where to find the modules. The linker will not use exploded modules or JAR/JMOD files.

The output path simply informs the linker where to save the custom run-time image.

Encapsulating most internal APIs [JEP-260]

JEP-260 was implemented to make the Java platform more secure. The core of this JEP's goal was to encapsulate the majority of internal APIs. Specifically, most of the JDK's internal APIs are no longer accessible by default. Currently, internal APIs deemed to be *critical* and *widely-used* remain accessible. In the future, we are likely to see functionality to replace them, and at that time, those internal APIs will not be accessible by default.

So, why is this change necessary? There are a few widely-used APIs that are unstable and, in some cases, not standardized. Unsupported APIs should not have access to internal details of the JDK. Therefore, JEP-260 resulted in increased security of the Java platform. Generally speaking, you should not use unsupported APIs in your development projects.

The aforementioned critical APIs (internal to the JDK) are:

- `sun.misc`
- `sun.misc.Unsafe`
- `sun.reflect.Reflection`
- `sun.reflect.ReflectionFactory.newConstrutorForSerialization`

The aforementioned critical internal APIs are still accessible in JDK 9. They will be accessible with the `jdk.unsupported` JDK module. Full JRE and JDK images will contain the `jdk.unsupported` module.

> You can use the Java Dependency Analysis Tool, `jdeps`, to help determine if your Java program has any dependencies on JDK internal APIs.

This is an interesting change to watch. It is likely that the currently accessible internal APIs will not be accessible by default when Java 10 is released.

Summary

In this chapter, we examined the structure of Java modules as specified by *Project Jigsaw* and took an in-depth look at how *Project Jigsaw* was implemented to improve the Java platform. We also reviewed key internal changes to the Java platform as they relate to the modular system. Our review started with a modular primer where we learned about Java 9's modular system in terms of benefits and requirements.

We explored how Java 9 introduced modularity to the JDK including its source code and organization of the same. The seven primary tool categories that make up the JDK were also explored. As we learned, modularity in Java 9 also extends to runtime images resulting in more maintainability, better performance, and increased security. The concept of **link time** was introduced as an optional phase between compile-time and runtime. We concluded the chapter with a look at the Java Linker and how Java 9 encapsulates internal APIs.

In the next chapter, we will explore how to migrate our existing applications to the Java 9 platform. We will look at both manual and semi-automated migration processes.

Migrating Applications to Java 9 **5**

In the previous chapter, we took a close look at the structure of Java modules as specified by Project Jigsaw and examined how Project Jigsaw was implemented to improve the Java platform. We also reviewed key internal changes to the Java platform with specific focus on the new modular system. We started with a modular primer where we learned about Java 9's modular system in terms of benefits and requirements. Next, we explored how Java 9 introduced modularity to the JDK. This included a look at how the source code was reorganized for Java 9. We also explored the JDK's seven primary tool categories and learned that Java 9 modularity extends to runtime images resulting in more maintainability, better performance, and increased security. The concept of **link time** was introduced as an optional phase between compile-time and runtime. We concluded the chapter with a look at the **Java linker** and how Java 9 encapsulates internal APIs.

In this chapter, we will explore how to migrate our existing applications to the Java 9 platform. We will look at both manual and semi-automated migration processes. Java 9 is a major release with numerous changes to the JDK so developers should not be surprised if their Java 8 code no longer works with Java 9. This chapter aims to provide you with insights and processes to get your Java 8 code working with Java 9.

The topics we will cover in this chapter are:

- Quick review of Project Jigsaw
- How modules fit into the Java landscape
- Migration planning
- Advice from Oracle
- Useful tools

Quick review of Project Jigsaw

Project Jigsaw is the Java project that encompasses several change recommendations to the Java platform. As you have read in earlier chapters, Java 9's greatest changes involve modules and modularity. The initiative to move to modules in Java was driven by Project Jigsaw. The need for modularity stemmed from two major challenges with Java:

- Classpath
- JDK

Next, we will review both of those challenges and see how they were addressed and overcome with the new release to the Java platform, Java 9.

Classpath

Prior to Java 9, the classpath was problematic and the source of developer anguish. This was evident in the numerous developer forums and, fortunately, Oracle was paying attention. Here are the several instances in which the classpath can be problematic; here are two primary cases:

- The first case involves having two or more versions of a library on your development computer. The way this was previously handled by the Java system was inconsistent. Which library was used during the class loading process was anyone's guess. This resulted in an undesired lack of specificity--not enough details regarding which library was loaded.
- The second case is in exercising the most advanced features of the class loader. Often times, this type of class loader usage resulted in the most errors and bugs. These were not always easy to detect and resulted in a lot of extra work for developers.

Classpaths, before Java 9, were almost always very lengthy. Oracle, in a recent presentation, shared a classpath that contained 110 JAR files. This type of unwieldy classpath makes it difficult to detect conflicts or even determine if anything was missing and if so, what might be missing. The re-envisioning of the Java platform as a modular system made these classpath issues a thing of the past.

> Modules solve the pre-Java 9 classpath problem by providing reliable configuration.

The monolithic nature of the JDK

Java has continually evolved in an impressive fashion since 1995 and with each evolutionary step, the JDK grew larger. As with Java 8, the JDK had become prohibitively large. Prior to Java 9, there were several problematic issues stemming from the monolithic nature of the JDK, including:

- Because the JDK is so large, it does not fit on very small devices. In some development sectors this is enough reason to find a non-Java solution for software engineering problems.
- The oversized JDK resulted in waste. It was wasteful in terms of processing and memory when running on devices, networks, and the cloud. This stems from the fact that the entire JDK is loaded, even when only a small subset of the JDK is required.
- While the Java platform has great performance when running, the startup performance, in terms of load and launch times, leaves much to be desired.
- The vast number of internal APIs has also been a pain point. Because so many internal APIs existed and were used by developers, the system has been difficult to evolve.
- The existence of internal APIs has made it difficult to make the JDK secure and scalable. With so many internal dependencies, isolating security and scalability issues has been overly problematic.

The answer to the monolithic woes of the JDK is the module. Java 9 introduced the module and its own modular system. One of the great updates to the platform is that only the modules needed are compiled, as opposed to the entire JDK. This modular system is covered throughout this book.

> Modules solve the pre-Java 9 JDK monolithic issue by providing strong encapsulation.

How modules fit into the Java landscape

As you can see from the following illustration, packages are comprised of classes and interfaces, and modules are comprised of packages. Modules are a container of packages. This is the basic premise, at a very high level, of Java 9's new modular system. It is important to view modules as part of the modular system and not simply as a new level of abstraction above packages, as the illustration might suggest.

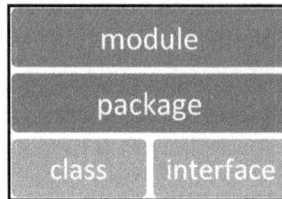

So, modules are new to Java 9 and they, as you would expect, require declaration before they can be used. A module's declaration includes names of other modules in which it has a dependency. It also exports packages for other modules that have dependencies to it. Modular declarations are arguably the most important modular issue to address as you start developing with Java 9. Here is an example:

```
module com.three19.irisScan
{
   // modules that com.three19.irisScan depends upon
   requires com.three19.irisCore;
   requires com.three19.irisData;

   // export packages for other modules that are dependent
      upon com.three19.irisScan
   exports com.three19.irisScan.biometric;
}
```

When programming a Java 9 application, your module declarations will be placed in a `module-info.java` file. Once this file is completed, you simply run `javac`, the Java Compiler, to generate the `module-info.class` Java class file. You accomplish this task in the same manner that you currently compile your `.java` files into `.class` files.

You can also create modular JAR files that have your `module-info.class` file at its root. This represents a great level of flexibility.

Base module

When programming Java 9 applications, or porting existing applications programmed with older versions of Java, the base module (`java.base`) must be used. Every module requires the `java.base` module because it defines the critical, or foundational, Java platform APIs. Here are the contents of the `java.base` module:

```
module java.base
{
  exports java.io;
  exports java.lang;
  exports java.lang.annotation;
  exports java.lang.invoke;
  exports java.lang.module;
  exports java.lang.ref;
  exports java.lang.reflect;
  exports java.math;
  exports java.net;
  exports java.net.spi;
  exports java.nio;
  exports java.nio.channels;
  exports java.nio.channels.spi;
  exports java.nio.charset;
  exports java.nio.charset.spi;
  exports java.nio.file;
  exports java.nio.file.attribute;
  exports java.nio.file.spi;
  exports java.security;
  exports java.security.aci;
  exports java.security.cert;
  exports java.security.interfaces;
  exports java.security.spec;
  exports java.text;
  exports java.text.spi;
  exports java.time;
  exports java.time.chrono;
  exports java.time.format;
  exports java.time.temporal;
  exports java.time.zone;
  exports java.util;
  exports java.util.concurrent;
  exports java.util.concurrent.atomic;
  exports java.util.concurrent.locks;
  exports java.util.function;
  exports java.util.jar;
  exports java.util.regex;
  exports java.util.spi;
```

```
    exports java.util.stream;
    exports java.util.zip;
    exports java.crypto;
    exports java.crypto.interfaces;
    exports java.crytpo.spec;
    exports java.net;
    exports java.net,ssi;
    exports java.security.auth;
    exports java.security.auth.callbak;
    exports java.security.auth.login;
    exports java.security.auth.spi;
    exports java.security.auth.x500;
    exports java.security.cert;
}
```

As you can see, the `java.base` module does not require any modules and it exports numerous packages. It can be useful to have a list of these exports handy so you know what is available to you as you start creating applications using the new Java platform, Java 9.

You will notice that in the previous section, we did not include the `requires java.base;` line of code in our declaration of our `com.three19.irisScan` module. The updated code is provided as follows and now includes the `requires java.base;` line of code:

```
module com.three19.irisScan
{
  // modules that com.three19.irisScan depends upon
  requires java.base; // optional inclusion
  requires com.three19.irisCore;
  requires com.three19.irisData;

  // export packages for other modules that are dependent
     upon com.three19.irisScan
  exports com.three19.irisScan.biometric;
}
```

If you do not include the `requires java.base;` line of code in your module declarations, the Java Compiler will automatically include it.

Reliable configuration

As suggested earlier in this chapter, modules provide a reliable configuration of our Java 9 applications that solves the classpath problem in earlier versions of the Java platform.

Java reads and interprets modular declarations making the modules readable. These readable modules permit the Java platform to determine if any modules are missing, if there are duplicate libraries declared, or there are any other conflicts. In Java 9, very specific error messages will be generated and output by the compiler or at runtime. Here is an example of a compile-time error:

```
src/com.three19.irisScan/module-info.java: error: module not found:
com.three19.irisScan
requires com.three19.irisCore;
        ^
1 error
```

Here is an example of a runtime error that would occur if the module `com.three19.isrisCore` was not found, but required by the `com.three19.irisScan` app:

```
Error occurred during initialization of VM
java.lang.module.ResolutionException: Module com.three19.irisCore not
found, required by com.three19.irisScan app
```

Strong encapsulation

Earlier in this chapter, you read that Java 9's strong encapsulation remedied the monolithic JDK issue. Encapsulation, in Java 9, is driven by the information in the `module-info.java` file. The information in this file lets Java know what modules are dependent upon others and what each of them exports. This underscores the importance of ensuring our `module-info-java` files are properly configured. Let's look at an example written with standard Java code, nothing new in Java 9 in the way this was coded:

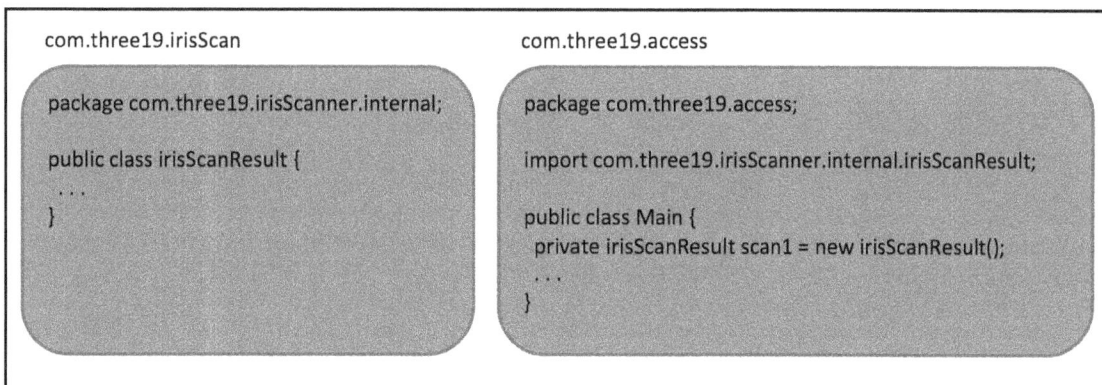

```
com.three19.irisScan

package com.three19.irisScanner.internal;

public class irisScanResult {
...
}
```

```
com.three19.access

package com.three19.access;

import com.three19.irisScanner.internal.irisScanResult;

public class Main {
  private irisScanResult scan1 = new irisScanResult();
...
}
```

In the preceding example, the `com.three19.irisScan` module has an `irisScanner` package intended for internal use and an `irisScanResult` class. If the `com.three19.access` application tries to import and use the `irisScanResult` class, the following error message will be produced by the Java Compiler:

```
src/com.three19.access/com/three19/access/Main.java: error: irisScanResult
is not accessible because package com.three19.irisScanner.internal is not
exported
  private irisSanResult scan1 = new irisScanResult();
                                    ^
1 error
```

If for some reason the compiler does not catch this error, although it would be very unlikely, the following runtime error would occur:

```
Exception in thread "main" java.lang.IllegalAccessError: class
com.three19.access.Main (in module: com.three19.access) cannot access class
com.three19.irisScanner.internal.irisScanResult (in module:
com.three19.irisScan), com.three19.irisScanner.internal is not exported to
com.three19.access.
```

The detailed error messages will make debugging and troubleshooting much easier.

Migration planning

The changes to the Java platform are significant and Java 9 is considered a major release. It would be naive to think our current Java applications will work seamlessly on Java 9. While that might be the case, at least for simple programs, it is prudent to plan ahead and consider the issues you are most likely to encounter. Before we look at these issues, let's test a simple Java application in the next section.

Testing a simple Java application

The following code consists of a single Java class, `GeneratePassword`. This class prompts the user for a desired password length and then generates a password based on the user's requested length. If the user asks for a length shorter than 8, the default length of 8 will be used. This code was written with the Java SE 1.7 JRE System Library:

```
/*
 * This is a simple password generation app
 */
```

```java
import java.util.Scanner;

public class GeneratePassword
{
  public static void main(String[] args)
  {
    // passwordLength int set up to easily change the schema
    int passwordLength = 8; //default value

    Scanner in = new Scanner(System.in);
    System.out.println("How long would you like your
     password (min 8)?");
    int desiredLength;
    desiredLength = in.nextInt();

    // Test user input
    if (desiredLength >8)
    {
      passwordLength = desiredLength;
    }

    // Generate new password
    String newPassword = createNewPassword(passwordLength);

    // Prepare and provide output
    String output = "nYour new " + passwordLength
     + "-character password is: ";
    System.out.println(output + newPassword);
  }

  public static String createNewPassword(int lengthOfPassword)
  {
    // Start with an empty String
    String newPassword = "";

    // Populate password
    for (int i = 0; i < lengthOfPassword; i++)
    {
      newPassword = newPassword + randomizeFromSet(
        "aAbBcCdDeEfFgGhHiIjJkKlLmMnNoOpPqQrRsStTuUvVwWxXyYzZ
        0123456789+-*/?!@#$%&");
    }

    return newPassword;
  }

  public static String randomizeFromSet(String characterSet)
  {
```

```
        int len = characterSet.length();
        int ran = (int)(len * Math.random());
        return characterSet.substring(ran, ran + 1);
    }
}
```

In the following screenshot, we test the `GeneratePassword` app on a Mac running Java 8. As you can see, we start by querying Java to verify the current version. In this test, Java `1.8.0_121` was used. Next, we compile the `GeneratePassword` Java file using the `javac` utility. Lastly, we run the app:

```
● ● ●                    🏠 edljr — -bash — 80×24
Edwards-iMac:~ edljr$ java -version
java version "1.8.0_121"
Java(TM) SE Runtime Environment (build 1.8.0_121-b13)
Java HotSpot(TM) 64-Bit Server VM (build 25.121-b13, mixed mode)
Edwards-iMac:~ edljr$
Edwards-iMac:~ edljr$
Edwards-iMac:~ edljr$ javac GeneratePassword.java
Edwards-iMac:~ edljr$
Edwards-iMac:~ edljr$
Edwards-iMac:~ edljr$ java GeneratePassword
How long would you like your password (min 8)?
32

Your new 32-character password is: B#CZy0z1Mq0WI@dkFfiuG9BrHw$w9KFg
Edwards-iMac:~ edljr$ ▮
```

As you can see from the preceding test, `GeneratePassword.java` was successfully compiled with the `GeneratePassword.class` file resulting. The application was run using the `java GeneratePassword` command. The user was prompted for a desired password length and `32` was entered. The application then successfully generated a 32-character random password and provided the appropriate output.

This test demonstrated the example application works successfully using JDK 1.8. Next, let's test the same application using JDK 9.

We start with the `java -version` command to show that we are using JDK 9 on this computer. The following screenshot shows that we successfully compiled the `.java` file to a `.class` file. When the application was run, it functioned as expected and provided the proper results:

```
C:\Users\elavi\Desktop>java -version
java version "9"
Java(TM) SE Runtime Environment (build 9+175)
Java HotSpot(TM) 64-Bit Server VM (build 9+175, mixed mode)

C:\Users\elavi\Desktop>javac GeneratePassword.java

C:\Users\elavi\Desktop>java GeneratePassword
How long would you like your password (min 8)?
32

Your new 32-character password is: t-Cu9%siptpw$sPlYVuDQnThuiEh#4vC

C:\Users\elavi\Desktop>
```

As you can see, we clearly demonstrated that a pre-Java 9 application has the potential to successfully run on Java 9 without having to make any modifications. This is a simple case study and featured a very basic Java program. This is, of course, the best case scenario, and cannot be assumed. You will want to test your applications to ensure they run as expected on the Java 9 platform.

In the next section, we will review some potential issues you might encounter when testing your pre-Java 9 applications using the new Java platform with JDK 9.

Potential migration issues

The potential migration issues featured in this section include direct access to the JRE, access to internal APIs, accessing internal JARs, JAR URL depreciation, the extension mechanism, and the JDK's modularization. Let's look at each of these potential migration issues.

The JRE

Creating the Java 9's modular system resulted in some simplification in respect to the number and location of development and utility tools. One such example is the JDK's consumption of the JRE. In all pre-Java 9 versions, the Java platform included the JDK and JRE as two separate components. In Java 9, these components have been combined. This is a significant change and one that developers should be keenly aware of. If you have an application that specifically points to the JRE directory, you will need to make changes to avoid problems. The JRE contents are shown as follows:

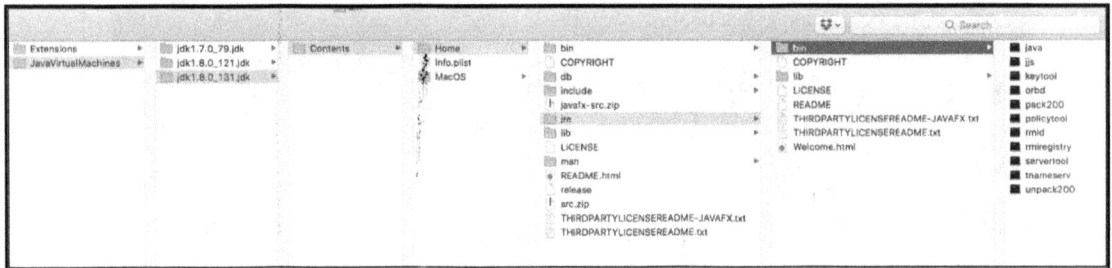

Access to internal APIs

The Java 9 platform has encapsulated internal APIs to increase security of the platform and applications written in Java. Applications that you program in Java 9 will not have default access to the JDK's internal APIs, unlike with previous versions of the Java platform. Oracle has identified some internal APIs as critical; those APIs remain accessible via the `jdk.unsupported` JDK module.

The aforementioned critical APIs (internal to the JDK) are:

- `sun.misc`
- `sun.misc.Unsafe`
- `sun.reflect.Reflection`
- `sun.reflect.ReflectionFactory.newConstrutorForSerialization`

If you have pre-Java 9 applications that implement any `sun.*` or `com.sun.*` package, you will likely run into problems migrating your applications to Java 9. In order to address this issue, you should review your class files for use of `sun.*` and `com.sun.*` packages. Alternatively, you can use the Java dependency analysis tool, `jdeps`, to help determine if your Java program has any dependencies on JDK internal APIs.

> The `jdeps` tool is the Java dependency analysis tool, that can be used to help determine if your Java program has any dependencies on JDK internal APIs.

Accessing internal JARs

Java 9 does not permit access to internal JARs such as `lib/ant-javax.jar`, `lib/dt.jar`, and others listed in the `lib` directory shown here:

```
ant-javafx.jar
ct.sym
dt.jar
ir.idl
javafx-mx.jar
jconsole.jar
missioncontrol
orb.idl
packager.jar
sa-jdi.jar
tools.jar
visualvm
```

The key thing to note here is that if you have Java applications that are dependent on one of these tools residing in the `lib` folder, you will need to modify your code accordingly.

> It is recommended that you test your IDE once you start using Java 9 to ensure the IDE is updated and officially supports Java 9. If you use more than one IDE for Java development, test each one to avoid surprises.

JAR URL depreciation

JAR file URLs were, prior to Java 9, used by some APIs to identify specific files in the runtime image. These URLs contain a `jar:file:` prefix with two paths; one to the `jar` and one to the specific resource file within the `jar`. Here is the syntax for the pre-Java 9 JAR URL:

```
jar:file:<path-to-jar>!<path-to-file-in-jar>
```

With the advent of Java 9's modular system, containers will house resource files instead of individual JARs. The new syntax for accessing resource files is as follows:

```
jrt:/<module-name>/<path-to-file-in-module>
```

A new URL schema, `jrt`, is now in place for naming resources within a runtime image. These resources include classes and modules. The new schema allows for the identification of a resource without introducing a security risk to the runtime image. This increased security ensures that the runtime image's form and structure remain concealed. Here is the new schema:

```
jrt:/[$MODULE[/$PATH]]
```

Interestingly, a `jrt` URL's structure determines its meaning, suggesting that the structure can take one of several forms. Here are three examples of different `jrt` URL structures:

- `jrt:/$MODULE/$PATH`: This structure provides access to the resource file, identified with the `$PATH` parameter, within the module specified with the `$MODULE` parameter
- `jrt:/$MODULE`: This structure provides reference to all resource files within the module specified with the `$MODULE` parameter
- `jrt:/`: This structure provides reference to all resource files in the runtime image

If you have preexisting code that uses URL instances, returned by APIs, you should not have any problems. On the other hand, if your code is dependent on the `jar` URL structure, you will have problems.

Extension mechanism

The Java platform previously had an extension mechanism that gave developers the ability to make custom APIs available to all applications. As you can see in the following illustration, extensions are plugins of sorts, or add-ons to the Java platform. The APIs and classes in each extension are, by default, automatically available:

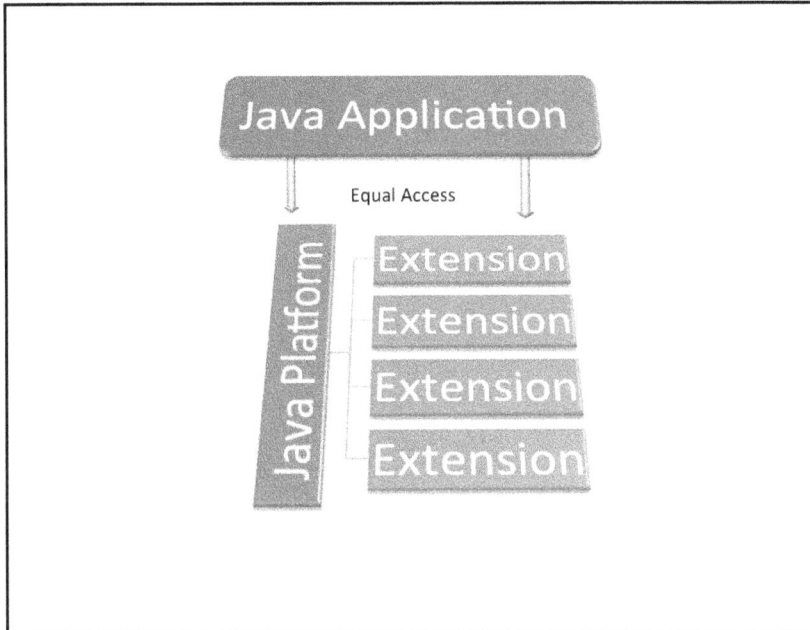

As the illustration suggests, Java applications have access both to the Java platform and extensions without requiring classpaths. This feature was depreciated in Java 8 and no longer exists in Java 9.

The JDK's modularization

By now, you have a firm appreciation of Java 9's modularization. The old adage in Java, and other object-oriented programming language, is *everything is a class*. Now, with Java 9, *everything is a module* is the new adage. There are three type of modules as explained as follows:

Module type	Description
Automatic	When a JAR is placed on a new module path, modules are automatically created
Explicit/Named	These modules are manually defined by editing the `module-info.java` file
Unnamed	When a JAR is placed on a classpath, unnamed modules are created

When you migrate your applications to Java 9, your application and its libraries become unnamed modules. So, you will need to ensure all the modules are in the module path.

Another thing to be aware of is that your runtime image will not contain the entire JDK. Instead, it will only contain the modules your application requires. It is worth reviewing how the JDK is modularized in Java 9. The following table contains the API specification for the JDK in Java 9:

`jdk.accessibility`	`jdk.attach`	`jdk.charsets`	`jdk.compiler`
`jdk.crypto.cryptoki`	`jdk.crypto.ec`	`jdk.dynalink`	`jdk.editpad`
`jdk.hotspot.agent`	`jdk.httpserver`	`jdk.incubator.httpclient`	`jdk.jartool`
`jdk.javadoc`	`jdk.jcmd`	`jdk.jconsole`	`jdk.jdeps`
`jdk.jdi`	`jdk.jdwp.agent`	`jdk.jlink`	`jdk.jshell`
`jdk.jsobject`	`jdk.jstatd`	`jdk.localedata`	`jdk.management`
`jdk.management.agent`	`jdk.naming.dns`	`jdk.naming.rmi`	`jdk.net`
`jdk.pack`	`jdk.packager.services`	`jdk.policytool`	`jdk.rmic`
`jdk.scripting.nashorn`	`jdk.sctp`	`jdk.security.auth`	`jdk.security.jgss`
`jdk.snmp`	`jdk.xml.dom`	`jdk.zipfs`	

The following table contains the API specification for Java SE in Java 9:

java.activation	java.base	java.compiler	java.cobra
java.datatransfer	java.desktop	java.instrument	java.logging
java.management	java.management.rmi	java.naming	java.prefs
java.rmi	java.scripting	java.se	java.se.ee
java.security.jgss	java.security.sasi	java.sql	java.sql.rowset
java.transaction	java.xml	java.xml.bind	java.xml.crypto
java.xml.ws	java.xml.ws	java.xml.ws.annotation	

> Remember, all applications will have access to `java.base` as it is in the module path by default.

The following table contains the API specification for JavaFX in Java 9:

javafx.base	javafx.controls	javafx.fxml	javafx.graphics
javafx.media	javafx.swing	javafx.web	

There are two additional modules:

- `java.jnlp` defines the API for **JNLP (Java Network Launch Protocol)**
- `java.smartcardio` defines the API for the Java Smart Card Input/Output

> For details on any of these modules, visit Oracle's *Java® Platform, Standard Edition & Java Development Kit Version 9 API Specification* website: `http://download.java.net/java/jdk9/docs/api/overview-summary.html`.

Advice from Oracle

Oracle has done a great job in bringing us this major update, version 9, to the Java platform. Their insights into getting ready for Java 9 and how to migrate to the new JDK is worth reviewing. In this section, we will look at preparatory steps, breaking encapsulation, changes to the runtime image, components such as tools and APIs that have been removed, changes to garbage collection, and deployment.

Preparatory steps

Oracle provides a five-step process to help developers migrate their Java applications to version 9. These steps are listed as follows and then covered in subsequent sections:

1. Get the JDK 9 early access build.
2. Run your program before recompiling.
3. Update third-party libraries and tools.
4. Compile your application.
5. Run `jdeps` on your code.

Getting the JDK 9 early access build

If you are reading this book before Java 9 is officially released, then you can obtain a JDK 9 early access build from here--`http://jdk.java.net/9/`. Early release builds are available for Windows (32 and 64), macOS (64), Linux (32 and 64) and various Linux ARM, Solaris, and Alpine Linux versions.

Taking the time to test your applications for Java 9 and get them migrated before Java 9 is officially released, helps ensure you will not experience any downtime for services that rely on your Java applications.

Running your program before recompiling

As indicated earlier in this chapter, there is a chance that your existing Java applications will run without modification on the Java 9 platform. So, before you make any changes, try running your current application on the Java 9 platform. If your application works fine on Java 9, that is great, but your work is not complete. Review the next three sections on updating third-party libraries and tools, compiling your application, and running `jdeps` on your code.

Updating third-party libraries and tools

Third-party libraries and tools can help extend our applications and shorten development time. For Java 9 compatibility, it is important to ensure that each third-party library and tool you use is compatible with and supports version 9 of the JDK. Running your application on Java 9 will not provide you with the level of insight you need to ensure you do not have compatibility issues down the road. It is recommended that you review the official website for each library and tool to verify compatibility with and support of JDK 9.

If a library or tool that you use does have a version that supports JDK 9, download and install it. If you find one that does not yet support JDK 9, consider finding a replacement for it.

In our context, tools includes **Integrated Development Environments** (**IDE**). NetBeans, Eclipse, and IntelliJ all have IDE versions that support JDK 9. Links to those sites are provided as follows:

- **NetBeans**: http://bits.netbeans.org/download/trunk/nightly/latest/
- **Eclipse**: https://www.eclipse.org/community/eclipse_newsletter/2015/june/article4.php
- **IntelliJ**: https://www.jetbrains.com/idea/nextversion/

Compiling your application

Your next step is to compile your application using JDK 9's `javac`. This is important, even if your app works fine on JDK 9. You might not receive compiler errors, but watch for warnings too. Here are the most common reasons your applications might not compile with JDK 9, assuming they compiled fine prior to Java 9.

First, as indicated earlier in this chapter, most of the JDK 9 internal APIs are not accessible by default. Your indication will be an `IllegalAccessErrors` error at runtime or compile time. You will need to update your code so that you are using accessible APIs.

A second reason your pre-Java 9 applications might not compile with JDK 9 is if you use the underscore character as a single character identifier. According to Oracle, this practice generates a warning in Java 8 and an error in Java 9. Let's look at an example. The following Java class instantiates an Object named _ and prints a singular message to the console:

```java
public class Underscore
{
  public static void main(String[] args)
  {
    Object _ = new Object();
    System.out.println("This ran successfully.");
  }
}
```

When we compile this program with Java 8, we receive a warning that use of '_' as an identifier might not be supported in releases after Java SE 8:

```
● ● ●                    🏠 edljr — -bash — 80×9
Edwards-iMac:~ edljr$ javac Underscore.java
Underscore.java:6: warning: '_' used as an identifier
                Object _ = new Object();
                       ^
   (use of '_' as an identifier might not be supported in releases after Java SE
8)
1 warning
Edwards-iMac:~ edljr$
```

As you can see in the following screenshot, that is just a warning and the application runs fine:

```
● ● ●                🏠 edljr — -bash — 46×5


Edwards-iMac:~ edljr$ java Underscore
This ran successfully.
Edwards-iMac:~ edljr$
```

Now, let's try compiling the same class using JDK 9:

```
■ Command Prompt                                              —    □    ×

C:\Users\elavi\Desktop>javac Underscore.java
Underscore.java:6: warning: '_' used as an identifier
                Object _ = new Object();
                       ^
   (use of '_' as an identifier might not be supported in releases after Java SE 8)
1 warning

C:\Users\elavi\Desktop>Java Underscore
This ran successfully.

C:\Users\elavi\Desktop>
```

As you can see, use of the underscore as a single character identifier still only resulted in a warning and not an error. The application ran successfully. This test was run when JDK 9 was still in early release. It is assumed that running this test once JDK 9 has been officially released will result in an error instead of just a warning. The error that would likely be thrown is as follows:

```
Underscore.java:2: error: as of release 9, '_' is a keyword, and may not be
used as a legal identifier.
```

Even if this issue is not resolved with the formal release of JDK 9, use of an underscore as a single character identifier is not good programming practice, so you should steer away from using it.

A third potential reason for your pre-Java 9 programmed application not to compile with JDK 9 is if you are using the -source and -target compiler options. Let's take a look at the -source and -target compiler options pre-Java 9 and with Java 9.

Pre-Java 9 -source and -target options

The -source option specifies the Java SE version and has the following acceptable values:

Value	Description
1.3	javac does not support features introduced after Java SE 1.3.
1.4	javac accepts code with language features introduced in Java SE 1.4.
1.5 or 5	javac accepts code with languages features introduced in Java SE 1.5.
1.6 or 6	javac reports encoding errors as errors instead of warnings. Of note, no new language features were intruded with Java SE 1.6.
1.7 or 7	javac accepts code with language features introduced in Java SE 1.7. This is the default value if the -source option is not used.

The -target option tells javac what version of the JVM to target. The acceptable values for the -target option are--1.1, 1.2, 1.3, 1.4, 1.5 or 5, 1.6 or 6 and 1.7 or 7. If the -target option is not used, the default JVM target is dependent on the value used with the -source option. Here is a table of -source values with their associated -target:

-source value	default -target
unspecified	1.7
1.2	1.4
1.3	1.4
1.4	1.4
1.5 or 5	1.7
1.6 or 6	1.7
1.7	1.7

Java 9 -source and -target options

In Java 9, the supported values are shown as follows:

Supported values	Remarks
9	This is the default, should no value be specified
8	Sets support to 1.8
7	Sets support to 1.7
6	Sets support to 1.6 and generates a warning (not an error) to indicate JDK 6 is depreciated

Running jdeps on your code

The jdeps class dependency analysis tool is not new to Java 9, but perhaps has never been as important to developers with the advent of Java 9. An important step to migrating your applications to Java 9 is to run the jdeps tool to determine the dependencies your applications and its libraries have. The jdeps tool does a great job of suggesting replacements if your code has dependencies on any internal APIs.

The following screenshot shows the options available to you when using the `jdeps` analyzer:

```
Command Prompt                                                    —    □    ×

C:\Users\elavi\Desktop>jdeps -help
Usage: jdeps <options> <classes...>
where <classes> can be a pathname to a .class file, a directory, a JAR file,
or a fully-qualified class name.  Possible options include:
  -dotoutput <dir>                    Destination directory for DOT file output
  -s             -summary             Print dependency summary only
  -v             -verbose             Print all class level dependencies
                                      Equivalent to -verbose:class -filter:none.
  -verbose:package                    Print package-level dependencies excluding
                                      dependencies within the same package by default
  -verbose:class                      Print class-level dependencies excluding
                                      dependencies within the same package by default
  -cp <path>     -classpath <path>    Specify where to find class files
  -p <pkgname> -package <pkgname>     Finds dependences matching the given package name
                                      (may be given multiple times)
  -e <regex>     -regex <regex>       Finds dependences matching the given pattern
                                      (-p and -e are exclusive)
  -f <regex>     -filter <regex>      Filter dependences matching the given pattern
                                      If given multiple times, the last one will be used.
  -filter:package                     Filter dependences within the same package (default)
  -filter:archive                     Filter dependences within the same archive
  -filter:none                        No -filter:package and -filter:archive filtering
                                      Filtering specified via the -filter option still applies.
  -include <regex>                    Restrict analysis to classes matching pattern
                                      This option filters the list of classes to
                                      be analyzed.  It can be used together with
                                      -p and -e which apply pattern to the dependences
  -P             -profile             Show profile or the file containing a package
  -apionly                            Restrict analysis to APIs i.e. dependences
                                      from the signature of public and protected
                                      members of public classes including field
                                      type, method parameter types, returned type,
                                      checked exception types etc
  -R             -recursive           Recursively traverse all dependencies.
                                      The -R option implies -filter:none.  If -p, -e, -f
                                      option is specified, only the matching dependences
                                      are analyzed.
  -jdkinternals                       Finds class-level dependences on JDK internal APIs.
                                      By default, it analyzes all classes on -classpath
                                      and input files unless -include option is specified.
                                      This option cannot be used with -p, -e and -s options.
                                      WARNING: JDK internal APIs may not be accessible in
                                      the next release.
  -version                            Version information

C:\Users\elavi\Desktop>
```

Let's take a look at an example. Here is a simple Java class called `DependencyTest`:

```java
import sun.misc.BASE64Encoder;

public class DependencyTest
{
    public static void main(String[] args) throws
     InstantiationException, IllegalAccessException
    {
      BASE64Encoder.class.newInstance();
      System.out.println("This Java app ran successfully.");
    }
}
```

Now, let's use javac to compile this class using Java 8:

```
                          ⬆ edljr — -bash — 85×14
Edwards-iMac:~ edljr$ javac DependencyTest.java
DependencyTest.java:1: warning: BASE64Encoder is internal proprietary API and may be
removed in a future release
import sun.misc.BASE64Encoder;
               ^
DependencyTest.java:6: warning: BASE64Encoder is internal proprietary API and may be
removed in a future release
               BASE64Encoder.class.newInstance();
               ^
2 warnings
Edwards-iMac:~ edljr$ java DependencyTest
This Java app ran successfully.
Edwards-iMac:~ edljr$
```

As you can see, Java 8 successfully compiled the class and the application ran. The compiler did give us a `DependencyTest.java:6: warning: BASE64Encoder is internal proprietary API and may be removed in a future release` warning. Now, let's see what happens when we try to compile this class using Java 9:

```
Command Prompt                                                          —  □  ×
C:\Users\elavi\Desktop>javac DependencyTest.java
DependencyTest.java:1: warning: BASE64Encoder is internal proprietary API and may be removed in a
 future release
import sun.misc.BASE64Encoder;
               ^
DependencyTest.java:6: warning: BASE64Encoder is internal proprietary API and may be removed in a
 future release
               BASE64Encoder.class.newInstance();
               ^
2 warnings
```

In this case, with Java 9, the compiler gave us two warnings instead of one. The first warning is for the `import sun.misc.BASE64Encoder;` statement and the second for the `BASE64Encoder.class.newInstance();` method call. As you can see, these are just warnings and not errors, so the `DependencyTest.java` class file is successfully compiled. Next, let's run the application:

```
Command Prompt                                                    —    □    ×

C:\Users\elavi\Desktop>java DependencyTest
Exception in thread "main" java.lang.NoClassDefFoundError: sun/misc/BASE64Encoder
        at DependencyTest.main(DependencyTest.java:6)
Caused by: java.lang.ClassNotFoundException: sun.misc.BASE64Encoder
        at java.base/jdk.internal.loader.BuiltinClassLoader.loadClass(Unknown Source)
        at java.base/jdk.internal.loader.ClassLoaders$AppClassLoader.loadClass(Unknown Source)
        at java.base/java.lang.ClassLoader.loadClass(Unknown Source)
        ... 1 more

C:\Users\elavi\Desktop>
```

Now, we can clearly see that Java 9 will not allow us to run the application. Next, let's run a dependency test using the `jdeps` analyzer tool. We will use the following command line syntax--`jdeps DependencyTest.class`:

```
Command Prompt                                                    —    □    ×

C:\Users\elavi\Desktop>jdeps DependencyTest.class
DependencyTest.class -> C:\Program Files\Java\jdk1.8.0_121\jre\lib\rt.jar
   <unnamed> (DependencyTest.class)
      -> java.io
      -> java.lang
      -> sun.misc                                    JDK internal API (rt.jar)

C:\Users\elavi\Desktop>
```

As you can see, we have three dependencies: `java.io`, `java.lang`, and `sun.misc`. Here we are given the suggestion to replace our `sun.misc` dependency with `rt.jar`.

Breaking encapsulation

The Java 9 platform is more secure than its predecessor versions due to, in part, the increased encapsulation that resulted from the modular reorganization. That being said, you might have a requirement to break through the modular system's encapsulation. Breaking through these access control boundaries is permitted by Java 9.

As you read earlier in this chapter, most internal APIs are strongly encapsulated. As previously suggested, you might look for replacement APIs when updating your source code. Of course, that is not always feasible. There are three additional approaches you can take--using the `--add-opens` option at runtime; employing the `--add-exports` option; and `--permit-illegal-access` command-line option. Let's look at each of those options.

The --add-opens option

You can use the `--add-opens` runtime option to allow your code to access non-public members. This can be referred to as deep reflection. Libraries that do this deep reflection are able to access all members, private and public. To grant this type of access to your code, you use the `--add-opens` option. Here is the syntax:

```
--add-opens module/package=target-module(,target-module)*
```

This allows the given module to open the specified package. The compiler will not produce any errors or warnings when this is used.

The --add-exports option

You can use `--add-exports` to break encapsulation so that you can use an internal API whose default is to be inaccessible. Here is the syntax:

```
--add-exports <source-module>/<package>=<target-module>(
,<target-module>)*
```

This command-line option gives code in the `<target-module>` access to types in the `<source-module>` package.

Another method of breaking encapsulation is with a JAR file's manifest. Here is an example:

```
--add-exports:java.management/sun.management
```

> The `--add-exports` command-line option should only be used if deemed absolutely necessary. It is not advisable to use this option except for short-term solutions. The danger of using it routinely is that any updates to referenced Internal APIs could result in your code not working properly.

The --permit-illegal-access option

A third option for breaking encapsulation is to use the `--permit-illegal-access` option. Of course, it is prudent to check with third-party library creators to see if they have an updated version. If that is not an option, you use `--permit-illegal-access` to gain illegal access to operations to be implemented on the classpath. Due to the significantly illegal operation here, you will receive warnings each time one of these operations occurs.

Runtime image changes

Java 9 represents a major change to the JDK and the JRE. Much of these changes are related to modularity and have been covered in other chapters. There are still a few more things you should consider.

Java version schema

With Java 9, the way the Java platform's version is displayed has changed. Here is an example of a pre-Java 9 version format:

```
Last login: Sat Jul 15 15:04:45 on ttys000
Edwards-iMac:~ edljr$ java -version
java version "1.8.0_121"
Java(TM) SE Runtime Environment (build 1.8.0_121-b13)
Java HotSpot(TM) 64-Bit Server VM (build 25.121-b13, mixed mode)
Edwards-iMac:~ edljr$
```

Now, let's look at how Java 9 reports its version:

```
C:\Users\elavi\Desktop>java -version
java version "9"
Java(TM) SE Runtime Environment (build 9+175)
Java HotSpot(TM) 64-Bit Server VM (build 9+175, mixed mode)

C:\Users\elavi\Desktop>
```

As you can see, with Java 9, the version schema is now `$MAJOR.$MINOR.$SECURITY.$PATCH`. This is markedly different than with previous versions of Java. This will only impact your applications if you have code that parses the string returned by the `java -version` command and option.

JDK and JRE layout

How files are organized in the JDK and the JRE have changed in the new version of Java. It is worth your time to familiarize yourself with the new filesystem layout. The following screenshot shows the file structure of the JDK's /bin folder:

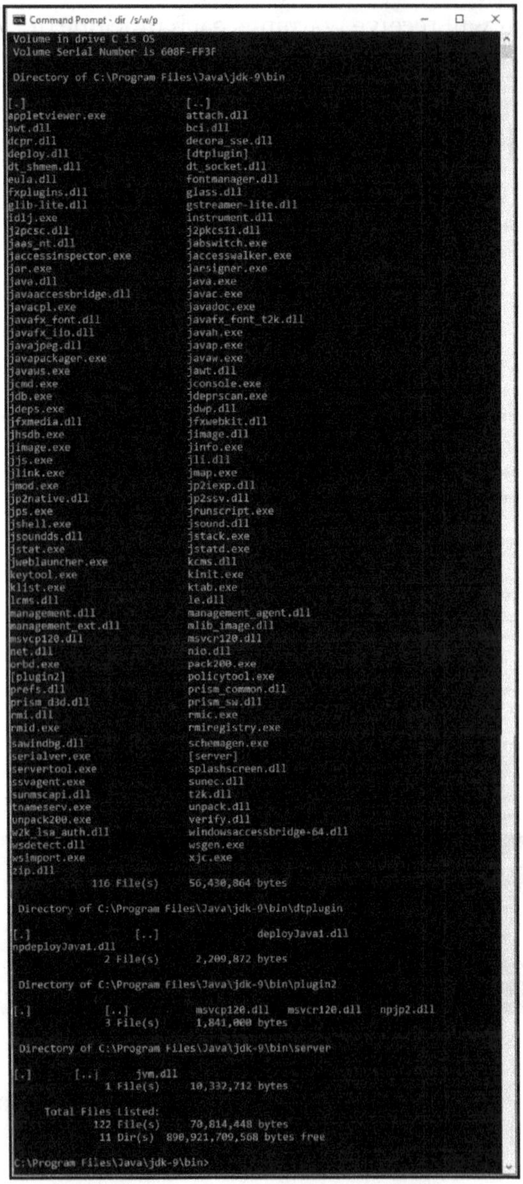

Here is the layout of the `lib` folder:

```
Command Prompt - dir /s/w/p                                          —    □    ×
 Volume in drive C is OS
 Volume Serial Number is 608F-FF3F

 Directory of C:\Program Files\Java\jdk-9\lib

[.]                             [..]
ant-javafx.jar                  classlist
ct.sym                          [deploy]
deploy.jar                      fontconfig.bfc
fontconfig.properties.src       [fonts]
java.jnlp.jar                   javacpl.cpl
javafx-swt.jar                  javafx.properties
javaws.jar                      jdk.deploy.jar
jdk.javaws.jar                  jdk.plugin.dom.jar
jdk.plugin.jar                  jrt-fs.jar
jvm.cfg                         jvm.lib
modules                         plugin-legacy.jar
plugin.jar                      psfont.properties.ja
psfontj2d.properties            sawindbg.dll.manifest
[security]                      [server]
src.zip                         tzdb.dat
tzmappings
            27 File(s)     249,507,799 bytes

 Directory of C:\Program Files\Java\jdk-9\lib\deploy

[.]                             [..]
messages.properties             messages_de.properties
messages_es.properties          messages_fr.properties
messages_it.properties          messages_ja.properties
messages_ko.properties          messages_pt_BR.properties
messages_sv.properties          messages_zh_CN.properties
messages_zh_HK.properties       messages_zh_TW.properties
splash.gif
            13 File(s)          60,861 bytes

 Directory of C:\Program Files\Java\jdk-9\lib\fonts

[.]                             [..]
LucidaBrightDemiBold.ttf        LucidaBrightDemiItalic.ttf
LucidaBrightItalic.ttf          LucidaBrightRegular.ttf
LucidaSansDemiBold.ttf          LucidaSansRegular.ttf
LucidaTypewriterBold.ttf        LucidaTypewriterRegular.ttf
             8 File(s)      2,068,932 bytes

 Directory of C:\Program Files\Java\jdk-9\lib\security

[.]                     [..]                    blacklist
blacklisted.certs       cacerts                 default.policy
public_suffix_list.dat  trusted.libraries
             6 File(s)        254,000 bytes

 Directory of C:\Program Files\Java\jdk-9\lib\server

[.]           [..]        Xusage.txt
             1 File(s)          1,383 bytes

    Total Files Listed:
            55 File(s)    251,892,975 bytes
            14 Dir(s)  890,920,189,952 bytes free

C:\Program Files\Java\jdk-9\lib>
```

What has been removed

Another area of change for the new version of the Java platform is that many platform components have been removed. The following sections represent the most significant components.

Notably, the rt.jar and tools.jar and dt.jar have been removed. These JAR files contained class and other resources files and all resided in the /lib directory.

The *endorsed standards override mechanism* has been removed. In Java 9, both javac and java will exit if they detect that mechanism. The mechanism was used for application servers to override some JDK components. In Java 9, you can use upgradeable modules to achieve the same result.

As previously covered in this chapter, the *extension mechanism* has also been removed.

The following listed APIs were previously depreciated and have been removed and are not accessible in Java 9. Removal of these APIs is the result of the modularization of the Java platform:

- apple.applescript
- com.apple.concurrent
- com.sun.image.codec.jpeg
- java.awt.dnd.peer
- java.awt.peer
- java.rmi.server.disableHttp
- java.util.logging.LogManager.addPropertyChangeListener
- java.util.logging.LogManager.removePropertyChangeListener
- java.util.jar.Pack200.Packer.addPropertyChangeListener
- java.util.jar.Pack200.Packer.removePropertyChangeListener
- java.util.jar.Pack200.Unpacker.addPropertyChangeListener
- java.util.jar.Pack200.Unpacker.removePropertyChangeListener
- javax.management.remote.rmi.RMIIIOPServerImpl
- sun.misc.BASE64Encoder
- sun.misc.BASE64Decoder
- sun.rmi.transport.proxy.connectTimeout

- `sun.rmi.transport.proxy.eagerHttpFallback`
- `sun.rmi.transport.proxy.logLevel`
- `sun.rmi.transport.tcp.proxy`

The following listed tools have been removed. In each case, the tool was previously depreciated or its functionality superseded by better alternatives:

- `hprof`
- `java-rmi.cgi`
- `java-rmi.exe`
- `JavaDB`
- `jhat`
- `native2ascii`

Two additional things that have been removed in Java 9 are:

- AppleScript engine. This engine was deemed as unusable and is dropped without replacement.
- Windows 32-bit client virtual machine. JDK 9 does support a 32-bit server JVM, but not a 32-bit client VM. This change was made to focus on the increased performance of 64-bit systems.

Updated garbage collection

Garbage collection has been one of Java's great claims to fame. In Java 9, the **Garbage-First** (**G1**) garbage collector is now the default garbage collector on both 32- and 64-bit servers. In Java 8, the default garbage collector was the parallel garbage collector. Oracle reports that there are three garbage collection combinations that will prohibit your application from starting in Java 9. Those combinations are:

- DefNew + CMS
- Incremental CMS
- ParNew + SerialOld

We will take an in-depth look at Java 9 garbage collection in `Chapter 7`, *Leveraging the New Default G1 Garbage Collector*.

Deployment

There are three issues that you should be aware of, in the context of migrating to Java 9, when you are deploying your applications. These issues are JRE version selection, serialized applets, and the update to the JNLP.

> **JNLP** is the acronym for **Java Network Launch Protocol** and is covered in a later section of this chapter.

JRE version selection

Prior to Java 9, developers could request a JRE version other than the version being launched when launching an application. This could be accomplished with a command-line option or with a proper JAR file manifest configuration. This feature has been removed in JDK 9 because of the way we typically deploy applications. Here are the three primary methods:

- Active installers
- **Java Web Start** using JNLP
- Native OS packaging systems

Serialized applets

Java 9 does not support the ability to deploy applets as serialized objects. In the past, applets were deployed as serialized objects to compensate for slow compression and JVM performance issues. With Java 9, compression techniques are advanced and the JVM has great performance.

If you attempt to deploy your applets as serialized objects, your object attributes and parameter tags will simply be ignored when your applet launches. Starting with Java 9, you can deploy your applets using standard deployment strategies.

JNLP update

The JNLP is used for launching applications on a desktop client using resources located on a web server. JNLP clients include Java Web Start and Java Plug-in software because they are able to launch applets that are remotely hosted. This protocol is instrumental in launching RIAs.

RIAs are **Rich Internet Applications** and when launched with JNLP have access to the various JNLP APIs that, with user permission, can access the user's desktop.

In Java 9, the JNLP specification has been updated. There are four specific updates as detailed in the next sections.

Nested resources

The ability to use component extensions with nest resources in Java or j2se elements was previously supported, but not documented in the specification. The specification has now been updated to reflect this support. The previous specification read:

No java elements can be specified as part of the resources.

The updated specification for Java 9 now reads:

A java element in a component extension will not govern what version of java is used, but may be used containing nested resource elements, and then those resources may be used only when using a Java version that matches the given version as specified in section 4.6

This specific change ensures that extension JLP files must have `java` or `j2se` resources and those resources will not dictate what JRE is used. Nested resources are permitted when using the specified version.

FX XML extension

When using the JNLP, you create a JNLP file. Here is an example:

```
<?xml version="1.0" encoding="UTF-8"?>
<jnlp spec="1.0+" codebase="" href="">
  <information>
    <title>Sample/title>
    <vendor>The Sample Vendor</vendor>
    <icon href="sample-icon.jpg"/>
    <offline-allowed/>
  </information>
  <resources>
```

```
    <!-- Application Resources -->
    <j2se version="1.6+"
     href="http://java.sun.com/products/autodl/j2se"/>
    <jar href="Sample-Set.jar" main="true" />
  </resources>
  <application-desc
    name="Sample Application"
    main-class="com.vendor.SampleApplication"
    width="800"
    height="500">
    <argument>Arg1</argument>
    <argument>Arg2</argument>
    <argument>Arg3</argument>
  </application-desc>
  <update check="background"/>
</jnlp>
```

Two changes have been made to the `<application-desc>` element. First, the optional `type` attribute has been added so the type of application can be annotated. The default type is `Java`, so if your program is a Java app, you need not include the `type` attribute. Alternatively, you can specify `Java` as your type as follows:

```
<application-desc
  name="Another Sample Application"
  type="Java" main-class="com.vendor.SampleApplication2"
  width="800"
  height="500">
  <argument>Arg1</argument>
  <argument>Arg2</argument>
  <argument>Arg3</argument>
</application-desc>
```

We can indicate other application types to include `JavaFX` as shown here:

```
<application-desc
  name="A Great JavaFX Application"
  type="JavaFX" main-class="com.vendor.GreatJavaFXApplication"
  width="800"
  height="500">
  <argument>Arg1</argument>
  <argument>Arg2</argument>
  <argument>Arg3</argument>
</application-desc>
```

If you indicate an application type that is not supported by the JNLP client, your application launch will fail. For more information about JNLP, you can consult the official documentation: `http://docs.oracle.com/javase/7/docs/technotes/guides/javaws/developersguide/faq.html`.

The second change to the `<application-desc>` element in Java 9 is the addition of the `param` sub-element. This allows us to provide the name of parameters along with their value using the `value` attribute. Here is an example of how an `<application-desc>` element of a JNLP file looks with the `param` sub-element and the `value` attribute included. This example shows three sets of parameters:

```
<application-desc
  name="My JRuby Application"
  type="JRuby"
  main-class="com.vendor.JRubyApplication"
  width="800"
  height="500">
  <argument>Arg1</argument>
  <argument>Arg2</argument>
  <argument>Arg3</argument>
  <param name="Parameter1" value="Value1"/>
  <param name="Parameter2" value="Value2"/>
  <param name="Parameter3" value="Value3"/>
</application-desc>
```

If the application `type` is Java, then any `param` sub-elements you use will be ignored.

JNLP file syntax

JNLP file syntax is now in complete compliance with XML specifications. Prior to Java 9, you could use `&` to create complex comparisons. That is not supported with standard XML. You can still create complex comparisons in JNLP files. Now you will use `&amp;` instead of `&`.

Numeric version comparison

The JNLP specification has been changed to reflect how numeric version elements were compared against non-numeric version elements. Previous to the change, version elements were compared lexicographically by ASCII value. With Java 9 and this JNLP specification change, elements are still compared lexicographically by ASCII value. The change is evident when the two strings have different lengths. In new comparisons, the shorter string will be padded with leading zeros to match the length of the longer string.

> Lexicographical comparisons use a mathematical model that is based on alphabetical order.

Useful tools

The first thing you will need to do before migrating your applications to Java 9 is to download JDK 9. You can download the early access builds at this URL--`http://jdk.java.net/9/`. You will need to accept the license agreement and then select which build to download. As you can see in the following screenshot, there are several options based on your operating system:

Builds		JRE	JDK
Windows	32	exe (sha256) 83.59 MB	exe (sha256) 298.30 MB
	64	exe (sha256) 88.62 MB	exe (sha256) 309.18 MB
Mac OS	64	dmg (sha256) 72.28 MB	dmg (sha256) 319.94 MB
Linux	32	tar.gz (sha256) 77.95 MB	tar.gz (sha256) 271.22 MB
	64	tar.gz (sha256) 78.96 MB	tar.gz (sha256) 279.76 MB
Linux ARM	32		tar.gz (sha256) 176.19 MB
	64		tar.gz (sha256) 176.06 MB
Solaris SPARC	64	tar.gz (sha256) 52.26 MB	tar.gz (sha256) 206.72 MB
Solaris x86	64	tar.gz (sha256) 51.94 MB	tar.gz (sha256) 205.77 MB
		Server JRE	**JDK**
Alpine Linux	64	tar.gz (sha256) 200.00 MB	tar.gz (sha256) 200.00 MB

Now that you have JDK 9 installed on your development computer, let's look at a couple of tools that can help facilitate migrating your applications to Java 9.

Java environment - jEnv

If you develop on a computer with Linux or macOS, you might consider using `jEnv`, an open source Java environment management tool. This is a command-line tool, so do not expect a GUI. You can download the tool at this URL--`https://github.com/gcuisinier/jenv`.

Here is the installation command for Linux:

```
$ git clone https://github.com/gcuisinier/jenv.git ~/.jenv
```

To download using macOS with Homebrew, use this command:

```
$ brew install jenv
```

You can also install on Linux or macOS using `Bash` as follows:

```
$ echo 'export PATH="$HOME/.jenv/bin:$PATH"' >> ~/.bash_profile
$ echo 'eval "$(jenv init -)"' >> ~/.bash_profile
```

Alternatively, you can install on Linux or macOS using `Zsh` as follows:

```
$ echo 'export PATH="$HOME/.jenv/bin:$PATH"' >> ~/.zshrc
$ echo 'eval "$(jenv init -)"' >> ~/.zshrc
```

After you have `jEnv` installed, you will need to configure it on your system as shown here. You will need to modify the script to reflect your actual path:

```
$ jenv add /Library/Java/JavaVirtualMachines/jdk17011.jdk/Contents/Home
```

You will want to repeat the `jenv add` command for each version of the JDK on your system. With each `jenv add` command, you will receive confirmation that the specific JDK version was added to `jEnv` as follows:

```
$ jenv add /System/Library/Java/JavaVirtualMachines/1.6.0.jdk/Contents/Home
oracle64-1.6.0.39 added
$ jenv add /Library/Java/JavaVirtualMachines/jdk17011.jdk/Contents/Home
oracle64-1.7.0.11 added
```

You can check to see what JDK versions you have added to your `jEnv` by using `$ jenv versions` at the Command Prompt. This will result in an output list.

Here are three additional `jEnv` commands:

- `jenv global <version>`: this sets the global version
- `jenv local <version>`: this sets the local version
- `jenv shell <version>`: this sets the instance version for the shell

Maven

Maven is an open source tool that can be used for building and managing Java-based projects. It already supports Java 9 and is part of the *Apache Maven Project*. If you are not already using Maven and you do a lot of Java development you might be enticed by the following Maven objectives:

- Making the build process easy
- Providing a uniform build system
- Providing quality project information
- Providing guidelines for best practices development
- Allowing transparent migration to new features

You can read more specifics about each of the Maven objectives at this site--`https://maven.apache.org/what-is-maven.html`. To download Maven, visit this site--`https://maven.apache.org/download.cgi`. Installation instructions for Windows, macOS, Linux, and Solaris are available here--`https://maven.apache.org/install.html`.

Maven can be integrated with Eclipse (M2Eclipse), JetBrains IntelliJ IDEA, and the Netbeans IDE. The M2Eclipse IDE, as an example, provides rich integration with Apache Maven and boasts the following features:

- You can launch Maven builds from within Eclipse
- Manage your dependencies for the Eclipse build path
- Easily resolve Maven dependencies (you can do this directly from Eclipse and not have to install a local Maven repository)
- Automatically download required dependencies (from remote Maven repositories)
- Use software wizards to create new Maven projects, create `pom.xml` files, and to enable Maven support for your plain Java projects
- Rapid dependency search of Maven remote repositories

Obtaining the M2Eclipse IDE

To obtain the M2Eclipse IDE, you must first have Eclipse installed. Here are the steps:

1. Start by opening your current Eclipse IDE. Next, select **Preferences** |
   Install/Update | **Available Software Sites** as shown in the following screenshot:

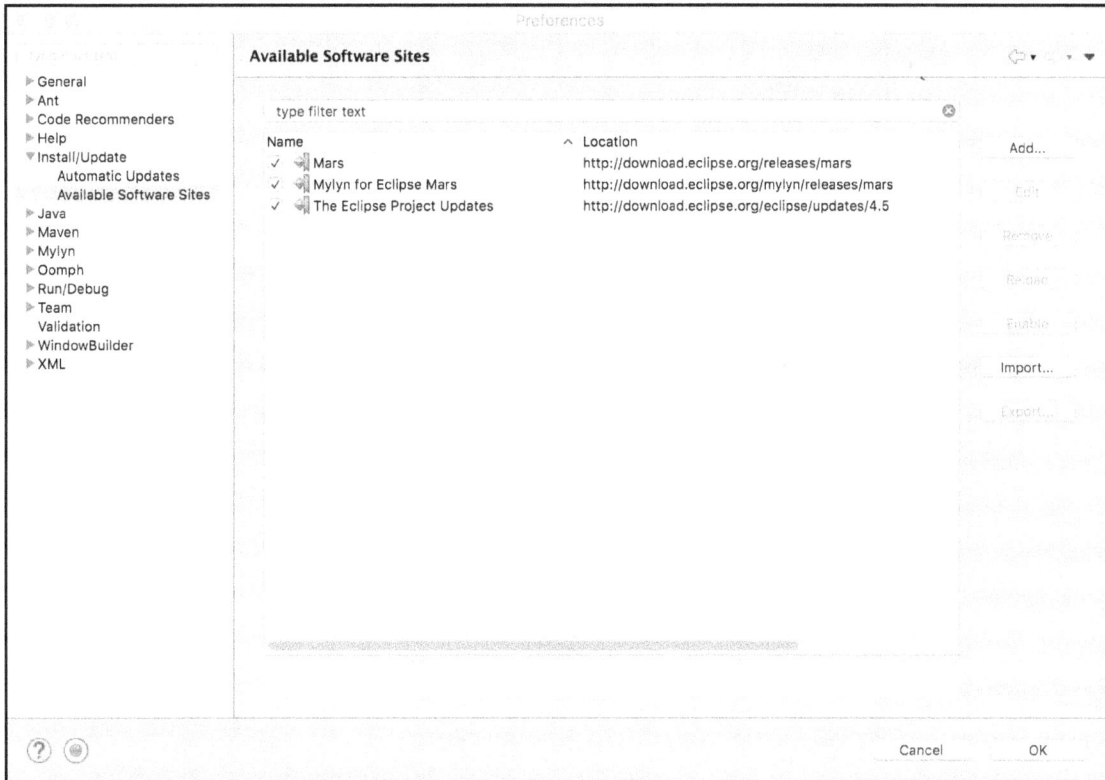

2. The next task is to add the M2Eclipse repository site to your list of **Available Software Sites**. To accomplish this, click the **Add** button and enter values in the **Name** and **Location** text input boxes. For **Name**, enter something to help you remember that M2Eclipse is available at this site. For **Location**, enter the URL-- `http://download.eclipse.org/technology/m2e/releases`. Then, click the **OK** button:

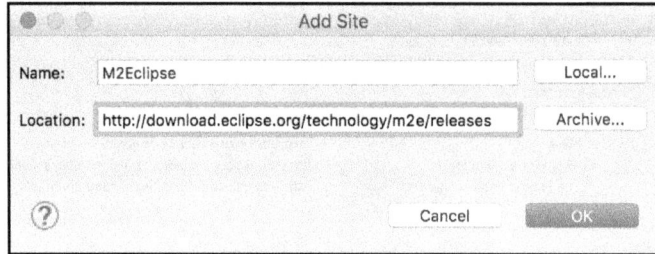

3. You should now see the **M2Eclipse** site listed in your list of **Available Software Sites** as shown in the following screenshot. Your final step is to click the **OK** button:

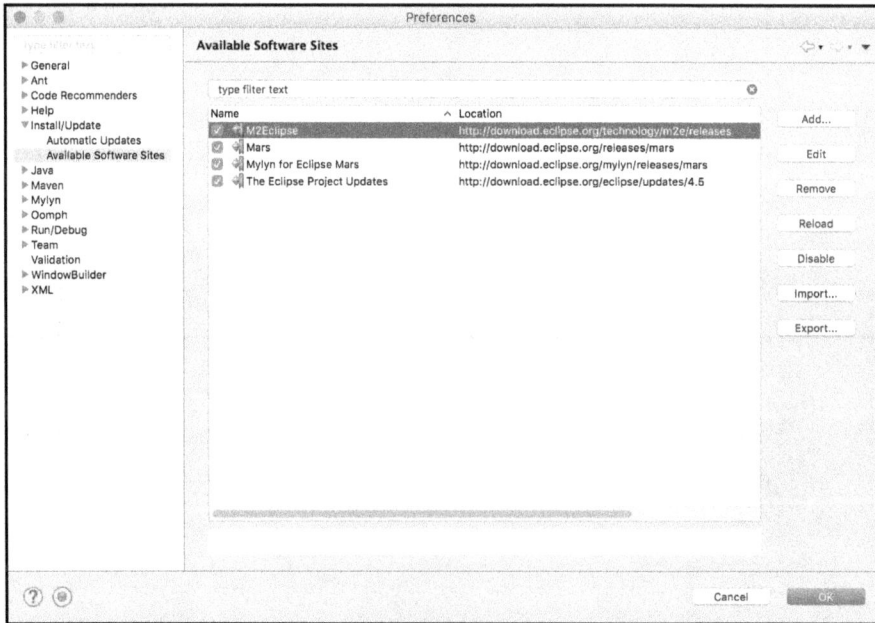

4. Now, when you start a new project, you will see `Maven Project` as an option:

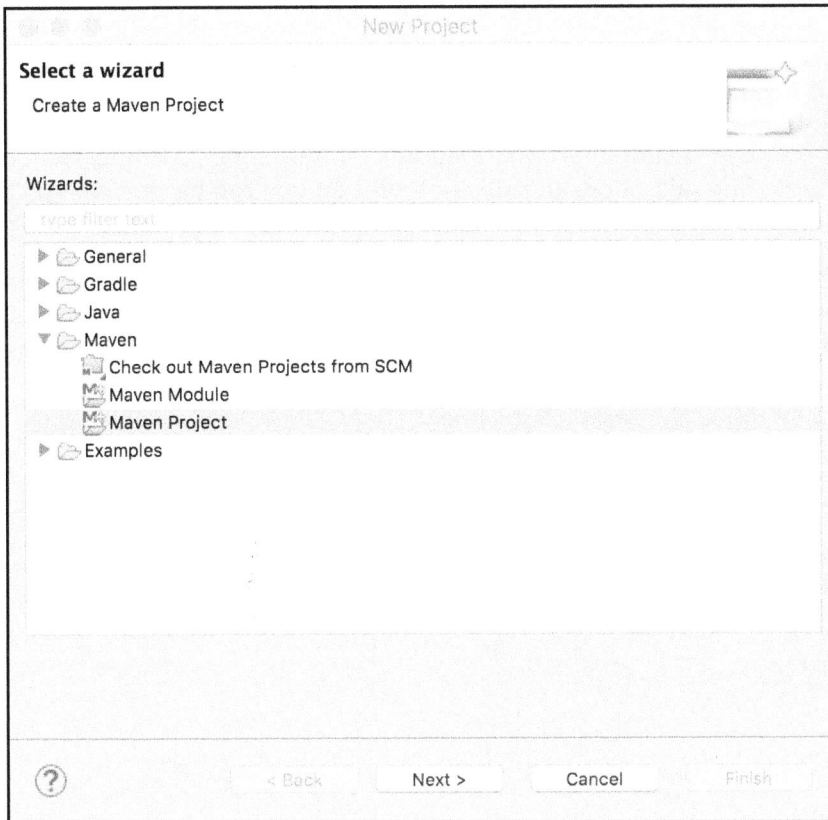

Maven is a proven tool for Java developers. You might consider obtaining additional information on Maven with one of the following resources:

*   *Apache Maven Project*: `https://maven.apache.org/index.html`
*   *Apache Maven Cookbook*: `https://www.packtpub.com/application-development/apache-maven-cookbook`
*   *Apache Maven 3.0 Cookbook*: `https://www.packtpub.com/application-development/apache-maven-3-cookbook`
*   *Getting Started with Apache Maven [Video]*: `https://www.packtpub.com/application-development/getting-started-apache-maven-video`

Summary

In this chapter, we explored potential issues involved in migrating our existing applications to the Java 9 platform. We looked at both manual and semi-automated migration processes. This chapter provided you with insights and processes to get your Java 8 code working with Java 9. Specifically, we conducted a quick review of Project Jigsaw, looked at how modules fit into the Java landscape, provided tips for migration planning, shared advice from Oracle regarding migration, and shared tools that you can use to help you as you get started with Java 9.

In the next chapter, we will take a close look at the Java shell and the JShell API. We demonstrate the JShell API and the JShell tool's ability to interactively evaluate declarations, statements, and expressions of the Java programming language. We will demonstrate features and use of this command-line tool.

6
Experimenting with the Java Shell

In the previous chapter, we explored how to migrate pre-Java 9 applications to the new Java platform. We examined several issues that might cause your current applications to have problems running on Java 9. We started with a review of Project Jigsaw and then looked at how modules fit into the new Java platform. We provided you with insights and processes to get your Java 8 code working with Java 9. Specifically, we provided tips for migration planning, shared advice from Oracle regarding migration, and shared tools that you can use to help you as you get started with Java 9.

In this chapter, we will take our first look at the new command line, **read-eval-print loop** (also referred to as **REPL**) tool in Java 9, the **Java Shell** (**JShell**). We will start with introductory information regarding the tool, the read-eval-print loop concept, and move into the commands and command-line options for use with JShell. We will take a practitioner's approach to our review of the Java Shell and include examples you can try on your own.

The following topics are covered in this chapter:

- What is JShell?
- Getting started with JShell
- Practical uses of JShell
- Working with scripts

What is JShell?

JShell is a new tool introduced with Java 9. It is an interactive read-eval-print loop tool that is used to evaluate the following Java programming language components--declarations, statements, and expressions. It has its own API so that it can be used by external applications.

> Read-Eval-Print Loop is often referred to as REPL, taking the first letter from each word in the phrase. It is also knows language shell or interactive top-level.

The introduction of JShell was a result of **Java Enhancement Program (JEP)** 222. Here are the stated goals of this JEP in regards to the Java Shell command-line tool:

- Facilitate rapid investigation
- Facilitate rapid coding
- Provide an edit history

The rapid investigation and coding listed previously includes statements and expressions. Impressively, these statements and expressions do not need to be part of a method. Furthermore, variables and methods are not required to be part of a class, making this tool especially dynamic.

In addition, the following listed features were included to make JShell much easier to use and to make your time using JShell as time-efficient as possible:

- Tab-completion
- Auto-completion for end-of-statement semicolons
- Auto-completion for imports
- Auto-completion for definitions

Getting Started with JShell

JShell is a command-line tool that is located in the `/bin` folder. The syntax for this tool is `jshell <options> <load files>`. As you can see here, there are several options that can be used with this tool:

```
Command Prompt                                          —    □    ×
C:\Program Files\Java\jdk-9\bin>jshell -h
Usage:    jshell <options> <load files>
where possible options include:
    --class-path <path>   Specify where to find user class files
    --module-path <path>  Specify where to find application modules
    --add-modules <module>(,<module>)*
                          Specify modules to resolve, or all modules on the
                             module path if <module> is ALL-MODULE-PATHs
    --startup <file>      One run replacement for the start-up definitions
    --no-startup          Do not run the start-up definitions
    --feedback <mode>     Specify the initial feedback mode. The mode may be
                             predefined (silent, concise, normal, or verbose) or
                             previously user-defined
    -q                    Quiet feedback.  Same as: --feedback concise
    -s                    Really quiet feedback.  Same as: --feedback silent
    -v                    Verbose feedback.  Same as: --feedback verbose
    -J<flag>              Pass <flag> directly to the runtime system.
                             Use one -J for each runtime flag or flag argument
    -R<flag>              Pass <flag> to the remote runtime system.
                             Use one -R for each remote flag or flag argument
    -C<flag>              Pass <flag> to the compiler.
                             Use one -C for each compiler flag or flag argument
    --version             Print version information and exit
    --show-version        Print version information and continue
    --help                Print this synopsis of standard options and exit
    --help-extra, -X      Print help on non-standard options and exit

C:\Program Files\Java\jdk-9\bin>
```

You have already seen the -h option, that we executed with jshell -h. This provided the listing of JShell options.

To log into your JShell, you simply use the jshell command. You will see that the prompt in the command window changes accordingly:

```
Command Prompt - jshell              —    □    ×

C:\Program Files\Java\jdk-9\bin>jshell
|  Welcome to JShell -- Version 9
|  For an introduction type: /help intro

jshell>
```

Exiting the shell is as easy as entering /exit. Once inside the JShell, you can enter any of the following commands:

Command	Functionality
/drop	Use this command to delete a source entry that is referenced by name or id. Here is the syntax: 　　/drop <name or id>
/edit	With this command, you can edit a source entry using a name or id reference. Here is the syntax: 　　/edit <name or id>
/env	This powerful command allows you to view or change the evaluation context. Here is the syntax: 　　/env [-class-path <path>] [-module-path <path>] 　　[-add-modules <modules]
/exit	This command is used to exit the JShell. The syntax is simply /exit without any options or parameters available.
/history	The history command provides a history of what you have typed. The syntax is simply /history without any options or parameters available.
/<id>	This command is used to rerun a previous snippet by referencing the id. Here is the syntax: /<id> You can also run a specific snippet by referencing the nth previous snippet with /-<n>.
/imports	You can use this command to list the imported items. The syntax is /imports and it does not accept any options or parameters.
/list	This command will list the source you typed. Here is the syntax: 　　/list [<name or id> | -all | -start]
/methods	This command lists all declared methods as well as their signatures. Here is the syntax: 　　/methods [<name or id> | -all | -start]
/open	Using this command, you can open a file as source input. Here is the syntax: 　　/open <file>
/reload	The reload command gives you the ability to reset and replay relevant history. Here is the syntax: 　　/reload [-restore] [-quiet]　[-class-path 　　<path>] [-module-path <path>]

`/reset`	This command resets the JShell. Here is the syntax:
	`/reset [-class-path <path>] [-module-path`
	`    <path>] [-add-modules <modules]`

`/save`	This command saves the snippet source to a file specified by you. Here is the syntax: `/save [-all	-history	-start] <file>`
`/set`	This command is used to set the JShell configuration information. Here is the syntax: `/set editor	start	feedback	mode	prompt |` ` truncation	format`
`/types`	This command simply lists declared types. Here is the syntax: `/types [<name or id>	-all	-start]`
`/vars`	This command lists all declared variables as well as their values. Here is the syntax: `/vars [<name or id>	-all	-start]`
`/!`	This command will rerun the last snippet. The syntax is simply / !

Several of the previously listed commands use the term **snippet**. In the context of Java 9 and JShell, a snippet is one of the following:
- ClassDeclaration
- Expression
- FieldDeclaration
- ImportDeclaration
- InterfaceDeclaration
- MethodDeclaration

Entering the `/help` or `/?` command in the JShell provides a complete list of commands and syntax that can be used in the shell. That list is provided as follows:

```
Command Prompt - jshell                                                  —    □    ×

jshell> /?
   Type a Java language expression, statement, or declaration.
   Or type one of the following commands:
   /list [<name or id>|-all|-start]
        list the source you have typed
   /edit <name or id>
        edit a source entry referenced by name or id
   /drop <name or id>
        delete a source entry referenced by name or id
   /save [-all|-history|-start] <file>
        Save snippet source to a file.
   /open <file>
        open a file as source input
   /vars [<name or id>|-all|-start]
        list the declared variables and their values
   /methods [<name or id>|-all|-start]
        list the declared methods and their signatures
   /types [<name or id>|-all|-start]
        list the declared types
   /imports
        list the imported items
   /exit
        exit jshell
   /env [-class-path <path>] [-module-path <path>] [-add-modules <modules>] ...
        view or change the evaluation context
   /reset [-class-path <path>] [-module-path <path>] [-add-modules <modules>]...
        reset jshell
   /reload [-restore] [-quiet] [-class-path <path>] [-module-path <path>]...
        reset and replay relevant history -- current or previous (-restore)
   /history
        history of what you have typed
   /help [<command>|<subject>]
        get information about jshell
   /set editor|start|feedback|mode|prompt|truncation|format ...
        set jshell configuration information
   /? [<command>|<subject>]
        get information about jshell
   /!
        re-run last snippet
   /<id>
        re-run snippet by id
   /-<n>
        re-run n-th previous snippet

   For more information type '/help' followed by the name of a
   command or a subject.
   For example '/help /list' or '/help intro'.

   Subjects:

   intro
        an introduction to the jshell tool
   shortcuts
        a description of keystrokes for snippet and command completion,
        information access, and automatic code generation
   context
        the evaluation context options for /env /reload and /reset

jshell>
```

The `/help` command can be especially helpful if you are still new to JShell. As you can see in the following screenshot, we can obtain an introduction to JShell by simply entering the `/help intro` command:

```
Command Prompt - jshell                                              —    □    ×

jshell> /help intro

  intro

  The jshell tool allows you to execute Java code, getting immediate results.
  You can enter a Java definition (variable, method, class, etc), like:  int x = 8
  or a Java expression, like:  x + x
  or a Java statement or import.
  These little chunks of Java code are called 'snippets'.

  There are also jshell commands that allow you to understand and
  control what you are doing, like:  /list

  For a list of commands: /help

jshell>
```

If you find yourself using JShell often you might benefit from one or more of the following listed shortcuts. These can be listed at any time from within JShell by using the `/help shortcuts` command:

```
Command Prompt - jshell                                              —    □    ×

jshell> /help shortcuts

  shortcuts

  Supported shortcuts include:

  <tab>
          After entering the first few letters of a Java identifier,
          a jshell command, or, in some cases, a jshell command argument,
          press the <tab> key to complete the input.
          If there is more than one completion, then possible completions will be shown.
          Will show documentation if available and appropriate.

  Shift-<tab> v
          After a complete expression, hold down <shift> while pressing <tab>,
          then release and press "v", the expression will be converted to
          a variable declaration whose type is based on the type of the expression.

  Shift-<tab> i
          After an unresolvable identifier, hold down <shift> while pressing <tab>,
          then release and press "i", and jshell will propose possible imports
          which will resolve the identifier based on the content of the specified classpath.

jshell>
```

Additional help can be obtained from within the JShell by using the `/help` command followed by the command you want additional help on. For example, entering `/help reload` provides detailed information regarding the `/reload` command. That information is provided as follows:

```
Command Prompt - jshell                                          —    □    ×

jshell> /help reload

  /reload

  Reset the jshell tool code and execution state then replay each valid snippet
  and any /drop commands in the order they were entered.

  /reload
        Reset and replay the valid history since jshell was entered, or
        a /reset, or /reload command was executed -- whichever is most
        recent.

  /reload -restore
        Reset and replay the valid history between the previous and most
        recent time that jshell was entered, or a /reset, or /reload
        command was executed. This can thus be used to restore a previous
        jshell tool session.

  /reload [-restore] -quiet
        With the '-quiet' argument the replay is not shown.  Errors will display.

  Each of the above accepts context options, see:

        /help context

  For example:

        /reload -add-modules com.greetings -restore

jshell>
```

Practical uses of JShell

Whether you are a new or seasoned developer or just new to Java, you are bound to find the JShell very useful. In this section, we will look at some practical uses of JShell. Specifically, we will cover:

- Feedback modes
- Listing your assets
- Editing in the JShell

Feedback modes

Command-line tools usually provide relatively sparse feedback in an effort to not overcrowd the screen or otherwise become a nuisance to developers. JShell has several feedback modes in addition to giving developers the ability to create their own custom modes.

As you can see from the following screenshot, there are four feedback modes--`concise`, `normal`, `silent`, and `verbose`. Here, we entered the `/set feedback` command without any parameters to list the feedback modes as well as to identify what the current feedback mode is. The first line of output displays the command-line command and argument set that would be used to set the mode to the currently set mode. So, in the following screenshot, the current feedback mode is set to `verbose` and the other three modes are listed:

We can dictate which mode we want to enter when we first enter JShell by including an option when we launch JShell. Here are the command-line options:

Command-line command and option	Feedback mode
jshell -q	concise
jshell -n	normal
jshell -s	silent
jshell -v	verbose

You will notice that we use `-q` for `concise` mode instead of `-c`. The `-c` option has the `-c<flag>` syntax and is used to pass `<flag>` to the compiler.

The best way to review the differences between the feedback modes is to use examples. Starting with the `normal` mode, we will execute command-line commands to accomplish the following ordered feedback demonstration:

1. Create a variable.
2. Update the variable's value.
3. Create a method.
4. Update the method.
5. Run the method.

To start our first test, we will execute the `/set feedback normal` command at the `jshell>` prompt, which sets the JShell feedback mode to `normal`. After entering the `normal` feedback mode, we will enter the necessary commands to run our demonstration:

```
Command Prompt - jshell                                          —    □    ✕

C:\Program Files\Java\jdk-9\bin>jshell
|  Welcome to JShell -- Version 9
|  For an introduction type: /help intro

jshell> /set feedback normal
|  Feedback mode: normal

jshell> int myVar = 3
myVar ==> 3

jshell> int myVar = 10
myVar ==> 10

jshell> void quickMath() {System.out.println("Your result is " + (x*30 + 19));}
|  created method quickMath(), however, it cannot be invoked until variable x is declared

jshell> void quickMath() {System.out.println("Your result is " + (myVar*30 + 19));}
|  modified method quickMath()

jshell> quickMath();
Your result is 319

jshell>
```

After entering `normal` feedback mode, we entered `int myVar = 3` to and received `myVar ==> 3` as feedback. In our next command, we changed the value of the same variable and received the same output with the new value. Our next statement, `void quickMath() {System.out.println("Your result is " + (x*30 + 19));}`, used a variable that was not declared and you see the resulting two-part feedback--one part indicating that the method was created and the other to inform that the method cannot be invoked until the undeclared variable is declared. Next, we changed our method to include the `myVar` variable and the feedback reported that the method was modified. Our last step was to run the method using `quickMath();` and the results are as we expected.

Let's try this same feedback demonstration in `concise` mode:

```
Command Prompt - jshell                                                    —   □   ×

C:\Program Files\Java\jdk-9\bin>jshell
|  Welcome to JShell -- Version 9
|  For an introduction type: /help intro

jshell> /set feedback concise
jshell> int myVar = 3
jshell> int myVar = 10
jshell> void quickMath() {System.out.println("Your result is " + (x*30 + 19));}
|  created method quickMath(), however, it cannot be invoked until variable x is declared
jshell> void quickMath() {System.out.println("Your result is " + (myVar*30 + 19));}
jshell> quickMath();
Your result is 319
jshell>
```

As you can see from the preceding screenshot, the `concise` feedback mode provides us with much less feedback. We created and modified the variables and received no feedback. When we created the method with an undeclared variable, we received the same feedback that we did in `normal` mode. We updated the method without confirmation or other feedback.

Our next use of the feedback demonstration will be in `silent` mode:

```
Command Prompt - jshell                                                    —    □    ×

C:\Program Files\Java\jdk-9\bin>jshell
|   Welcome to JShell -- Version 9
|   For an introduction type: /help intro

jshell> /set feedback silent
-> int myVar = 3
-> int myVar = 10
-> void quickMath() {System.out.println("Your result is " + (x*30 + 19));}
-> quickMath();
-> void quickMath() {System.out.println("Your result is " + (myVar*30 + 19));}
-> quickMath();
Your result is 319
->
```

When we entered `silent` feedback mode, as you can see in the preceding screenshot, the
JShell prompt changed from `jshell>` to `->`. There was no feedback provided when we
created the `myVar` variable, modified the `myVar` variable, or created the `quickMath()`
method. We intentionally created the `quickMath()` method to use an undeclared variable.
Because we were in `silent` feedback mode, we were not informed that the method had an
undeclared variable. Based on this lack of feedback, we ran the method and were not
provided any output or feedback. Next, we updated the method to include the `myVar`
declared variable and then ran the method.

> The `silent` feedback mode might seem pointless as no feedback is
> provided, but there is a great utility with this mode. Using the `silent`
> mode might be appropriate for pipelining or simply when you want to
> minimize the amount of terminal output. You can include specific,
> conditional, outputs with implicit `System.out.println` commands, as
> an example.

Our last use of the feedback demonstration is in `verbose` feedback mode. This feedback mode, as you would assume from its name, provides the most amount of feedback. Here are our test results:

```
Command Prompt - jshell                                        —    □    ×

C:\Program Files\Java\jdk-9\bin>jshell
|  Welcome to JShell -- Version 9
|  For an introduction type: /help intro

jshell> /set feedback verbose
|  Feedback mode: verbose

jshell> int myVar = 3
myVar ==> 3
|  created variable myVar : int

jshell> int myVar = 10
myVar ==> 10
|  modified variable myVar : int
|    update overwrote variable myVar : int

jshell> void quickMath() {System.out.println("Your result is " + (x*30 + 19));}
|  created method quickMath(), however, it cannot be invoked until variable x is declared

jshell> void quickMath() {System.out.println("Your result is " + (myVar*30 + 19));}
|  modified method quickMath()
|    update overwrote method quickMath()

jshell> quickMath();
Your result is 319

jshell>
```

In our feedback demonstration, using `verbose` feedback mode, we receive a bit more feedback as well as a nicer format for the feedback.

Creating a custom feedback mode

While the internal feedback modes (normal, concise, silent, and verbose) cannot be modified, you can create your own custom feedback mode. The first step in this process is to copy an existing mode. The following example demonstrates how to copy the verbose mode to a myCustom mode with the /set mode myCustom verbose -command command string:

```
Command Prompt - jshell                                   —    □    ×

jshell> /set mode myCustom verbose -command
|    Created new feedback mode: myCustom

jshell>
```

We used the -command option to ensure we would receive the command feedback. You can make various changes to your feedback mode using the /set command along with one of the options listed in the following screenshot:

```
Command Prompt - jshell                                              —    □    ×

/set

Set jshell configuration information, including:
the external editor to use, the start-up definitions to use, a new feedback mode,
the command prompt, the feedback mode to use, or the format of output.

/set editor [-wait] <command> <optional-arg>...
    Specify the command to launch for the /edit command.
    The <command> is an operating system dependent string.

/set start <file>
    The contents of the specified <file> become the default start-up snippets and commands.

/set feedback <mode>
    Set the feedback mode describing displayed feedback for entered snippets and commands.

/set mode <mode> [<old-mode>] -command|-quiet|-delete
    Create or update a user-defined feedback mode, optionally copying from an existing mode.

/set prompt <mode> "<prompt>" "<continuation-prompt>"
    Set the displayed prompts for a given feedback mode.

/set truncation <mode> <length> <selector>...
    Set the maximum length of a displayed value.

/set format <mode> <field> "<format>" <selector>...
    Configure a feedback mode by setting the format of a field when the selector matches.

/set
    Show editor, start, and feedback settings as /set commands.
    To show the settings of any of the above, omit the set value.
```

As an example, let's walk through the truncation setting that mandates how many characters are displayed on each output line. Using the /set truncation command, as illustrated in the following screenshot, shows the current truncation settings:

```
Command Prompt - jshell                                    —    □    ×

jshell> /set truncation
|   /set truncation myCustom 80
|   /set truncation myCustom 1000 expression,varvalue
|   /set truncation normal 80
|   /set truncation normal 1000 expression,varvalue
|   /set truncation silent 80
|   /set truncation silent 1000 expression,varvalue
|   /set truncation concise 80
|   /set truncation concise 1000 expression,varvalue
|   /set truncation verbose 80
|   /set truncation verbose 1000 expression,varvalue

jshell>
```

As you can see, our myCustom feedback mode has a truncation of 80. We will change that to 60 with the /set truncation myCustom 60 command and then use the /set truncation command for verification:

```
Command Prompt - jshell                                    —    □    ×

jshell> /set truncation myCustom 60

jshell> /set truncation
|   /set truncation myCustom 60
|   /set truncation normal 80
|   /set truncation normal 1000 expression,varvalue
|   /set truncation silent 80
|   /set truncation silent 1000 expression,varvalue
|   /set truncation concise 80
|   /set truncation concise 1000 expression,varvalue
|   /set truncation verbose 80
|   /set truncation verbose 1000 expression,varvalue

jshell>
```

As you can see in the previous screenshot, the truncation for our myCustom feedback mode was successfully changed from the 80 inherited from the verbose mode to 60, based on our use of the /set truncation myCustom 60 JShell command.

Listing your assets

There are a few JShell commands that are convenient for listing assets that you have created. Using the feedback demonstration from the previous section, we executed the /vars, /methods, and /list commands to provide a list of variables, methods, and all sources respectively:

```
Command Prompt - jshell                                                    —    □    ×

jshell> /vars
|    int myVar = 10

jshell> /methods
|    void quickMath()

jshell> /list

   2 : int myVar = 10;
   4 : void quickMath() {System.out.println("Your result is " + (myVar*30 + 19));}
   5 : quickMath();

jshell>
```

We can also use the /list -all command and option combination to see what packages the JShell imported. As you can see in the following screenshot, JShell imported several packages that make our work within the shell more convenient, saving us time from having to import these standard packages in our methods:

```
Command Prompt - jshell                                                    —    □    ×

jshell> /list -all

  s1 : import java.io.*;
  s2 : import java.math.*;
  s3 : import java.net.*;
  s4 : import java.nio.file.*;
  s5 : import java.util.*;
  s6 : import java.util.concurrent.*;
  s7 : import java.util.function.*;
  s8 : import java.util.prefs.*;
  s9 : import java.util.regex.*;
 s10 : import java.util.stream.*;
   1 : int myVar = 3;
   2 : int myVar = 10;
   3 : void quickMath() {System.out.println("Your result is " + (x*30 + 19));}
   4 : void quickMath() {System.out.println("Your result is " + (myVar*30 + 19));}
   5 : quickMath();

jshell>
```

If you just want to list the startup imports, you can use the `/list -start` command and option combination. As you can see in the following screenshot, each start up import has an "s" prefix and is numerically ordered:

Editing in the JShell

JShell is not a full-featured text editor, but there are several things you can do within the shell. This section provides you with the editing techniques grouped into modifying text, basic navigation, historical navigation, and advanced editing commands.

Modifying text

The default text edit/entry mode is that the text you type will appear at the current cursor position. You have several options available to you when you want to delete text. Here is a complete list:

Delete action	PC keyboard combination	Mac keyboard combination
Delete the character at the current cursor location	*Delete*	*Delete*
Delete the character to the left of the cursor	*Backspace*	*Backspace*
Delete the text from the cursor location to the end of the line	*Ctrl + K*	*Cmd + K*
Delete the text from the cursor location to the end of the current word	*Alt + D*	*Alt/Opt + D*

Delete from the cursor location to the previous white space	Ctrl + W	Cmd + W
Paste the most recently deleted text at the cursor location	Ctrl + Y	Cmd + Y
When the *Ctrl + Y* (or *Cmd + Y* on Mac) is used, you will be able to use the *Alt + Y* keyboard combination to cycle through previously deleted text	Alt + Y	Alt/Opt + Y

Basic navigation

While navigational control inside the JShell is similar to most command-line editors, it is helpful to have a list of basic navigational controls:

Key/Key combination	Navigation action
Left arrow	Move backward one character
Right arrow	Move forward one character
Up arrow	Move up one line through history
Down arrow	Move down one line forward through history
Return	Enter (submit) the current line
Ctrl + A (*cmd - A* on Mac)	Jump to the beginning of the current line
Ctrl + E (*cmd - E* on Mac)	Jump to the end of the current line
Alt + B	Jump back one word
Alt + F	Jump forward one word

Historical navigation

JShell remembers the snippets and commands that you enter. It maintains this history so that you can reuse snippets and commands you already entered. To cycle through snippets and commands, you can hold down the *Ctrl* key (*cmd* on Mac) and then use the up and down arrow keys until you see the snippet or command you want.

Advanced editing commands

There are several more editing options to include search functionality, macros creation and use, and more. JShell's editor is based on JLine2, a Java library for parsing console input and editing. You can learn more about JLine2 at this URL: `https://github.com/jline/jline2/wiki/JLine-2.x-Wiki`.

Working with scripts

Up to this point, you have entered data directly into JShell from the keyboard. You also have the ability to work with JShell scripts which are a sequence of JShell commands and snippets. The format is the same as other scripting formats with one command per line.

In this section, we will look at start up scripts, examine how to load scripts, how to save scripts, and then end with a look at advanced scripting with JShell.

Start up scripts

Each time the JShell is launched, the start up scripts are loaded. This also occurs each time the `/reset`, `/reload`, and `/env` commands are used.

By default, the DEFAULT start up script is used by JShell. If you want to use a different start up script, you merely need to use the `/set start <script>` command. Here is an example--`/set start MyStartupScript.jsh`. Alternatively, you can use the `jshell --start MyStartupScript.jsh` command at the Command Prompt to launch JShell and load the `MyStartupScript.jsh` JShell start up script.

When you use the `/set start <script>` command with the `-retain` option, you are telling JShell to use the new start up script the next time you launch JShell.

Loading scripts

Loading scripts in the JShell can be accomplished with one of the following methods:

- You can use the /open command along with the name of the script as a parameter. For example, if our script name is MyScript, we would use /open MyScript.
- A second option for loading scripts is to use the jshell MyScript.jsh at the Command Prompt. This will launch JShell and load the MyScript.jsh JShell script.

Saving scripts

In addition to creating JShell scripts in external editors, we can create them within the JShell environment as well. When taking this approach, you will need to use the /save command to save your scripts. As you can see in the following screenshot, the /save command requires, at a minimum, a file name argument:

```
jshell> /help save

/save

Save the specified snippets and/or commands to the specified file.

/save <file>
     Save the source of current active snippets to the file.

/save -all <file>
     Save the source of all snippets to the file.
     Includes source including overwritten, failed, and start-up code.

/save -history <file>
     Save the sequential history of all commands and snippets entered since jshell was launched.

/save -start <file>
     Save the current start-up definitions to the file.

jshell>
```

There are three options available to you with the /save command:

- The -all option can be used to save the source of all snippets to the specified file.
- The -history option saves a sequential history of all commands and snippets you entered since JShell was launched. JShell's ability to perform this operation informs you that it maintains a history of everything you enter.
- The -start option saves the current start up definitions to the specified file.

Advanced scripting with JShell

What are the limits of JShell? There is so much you can do with this tool, and you are virtually only limited by your imagination and programming abilities.

Let's look at an advanced code base that can be used to compile and run Java programs from a JShell script:

```java
import java.util.concurrent.*
import java.util.concurrent.*
import java.util.stream.*
import java.util.*

void print2Console(String thetext)
{
  System.out.println(thetext);
  System.out.println("");
}

void runSomeProcess(String... args) throws Exception
{
  String theProcess =
    Arrays.asList(args).stream().collect(
     Collectors.joining(" "));
    print2Console("You asked me to run: '"+theProcess+"'");
    print2Console("");
    ProcessBuilder compileBuilder = new
      ProcessBuilder(args).inheritIO();
    Process compileProc = compileBuilder.start();
    CompletableFuture<Process> compileTask =
     compileProc.onExit();
    compileTask.get();
}

print2Console("JShell session launched.")
print2Console("Preparing to compile Sample.java. . . ")
```

```
// run the Java Compiler to complete Sample.java
runSomeProcess("javac", "Sample.java")
print2Console("Compilation complete.")
print2Console("Preparing to run Sample.class...")

// run the Sample.class file
runSomeProcess("java", "Sample")
print2Console("Run Cycle compete.")

// exit JShell
print2Console("JShell Termination in progress...")
print2Console("Session ended.")

/exit
```

As you can see with this script, we created a `runSomeProcess()` method and can use it to explicitly compile and run external Java files.

Summary

In this chapter, we examined JShell, Java 9's new read-eval-print loop command-line tool. We started with introductory information regarding the tool and looked closely at the read-eval-print loop concept. We spent considerable time reviewing JShell commands and command-line options. Our coverage included practical guides to feedback modes, asset listing, and editing in the shell. We also gained experience working with scripts.

In the next chapter, we will look at Java 9's new default garbage collector. Specifically, we will look at the default garbage collection, depreciated garbage collection combinations, and examine garbage collection logging.

Leveraging the New Default G1
Garbage Collector

7

In the previous chapter, we examined **Java Shell (JShell)**, Java 9's new **read-eval-print loop (REPL)** command-line tool. We started with introductory information regarding the tool and looked closely at the read-eval-print loop concept. We spent considerable time reviewing JShell commands and command-line options. Our coverage included practical guides to feedback modes, asset listing, and editing in the shell. We also gained experience working with scripts.

In this chapter, we will take an in-depth look at **garbage collection** and how it is handled in Java 9. We will start with an overview of garbage collection, and then look at specifics in the pre-Java 9 realm. Armed with that foundational information, we will look at specific garbage collection changes in the Java 9 platform. Lastly, we will look at some garbage collection issues that persist, even after Java 9.

The following topics are covered in this chapter:

- Overview of garbage collection
- The pre-Java 9 garbage collection schema
- Collecting garbage with the new Java platform
- Persistent issues

Overview of garbage collection

Garbage collection is the mechanism used in Java to deallocate unused memory. Essentially, when an object is created, memory space is allocated and dedicated to that object until it no longer has any references pointing to it. At that time, the system deallocates the memory. Java performs this garbage collection automatically for us, which can lead to a lack of attention to memory usage and poor programming practices in the area of memory management and system performance.

Java's garbage collection is considered an automatic memory management schema because programmers do not have to designate objects as ready to be deallocated. The garbage collection runs on a low-priority thread and, as you will read later in this chapter, has variable execution cycles.

In our overview of garbage collection, we will look at the following concepts:

- Object life cycle
- Garbage collection algorithms
- Garbage collection options
- Java methods relevant to garbage collection

We will look at each of these concepts in the sections that follow.

Object life cycle

In order to fully understand Java's garbage collection, we need to look at the entire life cycle of an object. Because the core of garbage collection is automatic in Java, it is not uncommon to see the terms *garbage collection* and *memory management* as assumed components of the object life cycle.

We will start our review of the object life cycle with object creation.

Object creation

Objects are declared and created. When we write an object declaration, or declare an object, we are declaring a name or identifier so that we can refer to an object. For example, the following line of code declares `myObjectName` as the name of an object of type `CapuchinMonkey`. At this point, no object was created and no memory allocated for it:

```
CapuchinMonkey myObjectName;
```

We use the `new` keyword to create an object. The following example illustrates how to invoke the `new` operation to create an object. This operation results in:

```
myObjectName = new CapuchinMonkey();
```

Of course, we can combine the declaration and creation statements together by using `CapuchinMonkey myObjectName = new CapuchinMonkey();` instead of `CapuchinMonkey myObjectName;` and `myObjectName = new CapuchinMonkey();`. They were separated in the preceding example for illustrative purposes.

When an object is created, a specific amount of memory is allocated for storing that object. The amount of memory allocated can differ based on architecture and JVM.

Next look at the mid-life of an object.

Object mid-life

Objects are created and Java allocates system memory for storing that object. If the object is not used, the memory allocated to it is considered wasted. This is something we want to avoid. Even with small applications, this type of wasted memory can lead to poor performance and even out-of-memory issues.

Our goal is to deallocate or release the memory, any previously allocated memory that we no longer need. Fortunately, with Java, there is a mechanism for handling this issue. It is called garbage collection.

When an object, such as our `myObjectName` example, no longer has any references pointing to it, the system will reallocate the associated memory.

Object destruction

The idea of Java having a garbage collector running in the dark shadows of your code (usually a low-priority thread) and deallocating memory currently allocated to unreferenced objects, is appealing. So, how does this work? The garbage collection system monitors objects and, as feasible, counts the number of references to each object.

When there are no references to an object, there is no way to get to it with the currently running code, so it makes perfect sense to deallocate the associated memory.

> The term **memory leak** refers to small memory chunks to be lost or improperly deallocated. These leaks are avoidable with Java's garbage collection.

Garbage collection algorithms

There are several garbage collection algorithms, or types, for use by the Java virtual machine. In this section, we will cover the following garbage collection algorithms:

- Mark and sweep
- CMS garbage collection
- Serial garbage collection
- Parallel garbage collection
- G1 garbage collection

Mark and sweep

Java's initial garbage collection algorithm, *mark and sweep*, used a simple two-step process:

1. Java first step, mark, is to step through all objects that have accessible references, marking those objects as alive.
2. The second step, sweep, involves scanning the sea for any object that is not marked.

As you can readily determine, the mark and sweep algorithm seems effective, but probably not very efficient due to the two-step nature of this approach. This eventually lead to a Java garbage collection system with vastly improved efficiencies.

Concurrent mark sweep (CMS) garbage collection

The **concurrent mark sweep** (**CMS**) algorithm for garbage collection scans heap memory using multiple threads. Similar to the mark and sweep method, it marks objects for removal and then makes a sweep to actually remove those objects. This method of garbage collection is essentially an upgraded mark and sweep method. It was modified to take advantage of faster systems and had performance enhancements.

To manually invoke the concurrent mark sweep garbage collection algorithm for your application, use the following command-line option:

```
-XX:+UseConcMarkSweepGC
```

If you want to use the concurrent mark sweep garbage collection algorithm and dictate the number of threads to use, you can use the following command-line option. In the following example, we are telling the Java platform to use the concurrent mark sweep garbage collection algorithm with eight threads:

```
-XX:ParallelCMSThreads=8
```

Serial garbage collection

Java's serial garbage collection works on a single thread. When executing, it freezes all other threads until garbage collection operations have concluded. Due to the thread-freezing nature of serial garbage collection, it is only feasible for very small programs.

To manually invoke the serial garbage collection algorithm for your application, use the following command-line option:

```
-XX:+UseSerialGC
```

Parallel garbage collection

Prior to Java 9, the parallel garbage collection algorithm was the default garbage collector. It uses multiple threads but freezes all non-garbage collection threads in the application until garbage collection functions have completed, just like the serial garbage collection algorithm.

G1 garbage collection

The G1 garbage collection algorithm was created for use with large memory heaps. This approach involves segmenting the memory heap into regions. Garbage collection, using the G1 algorithm, takes place in parallel with each heap region.

Another part of the G1 algorithm is that when memory is deallocated, the heap space is compacted. Unfortunately, the compacting operation takes place using the *Stop the World* approach.

The G1 garbage collection algorithm also prioritizes the regions based on those that have the most garbage to be collected.

The G1 name refers to Garbage First.

To manually invoke the G1 garbage collection algorithm for your application, use the following command-line option:

```
-XX:+UseG1GC
```

Garbage collection options

Here is a list of JVM sizing options:

Sizing description	JVM option flag
Sets the initial heap size (young space plus tenured space).	`-XX:InitialHeapSize=3g`
Sets the maximum heap size (young space plus tenured space).	`-XX:MaxHeapSize=3g`
Sets the initial and maximum heap size (young space plus tenured space).	`-Xms2048m -Xmx3g`
Sets the initial size of young space.	`-XX:NewSize=128m`
Sets the maximum size of young space.	`-XX:MaxNewSize=128m`
Sets young space size. Uses ration of young verses tenured space. In the sample flag to the right, 3 means that young space will be three times smaller than tenured space.	`-XX:NewRation=3`
Sets the size of single survivor space as a portion of Eden space size.	`-XX:SurvivorRatio=15`
Sets the initial size of the permanent space.	`-XX:PermSize=512m`
Sets the maximum size of the permanent space.	`-XX:MaxPermSize=512m`
Sets the size of the stack area dedicated to each thread in bytes.	`-Xss512k`

| Sets the size of the stack area dedicated to each thread in Kbytes. | `-XX:ThreadStackSize=512` |
| Sets the maximum size of off-heap memory available to the JVM. | `-XX:MaxDirectMemorySize=3g` |

Here is a list of young garbage collection options:

Young garbage collection tuning option	Flag
Sets the initial value for the number of collections before an object will be promoted from young to tenured space. This is referred to as the **tenuring threshold**.	`-XX:InitialTenuringThreshold=16`
Sets the maximum value for tenuring threshold.	`-XX:MaxTenuringThreshold=30`
Sets the maximum object size allowed to be allocated in young space. If an object is larger than the maximum size it will be allocated to tenured space and bypass young space.	`-XX:PretenureSizeThreshold=3m`
This can be used to promote all young objects surviving the young collection to tenured space.	`-XX:+AlwaysTenure`
With this tag, objects from young space never get promoted to tenured space as long as the survivor space has sufficient room for them.	`-XX:+NeverTenure`
We can indicate that we want to use thread local allocation blocks in the young space. This is enabled by default.	`-XX:+UseTLAB`
Toggle this to allow the JVM to adaptively resize the **TLAB** (**Thread Local Allocation Blocks**) for threads.	`-XX:+ResizeTLAB`
Sets the initial size of TLAB for a thread.	`-XX:TLABSize=2m`
Sets the minimum allowable size of TLAB.	`-XX:MinTLABSize=128k`

Here is a list of **concurrent mark sweep (CMS)** tuning options:

CMS tuning option	Flag
Indicates that you want to solely use occupancy as a criterion for starting a CMS collection operation.	`-XX:+UseCMSInitiatingOccupancyOnly`
Sets the percentage CMS generation occupancy to start a CMS collection cycle. If you indicate a negative number, you are telling the JVM you want to use `CMSTriggerRatio`.	`-XX:CMSInitiatingOccupancyFraction=70`
Sets the percentage CMS generation occupancy that you want to initiate a CMS collection for bootstrapping collection statistics.	`-XX:CMSBootstrapOccupancy=10`
This is the percentage of `MinHeapFreeRatio` in CMS generation that is allocated prior to a CMS cycle starts.	`-XX:CMSTriggerRatio=70`
Sets the percentage of `MinHeapFreeRatio` in the CMS permanent generation that is allocated before starting a CMS collection cycle.	`-XX:CMSTriggerPermRatio=90`
This is the wait duration after a CMS collection is triggered. Use the parameter to specify how long the CMS is allowed to wait for young collection.	`-XX:CMSWaitDuration=2000`
Enables parallel remark.	`-XX:+CMSParallelRemarkEnabled`

Enables parallel remark of survivor space.	`-XX:+CMSParallelSurvivorRemarkEnabled`
You can use this to force young collection before the remark phase.	`-XX:+CMSScavengeBeforeRemark`
Use this to prevent scheduling remark if Eden used is below the threshold value.	`-XX:+CMSScheduleRemarkEdenSizeThreshold`
Sets the Eden occupancy percentage that you want CMS to try and schedule a remark pause.	`-XX:CMSScheduleRemarkEdenPenetration=20`
This is where you want to start sampling Eden top at least before young generation occupancy reaches $1/4^{th}$ (in our sample to the right) of the size at which you want to schedule remark.	`-XX:CMSScheduleRemarkSamplingRatio=4`
You can select `variant=1` or `variant=2` of verification following remark.	`-XX:CMSRemarkVerifyVariant=1`
Elects to use the parallel algorithm for young space collection.	`-XX:+UseParNewGC`
Enables the use of multiple threads for concurrent phases.	`-XX:+CMSConcurrentMTEnabled`
Sets the number of parallel threads used for the concurrent phases.	`-XX:ConcGCThreads=2`
Sets the number of parallel threads you want used for *stop-the-world* phases.	`-XX:ParallelGCThreads=2`

You can enable **incremental CMS (iCMS)** mode.	`-XX:+CMSIncrementalMode`
If this is not enabled, CMS will not clean permanent space.	`-XX:+CMSClassUnloadingEnabled`
This allows `System.gc()` to trigger concurrent collection instead of a full garbage collection cycle.	`-XX:+ExplicitGCInvokesConcurrent`
This allows `System.gc()` to trigger concurrent collection of permanent space.	`-XX:+ExplicitGCInvokesConcurrentAndUnloadsClasses`

> **TIP**
>
> **iCMS (incremental concurrent mark sweep**) mode is intended for servers with a small number of CPUs. It should not be employed on modern hardware.

Here are some miscellaneous garbage collection options:

Miscellaneous garbage collection options	Flag
This will cause the JVM to ignore any `System.gc()` method invocations by an application.	`-XX:+DisableExplicitGC`
This is the (soft reference) time to live in milliseconds per MB of free space in the heap.	`-XX:SoftRefLRUPolicyMSPerMB=2000`
This is the **use policy** used to limit the time spent in garbage collection before an `OutOfMemory` error is thrown.	`-XX:+UseGCOverheadLimit`
This limits the proportion of time spent in garbage collection before an `OutOfMemory` error is thrown. This is used with `GCHeapFreeLimit`.	`-XX:GCTimeLimit=95`

This sets the minimum percentage of free space after a full garbage collection before an `OutOfMemory` error is thrown. This is used with `GCTimeLimit`.	`-XX:GCHeapFreeLimit=5`

Finally, here are some G1 specific options. Note that, these are all supported starting with JVM 6u26:

G1 garbage collection options	Flag
Size of the heap region. The default is 2,048 and the acceptable range is 1 MiB to 32 MiB.	`-XX:G1HeapRegionSize=16m`
This is the confidence coefficient pause prediction heuristics.	`-XX:G1ConfidencePercent=75`
This determines the minimum reserve in the heap.	`-XX:G1ReservePercent=5`
This is the garbage collection time per MMU--time slice in milliseconds.	`-XX:MaxGCPauseMillis=100`
This is the pause interval time slice per MMU in milliseconds.	`-XX:GCPauseIntervalMillis=200`

MiB stands for **Mebibyte** which is a multiple of bytes for digital information.

Java methods relevant to garbage collection

Let's look at two specific methods associated with garbage collection.

The System.gc() method

Although garbage collection is automatic in Java, you can make explicit calls to the `java.lang.System.gc()` method to aid in the debugging process. This method does not take any parameters and does not return any value. It is an explicit call that runs Java's garbage collector. Here is a sample implementation:

```
System.gc();
System.out.println("Garbage collected and unused
 memory has been deallocated.");
```

Let's look at a more in-depth example. In the following code, we start by creating an instance of the `Runtime`, using `Runtime myRuntime = Runtime.getRuntime();` which returns a singleton. This gives us access to the JVM. After printing some header information and initial memory stats, we create an `ArrayList` with a size of `300000`. Then, we create a loop that generates `100000` array list objects. Lastly, we provide output in three passes, asking the JVM to invoke the garbage collector with `1` second pauses in between. Here is the source code:

```
package MyGarbageCollectionSuite;

import java.util.ArrayList;
import java.util.concurrent.TimeUnit;

public class GCVerificationTest
{
  public static void main(String[] args) throws
    InterruptedException
    {
      // Obtain a Runtime instance (to communicate
       with the JVM)
      Runtime myRuntime = Runtime.getRuntime();

      // Set header information and output initial
       memory stats
      System.out.println("Garbage Collection
       Verification Test");
      System.out.println("-----------------------------
       ----------------------------");
      System.out.println("Initial JVM Memory: " +
       myRuntime.totalMemory() +
          "tFree Memory: " + myRuntime.freeMemory());
      // Use a bunch of memory
      ArrayList<Integer> AccountNumbers = new
       ArrayList<>(300000);
      for (int i = 0; i < 100000; i++)
```

```
{
  AccountNumbers = new ArrayList<>(3000);
  AccountNumbers = null;
}

// Provide update with with three passes
for (int i = 0; i < 3; i++)
{
  System.out.println("----------------------------
    -----------");
  System.out.println("Free Memory before
    collection number " +
      (i+1) + ": " + myRuntime.freeMemory());
  System.gc();
  System.out.println("Free Memory after
    collection number " +
      (i+1) + ": " + myRuntime.freeMemory());
  TimeUnit.SECONDS.sleep(1); // delay thread
    1 second
}


}

}
```

As you can see from the following output, the garbage collector did not reallocate all of the 'garbage' during the first or even the second pass:

```
Garbage Collection Verification Test
-----------------------------------------------------------
Initial JVM Memory: 514850816    Free Memory: 509439928
--------------------------------------
Free Memory before collection number 1: 768241776
Free Memory after collection number 1: 888052656
--------------------------------------
Free Memory before collection number 2: 888052656
Free Memory after collection number 2: 887536992
--------------------------------------
Free Memory before collection number 3: 887536992
Free Memory after collection number 3: 888061280
```

There is an alternative to using the `System.gc()` method to invoke the garbage collector. In our example, we could have used `myRuntime.gc()`, our earlier singleton example.

The finalize() method

You can think of Java's garbage collector as a death dealer. When it removes something from memory, it is gone. This so-called death dealer is not without compassion as it provides each method with their final last words. The objects give their *last words* through a `finalize()` method. If an object has a `finalize()` method, the garbage collector invokes it before the object is removed and the associated memory deallocated. The method takes no parameters and has a return type of `void`.

The `finalize()` method is only called once and there can be variability when it is run. Certainly, the method is invoked before it is removed, but when the garbage collector runs is dependent on the system. If, as an example, you have a relatively small app that is running a memory-rich system, the garbage collector might not run at all. So, why include a `finalize()` method at all? It is considered poor programming practice to override the `finalize()` method. That being said, you can use the method if needed. In fact, you can add code there to add a reference to your object to ensure it is not removed by the garbage collector. Again, this is not advisable.

Because all objects in Java, even the ones you create yourself are child classes of `java.lang.Object`, every object in Java has a `finalize()` method.

The garbage collector, as sophisticated as it is, might not close databases, files, or network connections the way you want it done. If your application requires specific considerations when its objects are collected, you can override the object's `finalize()` method.

Here is an example implementation that demonstrates a use case for when you might want to override an object's `finalize()` method:

```
public class Animal
{
  private static String animalName;
  private static String animalBreed;
  private static int objectTally = 0;

  // constructor
  public Animal(String name, String type)
  {
    animalName = name;
    animalBreed = type;

    // increment count of object
    ++objectTally;
  }
```

```
protected void finalize()
{
  // decrement object count each time this method
  // is called by the garbage collector
  --objectTally;

  //Provide output to user
  System.out.println(animalName + " has been
   removed from memory.");

  // condition for 1 animal (use singular form)
  if (objectTally == 1)
  {
    System.out.println("You have " + objectTally + "
     animal remaining.");
  }

  // condition for 0 or greater than 1
   animals (use plural form)
  else
  {
    System.out.println("You have " + objectTally + "
     animals remaining.");
  }

}

}
```

As you can see in the preceding code, the objectTally count is incremented each time an object of type Animal is created and decremented when one is removed by the garbage collector.

> Overriding an object's finalize() method is usually discouraged. The finalize() method should normally be declared as protected.

Pre-Java 9 garbage collection

Java's garbage collection is not new to Java 9, it has existed since the initial release of Java. Java has long had a sophisticated garbage collection system that is automatic and runs in the background. By running in the background, we are referring to garbage collection processes running during idle times.

Idle times refer to the time in between input/output such as between keyboard input, mouse clicks, and output generation.

This automatic garbage collection has been one of the key factors in developers selecting Java for their programming solutions. Other programming languages such as C# and Objective-C have implemented garbage collection following the success of the Java platform.

Let's next take a look at the following listed concepts before we look at the changes to garbage collection in the Java 9 platform:

- Visualizing garbage collection
- Garbage collection upgrades in Java 8
- Case study - Games written with Java

Visualizing garbage collection

It can be helpful to visualize how garbage collection works and, perhaps more importantly, the need for it. Consider the following code snippet that progressively creates the string Garbage:

```
001 String var = new String("G");
002 var += "a";
003 var += "r";
004 var += "b";
005 var += "a";
006 var += "g";
007 var += "e";
008 System.out.println("Your completed String
 is: " + var + ".");
```

Clearly, the preceding code generates the output provided as follows:

```
Your completed String is Garbage.
```

What might not be clear is that the sample code results in five unreferenced string objects. This is due, in part, because strings are immutable. As you can see in the following illustration, with each successive line of code, the referenced object is updated and an additional object becomes unreferenced:

Line of Code	001	002	003	004	005	006	007
Code	String var = new String("G");	var+="a";	var+="r";	var+="b";	var+="a";	var+="g";	var+="e";
Referenced memory	var → "G"	var → "Ga"	var → "Gar"	var → "Garb"	var → "Garba"	var → "Garbag"	var → "Garbage"
Unreferenced memory		"G"	"G" "Ga"	"G" "Ga" "Gar"	"G" "Ga" "Gar" "Garb"	"G" "Ga" "Gar" "Garb" "Garba"	"G" "Ga" "Gar" "Garb" "Garbag"

The preceding unreferenced objects listed certainly will not break the memory bank, but it is indicative of how quickly a large number of unreferenced objects can accumulate.

Garbage collection upgrades in Java 8

As of Java 8, the default garbage collection algorithm was the parallel garbage collector. Java 8 was released with some improvements to the G1 garbage collection system. One of these improvements was the ability to use the following command-line option to optimize the heap memory by removing duplicative string values:

```
-XX:+UseStringDeduplication
```

The G1 garbage collector can view the character arrays when it sees a string. It then takes the value and stores it with a new, weak reference to the character array. If the G1 garbage collector finds a string with the same hash code, it will compare the two strings with a character-by-character review. If a match is found, both strings end up pointing to the same character array. Specifically, the first string will point to the character array of the second string.

This method can require substantial processing overhead and should only be used if deemed beneficial or absolutely necessary.

Case study - Games written with Java

Multiplayer games require extensive management techniques, both for server and client systems. The JVM runs the garbage collection thread in a low-priority thread and periodically runs. Server administrators previously used an incremental garbage collection schema using the now depreciated -Xincgc command-line option to avoid **server stalls** that occur when the server is overloaded. The goal is to have garbage collection run more frequently and with much shorter execution cycles each time.

> **TIP**
>
> When considering memory usage and garbage collection, it is important to use as little memory on the target system as possible and to limit pauses for garbage collection to the extent feasible. These tips are especially important for games, simulations, and other applications that require real-time performance.

The JVM manages the heap where Java memory is stored. The JVM starts with a small heap by default and grows as additional objects are created. The heap has two partitions--young and tenured. When objects are initially created, they are created in the young partition. Persistent objects are moved to the tenure partition. The creation of objects is usually very quick with not much more than pointer incrementation. Processing in the young partition is much faster than that of the tenured partition. This is important because it applies to the overall app, or in our case, a game's efficiency.

It becomes important for us to monitor our game's memory usage and when garbage collection occurs. To monitor garbage collection, we can add the verbose flag (-verbose:gc) when we launch our game such as with the following example:

```
java -verbose:gc MyJavaGameClass
```

The JVM will then provide a line of formatted output for each garbage collection. Here is the format of the verbose GC output:

```
[<TYPE> <MEMORY USED BEFORE> -> MEMORY USED AFTER
(TOTAL HEAP SIZE), <TIME>]
```

Let's look at two examples. In this first example, we see GC for type which refers to the young partition we previously discussed:

```
[GC 31924K -> 29732K(42234K), 0.0019319 secs]
```

In this second example, `Full GC` indicates that the garbage collection action was taken on the tenured partition of the memory heap:

```
[Full GC 29732K -> 10911K(42234K), 0.0319319 secs]
```

You can obtain more detailed information from the garbage collector using the `-XX:+PrintGCDetails` option as shown here:

```
java -verbose:gc -XX:+PrintGCDetails MyJavaGameClass
```

Collecting garbage with the new Java platform

Java came out of the gate with automatic garbage collection, making it a development platform of choice for many programmers. It was commonplace to want to avoid manual memory management in other programming languages. We have looked in-depth at the garbage collection system to include the various approaches, or algorithms, used by the JVM. Java 9 includes some relevant changes to the garbage collection system and was the focus of three **Java Enhancement Program** (JEP) issues. Those issues are listed here:

- Default garbage collection (JEP 248)
- Depreciated garbage collection combinations (JEP 214)
- Unified garbage collection logging (JEP 271)

We will review each one of these garbage collection concepts and their corresponding **Java Enhancement Plan** (**JEP**) issue in the following sections.

Default garbage collection

We previously detailed the following garbage collection approaches used by the JVM prior to Java 9. These are still plausible garbage collection algorithms:

- CMS garbage collection
- Serial garbage collection
- Parallel garbage collection
- G1 garbage collection

Let's briefly recap each of these approaches:

- **CMS garbage collection**: The CMS garbage collection algorithm scans heap memory using multiple threads. Using this approach, the JVM marks objects for removal and then makes a sweep to actually remove them.
- **Serial garbage collection**: This approach uses a thread-freezing schema on a single thread. When the garbage collection is in progress, it freezes all other threads until garbage collection operations have concluded. Due to the thread-freezing nature of serial garbage collection, it is only feasible for very small programs.
- **Parallel garbage collection**: This approach uses multiple threads but freezes all non-garbage collection threads in the application until garbage collection functions have completed, just like the serial garbage collection algorithm.
- **G1 garbage collection**: This is the garbage collection algorithm with the following characteristics:
    - Is used with large memory heaps
    - Involves segmenting the memory heap into regions
    - Takes place in parallel with each heap region
    - Compacts the heap space when memory is deallocated
    - Compacting operations take place using the *Stop the World* approach
    - Prioritizes the regions based on those that have the most garbage to be collected

Prior to Java 9, the parallel garbage collection algorithm was the default garbage collector. In Java 9, the G1 garbage collector is the new default implementation of Java's memory management system. This is true for both 32 and 64-bit server configurations.

Oracle assessed that the G1 garbage collector, mostly due to its low-pause nature, was a better performing garbage collection method than the parallel approach. This change was predicated on the following concepts:

- It is important to limit latency
- Maximizing throughput is less important than limiting latency
- The G1 garbage collection algorithm is stable

There are two assumptions involved with making the G1 garbage collection method the default method over the parallel approach:

- Making G1 the default garbage collection method will significantly increase its use. This increased usage might unveil performance or stability issues not realized before Java 9.
- The G1 approach is more processor-intensive than the parallel approach. In some use cases, this could be somewhat problematic.

On the surface this change might seem like a great step for Java 9 and that very well might be the case. Caution, however, should be used when blindly accepting this new default collection method. It is recommended that systems be tested if switching to G1 to ensure your applications do not suffer from performance degradation or have unexpected issues that are caused by the use of G1. As previously suggested, G1 has not benefited from the widespread testing that the parallel method has.

This last point about the lack of widespread testing is significant. Making G1 the default automatic memory management (garbage collection) system with Java 9 is tantamount to turning developers into unsuspecting testers. While no major problems are expected, knowing that there is potential for performance and stability issues when using G1 with Java 9 will place greater emphasis on testing your Java 9 applications.

Depreciated garbage collection combinations

Oracle has been great about depreciating features, APIs, and libraries before removing them from a new release to the Java platform. With this schema in place, language components that were depreciated in Java 8 are subject for removal in Java 9. There are a few garbage collection combinations that were deemed to be rarely used and depreciated in Java 8. Those combinations, listed here, have been removed in Java 9:

- DefNew + CMS
- ParNew + SerialOld
- Incremental CMS

These combinations, in addition to having been rarely used, introduced an unneeded level of complexity to the garbage collection system. This resulted in an extra drain on system resources without providing a commensurate benefit to the user or developer.

The following listed garbage collection configurations were affected by the aforementioned depreciation in the Java 8 platform:

Garbage collection configuration	Flag(s)
DefNew + CMS	`-XX:+UseParNewGC` `-XX:UseConcMarkSweepGC`
ParNew + SerialOld	`-XX:+UseParNewGC`
ParNew + iCMS	`-Xincgc`
ParNew + iCMS	`-XX:+CMSIncrementalMode` `-XX:+UseConcMarkSweepGC`

Defnew + ICMS	`-XX:+CMSIncrementalMode`
	`-XX:+UseConcMarkSweepGC`
	`-XX:-UseParNewGC`

The **Java Enhancement Program 214 (JEP 214)** removed garbage collection combinations depreciated in JDK 8. Those combinations are listed above along with the flags that control those combinations. In addition, the flags to enable CMS foreground collections were removed and are not present in JDK 9. Those flags are listed as follows:

Garbage collection combinations	Flag
CMS foreground	`-XX:+UseCMSCompactAtFullCollection`
CMS foreground	`-XX+CMSFullGCsBeforeCompaction`
CMS foreground	`-XX+UseCMSCollectionPassing`

The only assessed downside to the removal of the depreciated garbage collection combinations is that applications that use JVM start up files with any of the flags listed in this section, will need to have their JVM start up files modified to remove or replace the old flags.

Unified garbage collection logging

The **Java Enhancement Program #271 (JEP-271)** titled, *Unified GC Logging*, is intended to re-implement garbage collection logging using the unified JVM logging framework that was previously introduced with JEP-158. So, let's first review the Unified JVM Logging (JEP-158).

Unified JVM logging (JEP-158)

Creating a unified logging schema for the JVM was the central goal of JEP-158. Here is a high-level list of the goals of the JEP:

- Create a JVM-wide set of command-line options for all logging operations
- Use categorized tags for logging
- Provide six levels of logging:
    - Error
    - Warning
    - Information
    - Debug
    - Trace
    - Develop

> This is not an exhaustive list of goals. We will discuss JEP-158 in greater detail in `Chapter 14`, *Command Line Flags*.

The changes to the JVM, in the context of logging, can be categorized into:

- Tags
- Levels
- Decorations
- Output
- Command-line options

Let's briefly look at these categories.

Tags

Logging tags are identified in the JVM and can be changed in source code if needed. The tags should be self-identifying, such as `gc` for garbage collection.

Levels

Each log message has an associated level. As previously listed, the levels are error, warning, information, debug, trace, and develop. The following chart shows how the levels have an increasing level of verbosity in respect to how much information is logged:

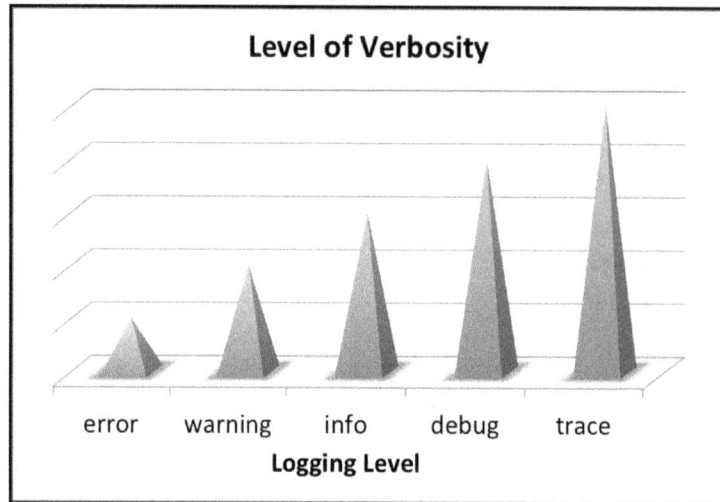

Decorations

In the context of Java 9's logging framework, decorations is metadata about the log message. Here is the alphabetic list of decorations that are available:

- level
- pid
- tags
- tid
- time
- timemillis
- timenanos
- uptime
- uptimemillis
- uptimenanos

For an explanation of these decorations, please refer to Chapter 14, *Command Line Flags*.

Output

The Java 9 logging framework supports three types of output:

- stderr: Provides output to stderr
- stdout: Provides output to stdout
- text file: Writes the output to text files

Command-line options

A new command-line option was added to the logging framework to provide overall control of the JVM's logging operations. The -Xlog command-line option has an extensive array of parameters and possibilities. Here is one example:

```
-Xlog:gc+rt*=debug
```

In this example, we are telling the JVM to take the following actions:

- Log all messages tagged with, at a minimum, the gc and rt tags
- Use the debug level
- Provide output to stdout

Unified GC logging (JEP-271)

Now that we have a general understanding of the changes to Java 9's logging framework, let's look at what changes JEP-271 introduced. In this section we will look at the following areas:

- Garbage collection logging options
- The gc tag
- Macros
- Additional considerations

Garbage collection logging options

Here is a list of garbage collection logging options and flags we had available to us before the introduction of Java 9's logging framework:

Garbage collection logging option	JVM option flag(s)
This prints the basic garbage collection information.	`-verbose:gc` or `-XX:+PrintGC`
This will print more detailed garbage collection information.	`-XX:+PrintGCDetails`
You can print timestamps for each garbage collection event. The seconds are sequential and begin from the JVM start time.	`-XX:+PrintGCTimeStamps`
You can print date stamps for each garbage collection event. Sample format: `2017-07-26T03:19:00.319+400:[GC . . . ]`	`-XX:+PrintGCDateStamps`
You can use this flag to print timestamps for individual garbage collection work thread tasks.	`-XX:+PrintGCTaskTimeStamps`
Using this you can redirect garbage collection output to a file instead of the console.	`-Xloggc:`
You can print detailed information regarding young space following each collection cycle.	`-XX:+PrintTenuringDistribution`
You can use this flag to print TLAB allocation statistics.	`-XX:+PrintTLAB`
Using this flag, you can print the times for reference processing (that is, weak, soft, and so on) during *stop-the-world* pauses.	`-XX:+PrintReferenceGC`
This reports if the garbage collection is waiting for native code to unpin objects in memory.	`-XX:+PrintJNIGCStalls`
This will print a pause summary after each *stop-the-world* pause.	`-XX:+PrintGCApplicationStoppedTime`

This flag will print time for each concurrent phase of garbage collection.	`-XX:+PrintGCApplicationConcurrentTime`
Using this flag will print a class histogram after a full garbage collection.	`-XX:+PrintClassHistogramAfterFullGC`
Using this flag will print a class histogram before a full garbage collection.	`-XX:+PrintClassHistogramBeforeFullGC`
This creates a heap dump file after full garbage collection.	`-XX:+HeapDumpAfterFullGC`
This creates a heap dump file before full garbage collection.	`-XX:+HeapDumpBeforeFullGC`
This creates a heap dump file in an out-of-memory condition.	`-XX:+HeapDumpOnOutOfMemoryError`
You use this flag to specify the path where you want your heap dumps saved on your system.	`-XX:HeapDumpPath=<path>`
You can use this to print CMS statistics, `if n >= 1`. Applies specifically to CMS only.	`-XX:PrintCMSStatistics=2`
This will print CMS initialization details. Applies specifically to CMS only.	`-XX:+PrintCMSInitiationStatistics`
You can use this flag to print additional information concerning free lists. Applies specifically to CMS only.	`-XX:PrintFLSStatistics=2`
You can use this flag to print additional information concerning free lists. Applies specifically to CMS only.	`-XX:PrintFLSCensus=2`
You can use this flag to print detailed diagnostic information following a promotion (young to tenure) failure. Applies specifically to CMS only.	`-XX:+PrintPromotionFailure`
This flag allows you to dump useful information regarding the state of the CMS old generation when a promotion (young to tenure) failure occurs. Applies specifically to CMS only.	`-XX:+CMSDumpAtPromotionFailure`

When the –XX:+CMSDumpAtPromotionFailure flag is used, you can use –XX:+CMSPrintChunksInDump to include additional details regarding free chunks. Applies specifically to CMS only.	-XX:+CMSPrintChunksInDump
When using the –XX:+CMSPrintChunksInDump flag, you can include additional information about the allocated objects using the –XX:+CMSPrintObjectsInDump flag. Applies specifically to CMS only.	-XX:+CMSPrintObjectsInDump

The gc tag

We can use the gc tag with the -Xlog option to inform the JVM to only log gc tagged items at the info level. As you will recall, this is similar to using -XX:+PrintGC. With both options, the JVM will log one line for each garbage collection operation.

It is important to note that the gc tag was not intended to be used on its own; rather, it is recommended that it be used in conjunction with other tags.

Macros

We can create macros to add logic to our garbage collection logging. Here is the general syntax for the log macro:

```
log_<level>(Tag1[,...])(fmtstr, ...)
```

Here is an example of a log macro:

```
log_debug(gc, classloading)("Number of objects
 loaded: %d.", object_count)
```

The following example skeleton log macro shows how you can use the new Java 9 logging framework to create scripts for greater fidelity in logging:

```
LogHandle(gc, rt, classunloading) log;
if (log.is_error())
{
  // do something specific regarding the 'error' level
}

if (log.is_warning())
{
  // do something specific regarding the 'warning'
  level
}

if (log.is_info())
{
  // do something specific regarding the 'info' level
}

if (log.is_debug())
{
  // do something specific regarding the 'debug' level
}

if (log.is_trace())
{
  // do something specific regarding the 'trace' level
}
```

Additional considerations

Here are some additional items to be considered in regards to garbage collection logging:

- Using the new -Xlog:gc should produce similar results to the -XX:+PrintGCDetails command-line option and flag pairing
- The new trace level provides the level of detail previously provided with the verbose flag

Persistent issues

Even with the advent of Java 9, there were downsides to Java's garbage collection system. Because it is an automatic process, we do not have complete control of when the collector runs. We, as developers, are not in control of garbage collection, the JVM is. The JVM makes the decision when to run garbage collection. As you have seen earlier in this chapter, we can ask the JVM to run garbage collection using the `System.gc()` method. Despite our use of this method, we are guaranteed that our request will be honored or that it will be complied with in a timely manner.

Earlier in this chapter, we reviewed several approaches and algorithms for garbage collection. We discussed how we, as developers, can take control of the process. That assumes that we have the ability to take control of garbage collection. Even when we specify a specific garbage collection technique, for example using –
`XX:+UseConcMarkSweepGC` for CMS garbage collection, we are not guaranteed that the JVM will use that implementation. So, we can do our best to control how the garbage collector works, but should remember that the JVM has the ultimate authority regarding how, when, and if garbage collection occurs.

Our lack of complete control over garbage collection underscores the importance of writing efficient code with memory management in mind. In the next sections, we will examine how to write code to explicitly make objects eligible for garbage collection by the JVM.

Making objects eligible for garbage collection

An easy method for making objects available for garbage collection is to assign `null` to the reference variable that refers to the object. Let's review this example:

```java
package MyGarbageCollectionSuite;

public class GarbageCollectionExperimentOne
{
  public static void main(String[] args)
  {

    // Declare and create new object.
    String junk = new String("Pile of Junk");

    // Output to demonstrate that the object
    has an active reference
    // and is not eligible for garbage collection.
    System.out.println(junk);
```

```
// Set the reference variable to null.
junk = null;

// The String object junk is now eligible
for garbage collection.

}

}
```

As indicated in the in-code comments, once the string object reference variable is set to null, in this case using the `junk = null;` statement, the object becomes available for garbage collection.

In our next example, we will abandon an object by setting its reference variable to point to a different object. As you can see in the following code, that results in the first object being available for garbage collection:

```
package MyGarbageCollectionSuite;

public class GarbageCollectionExperimentTwo
{
  public static void main(String[] args)
  {
    // Declare and create the first object.
    String junk1 = new String("The first pile of
     Junk");

    // Declare and create the second object.
    String junk2 = new String("The second pile of
     Junk");

    // Output to demonstrate that both objects have
    active references
    // and are not eligible for garbage collection.
    System.out.println(junk1);
    System.out.println(junk2);

    // Set the first object's reference to the
     second object.
    junk1 = junk2;

    // The String "The first pile of Junk" is now
     eligible for garbage collection.

  }
```

```
        }
```

Let's review one final method of making objects available for garbage collection. In this example, we have a single instance variable (objectNbr) that is a reference variable to an instance of the GarbageCollectionExperimentThree class. The class does not do anything interesting other than create additional reference variables to instances of the GarbageCollectionExperimentThree class. In our example, we set the objectNbr2, objectNbr3, objectNbr4, and objectNbr5 references to null. Although these objects have instance variables and can refer to each other, their accessibility outside of the class has been terminated by setting their references to null. This makes them (objectNbr2, objectNbr3, objectNbr4, and objectNbr5) eligible for garbage collection:

```
package MyGarbageCollectionSuite;
{

  // instance variable
  GarbageCollectionExperimentThree objectNbr;

  public static void main(String[] args)
  {
    GarbageCollectionExperimentThree objectNbr2 = new
     GarbageCollectionExperimentThree();
    GarbageCollectionExperimentThree objectNbr3 = new
     GarbageCollectionExperimentThree();
    GarbageCollectionExperimentThree objectNbr4 = new
     GarbageCollectionExperimentThree();
    GarbageCollectionExperimentThree objectNbr5 = new
     GarbageCollectionExperimentThree();
    GarbageCollectionExperimentThree objectNbr6 = new
     GarbageCollectionExperimentThree();
    GarbageCollectionExperimentThree objectNbr7 = new
     GarbageCollectionExperimentThree();

    // set objectNbr2 to refer to objectNbr3
    objectNbr2.objectNbr = objectNbr3;

    // set objectNbr3 to refer to objectNbr4
    objectNbr3.objectNbr = objectNbr4;

    // set objectNbr4 to refer to objectNbr5
    objectNbr4.objectNbr = objectNbr5;

    // set objectNbr5 to refer to objectNbr2
    objectNbr5.objectNbr = objectNbr2;

    // set selected references to null
```

```
        objectNbr2 = null;
        objectNbr3 = null;
        objectNbr4 = null;
        objectNbr5 = null;

    }

}
```

Summary

In this chapter we took an in-depth review of garbage collection as a critical pre-Java 9 platform component. Our review included object life cycle, garbage collection algorithms, garbage collection options, and methods related to garbage collection. We looked at upgrades to garbage collection in Java 8 and looked at a case study to help our understanding of modern garbage collection. We then turned our focus to the changes to garbage collection with the new Java 9 platform. Our exploration of garbage collection in Java 9 included looks at default garbage collection, depreciated garbage collection combinations, and unified garbage collection logging. We concluded our exploration of garbage collection by looking at a few garbage collection issues that persist, even after Java 9.

In the next chapter we will look at how to write performance tests using the **Java Microbenchmark Harness (JMH)**, a Java harness library for writing benchmarks for the JVM.

8
Microbenchmarking Applications with JMH

In the previous chapter, we took an in-depth review of **garbage collection** to include an object life cycle, garbage collection algorithms, garbage collection options, and methods related to garbage collection. We took a brief look at upgrades to garbage collection in Java 8 and focused on changes with the new Java 9 platform. Our exploration of garbage collection in Java 9 included looks at default garbage collection, depreciated garbage collection combinations, unified garbage collection logging, and garbage collection issues that persist, even after Java 9.

In this chapter, we will look at how to write performance tests using the **Java Microbenchmark Harness** (**JMH**), a Java harness library for writing benchmarks for the **Java Virtual Machine** (**JVM**). We will use Maven along with JMH to help illustrate the power of microbenchmarking with the new Java 9 platform.

Specifically, we will cover the following topics:

- Microbenchmarking overview
- Microbenchmarking with Maven
- Benchmarking options
- Techniques for avoiding microbenchmarking pitfalls

Microbenchmarking overview

Microbenchmarking is used to test the performance of a system. This differs from macrobenchmarking which runs tests on different platforms for efficiency comparison and subsequent analysis. With microbenchmarking, we typically target a specific slice of code on one system such as a method or loop. The primary purpose of microbenchmarking is to identify optimization opportunities in our code.

There are multiple approaches to benchmarking and we will focus on using the JMH tool. So, why benchmark at all? Developers do not always concern themselves with performance issues unless performance is a stated requirement. This can lead to post-deployment surprises that could have been avoided if microbenchmarking was conducted as part of the development process.

Microbenchmarking takes place across several phases of a process. As shown in the following diagram, the process involves design, implementation, execution, analysis, and enhancement:

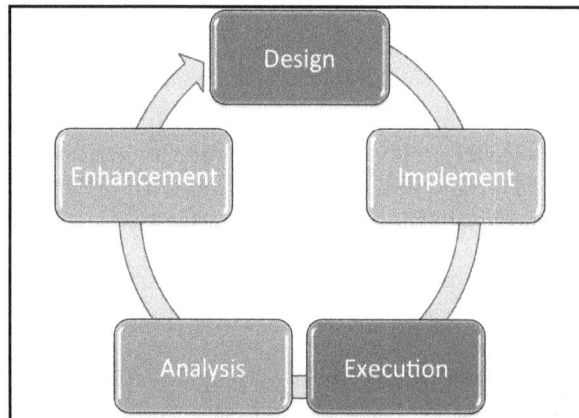

In the **Design** phase, we determine our goals and design our microbenchmark accordingly. In the **Implement** phase, we are writing the microbenchmark and then, in the **Execution** phase, we actually run the test. With microbenchmarking results in hand, we interpret and analyze the results in the **Analysis** phase. This leads to code improvements in the **Enhancement** phase. Once our code has been updated, we redesign the microbenchmarking test, adjust the implementation, or go straight to the **Execution** phase. This is a cyclical process that continues until we have achieved the performance optimization we identified in our goals.

Approach to using JMH

Oracle's documentation indicates that the most ideal JMH use case is to use a Maven project that is dependent on the application's JAR files. They further recommend that microbenchmarking take place via the command-line and not from within an **Integrated Development Environment** (**IDE**), as that could impact the results.

> Maven, also referred to as Apache Maven, is a project management and comprehension tool that we can use to manage our application project build, reporting, and documentation.

To use JMH, we will use bytecode processors (annotations) to generate the benchmark code. We use Maven archetypes to enable JMH.

In order to test the JMH, we require an IDE with support for Maven and Java 9. If you do not yet have Java 9 or an IDE with Java 9 support, you can follow the steps in the next section.

Installing Java 9 and Eclipse with Java 9 support

You can download and install Java 9 from the JDK 9 early access builds page--`http://jdk.java.net/9/`.

Once you have Java 9 installed, download the latest version of Eclipse. At the time of writing this book, that was Oxygen. Here is the relevant link--`https://www.eclipse.org/downloads/`.

The next step is to enable Java 9 support in your IDE. Launch Eclipse Oxygen and select **Help | Eclipse Marketplace...** , as shown in the following screenshot:

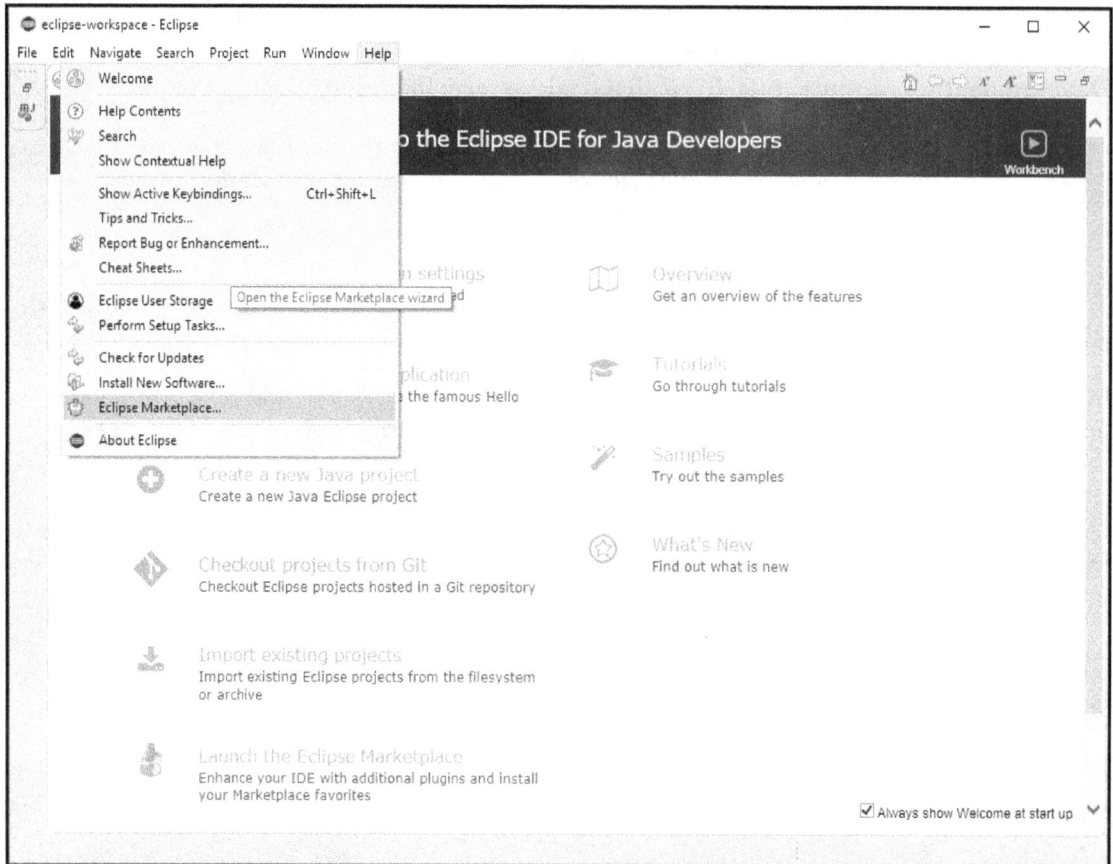

With the **Eclipse Marketplace** dialog window present search for `Java 9 support` using the search box. As you can see in the following screenshot, you will be presented with an **Install** button:

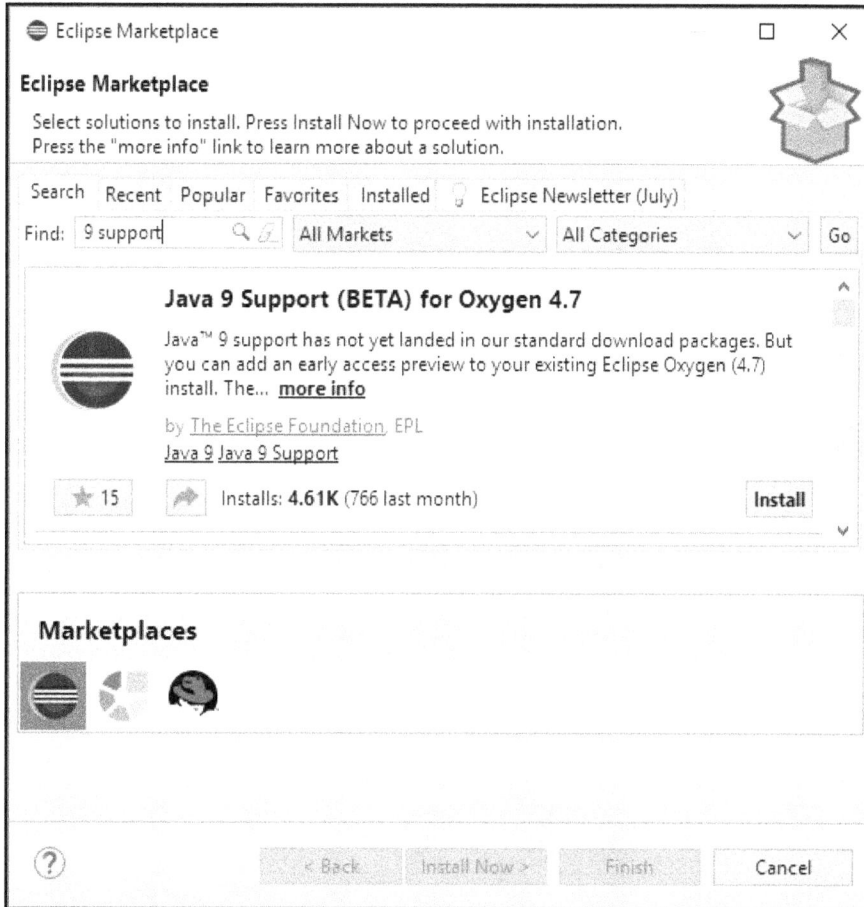

During the installation process, you will be required to accept the license agreement and, upon completion, you will be required to restart Eclipse.

Hands-on experiment

Now that we have Eclipse updated to support Java 9, you can run a quick test to determine if JMH is working on your development computer. Start by creating a new Maven project as illustrated in the following screenshot:

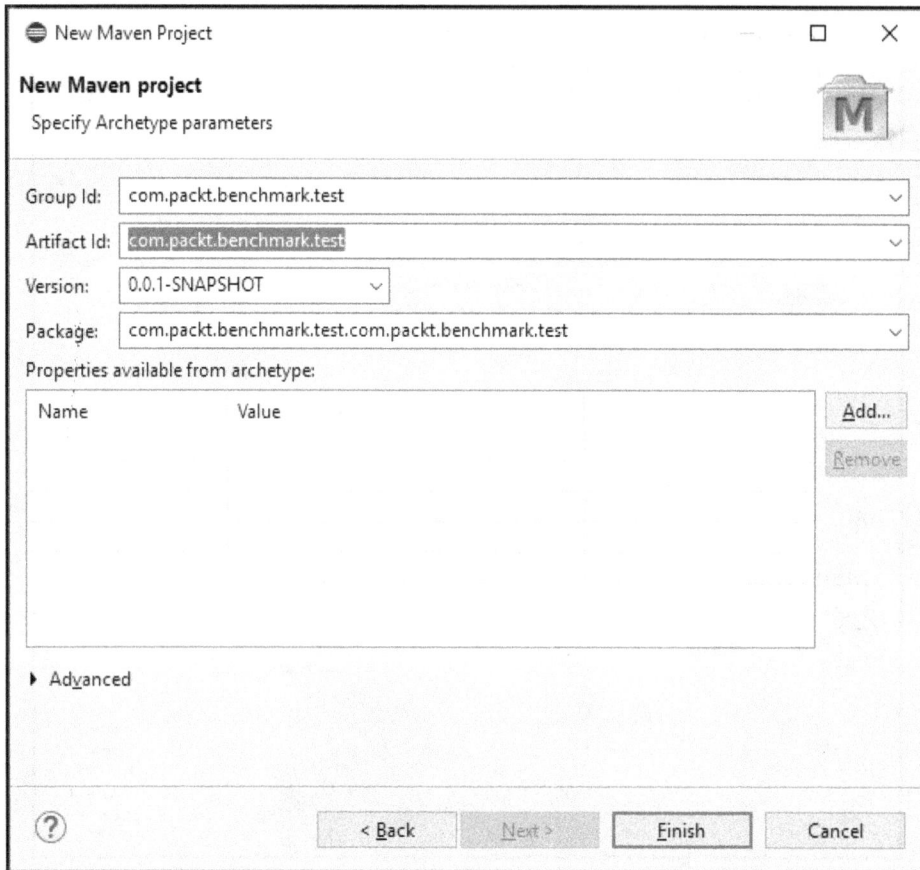

Next, we need to add a dependency. We can do this by editing the `pom.xml` file directly with the following code:

```
<dependency>
   <groupId>org.openjdk.jmh</groupId>
   <artifactId>jmh-core</artifactId>
   <version>0.1</version>
</dependency>
```

Alternatively, we can use the dependencies tab to enter the data in a dialog window, as shown in the following screenshot. Using this form updates the pom.xml file with the preceding code:

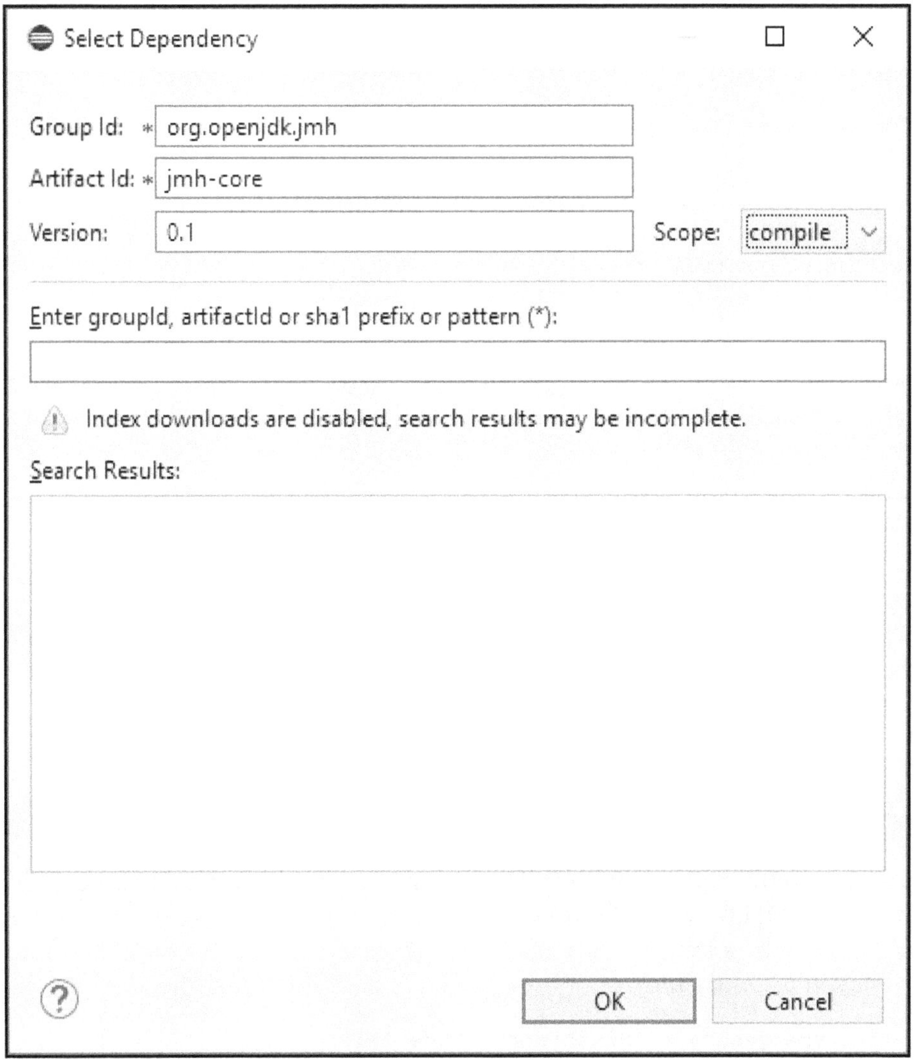

Next, we need to write a class that contains a JMH method. This is just as an initial test to confirm our recently updated development environment. Here is sample code you can use for your test:

```
package com.packt.benchmark.test.com.packt.benchmark.test;

import org.open.jdk.jmh.Main;

public class Test
{

  public static void main(String[] args)
  {
    Main.main(args);
  }
}
```

We can now compile and run our very simple test program. The results are provided in the Console tab, or the actual console if you are using the command-line. Here is what you will see:

```
<terminated> Test [Java Application] C:\Program Files\Java\jre1.8.0_131\bin\javaw.exe (Jul 30, 2017, 8:04:30 PM)
No matching benchmarks. Miss-spelled regexp? Use -v for verbose output.
```

You can see that the program worked sufficiently to let us know that JMH is working. Of course, there was, as the output indicates, no benchmarks set up. We will take care of that in the next section.

Microbenchmarking with Maven

One approach to getting started with JMH is to use the JMH Maven archetype. The first step is to create a new JMH project. At our system's command prompt, we will enter the mvn command followed by a long set of parameters to create a new Java project and the necessary Maven pom.xml file:

```
mvn archetype:generate -DinteractiveMode=false -
DarchetypeGroupId=org.openjdk.jmh -DarchetypeArtifactId=jmh -java-
benchmark-archetype -DgroupId=com.packt -DartifactId=chapter8-benchmark -
Dversion=1.0
```

Once you enter the `mvn` command and the preceding detailed parameters, you will see the results reported to you via the Terminal. Depending on your level of use, you might see a large number of downloads from `https://repo.maven.apache.org/maven2/org/apache/mave/plugins` and other similar repository sites.

You will also see an information section that informs you about the project build process:

```
[INFO]
[INFO] ------------------------------------------------------------------------
[INFO] Building Maven Stub Project (No POM) 1
[INFO] ------------------------------------------------------------------------
[INFO]
[INFO]
[INFO] >>> maven-archetype-plugin:3.0.1:generate (default-cli) > generate-sources @ standalone-pom >>>
[INFO]
[INFO] <<< maven-archetype-plugin:3.0.1:generate (default-cli) < generate-sources @ standalone-pom <<<
[INFO]
[INFO]
[INFO] --- maven-archetype-plugin:3.0.1:generate (default-cli) @ standalone-pom ---
```

There will likely be additional plugin and other resources downloaded from the `https://repo.maven.apache.org` repositories. Then, you will see an informational feedback component that lets you know the project is being generated in batch mode:

```
[INFO] Generating project in Batch mode
[INFO] Archetype [org.openjdk.jmh:jmh-java-benchmark-archetype:1.19] found in catalog remote
```

Finally, you will be presented with a set of parameters and a note that your project build was successful. As you can see with the following example, the process took less than 21 seconds to complete:

```
[INFO] ------------------------------------------------------------------------
[INFO] Using following parameters for creating project from Archetype: jmh-java-benchmark-archetype:1.19
[INFO] ------------------------------------------------------------------------
[INFO] Parameter: groupId, Value: com.packt
[INFO] Parameter: artifactId, Value: chapter8-benchmark
[INFO] Parameter: version, Value: 1.0
[INFO] Parameter: package, Value: com.packt
[INFO] Parameter: packageInPathFormat, Value: com/packt
[INFO] Parameter: package, Value: com.packt
[INFO] Parameter: groupId, Value: com.packt
[INFO] Parameter: artifactId, Value: chapter8-benchmark
[INFO] Parameter: version, Value: 1.0
[INFO] Project created from Archetype in dir: C:\chapter8-benchmark
[INFO] ------------------------------------------------------------------------
[INFO] BUILD SUCCESS
[INFO] ------------------------------------------------------------------------
[INFO] Total time: 20.753 s
[INFO] Finished at: 2017-07-31T18:03:27-05:00
[INFO] Final Memory: 18M/62M
[INFO] ------------------------------------------------------------------------
C:\>
```

A folder will be created based on the parameter we included in the -DartifactId option. In our example, we used -DartifactId=chapter8-benchmark, and Maven created a chapter8-benchmark project folder:

```
Command Prompt                                        —     □     ×

C:\chapter8-benchmark>dir
 Volume in drive C is OS
 Volume Serial Number is 608F-FF3F

 Directory of C:\chapter8-benchmark

07/31/2017  06:03 PM    <DIR>          .
07/31/2017  06:03 PM    <DIR>          ..
07/31/2017  06:03 PM             7,062 pom.xml
07/31/2017  06:03 PM    <DIR>          src
               1 File(s)          7,062 bytes
               3 Dir(s)  895,571,656,704 bytes free

C:\chapter8-benchmark>
```

You will see that Maven created the pom.xml file as well as a source (src) folder. In that folder, under the subdirectory structure of C:chapter8-benchmarksrcmainjavacompackt, is the MyBenchmark.java file. Maven created a benchmark class for us:

```
Command Prompt                                        —     □     ×

C:\chapter8-benchmark\src\main\java\com\packt>dir
 Volume in drive C is OS
 Volume Serial Number is 608F-FF3F

 Directory of C:\chapter8-benchmark\src\main\java\com\packt

07/31/2017  06:03 PM    <DIR>          .
07/31/2017  06:03 PM    <DIR>          ..
07/31/2017  06:03 PM             1,906 MyBenchmark.java
               1 File(s)          1,906 bytes
               2 Dir(s)  895,459,594,240 bytes free
```

Here are the contents of the `MyBenchmark.java` class created by the JMH Maven project creation process:

```
/*
 * Copyright (c) 2014, Oracle America, Inc.
 * All rights reserved.
 *
 * Redistribution and use in source and binary forms, with or
   without
 * modification, are permitted provided that the following
   conditions are met:
 *
 *  * Redistributions of source code must retain the above
     copyright notice,
 * this list of conditions and the following disclaimer.
 *
 *  * Redistributions in binary form must reproduce the above
     copyright
 * notice, this list of conditions and the following
   disclaimer in the
 * documentation and/or other materials provided with the
   distribution.
 *
 *  * Neither the name of Oracle nor the names of its
     contributors may be used
 * to endorse or promote products derived from this software
   without
 * specific prior written permission.
 *
 * THIS SOFTWARE IS PROVIDED BY THE COPYRIGHT HOLDERS AND
   CONTRIBUTORS "AS IS"
 * AND ANY EXPRESS OR IMPLIED WARRANTIES, INCLUDING, BUT NOT
   LIMITED TO, THE
 * IMPLIED WARRANTIES OF MERCHANTABILITY AND FITNESS FOR A
   PARTICULAR PURPOSE
 * ARE DISCLAIMED. IN NO EVENT SHALL THE COPYRIGHT HOLDER OR
   CONTRIBUTORS BE
 * LIABLE FOR ANY DIRECT, INDIRECT, INCIDENTAL, SPECIAL,
   EXEMPLARY,
   OR
 * CONSEQUENTIAL DAMAGES (INCLUDING, BUT NOT LIMITED TO,
   PROCUREMENT OF
 * SUBSTITUTE GOODS OR SERVICES; LOSS OF USE, DATA, OR PROFITS;
   OR BUSINESS
 * INTERRUPTION) HOWEVER CAUSED AND ON ANY THEORY OF LIABILITY,
   WHETHER IN
 * CONTRACT, STRICT LIABILITY, OR TORT (INCLUDING NEGLIGENCE OR
```

```
      OTHERWISE)
  * ARISING IN ANY WAY OUT OF THE USE OF THIS SOFTWARE, EVEN IF
    ADVISED OF
  * THE POSSIBILITY OF SUCH DAMAGE.
  */

package com.packt;

import org.openjdk.jmh.annotations.Benchmark;

public class MyBenchmark
{
  @Benchmark
  public void testMethod()
  {

    // This is a demo/sample template for building your JMH
       benchmarks.
    //Edit as needed.
    // Put your benchmark code here.
  }
}
```

Our next step is to modify the testMethod() so that there is something to test. Here is the modified method we will use for the benchmark test:

```
@Benchmark
public void testMethod()
{
  int total = 0;
  for (int i=0; i<100000; i++)
  {
    total = total + (i * 2 );
  }
  System.out.println("Total: " + total);
}
```

With our code edited, we will navigate back to the project folder, C:chapter8-benchmark, in our example, and execute mvn clean install at the command prompt.

You will see several repository downloads, source compilations, plugin installations and, finally the Build Success indicator, as shown here:

```
Command Prompt                                              —    □    ×
[INFO] -------------------------------------------------------------------
[INFO] BUILD SUCCESS
[INFO] -------------------------------------------------------------------
[INFO] Total time: 10.811 s
[INFO] Finished at: 2017-07-31T19:09:41-05:00
[INFO] Final Memory: 24M/82M
[INFO] -------------------------------------------------------------------

C:\chapter8-benchmark>
```

You will now see `.classpath` and `.project` files as well as a new `.settings` and target subfolders in the project directory:

```
Command Prompt                                              —    □    ×
C:\chapter8-benchmark>dir
 Volume in drive C is OS
 Volume Serial Number is 608F-FF3F

 Directory of C:\chapter8-benchmark

07/31/2017  07:09 PM    <DIR>          .
07/31/2017  07:09 PM    <DIR>          ..
07/31/2017  07:02 PM             1,024 .classpath
07/31/2017  07:02 PM               570 .project
07/31/2017  07:02 PM    <DIR>          .settings
07/31/2017  07:02 PM    <DIR>          bin
07/31/2017  06:03 PM             7,062 pom.xml
07/31/2017  06:03 PM    <DIR>          src
07/31/2017  07:09 PM    <DIR>          target
               3 File(s)          8,656 bytes
               6 Dir(s)  895,323,013,120 bytes free

C:\chapter8-benchmark>
```

If you navigate to the `target` subfolder, you will see that our `benchmarks.jar` file was created. This JAR contains what we need to run our benchmarks.

We can update our `MyBenchmark.java` file in an IDE, such as Eclipse. Then, we can execute `mvn clean install` again to overwrite our files. After the initial time, our builds will be much faster, as nothing will need to be downloaded. Here is a look at the output from the build process other than the first time:

```
C:\chapter8-benchmark>mvn clean install
[INFO] Scanning for projects...
[INFO]
[INFO]
[INFO] ------------------------------------------------------------------------
[INFO] Building JMH benchmark sample: Java 1.0
[INFO] ------------------------------------------------------------------------
[INFO]
[INFO] --- maven-clean-plugin:2.5:clean (default-clean) @ chapter8-benchmark ---
[INFO] Deleting C:\chapter8-benchmark\target
[INFO]
[INFO] --- maven-resources-plugin:2.6:resources (default-resources) @ chapter8-benchmark ---
[INFO] Using 'UTF-8' encoding to copy filtered resources.
[INFO] skip non existing resourceDirectory C:\chapter8-benchmark\src\main\resources
[INFO]
[INFO] --- maven-compiler-plugin:3.1:compile (default-compile) @ chapter8-benchmark ---
[INFO] Changes detected - recompiling the module!
[INFO] Compiling 1 source file to C:\chapter8-benchmark\target\classes
[INFO]
[INFO] --- maven-resources-plugin:2.6:testResources (default-testResources) @ chapter8-benchmark ---
[INFO] Using 'UTF-8' encoding to copy filtered resources.
[INFO] skip non existing resourceDirectory C:\chapter8-benchmark\src\test\resources
[INFO]
[INFO] --- maven-compiler-plugin:3.1:testCompile (default-testCompile) @ chapter8-benchmark ---
[INFO] No sources to compile
[INFO]
[INFO] --- maven-surefire-plugin:2.17:test (default-test) @ chapter8-benchmark ---
[INFO] No tests to run.
[INFO]
[INFO] --- maven-jar-plugin:2.4:jar (default-jar) @ chapter8-benchmark ---
[INFO] Building jar: C:\chapter8-benchmark\target\chapter8-benchmark-1.0.jar
[INFO]
[INFO] --- maven-shade-plugin:2.2:shade (default) @ chapter8-benchmark ---
[INFO] Including org.openjdk.jmh:jmh-core:jar:1.19 in the shaded jar.
[INFO] Including net.sf.jopt-simple:jopt-simple:jar:4.6 in the shaded jar.
[INFO] Including org.apache.commons:commons-math3:jar:3.2 in the shaded jar.
[INFO] Replacing C:\chapter8-benchmark\target\benchmarks.jar with C:\chapter8-benchmark\target\chapter8-benchmark-1.0-shaded.jar
[INFO]
[INFO] --- maven-install-plugin:2.5.1:install (default-install) @ chapter8-benchmark ---
[INFO] Installing C:\chapter8-benchmark\target\chapter8-benchmark-1.0.jar to C:\Users\elavi\.m2\repository\com\packt\chapter8-benchmark\1.0\chapter8-benchmark-1.0.jar
[INFO] Installing C:\chapter8-benchmark\pom.xml to C:\Users\elavi\.m2\repository\com\packt\chapter8-benchmark\1.0\chapter8-benchmark-1.0.pom
[INFO] ------------------------------------------------------------------------
[INFO] BUILD SUCCESS
[INFO] ------------------------------------------------------------------------
[INFO] Total time: 3.388 s
[INFO] Finished at: 2017-07-31T19:26:01-05:00
[INFO] Final Memory: 22M/73M
[INFO] ------------------------------------------------------------------------

C:\chapter8-benchmark>
```

Our last step is to run the benchmark tool. We can do that with the following command--
`java -jar benchmarks.jar`. Even for small benchmarks on simplistic code, as with our
example, the benchmarks could take some time to run. There will likely be several iterations
including warmups to provide a more concise and valid set of benchmark results.

Our benchmark results are provided here. As you can see, the test ran for 8 minutes and 8
seconds:

```
Command Prompt                                        —  □  ×

Total: 319
24676.388 ops/s


Result "com.packt.MyBenchmark.testMethod":
  23847.961 ±(99.9%) 772.746 ops/s [Average]
  (min, avg, max) = (14864.509, 23847.961, 35528.242), stdev = 3271.857
  CI (99.9%): [23075.215, 24620.708] (assumes normal distribution)


# Run complete. Total time: 00:08:08

Benchmark                 Mode  Cnt      Score     Error  Units
MyBenchmark.testMethod    thrpt  200  23847.961 ± 772.746  ops/s

C:\chapter8-benchmark\target>
```

Benchmarking options

In the previous section, you learned how to run a benchmark test. In this section, we will
look at the following configurable options for running our benchmarks:

- Modes
- Time units

Modes

The output of our benchmark results, from the previous section, included a **Mode** column that had the value of **thrpt** which is short for **throughput**. This is the default mode and there are an additional four modes. All JMH benchmark modes are listed and described as follows:

Mode	Description
All	Measures all other modes inclusively.
Average	This mode measures the average time for a single benchmark to run.
Sample Time	This mode measures the benchmark execution time and includes min and max times.
Single Shot Time	With this mode, there is no JVM warm up and the test is to determine how long a single benchmark method takes to run.
Throughput	This is the default mode and measures the number of operations per second the benchmark could be run.

To dictate which benchmark mode to use, you will modify your @Benchmark line of code to one of the following:

```
@Benchmark @BenchmarkMode(Mode.All)
@Benchmark @BenchmarkMode(Mode.Average)
@Benchmark @BenchmarkMode(Mode.SamplmeTime)
@Benchmark @BenchmarkMode(Mode.SingleShotTime)
@Benchmark @BenchmarkMode(Mode.Throughput)
```

Time units

In order to gain greater fidelity in benchmark output, we can designate a specific unit of time, listed here from shortest to longest:

- NANOSECONDS
- MICROSECONDS
- MILLISECONDS
- SECONDS
- MINUTES
- HOURS
- DAYS

In order to make this designation, we simply add the following code to our `@Benchmark` line:

```
@Benchmark @BenchmarkMode(Mode.Average)
@OutputTimeUnit(TimeUnit.NANOSECONDS)
```

In the preceding example, we have designated the average mode and nanoseconds as the time unit.

Techniques for avoiding microbenchmarking pitfalls

Microbenchmarking is not something that every developer will have to worry about, but for those that do, there are several pitfalls that you should be aware of. In this section we will review the most common pitfalls and suggest strategies for avoiding them.

Power management

There are many subsystems that can be used to help you manage the balance between power and performance (that is, `cpufreq`). These systems can alter the state of time during benchmarks.

There are two suggested strategies to this pitfall:

- Disable any power management systems before running tests
- Run the benchmarks for longer periods

OS schedulers

Operating system schedulers, such as Solaris schedulers, help determine which software processes gain access to a system's resources. Use of these schedulers can result in unreliable benchmarking results.

There are two suggested strategies to this pitfall:

- Refine your system scheduling policies
- Run the benchmarks for longer periods

Time sharing

Time-sharing systems are used to help balance system resources. Use of these systems often results in irregular gaps between a thread's start and stop time. Also, CPU load will not be uniform and our benchmarking data will not be as useful to us.

There are two suggested strategies to avoid this pitfall:

- Test all code before running benchmarks to ensure things work as they should
- Use JMH to measure only after all threads have started or all threads have stopped

Eliminating dead-code and constant folding

Dead-code and constant folding are often referred to as redundant code and our modern compilers are pretty good at eliminating them. An example of dead-code is code that will never be reached. Consider the following example:

```
. . .

int value = 10;

if (value != null)
{
  System.out.println("The value is " + value + ".");
} else
  {
    System.out.println("The value is null."); // This is
    a line of Dead-Code
}

. . .
```

In our preceding example, the line identified as dead-code is never reached since the variable value will never be equal to null. It is set to 10 immediately before the conditional if statement evaluates the variable.

The problem is that benchmarking code can sometimes be removed in the attempt to eliminate dead-code.

Constant folding is the compiler operation that occurs when compile-time constraints are replaced with actual results. The compiler performs constant folding to remove any redundant runtime computations. In the following example, we have a final int followed by a second int based on a mathematical calculation involving the first int:

```
. . .

static final int value = 10;

int newValue = 319 * value;

. . .
```

The constant folding operation would convert the two lines of the preceding code to the following:

```
int newValue = 3190;
```

There is one suggested strategy to this pitfall:

- Use the JMH API support to ensure your benchmarking code is not eliminated

Run-to-run variance

There are a plethora of issues that can drastically impact the run-to-run variance in benchmarking.

There are two suggested strategies to this pitfall:

- Run the JVM multiple times within every subsystem
- Use multiple JMH folks

Cache capacity

Dynamic randomly accessed memory (**DRAM**) is very slow. This can result in very different performance results during benchmarking.

There are two suggested strategies to this pitfall:

- Run multiple benchmarks with varying problem sets. Keep track of your memory footprint during tests.
- Use the `@State` annotation to dictate the JMH state. This annotation is sued to define the instance's scope. There are three states:
    - `Scope.Benchmark`: The instance is shared across all threads that are running the same test.
    - `Scope.Group`: One instance is allocated per thread group.
    - `Scope.Thread`: Each thread will have its own instance. This is the default state.

Summary

In this chapter, we learned that the JMH is a Java harness library for writing benchmarks for the JVM. We experimented with writing performance tests using Maven along with JMH to help illustrate the procedures of microbenchmarking with the new Java 9 platform. We started with a microbenchmarking overview, then dove deep into microbenchmarking with Maven, reviewed benchmarking options, and concluded with a few techniques for avoiding microbenchmarking pitfalls.

In the next chapter, we will learn to write an application that is managing other processes and utilizes the modern process management API of the Java 9 platform.

9
Making Use of the ProcessHandle API

In the previous chapter, we discovered the **Java Microbenchmark Harness (JMH)**. We explored performance tests and how to write them using JMH, the Java library for writing benchmarks for the Java Virtual Machine. We started with an overview of microbenchmarking, then looked at microbenchmarking with Maven, reviewed benchmarking options, and concluded with techniques for avoiding microbenchmarking pitfalls.

In this chapter, we will focus on the updates to the `Process` class and the new `java.lang.ProcessHandle` API. Prior to Java 9, managing processes in Java was never easy, because Java was rarely used to automate the controlling of other processes. The API was insufficient with some features lacking and some tasks needed to be solved in a system specific manner. For example, in Java 8, giving a process access to its own **process identifier (PID)** was an unnecessarily difficult task.

In this chapter, the reader will gain all the knowledge that is needed to write an application that manages other processes and utilizes the modern process management API of Java.

We will cover the following topics in this chapter:

- What is and how to use the new `ProcessHandle` interface
- How to get the PID of the current process
- How to list different processes that run in the operating system
- How to effectively wait for an external process to finish
- How to terminate external processes

What are processes?

In this section, we will review what processes are in the context of Java application programming. If you are already familiar with processes, you might consider skipping this section.

Processes are executional units in the operating system. When you start a program, you start a process. When the machine boots the code, the first thing it does is, execute the boot process. This process then starts other processes that become the child of the boot process. These child processes may start other processes. This way, when the machine runs there are trees of processes running. When the machine does something, it is done in some code executing inside some process. The operating system also runs as several processes that execute simultaneously. Applications are executed as one or more processes. Most of the applications run as a single process but as an example, the Chrome browser starts several processes to do all the rendering and network communication operations that finally function as a browser.

To get a better idea about what processes are, start the task manager on Windows or the **Activity Monitor** on OS X and click on the **Process** tab. You will see the different processes that currently exist on the machine. Using these tools, you can look at the parameters of the processes, or you can kill an individual process.

The individual processes have their memory allocated for their work and they are not allowed to freely access each other's memory.

The execution unit scheduled by the operating system is a thread. A process consists of one or more threads. These threads are scheduled by the operating system scheduler and are executed in time slots.

With every operating system, processes have a process identifier, which is a number that identifies the process. No two processes can be active at a time, sharing the same PID. When we want to identify an active process in the operating system we use the PID. On Linux and other Unix-like operating systems, the `kill` command terminates a process. The argument to be passed to this program is the PID of the process, to terminate. Termination can be graceful. It is something like asking the process to exit. If the process decides not to, it can keep running. Programs can be prepared to stop upon such requests. For example, a Java application may add a `Thread` object calling the `Runtime.getRuntime().addShutdownHook(Thread t)` method. The thread passed is supposed to start when the process is asked to stop and the thread can perform all tasks that the program has to do before it exits. However, there is no guarantee that it does start. It depends on the actual implementation.

The new ProcessHandle interface

There are two new interfaces and also their implementations in Java 9 supporting the handling of operating system processes. One of them is `ProcessHandle`, the other one is `ProcessHandle.Info`, a nested interface of the prior.

A `ProcessHandle` object identifies an operating system process and provides methods to manage the process. In prior versions of Java, this was possible only using operating system specific methods using the PID to identify the process. The major problem with this approach is that the PID is unique only while the process is active. When a process finishes, the operating system is free to reuse the PID for a new process. When we know only the PID of a process and check to see if the process is still running, what we are really doing is checking if there is an active process with that PID. Our process may be alive when we check it, but the next time our program queries the process state, it might be a different process.

The desktop and server operating systems try not to reuse the PID values for as long as possible. On some embedded systems the operating system may only use 16-bit to store the PID. When only 16-bit values are used, there is a greater chance that the PIDs will be reused. We can avoid this problem using the `ProcessHandle` API. We can receive a `ProcessHandle` and can call the `handle.isAlive()` method. This method will return `false` when the process finishes. This works even if the PID was reused.

Getting the PID of the current process

We can gain access to the PID of the processes via the handle. The `handle.getPid()` method returns a `Long` representing the numerical value of the PID. Since it is safer to access the processes through the handle, the importance of this method is limited. It may come in handy when our code wants to give information about itself to some other management tool. It is a common practice for programs to create a file that has the numeric PID as the name of the file. It may be a requirement that a certain program does not run in multiple processes. In that case, the code writes its own PID file to a specific directory. If a PID file with that name already exists, processing stops. If the previous process crashed and terminated without deleting the PID file, then the system manager can easily delete the file and start the new process. If the program hangs, then the system manager can easily kill the dead process if s/he knows the PID.

To get the PID of the current process, the call chain `ProcessHandle.current().getPid()` can be used.

Getting information about a process

To get information about a process, we need access to the `Info` object of the process. This is available through a `ProcessHandle`. We use a call to the `handle.info()` method to return it.

The `Info` interface defines query methods that deliver information about the process. These are:

- `command()` returns an `Optional<String>` containing the command that was used to start the process
- `arguments()` returns an `Optional<String[]>` that contains the arguments that were used on the command-line after the command to start the process
- `commandLine()` returns an `Optional<String>` that contains the whole command-line
- `startInstant()` returns an `Optional<Instant>`, which essentially represents the time the process was started
- `totalCpuDuration()` returns an `Optional<Duration>`, which represents the CPU time used by the process since it was started
- `user()` returns an `Optional<String>` that holds the name of the user the process belongs to

The values returned by these methods are all `Optional` because there is no guarantee that the actual operating system or the Java implementation can return the information. However, on most operating systems it should work and the returned values should be present.

The following sample code displays the information on a given process:

```
import java.io.IOException;
import java.time.Duration;
import java.time.Instant;
public class ProcessHandleDemonstration
{
  public static void main(String[] args) throws
    InterruptedException, IOException
  {
    provideProcessInformation(ProcessHandle.current());
    Process theProcess = new
     ProcessBuilder("SnippingTool.exe").start();
    provideProcessInformation(theProcess.toHandle());
    theProcess.waitFor();
    provideProcessInformation(theProcess.toHandle());
```

```
  }
  static void provideProcessInformation(ProcessHandle theHandle)
  {
    // get id
    long pid = ProcessHandle.current().pid();
    // Get handle information (if available)
    ProcessHandle.Info handleInformation = theHandle.info();
    // Print header
    System.out.println("|==============================|");
    System.out.println("| INFORMATION ON YOUR PROCESS |");
    System.out.println("|==============================|n");
    // Print the PID
    System.out.println("Process id (PID): " + pid);
    System.out.println("Process Owner: " +
      handleInformation.user().orElse(""));
    // Print additional information if available
    System.out.println("Command:" +
     handleInformation.command().orElse(""));
    String[] args = handleInformation.arguments().orElse
      (new String[]{});
    System.out.println("Argument(s): ");
    for (String arg: args) System.out.printf("t" + arg);
    System.out.println("Command line: " + handleInformation.
     commandLine().orElse(""));
    System.out.println("Start time: " +
      handleInformation.startInstant().
      orElse(Instant.now()).toString());
    System.out.printf("Run time duration: %sms%n",
      handleInformation.totalCpuDuration()
      .orElse(Duration.ofMillis(0)).toMillis());
  }
}
```

Here is the console output for the preceding code:

Listing processes

Prior to Java 9, we did not have the means to obtain a list of active processes. With Java 9 it is now possible to get the processes in a stream. There are three methods that return a Stream<ProcessHandle>. One lists the child processes. The other lists all the descendants; the children and the children of those recursively. The third lists all the processes.

Listing children

To get the stream of process handles that can be used to control the children, the static method processHandle.children() should be used. This will create a snapshot of the children processes of the process represented by processHandle and create the Stream. Since processes are dynamic there is no guarantee that during the code execution, while our program attends to the handles, that all children processes are still active. Some of them may terminate and our process may spawn new children, perhaps from a different thread. Thus the code should not assume that each of the ProcessHandle elements of the stream represents an active and running process.

The following program starts 10 command prompts in Windows and then counts the number of children processes and prints it to standard output:

```java
package packt.mastering.java9.process;
import java.io.IOException;

public class ChildLister {
  public static void main(String[] args) throws IOException {
    for (int i = 0; i < 10; i++) {
      new ProcessBuilder().command("cmd.exe").start();
    }
    System.out.println("Number of children :" +
      ProcessHandle.current().children().count());
  }
}
```

Executing the program will result in the following:

Listing descendants

Listing the descendants is very similar to listing children, but if we call the
`processHandle.descendants()` method then the `Stream` will contain all the children
processes and the children processes of those processes and so on. The following program
starts command prompts with command-line arguments so that they also spawn another
`cmd.exe` that terminates:

```
package packt.mastering.java9.process;

import java.io.IOException;
import java.util.stream.Collectors;

public class DescendantLister {
  public static void main(String[] args) throws IOException {
    for (int i = 0; i < 10; i++) {
      new ProcessBuilder().command("cmd.exe","/K","cmd").
        start();
    }
    System.out.println("Number of descendants: " +
     ProcessHandle.current().descendants().count();
  }
}
```

Running the command a few times will result in the following, non-deterministic output:

The output clearly demonstrates that when the Stream of the descendants is created not all processes are alive. The sample code starts 10 processes and each of them starts another. The Stream does not have 20 elements because some of these sub-processes were terminated during processing.

Listing all processes

Listing all the processes is slightly different from listing descendants and children. The method allProcess() is static and returns a Stream of handles of all processes that are active in the operating system at the time of execution.

The following sample code prints the process commands to the console that seem to be Java processes:

```
package packt.mastering.java9.process;
import java.lang.ProcessHandle.Info;
public class ProcessLister {
  private static void out(String format, Object... params) {
    System.out.println(String.format(format, params));
  }
  private static boolean looksLikeJavaProcess(Info info) {
    return info.command().isPresent() &&
    info.command().get().
    toLowerCase().indexOf("java") != -1;
  }

  public static void main(String[] args) {
    ProcessHandle.allProcesses().
     map(ProcessHandle::info).
     filter(info -> looksLikeJavaProcess(info)).
     forEach(
       (info) -> System.out.println(
         info.command().orElse("---"))
     );
  }

}
```

The output of the program lists all the process commands that have the string `java` inside:

Your actual output may, of course, be different.

Waiting for processes

When a process starts another process, it may wait for the process many times because it needs the result of the other program. If the structure of the task can be organized in a way that the parent program can do something else while waiting for the child process to finish, then the parent process can invoke the `isAlive()` method on the process handle. Many times, the parent process has nothing to do until the spawned process finishes. Old applications implemented loops that called the `Thread.sleep()` method so CPU was not excessively wasted and from time to time the process was checked to see if it was still alive. Java 9 offers a much better approach to the waiting process.

The `ProcessHandle` interface has a method called `onExit` that returns a `CompletableFuture`. This class was introduced in Java 8 and makes it possible to wait for a task to be finished without looping. If we have the handle to a process we can simply call the `handle.onExit().join()` method to wait until the process finishes. The `get()` method of the returned `CompletableFuture` will return the `ProcessHandle` instance that was used to create it in the first place.

We can call the `onExit()` method on the handle many times and each time it will return a different `CompletableFuture` object, each related to the same process. We can call the `cancel()` method on the object but it will only cancel the `CompletableFuture` object and not the process and also does not have any effect on the other `CompletableFuture` objects that were created from the same `ProcessHandle` instance.

Terminating processes

To terminate a process we can call the destroy() method or the destroyForcibly() method on the ProcessHandle instance. Both of these methods will terminate the process. The destroy() method is expected to terminate the process gracefully executing the process shutdown sequence. In this case the shutdown hooks added to the run time are executed if the actual implementation supports the graceful, normal termination of processes. The destroyForcibly() method will enforce process termination, and in this case the shutdown sequence will not be executed.

If the process managed by the handle is not alive then nothing happens when the code calls any of these methods. If there are any CompletableFuture objects created calling the onExit() method on the handle then they will be completed after the call to the destroy() or destroyForcefully() method when the process has terminated. This means that the CompletableFuture object will return from a join() or some similar method after some time when the process termination is complete and not immediately after destroy() or destroyForcefully() returned.

It is also important to note that process termination may depend on many things. If the actual process that is waiting to terminate another does not have the right to terminate the other process then the request will fail. In this case the return value of the method is false. It is also important to understand that a return value of true does not mean that the process has actually terminated. It only means that the termination request was accepted by the operating system and that the operating system will terminate the process at some point in the future. This will actually happen rather soon, but not instantaneously and thus it should not be a surprise if the method isAlive() returns true for some time after the method destroy() or destroyForcefully() returned the value true.

The difference between destroy() and destroyForcefully() is implementation specific. The Java standard does not state that destroy() does terminate the process letting the shutdown sequence be executed. It only *requests the process be killed. Whether the process represented by this ProcessHandle object is normally terminated or not is implementation dependent* (http://download.java.net/java/jdk9/docs/api/java/lang/ProcessHandle.html#supportsNormalTermination--).

> To learn more about ProcessHandle interface, visit http://download.java.net/java/jdk9/docs/api/java/lang/ProcessHandle.html.

This is because some operating systems do not implement the graceful process termination feature. In such situations, the implementation of `destroy()` is the same as calling `destroyForcefully()`. The system specific implementation of the interface `ProcessHandle` must implement the method `supportsNormalTermination()` that is `true` only if the implementation supports normal (not forceful) process termination. The method is expected to return the same value for all invocations in an actual implementation and should not change the return value during the execution of a JVM instance. There is no need to call the method multiple times.

The following examples demonstrate process starting, process termination, and waiting for the process to terminate. In our example, we use two classes. This first class demonstrates the `.sleep()` method:

```
package packt.mastering.java9.process;

public class WaitForChildToBeTerminated
{
  public static void main(String[] args)
   throws InterruptedException
  {
    Thread.sleep(10_000);
  }
}
```

The second class in our example calls the `WaitForChildToBeTerminated` class:

```
package packt.mastering.java9.process;

import java.io.IOException;
import java.util.Arrays;
import java.util.concurrent.CompletableFuture;
import java.util.stream.Collectors;

public class TerminateAProcessAfterWaiting {
  private static final int N = 10;

  public static void main(String[] args)
   throws IOException, InterruptedException {
     ProcessHandle ph[] = new ProcessHandle[N];

     for (int i = 0; i < N; i++)
     {
       final ProcessBuilder pb = ew ProcessBuilder().
        command("java", "-cp", "build/classes/main",
        "packt.mastering.java9.process.
        WaitForChildToBeTerminated");
```

```
    Process p = pb.start();
    ph[i] = p.toHandle();
}
long start = System.currentTimeMillis();
Arrays.stream(ph).forEach(ProcessHandle::destroyForcibly);


CompletableFuture.allOf(Arrays.stream(ph).
 map(ProcessHandle::onExit).
 collect(Collectors.toList()).
 toArray(new CompletableFuture[ph.length])).
 join();
long duration = System.currentTimeMillis() - start;
System.out.println("Duration " + duration + "ms");
  }
 }
```

The preceding code starts 10 processes, each executing the program that sleeps 10 seconds. Then it forcibly destroys the processes, more specifically, the operating system is asked to destroy them. Our example joins the `CompletableFuture` that is composed from the array of `CompletableFuture` objects, which are created using the handles of the individual processes.

When all the processes are finished then it prints out the measured time in milliseconds. The time interval starts when the processes are created and the process creation loop finished. The end of the measured time interval is when the processes are recognized by the JVM returning from the `join()` method.

The sample code sets the sleeping time to 10 seconds. This is a more noticeable time period. Running the code twice and deleting the line that destroys the processes can result a much slower printout. Actually the measured and printed elapsed times will also show that terminating the processes has an effect.

A small process controller application

To summarize and put into use all that we have learned in this chapter we look at a sample process control application. The functionality of the application is very simple. It reads from a series of configuration file(s) parameters how to start some processes and then if any of them stops, it tries to restart the process.

Even a real life application can be created from this demo version. You can extend the set of parameters of the process with environment variable specifications. You can add default directory for the process, input and output redirection or even how much CPU a process is allowed to consume without the controlling application killing and restarting it.

The application consists of four classes.

- `Main`: This class that contains the public static void main method and is used to start up the daemon.
- `Parameters`: This class contains the configuration parameters for a process. In this simple case it will only contain one field, the `commandLine`. If the application gets extended this class will contain the default directory, the redirections, and CPU use limiting data.
- `ParamsAndHandle`: This class that is nothing else than a data tuple holding a reference to a `Parameters` object and also a process handle. When a process dies and gets restarted the process handle is replaced by the new handle, but the reference to the `Parameters` object never changes, it is configuration.

- `ControlDaemon`: This class implements the interface `Runnable` and is started as a separate thread.

In the code we will use most of the process API we discussed in the previous sections, *Terminating processes* and we will use a lot of threading code and stream operations. Understanding the threading work of the JVM is important independent of the process management also. It has, however emphasized importance when used together with the process API.

Main class

The main method takes the name of the directory from the command line argument. It treats this as relative to the current working directory. It uses a separate method from the same class to read the set of configurations from the files in the directory and then starts the control daemon. The following code if the `main` method of the program:

```
public static void main(String[] args) throws IOException,
  InterruptedException
{
  // DemoOutput.out() simulated - implementation no shown
  DemoOutput.out(new File(".").getAbsolutePath().toString());
  if (args.length == 0)     {
    System.err.println("Usage: daemon directory");
```

```
        System.exit(-1);
    }
    Set<Parameters> params = parametersSetFrom(args[0]);
    Thread t = new Thread(new ControlDaemon(params));
    t.start();
}
```

Although this is a daemon, we are starting it as a normal thread and not as a daemon thread. When a thread is set to be a daemon thread it will not keep the JVM alive. When all other non-daemon threads stop, the JVM will just exit and the daemon threads will be stopped. In our case, the daemon thread we execute is the only one that keeps the code running. After that was started the main thread has nothing more to do, but the JVM should stay alive, until it is killed by the operator issuing a Unix `kill` command or pressing *Control* + *C* on the command line.

Getting the list of the files that are in the directory specified and getting the parameters from the file is simple using the new `Files` and `Paths` classes from the JDK:

```
private static Set<Parameters>
 GetListOfFilesInDirectory(String directory) throws IOException
{
  return Files.walk(Paths.get(directory))
    .map(Path::toFile)
    .filter(File::isFile)
    .map(file -> Parameters.fromFile(file))
    .collect(Collectors.toSet());
}
```

We get a stream of the files in the form of `Path` objects, map it to `File` objects, then we filter out the directories if there are any in the configuration directory and map the remaining plain files to `Parameters` objects using the static method `fromFile` of the `Parameters` class. Finally, we return a `Set` of the objects.

Parameters class

Our `Parameters` class has a field and a constructor as listed as follows:

```
final String[] commandLine;

public Parameters(String[] commandLine) {
  this.commandLine = commandLine;
}
```

The parameter class has two methods. The first method, `getCommandLineStrings`, gets the command line strings from the properties. This array contains the command and the command line parameters. If it was not defined in the file then we return an empty array:

```
private static String[] getCommandLineStrings(Properties props)
{
  return Optional
    .ofNullable(props.getProperty("commandLine"))
    .orElse("")
    .split("\s+");
}
```

The second method is the `static fromFile` that reads the properties from a properties file:

```
public static Parameters fromFile(final File file)
{
  final Properties props = new Properties();
  try (final InputStream is = new FileInputStream(file)) {
    props.load(is);
  } catch (IOException e) {
      throw new RuntimeException(e);
  }
  return new Parameters(getCommandLineStrings(props));
}
```

If the set of parameters handled by the program is extended then this class should also be modified.

The ParamsAndHandle class

The `ParamsAndHandle` is a very simple class that holds two fields. One for the parameters and the other is the handle to the process handle that is used to access the process started using the parameters:

```
public class ParamsAndHandle
{
  final Parameters params;
  ProcessHandle handle;

  public ParamsAndHandle(Parameters params,
    ProcessHandle handle) {
      this.params = params;
      this.handle = handle;
  }
```

```
    public ProcessHandle toHandle() {
       return handle;
    }
  }
```

Since the class is closely tied to the `ControlDaemon` class from where it is used there is no mutator or accessor associated with the field. We see the two classes as something inside the same encapsulation boundaries. The `toHandle` method is there so that we can use it as a method handle, as we will see in the next chapter.

The ControlDaemon class

The `ControlDaemon` class implements the `Runnable` interface and is started as a separate thread. The constructor gets the set of the parameters that were read from the properties files and converts them to a set of `ParamsAndHandle` objects:

```
private final Set<ParamsAndHandle> handlers;

public ControlDaemon(Set<Parameters> params) {
  handlers = params
  .stream()
  .map( s -> new ParamsAndHandle(s,null))
  .collect(Collectors.toSet());
}
```

Because the processes are not started at this point, the handles are all `null`. The `run()` method starts the processes:

```
@Override
public void run() {
  try {
    for (ParamsAndHandle pah : handlers) {
      log.log(DEBUG, "Starting {0}", pah.params);
      ProcessHandle handle = start(pah.params);
      pah.handle = handle;
    }
    keepProcessesAlive();
    while (handlers.size() > 0) {
      allMyProcesses().join();
    }
  } catch (IOException e)
    {
      log.log(ERROR, e);
    }
}
```

Processing goes through the set of parameters and uses the method (implemented in this class later) to start the processes. The handles to each process get to the `ParamsAndHandle` object. After that, the `keepProcessesAlive` method is called and waits for the processes to finish. When a process stops it gets restarted. If it cannot be restarted it will be removed from the set.

The `allMyProcesses` method (also implemented in this class) returns a `CompletableFuture` that gets completed when all the started processes have stopped. Some of the processes may have been restarted by the time the `join()` method returns. As long as there is at least one process running, the thread should run.

Using the `CompletableFuture` to wait for the processes and the `while` loop, we use minimal CPU to keep the thread alive so long as long there is at least one process we manage running, presumably even after a few restarts. We have to keep this thread alive even if it does not use CPU and executes no code most of the time to let the `keepProcessesAlive()` method do its work using `CompletableFutures`. The method is shown in the following code snippet:

```
private void keepProcessesAlive()
{
  anyOfMyProcesses()
    .thenAccept(ignore -> {
      restartProcesses();
      keepProcessesAlive();
    });
}
```

The `keepProcessesAlive()` method calls the `anyOfMyProcesses()` method that returns a `CompletableFuture`, which is completed when any of the managed processes exits. The method schedules to execute the lambda passed as an argument to the `thenAccept()` method for the time the `CompletableFuture` is completed. The lambda does two things:

- Restarts the processes that are stopped (probably only one)
- Calls the `keepProcessesAlive()` method

It is important to understand that this call is not performed from within the `keepProcessesAlive()` method itself. This is not a recursive call. This is scheduled as a `CompletableFuture` action. We are not implementing a loop in a recursive call, because we would run out of stack space. We ask the JVM executors to execute this method again when the processes are restarted.

It is important to know that the JVM uses the default `ForkJoinPool` to schedule these tasks and this pool contains daemon threads. That is the reason we have to wait and keep the method running because that is the only non-daemon thread that prevents the JVM from exiting.

The next method is `restartProcesses()`:

```
private void restartProcesses()
{
  Set<ParamsAndHandle> failing = new HashSet<>();
  handlers.stream()
   .filter(pah -> !pah.toHandle().isAlive())
   .forEach(pah -> {
     try {
       pah.handle = start(pah.params);
     } catch (IOException e) {
        failing.add(pah);
     }
   });
  handlers.removeAll(failing);
}
```

This method starts the processes that are in our set of managed processes and which are not alive. If any of the restarts fail it removes the failing processes from the set. (Be aware not to remove it in the loop to avoid `ConcurrentModificationException`.)

The `anyOfMyProcesses()` and `allMyProcesses()` methods are using the auxiliary `completableFuturesOfTheProcessesand()` method and are straight forward:

```
private CompletableFuture anyOfMyProcesses()
{
  return CompletableFuture.anyOf(
    completableFuturesOfTheProcesses());
}

private CompletableFuture allMyProcesses() {
  return CompletableFuture.allOf(
    completableFuturesOfTheProcesses());
}
```

The `completableFuturesOfTheProcesses()` method returns an array of
`CompletableFutures` created from the currently running managed processes calling their
`onExit()` method. This is done in a compact and easy to read functional programming
style, as shown here:

```
private CompletableFuture[] completableFuturesOfTheProcesses()
{
  return handlers.stream()
   .map(ParamsAndHandle::toHandle)
   .map(ProcessHandle::onExit)
   .collect(Collectors.toList())
   .toArray(new CompletableFuture[handlers.size()]);
}
```

The set is converted to a `stream`, mapped to a `stream` of `ProcessHandle` objects (this is
why we needed the `toHandle()` method in the `ParamsAndHandle` class). Then the handles
are mapped to `CompletableFuture` stream using the `onExit()` method and finally we
collect it to a list and convert to an array.

Our last method to complete our sample application is as follows:

```
private ProcessHandle start(Parameters params)
  throws IOException {
    return new ProcessBuilder(params.commandLine)
     .start()
     .toHandle();
}
```

This method starts the process using a `ProcessBuilder` and returns the `ProcessHandle`
so that we can replace the old one in our set and manage the new process.

Summary

In this chapter we discussed how Java 9 better enables us to manage processes. Prior to Java
9, process management from within Java required OS specific implementations and was
less than optimal in terms of CPU use and coding practice. The modern API, with new
classes like `ProcessHandle`, makes it possible to handle almost all aspects of processes.
We listed the new API, and had simple example codes for the use of each of them. In the
second half of the chapter we put together a whole application managing processes where
the learned API was put into practice.

In the next chapter, we will take a detailed look at the new Java Stack Walking API released
with Java 9. We will use code samples to illustrate how to use the API.

10
Fine-Grained Stack Tracing

Java 9 comes with a new stack walker API that lets the program walk the calling stack. This is a very special functionality that is rarely needed by ordinary programs. The API can be useful for some very special cases--for functionality that is delivered by framework. So, if you want an efficient means of stack walking that gives you filterable access to stack trace information, you will enjoy this new stack walker API.

The API gives fast and optimized access to the call stack, implementing lazy access to the individual frames.

In this chapter, we cover the following topics:

- Overview of the Java Stack
- The importance of stack information
- Using `StackWalker`
- The `StackFrame`
- Performance

Overview of the Java Stack

Before we dive into the stack walker, let's start by covering the Java Stack. This is basic stack information, not specific to the stack walker.

The Java runtime has a class named Stack, which can be used to store objects using the **last-in-first-out (LIFO)** policy.

When arithmetic expressions are calculated they are done using a stack. If we add *A* and *B* in our code first *A* is pushed on the **Operand Stack**, then *B* is pushed on the Operand Stack and finally the addition operation is executed, which fetches the two topmost elements of the Operand Stack and pushes the result, *A* + *B* there.

The JVM is written in C and executes calling C functions and returning from there. This call-return sequence is maintained using the Native Method Stack just like any other C program.

Finally, when the JVM creates a new thread it also allocates a call stack containing frames that in turn contain the local variables, reference to the previous frame, and reference to the class that contains the executing method. When a method is invoked a new frame is created. The frame is destroyed when a method finishes its execution, in other words, returns or throws an exception. This stack, the Java Virtual Machine Stack, is the one that the stack walker API manages.

The importance of stack information

Generally speaking we need the stack information when we want to develop caller dependent code. Having information about the caller allows our code to make decisions based on that information. In general practice, it is not a good idea to make functionality dependent on the caller. Information that affects the behavior of a method should be available via parameters. Caller dependent code development should be fairly limited.

The JDK accesses stack information with native methods that are not available to Java applications. The `SecurityManager` is a class that defines an application's security policy. This class checks that the caller of a reflection API is allowed to access the non-public members of another class. To do that it has to have access to the caller class and it does that through a protected native method.

This is an example of implementing some security measures without having to walk through a stack. We open our code for external developers to use it as a library. We also call methods of classes provided by the library user and they may call back to our code. There is some code that we want to allow library users to call but only if they were not called from our code. If we did not want to allow some of the code to be accessed directly by the library using code we could use Java 9's modular structure not exporting the package containing the classes not to be invoked. This is the reason we set the extra condition that the code is available for the callers from outside, except if they were called by our code:

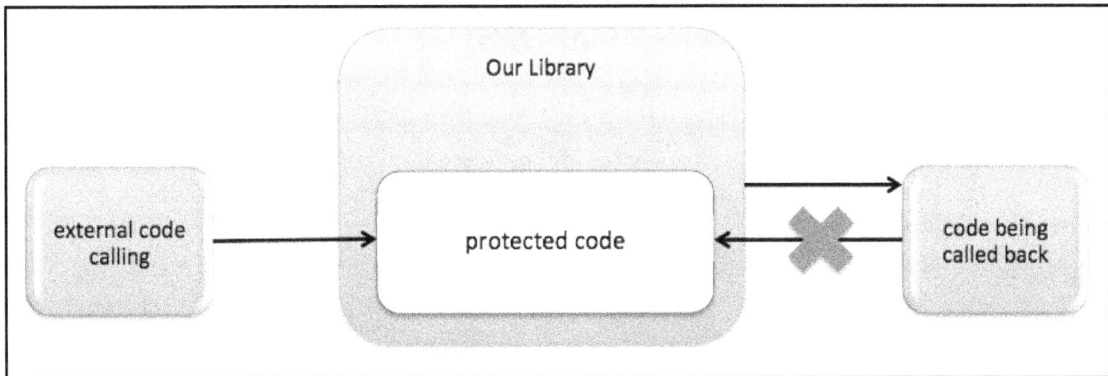

Another example is when we want to get access to a logger. Java applications use many different loggers and the logging system is usually very flexible so that the output of the different loggers can be switched on and off based on the actual need to introspect into the code. The most common practice is to use a different logger for each class and the name of the logger is usually the name of the class. The practice is so common that the logging framework even provides logger access methods that accept the reference to the class itself instead of the name. It essentially means that the call to get the handle of a logger looks something like the following:

```
private static final Logger LOG = Logger.getLogger(MyClass.class);
```

A problem can arise when we create new classes from existing classes if we forget to alter the name of the class name in the call for getting a new logger. This is not a serious problem, but it is common. In that case our code will use the logger of the other class and it will actually work, but may create confusion when we analyze the log files. It would be much nicer if we had a method that returns the logger that is named as the class of the caller.

Let's continue our exploration of stack information in the next two sections with code snippet examples.

Example - Restricting callers

In this section we develop a sample library with two methods. The `hello()` method prints `hello` to the standard output. The `callMe()` method accepts a `Runnable` as an argument and runs it. The first method however is restricted. It executes only if the caller is purely outside of the library. It throws an `IllegalCallerException` if the caller obtained the control in a way that the library was calling out, presumably via the second method invoking the passed `Runnable`. The implementation of the API is simple:

```
package packt.java9.deep.stackwalker.myrestrictivelibrary;
public class RestrictedAPI {
  public void hello(){
    CheckEligibility.itIsNotCallBack();
    System.out.println("hello");
  }
  public void callMe(Runnable cb){
    cb.run();
  }
}
```

The code that performs the eligibility checking is implemented in a separate class to keep things simple. We will examine that code shortly, but before that we look at the main code we use to start the demonstration. The main program code we use to demonstrate the functionality is the following:

```
package packt.java9.deep.stackwalker.externalcode;

import
 packt.java9.deep.stackwalker.myrestrictivelibrary.RestrictedAPI;

public class DirectCall {

  public static void main(String[] args) {
    RestrictedAPI api = new RestrictedAPI();
    api.hello();
    api.callMe(() -> {
        api.hello();
    });
  }
}
```

This code creates an instance of our API class and then directly invokes the `hello()` method. It should work and should print the characters `hello` on screen. The next code line asks the `callMe()` method to call back the `Runnable` provided in form of a lambda expression. In this case the call will fail, because the caller is outside but was called from inside the library.

Let's now look at how the eligibility check is implemented:

```
package packt.java9.deep.stackwalker.myrestrictivelibrary;

import static java.lang.StackWalker.Option.RETAIN_CLASS_REFERENCE;

public class CheckEligibility {
  private static final String packageName
    = CheckEligibility.class.getPackageName();

  private static boolean notInLibrary(StackWalker.StackFrame f) {
    return !inLibrary(f);
  }

  private static boolean inLibrary(StackWalker.StackFrame f) {
    return f.getDeclaringClass().getPackageName()
     .equals(packageName);
  }

  public static void itIsNotCallBack() {
    boolean eligible = StackWalker
     .getInstance(RETAIN_CLASS_REFERENCE)
     .walk(s -> s.dropWhile(CheckEligibility::inLibrary)
       .dropWhile(CheckEligibility::notInLibrary)
       .count() == 0
    );
    if (!eligible) {
      throw new IllegalCallerException();
    }
  }
}
```

The `itIsNotCallBack()` method is the one called from the `hello()` method. This method creates a stack walker and invokes the `walk()` method. The argument of the `walk()` method is a `Function` that converts a `Stream` of `StackFrame` objects to some other value that the `walk()` method will return.

At first this argument setting might seem complex and difficult to understand. It would be more logical to return a `Stream` that provides the `StackFrame` objects instead of forcing the caller to define a `Function` that will get this as an argument.

The sample code uses a lambda expression to define the `Function` as an argument to the `walk()` method. The argument to the lambda expression s is the stream. Since the first element of this stream is the actual call we drop it. Because these calls should also be refused if the caller is not eligible even though the call to method `hello()` was through some other class and method that is already inside the library, we drop all elements from the frame that belong to classes inside the package of the class `CheckEligibility`. This package is `packt.java9.deep.stackwalker.myrestrictivelibrary` and in the code this string is stored in the field `packageName`. The resulting stream contains only the `StackFrame` objects that are from outside of the library. We drop these also until the stream exhausts or until we find a `StackFrame` that again belongs to the library. If all elements were dropped we are good. In this case the result of `count()` is zero. If we find some class in the `StackFrame` that belongs to the library it means that the outside code was called from the library and in this case we have to refuse working. In this case the variable eligible will be `false` and we throw an exception, as can be seen in the following screenshot:

```
DirectCall.java        CheckEligibility.java

DirectCall   main()   -> Runnable
1    package packt.java9.deep.stackwalker.externalcode;
2
3    import packt.java9.deep.stackwalker.myrestrictivelibrary.RestrictedAPI;
4
5    public class DirectCall {
6
7        public static void main(String[] args) {
8            RestrictedAPI api = new RestrictedAPI();
9            api.hello();
10           api.callMe(() -> {
11               api.hello();
12           });
13       }
14   }
```

```
Run    DirectCall
    /Library/Java/JavaVirtualMachines/jdk-9.jdk/Contents/Home/bin/java "-javaagent:/Applications/IntelliJ IDEA CE
    Exception in thread "main" java.lang.IllegalCallerException
    hello
        at stackwalker/packt.java9.deep.stackwalker.myrestrictivelibrary.CheckEligibility.itIsNotCallBack(CheckEligibility.java:31)
        at stackwalker/packt.java9.deep.stackwalker.myrestrictivelibrary.RestrictedAPI.hello(RestrictedAPI.java:6)
        at stackwalker/packt.java9.deep.stackwalker.externalcode.DirectCall.lambda$main$0(DirectCall.java:11)
        at stackwalker/packt.java9.deep.stackwalker.myrestrictivelibrary.RestrictedAPI.callMe(RestrictedAPI.java:11)
        at stackwalker/packt.java9.deep.stackwalker.externalcode.DirectCall.main(DirectCall.java:10)

    Process finished with exit code 1
```

Example - Getting logger for caller

To get a logger, Java 9 has a new API. Using this API a module can provide an implementation for the service `LoggerFinder`, which in turn can return a `Logger` implementing the `getLogger()` method. This eliminates the dependency of libraries on specific loggers or logger facades, which is a huge advantage. The smaller but still annoying issue requiring us to write the name of the class again as the parameter to the method `getLogger()` is still there.

To avoid this cumbersome task, we create a helper class that looks up the caller class and retrieves the logger that is suitable for the caller class and module. Because in this case there is no need for all the classes referenced in the stack trace we will call the `getCallerClass()` method of the `StackWalker` class. We create a class named `Labrador` in the package `packt.java9.deep.stackwalker.logretriever`:

```
package packt.java9.deep.stackwalker.logretriever;

import java.lang.System.Logger;
import java.lang.System.LoggerFinder;

import static java.lang.StackWalker.Option.RETAIN_CLASS_REFERENCE;

public class Labrador {
  public static Logger retrieve() {
    final Class clazz = StackWalker
      .getInstance(RETAIN_CLASS_REFERENCE)
      .getCallerClass();
    return LoggerFinder.getLoggerFinder().getLogger(
      clazz.getCanonicalName(), clazz.getModule());
  }
}
```

Before Java 9 the solution for this issue was getting the `StackTrace` array from the `Thread` class and looking up the name of the caller class from there. Another approach was extending the `SecurityManager` that has a protected method `getClassContext()` that returns an array of all the classes on the stack. Both solutions walk through the stack and compose an array although we only need one element from the array. In case of logger retrieval it may not be a significant performance penalty since loggers are usually stored in `private static final` fields and thus are initialized once per class during class initialization. In other use cases the performance penalty may be significant.

After we have seen two examples we will look at the details of `StackWalker` inner working.

Working with StackWalker

In this section you will become more familiar with how to work with `StackWalker`. We will explore the following topics in this section:

- Getting an instance of `StackWalker`
- Stack walking options

Getting an instance of StackWalker

To perform the walking over the stack elements we need an instance of the stack walker. To do that, we invoke the `getInstance()` method. As shown here, there are four overloaded versions of this method:

- `static StackWalker getInstance()`
- `static StackWalker getInstance(StackWalker.Option option)`
- `static StackWalker getInstance(Set<StackWalker.Option> options)`
- `static StackWalker getInstance(Set<StackWalker.Option> options, int estimateDepth)`

The first version does not take any arguments and returns a `StackWalker` instance that will let us walk through normal stack frames. This is usually what we would be interested in. The other versions of the method accept a `StackWalker.Option` value or values. The enum `StackWalker.Option`, as the name suggests, is inside the class `StackWalker` and has three values:

- `RETAIN_CLASS_REFERENCE`
- `SHOW_REFLECT_FRAMES`
- `SHOW_HIDDEN_FRAMES`

These `enum` options have self-descriptive names and are explained in the next sections.

RETAIN_CLASS_REFERENCE

If we specify the first option `enum` constant, `RETAIN_CLASS_REFERENCE`, as an argument to the `getInstance()` method then the returned instance grants us access to the classes that the individual stack frames reference during the walking.

SHOW_REFLECT_FRAMES

The SHOW_REFLECT_FRAMES enum constant will generate a walker that includes the frames that source from some reflective calling.

SHOW_HIDDEN_FRAMES

Finally the enum constant option, SHOW_HIDDEN_FRAMES will include all the hidden frames, which contain reflective calls as well as call frames that are generated for lambda function calls.

Here is a simple demonstration of reflective and hidden frames:

```
package packt;
import static java.lang.StackWalker.Option.SHOW_HIDDEN_FRAMES;
import static java.lang.StackWalker.Option.SHOW_REFLECT_FRAMES;
public class Main {
```

The main method allowing us to execute this code directly calls the method simpleCall():

```
public static void main(String[] args) {
  simpleCall();
}
```

The method simpleCall() simply calls on as the name suggests:

```
static void simpleCall() {
  reflectCall();
}
```

The next method in the chain is a bit more complex. Although this also only calls the next one, it does so using reflection:

```
static void reflectCall() {
  try {
    Main.class.getDeclaredMethod("lambdaCall",
      new Class[0])
        .invoke(null, new Object[0]);
  } catch (Exception e) {
    throw new RuntimeException();
  }
}
```

In this next example, we have a method that calls using a lambda:

```
static void lambdaCall() {
  Runnable r = () -> {
    walk();
  };
  r.run();
}
```

The last method before the actual walking is called `walk()`:

```
static void walk() {
  noOptions();
  System.out.println();
  reflect();
  System.out.println();
  hidden();
}
```

The preceding `walk()` method calls three methods, one after the other. These methods are very similar to each other and provided here:

```
static void noOptions() {
  StackWalker
    .getInstance()
    .forEach(System.out::println);
}

static void reflect() {
  StackWalker
    .getInstance(SHOW_REFLECT_FRAMES)
    .forEach(System.out::println);
}

static void hidden() {
  StackWalker
    // shows also reflect frames
    .getInstance(SHOW_HIDDEN_FRAMES)
    .forEach(System.out::println);
}
```

The preceding three methods print out the frames to the standard output. They use the `forEach()` method of the stack walker. Here is the output of the stack walking program:

```
stackwalker/packt.Main.noOptions(Main.java:45)
stackwalker/packt.Main.walk(Main.java:34)
stackwalker/packt.Main.lambda$lambdaCall$0(Main.java:28)
stackwalker/packt.Main.lambdaCall(Main.java:30)
stackwalker/packt.Main.reflectCall(Main.java:19)
stackwalker/packt.Main.simpleCall(Main.java:12)
stackwalker/packt.Main.main(Main.java:8)
```

This output only contains the frames that belong to calls that are in our code. The `main()` method calls `simpleCall()`, which calls `reflectCall()`, that in turn calls `lambdaCall()`, which calls a lambda expression, that calls `walk()` and so on. The fact that we did not specify any option does not delete the lambda call from the stack. We performed that call, thus it must be there. What it deletes are the extra stack frames that are needed by the JVM to implement the lambda. We can see on the next output, when the option was `SHOW_REFLECT_FRAMES`, that the reflective frames are already there:

```
stackwalker/packt.Main.reflect(Main.java:58)
stackwalker/packt.Main.walk(Main.java:36)
stackwalker/packt.Main.lambda$lambdaCall$0(Main.java:28)
stackwalker/packt.Main.lambdaCall(Main.java:30)
java.base/jdk.internal.reflect.NativeMethodAccessorImpl.invoke0(Native
Method)
java.base/jdk.internal.reflect.NativeMethodAccessorImpl.invoke(NativeMethod
AccessorImpl.java:62)
java.base/jdk.internal.reflect.DelegatingMethodAccessorImpl.invoke(Delegati
ngMethodAccessorImpl.java:43)
java.base/java.lang.reflect.Method.invoke(Method.java:547)
stackwalker/packt.Main.reflectCall(Main.java:19)
stackwalker/packt.Main.simpleCall(Main.java:12)
stackwalker/packt.Main.main(Main.java:8)
```

In this case the difference is that we can see that the call from the `reflectCall()` method to `lambdaCall()` method is not direct. The `reflectCall()` method calls the `invoke()` method that calls another method of the same name defined in a different class that in turn calls the `invoke0()` method, which is a native method provided by the JVM. After that we finally get to the `lambdaCall()` method.

In the output we can also see that these reflective calls belong to the module `java.base` and not our `stackwalker` module.

If we include the hidden frames in addition to the reflective frames, specifying the option `SHOW_HIDDEN_FRAMES`, then we will see the following output:

```
stackwalker/packt.Main.hidden(Main.java:52)
stackwalker/packt.Main.walk(Main.java:38)
stackwalker/packt.Main.lambda$lambdaCall$0(Main.java:28)
stackwalker/packt.Main$$Lambda$46/269468037.run(Unknown Source)
stackwalker/packt.Main.lambdaCall(Main.java:30)
java.base/jdk.internal.reflect.NativeMethodAccessorImpl.invoke0(Native
Method)
java.base/jdk.internal.reflect.NativeMethodAccessorImpl.invoke(NativeMethod
AccessorImpl.java:62)
java.base/jdk.internal.reflect.DelegatingMethodAccessorImpl.invoke(Delegati
ngMethodAccessorImpl.java:43)
java.base/java.lang.reflect.Method.invoke(Method.java:547)
stackwalker/packt.Main.reflectCall(Main.java:19)
stackwalker/packt.Main.simpleCall(Main.java:12)
stackwalker/packt.Main.main(Main.java:8)
```

This includes an extra hidden frame that the JVM is using to execute the lambda call. In addition, the reflective frames are also included.

Final thoughts on enum constants

We can also specify more than one option giving a set of the options. The simplest way of doing that is to use the static `of()` method of the `java.util.Set` interface. This way the `RETAIN_CLASS_REFERENCE` option can be combined with either the `SHOW_REFLECT_FRAMES` option or the `SHOW_HIDDEN_FRAMES` option.

Although it is technically possible to combine `SHOW_REFLECT_FRAMES` and `SHOW_HIDDEN_FRAMES` as an option set, there is really no advantage in doing that. The latter includes the first, so the combination of the two is exactly same as the second.

Accessing classes

When we want to access the class objects during a stack walk, we have to specify the `RETAIN_CLASS_REFERENCE` option. Although the `StackFrame` interface defines the `getClassName()` method, that could be used to access a class of the name using the `Class.forName()` method, doing so would not guarantee that the class the `StackFrame` object refers to was loaded by the same class loader as the code calling `Class.forName()`. In some special cases, we could end up with two different classes of the same name loaded by two different class loaders.

When the option is not used during the creation of the StackWalker instance then the methods that otherwise return a class object will throw an UnsupportedOperationException exception. That way getDeclaringClass() cannot be used on the StackFrame and getCallerClass() on the StackWalker.

Walking methods

The StackWalker defines the forEach() method that expects a Consumer (preferably in the form of a lambda expression) that is invoked for each element of the stack trace walking up the stack. The argument to the Consumer method is a StackFrame object.

Although a method named forEach is also defined by the Stream interface and the method walk() passes a Stream object to the Function it gets as argument, we should not confuse the two. The forEach() method of StackWalker is a simpler, and most of the time less effective way to get through all the elements of the stack trace.

It is less effective, in most cases, because it forces the StackWalker instance to get all the elements of the stack trace so that the forEach() method can traverse through each element to the end. If we know that we will not traverse through the stack trace to the end we should use the walk() method that is accessing the stack the lazy way and thus leave more room for performance optimization.

The StackWalker class has the walk() method, which is the defining method that makes it a walker. The method accepts a Function that is called by the StackWalker. The return value of the walk() method will be the object returned by the Function. The argument to the Function is a Stream<StackFrame> that delivers the stack frames. The first frame is the one that contains the walk() method call, the next is the one that was calling method that contains the call to walk(), and so on.

The Function can be used to calculate some value based on the StackFrame objects that come from the stream and decide if a caller is eligible calling our code or not.

You might ponder, after reviewing the `walk()` method that needs a `Function` that in turn gets a `Stream<StackFrame>` as argument, why it is so complicated. We might wish we could get a `Stream<StackFrame>` from the `StackWalter` instance directly. The simplest approach would be to pass the stream back from the `Function`. Consider the following example:

```
// EXAMPLE OF WHAT NOT TO DO!!!!
public static void itIsNotCallBack() {
  Stream<StackWalker.StackFrame> stream =
    StackWalker
      .getInstance(RETAIN_CLASS_REFERENCE)
      .walk(s -> s);
  boolean eligible = // YOU GET EXCEPTION!!!!
    stream.dropWhile(CheckEligibility::inLibrary)
      .dropWhile(CheckEligibility::notInLibrary)
      .count() == 0;
  if (!eligible) {
    throw new IllegalCallerException();
  }
}
```

What we were doing is simply returning the stream directly from the walker call and walking through it afterwards doing same calculation. Our results are an `IllegalStateException` exception instead of the eligibility check.

The reason for that is that the implementation of the `StackWalker` is highly optimized. It does not copy the whole stack to provide source information for the stream. It works from the actual, living stack. To do that it has to be sure that the stack is not modified while the stream is in use. This is something very similar to the `ConcurrentModificationException` that we might get if we alter a collection while we iterate over it. If we passed the stream up in the call stack and then wanted to get the `StackFrame` out of it, the stream would try to get the information from the stack frame that is long gone, since we returned from the method that it belonged to. That way the `StackWalker` does not make a snapshot of the whole stack but rather it works from the actual one and it must ensure that the part of the stack it needs does not change. We may call methods from the `Function` and that way we can dig deeper in the call chain but we cannot get higher while the stream is in use.

Also do not try to play other tricks, like extending the `StackWalker` class. You cannot. It is a `final` class.

StackFrame

In previous sections, we iterated through the StackFrame elements, and provided sample code snippets, but did not take the time to examine it more closely. StackFrame is an interface defined inside the StackWalker class. It defines accessors, and a converter that can be used to convert the information to StackTraceElement.

The accessors the interface defines are the following:

- getClassName() will return the binary name of the class of the method represented by the StackFrame.
- getMethodName() will return the name of the method represented by the StackFrame.
- getDeclaringClass() will return the class of the method represented by the StackFrame. If the Option.RETAIN_CLASS_REFERENCE was not used during the creation of the StackWalker instance then the method will throw UnsupportedOperationException.
- getByteCodeIndex() gets the index to the code array containing the execution point of the method represented by the StackFrame. The use of this value can be helpful during bug hunting when looking at the disassembled Java code that the command line tool javap can give us. The programmatic use of this value can only be valuable for applications that have direct access to the byte code of the code, java agents or libraries that generate byte code during run-time. The method will return a negative number in case the method is native.
- getFileName() returns the name of the source file the method represented by the StackFrame was defined.
- getLineNumber() returns the line number of the source code.
- isNativeMethod() returns true if the method represented by the StackFrame is native and false otherwise.

The StackFrame does not provide any means to access the object that the method belongs to. You cannot access the arguments and the local variables of the method represented by the StackFrame and there is no other way you can accomplish that. This is important. Such access would be too invasive and is not possible.

Performance

Our coverage of `StackWalker` would not be complete without a look at performance considerations.

`StackWalker` is highly optimized and does not create huge memory structures that go unused. That is the reason why we have to use that `Function` passed to the method `walker()` as an argument. This is also the reason why a `StackTrace` is not automatically converted to a `StackTraceElement` when created. This only happens if we query the method name, the line number of the specific `StackTraceElement`. It is important to understand that this conversion takes a significant amount of time and if it was used for some debug purpose in the code it should not be left there.

To make the `StackWalker` even faster we can provide an estimate about the number of `StackFrame` elements that we will work with in the stream. If we do not provide such an estimate, the current implementation in the JDK will use eight `StackFrame` objects pre-allocated and when that is exhausted, the JDK will allocate more. The JDK will allocate the number of elements based on our estimate unless we estimate a value larger than 256. In that case, the JDK will use 256.

Summary

In this chapter, we learned how to use the `StackWalker` and provided example code. Our detailed review of the API included different usage scenarios, options, and information. We explained the API's complexity and shared how and how not to use the class. We closed with some related performance issues that the user has to be aware of.

In our next chapter, we will cover over a dozen Java Enhancement Proposals that were incorporated in the Java 9 platform. The featured changes will cover a wide range of tools and updates to APIs that are aimed at making developing with Java easier and the ability to create optimized Java applications. We will look at the new HTTP client, changes to the Javadoc and Doclet API, the new JavaScript parser, JAR and JRE changes, the new Java-level JVM compiler interface, support for TIFF images, platform logging, XML catalog support, collections, new platform-specific desktop features, and enhancements to method handling and the depreciation annotation.

11
New Tools and Tool Enhancements

In the previous chapter, we explored Java 9's new stack walker API and learned how it enables Java applications to walk the calling stack. This is a specialized functionality that is not often implemented in Java applications. That being said, the API may be good for some very special cases, such as for functionality that is delivered by a framework. You learned that if you develop framework-supporting application programming and you want code that depends on the caller context, then the stack walker API is for you. We also discovered that the API gives fast and optimized access to the call stack, implementing lazy access to the individual frames.

In this chapter, we will cover 16 **Java Enhancement Proposals (JEPs)** that were incorporated into the Java 9 platform. These JEPs cover a wide range of tools and updates to APIs to make developing with Java easier, with greater optimization possibilities for our resulting programs.

Our review of new tools and tool enhancements will include the following:

- The new HTTP client
- Javadoc and the Doclet API
- mJRE changes
- JavaScript parser
- Multi-release JAR files
- The Java-level JVM compiler interface
- TIFF support
- Platform logging
- XML Catalogs

- Collections
- Platform-specific desktop features
- Enhanced method handling
- Enhanced deprecation

The new HTTP client [JEP-110]

In this section, we will review Java's **Hypertext Transfer Protocol** (**HTTP**) client, starting with a pre-Java 9 look and then diving into the new HTTP client that is part of the Java 9 platform. This approach is needed to support an understanding of the changes made in Java 9.

The HTTP client before Java 9

JDK version 1.1 introduced the `HttpURLConnection` API that supported HTTP-specific features. This was a robust class that included the fields listed here:

- `chunkLength`
- `fixedContentLength`
- `fixedContentLengthLong`
- `HTTP_ACCEPTED`
- `HTTP_BAD_GATEWAY`
- `HTTP_BAD_METHOD`
- `HTTP_BAD_REQUEST`
- `HTTP_CLIENT_TIMEOUT`
- `HTTP_CONFLICT`
- `HTTP_CREATED`
- `HTTP_ENTITY_TOO_LARGE`
- `HTTP_FORBIDDEN`
- `HTTP_GONE`
- `HTTP_INTERNAL_ERROR`
- `HTTP_LENGTH_REQUIRED`
- `HTTP_MOVED_PERM`
- `HTTP_MOVED_TEMP`

- HTTP_MULT_CHOICE
- HTTP_NO_CONTENT
- HTTP_NOT_ACCEPTABLE
- HTTP_NOT_AUTHORITATIVE
- HTTP_NOT_FOUND
- HTTP_NOT_IMPLEMENTED
- HTTP_NOT_MODIFIED
- HTTP_OK
- HTTP_PARTIAL
- HTTP_PAYMENT_REQUIRED
- HTTP_PRECON_FAILED
- HTTP_PROXY_AUTH
- HTTP_REQ_TOO_LONG
- HTTP_RESET
- HTTP_SEE_OTHER
- HTTP_SERVER_ERROR
- HTTP_UNAUTHORIZED
- HTTP_UNAVAIABLE
- HTTP_UNSUPPORTED_TYPE
- HTTP_USE_PROXY
- HTTP_VERSION
- instanceFollowRedirects
- method
- responseCode
- responseMessage

As you can see from the list of fields, there was a great support for HTTP. In addition to a constructor, there are a plethora of available methods, including the following ones:

- disconnect()
- getErrorStream()
- getFollowRedirects()
- getHeaderField(int n)
- getHeaderFieldDate(String name, long Default)
- getHeaderFieldKey(int n)

- `getInstanceFollowRedirects()`
- `getPermission()`
- `getRequestMethod()`
- `getResponseCode()`
- `getResponseMessage()`
- `setChunkedStreamingMode(int chunklen)`
- `setFixedLengthStreamingMode(int contentLength)`
- `setFixedlengthStreamingMode(long contentLength)`
- `setFollowRedirects(boolean set)`
- `setInstanceFollowRedircts(boolean followRedirects)`
- `setRequestMethod(String method)`
- `usingProxy()`

The class methods listed earlier are in addition to the methods inherited from the `java.net.URLConnection` class and the `java.lang.Object` class.

There were problems with the original HTTP client that made it ripe for updating with the new Java platform. Those problems were as follows:

- The base `URLConnection` API had, defunct protocols such as Gopher and FTP increasingly over the years
- The `HttpURLConnection` API predated HTTP 1.1 and was overly abstract, making it less usable
- The HTTP client was woefully under documented, making the API frustrating and difficult to use
- The client only functioned on one thread at a time
- The API was extremely difficult to maintain due to the above points about it predating HTTP 1.1 and it lacking sufficient documentation

Now that we know what was wrong with the HTTP client, let's look at what's in store for Java 9.

Java 9's new HTTP client

There were several goals associated with creating the new HTTP client for the Java 9 platform. JEP-110 was the organizing proposal for the new HTTP client. The primary goals of JEP-110 are listed here and featured the creation of the new HTTP client presented. These goals are presented in the broad categories of ease of use, core capabilities, additional capabilities, and performance:

- Ease of use:
    - The API was designed to provide up to 90 percent of HTTP-related application requirements.
    - The new API is usable, without unnecessary complexity, for the most common use cases.
    - A simplistic blocking mode is included.
    - The API supports modern Java language features. Lambda expressions, a major new introduction released with Java 8, are an example.

- Core capabilities:
    - Supports HTTPS/TLS
    - Supports HTTP/2
    - Provides visibility on all details related to HTTP protocol requests and responses
    - Supports standard/common authentication mechanisms
    - Provides **headers received** event notifications
    - Provides **response body received** event notifications
    - Provides error event notifications

- Additional capabilities:
    - The new API can be used for WebSocket handshakes
    - It performs security checks in concert with the current networking API

- Performance:
    - For HTTP/1.1:
        - The new API must perform at least as efficiently as the previous API.
        - Memory consumption must not exceed that of Apache HttpClient, Netty, and Jetty, when being used as a client API.

- For HTTP/2:
  - Performance must exceed that of HTTP/1.1.
  - The new performance must match or exceed that of Netty and Jetty when being used as a client API. No performance degradation should be a result of the new client.
  - Memory consumption must not exceed that of Apache HttpClient, Netty, and Jetty, when being used as a client API.
- Avoids running timer threads

New API limitations

There are some intentional shortcomings of the new API. While this might sound counter-intuitive, the new API was not intended to completely replace the current `HttpURLConnection` API. Instead, the new API is intended to eventually replace the current one.

The following code snippet provides an example of how to implement the `HttpURLConnect` class to open and read a URL in a Java application:

```
/*
import statements
*/

public class HttpUrlConnectionExample
{
  public static void main(String[] args)
  {
    new HttpUrlConnectionExample();
  }
  public HttpUrlConnectionExample()
  {
    URL theUrl = null;
    BufferedReader theReader = null;
    StringBuilder theStringBuilder;

    // put the URL into a String
    String theUrl = "https://www.packtpub.com/";

    // here we are creating the connection
    theUrl = new URL(theUrl);
```

```
HttpURLConnection theConnection = (HttpURLConnection)
 theUrl.openConnection();

theConnection.setRequestedMethod("GET");

// add a delay
theConnection.setReadTimeout(30000); // 30 seconds
theConnection.connect();

// next, we can read the output
theReader = new BufferedReader(
  new InputStreamReader(theConnection.getInputStream()));
theStringBuilder =  new StringBuilder();

// read the output one line at a time
String theLine = null;
while ((theLine = theReader.readLine() != null)
{
  theStringBUilder.append(line + "n");
}

// echo the output to the screen console
System.out.println(theStringBuilder.toString());
// close the reader
theReader.close();
  }
 }
 . . .
```

The preceding code does not include exception handling for brevity.

Here are some specific limitations of the new API:

- Not all HTTP-related functionality is supported. It is estimated that about 10 percent of the HTTP's protocol is not exposed by the API.
- Standard/common authentication mechanisms have been limited to basic authentication.
- The overarching goal of the new API was the simplicity of use, which means that performance improvements might not be realized. Certainly, there will be no performance degradation, but there is not likely to be an overwhelming level of improvement, either.
- There is no support for filtering on requests.

- There is no support for filtering on responses.
- The new API does not include a pluggable connection cache.
- There is a lack of a general upgrade mechanism.

The new API is delivered as part of the Java 9 platform in the incubator mode. This suggests that the API will be standardized in a future Java platform, perhaps with Java 10.

Simplified Doclet API [JEP-221]

The Doclet API and Javadoc are closely related. Javadoc is a documentation tool and the Doclet API provides functionality so that we can inspect the javadoc comments embedded at the source-levels of libraries and programs. In this section, we will review the pre-Java 9 status of the Doclet API and then explore the changes introduced to the Doclet API in the Java 9 platform. In the following section, we will review Javadoc.

The pre-Java 9 Doclet API

The pre-Java 9 Doclet API, or the `com.sun.javadoc` package, gives us access to look at javadoc comments located in the source code. Invoking a Doclet is accomplished by using the `start` method. That method's signature is `public static boolean start(RootDoc root)`. We will use the `RootDoc` instance as a container for the program structure information.

In order to call javadoc, we need to pass the following:

- Package names
- Source file names (for classes and interfaces)
- An access control option--one of the following:
    - `package`
    - `private`
    - `protected`
    - `public`

When the preceding listed items are used to call javadoc, a **documented set** is provided as a filtered list. If our aim is to obtain a comprehensive, unfiltered list, we can use `allClasses(false)`.

Let's review an example Doclet:

```java
// Mandatory import statement.
import com.sun.javadoc.*;

// We will be looking for all the @throws documentation tags.
public class AllThrowsTags extends Doclet
{
  // This is used to invoke the Doclet.
  public static boolean start(Rootdoc myRoot)
  {
    // "ClassDoc[]" here referes to classes and interfaces.
    ClassDoc[] classesAndInterfaces =
     myRoot.classesAndInterfaces();
    for (int i = 0; i < classesAndInterfaces.length; ++i)
    {
      ClassDoc tempCD = classesAndInterfaces[i];
      printThrows(tempCD.contructors());
      printThrows(tempCD.methods());
    }
    return true;
  }

  static void printThrows(ExecutableMemberDoc[] theThrows)
  {
    for (int i = 0; i < theThrows.length; ++i)
    {
      ThrowsTag[] throws = theThrows[i].throwsTags();

      // Print the "qualified name" which will be a the
         class or
      // interface name.
      System.out.println(theThrows[i].qualifiedName());

      // A loop to print all comments with the Throws Tag that
      // belongs to the previously printed class or
         interface name
      for (int j = 0; j < throws.length; ++j)
      {
        // A println statement that calls three methods
           from the
        // ThrowsTag Interface: exceptionType(),
           exceptionName(),
        // and exceptionComment().
        System.out.println("--> TYPE: " +
          throws[j].exceptionType() +
          " | NAME: " + throws[j].exceptionName() +
          " | COMMENT: " + throws[j].exceptionComment());
```

```
            }
        }
    }
}
```

As you can see by the thoroughly commented code, gaining access to the javadoc content is relatively easy. In our preceding example, we would invoke the AllThrows class using the following code in the command line:

```
javadoc -doclet AllThrowsTags -sourcepath <source-location> java.util
```

The output of our result will consist of the following structure:

```
<class or interface name>
    TYPE: <exception type> | NAME: <exception name> | COMMENT: <exception
comment>
    TYPE: <exception type> | NAME: <exception name> | COMMENT: <exception
comment>
    TYPE: <exception type> | NAME: <exception name> | COMMENT: <exception
comment>
<class or interface name>
    TYPE: <exception type> | NAME: <exception name> | COMMENT: <exception
comment>
    TYPE: <exception type> | NAME: <exception name> | COMMENT: <exception
comment>
```

API enums

The API consists of one enum, LanguageVersion, which provides the Java programming language version. The constants for this enum are Java_1_1 and Java_1_5.

API classes

The Doclet class provides an example of how to create a class to start a Doclet. It contains an empty Doclet() constructor and the following methods:

- languageVersion()
- optionLength(String option)
- start(RootDoc root)
- validOptions(String[][] options, DocErrorReporter reporter)

API interfaces

The Doclet API contains the following listed interfaces. The interface names are self-describing. You can consult the documentation for additional details:

- `AnnotatedType`
- `AnnotationDesc`
- `AnnotationDesc.ElementValuePair`
- `AnnotationTypeDoc`
- `AnnotationTypeElementDoc`
- `AnnotationValue`
- `ClassDoc`
- `ConstructorDoc`
- `Doc`
- `DocErrorReporter`
- `ExecutableMemberDoc`
- `FieldDoc`
- `MemberDoc`
- `MethodDoc`
- `PackageDoc`
- `Parameter`
- `ParameterizedType`
- `ParamTag`
- `ProgramElementDoc`
- `RootDoc`
- `SeeTag`
- `SerialFieldTag`
- `SourcePosition`
- `Tag`
- `ThrowsTag`
- `Type`
- `TypeVariable`
- `WildcardType`

Problems with the pre-existing Doclet API

Fueling the need for a new Doclet API were several issues with the pre-existing Doclet API:

- It was not ideal for testing or concurrent usage. This stemmed from its implementation of static methods.
- The language model used in the API had several limitations and became more problematic with each successive Java upgrade.
- The API was inefficient, largely due to its heavy use of substring matching.
- There was no reference provided regarding the specific location of any given comment. This made diagnostics and troubleshooting difficult.

Java 9's Doclet API

Now that you have a good handle on the Doclet API as it existed prior to Java 9, let's look at what changes have been made and delivered with the Java 9 platform. The new Doclet API is in the `jdk.javadoc.doclet` package.

At a high level, the changes to the Doclet API are as follows:

- Updates the `com.sun.javadoc` Doclet API to take advantage of several Java SE and JDK APIs
- Updates the `com.sun.tools.doclets.standard.Standard` Doclet to use the new API
- Supports the updated Taglet API that is used to create custom javadoc tags

In addition to the changes listed earlier, the new API uses the two APIs listed here:

- Compiler tree API
- Language model API

Let's explore each of these in the following sections.

Compiler tree API

The compiler tree API is in the `com.sun.source.doctree` package. It provides several interfaces to document source-level comments. These APIs are represented as **Abstract Syntax Trees (ASTs)**.

There are two enums:

- `AttributeTree.ValueKind` with the following constants:
  - DOUBLE
  - EMPTY
  - SINGLE
  - UNQUOTED
- `DocTree.Kind` with the following constants:
  - ATTRIBUTE
  - AUTHOR
  - CODE
  - COMMENT
  - DEPRECATED
  - DOC_COMMENT
  - DOC_ROOT
  - END_ELEMENT
  - ENTITY
  - ERRONEOUS
  - EXCEPTION
  - IDENTIFIER
  - INHERIT_DOC
  - LINK
  - LINK_PLAIN
  - LITERAL
  - OTHER
  - PARAM
  - REFERENCE
  - RETURN
  - SEE
  - SERIAL
  - SERIAL_DATA
  - SERIAL_FIELD
  - SINCE
  - START_ELEMENT

- TEXT
- THROWS
- UNKNOWN_BLOCK_TAG
- UNKNOWN_INLINE_TAG
- VALUE
- VERSION

The `com.sun.source.doctree` package contains several interfaces. They are detailed in the following table:

Interface name	Extends	A tree node for:	Non-inherited methods
AttributeTree	DocTree	HTML element	getName(), getValue(), getValueKind()
AuthorTree	BlockTagTree, DocTree	@author block tag	getName()
BlockTagTree	DocTree	Base class for different types of block tags	getTagName()
CommentTree	DocTree	An embedded HTML comment with the following HTML tags--<!--text-->	getBody()
DeprecatedTree	BlockTagTree	@deprecated block tag	getBody()
DocCommentTree	DocTree	Body block tags	getBlockTags(), getBody(), getFirstSentence()
DocRootTree	InlineTagTree	@docroot inline tag	N/A
DocTree	N/A	Common interface for all	accept(DocTreeVisitor<R,D>visitor,Ddata), getKind()

DocTreeVisitor<R,P>	N/A	R = return type of visitor's methods; P = type of the additional parameter	visitAttribute(AttributeTree node, P p), visitAuthor(AuthorTree node, P p), visitComment(CommentTree node, P p), visitDeprecated(DeprecatedTree node, P p), visitDocComment(DocCommentTree node, P p), visitDocRoot(DocRootTree node, P p), visitEndElement(EndElementTree node, P p), visitEntity(EntityTree node, P p), visitErroneous(ErroneousTree node, P p), visitIdentifier(IdentifierTree node, P p), visitInheritDoc(InheritDocTree node, P p), visitLink(LinkTree node, P p), visitLiteral(LiteralTree node, P p), visitOther(DocTree node, P p), visitParam(ParamTree node, P p), visitReference(ReferenceTree node, P p), visitReturn(ReturnTree node, P p), visitSee(SeeTree node, P p), visitSerial(SerialTree node, P p), visitSerialData(SerialDataTree node, P p), visitSerialField(SerialFieldTree node, P p),visitSince(SinceTree node, P p), visitStartElement(StartElementTree node, P p),visitText(TextTree node, P p), visitThrows(ThrowsTree node, P p), visitUnknownBlockTag(UnknownBlockTagTree node, P p), visitUnknownInlineTag(UnknownInlineTagTree node, P p),visitValue(ValueTree node, P p),visitVersion(VersionTree node, P p)
EndElementTree	DocTree	End of an HTML element </name>	getName()
EntityTree	DocTree	An HTML entity	getName()
ErroneousTree	TextTree	This is for malformed text	getDiagnostic()
IdentifierTree	DocTree	An identifier in a comment	getName()
InheritDocTree	InlineTagTree	@inheritDoc inline tag	N/A
InlineTagTree	DocTree	Common interface for inline tags	getTagName()
LinkTree	InlineTagTree	@link or @linkplan inline tags	getLabel(), getReference()
LiteralTree	InlineTagTree	@literal or @code inline tags	getBody()
ParamTree	BlockTagTree	@param block tags	getDescription(), getName(), isTypeParameter()

`ReferenceTree`	`DocTree`	Used to reference a Java lang element	`getSignature()`
`ReturnTree`	`BlockTagTree`	`@return` block tags	`getDescription()`
`SeeTree`	`BlockTagTree`	`@see` block tags	`getReference()`
`SerialDataTree`	`BlockTagTree`	`@serialData` block tags	`getDescription()`
`SerialFieldTree`	`BlockTagTree`	`@serialData` block tags and `@serialField` field names and descriptions	`getDescription()`, `getName()`, `getType()`
`SerialTree`	`BlockTagTree`	`@serial` block tags	`getDescription()`
`SinceTree`	`BlockTagTree`	`@since` block tags	`getBody()`
`StartElementTree`	`DocTree`	Start of an HTML element `< name [attributes] [/] >`	`getAttributes()`, `getName()`, `isSelfClosing()`
`TextTree`	`DocTree`	Plain text	`getBody()`
`ThrowsTree`	`BlockTagTree`	`@exception` or `@throws` block tags	`getDescription()`, `getExceptionname()`
`UnknownBlockTagTree`	`BlockTagTree`	Unrecognized inline tags	`getContent()`
`UnknownInlineTagTree`	`InlineTagTree`	Unrecognized inline tags	`getContent()`
`ValueTree`	`InlineTagTree`	`@value` inline tags	`getReference()`
`VersionTree`	`BlockTagTree`	`@version` block tags	`getBody()`

Language model API

The language model API is in the `java.lang.model` package. It includes packages and classes that are used for language processing and language modeling. It consists of the following components:

- `AnnotatedConstruct` interface
- `SourceVersion` enum
- `UnknownEntityException` exception

Each of these language model API components is further explored in the next three sections.

The AnnotatedConstruct interface

The `AnnotatedConstruction` interface provides an annotatable construct to the language model API that has been part of the Java platform since version 1.8. It is applicable to constructs that are either an element (Interface `Element`) or a type (Interface `TypeMirror`). The annotations for each of these constructs differ, as shown in this table:

Construct type	Interface	Annotation
element	Element	Declaration
type	TypeMirror	Based on use of a type name

The `AnnotatedConstruction` interface has three methods:

- `getAnnotation(Class<A> annotationType)`: This method returns the type of the construct's annotation

- `getAnnotationMirrors()`: This method returns a list of annotations that are on the construct

- `getAnnotationsByType(Class<A> annotationType)`: This method returns the construct's associated annotations

The SourceVersion enum

The `SourceVersion` enum consists of the following constants:

- RELEASE_0
- RELEASE_1
- RELEASE_2
- RELEASE_3
- RELEASE_4
- RELEASE_5
- RELEASE_6
- RELEASE_7
- RELEASE_8

It is anticipated that the `SourceVersion` enum will be updated to include RELEASE_9 once the Java 9 platform has been officially released.

This enum also contains several methods, which are as follows:

Method name: `isIdentifier`

```
public static boolean isIdentifier(CharSequence name)
```

This method returns `true` if the parameter string is a Java identifier or keyword.

Method name: `isKeyword`

```
public static boolean isKeyword(CharSequence s)
```

This method returns `true` if the given `CharSequence` is a literal or keyword.

Method name: `isName`

```
public static boolean isName(CharSequence name)
```

This method returns `true` if the `CharSequence` is a valid name.

Method name: `latest`

```
public static SourceVersion latest()
```

This method returns the latest source version for modeling purposes.

Method name: `latestSupported`

```
public static SourceVersion latestSupported()
```

This method returns the latest source version that can be fully supported for modeling.

Method name: `valueOf`

```
public static SourceVersion valueOf(String name)
```

This method returns the enum constant based on the parameter string provided.

> You should be aware that the `value(String name)` method throws two exceptions: `IllegalArgumentException` and `NullPointerException`.

Method name: `values`

```
public static SourceVersion[] values()
```

This method returns an array of the enum constants.

The UnknownEntityException exception

The `UnknownEntityException` class extends `RuntimeException` and is a superclass of unknown exceptions. The class constructor is as follows:

```
protected UnknownEntityException(String message)
```

The constructor creates a new instance of `UnknownEntityException` with the message provided as a string argument. The method does not take additional arguments.

This class does not have its own methods, but inherits methods from both `java.lang.Throwable` and `class.java.lang.Object` classes as shown here:

The `java.lang.Throwable` class methods:

- `addSuppressed()`
- `fillInStackTrace()`
- `getCause()`
- `getLocalizedMessage()`
- `getMessage()`
- `getStackTrace()`
- `getSuppressed()`
- `initCause()`
- `printStackTrace()`
- `setStackTrace()`
- `toString()`

The `java.lang.Object` class methods:

- `clone()`
- `equals()`
- `finalize()`
- `getClass()`
- `hashCode()`
- `notify()`
- `notifyAll()`
- `wait()`

HTML5 Javadoc [JEP-224]

The Javadoc tool has been updated for the Java 9 platform. It can now generate HTML 5 markup output in addition to HTML 4. The new Javadoc tool provides support for both HTML 4 and HTML 5.

HTML 4 will continue, even with the advent of the Java 9 platform, to be the default Javadoc output format. HTML 5 will be an option and will not become the default output markup format until Java 10.

The following short Java application simply generates a 319-wide by 319-high frame. It is shown here without any Javadoc tags, which we will discuss later in this section:

```
/import javax.swing.JFrame;
import javax.swing.WindowConstants;

public class JavadocExample
{

  public static void main(String[] args)
  {
    drawJFrame();
  }

  public static void drawJFrame()
  {
    JFrame myFrame = new JFrame("Javadoc Example");
    myFrame.setSize(319,319);
    myFrame.setDefaultCloseOperation(
      WindowConstants.EXIT_ON_CLOSE);
```

```
        myFrame.setVisible(true);
    }
}
```

Once your package or class is completed, you can generate a Javadoc using the Javadoc tool. You can run the Javadoc tool, located in your JDK /bin directory, from the command line or from within your **Integrated Development Environment** (**IDE**). Each IDE handles Javadoc generation differently. For example, in Eclipse, you would select **Project** from the pull-down menu and then **Generate Javadoc**. In the IntelliJ IDEA IDE, you select the **Tools** pull-down menu and then **Generate Javadoc**.

The following screenshot shows the IntelliJ IDEA interface for the Generate Javadoc functionality. As you can see, the -html5 command-line argument has been included:

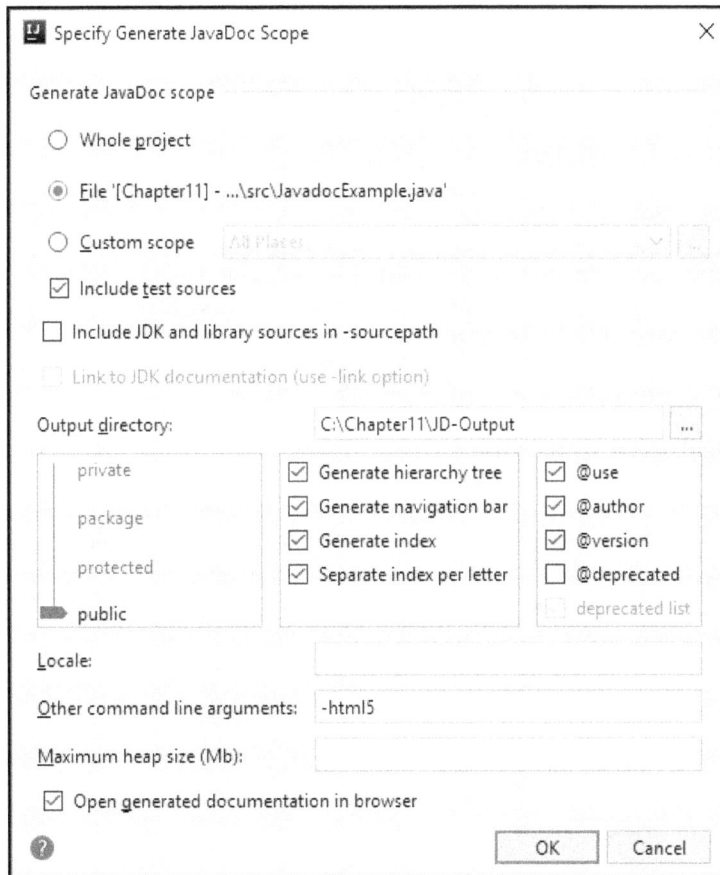

When the **OK** button is clicked, you will see a series of status messages, as shown in the following example:

```
"C:Program FilesJavajdk-9binjavadoc.exe" -public -splitindex -use -author -
version -nodeprecated -html5
@C:UserselaviAppDataLocalTempjavadoc1304args.txt -d C:Chapter11JD-Output
Loading source file C:Chapter11srcJavadocExample.java...
Constructing Javadoc information...
Standard Doclet version 9
Building tree for all the packages and classes...
Generating C:Chapter11JD-OutputJavadocExample.html...
Generating C:Chapter11JD-Outputpackage-frame.html...
Generating C:Chapter11JD-Outputpackage-summary.html...
Generating C:Chapter11JD-Outputpackage-tree.html...
Generating C:Chapter11JD-Outputconstant-values.html...
Generating C:Chapter11JD-Outputclass-useJavadocExample.html...
Generating C:Chapter11JD-Outputpackage-use.html...
Building index for all the packages and classes...
Generating C:Chapter11JD-Outputoverview-tree.html...
Generating C:Chapter11JD-Outputindex-filesindex-1.html...
Generating C:Chapter11JD-Outputindex-filesindex-2.html...
Generating C:Chapter11JD-Outputindex-filesindex-3.html...
Building index for all classes...
Generating C:Chapter11JD-Outputallclasses-frame.html...
Generating C:Chapter11JD-Outputallclasses-frame.html...
Generating C:Chapter11JD-Outputallclasses-noframe.html...
Generating C:Chapter11JD-Outputallclasses-noframe.html...
Generating C:Chapter11JD-Outputindex.html...
Generating C:Chapter11JD-Outputhelp-doc.html...

javadoc exited with exit code 0
```

Once the Javadoc tool exits, you are ready to view the Javadoc. Here is a screenshot of what was generated based on the previously provided code. As you can see, it is formatted in the same manner in which the formal Java documentation from Oracle is documented:

PACKAGE CLASS USE TREE INDEX HELP

PREV CLASS NEXT CLASS   FRAMES NO FRAMES   ALL CLASSES   SEARCH: Search   ×
SUMMARY: NESTED | FIELD | CONSTR | METHOD   DETAIL: FIELD | CONSTR | METHOD

Class JavadocExample

java.lang.Object
    JavadocExample

```
public class JavadocExample
extends java.lang.Object
```

Constructor Summary

Constructors

Constructor	Description
JavadocExample()	

Method Summary

All Methods   Static Methods   Concrete Methods

Modifier and Type	Method	Description
static void	drawJFrame()	
static void	main(java.lang.String[] args)	

Methods inherited from class java.lang.Object

equals, getClass, hashCode, notify, notifyAll, toString, wait, wait, wait

Constructor Detail

JavadocExample

```
public JavadocExample()
```

Method Detail

drawJFrame

```
public static void drawJFrame()
```

main

```
public static void main(java.lang.String[] args)
```

PACKAGE CLASS USE TREE INDEX HELP

PREV CLASS NEXT CLASS   FRAMES NO FRAMES   ALL CLASSES
SUMMARY: NESTED | FIELD | CONSTR | METHOD   DETAIL: FIELD | CONSTR | METHOD

When we generated the Javadoc, multiple documents were created, as illustrated by the directory tree provided in the following screenshot:

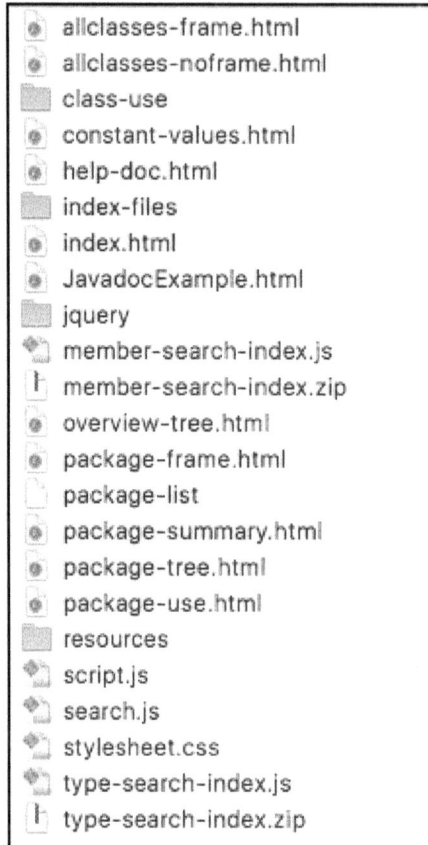

You can also add optional tags that are recognized by the Javadoc tool. Those tags are provided here:

- @author
- @code
- @deprecated
- @docRoot
- @exception
- @inheritDoc
- @link

- @linkplain
- @param
- @return
- @see
- @serial
- @serialData
- @serialField
- @since
- @throws
- @value
- @version

> **TIP**
>
> For more information on how to write document comments for the Javadoc tool, you can visit Oracle's official instructions at http://www.oracle.com/technetwork/articles/java/index-137868.html.

Javadoc search [JEP-225]

Prior to Java 9, the standard Doclet generated API documentation pages that made navigating them difficult. Unless you are very familiar with the layout of these documentation pages, you will likely use browser-based find functionality to search text. This is considered clunky and suboptimal.

The Java 9 platform includes a search box as part of the API documentation. This search box is granted by the standard Doclet and can be used to search for text within the documentation. This represents a great convenience for developers and is likely to change our usage of Doclet-generated documentation.

With the new Javadoc search functionality, we have the ability to search for the following indexed components:

- Module names
- Package names
- Types
- Members
- Terms/phrases indexed using the new @index inline tag

Introducing camel case search

The new Javadoc search functionality includes a great shortcut using camel case search. As an example, we can search for `openED` to find the `openExternalDatabase()` method.

Remove launch-time JRE version selection [JEP-231]

Prior to Java 9, we could use the **mJRE** (**Multiple JRE**) feature to specify a specific JRE version, or range of versions, for launching our applications. We would accomplish this via the command-line option `-version` or with an entry in the JAR file's manifest. The following flowchart illustrates what happens based on our selection:

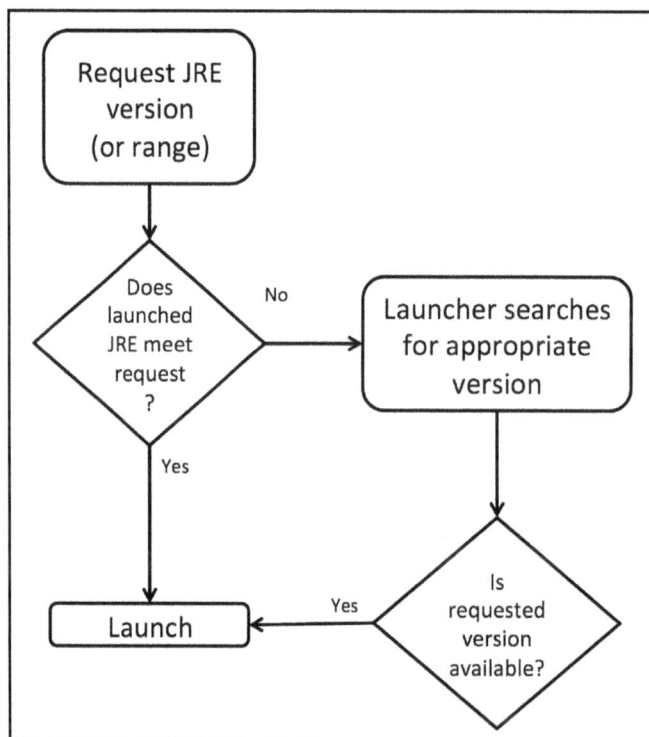

This functionality was introduced with JDK 5 and was not fully documented in that release or any subsequent release prior to JDK 9.

The following specific changes were introduced with the Java 9 platform:

- The mJRE feature has been removed.
- The launcher will now produce an error whenever the `-version` command-line option is used. This is a terminal errors in that processing will not continue.
- A warning will be produced if there is a `-version` entry in a JARs manifest. The warning will not stop execution.

Interestingly, the presence of a `-version` entry in a manifest file will only generate a warning. This is by design, to take into account the likelihood of the entry being in older JAR file. It is estimated that this warning will be changed into a terminal error when the Java 10 platform is released.

Parser API for Nashorn [JEP-236]

The focus of JEP 236 was to create an API for Nashorn's EMCAScript abstract syntax tree. In this section, we will individually look at Nashorn, EMCAScript and then the Parser API.

Nashorn

Oracle Nashorn is a JavaScript engine for the JVM developed in Java by Oracle. It was released with Java 8. It was created to provide developers with a highly efficiently and lightweight JavaScript runtime engine. Using this engine, developers were able to embed JavaScript code in their Java applications. Prior to Java 8, developers had access to the JavaScript engine created by Netscape. That engine, introduced in 1997, was maintained by Mozilla.

Nashorn can be used both as a command-line tool and as an embedded interpreter in Java applications. Let's look at examples of both.

> Nashorn is the German word for rhinoceros. The name spawned from the Rhino-named JavaScript engine from the Mozilla Foundation. Rhino is said to have originated from the picture of the animal on a JavaScript book cover. File this one under **interesting facts**.

Using Nashorn as a command-line tool

The Nashorn executable file, `jjs.exe`, resides in the `bin` folder. To access it, you can navigate to that folder or, if your system path is set up appropriately, you can launch into the shell by entering the `jjs` command in a Terminal / Command Prompt window on your system:

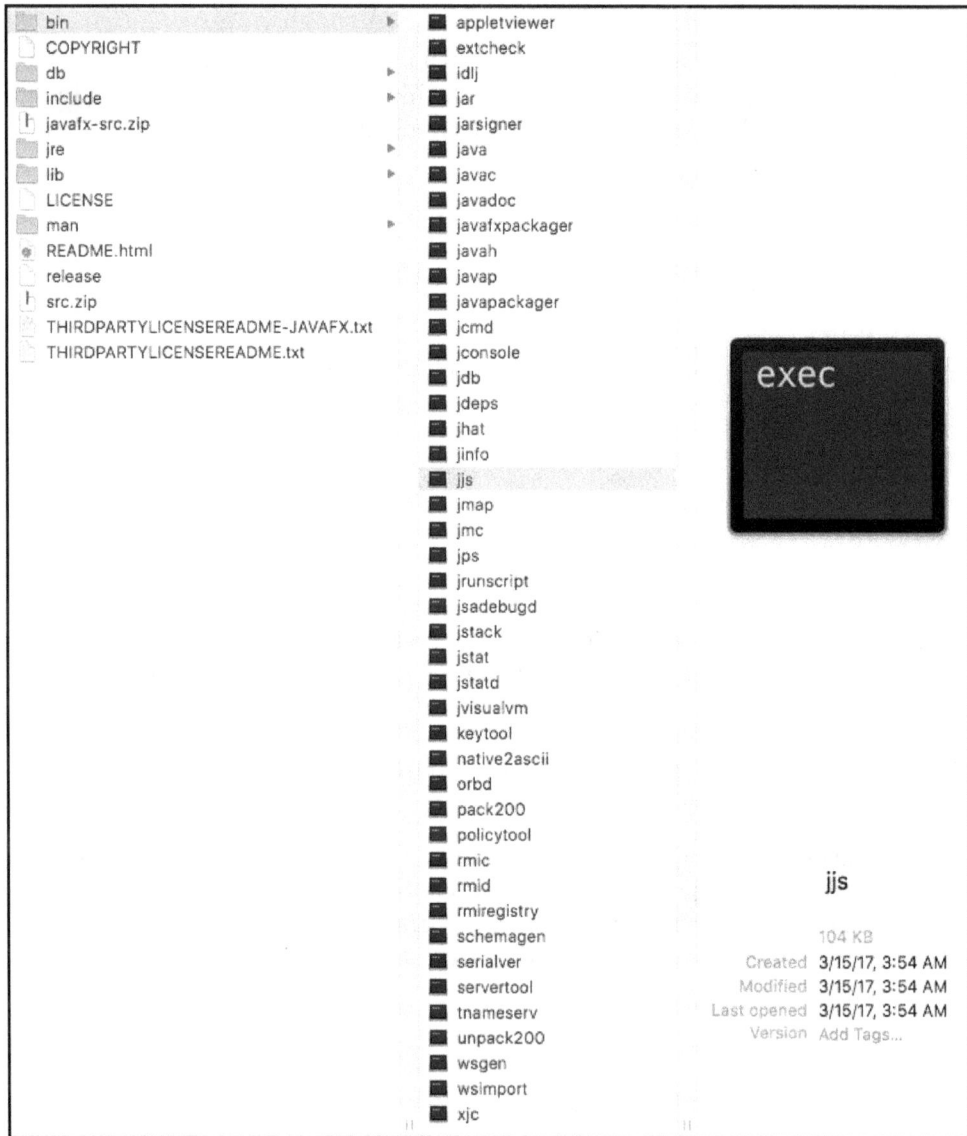

bin	▶	appletviewer	
COPYRIGHT		extcheck	
db	▶	idlj	
include	▶	jar	
javafx-src.zip		jarsigner	
jre	▶	java	
lib	▶	javac	
LICENSE		javadoc	
man	▶	javafxpackager	
README.html		javah	
release		javap	
src.zip		javapackager	
THIRDPARTYLICENSEREADME-JAVAFX.txt		jcmd	
THIRDPARTYLICENSEREADME.txt		jconsole	
		jdb	**exec**
		jdeps	
		jhat	
		jinfo	
		jjs	
		jmap	
		jmc	
		jps	
		jrunscript	
		jsadebugd	
		jstack	
		jstat	
		jstatd	
		jvisualvm	
		keytool	
		native2ascii	
		orbd	
		pack200	
		policytool	
		rmic	
		rmid	**jjs**
		rmiregistry	
		schemagen	104 KB
		serialver	Created 3/15/17, 3:54 AM
		servertool	Modified 3/15/17, 3:54 AM
		tnameserv	Last opened 3/15/17, 3:54 AM
		unpack200	Version Add Tags...
		wsgen	
		wsimport	
		xjc	

Here, you can see an open terminal window that first checks the version of Java and then uses the `jjs -version` command to launch the Nashorn shell. In this example, both Java and Nashorn are version 1.8.0.121. Alternatively, we can simply launch Nashorn with the `jjs` command, and the shell will open without the version identification:

```
⬆ edljr — jjs -version — 76×10

Edwards-iMac:~ edljr$ java -version
java version "1.8.0_121"
Java(TM) SE Runtime Environment (build 1.8.0_121-b13)
Java HotSpot(TM) 64-Bit Server VM (build 25.121-b13, mixed mode)
Edwards-iMac:~ edljr$ jjs -version
nashorn 1.8.0_121
jjs>
```

Next, let's create a short JavaScript and run it using Nashorn. Consider the following simple JavaScript code that has three simple lines of output.

```
var addtest = function()
{
    print("Simple Test");
    print("This JavaScript program adds the numbers 300
      and 19.");
    print("Addition results = " + (300 + 19));
}
addtest();
```

To have Java run this JavaScript application, we will use the `jjs address.js` command. Here is the output:

```
⬆ edljr — -bash — 71×7

Edwards-iMac:~ edljr$ jjs addtest.js
Simple Test
This JavaScript program adds the numbers 300 and 19.
Addition results = 319
Edwards-iMac:~ edljr$
```

There is a lot you can do with Nashorn. From the Command Prompt/Terminal window, we can execute `jjs` with the `-help` option to see a full list of command-line commands:

```
● ● ●                              🏠 edljr — -bash — 105×47
Edwards-iMac:~ edljr$ jjs -help
jjs [<options>] <files> [-- <arguments>]
        -D (-Dname=value. Set a system property. This option can be repeated.)

        -cp, -classpath (-cp path. Specify where to find user class files.)

        -doe, -dump-on-error (Dump a stack trace on errors.)
                param: [true|false]   default: false

        -fv, -fullversion (Print full version info of Nashorn.)
                param: [true|false]   default: false

        -fx (Launch script as an fx application.)
                param: [true|false]   default: false

        -h, -help (Print help for command line flags.)
                param: [true|false]   default: false

        --language (Specify ECMAScript language version.)
                param: [es5|es6]   default: es5

        -ot, --optimistic-types (Use optimistic type assumptions with deoptimizing recompilation.
                                 This makes the compiler try, for any program symbol whose type cannot
                                 be proven at compile time, to type it as narrow and primitive as
                                 possible. If the runtime encounters an error because symbol type
                                 is too narrow, a wider method will be generated until steady stage
                                 is reached. While this produces as optimal Java Bytecode as possible,
                                 erroneous type guesses will lead to longer warmup. Optimistic typing
                                 is currently disabled by default, but can be enabled for significantly
                                 better peak performance.)
                param: [true|false]   default: false

        -scripting (Enable scripting features.)
                param: [true|false]   default: false

        -strict (Run scripts in strict mode.)
                param: [true|false]   default: false

        -t, -timezone (Set timezone for script execution.)
                param: <timezone>   default: America/Chicago

        -v, -version (Print version info of Nashorn.)
                param: [true|false]   default: false

Edwards-iMac:~ edljr$
```

As you can see, using the `-scripting` option gives us the ability to create scripts using Nashorn as a text editor. There are several built-in functions that are useful when using Nashorn:

- `echo()`: This is similar to a `System.out.print()` Java method
- `exit()`: This exits Nashorn

- `load()`: This loads a script from a given path or URL
- `print()`: This is similar to a `System.out.print()` Java method
- `readFull()`: This reads a file's contents
- `readLine()`: This reads a single line from `stdin`
- `quit()`: This exits Nashorn

Using Nashorn as an embedded interpreter

A more common use of Nashorn, compared to using it as a command-line tool, is using it as an embedded interpreter. The `javax.script` API is public and can be accessed via the `nashorn` identifier. The following code demonstrates how we can gain access to Nashorn, define a JavaScript function, and obtain the results--all from within a Java application:

```
// required imports
import javax.script.ScriptEngine;
import javax.script.ScriptEngineManager;

public class EmbeddedAddTest
{
  public static void main(String[] args) throws Throwable
  {
    // instantiate a new ScriptEngineManager
    ScriptEngineManager myEngineManager =
      new ScriptEngineManager();

    // instantiate a new Nashorn ScriptEngine
    ScriptEngine myEngine = myEngineManager.getEngineByName(
      "nashorn");

    // create the JavaScript function
    myEngine.eval("function addTest(x, y) { return x + y; }");

    // generate output including a call to the addTest function
       via the engine
    System.out.println("The addition results are:
      " + myEngine.eval("addTest(300, 19);"));
  }
}
```

Here is the output provided in the console window:

```
  Problems    Javadoc    Declaration    Console  ⊠
<terminated> EmbeddedAddTest [Java Application] /Library/Java/JavaVirtualMachines/jdk1.8.0_131.jdk/Contents/Home/bin/java (Aug 8, 2017, 1:44:24 PM)
The addition results are: 319.0
```

This is a simplistic example to give you an idea of what is possible with embedded use of Nashorn. There are ample examples in Oracle's official documentation.

EMCAScript

EMCA (European Computer Manufacturers Association) was formed in 1961 as a standards organization for both information systems and communications systems. Today, the EMCA continues to develop standards and issue technical reports to help standardize how consumer electronics, information systems, and communications technology are used. They are over 400 ECMA standards, most of which have been adopted.

> You will notice that EMCA is not spelled with all capital letters as it is no longer considered an acronym. In 1994, the European Computer Manufacturers Association formally changed its name to EMCA.

EMCAScript, also referred to as ES, was created in 1997 as a scripted-language specification. JavaScript implements this specification. The specification includes the following:

- Complementary technologies
- Libraries
- Scripting language syntax
- Semantics

Parser API

One of the changes in the Java platform with version 9 is to provide specific support for Nashorn's EMCAScript abstract syntax tree. The goals of the new API are to provide the following:

- Interfaces to represent Nashorn syntax tree nodes
- The ability to create parser instances that can be configured with command-line options
- A visitor pattern API for interfacing with AST nodes
- Test programs to use the API

The new API, `jdk.nashorn.api.tree`, was created to permit future changes to the Nashorn classes. Prior to the new Parser API, IDEs used Nashorn's internal AST representations for code analysis. According to Oracle, use of the `idk.nashorn.internal.ir` package prevented the modernization of Nashorn's internal classes.

Here is a look at the the class hierarchy of the new `jdk.nashorn.api.tree` package:

Class Hierarchy

- java.lang.**Object**
  - jdk.nashorn.api.tree.**SimpleTreeVisitorES5_1**<R,P> (implements jdk.nashorn.api.tree.TreeVisitor<R,P>)
    - jdk.nashorn.api.tree.**SimpleTreeVisitorES6**<R,P>
  - java.lang.**Throwable** (implements java.io.Serializable)
    - java.lang.**Exception**
      - java.lang.**RuntimeException**
        - jdk.nashorn.api.tree.**UnknownTreeException**

The following graphic illustrates the complexity of the new API, featuring a full interface hierarchy:

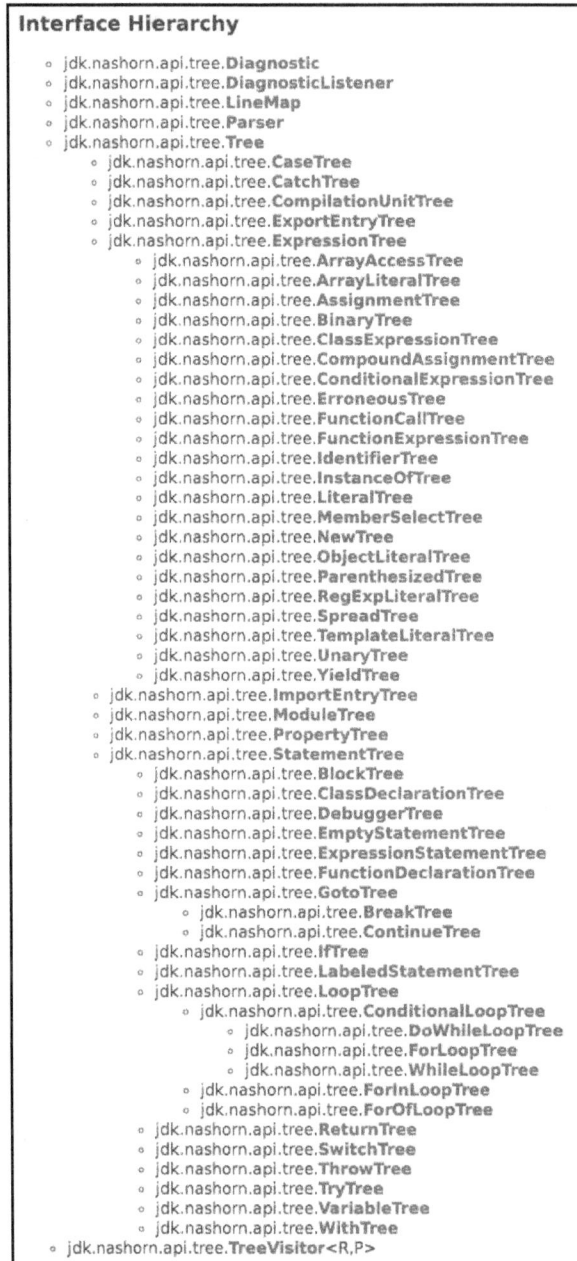

```
Interface Hierarchy
  ○ jdk.nashorn.api.tree.Diagnostic
  ○ jdk.nashorn.api.tree.DiagnosticListener
  ○ jdk.nashorn.api.tree.LineMap
  ○ jdk.nashorn.api.tree.Parser
  ○ jdk.nashorn.api.tree.Tree
      ○ jdk.nashorn.api.tree.CaseTree
      ○ jdk.nashorn.api.tree.CatchTree
      ○ jdk.nashorn.api.tree.CompilationUnitTree
      ○ jdk.nashorn.api.tree.ExportEntryTree
      ○ jdk.nashorn.api.tree.ExpressionTree
          ○ jdk.nashorn.api.tree.ArrayAccessTree
          ○ jdk.nashorn.api.tree.ArrayLiteralTree
          ○ jdk.nashorn.api.tree.AssignmentTree
          ○ jdk.nashorn.api.tree.BinaryTree
          ○ jdk.nashorn.api.tree.ClassExpressionTree
          ○ jdk.nashorn.api.tree.CompoundAssignmentTree
          ○ jdk.nashorn.api.tree.ConditionalExpressionTree
          ○ jdk.nashorn.api.tree.ErroneousTree
          ○ jdk.nashorn.api.tree.FunctionCallTree
          ○ jdk.nashorn.api.tree.FunctionExpressionTree
          ○ jdk.nashorn.api.tree.IdentifierTree
          ○ jdk.nashorn.api.tree.InstanceOfTree
          ○ jdk.nashorn.api.tree.LiteralTree
          ○ jdk.nashorn.api.tree.MemberSelectTree
          ○ jdk.nashorn.api.tree.NewTree
          ○ jdk.nashorn.api.tree.ObjectLiteralTree
          ○ jdk.nashorn.api.tree.ParenthesizedTree
          ○ jdk.nashorn.api.tree.RegExpLiteralTree
          ○ jdk.nashorn.api.tree.SpreadTree
          ○ jdk.nashorn.api.tree.TemplateLiteralTree
          ○ jdk.nashorn.api.tree.UnaryTree
          ○ jdk.nashorn.api.tree.YieldTree
      ○ jdk.nashorn.api.tree.ImportEntryTree
      ○ jdk.nashorn.api.tree.ModuleTree
      ○ jdk.nashorn.api.tree.PropertyTree
      ○ jdk.nashorn.api.tree.StatementTree
          ○ jdk.nashorn.api.tree.BlockTree
          ○ jdk.nashorn.api.tree.ClassDeclarationTree
          ○ jdk.nashorn.api.tree.DebuggerTree
          ○ jdk.nashorn.api.tree.EmptyStatementTree
          ○ jdk.nashorn.api.tree.ExpressionStatementTree
          ○ jdk.nashorn.api.tree.FunctionDeclarationTree
          ○ jdk.nashorn.api.tree.GotoTree
              ○ jdk.nashorn.api.tree.BreakTree
              ○ jdk.nashorn.api.tree.ContinueTree
          ○ jdk.nashorn.api.tree.IfTree
          ○ jdk.nashorn.api.tree.LabeledStatementTree
          ○ jdk.nashorn.api.tree.LoopTree
              ○ jdk.nashorn.api.tree.ConditionalLoopTree
                  ○ jdk.nashorn.api.tree.DoWhileLoopTree
                  ○ jdk.nashorn.api.tree.ForLoopTree
                  ○ jdk.nashorn.api.tree.WhileLoopTree
              ○ jdk.nashorn.api.tree.ForInLoopTree
              ○ jdk.nashorn.api.tree.ForOfLoopTree
          ○ jdk.nashorn.api.tree.ReturnTree
          ○ jdk.nashorn.api.tree.SwitchTree
          ○ jdk.nashorn.api.tree.ThrowTree
          ○ jdk.nashorn.api.tree.TryTree
          ○ jdk.nashorn.api.tree.VariableTree
          ○ jdk.nashorn.api.tree.WithTree
  ○ jdk.nashorn.api.tree.TreeVisitor<R,P>
```

The last component of the `jdk.nashorn.api.tree` package is the enum hierarchy, shown here:

Enum Hierarchy

- java.lang.**Object**
  - java.lang.**Enum**<E> (implements java.lang.Comparable<T>, java.io.Serializable)
    - jdk.nashorn.api.tree.**Diagnostic.Kind**
    - jdk.nashorn.api.tree.**Tree.Kind**

Multi-release JAR files [JEP-238]

The JAR file format has been extended in the Java 9 platform and now permits multiple versions of class files to exist in a single JAR file. The class versions can be specific to a Java release version. This enhancement allows developers to use a single JAR file to house multiple releases of their software.

The JAR file enhancement includes the following:

- Support for the `JarFile` API
- Support for standard class loaders

The changes to the JAR file format resulted in necessary changes to core Java tools so that they are able to interpret the new multiple-release JAR files. These core tools include the following:

- javac
- javap
- jdeps

Finally, the new JAR file format supports modularity as the key characteristic of the Java 9 platform. The changes to the JAR file format have not resulted in reduced performance of related tools or processes.

Identifying multi-release JAR files

Multi-release JAR files will have a new attribute, `Multi-Release: true`. This attribute will be located in the JAR `MANIFEST.MF` main section.

The directory structure will differ between standard JAR files and multi-release JAR files. Here is a look at a typical JAR file structure:

```
jar root
      Apple.class
      Banana.class
      Coconut.class
      Dragonfruit.class
      Elderberry.class
```

This illustration shows the new multi-release JAR file structure with Java version-specific class files for both Java 8 and Java 9:

```
jar root
      Apple.class
      Banana.class
      Coconut.class
      Dragonfruit.class
      Elderberry.class
      META-INF
            versions
                  8
                        Apple.class
                        Banana.class
                        Coconut.class
                        Dragonfruit.class
                        Elderberry.class
                  9
                        Apple.class
                        Banana.class
                        Coconut.class
                        Dragonfruit.class
                        Elderberry.class
```

Related JDK changes

Several changes had to be made to the JDK to support the new multi-release JAR file format. These changes include the following:

- The `URLClassLoader` is JAR-based and was modified so that it can read class files from the specified version.
- The new module-based class loader, new to Java 9, was written so that it can read class files from the specified version.
- The `java.util.jar.JarFile` class was modified so that it selects the appropriate class version from the multi-release JAR files.
- The JAR URL scheme's protocol handler was modified so that it selects the appropriate class version from the multi-release JAR files.
- The Java Compiler, `javac`, was made to read identified versions of the class files. These version identifications are made using the `-target` and `-release` command-line options with the `JavacFileManager` API and the `ZipFileSystem` API.
- The following tools were modified to take advantage of the changes to the `JavacFileManager` API and the `ZipFileSystem` API:
  - `javah`: This generates C header and source files
  - `schemagen`: This is the schema generator for namespaces in Java classes
  - `wsgen`: This is the parser for web service deployment
- The javap tool was updated to support the new versioning schema.
- The jdeps tool was modified to support the new versioning schema.
- The JAR packing tool set was updated accordingly. This tool set consists of `pack200` and `unpack200`.
- Of course, the JAR tool was enhanced so that it can create the multi-release JAR files.

All related documentation has been updated to support all the changes involved in establishing and supporting the new multi-release JAR file format.

Java-level JVM compiler interface [JEP-243]

The JEP-243 was to create a Java-based **JVM Compiler Interface** (**JVMCI**). The JVMCI enables a Java compiler (which must have been written in Java) to be used as a dynamic compiler by the JVM.

The reasoning behind the desire for the JVMCI is that it would be a highly optimized compiler that does not require low-level language features. Some JVM subsystems require low-level functionality, such as with garbage collection and bytemode interpretation. So, the JVMCI was written in Java instead of C or C++. This provides the collateral benefit of some of Java's greatest features, such as the following ones:

- Exception handling
- IDEs that are both free and robust
- Memory management
- Runtime extensibility
- Synchronization
- Unit testing support

As JVMCI was written in Java, it will arguably be easier to maintain.

There are three primary components of the JVMCI API:

- Virtual machine data structure access
- Installing compiled code with its metadata
- Using the JVM's compilation system

The JVMCI actually existed, to some extent, in Java 8. The JVMCI API was only accessible via a class loader that worked for code on the boot class path. In Java 9, this changes. It will still be experimental in Java 9, but more accessible. In order to enable the JVMCI, the following series of command-line options must be used:

```
-XX:+UnlockExperimentalVMOptions -XX:+EnableJVMCI -XX:+UseJVMCICompiler -
Djvmci.Compiler=<name of compiler>
```

Oracle is keeping the JVMCI experimental in Java 9 to permit further testing and to afford the greatest level of protection for developers.

BeanInfo annotations [JEP-256]

The JEP-256 focused on replacing @beanifo javadoc tags with more appropriate annotations. Furthermore, these new annotations are now processed at runtime so that BeanInfo classes can be generated dynamically. The modularity of Java 9 resulted in this change. The creation of custom BeanInfo classes has been simplified and the client library has been modularized.

In order to fully grasp this change, we will review JavaBean, BeanProperty, and SwingContainer before going any further into this JEP.

JavaBean

A JavaBean is a Java class. Like other Java classes, JavaBeans are reusable code. They are unique in their design because they encapsulate several objects into one. There are three conventions a JavaBean class must follow:

- The constructor should not take any arguments
- It must be serializable
- It must contain mutator and accessor methods for its properties

Here is an example JavaBean class:

```
public class MyBean implements java.io.Serializable
{
  // instance variables
  private int studentId;
  private String studentName;

  // no-argument constructor
  public MyBean()
  {
  }
  // mutator/setter
  public void setStudentId(int theID)
  {
    this.studentId = theID;
  }

  // accessor/getter
  public int getStudentId()
  {
    return studentId;
```

```
      }

      // mutator/setter
      public void setStudentName(String theName)
      {
        this.studentName = theName;
      }

      // accessor/getter
      public String getStudentName()
      {
        return studentName;
      }

    }
```

Accessing `JavaBean` classes is as simple as using the mutator and accessor methods. This is likely not new to you, but there is a good chance you did not know that those carefully coded classes you created were called `JavaBean` classes.

BeanProperty

`BeanProperty` is an annotation type. We use this annotation to specify a property so that we can automatically generate `BeanInfo` classes. This is a new annotation for Java 9.

The `BeanProperty` annotation has the following optional elements:

- `boolean bound`
- `String description`
- `String[] enumerationValues`
- `boolean expert`
- `boolean hidden`
- `boolean preferred`
- `boolean required`
- `boolean visualUpdate`

SwingContainer

SwingContainer is an annotation type. We use this annotation to specify a swing-related property so that we can automatically generate BeanInfo classes. This is a new annotation for Java 9.

The SwingContainer annotation has the following optional elements:

- String delegate
- boolean value

Now that we have reviewed JavaBean, BeanProperty, and SwingContainer, let's take a look at the BeanInfo classes.

BeanInfo classes

For the most part, BeanInfo classes are automatically generated at runtime. The exception is with Swing classes. Those classes generate BeanInfo classes based on the @beaninfo javadoc tags. This is done at compile time, not runtime. In Java 9, the @beaninfo tags have been replaced with @interface JavaBean, @interface BeanProperty, and @interface SwingContainer annotations.

These new annotations are used to set the corresponding attributes based on the optional elements noted in the previous sections. As an example, the following code snippet sets the attributes for a SwingContainer:

```
package javax.swing;

public @interface SwingContainer
{
  boolean value() default false;
  String delegate() default "";
}
```

This provides us with three benefits:

- It will be much easier to specify attributes in Bean classes instead of having to create individual BeanInfo classes
- We will be able to remove auto-generated classes
- The client library is much more easily modularized with this approach

TIFF image input/output [JEP-262]

JEP-262 is pretty straight forward. For Java 9, the image input/output plugins have been extended to include support for the TIFF image format. The `ImageIO` class extends the `Object` class and is part of Java SE. The class contains several methods for encoding and decoding images. Here is a list of static methods:

Method	Return value
`createImageInputStream(Object input)`	`ImageInputStream`
`createImageOutputStream(Object output)`	`ImageOutputStream`
`getCacheDirectory()`	Current value of the `CacheDirectory`
`getImageReader(ImageWriter writer)`	`ImageReader`
`getImageReaders(Object input)`	Iterator of current `ImageReaders`
`getImageReadersByFormatName(String formatName)`	Iterator of current `ImageReaders` with the specified format name
`getImageReadersByMIMEType(String MIMEType)`	Iterator of current `ImageReaders` of the specified MIME type
`getImageReadersBySuffix(String fileSuffix)`	Iterator of current `ImageReaders` with the specified suffix.
`getImageTranscoders(ImageReader reader)`	Iterator of current `ImageTranscoders`
`getImageWriter(ImageReader reader)`	`ImageWriter`
`getImageWriters(ImageTypeSpecifier type, String formatName)`	Iterator of current `ImageWriters` that can encode to the specified type
`getImageWritersByFormatName(String formatName)`	Iterator of current `ImageWriters` with the specified format name
`getImageWritersByMIMEType(String MIMEType)`	Iterator of current `ImageWriters` of the specified MIME type
`getImageWritersBySuffix(String fileSuffix)`	Iterator of current `ImageWriters` with the specified suffix.

`getReaderFileSuffixes()`	String array with file suffixes understood by current readers
`getReaderFormatNames()`	String array with format names understood by current readers
`getReaderMIMETypes()`	String array with MIME types understood by current readers
`getUseCache()`	`UseCache` value
`getWriterFileSuffixes()`	String array of file suffixes understood by current writers
`getWriterFormatNames()`	String array with format names understood by current writers
`getWriterMIMETypes()`	String array with MIME types understood by current writers
`read(File input)`	`BufferedImage` with an `ImageReader`
`read(ImageInputStream stream)`	`BufferedImage` with `ImageInputStream` and an `ImageReader`
`read(InputStream input)`	`BufferedImage` with `InputStream` and `ImageReader`
`read(URL input)`	`BufferedImage` with an `ImageReader`

There are also a few static methods that do not return a value or return a Boolean:

Method	Description
`scanForPlugins()`	Performs the following actions: • Scans the application classpath for plugins • Loads plugin service provider classes • Registers service provide instances in the IIORegistry
`setCacheDirectory(File cacheDirectory)`	This is where the cache files will be stored.

setUseCache(boolean useCache)	This method toggles if the cache will be disk-based or not. This applies to ImageInputStream and ImageOutputStream instances.
write(RenderedImage im, String formatName, File output)	Writes an image to the specified file.
write(RenderedImage im, String formatName, ImageOutputStream output)	Writes an image to an ImageOutputStream.
write(RenderedImage im, String formatName, OutputStream output)	Writes an image to an OutputStream.

As you can glean from the provided methods, the image input/output framework provides us with a convenient way of using image codecs. As of Java 7, the following image format plugins were implemented by javax.imageio:

- BMP
- GIF
- JPEG
- PNG
- WBMP

The TIFF is, as you can see, not on the list of image file formats. TIFFs are a common file format and, in 2001, macOS, with the release of MacOS X, used the format extensively.

The Java 9 platform includes ImageReader and ImageWriter plugins for the TIFFs. These plugins have been written in Java and have been bundled in the new javax.imageio.plugins.tiff package.

Platform logging API and service [JEP-264]

The Java 9 platform includes a new logging API enabling platform classes to log messages. It has a commensurate service for manipulating the logs. Before we go too far into what is new regarding the logging API and service, let's review java.util.logging.api which was introduced in Java 7.

The java.util.logging package

The `java.util.logging` package includes classes and interfaces that collectively comprise Java's core logging features. This functionality was created with the following goals:

- Problem diagnosis by end users and system administrators
- Problem diagnosis by field service engineers
- Problem diagnosis by the development organization

As you can see, the primary purpose was to enable maintenance of remote software.

The `java.util.logging` package has two interfaces:

- `public interface Filter`
    - Purpose: This provides fine-grain control over logged data
    - Method:
        - `isLoggable(LogRecord record)`
- `public interface LoggingMXBean`
    - Purpose: This is the logging facility's management interface
    - Methods:
        - `getLoggerLevel(String loggerName)`
        - `getLoggerNames()`
        - `getparentLoggerName(String loggerName)`
        - `setLoggerLevel(String loggerName, String levelName)`

The following table provides the `java.util.logging` package classes, along with a brief description regarding what each class provides in respect to logging functionality and management:

Class	Definition	Description
ConsoleHandler	`public class ConsoleHandler extends StreamHandler`	Publishes log records to `System.err`
ErrorManager	`public class ErrorManager extends Object`	Used to process errors during logging
FileHandler	`public class FileHandler extends StreamHandler`	File logging

Formatter	public abstract class Formatter extends Object	For formatting LogRecords
Handler	public abstract class Handler extends Object	Exports Logger messages
Level	public class Level extends Object implements Serializable	Controls level of logging. The levels, in descending order, are--severe, warning, info, config, fine, finer, and finest
Logger	public class Logger extends Object	Logs messages
LoggingPermission	public final class LoggingPermission extends BasicPermission	SecurityManager checks this
LogManager	public class LogManager	For maintaining shared state between loggers and logging services
LogRecord	public class LogRecord extends Object implements Serializable	Passed between handlers
MemoryHandler	public class MemoryHandler extends Handler	Buffers requests in memory
SimpleFormatter	public class SimpleFormatter extends Formatter	Provides human-readable LogRecord metadata
SocketHandler	public class SocketHandler extends StreamHandler	Network logging handler
StreamHandler	public class StreamHandler extends Handler	Stream-based logging handler
XMLFormatter	public class XMLFormatter extends Formatter	Formats logs into XML

Next, let's review what changes were made in Java 9.

Logging in Java 9

Prior to Java 9, there were multiple logging schemas available, including
`java.util.logging`, `SLF4J`, and `Log4J`. The latter two are third-party frameworks that
have separate facade and implementation components. This pattern has been replicated in
the new Java 9 platform.

Java 9 introduced changes to the `java.base` module so that it would handle logging
functions and not rely on the `java.util.logging` API. It has separate facade and
implementation components. This means that when using third-party frameworks, the JDK
only needs to provide the implementation component and return platform loggers that
work with the requesting logging framework.

As you can see in the following illustration, we use the `java.util.ServiceLoader` API to
load our `LoggerFinder` implementation. The JDK uses a default implementation if a
concrete implementation is not found using the system class loader:

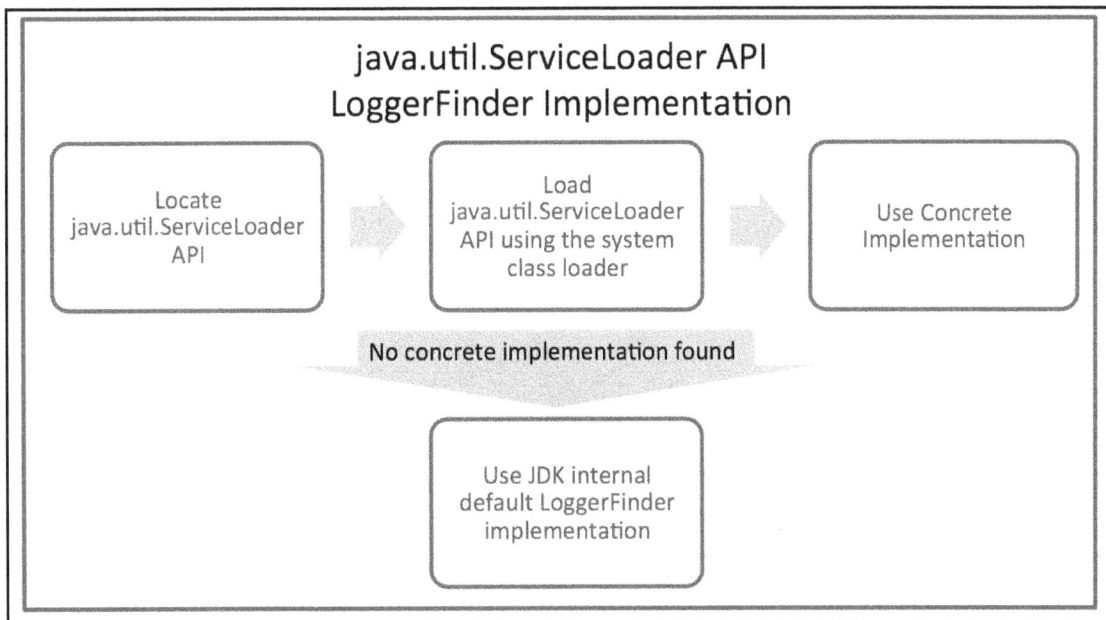

XML Catalogs [JEP-268]

JEP 268, titled XML Catalogs, focused on creating a standard XML Catalog API to support the OASIS XML Catalogs Standard v1.1. The new API defines catalog and catalog-resolve abstractions so that JAXP processors can use them. In this section, we will look at the following:

- The OASIS XML Catalog standard
- JAXP processors
- XML Catalogs prior to Java 9
- Java 9 platform changes

The OASIS XML Catalog standard

XML (eXtensible Markup Language) Catalogs are XML documents consisting of catalog entries. Each entry pairs an identifier to another location. OASIS is a not-for-profit consortium with the mission of advancing open standards. They published the XML catalog standard, version 1.1., in 2005. This standard has two basic use cases:

- Map an external identifier to a URI reference
- Map a URI reference to another URI reference

Here is a sample XML catalog entry:

```
<public publicId="-//Packt Publishing Limited//Mastering Java 9//EN"
uri="https://www.packtpub.com/application-development/mastering-java-9"/>
```

The complete OASIS XML Catalog standard can be found at the official site: `https://www.oasis-open.org/committees/download.php/14809/xml-catalogs.html`

JAXP processors

The Java API for XML processing is referred to as JAXP. As its name suggests, this API is used for parsing XML documents. There are four related interfaces:

- DOM: Document Object Model parsing
- SAX: Simple API for XML parsing
- StAX: Streaming API for XML parsing
- XSLT: Interface to transform XML documents

XML Catalogs prior to Java 9

The Java platform has had an internal catalog resolver since JDK 6. There was no public API, so external tools and libraries were used to access the functionality. Moving into Java 9, the goal was to make the internal catalog resolver a standard API for common use and ease of support.

Java 9 platform changes

The new XML Catalog API, delivered with Java 9, follows the OASIS XML Catalogs standard, v1.1. Here are the feature and capability highlights:

- Implements `EntityResolver`
- Implements `URIResolver`
- Creation of XML Catalogs is possible via the `CatalogManager`
- `CatalogManager` will be used to create `CatalogResolvers`
- OASIS open catalog file semantics will be followed
    - Map an external identifier to a URI reference
    - Map a URI reference to another URI reference
- `CatalogResolvers` will implement the JAXP `EntityResolver` interface
- `CatalogResolvers` will implement the JAXP `URIResolver` interface
- The SAX `XMLFilter` will be supported by the resolver.

Since the new XML Catalog API will be public, the pre-Java 9 internal catalog resolver will be removed, as it will no longer be necessary.

Convenience factory methods for collections [JEP-269]

The Java programming language does not support collection literals. Adding this feature to the Java platform was proposed in 2013 and revisited in 2016, but it only gained exposure as a research proposal, not for future implementation.

> Oracle's definition of a collection literal is "*a syntactic expression form that evaluates to an aggregate type, such as an array, list, or map*" (http://openjdk. java.net/jeps/186).

Of course, that is until Java 9 is released. Implementing collection literals in the Java programming language is reported to have the following benefits:

- Performance improvement
- Increased safety
- Reduction of boilerplate code

Even without being part of the research group, our knowledge of the Java programming language clues us in to additional benefits:

- Ability to write shorter code
- Ability to write space-efficient code
- Ability to make collection literals immutable

Let's look at two cases--using collections before Java 9, and then with the new support for collection literals in the new Java platform.

Using collections before Java 9

Here is an example of how we would create our own collections prior to Java 9. This first class defines the structure for `PlanetCollection`. It has the following components:

- A single instance variable
- A one argument constructor
- Mutator/setter method
- Accessor/getter method
- Method to print the object

Here is the code implementing the preceding listed constructor and methods:

```
public class PlanetCollection
{
  // Instance Variable
  private String planetName;

  // constructor
  public PlanetCollection(String name)
  {
    setPlanetName(name);
  }

  // mutator
  public void setPlanetName(String name)
  {
    this.planetName = name;
  }

  // accessor
  public String getPlanetName()
  {
    return this.planetName;
  }

  public void print()
  {
    System.out.println(getPlanetName());
  }
}
```

Now, let's look at the driver class that populates the collection:

```
import java.util.ArrayList;

public class OldSchool
{
  private static ArrayList<PlanetCollection> myPlanets =
    new ArrayList<>();

  public static void main(String[] args)
  {
    add("Earth");
    add("Jupiter");
    add("Mars");
    add("Venus");
    add("Saturn");
    add("Mercury");
```

```
        add("Neptune");
        add("Uranus");
        add("Dagobah");
        add("Kobol");
        for (PlanetCollection orb : myPlanets)
        {
          orb.print();
        }

    }

    public static void add(String name)
    {
      PlanetCollection newPlanet = new PlanetCollection(name);
      myPlanets.add(newPlanet);
    }
}
```

Here is the output from this application:

```
 Problems    Javadoc    Declaration    Console  
<terminated> OldSchool [Java Application] /Library/Java/JavaVirtualMachines/jdk1.8.0_131.jdk/Contents/Home/bin/java (Aug 9, 2017, 7:02:41 PM)
Earth
Jupiter
Mars
Venus
Saturn
Mercury
Neptune
Uranus
Dagobah
Kobol
```

This code is, unfortunately, very verbose. We populated our collection in static initializer blocks instead of using a field initializer. There are other methods of populating our list, but they are all more verbose than they should have to be. These other methods have additional problems, such as the need to create extra classes, the use of obscure code, and hidden references.

Let's now take a look at the solution to this problem, provided by the new Java 9 platform. We will look at what is new in the next section.

Using new collection literals

In order to rectify the currently required code verbosity in creating collections, we need library APIs for creating collection instances. Look at our pre-Java 9 code snippet in the previous section and then consider this possible refactoring:

```
PlanetCollection<String> myPlanets = Set.of(
    "Earth",
    "Jupiter",
    "Mars",
    "Venus",
    "Saturn",
    "Mercury",
    "Neptune",
    "Uranus",
    "Dagobah",
    "Kobol");
```

This code is highly human-readable and not verbose.

The new implementation will include static factory methods on the following interfaces:

- List
- Map
- Set

So, we are now able to create unmodifiable instances of List collections, Map collections, and Set collections. They can be instantiated with the following syntax:

- List.of(a, b, c, d, e);
- Set.of(a, b, c, d, e);
- Map.of();

The Map collections will have a set of fixed arguments.

Platform-specific desktop features [JEP-272]

The exciting JEP-272 was to create a new public API so that we can write applications with access to platform-specific desktop features. These features include interacting with task bars/docks and listening for application and system events.

The macOS X `com.apple.eawt` package was an internal API and, starting with Java 9, is no longer accessible. In support of Java 9's new embedded platform-specific desktop features, `apple.applescript` classes are being removed from the Java platform without replacement.

This effort had several objectives:

- Create a public API to replace the functionality in `com.apple.{east,eio}`
- Ensure OS X developers do not loose functionality. To this end, the Java 9 platform has replacements for the following packages:
    - `com.apple.eawt`
    - `com.apple.eio`
- Provide developers with a near-common set of features for platforms (that is, Windows and Linux) in addition to OS X. The common features include:
    - Login/logout handler with event listeners
    - Screen lock handler with event listeners
    - Task bar / dock actions to include:
        - Requesting user attention
        - Indicating task progress
        - Action shortcuts

The new API will be added to the `java.awt.Desktop` class.

Enhanced method handles [JEP-274]

The **Enhanced Method Handles** JEP-274 was to improve the following listed classes, to make common usage easier with improved optimizations:

- `MethodHandle` class
- `MethodHandles` class
- `MethodHandles.Lookup` class

The listed classes are all part of the `java.lang.invoke` package, which has been updated as part of the Java 9 platform. The improvements were made possible through the use of lookup refinement and `MethodHandle` combinations `for` loops and `try...finally` blocks.

In this section, we will look at the following regarding JEP-274:

- Reason for the enhancement
- Lookup functions
- Argument handling
- Additional combinations

Reason for the enhancement

This enhancement stemmed from developer feedback and the desire to make the `MethodHandle`, `MethodHandles`, and `MethodHandles.Lookup` classes much easier to use. There was also the call to add additional use cases.

The changes resulted in the following benefits:

- Enabled precision in the usage of the `MethodHandle` API
- Instantiation reduction
- Increased JVM compiler optimizations

Lookup functions

Changes regarding lookup functions, for the Java 9 platform, include the following:

- `MethodHandles` can now be bound to non-abstract methods in interfaces
- The lookup API allows class lookups from different contexts

The `MethodHandles.Lookup.findSpecial(Class<?> refs, String name, MethodType type, Class<?> specialCaller)` class has been modified to permit locating super-callable methods on interfaces.

In addition, the following methods have been added to the `MethodHandles.Lookup` class:

- `Class<?> findClass(String targetName)`
- `Class<?> accessClass(Class<?> targetClass)`

Argument handling

Three updates were made to improve `MethodHandle` argument handling for the Java 9 platform. These changes are highlighted as follows:

- Argument folding using `foldArguments(MethodHandle target, MethodHandle combinator)` did not previously have a position argument.
  - Argument collection using the `MethodHandle.asCollector(Class<?> arrayType, int arrayLength)` method did not previously support collecting the arguments into an array except for the trailing element. This has been changed, and there is now an additional `asCollector` method to support that functionality in Java 9.
- Argument spreading using the `MethodHandle.asSpreader(Class<?> arrayType, int arrayLength)` method spreads the contents of the trailing array to a number of arguments, in a reverse method of argument collection. Argument spreading has been modified to support the expansion of an array anywhere in the method signature.

> The new method definitions for the updated `asCollector` and `asSpreader` methods are provided in the next section.

Additional combinations

The following addition combinations have been added to support the ease of use and optimizations for the `MethodHandle`, `MethodHandles`, and `MethodHandles.Lookup` classes of the `java.lang.invoke` package in the Java 9 platform:

- Generic loop abstraction:
  - `MethodHandle loop(MethodHandle[] . . . clauses)`
- `While` loops:
  - `MethodHandle whileLoop(MethodHandle init, MethodHandle pred, MethodHandle body)`
- `Do...while` loops:
  - `MethodHandle doWhileLoop(MethodHandle init, MethodHandle body, MethodHandle pred)`

- Counting loops:
  - `MethodHandle countedLoop(MethodHandle iterations, MethodHandle init, MethodHandle body)`
- Data structure iteration:
  - `MethodHandle iteratedLoop(MethodHandle iterator, MethodHandle init, MethodHandle body)`
- `Try...finally` blocks:
  - `MethodHandle tryFinally(MethodHandle target, MethodHandle cleanup)`
- Argument handling:
  - Argument spreading:
    - `MethodHandle asSpreader(int pos, Class<?> arrayType, int arrayLength)`
  - Argument collection:
    - `MethodHandle asCollector(int pos, Class<?> arrayType, int arrayLength)`
  - Argument folding:
    - `MethodHandle foldArguments(MethodHandle target, int pos, MethodHandle combiner)`

Enhanced deprecation [JEP-277]

There are two facilities for expressing deprecation:

- `@Deprecated` annotation
- `@deprecated` javadoc tag

These facilities were introduced in Java SE 5 and JDK 1.1, respectively. The `@Deprecated` annotation was intended to annotate program components that should not be used because they were deemed dangerous and/or there was a better option. That was the intended use. Actual use varied including and because warnings were only provided at compile time; there was little reason to ignore the annotated code.

The **Enhanced Deprecation** JEP-277 was taken on to provide developers with clearer information regarding the intended disposition of the APIs in the specification documentation. Work on this JEP also resulted in a tool for analyzing a program's use of deprecated APIs.

To support this fidelity in information, the following components have been added to the `java.lang.Deprecated` annotation type:

- `forRemoval()`:
    - Returns Boolean `true` if the API element has been slated for future removal
    - Returns Boolean `false` if the API element has not been slated for future removal but is deprecated
    - Default is `false`
- `since()`:
    - Returns a string containing the release or version number, at which point the specified API was marked as deprecated

What the @Deprecated annotation really means

When an API, or methods within an API, has/have been marked with the `@Deprecated` annotation, one or more of the following conditions typically exists:

- There are errors in the API for which there is no plan to fix them
- Using the API is likely to result in errors
- The API has been replaced by another API
- The API is experimental

Summary

In this chapter, we covered 16 JEPs that were incorporated into the Java 9 platform. These JEPs cover a wide range of tools and updates to APIs to make developing with Java easier, with greater optimization possibilities for our resulting programs. Our review included a look at the new HTTP client, changes to Javadoc and the Doclet API, the new JavaScript parser, JAR and JRE changes, the new Java-level JVM compiler interface, the new support for TIFF images, platform logging, XML Catalog support, collections, and the new platform-specific desktop features. We also looked at enhancements to method handling and the deprecation annotation.

In the next chapter, we will cover concurrency enhancements introduced with the Java 9 platform. Our primary focus will be the support for reactive programming that is provided by the flow class API. We will also explore additional concurrency enhancements introduced in Java 9.

12
Concurrency and Reactive Programming

In the previous chapter, we covered several **Java Enhancement Proposals** (**JEPs**) that were incorporated into the Java 9 platform. These JEPs represented a wide range of tools and updates to APIs to make developing with Java easier, with greater optimization possibilities for our Java applications. We looked at the new HTTP client, changes to Javadoc and the Doclet API, the new JavaScript parser, JAR and JRE changes, the new Java-level JVM compiler interface, the new support for TIFF images, platform logging, XML catalog support, collections, and the new platform-specific desktop features. We also looked at enhancements to method handling and the deprecation annotation.

In this chapter we will cover concurrency enhancements introduced with the Java 9 platform. Our primary focus will be the support for reactive programming, a concurrency enhancement that is provided by the `Flow` class API. Reactive programming is a new concept for Java 9, so we will take an exploratory approach to the topic. We will also explore additional concurrency enhancements introduced in Java 9.

Specifically, we will cover the following topics:

- Reactive programming
- The new `Flow` API
- Additional concurrency updates
- Spin-wait hints

Reactive Programming

Reactive programming is when applications react to an asynchronous data stream as it occurs. The following image illustrates the flow:

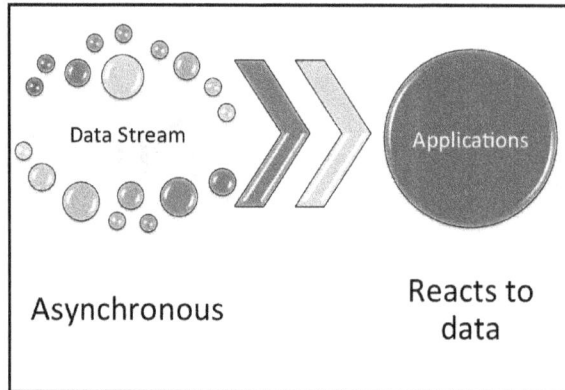

Reactive programming is not a fancy software engineering term only used by academics. It is, in fact, a programming model that can result in much greater efficiencies as opposed to the more common method of having applications iterate over data that is in memory.

There is more to reactive programming. First, let's consider that the data stream is provided by a publisher in an asynchronous manner to the subscriber.

> Data streams are a binary input/output of strings and primitive data types. The `DataInput` interface is used for an input stream and the `DataOutput` interface is used for output streams.

Processors, or a chain of processors, can be used to transform the data stream without the publisher or subscriber being impacted. In the following example, the **Processors** work on the stream of data without **Publisher** or **Subscriber** involvement, or even awareness:

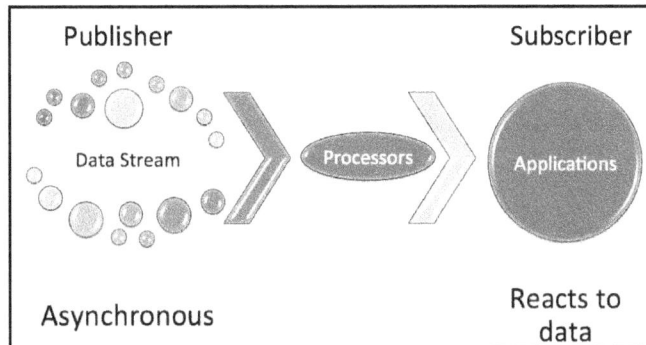

In addition to greater efficiency, reactive programming represents several additional benefits, which are highlighted here:

- The code base can be less verbose, making it:
    - Easier to code
    - Easier to maintain
    - Easier to read
- Stream processing results in memory efficiencies
- This is a solution for a variety of programming applications
- Less boiler-plate code needs to be written, so development time can be focused on programming core functionalities
- The following types of programming require less time and code:
    - Concurrency
    - Low-level threading
    - Synchronization

Reactive programming standardization

There are standards in many aspects of software development, and reactive programming has not escaped this. There is a **Reactive Streams** initiative to standardize asynchronous stream processing. The specific focus, in the context of Java, is with the JVM and JavaScript.

The Reactive Streams initiative aims at tackling the issue of governing how the data stream is exchanged between threads. As you will recall from the previous section, the idea of processors is predicated on there being no impact on the publisher or receiver. This no-impact mandate stipulates that the following are not required:

- Data buffering
- Data translation
- Conversion

The basic semantics of the standard define the regulation of data stream element transmission. This standard was specifically established for delivery with the Java 9 platform. Reactive Streams includes a library that will help developers convert from `org.reactivestreams` and `java.util.concurrent.Flow` namespaces.

The key to being successful with reactive programming and the Reactive Streams standardization is understanding the relevant terminology:

Term	Description
Demand	Demand refers to the subscriber's request for more elements as well as referring to the total number of elements requested that have not been fulfilled by the publisher yet.
Demand	Demand also refers to the total number of elements requested that have not been fulfilled by the publisher yet.
External synchronization	External access coordination for thread safety.
Non-obstructing	Methods are said to be non-obstructing if they rapidly execute without the requirement for heavy computations. Non-obstructing methods do not delay a subscriber's thread execution.
NOP	NOP execution is execution that can be called repeatedly without impact to the calling thread.
Responsivity	This term refers to a component's ability to respond.
Return normally	Return normally refers to when there are no errors--the normal condition. The `onError` method is the only way permitted by the standard to inform the subscriber of a failure.

Signal	One of the following methods: • `cancel` • `onComplete` • `onError` • `onNext` • `onSubscribe` • `request`

You can obtain the standard on Maven Central (`https://search.maven.org`). Here is the standard from Maven Central as of the publication date of this book:

```
<dependency>
    <groupId>org.reactivestreams</groupId>
    <artifactId>reative-streams</artifactId>
    <version>1.0.1</version>
</dependency>

<dependency>
    <groupId>org.reactivestreams</groupId>
    <artifact>reactive-streams-tck</artifactId>
    <version>1.0.0</version>
    <scope>test</scope>
</dependency>
```

In the next section, we will look at the Flow APIs in the Java 9 platform, as they correspond to the Reactive Streams specification.

The New Flow API

The `Flow` class is part of the `java.util.concurrent` package. It helps developers incorporate reactive programming in their applications. The class has one method, `defaultBufferSize()`, and four interfaces.

The `defaultBufferSize()` is a static method that returns the default buffer size for publishing and subscribing buffering. This default value is `256` and it is returned as an `int`. Let's look at the four interfaces.

The Flow.Publisher interface

The `Flow.Publisher` interface is a functional interface. A `Publisher` is a producer of data sent to subscribers:

```
@FunctionalInterface
public static interface Flow.Publisher<T>
```

This functional interface can serve as a lambda expression assignment target. It only takes one argument--the subscribed item type <T>. It has one method:

- void onSubscribe(Flow.Subscription subscription)

The Flow.Subscriber interface

The `Flow.Subscriber` interface is used to receive messages and its implementation is shown here:

```
public static interface Flow.Subscriber<T>
```

This interface is set up to receive messages. It only takes one argument--the subscribed item type <T>. It has the following methods:

- void onComplete()
- void onError(Throwable throwable)
- void onNext(T item)
- void onSubscribe(Flow.Subscription subscription)

The Flow.Subscription interface

The `Flow.Subscription` interface ensures that only subscribers receive what is requested. Also, as you will see here, a subscription can be cancelled at anytime:

```
public static interface Flow.Subscription
```

This interface does not take any arguments and is the linkage that controls the messages between instances of `Flow.Publisher` and `Flow.Subscriber`. It has the following methods:

- `void cancel()`
- `void request(long n)`

The Flow.Processor interface

The `Flow.Processor` interface can serve as both a `Subscriber` and a `Publisher`. The implementation is provided here:

```
static interface Flow.Processor<T,R> extends Flow.Subscriber<T>,
  Flow.Publisher<R>
```

This interface takes two arguments--the subscribed item type `<T>` and the published item type `<R>`. It does not have its own methods, but does inherit the following method from `java.util.concurrent.Flow.Publisher`:

- `void subscribe(Flow.Subscriber<? super T> subscriber)`

`Flow.Processor` also inherits the following methods from the `java.util.concurrent.Flow.Subscriber` interface:

- `void onComplete()`
- `void onError(Throwable throwable)`
- `void onNext(T item)`
- `void onSubscribe(Flow.Subscription subscription)`

Sample implementation

In any given implementation of reactive programming, we will have a `Subscriber` that requests data and a `Publisher` that provides the data. Let's first look at a sample `Subscriber` implementation:

```
import java.util.concurrent.Flow.*;

public class packtSubscriber<T> implements Subscriber<T>
{
  private Subscription theSubscription;
```

```
// We will override the four Subscriber interface methods

@Override
public void onComplete()
{
  System.out.println("Data stream ended");
}

@Override
public void onError(Throwable theError)
{
  theError.printStackTrace();
}

@Override
public void onNext(T theItem)
{
  System.out.println("Next item received: " + theItem);
  theSubscription.request(19);  // arbitrary number for
    example purposes
}

@Override
public void onSubscribe(Subscription theSubscription)
{
  this.theSubscription = theSubscription;
  theSubscription.request(19);
}

}
```

As you can see, implementing the Subscriber is not difficult. The heavy work is done with
the processors in-between the Subscriber and Publisher. Let's look at a sample
implementation where the Publisher publishes a data stream to subscribers:

```
import java.util.concurrent.SubmissionPublisher;

. . .

// First, let's create a Publisher instance
SubmissionPublisher<String> packtPublisher = new
 SubmissionPublisher<>();

// Next, we will register a Subscriber
PacktSubscriber<String> currentSubscriber = new
 PacktSubscriber<>();
packtPublisher.subscribe(currentSubscriber);
```

```
// Finally, we will publish data to the Subscriber and
    close the publishing effort
System.out.println("||---- Publishing Data Stream ----||");
. . .
packtPublisher.close();
System.out.println("||---- End of Data Stream Reached ----||");
```

Additional Concurrency Updates

The **More Concurrency Updates** Java Enhancement Proposal, JEP 266, aimed to improve the use of concurrency in Java. In this section, we will briefly explore the concept of Java concurrency and look at related enhancements to the Java 9 platform:

- Java concurrency
- Supporting Reactive Streams
- CompletableFuture API enhancements

Java concurrency

In this section, we will start with a brief explanation of concurrency, then look at system configurations, cover Java threads, and then look at the concurrency improvements.

Concurrency explained

Concurrent processing has been around since the 1960s. In those formative years, we already had systems that permitted multiple processes to share a single processor. These systems are more clearly defined as pseudo-parallel systems because it only appeared that multiple processes were being simultaneously executed. Our computers today still operate in this manner. The difference between the 1960s and current day is that our computers can have multiple CPUs, each with multiple cores, which better supports concurrency.

> Concurrency and parallelism are often used as interchangeable terms. Concurrency is when multiple processes overlap, although the start and stop times could be different. Parallelism occurs when tasks start, run, and stop at the same time.

System configurations

There are several different processor configurations that need to be considered. This section features two common configurations. The first configuration is that of shared memory and is illustrated here:

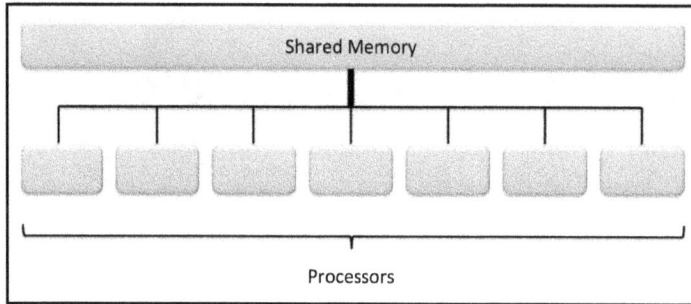

As you can see, the shared memory system configuration has multiple processors that all share a common system memory. The second featured system configuration is a distributed memory system:

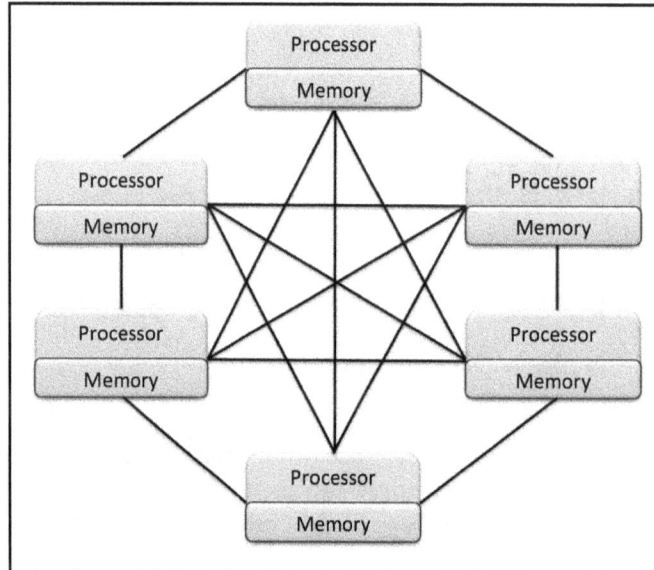

With the distributed memory system, each processor has its own memory and each individual processor is fully linked with the other processors, making for a distributed system that is fully linked.

Java threads

A thread in Java is a program execution and is built into the JVM. The Thread class is part of the java.lang package (java.lang.Thread). Threads have priorities that control in what order the JVM executes them. While the concept is simple, implementation is not. Let's start by taking a close look at the Thread class.

The Thread class has two nested classes:

- public static enum Thread.State
- public static interface Thread.UncaughtExceptionHandler

There are three instance variables for managing thread priorities:

- public static final int MAX_PRIORITY
- public static final int MIN_PRIORITY
- public static final int NORM_PRIORITY

The Thread class has eight constructors, all of which allocate a new Thread object. Here are the constructor signatures:

- public Thread()
- public Thread(Runnable target)
- public Thread(Runnable target, String name)
- public Thread(String name)
- public Thread(ThreadGroup group, Runnable target)
- public Thread(ThreadGroup group, Runnable target, String name)
- public Thread(ThreadGroup group, Runnable target, String name, long stackSize)
- public Thread(ThreadGroup group, String name)

The Thread class also has 43 methods, six of which have been deprecated. The remaining methods are listed here, save for the accessors and mutators which are listed separately. You can consult the documentation for details about each of these methods:

- public static int activeCount()
- public final void checkAccess()
- protected Object clone() throws CloneNotSupportedException
- public static Thread currentThread()

- `public static void dumpStack()`
- `public static int enumerate(Thread[] array)`
- `public static boolean holdsLock(Object obj)`
- `public void interrupt()`
- `public static boolean interrupted()`
- `public final boolean isAlive()`
- `public final boolean isDaemon()`
- `public boolean isInterrupted()`
- join methods:
    - `public final void join() throws InterruptedException`
    - `public final void join(long millis) throws InterruptedException`
    - `public final void join(long millis, int nano) throws InterruptedException`
- `public void run()`
- sleep methods:
    - `public static void sleep(long mills) throws InterruptedException`
    - `public static void sleep(long mills, int nano) throws InterruptedException`
- `public void start()`
- `public String toString()`
- `public static void yield()`

Here is the list of accessors/getters and mutators/setters for the `Thread` class:

- accessors/getters:
    - `public static Map<Thread, StackTraceElement[]> getAllStacktraces()`
    - `public ClassLoader getContextClassLoader()`
    - `public static Thread.UncaughtExceptionHandler getDefaultUncaughtExceptionHandler()`
    - `public long getId()`
    - `public final String getName()`
    - `public final int getPriority()`
    - `public StackTraceElement[] getStackTrace()`

- public Thread.State getState()
- public final ThreadGroup getThreadGroup()
- public Thread.UncaughtExceptionHandler getUncaughtExceptionHandler()

- mutators/setters:
  - public void setContextClassLoader(ClassLoader cl)
  - public final void setDaemon(boolean on)
  - public static void setDefaultUncaughtExceptionHandler(Thread.UncaughtExceptionHandler eh)
  - public final void setName(String name)
  - public final void setPriority(int newPriority)
  - public void setUncaughtExceptionHandler(Thread.UncaughtExceptionHandler eh)

In Java, concurrency is commonly referred to as multithreading. As indicated earlier, managing threads, and especially multithreads, requires great fidelity in control. Java employs a couple of techniques including the use of locks. Code segments can be locked to ensure that only a single thread can execute that code at any given time. We can lock classes and method with the use of the synchronized keyword. Here is an example of how to lock an entire method:

```
public synchronized void protectedMethod()
{
  . . .
}
```

The next code snippet demonstrates how to use the synchronized keyword to lock blocks of code within a method:

```
. . .
public class unprotectedMethod()
{
  . . .
  public int doSomething(int tValue)
  {
    synchronized (this)
    {
      if (tValue != 0)
      {
```

```
        // do something to change tValue
        return tValue;
      }
    }
  }
}
```

Concurrency improvements

The ability to employ multiple threads in our Java applications stands to greatly improve efficiency and leverage the increasing processing capabilities of modern computers. The use of threads in Java gives us great granularity in our concurrency controls.

Threads are at the core of Java's concurrency functionality. We can create a thread in Java by defining a `run` method and instantiating a `Thread` object. There are two methods of accomplishing this set of tasks. Our first option is to extend the `Thread` class and override the `Thread.run` method. Here is an example of that approach:

```
. . .
class PacktThread extends Thread
{
  . . .
  public void run()
  {
    . . .
  }
}

. . .

Thread varT = new PacktThread();

. . .

// This next line is start the Thread by executing
   the run() method.
varT.start();

. . .
```

A second approach is to create a class that implements the `Runnable` interface and passing an instance of the class to the constructor of the `Thread`. Here is an example:

```
. . .
class PacktRunner implements Runnable
{
  . . .
  public void run()
  {
    . . .
  }
}


. . .


PacktRunner varR = new PacktRunner();
Thread varT = new Thread(varR);


. . .


// This next line is start the Thread by executing the
    run() method.
varT.start();


. . .
```

Both of these methods work equally well, and which one you use is considered to be the developer's choice. Of course, if you are looking for additional flexibility, the second approach is probably a better one to use. You can experiment with both methods to help you make your determination.

CompletableFuture API enhancements

The `CompleteableFuture<T>` class is part of the `java.util.concurrent` package. The class extends the `Object` class and implements the `Future<T>` and `CompletionStage<T>` interfaces. This class is used to annotate threads that can be completed. We can use the `CompletableFuture` class to represent a future result. When the complete method is used, that future result can be completed.

It is important to realize that if multiple threads attempt to simultaneously complete (finish or cancel), all but one will fail. Let's look at the class and then look at the enhancements.

Class details

The `CompleteableFuture<T>` class has one internal class that marks asynchronous tasks:

```
public static interface
   CompletableFuture.AsynchronousCompletionTask
```

The constructor for the `CompleteableFuture<T>` class has to be in sync with the provided constructor signature, and it takes no arguments. The class has the following methods organized by what they return.

Returns a `CompletionStage`:

- `public CompletableFuture<Void> acceptEither(CompletionStage<? extends T> other, Consumer<? super T> action)`
- `public CompletableFuture<Void> acceptEitherAsync(CompletionStage<? extends T> other, Consumer<? super T> action)`
- `public CompletableFuture<Void> acceptEitherAsync(CompletionStage<? extends T> other, Consumer<? super T> action, Executor executor)`
- `public <U> CompletableFuture<U> applyToEither(CompletionStage<? extends T> other, Function<? super T, U> fn)`
- `public <U> CompletableFuture<U> applyToEitherAsync(CompletionStage<? extends T> other, Function<? super T, U> fn)`
- `public <U> CompletableFuture<U> applyToEitherAsync(CompletionStage<? extends T> other, Function<? super T, U> fn, Executor executor)`
- `public static <U> CompletedStage<U> completedStage(U value)`
- `public static <U> CompletionStage<U> failedStage(Throwable ex)`
- `public <U> CompletableFuture<U> handle(BiFunction<? super T, Throwable, ? extends U> fn)`
- `public <U> CompletableFuture<U> handleAsync(BiFunction<? super T, Throwable, ? extends U> fn)`
- `public <U> CompletableFuture<U> handleAsync(BiFunction<? super T, Throwable, ? extends U> fn, Executor executor)`
- `public CompletionStage<T> minimalCompletionStage()`
- `public CompletableFuture<Void> runAfterBoth(CompletionStage<?> other, Runnable action)`

- public CompletableFuture<Void>
  runAfterBothAsync(CompletionStage<?> other, Runnable action)
- public CompletableFuture<Void>
  runAfterBothAsync(CompletionStage<?> other, Runnable action,
  Executor executor)
- public CompletableFuture<Void>
  runAfterEither(CompletionStage<?> other, Runnable action)
- public CompletableFuture<Void>
  runAfterEitherAsync(CompletionStage<?> other, Runnable action)
- public CompletableFuture<Void>
  runAfterEitherAsync(CompletionStage<?> other, Runnable action,
  Executor executor)
- public CompletableFuture<T> whenComplete(BiConsumer<? super T,
  ? super Throwable> action)
- public CompletableFuture<T> whenCompleteAsync(BiConsumer<?
  super T, ? super Throwable> action)
- public CompletableFuture<T> whenCompleteAsync(BiConsumer<?
  super T, ? super Throwable> action, Executor executor)

These methods return a CompletionStage:

- public CompletableFuture<Void> thenAccept(Consumer<? super T>
  action)
- public CompletableFuture<Void> thenAcceptAsync(Consumer<? super
  T> action)
- public CompletableFuture<Void> thenAcceptAsync(Consumer<? super
  T> action, Executor executor)
- public <U> CompletableFuture<Void>
  thenAcceptBoth(CompletionStage<? extends U> other, BiConsumer<?
  super T, ? super U> action)
- public <U> CompletableFuture<Void>
  thenAcceptBothAsync(CompletionStage<? extends U> other,
  BiConsumer<? super T, ? super U> action)
- public <U> CompletableFuture<Void>
  thenAcceptBothAsync(CompletionStage<? extends U> other,
  BiConsumer<? super T, ? super U> action, Executor executor)
- public <U> CompletableFuture<U> thenApply(Function<? super T, ?
  extends U> fn)

- `public <U> CompletableFuture<U> thenApplyAsync(Function<? super T, ? extends U> fn)`
- `public <U> CompletableFuture<U> thenApplyAsync(Function<? super T, ? extends U> fn, Executor executor)`
- `public <U, V> CompletableFuture<V> thenCombine(CompletionStage<? extends U> other, BiFunction<? super T, ? super U, ? extends V> fn)`
- `public <U, V> CompletableFuture<V> thenCombineAsync(CompletionStage<? extends U> other, BiFunction<? super T, ? super U, ? extends V> fn)`
- `public <U, V> CompletableFuture<V> thenCombineAsync(CompletionStage<? extends U> other, BiFunction<? super T, ? super U, ? extends V> fn, Executor executor)`
- `public <U> CompletableFuture<U> thenCompose(Function<? super T, ? extends CompletionStage<U>> fn)`
- `public <U> CompletableFuture<U> thenComposeAsync(Function<? super T, ? extends CompletionStage<U>> fn)`
- `public <U> CompletableFuture<U> thenComposeAsync(Function<? super T, ? extends CompletionStage<U>> fn, Executor executor)`
- `public CompletableFuture<Void> thenRun(Runnable action)`
- `public CompletableFuture<Void>thenRunAsync(Runnable action)`
- `public CompletableFuture<Void>thenRunAsync(Runnable action, Executor executor)`

These methods return a `CompleteableFuture`:

- `public static CompletableFuture<Void> allOf(CompletableFuture<?>...cfs)`
- `public static CompletableFuture<Object> anyOf(CompletableFuture<?>... cfs)`
- `public CompletableFuture<T> completeAsync(Supplier<? extends T> supplier, Executor executor)`
- `public CompletableFuture<T> completeAsync(Supplier<? extends T> supplier)`
- `public static <U> CompletableFuture<U> completedFuture(U value)`

- `public CompletableFuture<T> completeOnTimeout(T value, long timeout, TimeUnit unit)`
- `public CompletableFuture<T> copy()`
- `public CompletableFuture<T> exceptionally(Function<Throwable, ? extends T> fn)`
- `public static <U> CompletableFuture<U> failedFuture(Throwable ex)`
- `public <U> CompletableFuture<U> newIncompeteFuture()`
- `public CompletableFuture<T> orTimeout(long timeout, TimeUnit unit)`
- `public static ComletableFuture<Void> runAsync(Runnable runnable)`
- `public static CompletableFuture<Void> runAsync(Runnable runnable, Executor executor)`
- `public static <U> CompletableFuture<U> supplyAsync(Supplier<U> supplier)`
- `public static <U> CompletableFuture<U> supplyAsync(Supplier<U. supplier, Executor executor)`
- `public CompletableFuture<T> toCompletableFuture()`

These methods return a `Executor`:

- `public Executor defaultExecutor()`
- `public static Executor delayedExecutor(long delay, Timeunit unit, Executor executor)`
- `public static Executor delayedExecutor(long delay, Timeunit unit)`

These methods return a `boolean`:

- `public boolean cancel(boolean mayInterruptIfRunning)`
- `public boolean complete(T value)`
- `public boolean completeExceptionally(Throwable ex)`
- `public boolean isCancelled()`
- `public boolean isCompletedExceptionally()`
- `public boolean isDone()`

No return type:

- `public void obtrudeException(Throwable ex)`
- `public void obtrudeValue(T value)`

Additional methods:

- `public T get(long timeout, TimeUnit unit) throws InterruptedException, ExecutionException, TimeoutException`
- `public T get() throws InterruptedException, ExecutionException`
- `public T getNow(T valueIfAbsent)`
- `public int getNumberOfDependents()`
- `public T join()`
- `public String toString()`

Enhancements

The `CompleteableFuture<T>` class received the following enhancements as part of the Java 9 platform:

- Added time-based enhancements:
    - This enables completions based on lapsed time
    - Delayed executions are now also supported
- Significant enhancement to subclasses:
    - Extending `CompletableFuture` is easier
    - Subclasses support alternative default executors

Specifically, the following methods were added in Java 9:

- `newIncompleteFuture()`
- `defaultExecutor()`
- `copy()`
- `minimalCompletionStage()`
- `completeAsync()`
- `orTimeout()`
- `completeOnTimeout()`

- delayedExecutor()
- completedStage()
- failedFuture()
- failedStage()

Spin-Wait Hints

With concurrency, we need to ensure that threads waiting to be executed actually get executed. The concept of spin-wait is a process that continually checks for a true condition. The aim of Java Enhancement Proposal 285 was to create an API that permits Java code to issue hints that a spin loop is currently being executed.

While this is not a feature that every Java developer will use, it can be useful for low-level programming. The hint system simply issues hints--indications, and performs no other actions. Justifications for adding these hints include the following assumptions:

- A spin loop's action time can be improved when using a spin hint
- Use of spin hints will reduce thread-to-thread latency
- CPU power consumption will be reduced
- Hardware threads will execute faster

This hint functionality will be contained in a new onSpinWait() method as part of the java.lang.Thread class. Here is an example of implementing the onSpinWait() method:

```
. . .

volatile boolean notInReceiptOfEventNotification;

. . .

while ( notInReceiptOfEventNotification );
{
  java.lang.Thread.onSpinWait();
}

// Add functionality here to read and process the event

. . .
```

Summary

In this chapter, we covered concurrency enhancements introduced with the Java 9 platform. We took a deep look at concurrency both as a core Java concept and with an eye to what Java 9 is delivering. We also explored the `Flow` class API that supports reactive programming, a new concept in Java 9. In addition, we explored concurrency enhancements and the new spin-wait hints introduced in Java 9.

In the next chapter, we will highlight the security enhancements introduced in Java 9 along with practical examples.

13
Security Enhancements

In the last chapter, we covered concurrency enhancements introduced with the Java 9 platform. We took an in-depth look at concurrency both as a core Java concept and as a series of enhancements for Java 9. We also explored the `Flow` class API that supports Reactive Programming, a new concept in Java 9. In addition, we explored concurrency enhancements and the new Spin-Wait hints introduced in Java 9.

In this chapter, we will look at several small changes made to the JDK that involve security. The size of these changes does not reflect their significance. The security enhancements introduced with the Java 9 platform provide developers with a greater ability to write and maintain applications that are more secure than previously possible.

Specifically, we will review the following content areas in this chapter:

- Datagram Transport Layer Security
- Creating PKCS12 keystores
- Improving security application performance
- TLS application-layer protocol negotiation extension
- Leveraging CPU instructions for GHASH and RSA
- OCSP stapling for TLS
- DRBG-based `SecureRandom` implementations

Datagram Transport Layer Security

Datagram Transport Layer Security (DTLS), is a communications protocol. The protocol provides a layer of security for datagram-based applications. DTLS permits secure communications and is based on the **Transport Layer Security (TLS)** protocol. Embedded security helps ensure messages are not forged, tampered with, or eavesdropped.

Let's review the relevant terminology:

- **Communication protocol**: A set of rules that govern how information is transmitted.
- **Datagram**: A structured transfer unit.
- **Eavesdropping**: Undetected listening to in-transit data packets.
- **Forgery**: Transmission of a packet with falsified sender.
- **Network packet**: A formatted unit of data for transmission.
- **Tampering**: The altering of data packets after the sender transmits them and before the intended receiver receives them.
- **TLS protocol**: The most common network security protocol. Uses, as an example, IMPA and POP for email.

The DTLS Java Enhancement Proposal 219 is aimed at creating an API for the DTLS versions 1.0 and 1.2.

In the sections that follow, we will look at each of the DTLS versions, 1.0 and 1.2, and then review the changes to the Java 9 platform.

DTLS protocol version 1.0

DTLS protocol version 1.0 was established in 2006 and provides communications security for datagram protocols. Here are the basic characteristics:

- Permits client/server applications to communicate without permitting:
  - Eavesdropping
  - Tampering
  - Message forgery
- Based on the TLS protocol
- Provides security guarantees
- The DLS protocol's datagram semantics are preserved

The following diagram illustrates where the **Transport Layer** fits into the overall schema of **SSL/TLS** protocol layers and protocols for each layer:

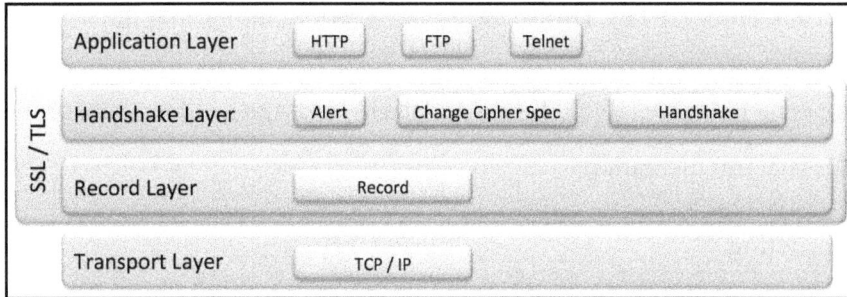

DTLS protocol version 1.0 provides detailed specifications with the major areas of coverage listed as follows:

- Ciphers:
  - Anti-replay block cipher
  - New cipher suites
  - Standard (or null) stream cipher
- Denial of service countermeasures
- Handshake:
  - Message format
  - Protocol
  - Reliability
- Messages:
  - Fragmentation and reassembly
  - Loss-insensitive messaging
  - Size
  - Timeout and retransmission
  - Packet loss
- **Path Maximum Transition Unit (PMTU)** discovery
- Record layer
- Record payload protection
- Reordering
- Replay detection
- Transport layer mapping

DTLS protocol version 1.2

DTLS protocol version 1.2 was published in January 2012 and is copyrighted by the **Internet Engineering Task Force** (**IETF**). This section shares code samples that illustrate the changes in version 1.2.

The following code illustrates the TLS 1.2 handshake message header. This format supports:

- Message fragmentation
- Message loss
- Reordering

```
// Copyright (c) 2012 IETF Trust and the persons identified as
    authors of the code. All rights reserved.

struct
{
  HandshakeType msg_type;
  uint24 length;
  uint16 message_seq;                      // New field
  uint24 fragment_offset;                  // New field
  uint24 fragment_length;                  // New field
  select (HandshakeType)
  {
    case hello_request: HelloRequest;
    case client_hello:  ClientHello;
    case hello_verify_request: HelloVerifyRequest;   // New type
    case server_hello:  ServerHello;
    case certificate:Certificate;
    case server_key_exchange: ServerKeyExchange;
    case certificate_request: CertificateRequest;
    case server_hello_done:ServerHelloDone;
    case certificate_verify:  CertificateVerify;
    case client_key_exchange: ClientKeyExchange;
    case finished: Finished;
  } body;
} Handshake;
```

The code presented in this section is from the DTLS protocol documentation and is republished here in accordance with IETF's *Legal Provisions Relating to IETF Documents.*

The record layer contains the information that we intend to send into records. The information starts off inside a DTLSPlaintext structure and then, after the handshake takes place, the records are encrypted and are eligible to be sent by the communication stream. The record layer format follows with new fields in version 1.2 annotated with the // New field in-code comments as follows:

```
// Copyright (c) 2012 IETF Trust and the persons identified
   as authors of the code. All rights reserved.


struct
{
  ContentType type;
  ProtocolVersion version;
  uint16 epoch;                                       // New field
  uint48 sequence_number;                             // New field
  uint16 length;
  opaque fragment[DTLSPlaintext.length];
} DTLSPlaintext;

struct
{
  ContentType type;
  ProtocolVersion version;
  uint16 epoch;                                       // New field
  uint48 sequence_number;                             // New field
  uint16 length;
  opaque fragment[DTLSCompressed.length];
} DTLSCompressed;

struct
{
  ContentType type;
  ProtocolVersion version;
  uint16 epoch;                                       // New field
  uint48 sequence_number;                             // New field
  uint16 length;
  select (CipherSpec.cipher_type)
  {
     case block:  GenericBlockCipher;
     case aead:   GenericAEADCipher;                  // New field
  } fragment;
} DTLSCiphertext;
```

Finally, here is the updated handshake protocol:

```
// Copyright (c) 2012 IETF Trust and the persons identified
   as authors of the code. All rights reserved.

enum {
  hello_request(0), client_hello(1),
   server_hello(2),
  hello_verify_request(3),                        // New field
  certificate(11), server_key_exchange (12),
  certificate_request(13), server_hello_done(14),
  certificate_verify(15), client_key_exchange(16),
  finished(20), (255) } HandshakeType;

struct {
  HandshakeType msg_type;
  uint24 length;
  uint16 message_seq;                             // New field
  uint24 fragment_offset;                         // New field
  uint24 fragment_length;                         // New field
  select (HandshakeType) {
    case hello_request: HelloRequest;
    case client_hello:  ClientHello;
    case server_hello:  ServerHello;
    case hello_verify_request: HelloVerifyRequest;  // New field
    case certificate:Certificate;
    case server_key_exchange: ServerKeyExchange;
    case certificate_request: CertificateRequest;
    case server_hello_done:ServerHelloDone;
    case certificate_verify:  CertificateVerify;
    case client_key_exchange: ClientKeyExchange;
    case finished: Finished;
  } body; } Handshake;

struct {
  ProtocolVersion client_version;
  Random random;
  SessionID session_id;
  opaque cookie<0..2^8-1>;                         // New field
  CipherSuite cipher_suites<2..2^16-1>;
  CompressionMethod compression_methods<1..2^8-1>; } ClientHello;

struct {
  ProtocolVersion server_version;
  opaque cookie<0..2^8-1>; } HelloVerifyRequest;
```

DTLS support in Java 9

Java 9's implementation of the DTLS API is transport-independent and light-weight. The design considerations for the API were as follows:

- Read timeouts will not be managed
- The implementation will use a single TLS record for each wrap/unwrap operation
- The application, not the API, will be required to:
  - Determine timeout values
  - Assemble out-of-order application data

The DTLS is a protocol used to secure data from the application layer before that data is passed to a transport layer protocol. DTLS is a good solution for encrypting and transmitting real-time data. Caution should be exercised so that we do not introduce vulnerabilities in our application's implementation. Here are security considerations specific to implementing DTLS in your Java 9 applications:

- Implement DTLS v1.2, since that is the latest version supported by Java 9.
- Avoid **Rivest-Shamir-Adleman** (**RSA**) encryption. If RSA must be used, add addition security to your private keys since this is a weak point for RSA.
- Use 192 bits or more when using the **Elliptic Curve Diffie-Hellman** (**ECDH**) anonymous key agreement protocol. The 192-bit value is based on a **National Institute of Standards and Technology** (**NIST**) recommendation.
- The use of **Authenticated Encryption with Associated Data** (**AEAD**), a form of encryption, is highly recommended. AEAD provides authenticity, confidentiality, and integrity assurances on the data being encrypted and decrypted.
- Always implement the `renegotiation_info` extension when implementing handshake renegotiation.
- Establish a **Forward Secrecy** (**FS**) capability in all Java applications using a communication protocol. Implementing FS ensures past session encryption keys are not compromised when long-term encryption keys are compromised. Ideally a **Perfect Forward Secrecy** (**PFS**), where each key is only valid for a single session, would be used in the Java applications that call for the greatest security of transmitted data.

Creating PKCS12 keystores

The Java 9 platform provides increased security for keystores. In order to appreciate the changes ushered in by Java Enhancement Proposal 229, create PKCS12 keystores by default, we will first review the concept of keystores, look at the `KeyStore` class, and then look at the changes.

Keystore primer

The concept of a `KeyStore` is relatively simple. It is essentially a database file, or data repository file, that stores public key certificates and private keys. The `Keystore` will be stored in the `/jre/lib/security/cacerts` folder. As you will see in the next section, this database is managed by Java's `java.security.KeyStore` class methods.

`KeyStore` features include:

- Contains one of the following entry types:
  - Private keys
  - Public key certificates
- Unique alias string names for every entry
- Password protection for each key

Java Keystore (JKS)

The `java.security.KeyStore` class is the storage facility for cryptographic keys and certificates. This class extends `java.lang.Object`, see as follows:

```
public class KeyStore extends Object
```

There are three types of entries managed by a `KeyStore`, each implements the `KeyStore.Entry` interface, one of the three interfaces provided by the `KeyStore` class. The Entry implementations are defined in the following table:

Implementation	Description
`KeyStore.PrivateKeyEntry`	• Contains the `PrivateKey` and can store it in a protected format • Contains the certificate chain for the public key

KeyStore.SecretKeyEntry	• Contains the SecretKey and can store it in a protected format
KeyStore.TrustedCertifcateEntry	• Contains a single public key Certificate from an external source

This class has been part of the Java platform since version 1.2. It has one constructor, three interfaces, six sub-classes, and several methods. The constructor definition is:

```
protected KeyStore(KeyStoreSpi keyStoresSpi,
  Provider provider, String type)
```

The KeyStore class contains the following interfaces:

- public static interface KeyStore.Entry:
  - This interface serves as a marker for KeyStore entry types and contains no methods.
- public static interface KeyStore.LoadStoreParameter:
  - This interface serves as a marker for load and store parameters and has the following method that returns null or the parameter used to protect the KeyStore data:
    - getProtectionParameter()
- public static interface KeyStore.ProtectionParameter:
  - This interface serves as a marker for KeyStore protection parameters and contains no methods.

The java.security.KeyStore class also contains the six nested classes listed as follows.

Builder

The KeyStore.Builder class is used when you want to defer the instantiation of a KeyStore:

```
public abstract static class KeyStore.Builder extends Object
```

This class provides the necessary information for instantiating a `KeyStore` object. The class has the following methods:

- `public abstract KeyStore getKeyStore() throws KeyStoreException`
- `public abstractKeyStore.ProtectionParameter getProjectionParameter(String alias) throws KeyStoreException`
- Three options for `newInstance`:
    - `public static KeyStore.Builder newInstance(KeyStore keyStore, KeyStore.ProtectionParameter protectionParameter)`
    - `public static KeyStore.Builder newInstance(String type, Provider provider, File file, KeyStore.ProtectionParameter protection)`
    - `public static KeyStore.Builder newInstance(String type, Provider provider, KeyStore.ProtectionParameter protection)`

The CallbackHandlerProtection class

The `KeyStore.CallbackHandlerProtection` class definition is as follows:

```
public static class KeyStore.CallbackHandlerProtection extends
  Object implements KeyStore.ProtectionParameter
```

This class provides a `ProtectionParameter` to encapsulate a `CallbackHandler` and has the following method:

```
public CallbackHandler getCallbackHandler()
```

The PasswordProtection class

The `KeyStore.PasswordProtection` class definition is as follows:

```
public static class KeyStore.PasswordProtection extends Object
  implements KeyStore.ProtectionParameter, Destroyable
```

This call provides an implementation of `ProtectionParameter` that is password-based. The class has the following methods:

- `public void destroy() throws DestroyFailedException`:
  - This method clears the password
- `public char[] getPassword()`:
  - Returns a reference to the password
- `public boolean isDestroyed()`:
  - Returns true if the password was cleared

The PrivateKeyEntry class

The `KeyStore.PrivateKeyEntry` class definition is as follows:

```
public static final class KeyStore.PrivateKeyEntry extends
  Object implements KeyStore.Entry
```

This creates an entry to hold a `PrivateKey` and the corresponding `Certificate` chain. This class has the following methods:

- `public Certificate getCertificate()`:
  - Returns the **end entity** `Certificate` from the `Certificate` chain
- `public Certificate[] getCertificateChain()`:
  - Returns the `Certificate` chain as an array of `Certificates`
- `public PrivateKey getPrivateKey()`:
  - Returns the `PrivateKey` from the current entry
- `public String toString()`:
  - Returns the `PrivateKeyEntry` as a `String`

The SecretKeyEntry class

The `KeyStore.SecretKeyEntry` class definition is as follows:

```
public static final class KeyStore.SecretKeyEntry extends
  Object implements KeyStore.Entry
```

This class holds a `SecretKey` and has the following methods:

- `public SecretKey getSecretKey()`:
    - Returns the entry's `SecretKey`
- `public String toString()`:
    - Returns the `SecretKeyEntry` as a `String`.

The TrustedCertificateEntry class

The `KeyStore.TrustedCertificateEntry` class definition is as follows:

```
public static final class KeyStore.TrustedCertificateEntry extends
  Object implements KeyStore.Entry
```

This class holds a trusted `Certificate` and has the following methods:

- `public Certificate getTrustedCertificate()`:
    - Returns the entry's trusted `Certificate`
- `public String toString()`:
    - Returns the entry's trusted `Certificate` as a `String`

The key to using this class is understanding the flow. First, we must load the `KeyStore`, using the `getInstance` method. Next we request access to the `KeyStore` instance. Then, we have access to read and write to the `Object`:

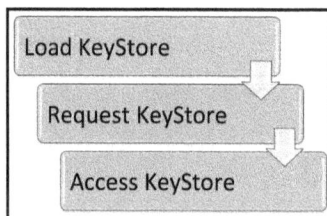

The following code snippet shows the load-request-access implementation:

```
   . . .

try {
   // KeyStore implementation will be returned for the default type
   KeyStore myKS = KeyStore.getInstance(KeyStore.getDefaultType());

   // Load
```

```
    myKS.load(null, null);
    // Instantiate a KeyStore that holds a trusted certificate
    TrustedCertificateEntry myCertEntry =
      new TrustedCertificateEntry(generateCertificate());

    // Assigns the trusted certificate to the "pack.pub" alias
    myKS.setCertificateEntry("packt.pub",
     myCertEntry.getTrustedCertificate());
    return myKS;
  }
  catch (Exception e) {
    throw new AssertionError(e);
  }
}
. . .
```

PKCS12 default in Java 9

Prior to Java 9, the default `KeyStore` type was **Java KeyStore** (**JKS**). The Java 9 platform now uses PKCS as the default `KeyStore` type, more specifically, PKCS12.

> PKCS is the acronym for **Public Key Cryptography Standards**.

This change to PKCS provides stronger cryptographic algorithms as compared to JKS. As you would expect, JDK 9 will still be compatible with JKS to support previously developed systems.

Improving security application performance

Java Enhancement Proposal 232, titled *Improving Security Application Performance,* was focused on performance improvements when running applications with a security manager installed. Security managers can result in processing overhead and less than ideal application performance.

This is an impressive undertaking as current CPU overhead when running security managers is estimated to result in 10-15% performance degradation. It is not feasible to completely remove the CPU overhead as some CPU processing is required to run the security manager. That being said, the intention of this proposal (JEP-232) was to decrease the overhead percentage as much as possible.

This effort resulted in the following optimizations, each detailed in subsequent sections:

- Security policy enforcement
- Permission evaluation
- Hash code
- Package checking algorithm

Security policy enforcement

JDK 9 uses `ConcurrentHashMap` for mapping `ProtectionDomain` to `PermissionCollection`. `ConcurrentHashMap` is typically used for high concurrency in applications. It has the following characteristics:

- Thread safe
- Enter map does not need to be synchronized
- Fast reads
- Writes use locks
- No object-level locking
- Locking at a very granular level

The `ConcurrentHashMap` class definition follows:

```
public class ConcurrentHashMap<K, V> extends AbstractMap<K, V>
    implements ConcurrentMap<K, V>, Serializable
```

In the preceding class definition, `K` refers to the type of keys maintained by the hash map and `V` indicates the type of mapped values. There is a `KeySetView` sub-class and several methods.

There are three additional classes related to enforcing security policy--`ProtectionDomain`, `PermissionCollection`, and `SecureClassLoader`:

- The `ProtectionDomain` class is used to encapsulate a group of classes so that permissions can be granted to the domain.
- The `PermissionCollection` class represents a collection of permission objects.
- The `SecureClassLoader` class, which extends the `ClassLoader` class, provides additional functionality for defining classes with permissions for retrieval by the system policy. In Java 9, this class uses `ConcurrentHashMap` for increased security.

Permission evaluation

Under the category of permission evaluation, three optimizations were made:

- The `identifyPolicyEntries` list previously had policy provider code for synchronization. This code has been removed in JDK 9.
- `PermissionCollection` entries are now stored in a `ConcurrentHashMap`. They were previously stored as a `HashMap` in a `Permission` class.
- Permissions are now stored in concurrent collections in subclasses of `PermissionCollection`.

The java.Security.CodeSource package

A hash code is an object-generated number that is stored in a hash table for rapid storage and retrieval. Every object in Java has a hash code. Here are some characteristics and rules for hash codes:

- Hash codes are the same for equal objects within a running process
- Hash codes can change between execution cycles
- Hash codes should not be used as keys

The Java 9 platform includes a modified `hashCode` method of `java.security.CodeSource` to optimize DNS lookups. These can be processor intensive, so a String version of the code source URL is used to compute hash codes.

The `CodeSource` class definition follows:

```
public class CodeSource extends Object implements Serializable
```

This class has the following methods:

- `public boolean equals(Object obj)`: Returns `true` if the objects are equal. This overrides the `equals` method in the `Object` class.
- `public final Certificate[] getCertificates()`: Returns an array of certificates.
- `public final CodeSigner[] getCodeSigners()`: Returns an array of the code signers associated with the `CodeSource`.
- `public final URL getLocation()`: Returns the URL.
- `public int hashCode()`: Returns the hash code value for the current object.
- `public boolean implies(CodeSource codesource)`: Returns true if the given code source meets the following criteria:
  - is not null
  - object's certificates are not null
  - object's location is not null
- `public String toString()`: Returns a `String` with information about the `CodeSource` to include the location and certificates.

Package checking algorithm

Java 9's final performance improvement when running applications with a security manager installed, came in the form of the `java.lang.SecurityManager` package enhancements. Specifically, the `checkPackageAccess` method's package checking algorithm was modified.

The `java.lang.SecurityManager` class allows applications to implement security policy on specific operations. The `public void checkPackageAccess(String pkg)` method, of this class receives a comma-delimited list of restricted packages from the the `getProperty` method. As illustrated here, depending on the evaluation, the `checkPackageAccess` method can throw one of two exceptions:

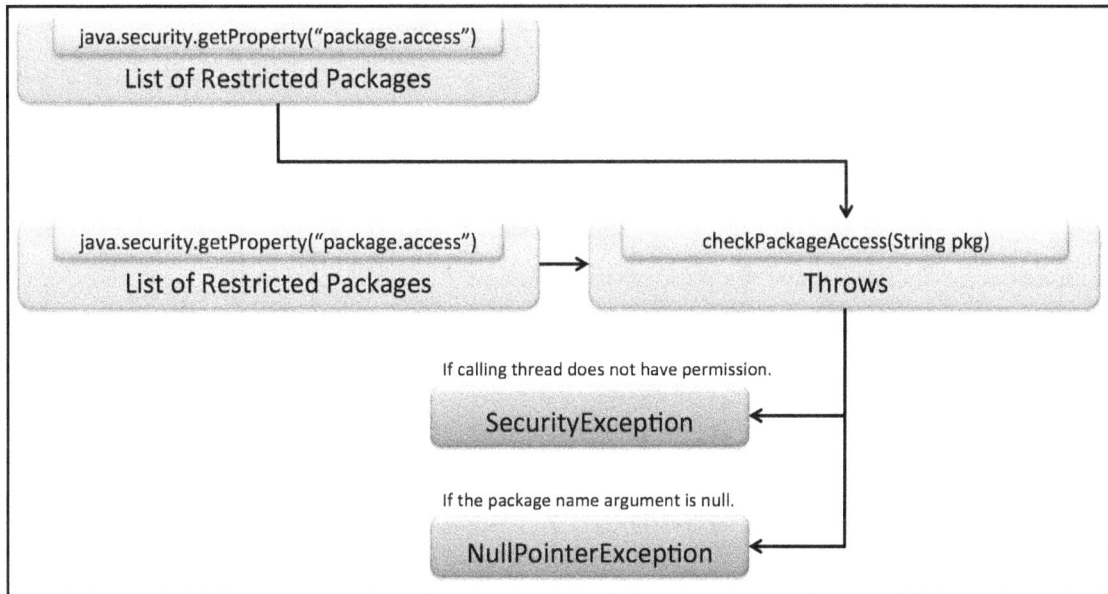

java.security.getProperty("package.access")
List of Restricted Packages

java.security.getProperty("package.access")
List of Restricted Packages

checkPackageAccess(String pkg)
Throws

If calling thread does not have permission.
SecurityException

If the package name argument is null.
NullPointerException

TLS application-layer protocol negotiation extension

Java Enhancement Proposal 244, simply enhanced the `javax.net.ssl` package so that it supports the **Transport Layer Security (TLS) ALPN (Application Layer Protocol Negotiation)** extension. This extension permits application protocol negotiation for TLS connections.

TLS ALPN extension

The ALPN is a TLS extension and can be used to negotiate which protocol to implement when using a secure connection. ALPN represents an efficient means of negotiating protocols. As indicated in the following diagram, there are five basic steps to TLS handshakes:

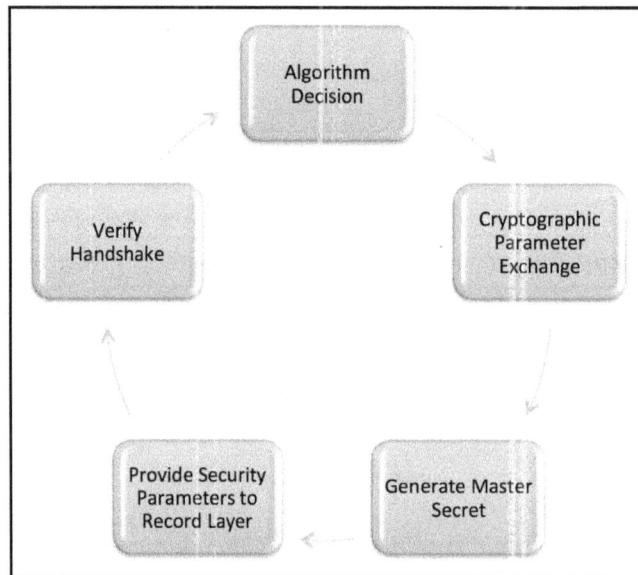

The javax.net.ssl package

The `java.net.ssl` package contains classes relating to secure socket packages. This permits us to use SSL as an example, for the reliable detection of errors introduced to the network byte stream. It also provides the ability to encrypt the data as well as provide authentication of client and server.

This package includes the following interfaces:

- `public interface HandshakeCompletedListener extends EventListener`
- `public interface HostnameVerifier`
- `public interface KeyManager`
- `public interface ManagerFactoryParameters`

- public interface SSLSession
- public interface SSLSessionBindingListener extends EventListener
- public interface SSLSessionContext
- public interace TrustManager
- public interface X509KeyManager extends KeyManager
- public interface X509TrustManager extends TrustManager

The `java.net.ssl` package also has the following sub-classes:

- public class CertPathTrustManagerParameters extends Object implements ManagerFactoryParameters
- public abstract class ExtendedSSLSession extends Object implements SSLSession
- public class HandshakeCompleteEvent extends EventObject
- public abstract class HttpsURLConnection extends HttpURLConnection
- public class KeyManagerFactory extends Object
- public abstract class KeyManagerFactorySpi
- public class KeyStoreBuilderParameters extends Object implements ManagerFactoryParameters
- public class SSLContext extends Object
- public abstract class SSLContextSpi extends Object
- public abstract class SSLEngine extends Object
- public class SSLEngineResult extends Object
- public class SSLParameters extends Object
- public final class SSLPermission extends BasicPermission
- public abstract class SSLServerSocket extends ServerSocket
- public abstract class SSLServerSocketFactory extends ServerSocketFactory
- public class SSLSessionBindingEvent extends EventObject
- public abstract class SSLSocket extends Socket
- public abstract class SSLSocketFactory extends SocketFactory
- public class TrustManagerFactory extends Object
- public abstract class TrustManagerFactorySpi extends Object

- `public abstract class X509ExtendedKeyManager extends Object implements X509KeyManager`
- `public abstract class X509ExtendedTrustManager extends Object implements x509TrustManager`

The java.net.ssl package extension

The change to the `java.net.ssl` package in the Java 9 platform is that it now supports the TLS ALPN extension. Key benefits of this change are:

- TLS clients and servers can now use multiple application-layer protocols, which may or may not use the same transport-layer port
- The ALPN extension permits clients to prioritize application-layer protocols it supports
- Servers can select a client protocol and for the TLS connection
- Supports HTTP/2

The following illustration was previously presented as the five basic steps to TLS handshakes. Updated for Java 9 and presented here, the illustration indicates where the protocol names are shared between the client and server:

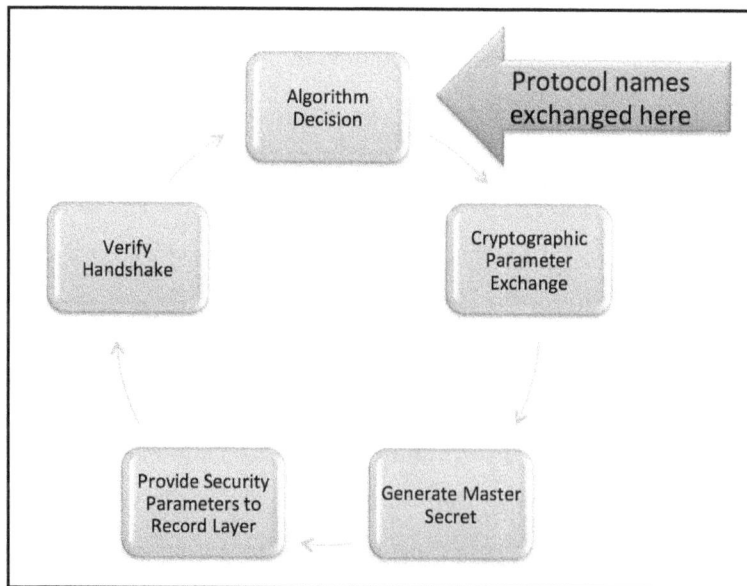

Once the client's list of application layer protocols is received, the server can select the server's preferred intersection value and externally scan initial plain text `ClientHellos` and select an ALPN protocol. An application server will do one of the following:

- Select any of the supported protocols
- Decide that the ALPN values (remotely offered and locally supported) are mutually exclusive
- Ignore the ALPN extension

Other key behaviors with regards to the ALPN extension:

- The server can alter connection parameters
- After the SSL/TLS handshake starts, the application can query to see if an ALPN value has been selected yet
- After the SSL/TLS handshake ends, the application can review which protocol was used

A `ClientHello` is the first message in the TLS handshake. It has the following structure:

```
struct {
    ProtocolVersion client_version;
    Random random;
    SessionID session_id;
    CipherSuite cipher_suites<2..2^16-1>;
    CompressionMethod compression_methods<1..2^8-1>;
    Extension extensions<0..2^16-1>;
} ClientHello;
```

Leveraging CPU instructions for GHASH and RSA

The self-descriptive title of Java Enhancement Proposal (JEP) 246, **Leverage CPU Instructions for GHASH and RSA**, provides great insight into its goal. The point of this JEP was to improve the performance of cryptographic operations, specifically GHASH and RSA. The performance improvement has been achieved in Java 9 by leveraging the newest SPARC and Intel x64 CPU instructions.

This enhancement did not require new or modified APIs as part of the Java 9 platform.

Hashing

Galois HASH (GHASH) and **Rivest-Shamir-Adleman (RSA)** are crypto systems hashing algorithms. Hashes are a fixed length string or number generated from a string of text. Algorithms, specifically hashing algorithms, are devised so that the resultant hashes cannot be reverse engineered. We use hashing to store passwords that are generated with a salt.

> ℹ️ Salts, in cryptology, are random data used as an input to a hashing function to generate a password. Salts help protect against rainbow table attacks and dictionary attacks.

The following graphic illustrates the basics of how hashing works:

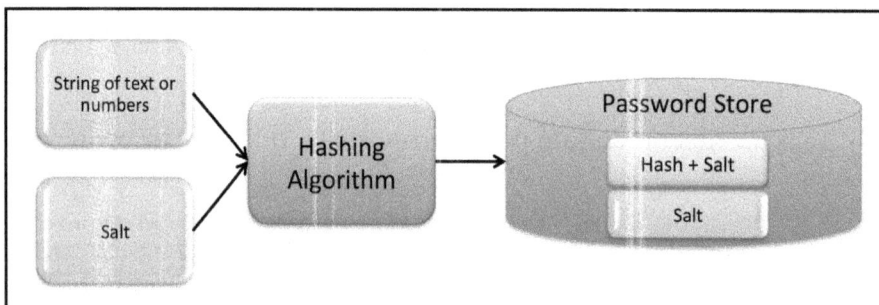

As you can see, the hashing algorithm is fed plain text and a salt resulting in a new hashed password and the salt being stored. Here is the same graphic with sample input/output to demonstrate the functionality:

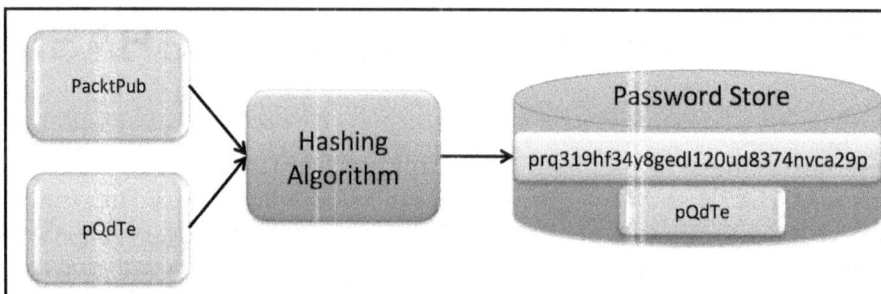

The validation process, the following diagram starts with the user entering their plain text password. The hashing algorithm takes that plain text and rehashes it with the stored salt. Then the resulting hashed password is compared to the stored one:

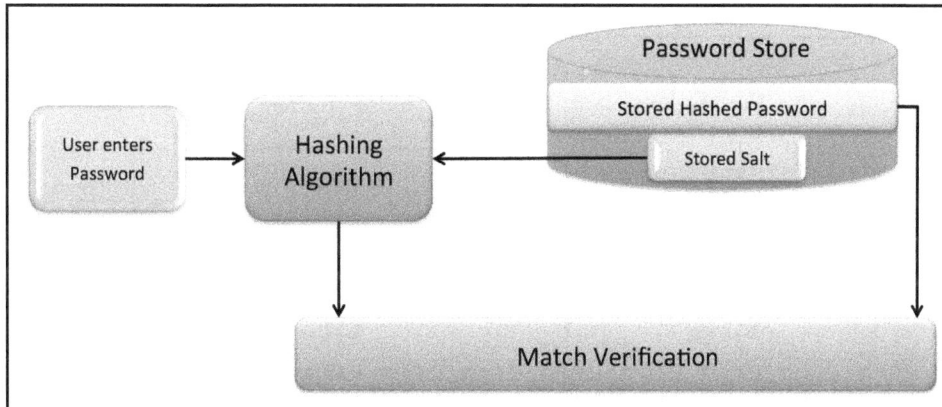

OCSP stapling for TLS

Online Certificate Status Protocol (**OCSP**) stapling is a method of checking the revocation status of digital certificates. The OCSP stapling approach for determining an SSL certificate's validity is assessed as being both safe and quick. The determination speed is achieved by permitting web servers to provide the validity information on its organic certificates instead of the lengthier process of requesting validating information from the certificate's issuing vendor.

> **Online Certificate Status Protocol** (**OCSP**) stapling was previously referred to as the **Transport Layer Security** (**TLS**) certificate status request extension.

OCSP stapling primer

THE OCSP stapling process involves several components and validity checks. The following graphic illustrates the OCSP stapling process:

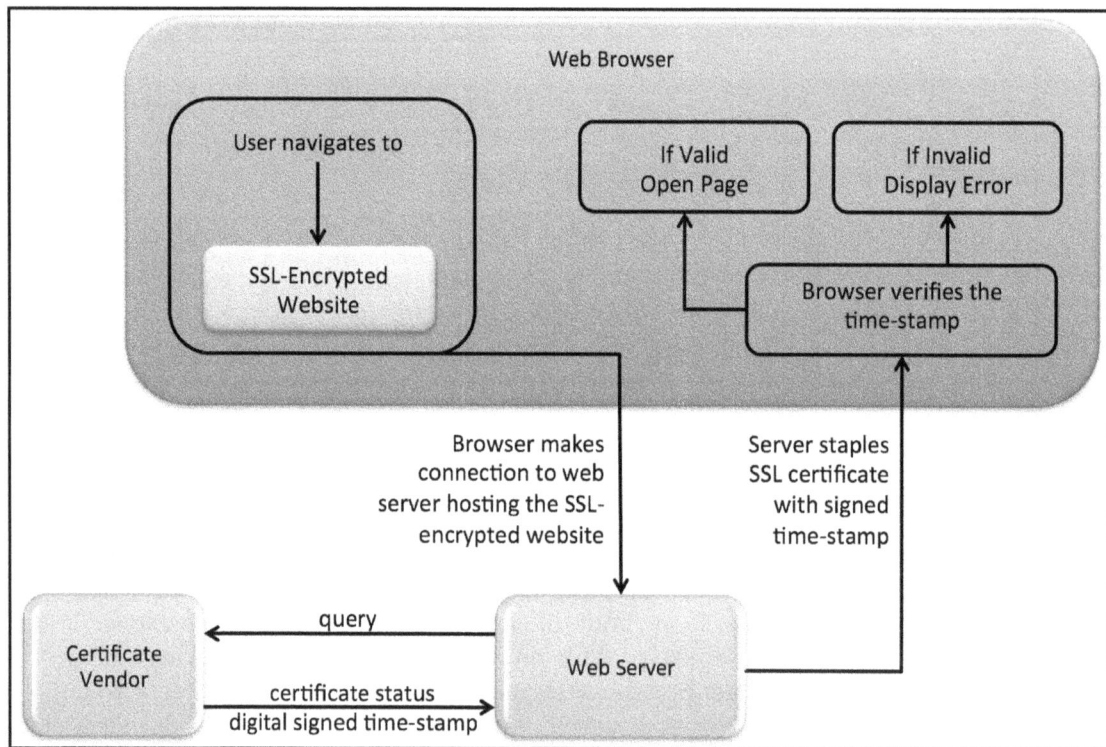

As you can see, the process starts when the user attempts to open an SSL-encrypted website via their browser. The browser queries the web server to ensure the SSL-encrypted website has a valid certificate. The web server queries the certificate's vendor and is provided with both the certificate status and the digital signed time-stamp. The web server takes those two components (certificate status and digital signed time-stamp), staples them together, and returns the stapled set to the requesting browser. The browser can then check the validity of the time-stamp and decide whether to display the SSL-encrypted website or to display an error.

Changes for the Java 9 platform

Java Enhancement Proposal 249, **OCSP Stapling for TLS**, implements OCSP stapling via the TLS certificate status request extension. OSCP stapling checks the validity of X.509 certificates.

> X.509 certificates are digital certificates that use the X509 **Public Key Infrastructure** (**PKI**).

Prior to Java 9, the certificate validity check (really, the check to see if the certificate has been revoked) can be enabled on the client side and has the following inefficiencies:

- OCSP responder performance bottlenecks
- Performance degradation based on multiple passes
- Additional performance degradation if OCSP checking is performed client side
- False **fails** when browsers do not connect to an OCSP responder
- Susceptibility of denial of service attacks on OCSP responders

The new OCSP stapling for TLS includes the following system property changes for the Java 9 platform:

- `jdk.tls.client.enableStatusRequestExtension`:
    - Default setting: true
    - Enables `status_request` extension
    - Enables `status_request_v2` extension
    - Enables processing `CertificateStatus` messages from server
- `jdk.tls.server.enableStatusRequestExtension`:
    - Default setting: false
    - Enables OCSP stapling support server-side
- `jdk.tls.stapling.responseTimeout`:
    - Default setting: 5000 milliseconds
    - Controls maximum time allocated by server to obtain OCSP responses
- `jdk.tls.stapling.cacheSize`:
    - Default setting: 256
    - Controls maximum number of cache entries
    - Can set maximum to zero eliminates ceiling

- `jdk.tls.stapling.cacheLifetime`:
    - Default setting: 3600 seconds (1 hour)
    - Controls maximum lifetime of a cached response
    - Can set value to zero in order to disable cache lifetime
- `jdk.tls.stapling.responderURI`:
    - Default setting: none
    - Can set a default URI for certificates without the **Authority Info Access (AIA)** extension
    - Does not override the AIA extension unless `jdk.tls.stapling.Override` property is set
- `jdk.tls.stapling.respoderOverride`:
    - Default setting: false
    - Allows a `jdk.tls.stapling.responderURI` provided property to override AIA extension values
- `jdk.tls.stapling.ignoreExtensions`:
    - Default setting: false
    - Disables OCSP extension forwarding as specified in `status_request` or `status_request_v2` TLS extensions.

The `status_request` and `status_request_v2` TLS hello extensions are now supported by both client and server-side Java implementations.

DRBG-based SecureRandom implementations

Prior to Java 9, the JDK had two approaches to generating secure random numbers. One method, written in Java, used SHA1-based random number generation and was not terribly strong. The other method was platform-dependent and used preconfigured libraries.

Deterministic Random Bit Generator (DRBG) is a method for generating random numbers. It has been approved by the **National Institute of Standards and Technology (NIST)**, a branch of the U.S. Department of Commerce. DRBG methodologies include modern and stronger algorithms for generating secure random numbers.

Java Enhancement Proposal 273, **DRBG-Based SecureRandom Implementations** aimed to implement three specific DRBG mechanisms. These mechanisms are listed as follows:

- Hash_DRBG
- HMAC_DRBG
- CTR_DRBG

> You can learn specifics about each of the DRBG mechanisms at http://nvlpubs.nist.gov/nistpubs/SpecialPublications/NIST.SP.800-90Ar1.pdf

Here are the three new APIs:

- SecureRandom: New methods allowing the configuration of SecureRandom objects with the below listed configurable properties:
    - seeding
    - reseeding
    - random-bit-generation
- SecureRandomSpi: new methods to implement the SecureRandom methods
- SecureRandomParameter: new interface so input can be passed to the new SecureRandom methods

Summary

In this chapter, we looked at several small, but significant changes to the JDK that involve security. The featured security enhancements that are part of the Java 9 platform provide developers with the distinct ability to write and maintain applications that implement security. Specifically, we covered DTLS, keystores, improving security application performance, the TLS application-layer protocol negotiation extension, leveraging CPU instructions for GHASH and RSA, OCSP stapling for TLS, and DRBG-based SecureRandom implementations.

In the next chapter we will explore the new command-line flags used in Java 9 as well as changes to various command-line tools. Our coverage will include managing the Java JVM run-time and compiler using the new command-line options and flags.

Command Line Flags

14

In the previous chapter, we looked at several security changes to the JDK. Java 9's security enhancements provide developers with the ability to write and maintain applications that implement security. Specifically, we covered datagram transport layer security, Keystores, improving security application performance, the TLS application-layer protocol negotiation extension, leveraging CPU instructions for GHASH and RSA, OCSP stapling for TLS, and DRBG-based `SecureRandom` implementations.

In this chapter, we will explore several changes to the Java 9 platform with the common theme of command-line flags. Specifically, we will cover the following concepts:

- Unified JVM logging
- Compiler control
- Diagnostic commands
- Heap profiling agent
- Removing your JHAT
- Command-line flag argument validation
- Compiling for older platform versions

Unified JVM Logging [JEP 158]

Creating a unified logging schema for the JVM was the central goal of JEP-158. Here is a comprehensive list of the goals of the JEP:

- Create a JVM-wide set of command-line options for all logging operations
- Use categorized tags for logging
- Permit messages to have multiple tags, also referred to as tag sets

- Provide six levels of logging:
    - Error
    - Warning
    - Information
    - Debug
    - Trace
    - Develop
- Select which messages are logged based on levels
- Optionally direct logging to the console or a file
    - Print one line at a time and do not support interleaving within the same line
- Permit output of multiple line logs (non-interleaved)
- Format all logging messages so that they are easily human-read
- Add decorations such as uptime, level, and tags
- Like levels, select which messages are logged based on decorations
- Convert pre-Java 9 `tty>print` logging to use unified logging as the output
- Permit dynamic message configuration using `jcmd` and `MBeans`
- Permit the ability to enable and disable individual log messages
- Add ability to determine the order in which decorations are printed

The unified logging changes to the JVM can be grouped into the five categories listed here:

- Command-line options
- Decorations
- Levels
- Output
- Tags

Let's briefly look at each of these categories.

Command-line options

The new command-line option, `-Xlog`, was added to the logging framework in Java 9. This command-line option has an extensive array of parameters and possibilities. The basic syntax is simply `-Xlog` followed by an option. Here is the formal basic syntax:

```
-Xlog[:option]
```

Here is a basic example with the `all` option:

```
-Xlog:all
```

Here is the extensive command-line syntax used to configure the new unified logging:

```
-Xlog[:option]

option              := [<what>][:[<output>][:[<decorators>][:<output-
options>]]]
                        'help'
                        'disable'

what                := <selector>[,...]

selector            := <tag-set>[*][=<level>]

tag-set             := <tag>[+..]
                        'all'

tag                 := name of tag

level               := trace
                        debug
                        info
                        warning
                        error

output              := 'stderr'
                        'stdout'
                        [file=]<filename>

decorators          := <decorator>[,...]
                        'none'

decorator           := time
                        uptime
                        timemillis
                        uptimemillis
                        timenanos
                        uptimenanos
                        pid
                        tid
                        level
                        tags

output-options      := <output_option>[,...]
```

```
output-option   := filecount=<file count>
                   filesize=<file size in kb>
                   parameter=value
```

The following `-Xlog` examples are followed by a description:

`-Xlog:all`

In the preceding example, we are telling the JVM to take the following actions:

- Log all messages
- Use the `info` level
- Provide output to `stdout`

> With this example, all `warning` messages will still be output to `stderr`.

The next example, shown here, logs messages at the `debug` level:

`-Xlog:gc+rt*=debug`

In the preceding example, we are telling the JVM to take the following actions:

- Log all messages tagged with, at a minimum, the `gc` and `rt` tags
- Use the `debug` level
- Provide output to `stdout`

The next example pushes the output to an external file:

`-Xlog:disable - Xlog:rt=debug:rtdebug.txt`

In the preceding example, we are telling the JVM to take the following actions:

- Disable all messages except those tagged with `rt` tags
- Use the `debug` level
- Provide output to a file named `rtdebug.txt`

Decorations

In the context of Java 9's logging framework, decorations are metadata about the log message. Here is the alphabetic list of decorations that are available:

- **level**: The level associated with the logged message
- **pid**: PID = Processor IDentifier
- **tags**: The tag-set associated with the logged message
- **tid**: TID = Thread IDentifier
- **time**: Refers to current date and time using ISO-8601 format
- **timemillis**: Current time in milliseconds
- **timenanos**: Current time in nanoseconds
- **uptime**: Time, in seconds and milliseconds, since the JVM started
- **uptimemillis**: Time, in milliseconds, since the JVM started
- **uptimenanos**: Time, in nanoseconds, since the JVM started

Decorations can be surpassed or included in unified logging output. Regardless of which decorations are used, they will appear in the output in the following order:

1. time
2. uptime
3. timemillis
4. uptimemillis
5. timenanos
6. uptimenanos
7. pid
8. tid
9. level
10. tags

Levels

Logged messages are individually associated with a verbosity level. As previously listed, the levels are **error**, **warning**, **information**, **debug**, **trace**, and **develop**. The following chart shows how the levels have an increasing level of verbosity in respect to how much information is logged. The **develop** level is for development purposes only and is not available in on-product application builds:

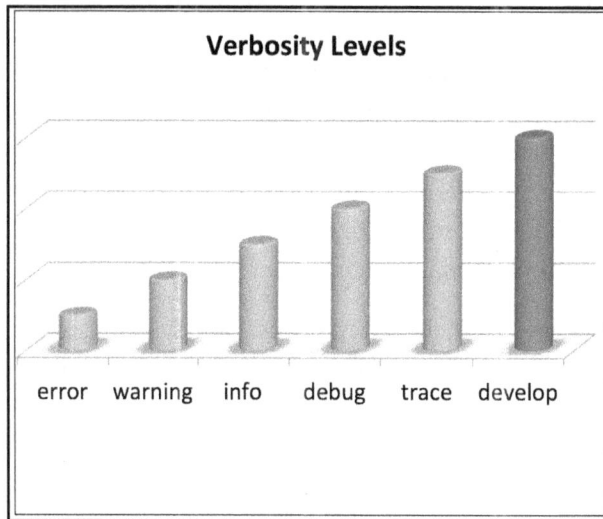

Verbosity Levels

error warning info debug trace develop

Output

The Java 9 logging framework supports three types of output with examples of direct use with the -Xlog command-line syntax:

In the following example, we provide output to stderr:

```
-Xlog:all=warning:stderr:none
```

The following example provides output to stdout:

```
-Xlog:all=warning:stdout:none
```

The following example writes the output to a text file:

```
-Xlog:all=warning:file=logmessages.txt:none
```

Tags

The new logging framework consists of a set of tags identified in the JVM. These tags can be changed in source code if needed. The tags should be self-identifying, such as gc for garbage collection.

When more than one tag is grouped together, they form a tag-set. When we add our own tags via source code, each tag should be associated with a tag-set. This will help ensure the tags stay organized and easily human-readable.

Compiler control [JEP 165]

Controlling Java Virtual Machine compilers might seem like an unnecessary task, but for many developers, this is an important aspect of testing. Java Enhancement Proposal 165 detailed a plan to implement runtime management of JVM compilers. This is accomplished with method-dependent compiler flags.

In this section, we will start with a look at JVM compilation modes, then look at the compiler that can be controlled using the Java 9 platform.

Compilation modes

The changes in the Java 9 platform include granular control of both the c1 and c2 JVM compliers. As you can see in the following illustration, the Java HotSpot JVM has two **Just-in-Time (JIT)** compilation modes--**c1** and **c2**:

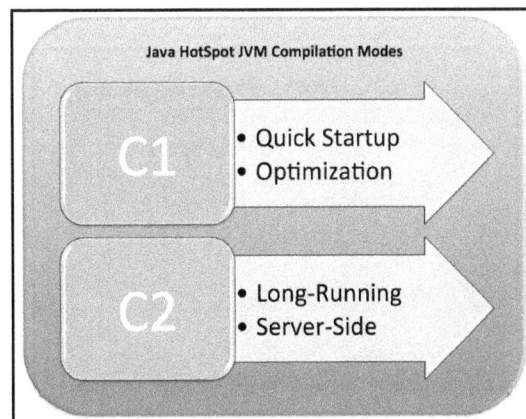

The **C1** and **C2** compilation modes use different compilation techniques and, if used on the same code base, can produce different sets of machine code.

C1 compilation mode

The C1 compilation mode inside Java HotSpot VM is typically used for applications that have the following characteristics:

- Quick startup
- Increased optimization
- Client-side

C2 compilation mode

The second compilation mode, C2, is used by applications with the following listed characteristics:

- Long runtimes
- Server-side

Tiered compilation

Tiered compilation allows us to use both **c1** and **c2** compilation modes. Starting with Java 8, tiered compilation is the default process. As illustrated here, the **c1** mode is used at startup to help provide greater optimization. Then, once the app has sufficiently warmed up, the **c2** mode is employed:

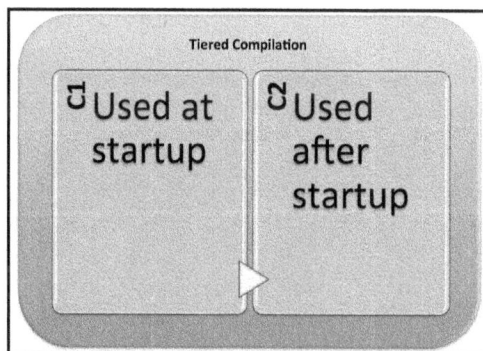

Compiler control in Java 9

Java 9 comes with the promise of the ability to have finite control over JVM compilers and to make changes at runtime. These additional abilities do not degrade performance. This permits greater fidelity of testing and testing optimization as we can run small compiler tests without having to relaunch the entire JVM.

To control compiler operations, we need to create a directives file. These files contain compiler directives which consist of a set of options with values. Directive files essentially use a subset of JSON:

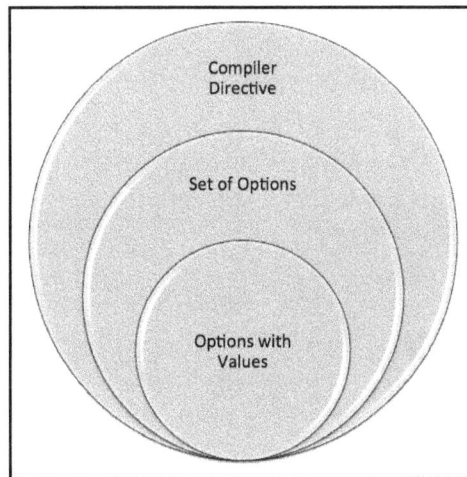

The **JavaScript Object Notation** (**JSON**) format is used for data-interchange. The directive files have the following formatting differences from JSON:

- `int` and `doubles` are the only supported number formats
- Double forward slash (`//`) can be used for comment lines
- Trailing commas (`,`) can be used in arrays and objects
- Escape characters are not supported
- Option names are formatted as strings and do not have to be quoted

> You can learn more about JSON at `http://www.json.org`.

We can add our directive file using the following syntax at the command line:

```
-XX:CompilerDirectivesFile=<file>
```

Here is a shell example of a directives file:

```
[   // Open square bracket marks the start of the directives file

{ // Open curly brace marks the start of a directive block

   // A directives block that applies specifically to the C1 mode
   c1: {
        // directives go here
      },
   // A directives block that applies specifically to the C2 mode
   c2: {
        // directives go here
      },

   // Here we can put a directives that do not apply to
   // a specific compiler mode

},

{   // can have multiple directive blocks

   c1: {
        // directives go here
      }

   c2: {
        // directives go here
      }
}

] // Close square bracket marks the start of the directives file
```

Diagnostic commands [JEP 228]

The Java Enhancement Proposal 228, **Add More Diagnostic Commands**, defined seven additional diagnostic commands to enhance the ability to diagnose the JDK and the JVM. The new diagnostic commands are detailed here.

The print_codegenlist command prints methods that are currently queued for compilation. Since c1 and c2 compilation modes are on separate queues, this command would need to be issued to a specific queue.

The dump_codelist diagnostic command will print the following listed information for the compiled methods:

- Full signature
- Address range
- State
    - Alive
    - Nonentrant
    - Zombie

In addition, the dump_codelist diagnostic command allows the output to be directed to stdout or to a specified file. Output can be in XML form or standard text.

The print_codeblocks command allows us to print:

- Code cache size
- Code cache list
- List of blocks in the code cache
- Addresses for code blocks

Th datadump_request diagnostic command sends a dump request to the **Java Virtual Machine Tool Interface (JVMTI)**. This replaces the **Java Virtual Machine Debug Interface (JVMDI)** and the **Java Virtual Machine Profiling Interface (JVMPI)** interfaces.

With the set_vmflag command, we can set a command-line flag or option in the JVM or the libraries.

Th print_class_summary diagnostic command prints a list of all loaded classes as well as the structure of their inheritance.

The print_utf8pool command prints all UTF-8 string constants.

Heap profiling agent [JEP 240]

Java Enhancement Proposal 240 is titled *Remove the JVM TI hprof Agent*. Here are the key terms associated with this JEP and referenced in the title that might be new to you:

- **Tool Interface (TI)**: This is a native programming interface that allows tools to control the execution of applications that are being run inside the Java Virtual Machine. The interface also permits state inquiries. The full nomenclature for this tool is the Java Virtual Machine Tool Interface, or JVM TI.
- **Heap Profiling (HPROF)**: This is an internal JDK tool used for profiling a JVM's use of CPUs and the heap. The most common exposure developers have to hprof is the file that is generated when following a crash. The generated file contains a heap dump.

The Java 9 JDK does not contain the hprof agent. It was removed largely because there are superior alternatives available. Here is a table of the related functionality:

HPROF Functionality	Alternative
Allocation Profiler (heap=sites)	Java VisualVM
CPU Profiler (cpu=samples) (cpu=times)	Java VisualVM Java Flight Recorder
Heap Dumps (heap=dump)	Internal JVM functionality: • GC.heap_dump(icmd <pid> GC.heap_dump) • jmap -dump

Interestingly, when HPROF was originally created, it was not intended to be used in production. In fact, it was only meant to test code for the JVM Tool Interface. So, with the advent of the Java 9 platform, the HPROF library (libhprof.so) will no longer be part of the JDK.

Removing your JHAT [JEP 241]

The **Java Heap Analysis Tool** (**JHAT**) is used to parse Java heap dump files. The syntax for this heap dump file parsing tool is as follows:

```
jhat
     [-stack <bool>]
     [-refs <bool>]
     [-port <port>]
     [-baseline <file>]
     [-debug <int>]
     [-version]
     [-h|-help]
     <file>
```

Here is a quick look at the options associated with the JHAT command:

Option	Description	Default
-J<flag>	This passes <flag> to the runtime system.	N/A
-stack<bool>	Toggles tracking of object allocation call stack.	true
-refs<bool>	Toggles tracking of references to objects.	true
-port<port>	Indicates the port for the JHAT HTTP server.	7000
-exclude<exclude-filename>	Exclude indicated file from reachable objects query.	N/A
-baseline<filename>	Specifies the baseline heap dump for use in comparisons.	N/A
-debug<int>	Sets verbosity of output.	N/A
-version	Simply outputs the JHAT release number.	N/A
-h -help	Provides help text.	N/A

JHAT has been part of the Java platform since JDK-6 in an experimental form. It was not supported and has been deemed to be outdated. Starting with Java 9, this tool will no longer be part of the JDK.

JVM command-line flag argument validation [JEP 245]

In this chapter, you have gained exposure to much of the command-line flag usage with the Java 9 platform. Java Enhancement Proposal 245, titled *Validate JVM Command-Line Flag Arguments*, was created to ensure all JVM command-line flags with arguments are validated. The primary goals of this effort were:

- Avoid JVM crashes
- Provide error messages to inform of invalid flag arguments

As you can see from the following graphic, there was no attempt to auto-correct the flag argument errors; rather, just to identify the errors and prevent the JVM from crashing:

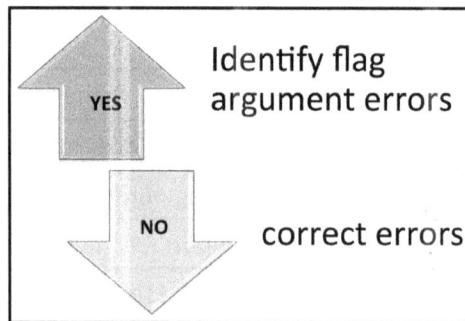

A sample error message is provided here and indicates that the flag argument was out of range. This error would be displayed during the flag argument range check performed during the JVM's initialization:

```
exampleFlag UnguardOnExecutionViolation = 4 is outside the allowed range [
0 . . . 3]
```

Here are some specifics regarding this change to the Java platform:

- Expand on the current `globals.hpp` source file to ensure complete flag default values and permissible ranges are documented
- Define a framework to support adding new JVM command-line flags in the future:
    - This will include value ranges and value sets
    - This will ensure the validity checking will apply to all newly added command-line flags
- Modify macro tables:
    - Add min/max for optional range
    - Add constraint entries for the following:
        - Ensure constraint checks are performed each time a flag changes
        - All manageable flags will continue to be checked while the JVM is running

Compile for older platform versions [JEP 247]

The Java Compiler, `javac`, has been updated for Java 9 to ensure it can be used to compile Java programs to run on user-selected older versions of the Java platform. This was the focus of Java Enhancement Proposal 247, **Compile for Older Platform Versions**.

As you can see in the following screenshot, `javac` has several options including `-source` and `-target`. The `javac` presented in the following screenshot is from Java 8:

```
● ◎ ●                           ⬆ edljr — -bash — 125×37

Edwards-iMac:~ edljr$ javac -help
Usage: javac <options> <source files>
where possible options include:
  -g                         Generate all debugging info
  -g:none                    Generate no debugging info
  -g:{lines,vars,source}     Generate only some debugging info
  -nowarn                    Generate no warnings
  -verbose                   Output messages about what the compiler is doing
  -deprecation               Output source locations where deprecated APIs are used
  -classpath <path>          Specify where to find user class files and annotation processors
  -cp <path>                 Specify where to find user class files and annotation processors
  -sourcepath <path>         Specify where to find input source files
  -bootclasspath <path>      Override location of bootstrap class files
  -extdirs <dirs>            Override location of installed extensions
  -endorseddirs <dirs>       Override location of endorsed standards path
  -proc:{none,only}          Control whether annotation processing and/or compilation is done.
  -processor <class1>[,<class2>,<class3>...] Names of the annotation processors to run; bypasses default discovery process
  -processorpath <path>      Specify where to find annotation processors
  -parameters                Generate metadata for reflection on method parameters
  -d <directory>             Specify where to place generated class files
  -s <directory>             Specify where to place generated source files
  -h <directory>             Specify where to place generated native header files
  -implicit:{none,class}     Specify whether or not to generate class files for implicitly referenced files
  -encoding <encoding>       Specify character encoding used by source files
  -source <release>          Provide source compatibility with specified release
  -target <release>          Generate class files for specific VM version
  -profile <profile>         Check that API used is available in the specified profile
  -version                   Version information
  -help                      Print a synopsis of standard options
  -Akey[=value]              Options to pass to annotation processors
  -X                         Print a synopsis of nonstandard options
  -J<flag>                   Pass <flag> directly to the runtime system
  -Werror                    Terminate compilation if warnings occur
  @<filename>                Read options and filenames from file

Edwards-iMac:~ edljr$ ▊
```

The `-source` option is used to dictate the Java version accepted by the compiler. The `-target` option informs which version of class files `javac` will produce. By default, `javac` generates class files in the most recent java version and that of the platform APIs. This can cause a problem when the compiled application uses APIs that are only available in the most recent platform version. This would render the application ineligible to run on older platform versions, despite what is dictated with the `-source` and `-target` options.

To address the aforementioned problem, a new command-line option is introduced with the Java 9 platform. This option is the `--release` option and, when used, will automatically configure javac to generate class files that link against a specific platform version. The following screenshot shows the `javac` options with the Java 9 platform. As you can see, the new `--release` option is included:

```
Command Prompt                                                    —    □    ×
C:\Users\elavi>javac -help
Usage: javac <options> <source files>
where possible options include:
  @<filename>                  Read options and filenames from file
  -Akey[=value]                Options to pass to annotation processors
  --add-modules <module>(,<module>)*
        Root modules to resolve in addition to the initial modules, or all modules
        on the module path if <module> is ALL-MODULE-PATH.
  --boot-class-path <path>, -bootclasspath <path>
        Override location of bootstrap class files
  --class-path <path>, -classpath <path>, -cp <path>
        Specify where to find user class files and annotation processors
  -d <directory>               Specify where to place generated class files
  -deprecation
        Output source locations where deprecated APIs are used
  -encoding <encoding>         Specify character encoding used by source files
  -endorseddirs <dirs>         Override location of endorsed standards path
  -extdirs <dirs>              Override location of installed extensions
  -g                           Generate all debugging info
  -g:{lines,vars,source}       Generate only some debugging info
  -g:none                      Generate no debugging info
  -h <directory>
        Specify where to place generated native header files
  --help, -help                Print this help message
  --help-extra, -X             Print help on extra options
  -implicit:{none,class}
        Specify whether or not to generate class files for implicitly referenced files
  -J<flag>                     Pass <flag> directly to the runtime system
  --limit-modules <module>(,<module>)*
        Limit the universe of observable modules
  --module <module-name>, -m <module-name>
        Compile only the specified module, check timestamps
  --module-path <path>, -p <path>
        Specify where to find application modules
  --module-source-path <module-source-path>
        Specify where to find input source files for multiple modules
  --module-version <version>
        Specify version of modules that are being compiled
  -nowarn                      Generate no warnings
  -parameters
        Generate metadata for reflection on method parameters
  -proc:{none,only}
        Control whether annotation processing and/or compilation is done.
  -processor <class1>[,<class2>,<class3>...]
        Names of the annotation processors to run; bypasses default discovery process
  --processor-module-path <path>
        Specify a module path where to find annotation processors
  --processor-path <path>, -processorpath <path>
        Specify where to find annotation processors
  -profile <profile>
        Check that API used is available in the specified profile
  --release <release>
        Compile for a specific VM version. Supported targets: 6, 7, 8, 9
  -s <directory>               Specify where to place generated source files
  -source <release>
        Provide source compatibility with specified release
  --source-path <path>, -sourcepath <path>
        Specify where to find input source files
  --system <jdk>|none          Override location of system modules
  -target <release>            Generate class files for specific VM version
  --upgrade-module-path <path>
        Override location of upgradeable modules
  -verbose                     Output messages about what the compiler is doing
  --version, -version          Version information
  -Werror                      Terminate compilation if warnings occur

C:\Users\elavi>
```

Here is the syntax for the new option:

```
javac --release <release> <source files>
```

Summary

In this chapter we explored several changes to the Java 9 platform with the common theme of command-line flags. Specifically, we covered unified JVM logging, compiler control, new diagnostic commands, removal of the HPROF heap profiling agent, the removal of the JHAT, command-line flag argument validation, and the ability to compile for older platform versions.

In the next chapter, we will focus on best practices with additional utilities provided with the Java 9 platform. These will include UTF-8, Unicode 7.0, Linux, and more.

Best Practices In Java 9

15

In the last chapter, we explored several changes regarding command-line flags in Java 9. Specifically, we covered unified JVM logging, compiler control, new diagnostic commands, removal of the HPROF heap profiling agent, the removal of the **Java Heap Analysis Tool** (**JHAT**), command-line flag argument validation, and the ability to compile for older platform versions.

In this chapter, we will focus on best practices with additional utilities provided with the Java 9 platform. Specifically, we will cover:

- Support for UTF-8
- Unicode 7.0.0
- Linux/AArch64 port
- Multi-resolution images
- Common Locale Data Repository

Support for UTF-8

Unicode Transformation Format-8 (**UTF-8**) is a character set that encapsulates all Unicode characters using one to four 8-bit bytes. It is the byte-oriented encoded form of Unicode. UTF-8 is and has been the predominant character set for encoding web pages since 2009. Here are some characteristics of UTF-8:

- Can encode all 1,112,064 Unicode code points
- Uses one to four 8-bit bytes

- Accounts for nearly 90% of all web pages
- Is backward compatible with ASCII
- Is reversible

The pervasive use of UTF-8 underscores the importance of ensuring the Java platform fully supports UTF-8. This mindset led to the Java Enhancement Proposal 226, **UTF-8 property resource bundles**. With Java 9 applications, we have the ability to specify property files that have UTF-8 encoding. The Java 9 platform includes changes to the `ResourceBundle` API to support UTF-8.

Let's take a look at the pre-Java 9 `ResourceBundle` class, followed by what changes were made to this class in the Java 9 platform.

The ResourceBundle class

The following class provides developers with the ability to isolate locale-specific resources from a resource bundle. This class significantly simplifies localization and translation:

```
public abstract class ResourceBundle extends Object
```

Creating resource bundles needs a purposeful approach. For example, let's imagine that we are creating a resource bundle that will support multiple languages for a business application. Our button labels, among other things, will be displayed differently depending on the current locale. So, for our example, we can create a resource bundle for our buttons. We can call it `buttonResources`. Then, for each locale, we can create a `buttonResource_<identifier>`. Here are some examples:

- `buttonResource_ja`: for Japanese
- `buttonResource_uk`: for UK English
- `buttonResource_it`: for Italian
- `buttonResource_lh`: for Lithuanian

We can use a resource bundle with the same name as the base name for our default bundle. So, `buttonResource` would contain our default bundle.

To obtain a locale-specific object, we make a call to the `getBundle` method. An example follows:

```
. . .

ResourceBundle = buttonResource =
```

```
ResourceBundle.getBundle("buttonResource", currentLocale);

. . .
```

In the next sections we will examine the ResourceBundle class by looking at its nested class, field and constructor, and included methods.

The nested class

There is one nested class associated with the ResourceBundle class, that is the ResourceBundle.Control class. It provides callback methods that are used when the ResourceBundle.getBundle method is used:

```
public static class ResourceBundle.Control extends Object
```

The ResourceBundle.Control class has the following fields:

- public static final List<String> FORMAT_CLASS
- public static final List<String> FORMAT_DEFAULT
- public static final List<String> FORMAT_PROPERTIES
- public static final long TTL_DONT_CACHE
- public static final long TTL_NO_EXPIRATION_CONTROL

The class has a single, empty constructor and the following methods:

- getCandidateLocales():

```
public List<Locale> getCandidateLocales(String baseName,
  Locale locale)
```

Component	Details
Throws	NullPointerException (if baseName or locale is null)
Parameters	baseName: a fully qualified class name locale: the desired locale
Returns	List of candidate locales

- getControl():

```
public static final ResourceBundle.Control getControl(
  List<String> formats)
```

Component	Details
Throws	IllegalArgumentException (if formats is unknown) NullPointerException (if formats is null)
Parameters	formats: These are the formats that will be returned by the ResourceBundle.Control.getFormats method
Returns	A ResourceBundle.Control that supports the formats specified

- getFallbackLocale():

```
public Locale getFallbackLocale(String baseName, Locale locale)
```

Component	Details
Throws	NullPointerException (if baseName or locale is null)
Parameters	baseName: a fully qualified class name locale: the desired locale that could not be found with the ResourceBundle.getBundle method
Returns	The fallback locale

- getFormats():

```
public List<String> getFormats(String baseName)
```

Component	Details
Throws	NullPointerException (if baseName is null)
Parameters	baseName: a fully qualified class name
Returns	A list of Strings with their formats so the resource bundles can be loaded

- `getNoFallbackControl():`

```
public static final ResourceBundle.Control
getNoFallbackControl(List<String> formats)
```

Component	Details
Throws	`IllegalArgumentException` (if `formats` is unknown) `NullPointerException` (if `formats` is null)
Parameters	`formats`: these are the formats that will be returned by the `ResourceBundle.Control.getFormats` method
Returns	A `ResourceBundle.Control` that supports the formats specified without a fallback locale.

- `getTimeToLive():`

```
public long getTimeToLive(String baseName, Locale locale)
```

Component	Details
Throws	`NullPointerException` (if `baseName` is null)
Parameters	`baseName`: a fully qualified class name `locale`: the desired locale
Returns	Zero or a positive millisecond that is offset from the cached time

- `needsReload():`

```
public boolean needsReload(String baseName, Locale locale,
  String format, ClassLoader loader, ResourceBundle bundle,
  long loadTime)
```

Component	Details
Throws	`NullPointerException` (if any of the following listed parameters are null): • `baseName` • `locale` • `format` • `loader` • `bundle`

Parameters	`baseName`: a fully qualified class name `locale`: the desired locale `format`: the resource bundle format `loader`: the `ClassLoader` that should be used to load the bundle `bundle`: the expired bundle `loadTime`: a time bundle was added to the cache
Returns	`true/false` to indicate if the expired bundle needs to be reloaded

- `newBundle()`:

```
public ResourceBundle newBundle(String baseName, Locale locale,
    String format, ClassLoader loader, boolean reload)
```

Component	Details
Throws	`ClassCastException` (if the loaded class cannot be cast to ResourceBundle) `ExceptionInInitializerError` (if initialization fails) `IllegalAccessException` (if the class or constructor is not accessible) `IllegalArgumentException` (if the format is unknown) `InstantiationException` (if the class instantiation fails) `IOException` (resource reading error) `NullPointerException` (if any of the following listed parameters are null): • `baseName` • `locale` • `format` • `loader` `SecurityException` (if access to new instances is denied)
Parameters	`baseName`: a fully qualified class name `locale`: the desired locale `format`: the resource bundle format `loader`: the `ClassLoader` that should be used to load the bundle `reload`: `true/false` flag indicating if the resource bundle has expired
Returns	Instance of the resource bundle

- `toBundleName():`

  ```
  public String toBundleName(String baseName, Locale locale)
  ```

Component	Details
Throws	`NullPointerException` (if `baseName` or `locale` is null)
Parameters	`baseName`: a fully qualified class name `locale`: the desired locale
Returns	The bundle name

- `toResourceName():`

  ```
  public final String toResourceName(String bundleName,
    String suffix)
  ```

Component	Details
Throws	`NullPointerException` (if `bundleName` or `suffix` is null)
Parameters	`bundleName`: the name of the bundle `suffix`: the suffix for the file name
Returns	The converted resource name

Fields and constructors

The `ResourceBundle` class has one field as described here:

```
protected Resourcebundle parent
```

The parent bundle is searched by the `getObject` method when a specified resource is not found.

The constructor for the ResourceBundle class is as shown here:

```
public ResourceBundle()
{
}
```

Methods

The `ResourceBundle` class has 18 methods, each described here:

- `clearCache():`

    public static final void clearCache()

Component	Details
Throws	None
Parameters	None
Returns	None

    public static final void clearCache(ClassLoader loader)

Component	Details
Throws	`NullPointerException` (if loader is null)
Parameters	`loader`: the class loader
Returns	None

- `containsKey():`

    public boolean containsKey(String key)

Component	Details
Throws	`NullPointerException` (if key is null)
Parameters	`key`: resource key
Returns	`true/false` depending on if the key is in the `ResourceBundle` or parent bundles

- `getBundle()`:

```
public static final ResourceBundle getBundle(String baseName)
```

Component	Details
Throws	`MissingResourceException` (if the resource bundle for the provided `baseName` is not found) `NullPointerException` (if `baseName` is null)
Parameters	`baseName`: fully qualified class name
Returns	Resource bundle based on the given `baseName` and the default locale

```
public static final ResourceBundle getBundle(String baseName,
    Resourcebundle.Control control)
```

Component	Details
Throws	`IllegalArgumentException` (if the passed control performs improperly) `MissingResourceException` (if the resource bundle for the provided `baseName` is not found) `NullPointerException` (if `baseName` is null)
Parameters	`baseName`: fully qualified class name `control`: the control provides information so the resource bundle can be loaded
Returns	Resource bundle based on the given `baseName` and the default locale

```
public static final ResourceBundle getBundle(String baseName,
    Locale locale)
```

Component	Details
Throws	`MissingResourceException` (if the resource bundle for the provided `baseName` is not found) `NullPointerException` (if `baseName` or `locale` is null)
Parameters	`baseName`: fully qualified class name `locale`: desired locale
Returns	Resource bundle based on the given `baseName` and `locale`

```
public static final ResourceBundle getBundle(String baseName,
    Locale targetLocale, Resourcebundle.Control control)
```

Component	Details
Throws	IllegalArgumentException (if the passed control performs improperly) MissingResourceException (if the resource bundle for the provided baseName is not found in any of the locales) NullPointerException (if baseName, control, or locale is null)
Parameters	baseName: fully qualified class name control: the control provides information so the resource bundle can be loaded targetLocale: desired locale
Returns	Resource bundle based on the given baseName and locale

```
public static final ResourceBundle getBundle(String baseName,
    Locale locale, ClassLoader loader)
```

Component	Details
Throws	MissingResourceException (if the resource bundle for the provided baseName is not found in any of the locales) NullPointerException (if baseName, loader, or locale is null)
Parameters	baseName: fully qualified class name locale: desired locale loader: class loader
Returns	Resource bundle based on the given baseName and locale

```
public static final ResourceBundle getBundle(String baseName,
    Locale targetLocale, ClassLoader loader,
    ResourceBundle.Control control)
```

Component	Details
Throws	IllegalArgumentException (if the passed control performs improperly) MissingResourceException (if the resource bundle for the provided baseName is not found in any of the locales) NullPointerException (if baseName, control, loader, or targetLocale is null)
Parameters	baseName: fully qualified class name control: the control providing information so the resource bundle can be loaded loader: class loader targetLocale: desired locale
Returns	Resource bundle based on the given baseName and locale

- getKeys():

```
public abstract Enumeration<String> getKeys()
```

Component	Details
Throws	None
Parameters	None
Returns	Enumeration of keys in the ResourceBundle and parent bundles

- getLocale():

```
public Locale getLocale()
```

Component	Details
Throws	None
Parameters	None
Returns	the locale of the current resource bundle

- `getObject()`:

  ```
  public final Object getObject(String key)
  ```

Component	Details
Throws	`MissingResourceException` (if the resource for the provided key is not found) `NullPointerException` (if key is null)
Parameters	key: this is the key for the desired object
Returns	The object for the key provided

- `getString()`:

  ```
  public final String getString(String key)
  ```

Component	Details
Throws	`ClassCastException` (if the found object is not a key) `MissingResourceException` (if the resource for the provided key is not found) `NullPointerException` (if key is null)
Parameters	key: this is the key for the desired `String`
Returns	The `String` for the key provided

- `getStringArray()`:

  ```
  public final String[] getStringArray(String key)
  ```

Component	Details
Throws	`ClassCastException` (if the found object is not a `String` array) `MissingResourceException` (if the resource for the provided key is not found) `NullPointerException` (if key is null)
Parameters	key: this is the key for the desired `String` array
Returns	The `String` array for the key provided

- handleGetObject():

```
protected abstract Object handleGetObject(String key)
```

Component	Details
Throws	NullPointerException (if key is null)
Parameters	key: key for the desired Object
Returns	The object for the given key

- handleKeySet():

```
protected Set<String> handleKeySet()
```

Component	Details
Throws	None
Parameters	None
Returns	Set of keys in ResourceBundle

- keySet():

```
public Set<String> keySet()
```

Component	Details
Throws	None
Parameters	None
Returns	Set of keys in ResourceBundle and its parent bundles

- setParent():

```
protected void setParent(ResourceBundle parent)
```

Component	Details
Throws	None
Parameters	parent: the parent bundle for the current bundle
Returns	None

Changes in Java 9

The properties file format, based on ISO-8859-1, was previously supported by the Java platform. That format does not easily support escape characters, although it does provide an appropriate escape mechanism. The use of ISO-8859-1 requires conversion between the text characters and their escaped form.

The Java 9 platform includes a modified `ResourceBundle` class with the default file encoding set to UTF-8 vice ISO-8859-1. This saves applications the time it takes to make the aforementioned escape mechanism conversions.

Unicode 7.0.0

Java Enhancement Proposal 227, titled Unicode 7.0, was created to indicate the need to update the appropriate APIs to support Unicode version 7.0. That version of Unicode was released on June 16, 2014. Previous to Java 9, Unicode version 6.2 was the latest version supported.

> You can learn more about **Unicode version 7.0.0** at the official specification page at: `http://unicode.org/versions/Unicode7.0.0/`.

At the time this book was published, the most recent Unicode standard was version 10.0.0, released on June 20, 2017. Interestingly, the Java 9 platform will support Unicode version 7.0.0, but not the more recent version 10.0.0 of the Unicode standard. In addition to the two Unicode specifications listed here, from version 7.0.0, will not be implemented by the Java 9 platform:

- **Unicode Technical Standard #10 (UTS #10)**
  - Unicode collation algorithm: details how to compare Unicode strings
- **Unicode Technical Standard #46 (UTS #46)**
  - **Unicode Internationalizing Domain Names for Applications (IDNA) Compatibility processing**: comprehensive mapping for text case and domain name variants

The core of the Java 9 platform changes, specific to Unicode 7.0.0 support, includes the following Java classes:

- `java.lang package`
  - Character
  - String
- `java.text.package`
  - Bidi
  - BreakIterator
  - Normalizer

Let's take a quick look at each of those classes to help solidify our comprehension of the broad impact that support for Unicode 7.0.0 has on the Java 9 platform.

The java.lang package

The `java.lang.package` provides fundamental classes used in nearly every Java application. In this section, we will look at the `Character` and `String` classes.

The `Character` class:

```
public final class Character extends Object implements
  Serializable, Comparable<Character>
```

This is one of the many core classes that has been around since the first version of Java. An object of the `Character` class consists of a single field of type `char`.

The `String` class:

```
public final class String extends Object implements
  Serializable, Comparable<String>, CharSequence
```

Strings, another core originating class, are immutable character strings.

Modifying the `Character` and `String` classes to support a newer version of Unicode, version 7.0 for Java 9, is an important step to help keep Java relevant as the premier programming language.

The java.text package

The `Bidi`, `BreakIterator`, and `Normalizer` classes are not as widely used as the `Character` and `String` classes. Here is a brief overview of those classes.

The `Bidi` class:

```
public final class Bidi extends Object
```

This class is used to implement Unicode's bidirectional algorithm. This is used to support Arabic or Hebrew.

> For specific information on the *Unicode Bidirectional Algorithm,* visit `http:/`
> `/unicode.org/reports/tr9/`.

The `BreakIterator` class:

```
public abstract class BreakIterator extends Object
  implements Cloneable
```

This class is used for finding text boundaries.

The `Normalizer` class:

```
public final class Normalizer extends Object
```

This method contains two methods:

- `isNormalized`: used to determine if `char` values of a given sequence are normalized
- `normalize`: normalizes a sequence of char values

Additional significance

As previously stated, JDK 8 supports Unicode 6.2. Version 6.3 was released on September 30, 2013 with the following listed highlights:

- Bidirectional behavior improvements
- Improved Unihan data
- Better support for Hebrew

Version 7.0.0, released on June 16, 2014, introduced the following changes:

- Added 2,834 characters
    - Increased support for Azerbaijan, Russian, and high German dialects
    - Pictographic symbols
    - Historic scripts for several countries and regions
- Updates to the Unicode bidirectional algorithm
- Nearly 3,000 new Cantonese pronunciation entries
- Major enhancements to the Indic script properties

The vast changes to Unicode with version 6.3 and 7.0.0 underscores the importance of the Java 9 platform supporting 7.0.0 as opposed to 6.2, as with Java 8.

The Linux/AArch64 port

Java Enhancement Proposal 237 (JEP 237) had a single goal of porting JDK 9 to Linux/AArch64. In order to understand what this means to us as Java 9 developers, let's talk a bit about hardware.

ARM is a British company that has been creating computing cores and architectures for over three decades. Their original name was **Acorn RISC Machine (ARM)**, with **RISC** standing for **Reduced Instruction Set Computing**. Somewhere along the way, they changed their name to **Advanced RISC Machine (ARM)**, and finally, to ARM Holdings or just ARM. They license their architectures to other companies. ARM reports that there have been over 100 billion ARM processors manufactured.

In late 2011, ARM came out with a new ARM architecture called ARMv8. This architecture included a 64-bit optional architecture called AArch64, which, as you would expect, came with a new instruction set. Here is an abbreviated list of AArch64 features:

- A64 instruction set:
  - 31 general purpose 64-bit registers
  - Dedicated zero or stack pointer registers
  - The ability to take 32-bit or 64-bit arguments
- Advanced SIMD (NEON) - enhanced:
  - 32x 128-bit registers
  - Supports double-precision floating points
  - AES encrypt/decrypt and SHA-1/SHA-2 hashing
- New exception system

Oracle did a great job of identifying this architecture as something that needs to be supported in the new Java 9 platform. The new AArch64 architecture is said to essentially be an entirely new design. JDK 9 has been successfully ported to Linux/AArch64 with the following implementations:

- Template interpreter
- C1 JIT compiler
- C2 JIT compiler

> For information about the C1 and C2 JIT compilers, refer to `Chapter 14`, *Command Line Flags*.

Multi-resolution Images

The purpose of Java Enhancement Proposal 251 was to create a new API that supports multi-resolution images. Specifically, to allow a multi-resolution image to encapsulate several resolution variants of the same image. This new API will be located in the `java.awt.image` package. The following diagram shows how multi-resolution can encapsulate a set of images, with different resolutions, into a single image:

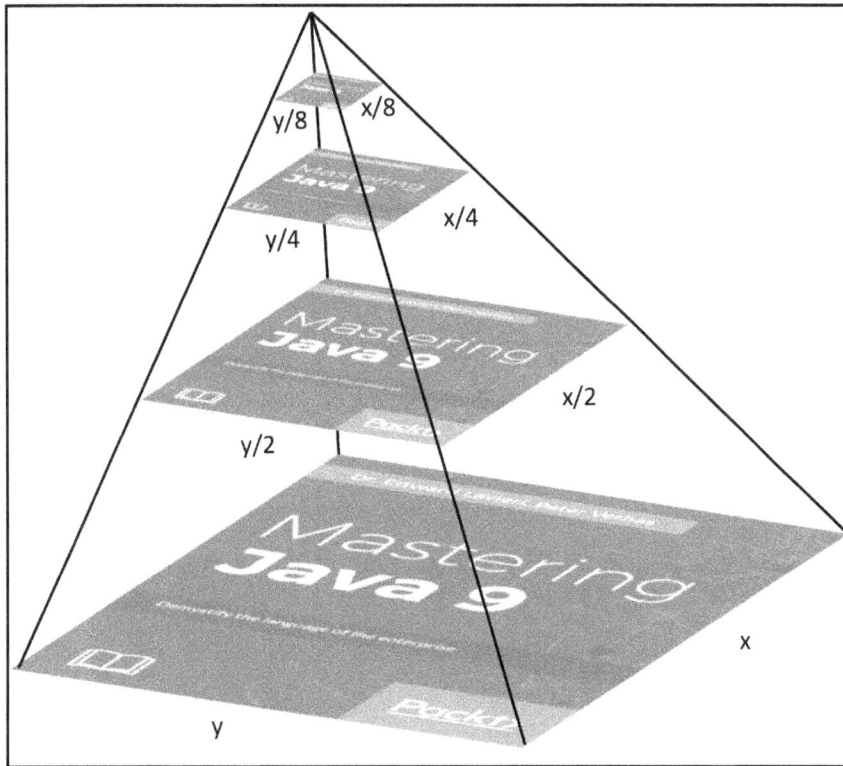

This new API will give developers the ability to retrieve all image variants or retrieve a resolution-specific image. This is a powerful set of capabilities. The `java.awt.Graphics` class will be used to retrieve the desired variant from the multi-resolution image.

Here is a quick look at the API:

```
package java.awt.image;

public interface MultiResolutionImage
{
  Image getResolutionVariant(float destinationImageWidth,
   float destinationImageHeight);

  public List <Image> getResolutionVariants();
}
```

As you can see in the preceding code example, the API contains the `getResolutionVariant` and `getResolutionVariants` that return an `Image` and a list of images respectively. Since `MultiResolutionImage` is an interface, we will need an abstract class to implement it.

Common Locale Data Repository (CLDR)

Java Enhancement Proposal 252, uses CLDR Locale Data by default, implements the decision to use locale data from the Unicode Common Locale Data Repository by default. CLDR is a key component of many software applications that supports multiple languages. It is touted as the largest locale data repository and is used by a plethora of large software providers to include Apple, Google, IBM, and Microsoft. The widespread use of CLDR has made it the unofficial industry standard repository for locale data. Making this the default repository in the Java 9 platform further solidifies it as the software industry standard.

Interestingly, CLDR was already part of JDK 8, but was not the default library. In Java 8, we had to enable CLDR by setting a system property as shown here:

```
java.locale.providers=JRE,CLDR
```

So, in Java 9, we no longer have to enable CLDR as it will be the default repository.

There are additional locale data repositories in the Java 9 platform. They are listed here in their default lookup order:

1. **Common Locale Data Repository (CLDR)**.
2. COMPAT - previously JRE.
3. **Service Provider Interface (SPI)**.

To change the lookup order, we can change the `java.locale.providers` setting as illustrated:

```
java.locale.providers=SPI,COMPAT,CLDR
```

In the preceding example, `SPI` would be first, followed by `COMPAT`, and then `CLDR`.

Summary

In this chapter, we focused on best practices with additional utilities provided by the Java 9 platform. Specifically, we covered UTF-8 property files, Unicode 7.0.0, Linux/AArch64 port, multi-resolution images, and Common Locale Data Repository.

In the next chapter, our final chapter, we will look at the future direction for the Java platform by looking ahead to what we can expect in Java 10.

16
Future Directions

In the last chapter, we focused on best practices with some exciting utilities provided by the Java 9 platform. Specifically, we covered UTF-8 Property Files, Unicode 7.0.0, Linux/AArch64 port, multi-resolution images, and common locale data repository.

This chapter provides an overview of the future development of the Java platform, beyond Java 9. We will look at what is planned for Java 10 and what further changes we are likely to see in the future. Each potential change to the Java platform will be characterized as targeted, submitted, or drafted. Targeted refers to changes that have been earmarked for Java 10. Submitted refers to a change that has been submitted but does not target a specific version of the Java platform. Changes that are drafted are still on the drawing board and are not ready to be submitted or designated as targeted.

Specifically, this chapter covers future changes to the Java platform grouped in the following categories:

- JDK changes
- Java Compiler
- Java Virtual Machine
- JavaX
- Special projects

Future Changes to the JDK

The Java Development Kit is at core of the Java platform and is continually being updated with new capabilities and efficiencies realized with each release. Looking beyond Java 9, we see a multitude of possible changes to the JDK. Many of these changes will be implemented in Java 10 and others might be saved for later releases.

The changes to the JDK in Java 10 and beyond are presented in the following proposal categories:

- Targeted for Java 10
- Submitted Proposals
- Drafted Proposals

JDK changes targeted for Java 10

At the time of this book's publication, the following listed **Java Development Kit (JDK)**-related changes were slated for inclusion in the Java 10 platform:

- Repository consolidation
- Native-Header Tool Removal

Repository consolidation

The Java 9 platform consists of eight distinct repositories as depicted in the following diagram. In Java 10, we should see all of these repositories combined into a single repository:

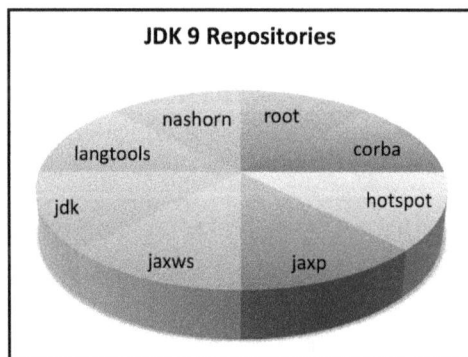

Repository consolidation should help streamline development. Moreover, it should increase the ease of maintaining and updating the Java platform.

> You can get an early look at this repository at `http://hg.openjdk.java.net/jdk10/consol-proto/`.

Native-header tool removal

The javah tool is used to generate C header files and C source files from Java classes. C programs can reference the generated header files and source files.

Here is a look at the life and death of the javah tool:

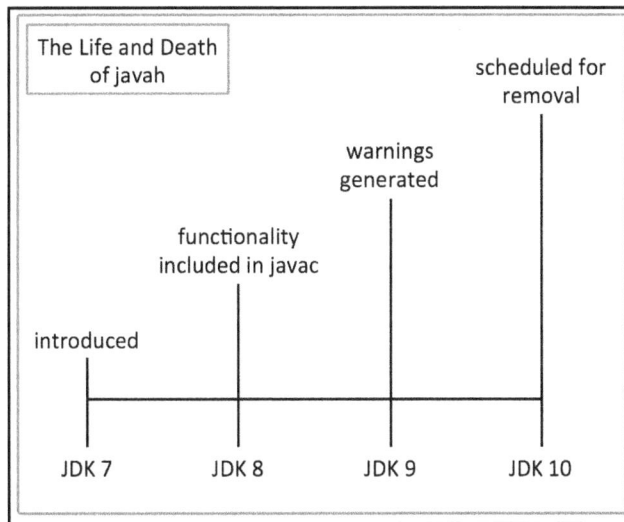

As illustrated earlier, the javah tool was introduced with Java 7 and its functionality was included in the javac that came with JDK8. This functionality was reportedly superior compared to that of the original tool. In JDK 9, developers received warnings each time the javah tool was used, informing them of its pending removal from the JDK. The tool is slated for removal in JDK 10.

JDK-related submitted proposals

The following Java Enhancement Proposals have been submitted, but have not yet been committed for delivery as part of the Java 10 platform. Oracle has set a two-year release plan, so it is safe to assume that, many if not all, of the proposals listed in this section and beyond have a chance of being part of the Java 10 platform:

- Parallelize the Full GC Phase in CMS
- REST APIs for JMX
- Support Heap Allocation

Parallelize the Full GC Phase in CMS

In `Chapter 7`, *Leveraging the New Default G1 Garbage Collector*, we reviewed the changes to the **Concurrent Mark Sweep** (**CMS**) garbage collector. CMS garbage collection involves scanning heap memory, marking objects for removal and then making a sweep to actually remove those objects. The CMS method of garbage collection is essentially an upgraded "Mark and Sweep" method; which you can refer to `Chapter 7`, *Leveraging the New Default G1 Garbage Collector*, for additional information.

The current downside to CMS garbage collection is that the serial mark and sweep is implemented using a single thread. This results in unwanted pause times. Currently, full garbage collection takes place in four phases:

- **Marking phase**: Mark objects for collection
- **Forwarding phase**: Determine where live objects will be relocated
- **Adjust pointer phase**: Updates points based on new locations of live objects
- **Compaction phase**: Moves objects to designated locations

The future plan for CMS is to implement the mark and sweep so they can be performed in parallel. The change is not to the garbage collection algorithm. Instead, each of the above listed phases will be parallelized. This will result in greater efficiencies for CMS garbage collection and hopefully eliminate, or significantly reduce, pause times.

REST APIs for JMX

Representational State Transfer (**REST**), RESTful programming, and RESTful API use a client/server cacheable communications protocol, usually HTTP. REST is a common software architecture for developing networked applications.

One of the future changes to the Java platform is to provide RESTful web interfaces to MBeans.

Managed Bean (**MBean**) is an object in Java that represents a resource to be managed. These resources could include a specific hardware device, an application, a service, or other component.

The interfaces will permit MBeans to use the following HTTP methods:

- CONNECT
- DELETE
- GET
- HEAD
- OPTIONS
- POST
- PUT
- TRACE

MBeans are managed using **Java Management Extensions** (**JMX**). The JMX architecture has three levels, as depicted in the following diagram:

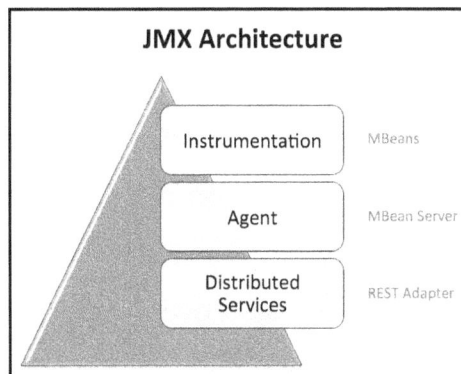

As you can see, the REST adapter is part of the **Distributed Services** level. That level contains both connectors and adapters. The connectors provide mirroring of agent level interfaces to remote clients. The adapters, on the other hand, convert the interfaces using a different protocol. The future change will be to transform the services at the **Agent** level to REST APIs.

Support heap allocation

A proposed future change is to allow developers to designate alternate memory devices for the Java heap. Specifically, the proposal is to permit developers to designate non-DRAM memory for the Java heap. This change takes advantage of the decreasing cost of memory and memory devices.

Implementation is likely to use an `AllocateHeapAt` flag.

JDK-related drafted proposals

This section covers several JDK-related proposals that, at the time of this book's publication, were in the draft phase. That suggests they might not be fully analyzed or might even be cancelled. That being said, it is likely that each of these will move from drafted, to submitted, and then to targeted for the Java 10 platform.

Draft proposals covered in this section are as follows:

- Finalization promptness
- Java memory model
- Foreign function interface
- Isolated methods
- Reduce metaspace waste
- Improve IPv6 support
- Unboxed argument lists for method handles
- Enhanced MandelblotSet Demo Using Value Types
- Efficient Array Comparison Intrinsics

Finalization promptness

The Java language includes finalization to clean up objects that were unreachable by garbage collection. The proposed change is to make this process quicker and will require modifications to the following:

- `ReferenceHandleThread`
- `FinalizerThread`
- `java.lang.ref.Reference`

Additional changes related to increasing the promptness of finalization includes the creation of a new API. The following graphic details how the API will be able to implement GC and runtime actions, and then inform that finalization needs to take place. This certainly should result in faster processing:

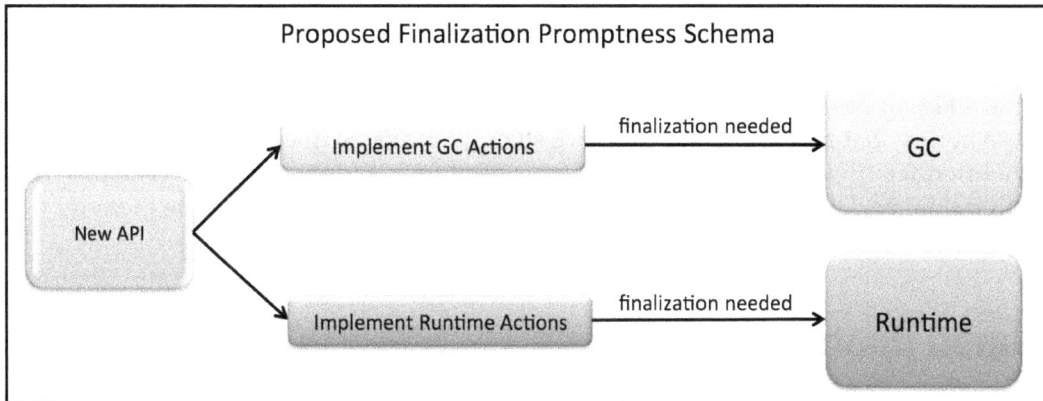

Java memory model

There is a continuing effort to keep **Java's memory model** (**JMM**) updated. Current efforts are focused on several areas to include:

- Shared memory concurrency
- JVM concurrency support
- JDK components
- Tools

Expected results of JMM-related engineering efforts are as follows:

- Improved formalization
- JVM voverage
- Extended scope
- C11/C++11 compatibility
- Implementation guidance
- Testing support
- Tool support

Foreign Function Interfaces

Foreign Function Interfaces (**FFI**) are software APIs that permits programs to call methods/functions from a program written in a different language. In an upcoming version of the JDK, we are apt to see an FFI that allows developers to call upon shared libraries and operating-system kernels directly from java methods. The proposed FFI will reportedly also enable developers to manage native memory blocks.

The new FFI will be similar to **Java Native Access** (**JNA**) and **Java Native Runtime** (**JNR**). JNA is a library that permits access to native shared libraries without having to use the **Java Native Interface** (**JNI**). JNR is a Java API that is used for calling native code. The proposed FFI will permit and optimize native method calls as well as optimized native memory management.

Isolated methods

The `MethodHandles.Lookup` class is part of the `java.lang.invoke` package. We use lookup objects to create method handles and a lookup class to access them. Here is the header for the lookup class:

```
public static final class MethodHandles.Lookup extends Object
```

Future changes to the `MethodHandles.Lookup` class will support the loading of method byte codes without the need for an attached class. Furthermore, these methods will be referenced using method handles. The class will have a new `loadCode` method.

Reducing metaspace waste

Currently, when metaspace chunks are freed, they cannot be used as different sized chunks. So, if metaspace chunk A was freed and was of size X, that space cannot be reused for a metaspace chunk greater than or less than size X. This results in a tremendous amount of unusable metaspace waste. This can also lead to out-of-memory errors.

A future change to the JDK will resolve this issue by increasing the reuse of metaspace chunks. The change will support the following cases:

- Allow neighboring chunks to form a larger chunk
- Allow larger chunks to be divided into smaller chunks

This proposed change resolves the issue by ensuring smaller chunks can be reused and that larger chunks are not wasted as they can be split to support the reuse of smaller chunks.

Improving IPv6 support

Internet Protocol version 6 (**IPv6**) is the current version of the Internet Protocol. The Internet Protocol provides the identification and location schema that enables Internet traffic routing. IPv6 is considered an Internet layer protocol that is sued by packet-switched networking.

The following diagram shows the history of the Internet Protocol:

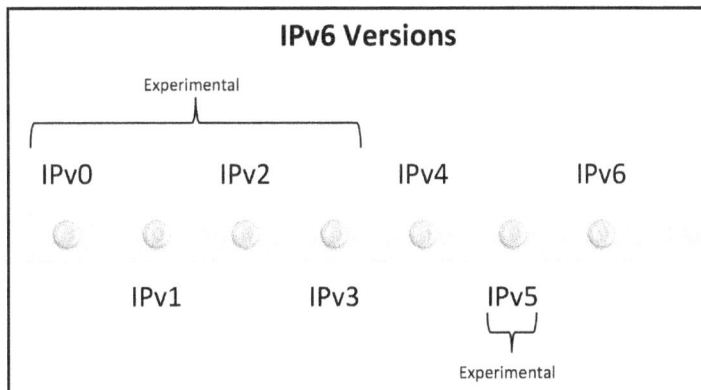

IPv6 is the replacement for IPv4 and has several changes that the Java platform should support. Key IPv6 changes from IPv4 are categorized as follows:

- Jumbograms
- Larger address space
- Mobility
- Multicasting
- Network-layer security
- Options extensibility
- Privacy
- Simplified router processing
- Stateless address auto-configuration

As the Internet continues to transition from IPv4 to IPv6, the following cases are possible and should all be supported in the Java 10 platform:

- Multiple versions of IPv4 exist
- One version of IPv6 exists
- Multiple versions of IPv6 exist
- Multiple versions of IPv4 and one version of IPv6 exist
- Multiple versions of IPv4 and IPv6 exist

Unboxed argument lists for method handles

The way in which unboxed argument lists are currently handled can lead to processing inefficiencies. This is especially true when we use `Object[]` or `List<object>` as variable-length argument lists. Java uses `java.lang.invoke` to transform the method calls using boxing. In Java, autoboxing is when the compiler automatically converts primitive types and their corresponding object wrapper classes. Here is the list of wrapper classes along with the corresponding primitive type:

Wrapper class	Primitive type
Boolean	boolean
Byte	byte
Character	char
Double	double
Float	float
Integer	int
Long	long
Short	short

As you can see from the following illustration autoboxing occurs when we go from primitive values to an object of the associated wrapper class and, when we go from an object of a wrapper class to primitive values it is called unboxing:

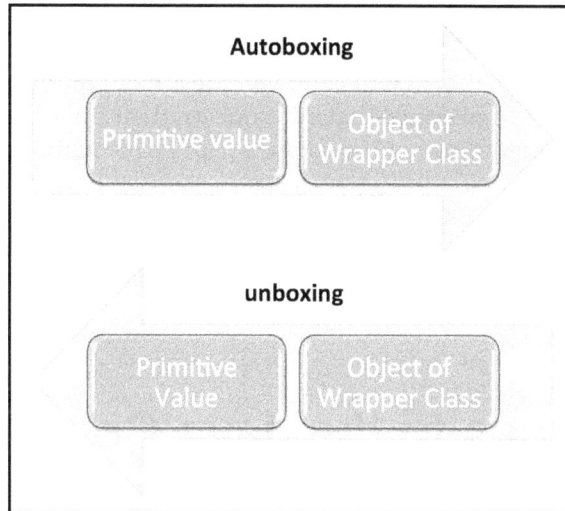

The inefficiencies are due to mismatches between the argument's list actual types and the array or list encasing them. In a future Java release, these inefficiencies will be removed. A new `ArgumentList` class will be added to the Java platform that polymorphically boxes valid arguments lists into a heap node.

Enhanced MandelblotSet demo using value types

This low priority Java Enhancement Proposal is likely to be implemented in Java 10 as its scope is limited. The plan is to develop a sample Java application that demonstrates improvements in memory and performance specific to using Valhalla project components, value types, and generics instead of primitive types.

> Valhalla project components refer to user-defined custom immutable primitive types as value types.

You can read more about value types in the Java Virtual Machine section of this chapter.

A Mandelbrot set is a specific example of fractal mathematics used in chaos theory. The sample MandelbrotSet that accompanied JDK 8 provides a comparison of parallel and sequential data streams. In Java 10 or beyond, the sample MandelbrotSet will be updated to show performance and memory efficiencies between using Valhalla project components, value types and generics as opposed to primitive types.

Efficient array comparison intrinsics

A future change to the Java platform will be to include a method for comparing arrays. Currently, this is something developers have to code on their own. The change will be incorporated by adding something similar to the `compareTo` method in `java.util.Arrays`.

Although specifics are not available, the prospect of being able to compare arrays using native functionality is exciting. This is a component that will save many developers time. This is likely to be realized in the Java 10 platform release.

Future changes to the Java Compiler

There are two notable draft changes to the Java platform, specifically the Java Compiler. These Java Enhancement Proposals are listed as follows and detailed in this section:

- Policy for retiring javac `-source` and `-target` options
- Pluggable static analyzers

Policy for retiring javac -source and -target options

A formal draft proposal has been submitted to define a policy for retiring `-source` and `-target` options. This effort is to help reduce maintenance costs of the compiler. The `-source` and `-target` options were provided to ease development efforts, but not formally required by any standards. Starting with the Java 9 platform, these target options are not recognized.

The new policy is called "one plus three back" which means that the current version will be supported as well as the three previous releases. This policy will persist with JDK 10.

Pluggable static analyzers

An ongoing research Java Enhancement Proposal was initiated in the summer of 2013 as an exploratory measure and future support for a full Java Enhancement Proposal to empower developers to define extensions that can, at compile time, conduct the arbitrary static analysis. The research is to see how a pluggable static type analyzer framework can be implemented for the Java Compiler.

The goals of the research are as follows:

- Collect static analyzer requirements
- Analyze static analyzers
- Determine the requirements for a framework that supports static analyzers
- Implement and test

The final outcome of the ongoing research will be either to submit a feature Java Enhancement Proposal or to make the recommendation that pursuit of the feature cease.

Future Changes to the Java Virtual Machine

Several new features and enhancements to the Java Virtual Machine (JVM) and core libraries have been submitted and drafted. It is likely that at least some of these features and enhancements will be realized in the Java 10 platform, and others will be saved for later releases.

JVM-related submitted proposals

There are three Java Enhancement Proposals that have been submitted. While, not currently earmarked for Java 10, it is likely that we will see the changes when Java 10 is released. The three proposals are listed as follows:

- Container aware Java
- Enable execution of Java methods on GPU
- Epsilon GC: The arbitrarily low overhead gGarbage (non-) collector

Container aware Java

An effort is being made so the JVM and core libraries are aware when they are running in a container. Moreover, to be adaptive in the use of available system resources. This feature is especially relevant with the ubiquitous nature of cloud computing.

There are two major components of the proposed feature:

- Detection:
  - Determine if Java is running inside a container
- Container resource exposure:
  - Expose container resources limits
  - Expose container resource configuration

Several configuration status points have been initially identified:

General	CPU-related	Memory-related
isContainerized	CPU Period	Block I/O Device Weight
	CPU Quota	Block I/O Weight
	CPU Set Memory Nodes	Current Memory Usage
	CPU Sets	Device I/O Read Rate
	CPU Usage	Device I/O Write Rate
	CPU Usage Per CPU	Max Memory Usage
	Number of CPUs	Maximum Kernal Memory
		Memory Swappiness
		OOM Kill Enabled
		OOM Score Adjustment
		Shared Memory Size
		Soft Memory Limit
		Total Memory Limit

Initially, this feature is scheduled to support Docker on Linux-64. A likely scenario is that this feature be released with Java 10 with sole support for Docker on Linux-64. Then, feature support will be expanded in subsequent releases of the Java platform.

Enable execution of Java methods on GPU

Enabling the seamless ability for Java applications to take advantage of GPUs is the subject of project Sumatra. The goal is to use Java's Stream API in parallel and the lambda programming model. It makes great sense for us to exploit the processing power and efficiency of GPUs.

The overarching goal is to make this feature easy to use for developers. The feature will be implemented with the following characteristics:

- Do not change the syntax of the Java parallel stream API
- Hardware and software stacks should be automatically detected
- Automatic detection and analysis to determine if using the GPU makes sense from a performance standard
- Provide CPU execution when offloading processing to a GPU fails
- There will be no performance degradation
- There will be no new security risks introduced by this feature
- There will be memory persistence between the CPU and GPU

The key benefit of this Java Enhancement Proposal will be performance improvements for our Java applications.

Epsilon GC - The arbitrarily low overhead garbage (non-) collector

In `Chapter 7`, *Leveraging the New Default G1 Garbage Collector*, we detailed the enhancements to Java's Garbage Collection with the release of the Java 9 platform. In the spirit of continuous improvement, a Java Enhancement Proposal has been submitted to develop a garbage collection to specifically handle memory allocation. This garbage collector will signal the JVM to shutdown when no more memory is available on the Java heap.

The goal is for this garbage collector to be passive and use very limited overhead. The introduction of this garbage collection is not intended to degrade performance.

This change will not impact current garbage collectors.

JVM-related drafted proposals

The following Java Enhancement Proposals have been drafted for a future version of the Java platform and are detailed in this section:

- Provide stable USDT probe points on JVM compiled methods
- Concurrent Monitor Deflation
- Low-overhead way of sampling Java heap allocations
- Diagnostic Command Framework
- Enhanced Class Redefinition
- Enable NUMA mode by default when appropriate
- Value objects
- Align JVM Access Checks

Provide stable USDT probe points on JVM compiled methods

User-level Statistically Defined Tracing (**USDT**) is used to insert probe points to mark the entry and exit of methods. Compilers then permit a handshake with tracing tools so that those tools can discover the probe points and manipulate them.

> Common tracing tools are Dtrace and **Berkeley Packet Filters** (**BPF**).

The Java Virtual Machine, even with JVM 9, does not support this technology set. The current lack of support stems from how the JVM generates compiled code; it does this dynamically without any static **Executable Linkable Files** (**ELFs**). Tracing tools need the ELFs to work. An additional mitigating factor is that the JVM dynamically patches its own generated code which does not support external patching.

In a future Java release, likely Java 10, the **JVMTI** (**JVM Tools Interface**) will be modified to support probe tools to perform their standard operations on the JVM's dynamically compiled code. Provisionally identified changes to JVMTI APIs include:

- Adding patch points or method entry and exit
- The enumeration of the compiled methods
- State change notifications on compiled method load
- Query support
- Toggle trace points on/off
- Making chunks of compiled methods inspectable

The good news is that there will not need to be any changes to how Java code is compiled. It can already be patched, so the required functionality will be created by modifying the USDT API as well as a few changes to the JVM.

Concurrent monitor deflation

A monitor, in our context, is a synchronized mechanism that controls concurrent access to an object. Monitors help prevent multiple threads from accessing a monitored object at the same time. The JVM automatically switches between three monitor implementation methods. The three implementation methods are illustrated as follows:

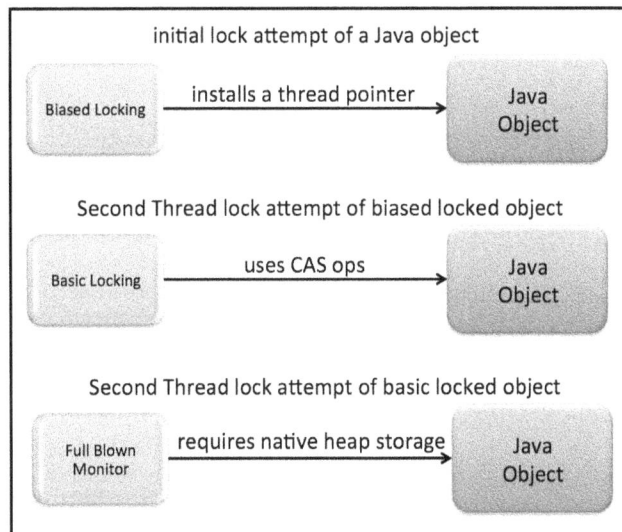

The initial lock of a Java object uses biased locking. That method ensures only the locking thread can lock the object. With this approach, the JVM installs a thread pointer in the Java object. When a second thread attempts to lock the Java object, the JVM switches to the basic locking monitor implementation method. This second method uses **compare-and-swap** (**CAS**) operations. When a CAS operation fails, such as when a second thread attempt to lock the Java object, the JVM switches to the third monitor implementation method. That method is a full-blown monitor. This method requires native heap storage which is referred to as the monitor being inflated.

The purpose of the Concurrent Monitor Deflation Java Enhancement Proposal is to perform monitor deflation while the threads are running. This will decrease the JVM-induced pause times.

Provide a low-overhead way of sampling Java heap allocations

Mismanagement of Java heaps can result in heap exhaustion, and insufficient memory due to memory fragmentation (GC thrashing). In a future release of Java, most likely Java 10, we will have a means of sampling Java heap allocations. This will be implemented by enhancing the **Java Virtual Machine Tools Interface** (**JVMTI**). The resulting functionality will provide an extremely low-overhead solution.

Diagnostic Command Framework

Java Enhancement Proposal 137, Diagnostic Command Framework, proposes a framework be created for sending diagnostic commands to the Java Virtual Machine.

The framework will include a **Java Management Extension** (JMX) interface, which will permit remote issuing of diagnostic commands via a JMX connection.

The JRocket Mission Control tools already have this feature successfully implemented. This served as proof of concept and it is therefore extremely likely that this enhancement will be part of the Java 10 platform.

Enhanced Class Redefinition

Java Enhancement Proposal 159, Enhanced Class Redefinition, calls for enhanced JVM capabilities in regards to class redefinition at runtime. Specifically the proposal includes the following class redefinition operations:

- Adding super types
- Adding methods
- Adding static fields
- Adding instance fields
- Removing methods
- Removing static fields
- Removing instance fields

Current JVM class redefinition capabilities are limited to method swapping. This is viewed as extremely restrictive. With the new proposed enhancement, developers will not have to restart their applications after changes. This is especially beneficial when dealing with large and distributed systems.

Enable NUMA mode by default when appropriate

Java Enhancement Proposal 163, enable NUMA mode by default when appropriate. This proposal is only applicable to NUMA hardware. The intent is to have the JVM enable the following flag when it detects NUMA hardware:

```
XX:+UseNUMA
```

This flag can currently be evoked manually. With the proposed enhancement, it will be evoked automatically by the JVM when it has detected that it is running on a NUMA piece of hardware.

> **Non-Uniform Memory Access (NUMA)** is a memory model used in computer multiprocessing. With this memory model, access time is dependent on the memory location relative to that of the processor.

This will be an easy enhancement to implement and is likely to be part of the Java 10 platform release.

Value objects

Java Enhancement Proposal 169, value objects, intended to provide the necessary JVM infrastructure to permit working with objects that are immutable as well as objects that are without reference. This new infrastructure will allow for the efficient by-value computation with non-primitive data types.

The set of goals for this proposal include the following:

- More closely align `java.lang.Integer` and `int` semantics.
- Make Java data structures more portable
- Support abstract data types with a performance similar to that of Java primitive data types:
    - User-defined
    - Library-defined
- Optimize parallel computations by enabling function-style computation with pure data
- Improve support for:
    - Complex numbers
    - Vector values
    - Tuples
- Increase safety and security
- Decrease "defensive copying"

One of the stated implementation strategies is to add a `lockPermanently` operation. It will get passed an Object and then mark that Object as both immutable and unaliasable. The concept of a permanently locked object stipulates that:

- Fields cannot be changed
- Elements of an array cannot be changed
- No synchronization is possible
- 'Waiting' methods cannot be evoked
- 'Notifying' methods cannot be evoked
- Identity hash codes inquiries are not permitted
- Pointer equality checks cannot be performed

This is likely to be one of the more popular additions to the Java 10 platform.

Align JVM Access Checks

Java Enhancement Proposal 181, Align JVM Checks with Java Language Rules for Nested Classes, focuses on the need to align JVM access checking rules with Java language rules, specifically for constructors, fields, and methods in nested classes. This will be accomplished by partitioning related classes in nests. Class files will be able to access private names of other class files in the same nest.

Nests will share an access control context. With the advent of nests, access bridges will not be required. The bulk of the change will be to the JVM's access rules.

Future Changes to JavaX

The `Javax.*` packages are the subject of two specific Java Enhancement Proposals that have been submitted for a future Java platform release. Those proposals are as follows:

- JMX specific annotations for registration of managed resources
- Modernize the GTK3 Look and Feel implementation

JMX specific annotations for registration of managed resources

The draft Java Enhancement Proposal titled, JMX specific annotations for registration of managed resources, will provide a set of annotations for registration and configuration of **MBeans** (**Managed Bean**).

An MBean is a Java Object representing a manageable resource (app, service, component, or device).

The goal of this proposal is to lessen the burden on developers in the registration and configuring of MBeans. In addition, the source code readability will increase by ensuring all MBean declaration components are co-located.

The JMX specific annotations will be located in the `javax.management.annotations` package.

This Java Enhancement Proposal has been specifically planned for Java 11. Although, there is a possibility that it could be redesigned for Java 10.

Modernize the GTK3 Look and Feel Implementation

GTK3 is a widget toolkit used for creating graphical user interfaces, formally known as the GIMP toolkit. The draft Java Enhancement Proposal titled, Modernize the GTK3 Look and Feel implementation, calls for the rewriting of the current GTK2 Look and Feel so that it uses GTK3 instead.

GTK3 implementation will not replace GTK2. It is important to note that one or the other, not both of these can be used at runtime.

> You can access the GTK3 reference manual at `https://developer.gnome.org/gtk3/stable/`.

Ongoing Special Projects

Java Enhancement Proposals present design and implementation changes to the Java platform. The criteria for a JEP being drafted is that the work must meet at least one of the following:

- At least two weeks of engineering work
- Signifies a significant change to the JDK
- Represents a high demand issue for developers or customers

Projects, on the other hand, represent collaborative efforts that are sponsored by one of the following groups:

- 2D Graphics
- Adoption
- AWT
- Build
- Compatibility and specification review
- Compiler
- Conformance
- Core Libraries
- Governing Board
- HotSpot
- Internationalization
- JMX
- Members
- Networking
- NetBeans Projects
- Porters
- Quality
- Security
- Serviceability
- Sound
- Swing
- Web

Groups are formal and new ones can be proposed.

The following listed active projects represent possible future enhancement areas to the Java platform. Brief information about each project is provided later in this section and provides insight into general areas of future changes:

- Annotations pipeline 2.0
- Audio Synthesis Engine
- Caciocavallo
- Common VM Interface

- Compiler Grammar
- Da Vinci Machine
- Device I/O
- Graal
- HarfBuzz Integration
- Kona
- OpenJFX
- Panama
- Shenandoah

Annotations pipeline 2.0

This project explores improvements to how annotations are handled within the Java compiler pipeline. There is no intention to propose changing specifications; rather, the focus is on performance enhancements.

Audio Synthesis Engine

This project is looking at the creation of a new midi synthesizer for the JDK. The current midi synthesizer belongs to a licensed library. The working group would like to see the new midi synthesizer as an open source JDK asset.

Caciocavallo

The Caciocavallo project aims to improve the OpenJDK **Abstract Windows Toolkit** (**AWT**) internal interfaces. This extends to 2D subsystems. The proposed improvement stands to ease the way AWT is ported to new platforms.

Common VM Interface

The Common VM Interface project has the goal of documenting the VM interface for OpenJDK. This should make it easier for Classpath VMs and other VMs to use OpenJDK.

Compiler Grammar

The Compiler Grammar project is working on an experimental Java Compiler that is based on ANTLR grammar. **ANTLR, Another Tool for Language Recognition**, is a parser that reads, processes, and executes structured text or binary files. The project team hopes this Java Compiler will replace the current one as it uses a hand-written parser, **LALR (Look-Ahead Left to Right)**. The LALR parser has been identified by the project group as fragile and difficult to extend.

Da Vinci Machine

The Da Vinci Machine Project, represents the effort to extend the JVM with support for non-Java languages. Current efforts are focused on allowing the new languages to exist alongside Java in the JVM. Performance and efficiency are key characteristics of the effort.

Device I/O

This project intends to provide access to generic peripheral devices via a Java-level API. The initial list of peripheral devices the project team wants to support include:

- GPIO (**General Purpose Input/Output**)
- I2C (**Inter-Integrated Circuit Bus**)
- SPI (**Serial Peripheral Interface**)
- UART (**Universal Asynchronous Receiver/Transmitter**)

Graal

The Graal project has the goal of exposing VM functionality via Java APIs. This exposure will permit developers to write, in Java, dynamic compilers for a given language runtime. This effort includes the development of a multi-language interpreter framework.

HarfBuzz Integration

The HarfBuzz Integration project hopes to integrate the HarfBuzz layout engine into the Java Development Kit. This is intended to replace the ICU layout engine with the HarfBuzz layout engine. The ICU layout engine has been deprecated, solidifying the importance of this project's future success.

Kona

The Kona project, is working to define and implement Java APIs to support the **Internet of Things (IoT)** domain. This includes networking technologies and protocols. Although not stated, safety and security will be paramount to this effort's implementation success.

OpenJFX

There are not many details available regarding the OpenJFX project. The stated goal of this project is to create the next-generation Java client toolkit. Based on the project title, it can be assumed that the group wants to create an OpenJFX version of JavaFX, which is a set of packages used to create rich internet applications.

Panama

Project panama is focused on enhancing the connections between JVM and non-Java APIs. The project includes the following selected components:

- Native function calls
- Native data access from JVM
- Native data access inside JVM heap
- New data layouts in JVM heap
- API extraction tools for header files

The project team has generated a repository tree that matches JDK 9's structure. This significantly increases the likelihood of the project's success.

Shenandoah

Project Shenandoah has the goal of significantly reducing the pause times with garbage collection operations. The approach is to have more garbage collection operations run concurrently with the Java application. In Chapter 7, *Leveraging the New Default G1 Garbage Collector* you read about CMS and G1. The Shenandoah project intends to add concurrent compaction to the possible garbage collection approaches.

Summary

In this chapter we provided an overview of the future developments of the Java platform, beyond Java 9. We looked at what is planned for Java 10 and what further changes we are likely to see beyond Java 10. Each potential change to the Java platform was characterized as targeted, submitted, or drafted. Specifically, we covered future changes to the Java platform grouped in the following categories: JDK Changes, Java Compiler, Java Virtual Machine, JavaX, and special projects.

Java 9 Programming Blueprints

2

*Implement new features such as modules, the process
handling API, REPL, and many more to build end-to-end
applications in Java 9*

17
Introduction

In the process of erecting a new building, a set of blueprints helps all related parties communicate--the architect, electricians, carpenters, plumbers, and so on. It details things such as shapes, sizes, and materials. Without them, each of the subcontractors would be left guessing as to what to do, where to do it, and how. Without these blueprints, modern architecture would be almost impossible.

What is in your hands--or on the screen in front of you--is a set of blueprints of a different sort. Rather than detailing exactly how to build your specific software system, as each project and environment has unique constraints and requirements, these blueprints offer examples of how to build a variety of Java-based systems, providing examples of how to use specific features in the **Java Development Kit**, or **JDK**, with a special focus on the new features of Java 9 that you can then apply to your specific problem.

Since it would be impossible to build an application using only the new Java 9 features, we will also be using and highlighting many of the newest features in the JDK. Before we get too far into what that entails, then, let's take a brief moment to discuss some of these great new features from recent major JDK releases. Hopefully, most Java shops are already on Java 7, so we'll focus on version 8 and, of course, version 9.

In this chapter, we will cover the following topics:

- New features in Java 8
- New features in Java 9
- Projects

New features in Java 8

Java 8, released on March 8, 2014, brought arguably two of the most significant features since Java 5, released in 2004--lambdas and streams. With functional programming gaining popularity in the JVM world, especially with the help of languages such as Scala, Java adherents had been clamoring for more functional-style language features for several years. Originally slated for release in Java 7, the feature was dropped from that release, finally seeing a stable release with Java 8.

While it can be hoped that everyone is familiar with Java's lambda support, experience has shown that many shops, for a variety of reasons, are slow to adopt new language versions and features, so a quick introduction might be helpful.

Lambdas

The term lambda, which has its roots in lambda calculus, developed by Alonzo Church in 1936, simply refers to an anonymous function. Typically, a function (or method, in more proper Java parlance), is a statically-named artifact in the Java source:

```
public int add(int x, int y) {
   return x + y;
}
```

This simple method is one named `add` that takes two `int` parameters as well as returning an `int` parameter. With the introduction of lambdas, this can now be written as follows:

```
(int x, int y) → x + y
```

Or, more simply as this:

```
(x, y) → x + y
```

This abbreviated syntax indicates that we have a function that takes two parameters and returns their sum. Depending on where this lambda is used, the types of the parameters can be inferred by the compiler, making the second, even more concise format possible. Most importantly, though, note that this method is no longer named. Unless it is assigned to a variable or passed as a parameter (more on this later), it can not be referenced--or used--anywhere in the system.

This example, of course, is absurdly simple. A better example of this might be in one of the many APIs where the method's parameter is an implementation of what is known as a **Single Abstract Method** (SAM) interface, which is, at least until Java 8, an interface with a single method. One of the canonical examples of a SAM is `Runnable`. Here is an example of the pre-lambda `Runnable` usage:

```
Runnable r = new Runnable() {
  public void run() {
    System.out.println("Do some work");
  }
};
Thread t = new Thread(r);
t.start();
```

With Java 8 lambdas, this code can be vastly simplified to this:

```
Thread t = new Thread(() ->
  System.out.println("Do some work"));
t.start();
```

The body of the `Runnable` method is still pretty trivial, but the gains in clarity and conciseness should be pretty obvious.

While lambdas are anonymous functions (that is, they have no names), Java lambdas, as is the case in many other languages, can also be assigned to variables and passed as parameters (indeed, the functionality would be almost worthless without this capability). Revisiting the `Runnable` method in the preceding code, we can separate the declaration and the use of `Runnable` as follows:

```
Runnable r = () {
  // Acquire database connection
  // Do something really expensive
};
Thread t = new Thread(r);
t.start();
```

This is intentionally more verbose than the preceding example. The stubbed out body of the `Runnable` method is intended to mimic, after a fashion, how a real-world `Runnable` may look and why one may want to assign the newly-defined `Runnable` method to a variable in spite of the conciseness that lambdas offer. This new lambda syntax allows us to declare the body of the `Runnable` method without having to worry about method names, signatures, and so on. It is true that any decent IDE would help with this kind of boilerplate, but this new syntax gives you, and the countless developers who will maintain your code, much less noise to have to parse when debugging the code.

Any SAM interface can be written as a lambda. Do you have a comparator that you really only need to use once?

```
List<Student> students = getStudents();
students.sort((one, two) -> one.getGrade() - two.getGrade());
```

How about `ActionListener`?

```
saveButton.setOnAction((event) -> saveAndClose());
```

Additionally, you can use your own SAM interfaces in lambdas as follows:

```
public <T> interface Validator<T> {
  boolean isValid(T value);
}
cardProcessor.setValidator((card)
card.getNumber().startsWith("1234"));
```

One of the advantages of this approach is that it not only makes the consuming code more concise, but it also reduces the level of effort, such as it is, in creating some of these concrete SAM instances. That is to say, rather than having to decide between an anonymous class and a concrete, named class, the developer can declare it inline, cleanly and concisely.

In addition to the SAMs Java developers have been using for years, Java 8 introduced a number of functional interfaces to help facilitate more functional style programming. The Java 8 Javadoc lists 43 different interfaces. Of these, there are a handful of basic function **shapes** that you should know of, some of which are as follows:

`BiConsumer<T,U>`	This represents an operation that accepts two input arguments and returns no result
`BiFunction<T,U,R>`	This represents a function that accepts two arguments and produces a result
`BinaryOperator<T>`	This represents an operation upon two operands of the same type, producing a result of the same type as the operands
`BiPredicate<T,U>`	This represents a predicate (Boolean-valued function) of two arguments
`Consumer<T>`	This represents an operation that accepts a single input argument and returns no result
`Function<T,R>`	This represents a function that accepts one argument and produces a result

`Predicate<T>`	This represents a predicate (Boolean-valued function) of one argument
`Supplier<T>`	This represents a supplier of results

There are a myriad of uses for these interfaces, but perhaps the best way to demonstrate some of them is to turn our attention to the next big feature in Java 8--Streams.

Streams

The other major addition to Java 8, and, perhaps where lambdas shine the brightest, is the new **Streams API**. If you were to search for a definition of Java streams, you would get answers that range from the somewhat circular **a stream of data elements** to the more technical **Java streams are monads**, and they're probably both right. The Streams API allows the Java developer to interact with a stream of data elements via a **sequence of steps**. Even putting it that way isn't as clear as it could be, so let's see what it means by looking at some sample code.

Let's say you have a list of grades for a particular class. You would like to know what the average grade is for the girls in the class. Prior to Java 8, you might have written something like this:

```
double sum = 0.0;
int count = 0;
for (Map.Entry<Student, Integer> g : grades.entrySet()) {
  if ("F".equals(g.getKey().getGender())) {
    count++;
    sum += g.getValue();
  }
}
double avg = sum / count;
```

We initialize two variables, one to store the sums and one to count the number of hits. Next, we loop through the grades. If the student's gender is female, we increment our counter and update the sum. When the loop terminates, we then have the information we need to calculate the average. This works, but it's a bit verbose. The new Streams API can help with that:

```
double avg = grades.entrySet().stream()
 .filter(e -> "F".equals(e.getKey().getGender())) // 1
 .mapToInt(e -> e.getValue()) // 2
 .average() // 3
 .getAsDouble(); //4
```

This new version is not significantly smaller, but the purpose of the code is much clearer. In the preceding pre-stream code, we have to play computer, parsing the code and teasing out its intended purpose. With streams, we have a clear, declarative means to express application logic. For each entry in the map do the following:

1. Filter out each entry whose `gender` is not `F`.
2. Map each value to the primitive int.
3. Average the grades.
4. Return the value as a double.

With the stream-based and lamba-based approach, we don't need to declare temporary, intermediate variables (grade count and total), and we don't need to worry about calculating the admittedly simple average. The JDK does all of the heavy-lifting for us.

The new java.time package

While lambdas and streams are extremely important game-changing updates, with Java 8, we were given another long-awaited change that was, at least in some circles, just as exciting: a new date/time API. Anyone who has worked with dates and times in Java knows the pain of `java.util.Calendar` and company. Clearly, you can get your work done, but it's not always pretty. Many developers found the API too painful to use, so they integrated the extremely popular Joda Time library into their projects. The Java architects agreed, and engaged Joda Time's author, Stephen Colebourne, to lead JSR 310, which brought a version of Joda Time (fixing various design flaws) to the platform. We'll take a detailed look at how to use some of these new APIs in our date/time calculator later in the book.

Default methods

Before turning our attention to Java 9, let's take a look at one more significant language feature: default methods. Since the beginning of Java, an interface was used to define how a class looks, implying a certain type of behavior, but was unable to implement that behavior. This made polymorphism much simpler in a lot of cases, as any number of classes could implement a given interface, and the consuming code treats them as that interface, rather than whatever concrete class they actually are.

One of the problems that have confronted API developers over the years, though, was how to evolve an API and its interfaces without breaking existing code. For example, take the `ActionSource` interface from the JavaServer Faces 1.1 specification. When the JSF 1.2 expert group was working on the next revision of the specification, they identified the need to add a new property to the interface, which would result in two new methods--the getters and setters. They could not simply add the methods to the interface, as that would break every implementation of the specification, requiring the maintainers of the implementation to update their classes. Obviously, this sort of breakage is unacceptable, so JSF 1.2 introduced `ActionSource2`, which extends `ActionSource` and adds the new methods. While this approach is considered ugly by many, the 1.2 expert group had a few choices, and none of them were very good.

With Java 8, though, interfaces can now specify a default method on the interface definition, which the compiler will use for the method implementation if the extending class does not provide one. Let's take the following piece of code as an example:

```
public interface Speaker {
  void saySomething(String message);
}
public class SpeakerImpl implements Speaker {
  public void saySomething(String message) {
    System.out.println(message);
  }
}
```

We've developed our API and made it available to the public, and it's proved to be really popular. Over time, though, we've identified an improvement we'd like to make: we'd like to add some convenience methods, such as `sayHello()` and `sayGoodbye()`, to save our users a little time. However, as discussed earlier, if we just add these new methods to the interface, we'll break our users' code as soon as they update to the new version of the library. Default methods allow us to extend the interface and avoid the breakage by defining an implementation:

```
public interface Speaker {
  void saySomething(String message);
  default public void sayHello() {
    System.out.println("Hello");
  }
  default public void sayGoodbye() {
    System.out.println("Good bye");
  }
}
```

Now, when users update their library JARs, they immediately gain these new methods and their behavior, without making any changes. Of course, to use these methods, the users will need to modify their code, but they need not do so until--and if--they want to.

New features in Java 9

As with any new version of the JDK, this release was packed with a lot of great new features. Of course, what is most appealing will vary based on your needs, but we'll focus specifically on a handful of these new features that are most relevant to the projects we'll build together. First up is the most significant, the Java Module System.

Java Platform Module System/Project Jigsaw

Despite being a solid, feature-packed release, Java 8 was considered by a fair number to be a bit disappointing. It lacked the much anticipated **Java Platform Module System (JPMS)**, also known more colloquially, though not quite accurately, as Project Jigsaw. The Java Platform Module System was originally slated to ship with Java 7 in 2011, but it was deferred to Java 8 due to some lingering technical concerns. Project Jigsaw was started not only to finish the module system, but also to modularize the JDK itself, which would help Java SE scale down to smaller devices, such as mobile phones and embedded systems. Jigsaw was scheduled to ship with Java 8, which was released in 2014, but it was deferred yet again, as the Java architects felt they still needed more time to implement the system correctly. At long last, though, Java 9 will finally deliver this long-promised project.

That said, what exactly is it? One problem that has long haunted API developers, including the JDK architects, is the inability to hide implementation details of public APIs. A good example from the JDK of private classes that developers should not be using directly is the `com.sun.*`/`sun.*` packages and classes. A perfect example of this--of private APIs finding widespread public use--is the `sun.misc.Unsafe` class. Other than a strongly worded warning in Javadoc about not using these internal classes, there's little that could be done to prevent their use. Until now.

With the JPMS, developers will be able to make implementation classes public so that they may be easily used inside their projects, but not expose them outside the module, meaning they are not exposed to consumers of the API or library. To do this, the Java architects have introduced a new file, `module-info.java`, similar to the existing `package-info.java` file, found at the root of the module, for example, at `src/main/java/module-info.java`. It is compiled to `module-info.class`, and is available at runtime via reflection and the new `java.lang.Module` class.

So what does this file do, and what does it look like? Java developers can use this file to name the module, list its dependencies, and express to the system, both compile and runtime, which packages are exported to the world. For example, suppose, in our preceding stream example, we have three packages: `model`, `api`, and `impl`. We want to expose the models and the API classes, but not any of the implementation classes. Our `module-info.java` file may look something like this:

```
module com.packt.j9blueprints.intro {
  requires com.foo;
  exports com.packt.j9blueprints.intro.model;
  exports com.packt.j9blueprints.intro.api;
}
```

This definition exposes the two packages we want to export, and also declares a dependency on the `com.foo` module. If this module is not available at compile-time, the project will not build, and if it is not available at runtime, the system will throw an exception and exit. Note that the `requires` statement does not specify a version. This is intentional, as it was decided not to tackle the version-selection issue as part of the module system, leaving that to more appropriate systems, such as build tools and containers.

Much more could be said about the module system, of course, but an exhaustive discussion of all of its features and limitations is beyond the scope of this book. We will be implementing our applications as modules, though, so we'll see the system used--and perhaps explained in a bit more detail--throughout the book.

> Those wanting a more in-depth discussion of the Java Platform Module System can search for the article, *The State of the Module System*, by Mark Reinhold.

Process handling API

In prior versions of Java, developers interacting with native operating system processes had to use a fairly limited API, with some operations requiring resorting to native code. As part of **Java Enhancement Proposal (JEP)** 102, the Java process API was extended with the following features (quoting from the JEP text):

- The ability to get the pid (or equivalent) of the current Java virtual machine and the pid of processes created with the existing API.
- The ability to enumerate processes on the system. Information on each process may include its pid, name, state, and perhaps resource usage.

- The ability to deal with process trees; in particular, some means to destroy a process tree.
- The ability to deal with hundreds of subprocesses, perhaps multiplexing the output or error streams to avoid creating a thread per subprocess.

We will explore these API changes in our first project, the Process Viewer/Manager (see the following sections for details).

Concurrency changes

As was done in Java 7, the Java architects revisited the concurrency libraries, making some much needed changes, this time in order to support the reactive-streams specification. These changes include a new class, `java.util.concurrent.Flow`, with several nested interfaces: `Flow.Processor`, `Flow.Publisher`, `Flow.Subscriber`, and `Flow.Subscription`.

REPL

One change that seems to excite a lot of people isn't a language change at all. It's the addition of a **REPL** (**Read-Eval-Print-Loop**), a fancy term for a language shell. In fact, the command for this new tool is `jshell`. This tool allows us to type or paste in Java code and get immediate feedback. For example, if we wanted to experiment with the Streams API discussed in the preceding section, we could do something like this:

```
$ jshell
|   Welcome to JShell -- Version 9-ea
|   For an introduction type: /help intro

jshell> List<String> names = Arrays.asList(new String[]{"Tom", "Bill",
"Xavier", "Sarah", "Adam"});
names ==> [Tom, Bill, Xavier, Sarah, Adam]

jshell> names.stream().sorted().forEach(System.out::println);
Adam
Bill
Sarah
Tom
Xavier
```

This is a very welcome addition that should help Java developers rapidly prototype and test their ideas.

Projects

With that brief and high-level overview of what new features are available to use, what do these blueprints we'll cover look like? We'll build ten different applications, varying in complexity and kind, and covering a wide range of concerns. With each project, we'll pay special attention to the new features we're highlighting, but we'll also see some older, tried and true language features and libraries used extensively, with any interesting or novel usages flagged. Here, then, is our project lineup.

Process Viewer/Manager

We will explore some of the improvements to the process handling APIs as we implement a Java version of the age old Unix tool--**top**. Combining this API with JavaFX, we'll build a graphical tool that allows the user to view and manage processes running on the system.

This project will cover the following:

- Java 9 Process API enhancements
- JavaFX

Duplicate File Finder

As a system ages, the chances of clutter in the filesystem, especially duplicated files, increases exponentially, it seems. Leveraging some of the new File I/O libraries, we'll build a tool to scan a set of user-specified directories to identify duplicates. Pulling JavaFX back out of the toolbox, we'll add a graphical user interface that will provide a more user-friendly means to interactively process the duplicates.

This project will cover the following:

- Java File I/O
- Hashing libraries
- JavaFX

Date Calculator

With the release of Java 8, Oracle integrated a new library based on a redesign of Joda Time, more or less, into the JDK. Officially known as JSR 310, this new library fixed a longstanding complaint with the JDK--the official date libraries were inadequate and hard to use. In this project, we'll build a simple command-line date calculator that will take a date and, for example, add an arbitrary amount of time to it. Consider the following piece of code for example:

```
$ datecalc "2016-07-04 + 2 weeks"
2016-07-18
$ datecalc "2016-07-04 + 35 days"
2016-08-08
$ datecalc "12:00CST to PST"
10:00PST
```

This project will cover the following:

- Java 8 Date/Time APIs
- Regular expressions
- Java command-line libraries

Social Media Aggregator

One of the problems with having accounts on so many social media networks is keeping tabs on what's happening on each of them. With accounts on Twitter, Facebook, Google+, Instagram, and so on, active users can spend a significant amount of time jumping from site to site, or app to app, reading the latest updates. In this chapter, we'll build a simple aggregator app that will pull the latest updates from each of the user's social media accounts and display them in one place. The features will include the following:

- Multiple accounts for a variety of social media networks:
  - Twitter
  - Pinterest
  - Instagram
- Read-only, rich listings of social media posts
- Links to the appropriate site or app for a quick and easy follow-up
- Desktop and mobile versions

This project will cover the following:

- REST/HTTP clients
- JSON processing
- JavaFX and Android development

Given the size and scope of this effort, we'll actually do this in two chapters: JavaFX in the first, and Android in the second.

Email filter

Managing email can be tricky, especially if you have more than one account. If you access your mail from more than one location (that is, from more than one desktop or mobile app), managing your email rules can be trickier still. If your mail system doesn't support rules stored on the server, you're left deciding where to put the rules so that they'll run most often. With this project, we'll develop an application that will allow us to author a variety of rules and then run them via an optional background process to keep your mail properly curated at all times.

A sample `rules` file may look something like this:

```
[
  {
    "serverName": "mail.server.com",
    "serverPort": "993",
    "useSsl": true,
    "userName": "me@example.com",
    "password": "password",
    "rules": [
      {"type": "move",
        "sourceFolder": "Inbox",
        "destFolder": "Folder1",
        "matchingText": "someone@example.com"},
      {"type": "delete",
        "sourceFolder": "Ads",
        "olderThan": 180}
    ]
  }
]
```

This project will cover the following:

- JavaMail
- JavaFX
- JSON Processing
- Operating System integration
- File I/O

JavaFX photo management

The Java Development Kit has a very robust assortment of image handling APIs. In Java 9, these were augmented with improved support for the TIFF specification. In this chapter, we'll exercise this API in creating an image/photo management application. We'll add support for importing images from user-specified locations into the configured official directory. We'll also revisit the duplicate file finder and reuse some of the code developed as a part of the project to help us identify duplicate images.

This project will cover the following:

- The new `javax.imageio` package
- JavaFX
- NetBeans Rich Client Platform
- Java file I/O

A client/server note application

Have you ever used a cloud-based note-taking application? Have you wondered what it would take to make your own? In this chapter, we'll create such an application, with complete front and backends. On the server side, we'll store our data in the ever popular document database, MongoDB, and we'll expose the appropriate parts of the business logic for the application via REST interfaces. On the client side, we'll develop a very basic user interface in JavaScript that will let us experiment with, and demonstrate how to use, JavaScript in our Java project.

This project will cover the following:

- Document databases (MongoDB)
- JAX-RS and RESTful interfaces
- JavaFX
- JavaScript and Vue 2

Serverless Java

Serverless, also known as **function as a service** (**FaaS**), is one of the hottest trends these days. It is an application/deployment model where a small function is deployed to a service that manages almost every aspect of the function--startup, shutdown, memory, and so on, freeing the developer from worrying about such details. In this chapter, we'll write a simple serverless Java application to see how it might be done, and how you might use this new technique for your own applications.

This project will cover the following:

- Creating an Amazon Web Services account
- Configuring AWS Lambda, Simple Notification Service, Simple Email Service, and DynamoDB
- Writing and deploying a Java function

Android desktop synchronization client

With this project, we'll change gears a little bit and focus specifically on a different part of the Java ecosystem: Android. To do this, we'll focus on a problem that still plagues some Android users--the synchronization of an Android device and a desktop (or laptop) system. While various cloud providers are pushing us to store more and more in the cloud and streaming that to devices, some people still prefer to store, for example, photos and music directly on the device for a variety of reasons, ranging from cost for cloud resources to unreliable wireless connectivity and privacy concerns.

In this chapter, we'll build a system that will allow users to synchronize music and photos between their devices and their desktop or laptop. We'll build an Android application that provides the user interface to configure and monitor synchronization from the mobile device side as well as the Android Service that will perform the synchronization in the background, if desired. We will also build the related components on the desktop--a graphical application to configure and monitor the process from the desktop as well as a background process to handle the synchronization from the desktop side.

This project will cover the following:

- Android
- User interfaces
- Services
- JavaFX
- REST

Getting started

We have taken a quick look at some of the new language features we will be using. We have also seen a quick overview of the projects we will be building. One final question remains: what tools will we be using to do our work?

The Java ecosystem suffers from an embarrassment of riches when it comes to development tools, so we have much to choose from. The most fundamental choice facing us is the build tool. For our work here, we will be using Maven. While there is a strong and vocal community that would advocate Gradle, Maven seems to be the most common build tool at the moment, and seems to have more robust, mature, and native support from the major IDEs. If you do not have Maven already installed, you can visit `http://maven.apache.org` and download the distribution for your operating system, or use whatever package management system is supported by your OS.

For the IDE, all screenshots, directions, and so forth will be using NetBeans--the free and open source IDE from Oracle. There are, of course, proponents of both IntelliJ IDEA and Eclipse, and they're both fine choices, but NetBeans offers a complete and robust development out-of-the-box, and it's fast, stable, and free. To download NetBeans, visit `http://netbeans.org` and download the appropriate installer for your operating system. Since we are using Maven, which IDEA and Eclipse both support, you should be able to open the projects presented here in the IDE of your choice. Where steps are shown in the GUI, though, you will need to adjust for the IDE you've chosen.

At the time of writing, the latest version of NetBeans is 8.2, and the best approach for using it to do Java 9 development is to run the IDE on Java 8, and to add Java 9 as an SDK. There is a development version of NetBeans that runs on Java 9, but, as it is a development version, it can be unstable from time to time. A stable NetBeans 9 should ship at roughly the same time as Java 9 itself. In the meantime, we'll push forward with 8.2:

1. To add Java 9 support, we will need to add a new Java platform, and we will do that by clicking on **Tools** | **Platforms**.
2. This will bring up the **Java Platform Manager** screen:

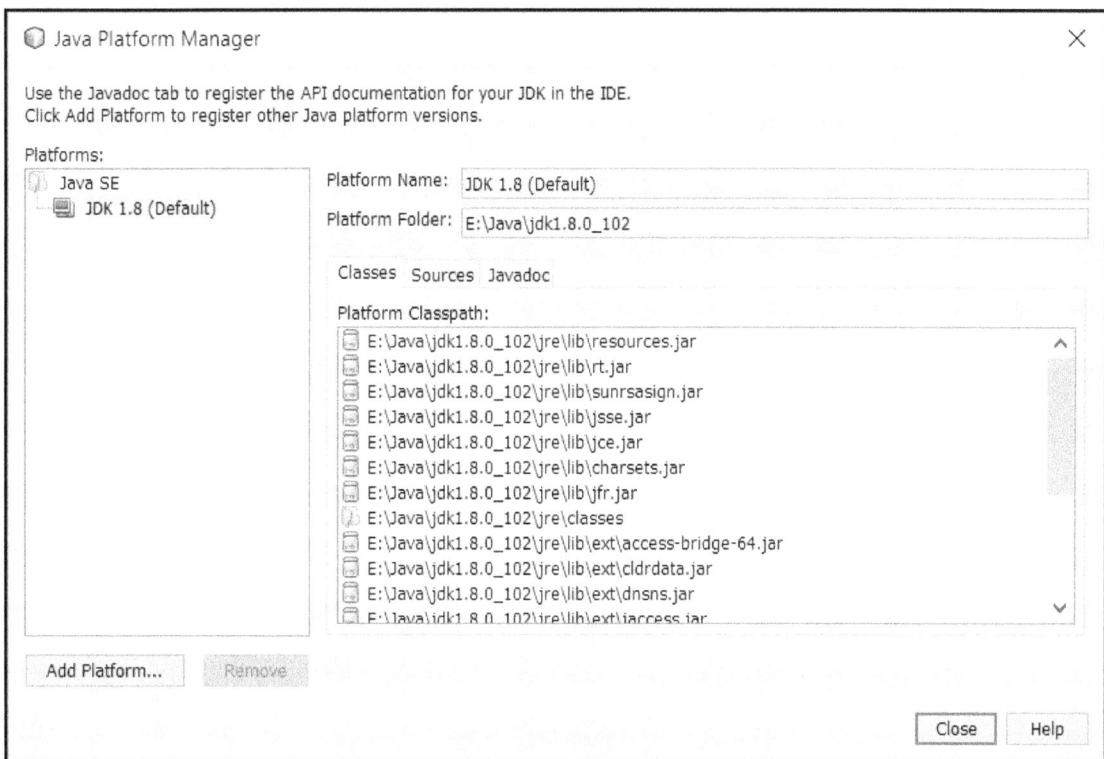

3. Click on **Add Platform...** on the lower left side of your screen.

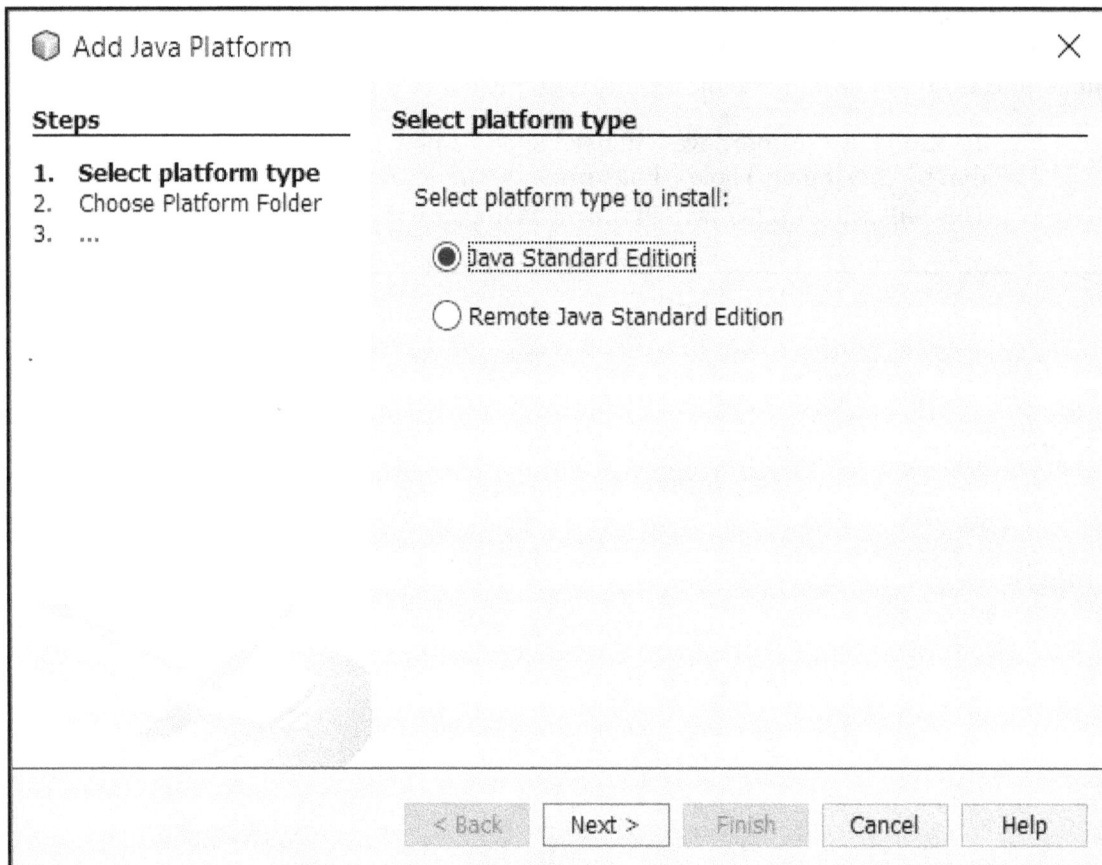

Add Java Platform   ✕

Steps   **Select platform type**

1. Select platform type   Select platform type to install:
2. Choose Platform Folder
3. ...   ⦿ Java Standard Edition

                                     ◯ Remote Java Standard Edition

                          < Back   Next >   Finish   Cancel   Help

---

4. We want to add a **Java Standard Edition** platform, so we will accept the default and click on **Next**.

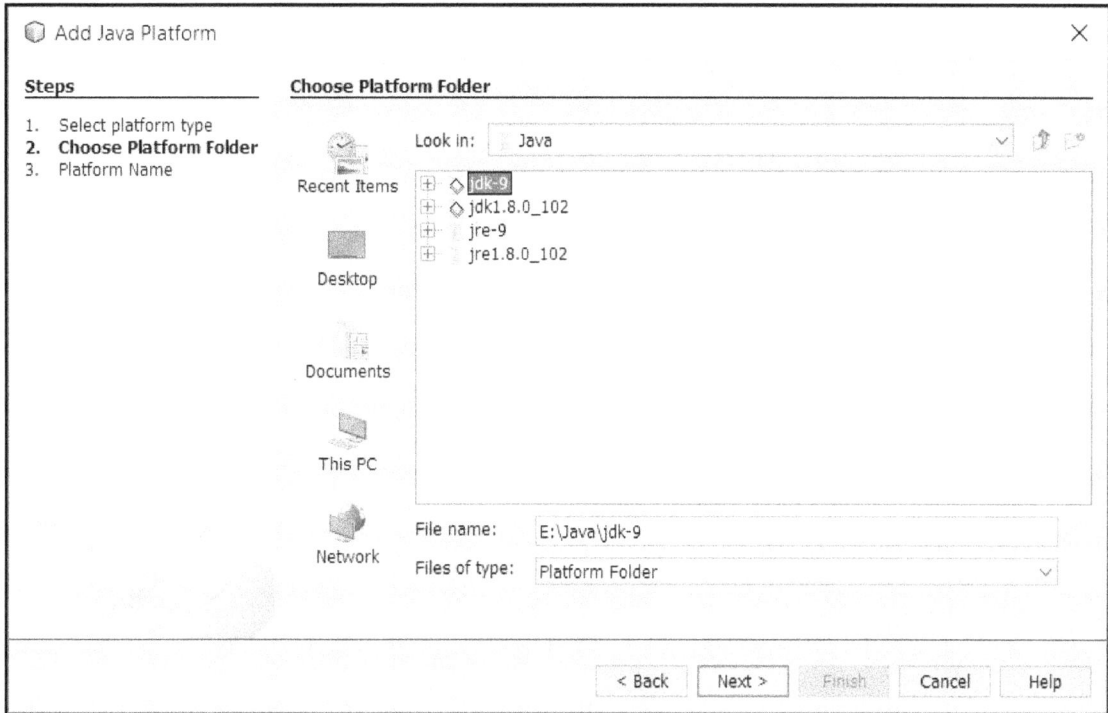

5. On the **Add Java Platform** screen, we will navigate to where we've installed Java 9, select the JDK directory, and click on **Next**.

6. We need to give the new Java Platform a name (NetBeans defaults to a very reasonable JDK 9) so we will click on **Finish** and can now see our newly added Java 9 option.

Java Platform Manager ✕

Use the Javadoc tab to register the API documentation for your JDK in the IDE.
Click Add Platform to register other Java platform versions.

Platforms:

- Java SE
  - JDK 1.8 (Default)
  - JDK 9

Platform Name: JDK 9

Platform Folder: E:\Java\jdk-9

Classes Sources Javadoc

Platform Modules:

- java.activation
- java.annotations.common
- java.base
- java.compact1
- java.compact2
- java.compact3
- java.compiler
- java.corba
- java.datatransfer
- java.desktop
- java.httpclient
- java.instrument

Add Platform...   Remove

Close   Help

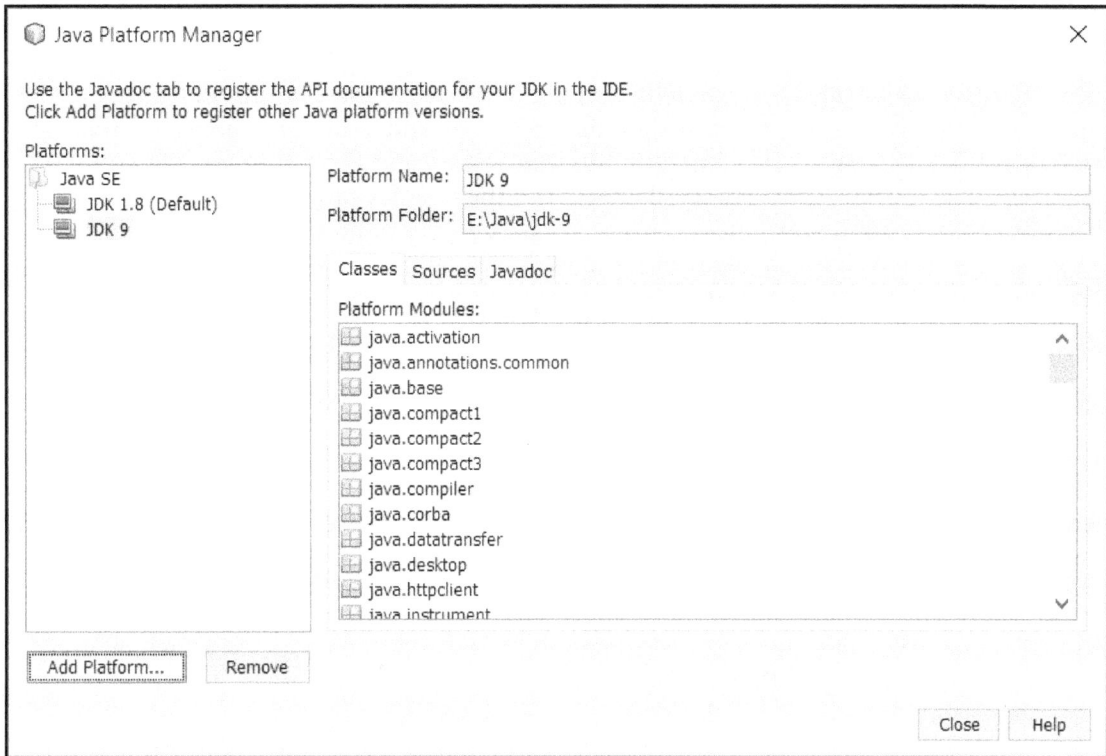

With the project SDK set, we're ready to take these new Java 9 features for a spin, which we'll start doing in `Chapter 18`, *Managing Processes in Java*.

> **TIP**
>
> If you do run NetBeans on Java 9, which should be possible by the time this book is published, you will already have Java 9 configured. You can, however, use the preceding steps to configure Java 8, should you need that version specifically.

Summary

In this chapter, we've taken a quick look at some of the great new features in Java 8, including lambdas, streams, the new date/time package, and default methods. From Java 9, we took a quick look at the Java Platform Module System and Project Jigsaw, the process handling APIs, the new concurrency changes, and the new Java REPL. For each, we've discussed the what and why, and looked at some examples of how these might affect the systems we write. We've also taken a look at the types of project we'll be building throughout the book and the tools we'll be using.

Before we move on, I'd like to restate an earlier point--every software project is different, so it is not possible to write this book in such a way that you can simply copy and paste large swathes of code into your project. Similarly, every developer writes code differently; the way I structure my code may be vastly different from yours. It is important, then, that you keep that in mind when reading this book and not get hung up on the details. The purpose here is not to show you the one right way to use these APIs, but to give you an example that you can look at to get a better sense of how they might be used. Learn what you can from each example, modify things as you see fit, and go build something amazing.

With all of that said, let's turn our attention to our first project, the Process Manager, and the new process handling APIs.

18
Managing Processes in Java

With a very quick tour through some of the big new features of Java 9, as well as those from a couple of previous releases, let's turn our attention to applying some of these new APIs in a practical manner. We'll start with a simple process manager.

While having your application or utility handle all of your user's concerns internally is usually ideal, occasionally you need to run (or **shell out to**) an external program for a variety of reasons. From the very first days of Java, this was supported by the JDK via the `Runtime` class via a variety of APIs. Here is the simplest example:

```
Process p = Runtime.getRuntime().exec("/path/to/program");
```

Once the process has been created, you can track its execution via the `Process` class, which has methods such as `getInputStream()`, `getOutputStream()`, and `getErrorStream()`. We have also had rudimentary control over the process via `destroy()` and `waitFor()`. Java 8 moved things forward by adding `destroyForcibly()` and `waitFor(long, TimeUnit)`. Starting with Java 9, these capabilities will be expanded. Quoting from the **Java Enhancement Proposal** (**JEP**), we see the following reasons for this new functionality:

Many enterprise applications and containers involve several Java virtual machines and processes and have long-standing needs that include the following:

- *The ability to get the pid (or equivalent) of the current Java virtual machine and the pid of processes created with the existing API.*
- *The ability to enumerate processes on the system. Information on each process may include its pid, name, state, and perhaps resource usage.*
- *The ability to deal with process trees, in particular, some means to destroy a process tree.*
- *The ability to deal with hundreds of sub-processes, perhaps multiplexing the output or error streams to avoid creating a thread per sub-process.*

In this chapter, we'll build a simple process manager application, akin to **Windows Task Manager** or *nix's top. There is, of course, little need for a process manager written in Java, but this will be an excellent avenue for us to explore these new process handling APIs. Additionally, we'll spend some time with other language features and APIs, namely, JavaFX and `Optional`.

The following topics are covered in this chapter:

- Creating the project
- Bootstrapping the application
- Defining the user interface
- Initializing the user interface
- Adding menus
- Updating the process list

With that said, let's get started.

Creating a project

Typically speaking, it is much better if a build can be reproduced without requiring the use of a specific IDE or some other proprietary tool. Fortunately, NetBeans offers the ability to create a Maven-based JavaFX project. Click on **File | New Project** and select Maven, then **JavaFX Application**:

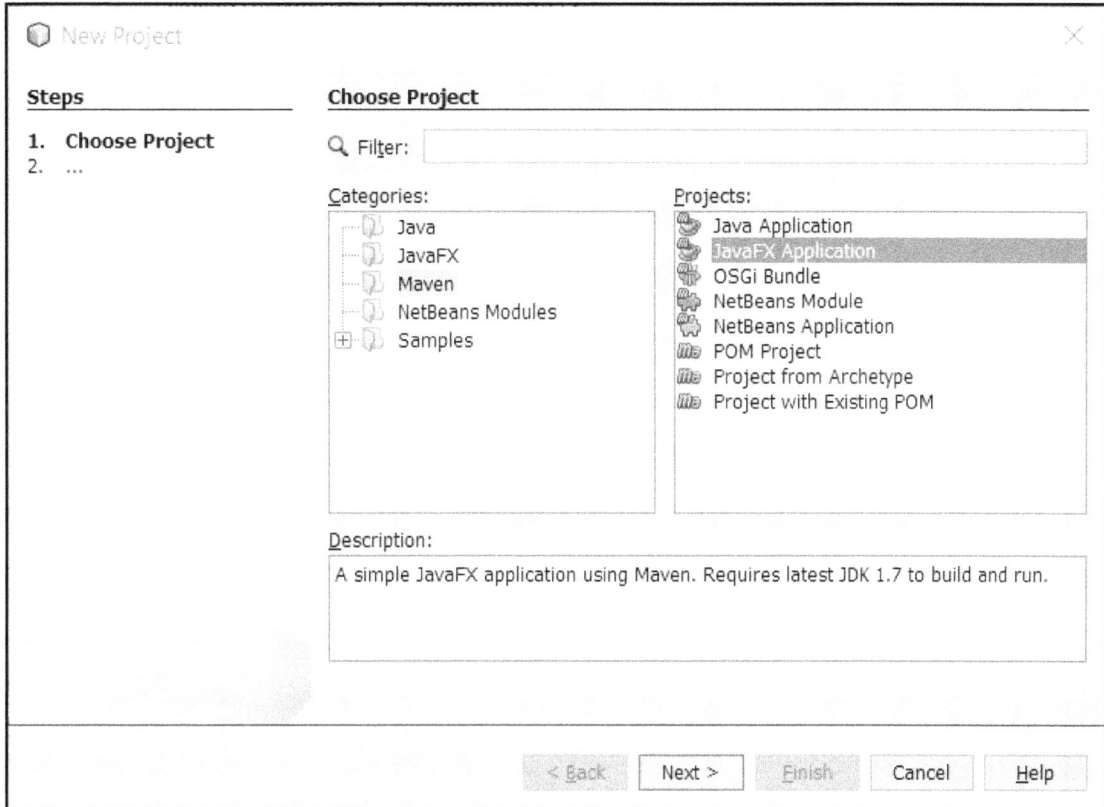

Next, perform the following steps:

1. Click on **Next**.
2. Enter **Project Name** as ProcessManager.
3. Enter **Group ID** as com.steeplesoft.
4. Enter **Package** as com.steeplesoft.processmanager.
5. Select **Project Location**.
6. Click on **Finish**.

Consider the following screenshot as an example:

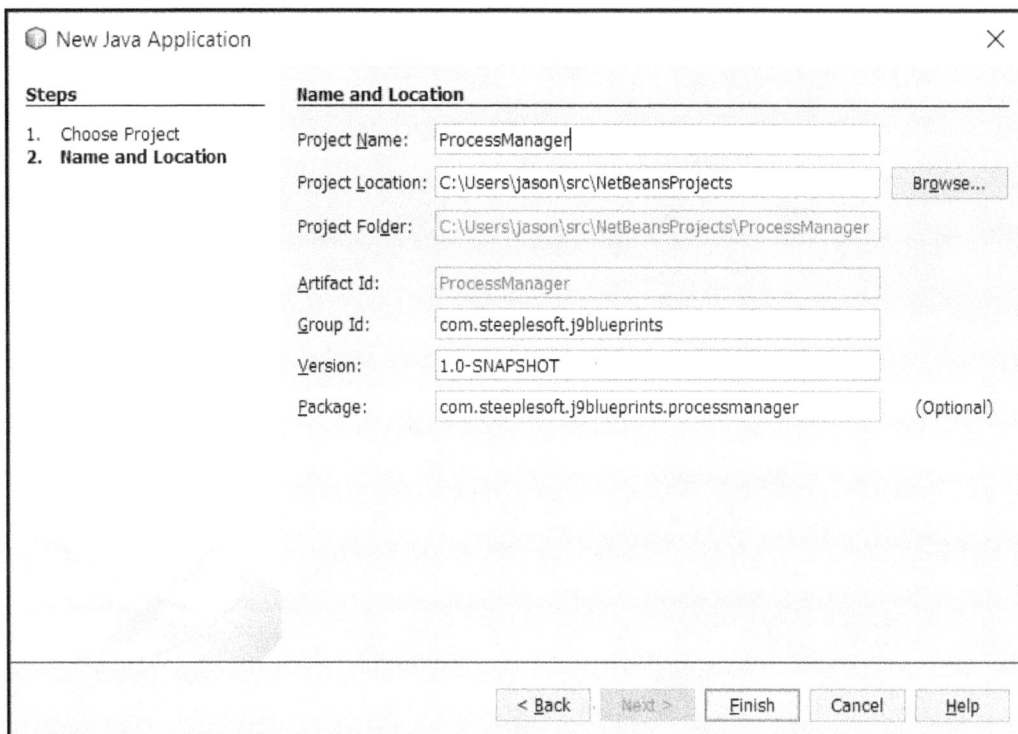

Once the new project has been created, we need to update the Maven pom to use Java 9:

```
<build>
  <plugins>
    <plugin>
      <groupId>org.apache.maven.plugins</groupId>
      <artifactId>maven-compiler-plugin</artifactId>
      <version>3.6.1</version>
      <configuration>
        <source>9</source>
        <target>9</target>
      </configuration>
    </plugin>
  </plugins>
</build>
```

Now, with both NetBeans and Maven configured to use Java 9, we're ready to start coding.

Bootstrapping the application

As noted in the introduction, this will be a JavaFX-based application, so we'll start by creating the skeleton for the application. This is a Java 9 application, and we intend to make use of the Java Module System. To do that, we need to create the module definition file, `module-info.java`, which resides in the root of our source tree. This being a Maven-based project, that would be `src/main/java`:

```
module procman.app {
    requires javafx.controls;
    requires javafx.fxml;
}
```

This small file does a couple of different things. First, it defines a new `procman.app` module. Next, it tells the system that this module `requires` two JDK modules: `javafx.controls` and `javafx.fxml`. If we did not specify these two modules, then our system, which we'll see below, would not compile, as the JDK would not make the required classes and packages available to our application. These modules are part of the standard JDK as of Java 9, so that shouldn't be an issue. However, that may change in future versions of Java, and this module declaration will help prevent runtime failures in our application by forcing the host JVM to provide the module or fail to start. It is also possible to build custom Java runtimes via the **J-Link** tool, so missing these modules is still a possibility under Java 9. With our module configured, let's turn to the application.

> The emerging standard directory layout seems to be something like src/main/java/*<module1>*, src/main/java/*<module2>*, and so on. At the time of writing this book, while Maven can be coaxed into such a layout, the plugins themselves, while they do run under Java 9, do not appear to be module-aware enough to allow us to organize our code in such a manner. For that reason, and for the sake of simplicity, we will treat one Maven module as one Java module and maintain the standard source layout for the projects.

The first class we will create is the `Application` descendant, which NetBeans created for us. It created the `Main` class, which we renamed to `ProcessManager`:

```
public class ProcessManager extends Application {
    @Override
    public void start(Stage stage) throws Exception {
        Parent root = FXMLLoader
          .load(getClass().getResource("/fxml/procman.fxml"));
        Scene scene = new Scene(root);
        scene.getStylesheets().add("/styles/Styles.css");
```

```
        stage.setTitle("Process Manager");
        stage.setScene(scene);
        stage.show();
    }

    public static void main(String[] args) {
        launch(args);
    }
}
```

Our `ProcessManager` class extends the JavaFX base class, `Application`, which provides a variety of functionality to start and stop the application. We see in the `main()` method that we simply delegate to `Application.launch(String[])`, which does the heavy lifting for us in starting our new application.

The more interesting part of this class is the `start()` method, which is where the JavaFX life cycle calls back into our application, giving us the opportunity to build the user interface, which we'll do next.

Defining the user interface

When building the user interface for a JavaFX application, you can do it in one of two ways: code or markup. To keep our code smaller and more readable, we'll build the user interface using FXML--the XML-based language created specifically for JavaFX to express user interfaces. This presents us with another binary choice--do we write the XML by hand, or do we use a graphical tool? Again, the choice is a simple one--we'll use a tool, **Scene Builder**, which is a WYSIWYG tool originally developed by Oracle and now maintained and supported by Gluon. We will, however, also be looking at the XML source so that we can understand what's being done, so if you don't like using a GUI tool, you won't be left out.

Installing and using Scene Builder is, as you would expect, pretty straightforward. It can be downloaded from `http://gluonhq.com/labs/scene-builder/`. Once installed, you need to tell NetBeans where to find it, which can be done in the Settings window, under **Java | JavaFX**, as you can see in the following screenshot:

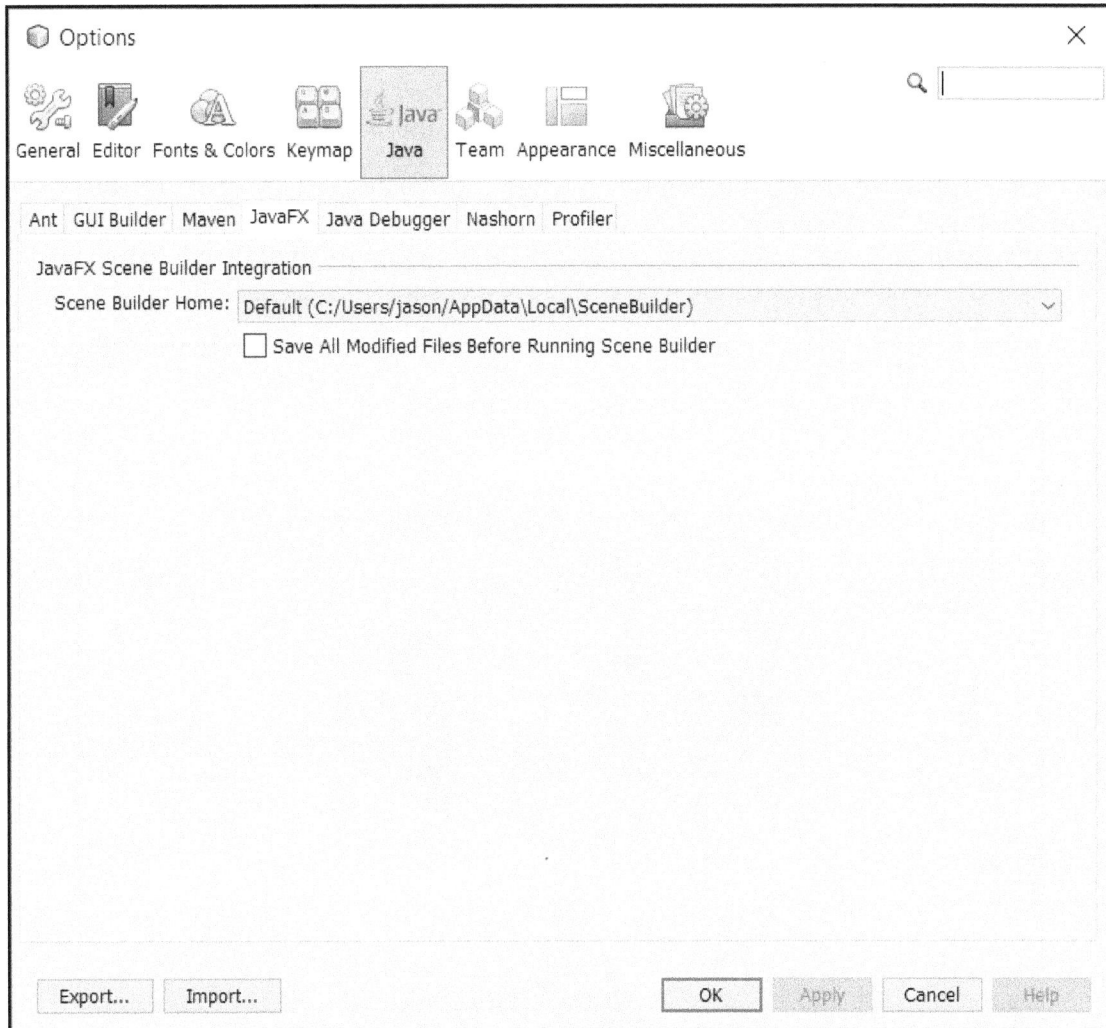

We are now ready to create the FXML file. Under the `resources` directory in the Project View, create a new folder called `fxml`, and in that folder, create a file called `procman.fxml`, as follows:

```
<BorderPane xmlns="http://javafx.com/javafx/8.0.60"
  xmlns:fx="http://javafx.com/fxml/1"
  fx:controller="com.steeplesoft.procman.Controller">
</BorderPane>
```

`BorderPane` is a container that defines five regions--`top`, `bottom`, `left`, `right`, and `center`, giving us a fairly coarsely-grained control over where on the form the controls should appear. Typically, with `BorderPane`, each area uses a nested container to provide the finer-grained control often necessary. For our needs, this level of control will be perfect.

The primary concern of the user interface is the list of processes, so we'll start with the controls for that. From Scene Builder, we want to click on the `Controls` section on the accordion on the left, then scroll down to `TableView`. Click on this and drag it to the `CENTER` region on the form, as shown here in this screenshot from Scene Builder:

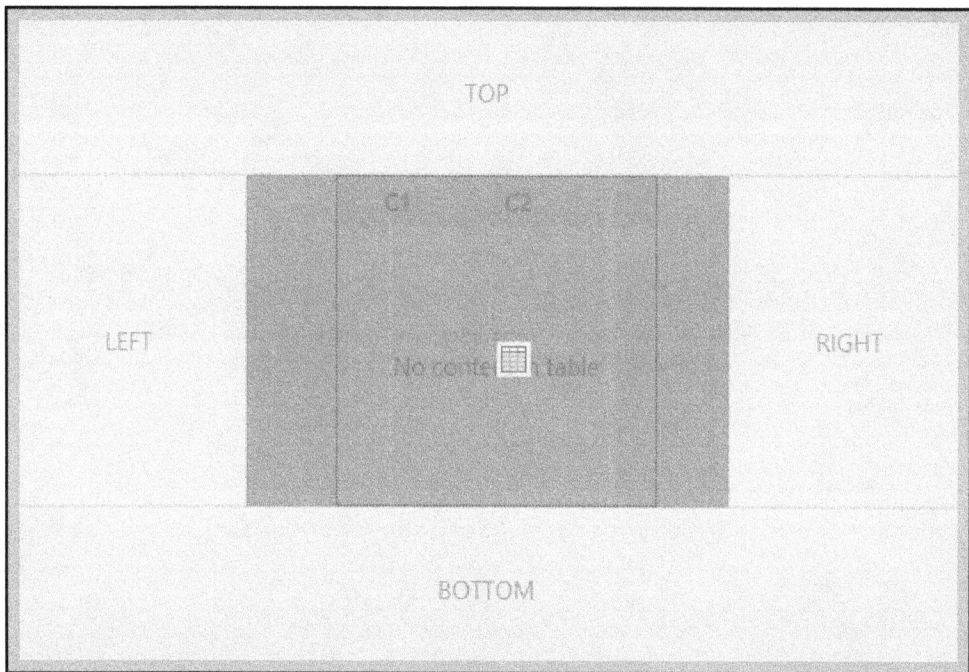

The resulting FXML should look something like this:

```
<center>
    <TableView fx:id="processList"
            BorderPane.alignment="CENTER">
    </TableView>
</center>
```

With no components in the other areas, `TableView` will expand to fill the window's full area, which is what we want for now.

Initializing the user interface

While the FXML defines the structure of the user interface, we do need some Java code to initialize various elements, respond to actions, and so forth. This class, referred to as the controller, is simply a class that extends `javafx.fxml.Initializable`:

```
public class Controller implements Initializable {
    @FXML
    private TableView<ProcessHandle> processList;
    @Override
    public void initialize(URL url, ResourceBundle rb) {
    }
}
```

The `initialize()` method comes from the interface, and is used by the JavaFX runtime to initialize the controller when it is created in the call to `FXMLLoader.load()` from the preceding `Application` class. Note the `@FXML` annotation on the instance variable `processList`. When JavaFX initializes the controller, before the `initialize()` method is called, the system looks for FXML elements that specify an `fx:id` attribute, and assigns that reference to the appropriate instance variable in the controller. To complete this connection, we must make one more change to our FXML file:

```
<TableView fx:id="processList" BorderPane.alignment="CENTER">
...
```

The change can also be made in Scene Builder as seen in this screenshot:

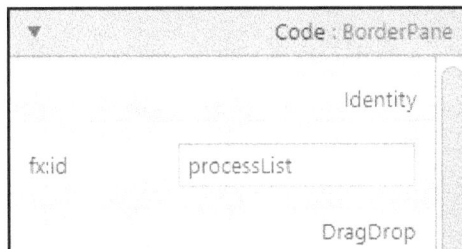

The value of the **fx:id** attribute must match the name of an instance variable that has been annotated with `@FXML`. When `initialize` is called, `processList` will have a valid reference to `TableView` that we can manipulate in our Java code.

The value of **fx:id** can be set via Scene Builder as well. To set the value, click on the control in the form editor, then expand the **Code** section in the accordion on the right. In the **fx:id** field, type in the name of the desired variable name.

The final piece of the puzzle is specifying the controller for the FXML file. In the XML source, you can set this via the `fx:controller` attribute on the root element of the user interface:

```
<BorderPane  xmlns="http://javafx.com/javafx/8.0.60"
   xmlns:fx="http://javafx.com/fxml/1"
   fx:controller="com.steeplesoft.procman.Controller">
```

This can also be set via Scene Builder. In the **Document** section of the accordion on the left, expand the **Controller** section and enter the desired fully-qualified class name in the **Controller class** field:

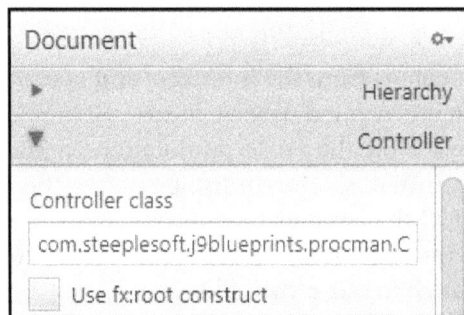

With those pieces in place, we can begin the work of initializing `TableView`, which gets us back to our primary interest, the process handling APIs. Our starting point is `ProcessHandles.allProcesses()`. From the Javadoc, you learn that this method returns **a snapshot of all processes visible to the current process**. From each `ProcessHandle` in the stream, we can get information about the process ID, its state, children, parents, and so on. Each `ProcessHandle` also has a nested object, `Info`, that contains a snapshot of information about the process. Since not all information is available across the various supported platforms and it is limited by the privileges of the current process, the properties on the `Info` object are the `Optional<T>` instances, indicating that the values may or may not be set. It's probably worth the time to take a quick look at what `Optional<T>` is.

The Javadoc describes `Optional<T>` as a **container object which may or may not contain a non-null value**. Inspired by Scala and Haskell, `Optional<T>` was introduced in Java 8 to allow API authors to provide a more null-safe interface. Prior to Java 8, a method on `ProcessHandle.Info` may be defined like this:

```
public String command();
```

To consume the API, the developer would likely write something like this:

```
String command = processHandle.info().command();
if (command == null) {
  command = "<unknown>";
}
```

If the developer fails to check for null explicitly, `NullPointerException` is almost certain to occur at some point. By using `Optional<T>`, the API author signals to the user that the return value may be null and should be handled carefully. The updated code, then, may look like this:

```
String command = processHandle.info().command()
  .orElse("<unknown>");
```

Now, in one concise line, we can get the value, if it is present, or a default if it is not. The `ProcessHandle.Info` API makes extensive use of this construct as we'll see later.

What else does `Optional` afford us as developers? There are a number of instance methods that can help clarify null-handling code:

- `filter(Predicate<? super T> predicate)`: With this method, we filter the contents of `Optional`. Rather than using an `if...else` block, we can pass the `filter()` method a `Predicate` and do the test inline. A `Predicate` is a `@FunctionalInterface` that takes an input and returns a Boolean. For example, some uses of the JavaFX `Dialog` may return `Optional<ButtonType>`. If we wanted to do something **only** if the user clicked a specific button, say, OK, we could filter `Optional` like this:

  ```
  alert.showAndWait()
    .filter(b -> b instanceof ButtonType.OK)
  ```

- `map(Function<? super T,? extends U> mapper)`: The `map` function allows us to pass the contents of `Optional` to a function, which will perform some processing on it, and return it. The return from the function, though, will be wrapped in an `Optional`:

  ```
  Optional<String> opts = Optional.of("hello");
  Optional<String> upper = opts.map(s ->
    s.toUpperCase());
  Optional<Optional<String>> upper2 =
    opts.map(s -> Optional.of(s.toUpperCase()));
  ```

Note the double wrapping in `Optional` for `upper2`. If `Function` returns `Optional`, it will be wrapped in another `Optional`, giving us this odd double wrap, which is less than desirable. Fortunately, we have an alternative.

- `flatMap(Function<? super T,Optional<U>> mapper)`: The `flatMap` function combines two functional ideas--maps and flatten. If the result of `Function` is an `Optional` object, rather than double wrapping the value, it is flattened to a single `Optional` object. Revisiting the preceding example, we get this:

```
Optional<String> upper3 = opts.flatMap(s ->
  Optional.of(s.toUpperCase()));
```

Note that `upper3`, unlike `upper2`, is a single `Optional`:

- `get()`: This returns the wrapped value, if present. If there is no value, a `NoSuchElementException` error is thrown.
- `ifPresent(Consumer<? super T> action)`: If the `Optional` object contains a value, it is passed to the `Consumer`. If there is no value present, nothing happens.
- `ifPresentOrElse(Consumer<? super T> action, Runnable emptyAction)`: Like `ifPresent()`, this will pass the value to the `Consumer` if there is one present. If no value is present, the `Runnable emptyAction` is executed.
- `isPresent()`: This simply returns true if the `Optional` object contains a value.
- `or(Supplier<Optional<T>> supplier)`: If the `Optional` object has a value, the `Optional` is described. If there is no value present, an `Optional` object produced by the `Supplier` is returned.
- `orElse(T other)`: If the `Optional` object contains a value, it is returned. If there is no value, `other` is returned.
- `orElseGet(Supplier<? extends T> supplier)`: This works just like `orElse()` mentioned earlier, but, if no value is present, the result of the `Supplier` is returned.

- orElseThrow(Supplier<? extends X> exceptionSupplier): If there is a value present, it is returned. If there is no value, the Exception provided by the Supplier is thrown.

Optional also has several static methods that facilitate the creation of the Optional instances, some of which are as follows:

- empty(): This returns an empty Optional object.
- of(T value): This returns an Optional object describing the non-null value. If the value is null, a NullPointerException is thrown.
- ofNullable(T value): This returns an Optional object describing the value. If the value is null, an empty Optional is returned.

With that very brief introduction to Optional<T> under our belts, let's see how its presence affects our application.

Returning our attention to the initialize() method, then, our first step is to get the list of processes to display. The streams API makes this extremely simple:

```
ProcessHandle.allProcesses()
  .collect(Collectors.toList());
```

The allProcesses() method returns Stream<ProcessHandle>, which allows us to apply the new stream operations to our problem. In this case, we just want to create a List of all of the ProcessHandle instances, so we call collect(), which is a stream operation that takes in a Collector. There are a number of options from which we could choose, but we want a List, so we use Collectors.toList(), which will collect each item in the stream and eventually return a List when the stream terminates. Note that the parameterized type of List will match that of Stream, which is ProcessHandle in this case.

This one line, then, gets us a List<ProcessHandle> of every process on the system that the current process can see, but that only gets us halfway. The TableView API doesn't accept a List<T>. It only supports ObservableList<T>, but what is that? Its Javadoc defines it very simply--*A list that allows listeners to track changes when they occur*. To put it another way, when this list changes, TableView will be told about it automatically and will redraw itself. Once we associate TableView with this list, all we have to worry about is the data, and the control will handle the rest. Creating ObservableList is pretty straightforward:

```
@FXML
private TableView<ProcessHandle> processView;
```

```
final private ObservableList<ProcessHandle> processList =
  FXCollections.observableArrayList();
// ...
processView.setItems(processList);
processList.setAll(ProcessHandle.allProcesses()
 .collect(Collectors.toList()));
```

In our case, the `TableView` instance is injected by the runtime (included here for clarity), and we create the `ObservableList` via `FXCollections.observableArrayList()`. In `initialize()`, we set the `ObservableList` on the `TableView` via `setItems()`, then populate the `ObservableList` via `setAll()`. With that, our `TableView` has all the data it needs to render itself. Almost. It has the **data** to render, but **how** does it do it? Where does each field of `ProcessHandle.Info` go? To answer that, we have to define the columns on the table, and tell each column where to get its data.

To do that, we need to create several `TableColumn<S, T>` instances. The `TableColumn` is responsible for displaying not only its column heading (as appropriate), but also the value of each cell. However, you have to tell it **how** to display the cell. That is done via a cell value factory. Under Java 7, that API would get us code like this:

```
TableColumn<ProcessHandle, String> commandCol =
 new TableColumn<>("Command");
commandCol.setCellValueFactory(new
  Callback<TableColumn.CellDataFeatures<ProcessHandle, String>,
   ObservableValue<String>>() {
     public ObservableValue<String> call(
      TableColumn.CellDataFeatures<ProcessHandle,
       String> p) {
         return new SimpleObjectProperty(p.getValue()
         .info()
         .command()
         .map(Controller::afterLast)
         .orElse("<unknown>"));
     }
   }
);
```

I'll go ahead and say it for you: that's really ugly. Fortunately, we can put lambdas and type inference to work for us, to make that a lot more pleasant to read:

```
TableColumn<ProcessHandle, String> commandCol =
 new TableColumn<>("Command");
commandCol.setCellValueFactory(data ->
 new SimpleObjectProperty(data.getValue().info().command()
  .map(Controller::afterLast)
  .orElse("<unknown>")));
```

That's fourteen lines of code replaced by six. Much prettier. Now, we just have to do that five more times, once for each column. As improved as the preceding code may be, there's still quite a bit of repeated code. Again, Java 8 functional interfaces can help us clean the code up a bit more. For each column, we want to specify the header, a width, and what to extract from `ProcessHandle.Info`. We can encapsulate that with this method:

```
private <T> TableColumn<ProcessHandle, T>
  createTableColumn(String header, int width,
    Function<ProcessHandle, T> function) {
      TableColumn<ProcessHandle, T> column =
        new TableColumn<>(header);

      column.setMinWidth(width);
      column.setCellValueFactory(data ->
       new SimpleObjectProperty<T>(
         function.apply(data.getValue())));
         return column;
}
```

The `Function<T,R>` interface is `FunctionalInterface`, which represents a function that takes in one type, `T`, and returns another, `R`. In our case, we're defining this method as one that takes as parameters a `String`, an `int`, and a function that takes in `ProcessHandle` and returns a generic type. That may be hard to picture, but with this method defined, we can replace the preceding code and the others like it with calls to this method. The same preceding code can now be condensed to this:

```
createTableColumn("Command", 250,
  p -> p.info().command()
  .map(Controller::afterLast)
  .orElse("<unknown>"))
```

Now we just need to add these columns to the control, which we can do with this:

```
processView.getColumns().setAll(
  createTableColumn("Command", 250,
  p -> p.info().command()
   .map(Controller::afterLast)
   .orElse("<unknown>")),
  createTableColumn("PID", 75, p -> p.getPid()),
  createTableColumn("Status", 150,
   p -> p.isAlive() ? "Running" : "Not Running"),
  createTableColumn("Owner", 150,
   p -> p.info().user()
    .map(Controller::afterLast)
    .orElse("<unknown>")),
  createTableColumn("Arguments", 75,
```

```
      p -> p.info().arguments().stream()
       .map(i -> i.toString())
       .collect(Collectors.joining(", "))));
```

Note that every method we're using on `ProcessHandle.Info` returns the `Optional<T>` we looked at in the preceding code. Since it does this, we have a very nice and clean API to get the information we want (or a reasonable default) without the specter of a `NullPointerException` in production.

If we run the application now, we should get something like this:

Command	PID	Status	Owner	Arguments
svchost.exe	11772	Running	jason	
taskhostw.exe	6332	Running	jason	
RuntimeBroker.exe	10900	Running	jason	
<unknown>	8032	Not Running	<unknown>	
ETDIntelligent.exe	9656	Running	jason	
explorer.exe	3204	Running	jason	
igfxEM.exe	11676	Running	jason	
igfxHK.exe	8536	Running	jason	
igfxTray.exe	3948	Running	jason	
NvBackend.exe	12016	Running	jason	
ShellExperienceHost.exe	10260	Running	jason	
<unknown>	12212	Not Running	<unknown>	
RAVCpl64.exe	5472	Running	jason	
RAVBg64.exe	6452	Running	jason	
RAVBg64.exe	2512	Running	jason	
RAVBg64.exe	5632	Running	jason	
utility.exe	7824	Running	jason	
StagelightUpdate.exe	9496	Running	jason	
DolbyDAX2TrayIcon.exe	1472	Running	jason	

It's looking good so far, but it's not quite ready yet. We want to be able to start new processes as well as kill existing ones. Both of those will require menus, so we'll add those next.

Adding menus

Menus in JavaFX start with a component called `MenuBar`. We want this menu to be at the top of the window, of course, so we add the component to the `top` section of our `BorderPane`. If you use Scene Builder, you will end up with something like this in your FXML file:

```
<MenuBar BorderPane.alignment="CENTER">
  <menus>
    <Menu mnemonicParsing="false" text="File">
      <items>
        <MenuItem mnemonicParsing="false" text="Close" />
      </items>
    </Menu>
    <Menu mnemonicParsing="false" text="Edit">
      <items>
        <MenuItem mnemonicParsing="false" text="Delete" />
      </items>
    </Menu>
    <Menu mnemonicParsing="false" text="Help">
      <items>
        <MenuItem mnemonicParsing="false" text="About" />
      </items>
    </Menu>
  </menus>
</MenuBar>
```

We won't be needing the edit menu, so we can remove that section from the FXML file (or by right-clicking on the second `Menu` entry in Scene Builder and clicking on **Delete**). To create the menu items we do want, we add the appropriate `MenuItem` entries to the `item` element under the `File` element:

```
<Menu mnemonicParsing="true" text="_File">
  <items>
    <MenuItem mnemonicParsing="true"
      onAction="#runProcessHandler"
      text="_New Process..." />
    <MenuItem mnemonicParsing="true"
      onAction="#killProcessHandler"
      text="_Kill Process..." />
    <MenuItem mnemonicParsing="true"
      onAction="#closeApplication"
      text="_Close" />
  </items>
</Menu>
```

Each of these `MenuItem` entries has three attributes defined:

- `mnemonicParsing`: This instructs JavaFX to use any letter prefixed with an underscore as a keyboard shortcut
- `onAction`: This identifies the method on the controller that will be called when `MenuItem` is activated/clicked
- `text`: This defines the label of `MenuItem`

The most interesting part is `onAction` and its relationship with the controller. JavaFX, of course, already knows that this form is backed by `com.steeplesoft.procman.Controller`, so it will look for a method with the following signature:

```
@FXML
public void methodName(ActionEvent event)
```

`ActionEvent` is a class that is used in a number of scenarios by JavaFX. In our case, we have methods specifically for each menu item, so the event itself isn't too terribly interesting. Let's take a look at each handler, starting with the simplest--`closeApplication`:

```
@FXML
public void closeApplication(ActionEvent event) {
  Platform.exit();
}
```

There's nothing much to see here; when the menu item is clicked, we exit the application by calling `Platform.exit()`.

Next up, let's see how to kill a process:

```
@FXML
public void killProcessHandler(final ActionEvent event) {
  new Alert(Alert.AlertType.CONFIRMATION,
  "Are you sure you want to kill this process?",
  ButtonType.YES, ButtonType.NO)
   .showAndWait()
   .filter(button -> button == ButtonType.YES)
   .ifPresent(response -> {
     ProcessHandle selectedItem =
      processView.getSelectionModel()
       .getSelectedItem();
     if (selectedItem != null) {
       selectedItem.destroy();
       processListUpdater.updateList();
     }
```

```
        });
    }
```

We have quite a bit going on here. The first thing we do is to create an `Alert` box of type `CONFIRMATION`, which asks the user to confirm the request. The dialog has two buttons: `YES` and `NO`. Once the dialog has been created, we call `showAndWait()`, which does as its name implies--it shows the dialog and waits for the user's response. It returns `Optional<ButtonType>`, which holds the type of the button that the user clicked on, which will either be `ButtonType.YES` or `ButtonType.NO`, given the type of `Alert` box we've created. With `Optional`, we can apply `filter()` to find only the type of button that we're interested in, which is `ButtonType.YES`, the result of which is another `Optional`. If the user clicked on yes, `ifPresent()` will return true (thanks to our filter), and the lambda we passed in will be executed. Very nice and concise.

The next area of interest is that lambda. Once we've identified **that** the user would like to kill a process, we need to identify **which** process to kill. To do that, we ask `TableView` which row is selected via `TableView.getSelectionModel() .getSelectedItem()`. We do need to check for null (alas, there's no `Optional` here) in the event that the user has not actually selected a row. If it is non-null, we can call `destroy()` on the `ProcessHandle` the `TableView` gives us. We then call `processListUpdater.updateList()` to refresh the UI. We'll take a look at that later.

Our final action handler has to run the following command:

```
@FXML
public void runProcessHandler(final ActionEvent event) {
    final TextInputDialog inputDlg = new TextInputDialog();
    inputDlg.setTitle("Run command...");
    inputDlg.setContentText("Command Line:");
    inputDlg.setHeaderText(null);
    inputDlg.showAndWait().ifPresent(c -> {
        try {
            new ProcessBuilder(c).start();
        } catch (IOException e) {
            new Alert(Alert.AlertType.ERROR,
                "There was an error running your command.")
                .show();
        }
    });
}
```

This is, in many ways, similar to the preceding `killProcessHandler()` method--we create a dialog, set some options, call `showAndWait()`, then process `Optional`. Unfortunately, the dialog doesn't support the builder pattern, meaning we don't have a nice, fluid API to build the dialog, so we do it in several discrete steps. Processing `Optional` is also similar. We call `ifPresent()` to see if the dialog returned a command line (that is, the user entered some text **and** pressed **OK**), and pass that to the lambda if present.

Let's take a quick look at the lambda. This is another example of a multiline lambda. Whereas most lambdas we've seen so far have been simple, one-line functions, remember that a lambda **can** span multiple lines. All that needs to be done to support that is to wrap the block in curly braces as we've done, and it's business as usual. Care must be taken with multiline lambdas like this, as any gains in readability and conciseness that lambdas give us can be quickly obscured or erased by a lambda body that grows too large. In those instances, extracting the code out to a method and using a method reference might be the wise thing to do. Ultimately, the decision is yours, but remember the words of Uncle Bob Martin--*Clarity is king*.

One final item on the topic of menus. To be even more useful, the application should provide a context menu that will allow the user to right-click on a process and kill it from there, as opposed to clicking on the row, moving the mouse to the `File` menu, and more. Adding a context menu is a simple operation. All we need to do is modify our `TableView` definition in FXML like this:

```
<TableView fx:id="processView" BorderPane.alignment="CENTER">
  <contextMenu>
    <ContextMenu>
      <items>
        <MenuItem onAction="#killProcessHandler"
          text="Kill Process..."/>
      </items>
    </ContextMenu>
  </contextMenu>
</TableView>
```

Here, we are adding a `contextMenu` child to our `TableView`. Much like its sibling, `MenuBar`, `contextMenu` has an `items` child, which, in turn, has 0 or more `MenuItem` children. In this case, the `MenuItem` for `Kill Process...` looks remarkably like that under `File`, with the only difference being the `mnemonicProcessing` information. We're even reusing the `ActionEvent` handler, so there's no extra coding, and the behavior for killing a process is always the same, regardless of which menu item you click on.

Updating the process list

If the application started and showed a list of processes, but never updated that list, it wouldn't be very useful at all. What we then need is a way to update the list periodically, and for that, we'll use a Thread.

As you may or may not know, a Thread is roughly a means to run a task in the background (the Javadoc describes it as a *thread of execution in a program*). A system can be single or multithreaded, depending on the needs and runtime environment of the system. And multithreaded programming is hard to get right. Luckily, our use case here is fairly simple, but we must still exercise caution, or we'll see some really unexpected behavior.

Ordinarily, the advice you would get when creating a Thread is to implement a Runnable interface, which you will then pass to the thread's constructor, and that's very good advice, as it makes your class hierarchy much more flexible, since you're not tied to a concrete base class (Runnable is an interface). In our case, however, we have a relatively simple system that has little to gain from that approach, so we'll extend Thread directly and simplify our code a little as well as encapsulating our desired behavior. Let's take a look at our new class:

```java
private class ProcessListUpdater extends Thread {
  private volatile boolean running = true;

  public ProcessListRunnable() {
    super();
    setDaemon(true);
  }

  public void shutdown() {
    running = false;
  }

  @Override
  public void run() {
    while (running) {
      updateList();
      try {
        Thread.sleep(5000);
      } catch (InterruptedException e) {
        // Ignored
      }
    }
  }

  public synchronized void updateList() {
```

```
    processList.setAll(ProcessHandle.allProcesses()
        .collect(Collectors.toList()));
    processView.sort();
  }
}
```

We have a pretty basic class, which we've given a reasonable and meaningful name that extends `Thread`. In the constructor, note that we call `setDaemon(true)`. This will allow our application to exit as expected and not block, waiting for the thread to terminate. We've also defined a `shutdown()` method, which we'll use from our application to stop the thread.

> The `Thread` class does have various state control methods, such as `stop()`, `suspend()`, `resume()`, and more, but these have all been deprecated as they are considered inherently unsafe. Search for the article, Why are `Thread.stop`, `Thread.suspend`, and `Thread.resume` deprecated? If you would like more details; however, the suggested best practice now is to use a control flag, like we've done with `running`, to signal to the `Thread` class that it needs to clean up and shut down.

Finally, we have the heart of our `Thread` class, `run()`, which loops infinitely (or until `running` becomes false), sleeping for five seconds after performing its work. The actual work is done in `updateList()`, which builds the list of processes, updates `ObservableList` we discussed earlier, and then instructs `TableView` to re-sort itself, based on the user's sort selection, if any. This is a public method, allowing us to call this at need, as we did in `killProcessHandler()`. That leaves us with the following block of code to set it up:

```
@Override
public void initialize(URL url, ResourceBundle rb) {
  processListUpdater = new ProcessListUpdater();
  processListUpdater.start();
  // ...
}
```

The following code will shut it down, which we've already seen in `closeHandler()`:

```
processListUpdater.shutdown();
```

The eagle-eyed will notice that `updateList()` has the `synchronized` keyword on it. This is to prevent any sort of race condition that might be caused by calling this method from multiple threads. Imagine the scenario where the user decides to kill a process and clicks on **OK** on the confirmation dialog at the exact moment the thread wakes up (this type of thing happens more often than you might think). We could conceivably have two threads calling `updateList()` at the same time, resulting in the first thread hitting `processView.sort()` just as the second is hitting `processList.setAll()`. What happens when `sort()` is called while another thread is rebuilding the list? It's hard to say for sure, but it could be catastrophic, so we want to disallow that. The `synchronized` keyword instructs the JVM to allow only one thread to execute the method at a time, causing all others to queue up, waiting their turn (note that their execution order is non-deterministic, so you can't base any expectations on the order in which threads get to run a `synchronized` method). This avoids the potential for a race condition, and ensures that our program doesn't crash.

While appropriate here, care must be taken with `synchronized` methods, as acquiring and releasing the locks can be expensive (though much less so with modern JVMs) and, more importantly, it forces threads to run sequentially when they hit this method call, which can cause a very undesirable lag in the application, especially in GUI applications. Keep that in mind when writing your own multithreaded applications.

Summary

With that in place, our application is complete. While not a terribly complex application, it does include several interesting technologies such as JavaFX, Lambdas, Streams, `ProcessHandle` plus related classes, and Threads.

In the next chapter, we'll build a simple command-line utility to find duplicate files. Through that, we'll get hands-on experience with the new File I/O APIs, the Java Persistence API (JPA), file hashing, and some more JavaFX.

19
Duplicate File Finder

Any system that's been running for a while starts to suffer from hard drive clutter. This is especially true, for example, with large music and photo collections. Except for the most fastidious files getting copied and moved, we end up with a copy here and a copy there. The question is, though, which of these are duplicates and which are not? In this chapter, we'll build a file-walking utility that will scan a set of directories looking for duplicate files. We'll be able to specify whether the duplicates should be deleted, **quarantined**, or simply reported.

In this chapter, we will cover the following topics:

- The Java Platform Module System
- The Java NIO (New I/O) File APIs
- File hashing
- **Java Persistence API (JPA)**
- The new Java Date/Time API
- Writing command-line utilities
- More JavaFX

Getting started

This application, while conceptually fairly simple, is a bit more complex than what we looked at in the last chapter, in that we will have both, a command line and a graphical interface. The experienced programmer is likely to immediately see the need to share the code between these two interfaces, as **DRY (Don't Repeat Yourself)** is one of the many hallmarks of a well-designed system. To facilitate this sharing of code, then, we will want to introduce a third module, which provides a library that can be consumed by the other two projects. We will call these modules `lib`, `cli`, and `gui`. Our first step in setting up the project is to create the various Maven POM files to describe the project's structure. The parent POM will look something like this:

```xml
<?xml version="1.0" encoding="UTF-8"?>
<project xmlns="http://maven.apache.org/POM/4.0.0"
  xmlns:xsi="http://www.w3.org/2001/XMLSchema-instance"
  xsi:schemaLocation="http://maven.apache.org/POM/4.0.0
  http://maven.apache.org/xsd/maven-4.0.0.xsd">
  <modelVersion>4.0.0</modelVersion>

 <groupId>com.steeplesoft.dupefind</groupId>
 <artifactId>dupefind-master</artifactId>
 <version>1.0-SNAPSHOT</version>
 <packaging>pom</packaging>

 <modules>
    <module>lib</module>
    <module>cli</module>
    <module>gui</module>
 </modules>

 <name>Duplicate Finder - Master</name>
</project>
```

This is a fairly typical POM file. We will start by identifying the project's parent that lets us inherit a number of settings, dependencies, and so on, and avoid having to repeat them in this project. Next, we will define the Maven coordinates for the project. Note that we don't define a version for this project, allowing the parent's version to cascade down. This will allow us to increase the version as needed in one place, and update all of the subprojects implicitly.

The last interesting part of this POM, for those who haven't seen a multi-module project before, is the `modules` section. The only thing to note here, for those who are new to this, is that each `module` element refers to a directory name, which is a direct child of the current directory, and should be declared in the order in which they are needed. In our case, the CLI and GUI both depend on the library, so `lib` goes first. Next, we'll need to create the POM files for each module. Each of these are typical POMs of type jar, so there's no need to include them here. There will be varying dependencies in each, but we'll cover those as the need arises.

Building the library

The foundational piece of this project is the library which both the CLI and the GUI will consume, so it makes sense to start here. When designing the library--its inputs, outputs, and general behavior--it helps to understand what exactly do we want this system to do, so let's take some time to discuss the functional requirements.

As stated in the introduction, we'd like to be able to search for duplicate files in an arbitrary number of directories. We'd also like to be able to restrict the search and comparison to only certain files. If we don't specify a pattern to match, then we want to check every file.

The most important part is how to identify a match. There are, of course, a myriad of ways in which this can be done, but the approach we will use is as follows:

- Identify files that have the same filename. Think of those situations where you might have downloaded images from your camera to your computer for safekeeping, then, later, perhaps you forgot that you had already downloaded the images, so you copied them again somewhere else. Obviously, you only want one copy, but is the file, for example, `IMG_9615.JPG`, in the temp directory the same as the one in your picture backup directory? By identifying files with matching names, we can test them to be sure.

- Identify files that have the same size. The likelihood of a match here is smaller, but there is still a chance. For example, some photo management software, when importing images from a device, if it finds a file with the same name, will modify the filename of the second file and store both, rather than stopping the import and requiring immediate user intervention. This can result in a large number of files such as `IMG_9615.JPG` and `IMG_9615-1.JPG`. This check will help identify these situations.

- For each match above, to determine whether the files are actually a match, we'll generate a hash based on the file contents. If more than one file generates the same hash, the likelihood of those files being identical is extremely high. These files we will flag as potential duplicates.

It's a pretty simple algorithm and should be pretty effective, but we do have a problem, albeit one that's likely not immediately apparent. If you have a large number of files, especially a set with a large number of potential duplicates, processing all of these files could be a very lengthy process, which we would like to mitigate as much as possible, which leads us to some non-functional requirements:

- The program should process files in a concurrent manner so as to minimize, as much as possible, the amount of time it takes to process a large file set
- This concurrency should be bounded so that the system is not overwhelmed by processing the request
- Given the potential for a large amount of data, the system must be designed in such a way so as to avoid using up all available RAM and causing system instability

With that fairly modest list of functional and non-functional requirements, we should be ready to begin. Like the last application, let's start by defining our module. In `src/main/java`, we will create this `module-info.java`:

```
module com.steeplesoft.dupefind.lib {
    exports com.steeplesoft.dupefind.lib;
}
```

Initially, the compiler--and the IDE--will complain that the `com.steeplesoft.dupefind.lib` package does not exist and won't compile the project. That's fine for now, as we'll be creating that package now.

The use of the word **concurrency** in the functional requirements, most likely, immediately brings to mind the idea of threads. We introduced the idea of threads in `Chapter 18`, *Managing Java Processes*, so if you are not familiar with them, review that section in the previous chapter.

Our use of threading in this project is different from that in the last, in that we will have a body of work that needs to be done, and, once it's finished, we want the threads to exit. We also need to wait for these threads to finish their work so that we can analyze it. In the `java.util.concurrent` package, the JDK provides several options to accomplish this.

Concurrent Java with a Future interface

One of the more common and popular APIs is the `Future<V>` interface. `Future` is a means to encapsulate an asynchronous calculation. Typically, the `Future` instance is returned by `ExecutorService`, which we'll discuss later. The calling code, once it has the reference to `Future`, can continue to work on other tasks while `Future` runs in the background in another thread. When the caller is ready for the results of `Future`, it calls `Future.get()`. If `Future` has finished its work, the call returns immediately with the results. If, however, `Future` is still working, calls to `get()` will block until `Future` completes.

For our uses, though, `Future` isn't the most appropriate choice. Looking over the non-functional requirements, we see the desire to avoid crashing the system by exhausting the available memory explicitly listed out. As we'll see later, the way this will be implemented is by storing the data in a lightweight on-disk database, and we will implement that--again, as we'll see later-by storing the file information as it is retrieved rather than by gathering the data, then saving it in a post-process method. Given that, our `Future` won't be returning anything. While there is a way to make that work (defining `Future` as `Future<?>` and returning `null`), it's not the most natural approach.

Perhaps the most appropriate approach is `ExecutorService`, which is `Executor` that provides additional functionality, such as the ability to create a `Future`, as discussed earlier, and manage termination of the queue. What, then, is `Executor`? `Executor` is a mechanism to execute `Runnable` that is more robust than simply calling `new Thread(runnable).start()`. The interface itself is very basic, consisting only of the `execute(Runnable)` method, so its value is not immediately apparent just from looking at the Javadoc. If, however, you look at `ExecutorService`, which is the interface that all `Executor` provided by the JDK implement, as well as the various `Executor` implementations, their value easily becomes more apparent. Let's take a quick survey now.

Looking at the `Executors` class, we can see five different types of `Executor` implementations: a cached thread pool, a fixed-size thread pool, a scheduled thread pool, a single thread executor, and a work-stealing thread pool. With the single thread `Executor` being the only exception, each of these can be instantiated directly (`ThreadPoolExecutor`, `ScheduledThreadPoolExecutor`, and `ForkJoinPool`), but users are urged by the JDK authors to use the convenience methods on the `Executors` class. That said, what are each of these options and why might you choose one?

- `Executors.newCachedThreadPool()`: This returns `Executor` that provides a pool of cached threads. As tasks come in, `Executor` will attempt to find an unused thread to execute the task with. If one cannot be found, a new `Thread` is created and the work begins. When a task is complete, `Thread` is returned to the pool to await reuse. After approximately 60 seconds, unused threads are destroyed and removed from the pool, which prevents resources from being allocated and never released. Care must be taken with this `Executor`, though, as the thread pool is unbounded, which means that under heavy use, the system could be overwhelmed by active threads.

- `Executors.newFixedThreadPool(int nThreads)`: This method returns an `Executor` similar to the one previously mentioned, with the exception that the thread pool is bounded to at most `nThreads`.

- `Executors.newScheduledThreadPool(int corePoolSize)`: This `Executor` is able to schedule tasks to run after an optional initial delay and then periodically, based on the delay and `TimeUnit` value. See, for example, the `schedule(Runnable command, long delay, TimeUnit unit)` method.

- `Executors.newSingleThreadExecutor()`: This method will return an `Executor` that will use a single thread to execute the tasks submitted to it. Tasks are guaranteed to be executed in the order in which they were submitted.

- `Executors.newWorkStealingExecutor()`: This method will return a so-called **work stealing** `Executor`, which is of type `ForkJoinPool`. The tasks submitted to this `Executor` are written in such a way as to be able to divide up the work to additional worker threads until the size of the work is under a user-defined threshold.

Given our non-functional requirements, the fixed-size `ThreadPoolExecutor` seems to be the most appropriate. One configuration option we'll need to support, though, is the option to force the generation of hashes for every file found. Based on the preceding algorithm, only files that have duplicate names or sizes will be hashed. However, users may want a more thorough analysis of their file specification and would like to force a hash on every file. We'll implement this using the work-stealing (or fork/join) pool.

With our threading approach selected, let's take a look at the entry point for the library, a class we'll call `FileFinder`. Since this is our entry point, it will need to know where we want to search and what we want to search for. That will give us the instance variables, `sourcePaths` and `patterns`:

```
private final Set<Path> sourcePaths = new HashSet<>();
private final Set<String> patterns = new HashSet<>();
```

We're declaring the variables as `private`, as that is a good object-oriented practice. We're also declaring them `final`, to help avoid subtle bugs where these variables are assigned new values, resulting in the unexpected loss of data. Generally speaking, I find it to be a good practice to mark variables as `final` by default to prevent such subtle bugs. In the case of instance variables in a class like this, a variable can only be declared `final` if it is either immediately assigned a value, as we are doing here, or if it is given a value in the class' constructors.

We also want to define our `ExecutorService` now:

```
private final ExecutorService es =
  Executors.newFixedThreadPool(5);
```

We have somewhat arbitrarily chosen to limit our thread pool to five threads, as it seems to be a fair balance between providing a sufficient number of worker threads for heavy requests, while not allocating a large number of threads that may not be used in most cases. In our case, it is probably a minor issue overblown, but it's certainly something to keep in mind.

Next, we need to provide a means to store any duplicates found. Consider the following lines of code as an example:

```
private final Map<String, List<FileInfo>> duplicates =
  new HashMap<>();
```

We'll see more details later, but, for now, all that we need to note is that this is a `Map` of `List<FileInfo>` objects, keyed by the file hash.

The final variable to make note of is something that might be a bit unexpected--an `EntityManagerFactory`. You might be asking yourself, what is that? The `EntityManagerFactory` is an interface to interact with a persistence unit as defined by the **Java Persistence API (JPA)**, which is part of the Java Enterprise Edition Specification. Fortunately, though, the specification was written in such a way to mandate that it be usable in a **Standard Edition (SE)** context like ours.

So, what are we doing with such an API? If you'll look back at the non-functional requirements, we've specified that we want to make sure that the search for duplicate files doesn't exhaust the available memory on the system. For very large searches, it is quite possible that the list of files and their hashes can grow to a problematic size. Couple that with the memory it will take to generate the hashes, which we'll discuss later, and we can very likely run into out-of-memory situations. We will, therefore, be using JPA to save our search information in a simple, light database (SQLite) that will allow us to save our data to the disk. It will also allow us to query and filter the results more efficiently than iterating over in-memory structures repeatedly.

Before we can make use of those APIs, we need to update our module descriptor to let the system know that we now require the persistence modules. Consider the following code snippet as an example:

```
module dupefind.lib {
    exports com.steeplesoft.dupefind.lib;
    requires java.logging;
    requires javax.persistence;
}
```

We've declared to the system that we require both `javax.persistence` and `java.logging`, which we'll be using later. As we discussed in Chapter 18, *Managing Processes in Java*, if any of these modules are not present, the JVM instance will fail to start.

Perhaps the more important part of the module definition is the `exports` clause. With this line (there can be 0 or more of them), we're telling the system that we are exporting all of the types in the specified package. This line will allow our CLI module, which we'll get into later, to use the classes (as well as interfaces, enums, and so on, if we were to add any) in that module. If a type's package does not `export`, consuming modules will be unable to see the type, which we'll also demonstrate later.

With that understanding, let's take a look at our constructor:

```
public FileFinder() {
    Map<String, String> props = new HashMap<>();
    props.put("javax.persistence.jdbc.url",
     "jdbc:sqlite:" +
     System.getProperty("user.home") +
     File.separator +
     ".dupfinder.db");
    factory = Persistence.createEntityManagerFactory
     ("dupefinder", props);
    purgeExistingFileInfo();
}
```

To configure the persistence unit, JPA typically uses a `persistence.xml` file. In our case, though, we'd like a bit more control over where the database file is stored. As you can see in the preceding code, we are constructing the JDBC URL using the `user.home` environment variable. We then store that in a `Map` using the JPA-defined key to specify the URL. This `Map` is then passed to the `createEntityManagerFactory` method, which overrides anything set in `persistence.xml`. This allows us to put the database in the home directory appropriate for the user's operating system.

With our class constructed and configured, it's time to take a look at how we'll find duplicate files:

```
public void find() {
    List<PathMatcher> matchers = patterns.stream()
      .map(s -> !s.startsWith("**") ? "**/" + s : s)
      .map(p -> FileSystems.getDefault()
      .getPathMatcher("glob:" + p))
      .collect(Collectors.toList());
```

Our first step is to create a list of the `PathMatcher` instances based on the patterns specified by the user. A `PathMatcher` instance is a functional interface that is implemented by objects that attempt to match files and paths. Our instances are retrieved from the `FileSystems` class.

When requesting `PathMatcher`, we have to specify the globbing pattern. As can be seen in the first call to `map()`, we have to make an adjustment to what the user specified. Typically, a pattern mask is specified simply as something like `*.jpg`. However, a pattern mask like this won't work in a way that the user expects, in that it will only look in the current directory and not walk down into any subdirectories. To do that, the pattern must be prefixed with `**/`, which we do in the call to `map()`. With our adjusted pattern, we request the `PathMatcher` instance from the system's default `FileSystem`. Note that we specify the matcher pattern as `"glob:" + p` because we need to indicate that we are, indeed, specifying a `glob` file.

With our matchers prepared, we're ready to start the search. We do that with this code:

```
sourcePaths.stream()
  .map(p -> new FindFileTask(p))
  .forEach(fft -> es.execute(fft));
```

Using the `Stream` API, we map each source path to a lambda that creates an instance of `FindFileTask`, providing it the source path it will search. Each of these `FileFindTask` instances will then be passed to our `ExecutorService` via the `execute()` method.

The `FileFindTask` method is the workhorse for this part of the process. It is a `Runnable` as we'll be submitting this to the `ExecutorService`, but it is also a `FileVisitor<Path>` as it will be used in walking the file tree, which we do from the `run()` method:

```
@Override
public void run() {
  final EntityTransaction transaction = em.getTransaction();
  try {
    transaction.begin();
    Files.walkFileTree(startDir, this);
    transaction.commit();
  } catch (IOException ex) {
    transaction.rollback();
  }
}
```

Since we will be inserting data into the database via JPA, we'll need to start a transaction as our first step. Since this is an application-managed `EntityManager`, we have to manage the transaction manually. We acquire a reference to the `EntityTransaction` instance outside the `try/catch` block to simplify referencing it. Inside the `try` block, we start the transaction, start the file walking via `Files.walkFileTree()`, then commit the transaction if the process succeeds. If it fails--if an `Exception` was thrown--we roll back the transaction.

The `FileVisitor` API requires a number of methods, most of which are not too terribly interesting, but we'll show them for clarity's sake:

```
@Override
public FileVisitResult preVisitDirectory(final Path dir,
final BasicFileAttributes attrs) throws IOException {
  return Files.isReadable(dir) ?
    FileVisitResult.CONTINUE : FileVisitResult.SKIP_SUBTREE;
}
```

Here, we tell the system that if the directory is readable, then we continue with walking down that directory. Otherwise, we skip it:

```
@Override
public FileVisitResult visitFileFailed(final Path file,
 final IOException exc) throws IOException {
    return FileVisitResult.SKIP_SUBTREE;
}
```

The API requires this method to be implemented, but we're not very interested in file read failures, so we simply return a skip result:

```
@Override
public FileVisitResult postVisitDirectory(final Path dir,
  final IOException exc) throws IOException {
    return FileVisitResult.CONTINUE;
}
```

Much like the preceding method, this method is required, but we're not interested in this particular event, so we signal the system to continue:

```
@Override
public FileVisitResult visitFile(final Path file, final
  BasicFileAttributes attrs) throws IOException {
    if (Files.isReadable(file) && isMatch(file)) {
      addFile(file);
    }
    return FileVisitResult.CONTINUE;
}
```

Now we've come to a method we're interested in. We will check to make sure that the file is readable, then check to see if it's a match. If it is, we add the file. Regardless, we continue walking the tree. How do we test if the file's a match? Consider the following code snippet as an example:

```
private boolean isMatch(final Path file) {
  return matchers.isEmpty() ? true :
    matchers.stream().anyMatch((m) -> m.matches(file));
}
```

We iterate over the list of `PathMatcher` instances we passed in to the class earlier. If the `List` is empty, which means the user didn't specify any patterns, the method's result will always be `true`. However, if there are items in the `List`, we use the `anyMatch()` method on the `List`, passing a lambda that checks the `Path` against the `PathMatcher` instance.

Adding the file is very straightforward:

```
private void addFile(Path file) throws IOException {
  FileInfo info = new FileInfo();
  info.setFileName(file.getFileName().toString());
  info.setPath(file.toRealPath().toString());
  info.setSize(file.toFile().length());
  em.persist(info);
}
```

We create a `FileInfo` instance, set the properties, then persist it to the database via `em.persist()`.

With our tasks defined and submitted to `ExecutorService`, we need to sit back and wait. We do that with the following two method calls:

```
es.shutdown();
es.awaitTermination(Integer.MAX_VALUE, TimeUnit.SECONDS);
```

The first step is to ask `ExecutorService` to shut down. The `shutdown()` method will return immediately, but it will instruct `ExecutorService` to refuse any new tasks, as well as shut down its threads as soon as they are idle. Without this step, the threads will continue to run indefinitely. Next, we will wait for the service to shut down. We specify the maximum wait time to make sure we give our tasks time to complete. Once this method returns, we're ready to process the results, which is done in the following `postProcessFiles()` method:

```
private void postProcessFiles() {
    EntityManager em = factory.createEntityManager();
    List<FileInfo> files = getDuplicates(em, "fileName");
```

Modern database access with JPA

Let's stop here for a moment. Remember our discussion of the **Java Persistence API (JPA)** and database? Here is where we see that coming in. With the JPA, interactions with the database are done via the `EntityManager` interface, which we retrieve from the cleverly named `EntityManagerFactory`. It is important to note that the `EntityManager` instances are not thread-safe, so they should not be shared between threads. That's why we didn't create one in the constructor and pass it around. This is, of course, a local variable, so we need not worry about that too much until, and if, we decide to pass it as a parameter to another method, which we are doing here. As we will see in a moment, everything happens in the same thread, so we will not have to worry about thread-safety issues as the code stands now.

With our `EntityManager,` we call the `getDuplicates()` method and pass the manager and field name, `fileName`. This is what that method looks like:

```
private List<FileInfo> getDuplicates(EntityManager em,
  String fieldName) {
    List<FileInfo> files = em.createQuery(
      DUPLICATE_SQL.replace("%FIELD%", fieldName),
        FileInfo.class).getResultList();
    return files;
}
```

This is a fairly straightforward use of the Java Persistence API--we're creating a query and telling it that we want, and getting a `List` of `FileInfo` references back. The `createQuery()` method creates a `TypedQuery` object, on which we will call `getResultList()` to retrieve the results, which gives us `List<FileInfo>`.

Before we go any further, we need to have a short primer on the Java Persistence API. JPA is what is known as an **object-relational mapping (ORM)** tool. It provides an object-oriented, type-safe, and database-independent way of storing data in, typically, a relational database. The specification/library allows application authors to define their data models using concrete Java classes, then persist and/or read them with little thought about the mechanics specific to the database currently being used. (The developer isn't completely shielded from database concerns--and it's arguable as to whether or not he or she should be--but those concerns are greatly lessened as they are abstracted away behind the JPA interfaces). The process of acquiring a connection, creating the SQL, issuing it to the server, processing results, and more are all handled by the library, allowing a greater focus on the business of the application rather than the plumbing. It also allows a high degree of portability between databases, so applications (or libraries) can be easily moved from one system to another with minimal change (usually restricted to configuration changes).

At the heart of JPA is `Entity`, the business object (or domain model, if you prefer) that models the data for the application. This is expressed in the Java code as a **plain old Java object (POJO)**, which is marked up with a variety of annotations. A complete discussion of all of those annotations (or the API as a whole) is outside the scope of this book, but we'll use enough of them to get you started.

With that basic explanation given, let's take a look at our one and only entity--the `FileInfo` class:

```
@Entity
public class FileInfo implements Serializable {
  @GeneratedValue
  @Id
  private int id;
```

```
        private String fileName;
        private String path;
        private long size;
        private String hash;
    }
```

This class has five properties. The only one that needs special attention is id. This property holds the primary key value for each row, so we annotate it with @Id. We also annotate this field with @GeneratedValue to indicate that we have a simple primary key for which we'd like the system to generate a value. This annotation has two properties: strategy and generator. The default value for strategy is GenerationType.AUTO, which we happily accept here. Other options include IDENTITY, SEQUENCE, and TABLE. In more complex uses, you may want to specify a strategy explicitly, which allows you to fine-tune how the key is generated (for example, the starting number, the allocation size, the name of the sequence or table, and so on). By choosing AUTO, we're telling JPA to choose the appropriate generation strategy for our target database. If you specify a strategy other than AUTO, you will also need to specify the details for the generator, using @SequenceGenerator for SEQUENCE and @TableGenerator for TABLE. You will also need to give the ID of the generator to the @GeneratedValue annotation using the generator attribute. We're using the default, so we need not specify a value for this attribute.

The next four fields are the pieces of data we have identified that we need to capture. Note that if we do not need to specify anything special about the mapping of these fields to the database columns, no annotations are necessary. However, if we would like to change the defaults, we can apply the @Column annotation and set the appropriate attribute, which can be one or more of columnDefinition (used to help generate the DDL for the column), insertable, length, name, nullable, precision, scale, table, unique, and updatable. Again, we're happy with the defaults.

JPA also requires each property to have a getter and a setter; the specification seems to be worded oddly, which has led to some ambiguity as to whether or not this is a hard requirement, and different JPA implementations handle this differently, but it's certainly safer to provide both as a matter of practice. If you need a read-only property, you can experiment with either no setter, or simply a no-op method. We haven't shown the getters and setters here, as there is nothing interesting about them. We have also omitted the IDE-generated equals() and hashCode() methods.

To help demonstrate the module system, we've put our entity in a
com.steeplesoft.dupefind.lib.model subpackage. We'll tip our hand a bit and go
ahead and announce that this class will be used by both our CLI and GUI modules, so we'll
need to update our module definition as follows:

```
module dupefind.lib {
    exports com.steeplesoft.dupefind.lib;
    exports com.steeplesoft.dupefind.lib.model;
    requires java.logging;
    requires javax.persistence;
}
```

That's all there is to our entity, so let's turn our attention back to our application logic. The
createQuery() call deserves a bit of discussion. Typically, when using JPA, queries are
written in what is called **JPAQL (Java Persistence API Query Language)**. It looks very
much like SQL, but has a more object-oriented feel to it. For example, if we wanted to query
for every FileInfo record in the database, we would do so with this query:

```
SELECT f FROM FileInfo f
```

I have put the keywords in all caps, with variable names in lower and the entity name in
camel case. This is mostly a matter of style, but while most identifiers are case-insensitive,
JPA does require that the case on the entity name matches that of the Java class it
represents. You must also specify an alias, or identification variable, for the entity, which
we simply call f.

To get a specific FileInfo record, you can specify a WHERE clause as follows:

```
SELECT f from FileInfo f WHERE f.fileName = :name
```

With this query, we can filter the query just as SQL does, and, just like SQL, we specify a
positional parameter. The parameter can either be a name, like we've done here, or simply a
?. If you use a name, you set the parameter value on the query using that name. If you use
the question mark, you must set the parameter using its index in the query. For small
queries, this is usually fine, but for larger, more complex queries, I would suggest using
names so that you don't have to manage index values, as that's almost guaranteed to cause a
bug at some point. Setting the parameter can look something like this:

```
Query query = em.createQuery(
    "SELECT f from FileInfo f WHERE f.fileName = :name");
query.setParameter("name", "test3.txt");
query.getResultList().stream() //...
```

With that said, let's take a look at our query:

```
SELECT f
FROM FileInfo f,
    (SELECT s.%FIELD%
     FROM FileInfo s
     GROUP BY s.%FIELD%
     HAVING (COUNT(s.%FIELD%) > 1)) g
WHERE f.%FIELD% = g.%FIELD%
AND f.%FIELD% IS NOT NULL
ORDER BY f.fileName, f.path
```

This query is moderately complicated, so let's break it down and see what's going on. First, in our SELECT query, we will specify only f, which is the identification variable of the entity for which we are querying. Next, we are selecting from a regular table and a temporary table, which is defined by the subselect in the FROM clause. Why are we doing it this way? We need to identify all of the rows that have a duplicate value (fileName, size, or hash). To do that, we use a HAVING clause with the COUNT aggregation function, HAVING (COUNT(fieldName > 1)) which says, in effect, give me all of the rows where this field occurs more than one time. The HAVING clause requires a GROUP BY clause, and once that's done, all of the rows with duplicate values are aggregated down to a single row. Once we have that list of rows, we will then join the real (or physical) table to those results to filter our physical table. Finally, we filter out the null fields in the WHERE clause, then order by fileName and path so that we don't have to do that in our Java code, which is likely to be less efficient than it would be if done by the database--a system designed for such operations.

You should also note the %FIELD% attribute in the SQL. We'll run the same query for multiple fields, so we've written the query once, and placed a marker in the text that we will replace with the desired field, which is sort of a *poor man's* template. There are, of course, a variety of ways to do this (and you may have one you find superior), but this is simple and easy to use, so it's perfectly acceptable in this environment.

We should also note that it is, generally speaking, a very bad idea to either concatenate SQL with values or do string replacements like we're doing, but our scenario is a bit different. If we were accepting user input and inserting that into the SQL this way, then we would certainly have a target for an SQL injection attack. In our use here, though, we aren't taking input from users, so this approach should be perfectly safe. In terms of database performance, this shouldn't have any adverse effects either. While we will require three different hard parses (one for each field by which we will filter), this is no different than if we were hardcoding the queries in our source file. Both of those issues, as well as many more, are always good to consider as you write your queries (and why I said the developer is mostly shielded from database concerns).

All of that gets us through the first step, which is identifying all of the files that have the same name. We now need to identify the files that have the same size, which can be done using the following piece of code:

```
List<FileInfo> files = getDuplicates(em, "fileName");
files.addAll(getDuplicates(em, "size"));
```

In our call to find duplicate filenames, we declared a local variable, `files`, to store those results. In finding files with duplicate sizes, we call the same `getDuplicates()` method, but with the correct field name, and simply add that to `files` via the `List.addAll()` method.

We now have a complete list of all of the possible duplicates, so we need to generate the hashes for each of these to see if they are truly duplicates. We will do that with this loop:

```
em.getTransaction().begin();
files.forEach(f -> calculateHash(f));
em.getTransaction().commit();
```

In a nutshell, we start a transaction (since we'll be inserting data into the database), then loop over each possible duplicate via `List.forEach()` and a lambda that calls `calculateHash(f)`, and then pass the `FileInfo` instance. Once the loop terminates, we commit the transaction to save our changes.

What does `calculateHash()` do? Let's a take a look:

```
private void calculateHash(FileInfo file) {
  try {
    MessageDigest messageDigest =
      MessageDigest.getInstance("SHA3-256");
    messageDigest.update(Files.readAllBytes(
      Paths.get(file.getPath())));
    ByteArrayInputStream inputStream =
      new ByteArrayInputStream(messageDigest.digest());
    String hash = IntStream.generate(inputStream::read)
     .limit(inputStream.available())
     .mapToObj(i -> Integer.toHexString(i))
     .map(s -> ("00" + s).substring(s.length()))
     .collect(Collectors.joining());
    file.setHash(hash);
  } catch (NoSuchAlgorithmException | IOException ex) {
    throw new RuntimeException(ex);
  }
}
```

This simple method encapsulates the work required to read the contents of a file and generate a hash. It requests an instance of `MessageDigest` using the `SHA3-256` hash, which is one of the four new hashes supported by Java 9 (the other three being `SHA3-224`, `SHA3-384`, and `SHA3-512`). Many developers' first thought is to reach for MD-5 or SHA-1, but those are no longer considered reliable. Using the new SHA-3 should guarantee we avoid any false positives.

The rest of the method is pretty interesting in terms of how it does its work. First, it reads all of the bytes of the specified file and passes them to `MessageDigest.update()`, which updates the internal state of the `MessageDigest` object to give us the hash we want. Next, we create a `ByteArrayInputStream` that wraps the results of `messageDigest.digest()`.

With our hash ready, we generate a string based on those bytes. We will do that by generating a stream via the `IntStream.generate()` method using the `InputStream` we just created as a source. We will limit the stream generation to the bytes available in the `inputStream`. For each byte, we will convert it to a string via `Integer.toHexString()`; then pad it with zero to two spaces, which prevents, for example, the single-digit hex characters `E` and `F` from being interpreted as `EF`; then collect them all into a string using `Collections.joining()`. Finally, we take that string value and update the `FileInfo` object.

The eagle-eyed might notice something interesting: we call `FileInfo.setHash()` to change the value of the object, but we never tell the system to persist those changes. This is because our `FileInfo` instance is a managed instance, meaning that we got it from JPA, which is keeping an eye on it, so to speak. Since we retrieved it via JPA, when we make any changes to its state, JPA knows it needs to persist those changes. When we call `em.getTransaction().commit()` in the calling method, JPA automatically saves those changes to the database.

> **TIP**
>
> There's a catch to this automatic persistence: if you retrieve an object via JPA, then pass it across some sort of barrier that serializes the object, for example, across a remote EJB interface, then the JPA entity is said to be "detached". To reattach it to the persistence context, you will need to call `entityManager.merge()`, after which this behavior will resume. There is no need to call `entityManager.flush()` unless you have some need to synchronize the in-memory state of the persistence context with the underlying database.

Once we've calculated the hashes for the potential duplicates (at this point, given that they have duplicate SHA-3 hashes, they are almost certainly actual duplicates), we're ready to gather and report them:

```
getDuplicates(em, "hash").forEach(f -> coalesceDuplicates(f));
em.close();
```

We call the same `getDuplicates()` method to find duplicate hashes, and pass each record to the `coalesceDuplicates()` method, which will group these in a manner appropriate to report upstream to our CLI or GUI layers, or, perhaps, to any other program consuming this functionality:

```
private void coalesceDuplicates(FileInfo f) {
  String name = f.getFileName();
  List<FileInfo> dupes = duplicates.get(name);
  if (dupes == null) {
    dupes = new ArrayList<>();
    duplicates.put(name, dupes);
  }
  dupes.add(f);
}
```

This simple method follows what is likely a very familiar pattern:

1. Get a `List` from a `Map` based on the key, the filename.
2. If the map doesn't exist, create it and add it to the map.
3. Add the `FileInfo` object to the list.

This completes the duplicate file detection. Back in `find()`, we will call `factory.close()` to be a good JPA citizen, then return to the calling code. With that, we're ready to build our CLI.

Building the command-line interface

The primary means to interact with our new library will be the command-line interface we will now develop. Unfortunately, the Java SDK has nothing built in to help make sophisticated command-line utilities. If you've been using Java for any time, you've seen the following method signature:

```
public static void main(String[] args)
```

Clearly, there is *a* mechanism to process command-line arguments. The `public static void main` method is passed string arrays that represent arguments provided by the user on the command line, but that's about as far as it goes. To parse the options, the developer is required to iterate over the array, analyzing each entry. It might look something like this:

```
int i = 0;
while (i < args.length) {
  if ("--source".equals(args[i])) {
    System.out.println("--source = " + args[++i]);
  } else if ("--target".equals(args[i])) {
    System.out.println("--target = " + args[++i]);
  } else if ("--force".equals(args[i])) {
    System.out.println("--force set to true");
  }
  i++;
}
```

This is an effective solution, if very naive and error-prone. It assumes that whatever follows `--source` and `--target` is that argument's value. If the user types `--source --target /foo`, then our processor breaks. Clearly, something better is needed. Fortunately, we have options.

If you were to search for Java command-line libraries, you'll find an abundance of them (at least 10 at last count). Our space (and time) is limited here, so we obviously can't discuss all of them, so I'll mention the first three that I'm familiar with: Apache Commons CLI, Airline, and Crest. Each of these has some fairly significant differences from its competitors.

Commons CLI takes a more procedural approach; the list of available options, its name, description, whether or not it has arguments, and so forth, are all defined using Java method calls. Once the list of `Options` has been created, the command-line arguments are then manually parsed. The preceding example could be rewritten as follows:

```
public static void main(String[] args) throws ParseException {
  Options options = new Options();
  options.addOption("s", "source", true, "The source");
  options.addOption("t", "target", true, "The target");
  options.addOption("f", "force", false, "Force");
  CommandLineParser parser = new DefaultParser();
  CommandLine cmd = parser.parse(options, args);
  if (cmd.hasOption("source")) {
    System.out.println("--source = " +
      cmd.getOptionValue("source"));
  }
  if (cmd.hasOption("target")) {
    System.out.println("--target = " +
```

```
        cmd.getOptionValue("target"));
   }
   if (cmd.hasOption("force")) {
      System.out.println("--force set to true");
   }
}
```

It's certainly more verbose, but it's also clearly, I think, more robust. We can specify long and short names for the option (`--source` versus `-s`), we can give it a description, and, best of all, we get built-in validation that an option has its required value. As much of an improvement as this is, I've learned from experience that the procedural approach here gets tedious in practice. Let's take a look at our next candidate to see how it fares.

Airline is a command-line library originally written as part of the airlift organization on GitHub. After languishing for some time, it was forked by Rob Vesse and given a new life (`http://rvesse.github.io/airline`). Airline's approach to command-line definition is more class-based--to define a command utility, you declare a new class, and mark it up appropriately with a number of annotations. Let's implement our preceding simple command line with Airline:

```
@Command(name = "copy", description = "Copy a file")
public class CopyCommand {
  @Option(name = {"-s", "--source"}, description = "The source")
  private String source;
  @Option(name = {"-t", "--target"}, description = "The target")
  private String target;
  @Option(name = {"-f", "--force"}, description = "Force")
  private boolean force = false;
  public static void main(String[] args) {
    SingleCommand<CopyCommand> parser =
      SingleCommand.singleCommand(CopyCommand.class);
    CopyCommand cmd = parser.parse(args);
    cmd.run();
  }

  private void run() {
    System.out.println("--source = " + source);
    System.out.println("--target = " + target);
    if (force) {
      System.out.println("--force set to true");
    }
  }
}
```

The options handling continues to grow in terms of code size, but we're also gaining more and more clarity as to what options are supported, and what they each mean. Our command is clearly defined via @Command on the class declaration. The possible options are delineated as @Option--annotated instance variables, and the business logic in run() is completely devoid of command-line parsing code. By the time this method is called, all the data has been extracted and we're ready to do our work. That looks very nice, but let's see what our last contender has to offer.

Crest is a library from Tomitribe, the company behind TomEE, the "all-Apache Java EE Web Profile certified stack" based on the venerable Tomcat Servlet container. Crest's approach to command definition is method based, where you define a method per command. It also uses annotations, and offers Bean Validation out of the box, as well as optional command discovery. Reimplementing our simple command, then, may look like this:

```
public class Commands {
  @Command
  public void copy(@Option("source") String source,
    @Option("target") String target,
    @Option("force") @Default("false") boolean force) {
      System.out.println("--source = " + source);
      System.out.println("--target = " + target);
      if (force) {
        System.out.println("--force set to true");
      }
    }
  }
}
```

That seems to be the best of both worlds: it's nice and concise, and will still keep the actual logic of the command free from any CLI-parsing concerns, unless you're bothered by the annotations on the method. Although the actual logic-implementing code is free from such concerns. While Airline and Crest both offer things the other does not, Crest wins for me, so that's what we'll use to implement our command-line interface.

With a library chosen, then, let's take a look at what our CLI might look like. Most importantly, we need to be able to specify the path (or paths) we want to search. Likely, most files in those paths will have the same extension, but that certainly won't always be the case, so we want to allow the user to specify only the file patterns to match (for example, .jpg). Some users might also be curious about how long it takes to run the scan, so let's throw in a switch to turn on that output. And finally, let's add a switch to make the process a bit more verbose.

With our functional requirements set, let's start writing our command. Crest is method-based in its command declarations, but we'll still need a class to put our method in. If this CLI were more complicated (or, for example, if you were writing a CLI for an application server), you could easily put several CLI commands in the same class, or group similar commands in several different classes. How you structure them is completely your concern, as Crest is happy with whatever you choose.

We'll start with our CLI interface declaration as follows:

```
public class DupeFinderCommands {
  @Command
  public void findDupes(
    @Option("pattern") List<String> patterns,
    @Option("path") List<String> paths,
    @Option("verbose") @Default("false") boolean verbose,
    @Option("show-timings")
    @Default("false") boolean showTimings) {
```

Before we can discuss the preceding code, we need to declare our Java module:

```
module dupefind.cli {
  requires tomitribe.crest;
  requires tomitribe.crest.api;
}
```

We've defined a new module, which is named similarly to our library's module name. We also declared that we `require` two Crest modules.

Back to our source code, we have the four parameters that we discussed in our functional requirements. Note that `patterns` and `paths` are defined as `List<String>`. When Crest is parsing the command line, if it finds multiple instances of one of these (for example, `--path=/path/one--path=/path/two`), it will collect all of these values and store them as a `List` for you. Also, note that `verbose` and `showTimings` are defined as `boolean`, so we see a nice example of the type coercion that Crest will do on our behalf. We also have default values for both of these, so we're sure to have sane, predictable values when our method executes.

The business logic of the method is pretty straightforward. We will handle the verbose flag upfront, printing a summary of the operation requested as follows:

```
if (verbose) {
  System.out.println("Scanning for duplicate files.");
  System.out.println("Search paths:");
  paths.forEach(p -> System.out.println("t" + p));
  System.out.println("Search patterns:");
  patterns.forEach(p -> System.out.println("t" + p));
  System.out.println();
}
```

Then we will perform the actual work. Thanks to the work we did building the library, all of the logic for the duplicate search is hidden away behind our API:

```
final Instant startTime = Instant.now();
FileFinder ff = new FileFinder();
patterns.forEach(p -> ff.addPattern(p));
paths.forEach(p -> ff.addPath(p));
ff.find();

System.out.println("The following duplicates have been found:");
final AtomicInteger group = new AtomicInteger(1);
ff.getDuplicates().forEach((name, list) -> {
  System.out.printf("Group #%d:%n", group.getAndIncrement());
  list.forEach(fileInfo -> System.out.println("t"
    + fileInfo.getPath()));
});
final Instant endTime = Instant.now();
```

This code won't compile at first, as we've not told the system we need it. We can do that now:

```
module dupefind.cli {
  requires dupefind.lib;
  requires tomitribe.crest;
  requires tomitribe.crest.api;
}
```

We can now import the `FileFinder` class. First, to demonstrate that the modules are, in fact, doing what they're supposed to do, let's try to import something that wasn't exported: `FindFileTask`. Let's create a simple class:

```
import com.steeplesoft.dupefind.lib.model.FileInfo;
import com.steeplesoft.dupefind.lib.util.FindFileTask;
public class VisibilityTest {
  public static void main(String[] args) {
    FileInfo fi;
    FindFileTask fft;
  }
}
```

If we try to compile this, Maven/javac will complain loudly with an error message like this:

```
[ERROR] Failed to execute goal org.apache.maven.plugins:maven-compiler-
plugin:3.6.1:compile (default-compile) on project cli: Compilation failure:
Compilation failure:
[ERROR] /C:/Users/jason/src/steeplesoft/DupeFinder/cli/src/main/java/com/
steeplesoft/dupefind/cli/VisibilityTest.java:[9,54]
com.steeplesoft.dupefind.lib.util.FindFileTask is not visible because
package com.steeplesoft.dupefind.lib.util is not visible
[ERROR] /C:/Users/jason/src/steeplesoft/DupeFinder/cli/src/main/java/com/
steeplesoft/dupefind/cli/VisibilityTest.java:[13,9] cannot find symbol
[ERROR] symbol:   class FindFileTask
[ERROR] location: class com.steeplesoft.dupefind.cli.VisibilityTest
```

We have successfully hidden our utility classes while exposing our public API. It may take some time for this practice to become widespread, but it should work wonders in preventing the crystallization of private APIs as pseudo-public.

Back on task, we create an instance of our `FileFinder` class, use `String.forEach` to pass our `paths` and `patterns` to the finder, then start the work with a call to `find()`. The work itself is threaded, but we've exposed a synchronous API, so our call here will block until the work has been completed. Once it returns, we start printing details to the screen. Since `FindFiles.getDuplicates()` returns `Map<String, List<FileInfo>>`, we call `forEach()` on the `Map` to iterate over each key, then we call `forEach()` on the `List` to print information about each file. We also use an `AtomicInteger` as the index, as the variable must be final or effectively final, so we just use a `final` instance of `AtomicInteger`. `BigInteger` may come to mind to more experienced developers, but it's immutable, so that makes it a poor choice for our use here.

The output of running the command will look something like this:

```
The following duplicates have been found:
Group #1:
    C:somepathtestset1file5.txt
    C:somepathtestset2file5.txt
Group #2:
    C:somepathtestset1file11.txt
    C:somepathtestset1file11-1.txt
    C:somepathtestset2file11.txt
```

Next, we handle showTimings. I didn't call it out in the preceding code, though I will now, but we get an Instant instance (from the Java 8 date/time library in java.time) before and after processing. Only when showTimings is true do we actually do anything with them. The code that does that looks like this:

```
if (showTimings) {
    Duration duration = Duration.between(startTime, endTime);
    long hours = duration.toHours();
    long minutes = duration.minusHours(hours).toMinutes();
    long seconds = duration.minusHours(hours)
        .minusMinutes(minutes).toMillis() / 1000;
    System.out.println(String.format(
      "%nThe scan took %d hours, %d minutes, and %d seconds.%n",
      hours, minutes, seconds));
}
```

With our two Instant, we get a Duration, then start calculating hours, minutes, and seconds. Hopefully, this never runs more than an hour, but it can't hurt to be ready for it. And that's all there is to the CLI, in terms of code. Crest did the heavy lifting for our command-line parameter parsing, leaving us with a straightforward and clean implementation of our logic.

There's one last thing we need to add, and that's the CLI help. It would be very helpful for the end user to be able to find out how to use our command. Fortunately, Crest has support built in to provide that information. To add the help information, we need to create a file called OptionDescriptions.properties in the same package as our command class (remember that since we're using Maven, this file should be under src/main/resource), as follows:

```
path = Adds a path to be searched. Can be specified multiple times.
pattern = Adds a pattern to match against the file names (e.g.,
"*.png").
Can be specified multiple times.
show-timings= Show how long the scan took
```

```
    verbose = Show summary of duplicate scan configuration
```

Doing so will produce an output like this:

```
$ java -jar cli-1.0-SNAPSHOT.jar help findDupes
Usage: findDupes [options]
Options:
  --path=<String[]>    Adds a path to be searched. Can be
                       specified multiple times.
  --pattern=<String[]> Adds a pattern to match against
                       the file names
                       (e.g., "*.png"). Can be specified
                        multiple times.
  --show-timings       Show how long the scan took
  --verbose            Show summary of duplicate scan configuration
```

You can be as verbose as you need to be without making your source code an unreadable mess.

With that, our CLI is feature-complete. Before we move on, we need to take a look at some build concerns for our CLI and see how Crest fits in. Obviously, we need to tell Maven where to find our Crest dependency, which is shown in the following piece of code:

```
<dependency>
  <groupId>org.tomitribe</groupId>
  <artifactId>tomitribe-crest</artifactId>
  <version>${crest.version}</version>
</dependency>
```

We also need to tell it where to find our duplicate finder library as follows:

```
<dependency>
  <groupId>${project.groupId}</groupId>
  <artifactId>lib</artifactId>
  <version>${project.version}</version>
</dependency>
```

Note groupId and version: since our CLI and library modules are part of the same parent multi-module build, we set groupId and version to that of the parent module, allowing us to manage that from a single location, which makes changing groups or bumping versions much simpler.

The more interesting part is the `build` section of our POM. First, let's start with `maven-compiler-plugin`. While we are targeting Java 9, `crest-maven-plugin`, which we'll look at in a moment, does not currently seem to like the classes generated for Java 9, so we instruct the compiler plugin to emit Java 1.8 bytecode:

```
<plugin>
  <groupId>org.apache.maven.plugins</groupId>
  <artifactId>maven-compiler-plugin</artifactId>
  <configuration>
     <source>1.8</source>
     <target>1.8</target>
  </configuration>
</plugin>
```

Next, we need to set up `crest-maven-plugin`. To expose our command classes to Crest, we have two options: we can use runtime scanning for the classes, or we can have Crest scan for commands at build time. In order to make this utility as small as possible, as well as reducing the startup time as much as possible, we will opt for the latter approach, so we will need to add another plugin to the build, as follows:

```
<plugin>
  <groupId>org.tomitribe</groupId>
  <artifactId>crest-maven-plugin</artifactId>
  <version>${crest.version}</version>
  <executions>
     <execution>
        <goals>
           <goal>descriptor</goal>
        </goals>
     </execution>
  </executions>
</plugin>
```

When this plugin runs, it will generate a file called `crest-commands.txt` that Crest will process to find classes when it starts. It may not save much time here, but it's definitely something to keep in mind for larger projects.

Finally, we don't want the user to have to worry about setting up the classpath (or module path!) each time, so we'll introduce the Maven Shade plugin, which will create a single, fat jar with all of our dependencies, transitive and otherwise:

```
<plugin>
  <artifactId>maven-shade-plugin</artifactId>
  <version>2.1</version>
  <executions>
    <execution>
      <phase>package</phase>
      <goals>
        <goal>shade</goal>
      </goals>
      <configuration>
        <transformers>
          <transformer implementation=
            "org.apache.maven.plugins.shade.resource
            .ManifestResourceTransformer">
            <mainClass>
              org.tomitribe.crest.Main
            </mainClass>
          </transformer>
        </transformers>
      </configuration>
    </execution>
  </executions>
</plugin>
```

After the build, we can then run a search with the following command:

```
java -jar targetcli-1.0-SNAPSHOT.jar findDupes
  --path=../test/set1 --path=../test/set2 -pattern=*.txt
```

Clearly, it can still be improved, so we would want to ship that, say, with script wrappers (shell, batch, and so on), but the number of jars is cut down from 18 or so to 1, so that's a big improvement.

With our CLI done, let's make a simple GUI that consumes our library as well.

Building the graphical user interface

For our GUI, we'd like to expose the same type of functionality as the command line, but, obviously, with a nice graphical interface. For this, we'll again reach for JavaFX. We'll give the user a means to select, using a chooser dialog, the directories to be searched, and a field by which to add the search patterns. Once the duplicates have been identified, we will display them in a list for the user to peruse. All of the duplicate groups will be listed and, when clicked, the files in that group will be displayed in another list. The user can right-click on the list and choose to either view the file (or files) or delete it (or them). When we are finished, the application will look like this:

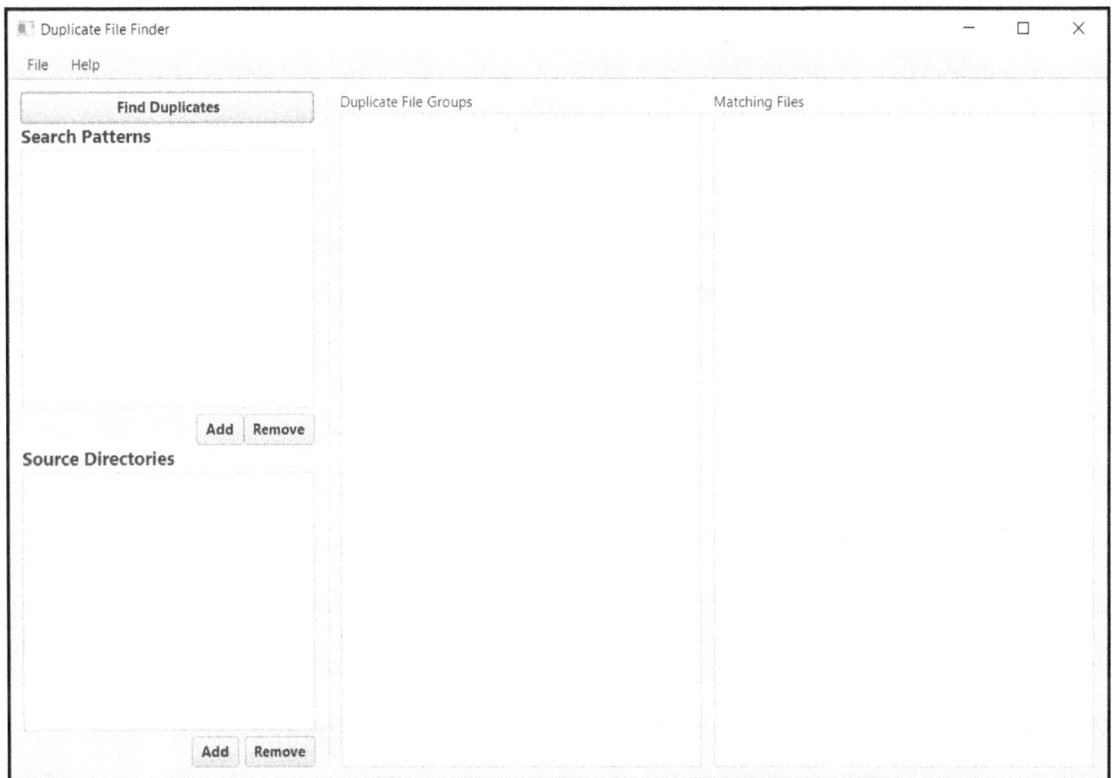

Let's start by creating our project. In NetBeans, go to **File | New Project** and select **Maven | JavaFX Application**. You can name it whatever you'd like, but we've used the name `Duplicate Finder - GUI`, groupId as `com.steeplesoft.dupefind`, and artifactId as `gui`.

Once you have your project, you should have two classes, `Main` and `FXMLController`, as well as the `fxml/Scene.fxml` resource. This may sound repetitive, but before we go any further, we need to set up our Java module as follows:

```
module dupefind.gui {
  requires dupefind.lib;
  requires java.logging;
  requires javafx.controls;
  requires javafx.fxml;
  requires java.desktop;
}
```

Then, to create the interface we saw, we will use `BorderPane`, to which we'll add `MenuBar` to the `top` section, as follows:

```
<top>
  <MenuBar BorderPane.alignment="CENTER">
    <menus>
      <Menu mnemonicParsing="false"
        onAction="#closeApplication" text="File">
        <items>
          <MenuItem mnemonicParsing="false" text="Close" />
        </items>
      </Menu>
      <Menu mnemonicParsing="false" text="Help">
        <items>
          <MenuItem mnemonicParsing="false"
            onAction="#showAbout" text="About" />
        </items>
      </Menu>
    </menus>
  </MenuBar>
</top>
```

When you add `MenuBar` with Scene Builder, it automatically adds several sample `Menu` entries for you. We've removed the unwanted entries, and tied the remaining to Java methods in the controller class. Specifically, the `Close` menu will call `closeApplication()` and `About` will call `showAbout()`. This looks just like the menu markup seen previously in the book, so there's not much to talk about.

The rest of the layout is a bit more complex. In the `left` section, we have a number of controls stacked vertically. JavaFX has a built-in container that makes that easy to do: `VBox`. We'll get to its contents in a moment, but its usage looks like this:

```
<VBox BorderPane.alignment="TOP_CENTER">
  <children>
```

```
            <HBox... />
            <Separator ... />
            <Label .../>
            <ListView ... />
            <HBox ... />
            <Label ... />
            <ListView... />
            <HBox ... />
        </children>
        <padding>
            <Insets bottom="10.0" left="10.0" right="10.0"
              top="10.0" />
        </padding>
    </VBox>
```

That's not valid FXML, so don't try to copy and paste that. I've omitted the details of the children for clarity. As you can see, VBox has a number of children, each of which will be stacked vertically, but, as we can see from the preceding screenshot, there are some we want to be lined up horizontally. To achieve that, we nest an HBox instance where needed. Its markup looks just like VBox.

There's not much of interest in this part of the FXML, but there are a couple of things to note. We want certain parts of the user interface to shrink and grow as the window is resized, namely ListView. By default, each component's various height and width properties--minimum, maximum, and preferred--will use the computed size, which means, roughly, that they'll be as big as they need to be to render themselves, and, in most cases, that's fine. In our situation, we want the two ListView instances to grow as much as possible inside their respective containers, which, in this case, is VBox we discussed earlier. To make that happen, we need to modify our two ListView instances like this:

```
    <ListView fx:id="searchPatternsListView" VBox.vgrow="ALWAYS" />
    ...
    <ListView fx:id="sourceDirsListView" VBox.vgrow="ALWAYS" />
```

With both the ListView instances set to ALWAYS grow, they will compete with each other for the available space, and end up sharing it. The available space, of course, is dependent on the height of the VBox instance, as well as the computed height of the other components in the container. With that property set, we can increase or decrease the size of the window, and watch the two ListView instances grow and shrink, while everything else remains the same.

For the rest of the user interface, we'll apply the same tactic to arrange components, but, this time, we'll start with an HBox instance, and divide that up as necessary. We have two ListView instances that we also want to fill all the available space with, so we mark those up in the same way we did the last two. Each ListView instance also has a Label, so we wrap each Label/ListView pair in a VBox instance to get our vertical distribution. In pseudo-FXML, this would look like this:

```
<HBox>
  <children>
      <Separator orientation="VERTICAL"/>
      <VBox HBox.hgrow="ALWAYS">
        <children>
          <VBox VBox.vgrow="ALWAYS">
              <children>
                <Label ... />
                <ListView ... VBox.vgrow="ALWAYS" />
              </children>
          </VBox>
        </children>
      </VBox>
      <VBox HBox.hgrow="ALWAYS">
        <children>
          <Label ... />
          <ListView ... VBox.vgrow="ALWAYS" />
        </children>
      </VBox>
  </children>
</HBox>
```

There is one item of interest in this part of the user interface, and that is the context menu we discussed earlier. To add a context to a control, you nest a contextMenu element in the target control's FXML like this:

```
<ListView fx:id="matchingFilesListView" VBox.vgrow="ALWAYS">
  <contextMenu>
    <ContextMenu>
      <items>
        <MenuItem onAction="#openFiles" text="Open File(s)..." />
        <MenuItem onAction="#deleteSelectedFiles"
          text="Delete File(s)..." />
      </items>
    </ContextMenu>
  </contextMenu>
</ListView>
```

We've defined a content menu with two `MenuItem`: `"Open File(s)..."` and `"Deleted File(s)..."`. We've also specified the action for the two `MenuItem` using the `onAction` attribute. We'll look at these following methods.

This marks the end of our user interface definition, so now we turn our attention to the Java code, in which we will finish preparing the user interface for use, as well as implement our application's logic.

While we didn't show the FXML that accomplishes this, our FXML file is tied to our controller class: `FXMLController`. This class can be called anything, of course, but we've opted to use the name generated by the IDE. In a larger application, more care will need to be given in the naming of this class. To allow the injection of our user interface components into our code, we need to declare instance variables on our class, and mark them up with the `@FXML` annotation. Some examples include the following:

```
@FXML
private ListView<String> dupeFileGroupListView;
@FXML
private ListView<FileInfo> matchingFilesListView;
@FXML
private Button addPattern;
@FXML
private Button removePattern;
```

There are several others, but this should be sufficient to demonstrate the concept. Note that rather than declaring a plain `ListView`, we've parameterized our instances as `ListView<String>` and `ListView<FileInfo>`. We know this is what we're putting into the control, so specifying that the type parameter gets us a measure of type safety at compile time, but also allows us to avoid having to cast the contents every time we interact with them.

Next, we need to set up the collections that will hold the search paths and patterns that the user will enter. We'll use the `ObservableList` instances for that. Remember that with an `ObservableList` instance, the container can automatically rerender itself as needed when the `Observable` instance is updated:

```
final private ObservableList<String> paths =
  FXCollections.observableArrayList();
final private ObservableList<String> patterns =
  FXCollections.observableArrayList();
```

In the `initialize()` method, we can start tying things together. Consider the following code snippet as an example:

```
public void initialize(URL url, ResourceBundle rb) {
  searchPatternsListView.setItems(patterns);
  sourceDirsListView.setItems(paths);
```

Here, we associate our `ListView` instances with our `ObservableList` instances. Now, at any point that these lists are updated, the user interface will immediately reflect the change.

Next, we need to configure the duplicate file group `ListView`. The data coming back from our library is a `Map` of a `List<FileInfo>` object, keyed by the duplicate hashes. Clearly, we don't want to show the user a list of hashes, so, like the CLI, we want to denote each group of files with a more friendly label. To do that, we need to create a `CellFactory`, which will, in turn, create a `ListCell` that is responsible for rendering the cell. We will do that as follows:

```
dupeFileGroupListView.setCellFactory(
  (ListView<String> p) -> new ListCell<String>() {
    @Override
    public void updateItem(String string, boolean empty) {
      super.updateItem(string, empty);
      final int index = p.getItems().indexOf(string);
      if (index > -1) {
        setText("Group #" + (index + 1));
      } else {
        setText(null);
      }
    }
  }
});
```

While lambdas can be great, in that they tend to make code more concise, they can also obscure some details. In a non-lambda code, the lambda above might look like this:

```
dupeFileGroupListView.setCellFactory(new
  Callback<ListView<String>, ListCell<String>>() {
    @Override
    public ListCell<String> call(ListView<String> p) {
      return new ListCell<String>() {
        @Override
        protected void updateItem(String t, boolean bln) {
          super.updateItem(string, empty);
          final int index = p.getItems().indexOf(string);
          if (index > -1) {
            setText("Group #" + (index + 1));
          } else {
```

```
                    setText(null);
                }
            }
        };
    }
});
```

You certainly get more detail, but it's also much harder to read. The main point in including both here is twofold: to show why lambdas are often so much better, and to show the actual types involved, which helps the lambdas make sense. With that understanding of the lambdas under our belts, what is the method doing?

First, we call `super.updateItem()`, as that's simply good practice. Next, we find the index of the string being rendered. The API gives us the string (since it's a `ListView<String>`), so we find its index in our `ObservableList<String>`. If it's found, we set the text of the cell to `Group #` plus the index plus one (since indexes in Java are typically zero-based). If the string isn't found (`ListView` is rendering an empty cell), we set the text to null to ensure that the field is blank.

Next, we need to perform a similar procedure on `matchingFilesListView`:

```
matchingFilesListView.getSelectionModel()
    .setSelectionMode(SelectionMode.MULTIPLE);
matchingFilesListView.setCellFactory(
    (ListView<FileInfo> p) -> new ListCell<FileInfo>() {
        @Override
        protected void updateItem(FileInfo fileInfo, boolean bln) {
            super.updateItem(fileInfo, bln);
            if (fileInfo != null) {
                setText(fileInfo.getPath());
            } else {
                setText(null);
            }
        }
    }
});
```

This is almost identical, but with a couple of exceptions. First, we're setting the selection mode of `ListView` to `MULTIPLE`. This will allow the user to control-click on items of interest, or shift-click on a range of rows. Next, we set up `CellFactory` in an identical fashion. Note that since the `ListView` instance's parameterized type is `FileInfo`, the types in the method signature of `ListCell.updateItem()` are different.

We have one last user interface setup step. If you look back at the screenshot, you will notice that the **Find Duplicates** button is the same width as `ListView`, unlike the other buttons, which are just wide enough to render their content. We do that by binding the width of the `Button` element to that of its container, which is an `HBox` instance:

```
findFiles.prefWidthProperty().bind(findBox.widthProperty());
```

We are getting the preferred width property, which is a `DoubleProperty`, and binding that to the width property (also a `DoubleProperty`) of `findBox`, the control's container. `DoubleProperty` is an `Observable` instance, just as `ObservableListView` is, so we're telling the `findFiles` control to observe its container's width property, and set its own value accordingly when the other changes. This lets us set the property, after a fashion, and then forget about it. Unless we want to break the binding between these two properties, we never again have to think about it, and we certainly don't need to manually watch one property to update the author. The framework does that for us.

Now, how about those buttons? How do we make them do something? We do that by setting the `onAction` property of the `Button` element to a method in our controller: `#someMethod` translates to `Controller.someMethod(ActionEvent event)`. We can handle this in one of at least two ways: we can create a separate handler method for each button, or, as we've done here, we can create one, then delegate to another method as appropriate; either is fine:

```java
@FXML
private void handleButtonAction(ActionEvent event) {
  if (event.getSource() instanceof Button) {
    Button button = (Button) event.getSource();
    if (button.equals(addPattern)) {
      addPattern();
    } else if (button.equals(removePattern)) {
    // ...
```

We have to make sure we're actually getting a `Button` element, then we cast it and compare it to the instances that were injected. The actual handlers for each button are as follows:

```java
private void addPattern() {
  TextInputDialog dialog = new TextInputDialog("*.*");
  dialog.setTitle("Add a pattern");
  dialog.setHeaderText(null);
  dialog.setContentText("Enter the pattern you wish to add:");

  dialog.showAndWait()
  .filter(n -> n != null && !n.trim().isEmpty())
  .ifPresent(name -> patterns.add(name));
}
```

To add a pattern, we create a `TextInputDialog` instance with the appropriate text, then call `showAndWait()`. The beauty of this method in JavaFX 8 is that it returns `Optional<String>`. If the user enters text in the dialog, and if the user clicks on OK, the `Optional` will have content. We identify that with the call to `ifPresent()`, passing it a lambda that adds the new pattern to `ObservableList<String>`, which automatically updates the user interface. If the user doesn't click on **OK**, the `Optional` will be empty. If the user didn't enter any text (or entered a bunch of spaces), the call to `filter()` will prevent the lambda from ever running.

Removing an item is similar, though we get to hide some of the details in a utility method, since we have two needs for the functionality. We make sure something is selected, then show a confirmation dialog, removing the pattern from the `ObservableList<String>` if the user clicks on **OK**:

```
private void removePattern() {
  if (searchPatternsListView.getSelectionModel()
  .getSelectedIndex() > -1) {
    showConfirmationDialog(
      "Are you sure you want to remove this pattern?",
      (() -> patterns.remove(searchPatternsListView
      .getSelectionModel().getSelectedItem())));
  }
}
```

Let's take a look at the `showConfirmationDialog` method:

```
protected void showConfirmationDialog(String message,
 Runnable action) {
  Alert alert = new Alert(Alert.AlertType.CONFIRMATION);
  alert.setTitle("Confirmation");
  alert.setHeaderText(null);
  alert.setContentText(message);
  alert.showAndWait()
  .filter(b -> b == ButtonType.OK)
  .ifPresent(b -> action.run());
}
```

Again, this is much like the dialogs earlier, and should be self-explanatory. The interesting part here is the use of a lambda as a method parameter that makes this, by the way, a higher order function--meaning it takes in a function as a parameter, returns a function as its result, or both. We pass in `Runnable`, as we want a lambda that takes in nothing and returns nothing, and `Runnable` is a `FunctionalInterface` that matches that description. After we show the dialog and get the user's response, we will filter for only responses where the button clicked on was `OK`, and, if present, we execute `Runnable` via `action.run()`. We have to specify `b -> action.run()` as `ifPresent()` takes a `Consumer<? super ButtonType>`, so we create one and ignore the value passed in, allowing us to shield our calling code from that detail.

Adding a path requires a `DirectoryChooser` instance:

```
private void addPath() {
    DirectoryChooser dc = new DirectoryChooser();
    dc.setTitle("Add Search Path");
    dc.setInitialDirectory(new File(lastDir));
    File dir = dc.showDialog(null);
    if (dir != null) {
        try {
            lastDir = dir.getParent();
            paths.add(dir.getCanonicalPath());
        } catch (IOException ex) {
            Logger.getLogger(FXMLController.class.getName()).log(
                Level.SEVERE, null, ex);
        }
    }
}
```

When creating the `DirectoryChooser` instance, we set the initial directory to the last directory used as a convenience for the user. When the application starts, this defaults to the user's home directory, but once a directory is successfully chosen, we set `lastDir` to the added directory's parent, allowing the user to start where he or she left off should there be a need to enter multiple paths. `DirectoryChooser.showDialog()` returns a file, so we get its canonical path and store that in paths, which, again, causes our user interface to be updated automatically.

Removing a path looks very similar to removing a pattern, as you can see in the following code snippet:

```
private void removePath() {
  showConfirmationDialog(
    "Are you sure you want to remove this path?",
    (() -> paths.remove(sourceDirsListView.getSelectionModel()
    .getSelectedItem()))));
}
```

Same basic code, just a different lambda. Aren't lambdas just the coolest?

The handler for the `findFiles()` button is a bit different, but looks a lot like our CLI code, as you can see here:

```
private void findFiles() {
    FileFinder ff = new FileFinder();
    patterns.forEach(p -> ff.addPattern(p));
    paths.forEach(p -> ff.addPath(p));

    ff.find();
    dupes = ff.getDuplicates();
    ObservableList<String> groups =
      FXCollections.observableArrayList(dupes.keySet());

    dupeFileGroupListView.setItems(groups);
}
```

We create our `FileFinder` instance, set the paths and patterns using streams and lambdas, then start the search process. When it completes, we get the list duplicate file information via `getDuplicates()`, then create a new `ObservableList<String>` instance using the keys of the map, which we then set on `dupeFileGroupListView`.

Now we need to add the logic to handle mouse clicks on the group list, so we will set the
onMouseClicked property on ListView in the FXML file to #dupeGroupClicked, as you
can see in the following code block:

```
@FXML
public void dupeGroupClicked(MouseEvent event) {
  int index = dupeFileGroupListView.getSelectionModel()
    .getSelectedIndex();
  if (index > -1) {
    String hash = dupeFileGroupListView.getSelectionModel()
    .getSelectedItem();
    matchingFilesListView.getItems().clear();
    matchingFilesListView.getItems().addAll(dupes.get(hash));
  }
}
```

When the control is clicked on, we get the index and make sure it is non-negative, so as to
ensure that the user actually clicked on something. We then get the hash of the group by
getting the selected item from ListView. Remember that while ListView may show
something like Group #2, the actual content of that row is the hash. We just used a custom
CellFactory to give it a prettier label. With the hash, we clear the list of items in
matchingFilesListView, then get the control's ObservableList and add all of the
FileInfo objects in the List keyed by the hash. And, again, we get an automatic user
interface update, thanks to the power of Observable.

We also want the user to be able to navigate the list of duplicate groups using the keyboard
to update the matching file list. We do that by setting the onKeyPressed attribute on our
ListView to point to this rather simple method:

```
@FXML
public void keyPressed(KeyEvent event) {
  dupeGroupClicked(null);
}
```

It just so happens that we're not too terribly interested in the actual Event in either of these
methods (they're never actually used), so we can naively delegate to the mouse-click
method discussed earlier.

There are two more minor pieces of functionality we need to implement: viewing the
matching files and deleting matching files.

We've already created the context menu and menu entries, so all we need to do is implement the handler methods as follows:

```
@FXML
public void openFiles(ActionEvent event) {
  matchingFilesListView.getSelectionModel().getSelectedItems()
  .forEach(f -> {
    try {
      Desktop.getDesktop().open(new File(f.getPath()));
    } catch (IOException ex) {
      // ...
    }
  });
}
```

The matching file list allows multiple selections, so we need to get List<FileInfo> from the selection model instead of the single object we've already seen. We then call forEach() to process the entry. We want to open the file in whatever application the user has configured in the operating system to handle that file type. To do this, we use an AWT class introduced in Java 6: Desktop. We get the instance via getDesktop(), then call open(), passing it File that points to our FileInfo target.

Deleting a file is similar:

```
@FXML
public void deleteSelectedFiles(ActionEvent event) {
  final ObservableList<FileInfo> selectedFiles =
    matchingFilesListView.getSelectionModel()
    .getSelectedItems();
  if (selectedFiles.size() > 0) {
    showConfirmationDialog(
      "Are you sure you want to delete the selected files",
      () -> selectedFiles.forEach(f -> {
        if (Desktop.getDesktop()
        .moveToTrash(new File(f.getPath()))) {
          matchingFilesListView.getItems()
          .remove(f);
          dupes.get(dupeFileGroupListView
            .getSelectionModel()
            .getSelectedItem()).remove(f);
        }
      }));
  }
}
```

Similarly to open files, we get all of the selected files. If there's at least one, we confirm the user's intent via `showConfirmationDialog()`, and pass in a lambda that handles the deleting. We do the actual file deletion using the `Desktop` class again to move the file to the trash can provided by the filesystem to provide the user with a safe delete option. If the file is successfully deleted, we remove its entry from `ObservableList`, as well as our cache duplicate file `Map`, so that it isn't shown should the user click on this file group again.

Summary

With that, our application is done. So, what have we covered? From the project description, this seemed like a pretty simple application, but as we started breaking down the requirements and delving into the implementation, we ended up covering a lot of territory-- a scenario that is not at all uncommon. We built another multi-module Maven project. We introduced Java concurrency, including basic `Thread` management and `ExecutorService` usage, as well as the Java Persistence API, showing basic `@Entity` definition, `EntityManagerFactory`/`EntityManager` usage, and JPAQL query authoring. We discussed creating file hashes using the `MessageDigest` classes, and demonstrated the new file I/O APIs, including the directory tree walking APIs. We also built a more complex user interface in JavaFX using nested containers, "linked" `ListView` instances, and bound properties.

That's quite a bit for such a "simple" project. Our next project will also be relatively simple, as we build a command-line date calculator that will allow us to explore the `java.time` package and see some of what this new date/time API offers.

20
Date Calculator

If you've been developing in Java for any serious length of time, you know one thing to be true--working with dates is awful. The `java.util.Date` class, with its related classes, shipped with 1.0, and `Calendar` and its related classes coming along in 1.1. Even early on, problems were apparent. For example, the Javadoc on `Date` says this--*Unfortunately, the API for these functions was not amenable to internationalization*. As a result, `Calendar` was introduced in 1.1. Sure, there have been other enhancements down through the years, but given Java's strict adherence to backwards compatibility, there's only so much the language architects can do. As much as they may want to fix those APIs, their hands are tied.

Fortunately, **Java Specification Request** (JSR 310) was filed. Led by Stephen Colebourne, an effort was begun to create a new API, based on the very popular open source library, Joda-Time. In this chapter, we'll take an in-depth look at this new API, then build a simple command-line utility to perform date and time math, which will give us an opportunity to see some of this API in action.

This chapter, then, will be covering the following topics:

- The Java 8 Date/Time API
- Revisiting command-line utilities
- Text parsing

Getting started

Like the project in `Chapter 18`, *Managing Processes in Java*, this project is fairly simple, conceptually. The end goal is a command-line utility to perform various date and time calculations. However, while we're at it, it would be very nice if the actual date/time work were to be put in a reusable library, so that's what we'll do. This leaves us with two projects, which we'll set up, like last time, as a multi-module Maven project.

The parent POM will look something like this:

```xml
<?xml version="1.0" encoding="UTF-8"?>
<project xmlns="http://maven.apache.org/POM/4.0.0"
  xmlns:xsi="http://www.w3.org/2001/XMLSchema-instance"
  xsi:schemaLocation="http://maven.apache.org/POM/4.0.0
  http://maven.apache.org/xsd/maven-4.0.0.xsd">
  <modelVersion>4.0.0</modelVersion>

  <artifactId>datecalc-master</artifactId>
  <version>1.0-SNAPSHOT</version>
  <packaging>pom</packaging>
  <modules>
    <module>datecalc-lib</module>
    <module>datecalc-cli</module>
  </modules>
</project>
```

If you read `Chapter 18`, *Managing Processes in Java*, or have worked with multi-module Maven builds before, there's nothing new here. It's included simply for completeness. If this is foreign to you, take a moment to review the first few pages of Chapter 18 before continuing.

Building the library

Since we'd like to be able to reuse this tool in other projects, we'll start by building a library that exposes its functionality. All of the functionality we'll need is built into the platform, so our POM file is very simple:

```xml
<?xml version="1.0" encoding="UTF-8"?>
<project xmlns="http://maven.apache.org/POM/4.0.0"
  xmlns:xsi="http://www.w3.org/2001/XMLSchema-instance"
  xsi:schemaLocation="http://maven.apache.org/POM/4.0.0
  http://maven.apache.org/xsd/maven-4.0.0.xsd">
  <modelVersion>4.0.0</modelVersion>
```

```
  <parent>
    <groupId>com.steeplesoft</groupId>
      <artifactId>datecalc-master</artifactId>
      <version>1.0-SNAPSHOT</version>
  </parent>
  <artifactId>datecalc-lib</artifactId>
  <packaging>jar</packaging>
  <dependencies>
    <dependency>
      <groupId>org.testng</groupId>
      <artifactId>testng</artifactId>
      <version>6.9.9</version>
      <scope>test</scope>
    </dependency>
  </dependencies>
</project>
```

There are **almost** no external dependencies. The only dependency listed is on the testing library, TestNG. We didn't talk much about testing in the last chapter (rest assured, there are tests in the project). In this chapter, we'll introduce the topic of testing and show some examples.

Now we need to define our module. Remember that these are Java 9 projects, so we want to make use of the module functionality to help protect our internal classes from accidental public exposure. Our module is very simple. We need to give it a name, then export our public API package, as follows:

```
module datecalc.lib {
  exports com.steeplesoft.datecalc;
}
```

Since everything we need is already in the JDK, we have nothing to declare beyond what we export.

With our project set up, let's take a quick look at the functional requirements. Our intent with this project is to build a system that allows the user to provide an arbitrary string representing a date or time calculation expression and get a response. The string may look something like "today + 2 weeks" to find out the date 2 weeks from today, "now + 3 hours 15 minutes" to find out what time it is in 3 hours and 15 minutes, or "2016/07/04 - 1776/07/04" to find out how many years, months, and days are between the two dates. The processing of these expressions will be one line at a time, so the ability to pass in, for example, a text document with multiple expressions and get multiple results is explicitly excluded from the scope. This can be implemented easily enough, of course, by any consuming application or library.

So, now we have a project set up and ready to go, and we have a rough sketch of its fairly simple functional requirements. We're ready to start coding. Before we do that, let's take a quick tour of the new `java.time` package to get a better sense of what we'll be seeing in this project, as well as some of the functionality we **won't** be using in this simple project.

A timely interlude

Prior to Java 8, two primary date-related classes were `Date` and `Calendar` (and, of course, `GregorianCalendar`). The new `java.time` package offers several new classes, such as `Duration`, `Period`, `Clock`, `Instant`, `LocalDate`, `LocalTime`, `LocalDateTime`, and `ZonedDateTime`. There is a plethora of supporting classes, but these are the primary starting points. Let's take a quick look at each.

Duration

`Duration` is a **time-based unit of time**. While it may sound odd to phrase it that way, the wording was chosen to distinguish it from a date-based unit of time, which we'll look at next. In plain English, it's a measurement of time, such as **10 seconds**, **1 hour**, or **100 nanoseconds**. `Duration` is measured in seconds, but there are a number of methods to get a representation of the duration in other units of measure, which are as follows:

- `getNano()`: This is `Duration` in nanosecods
- `getSeconds()`: This is `Duration` in seconds
- `get(TemporalUnit)`: This is `Duration` in a unit of measure specified

There are also a variety of arithmetic methods, which are mentioned as follows:

- `add/minus (int amount, TemporalUnit unit)`
- `add/minus (Duration)`
- `addDays/minusDays(long)`
- `addHours/minusHours(long)`
- `addMillis/minusMillis(long)`
- `addMinutes/minusMinutes(long)`
- `addNanos/minusNanos(long)`
- `addSeconds/minusSeconds(long)`
- `dividedBy/multipliedBy`

We also have a number of convenient factory and extraction methods, such as the following:

- `ofDays(long)/toDays()`
- `ofHours(long)/toHours()`
- `ofMinutes(long)/toMinutes()`
- `ofSeconds(long)/toSeconds()`

A `parse()` method is also supplied. Unfortunately, perhaps, for some, the input for this method may not be what you might expect. Since we're dealing with a duration that is often, say, in hours and minutes, you might expect the method to accept something like "1:37" for 1 hour and 37 minutes. However, that will cause the system to throw `DateTimeParseException`. What the method expects to receive is a string in an ISO-8601 format, which looks like this--`PnDTnHnMn.nS`. That's pretty fantastic, isn't it? While it may be confusing at first, it's not too bad once you understand it:

- The first character is an optional + (plus) or – (minus) sign.
- The next character is `P` and can be either uppercase or lowercase.
- What follows is at least one of four sections indicating days (`D`), hours (`H`), minutes (`M`), and seconds (`S`). Again, case doesn't matter.
- They must be declared in this order.
- Each section has a numeric part that includes an optional + or – sign, one or more ASCII digits, and the unit of measure indicator. The seconds amount may be fractional (expressed as a floating point number) and may use a period or a comma.
- The letter `T` must come before the first instance of hours, minutes, or seconds.

Simple, right? It may not be very friendly to a non-technical audience, but that it supports encoding a duration in a string that allows unambiguous parsing is a huge step forward.

Period

`Period` is a date-based unit of time. Whereas `Duration` was about time (hours, minutes, seconds, and so on), `Period` is about years, weeks, months, and so forth. Like `Duration`, it exposes several arithmetic methods to add and subtract, though these deal with years, months, and days. It also offers `plus(long amount, TemporalUnit unit)` (and the equivalent `minus`) as well.

Also, like `Duration`, `Period` has a `parse()` method, which also takes an ISO-8601 format that looks like this--`PnYnMnD` and `PnW`. Based on the discussion earlier, the structure is probably pretty obvious:

- The string starts with an optional sign, followed by the letter `P`.
- After that, for the first form, come three sections, at least one of which must be present--years (`Y`), months(`M`), and days (`D`).
- For the second form, there is only one section--weeks (`W`).
- The amount in each section can have a positive or negative sign.
- The `W` unit can't be combined with the others. Internally, the amount is multiplied by `7` and treated as days.

Clock

`Clock` is an abstract class that provides access to the current instant (which we will see next), date, and time using a timezone. Prior to Java 8, we would have to call `System.currentTimeInMillis()` and `TimeZone.getDefault()` to calculate these values. `Clock` provides a nice interface to get that from one object.

The Javadoc states that the use of `Clock` is purely optional. In fact, the major date/time classes have a `now()` method that uses the system clock to get their value. If, however, you need to provide an alternate implementation (say, in testing, you need the `LocalTime` in another timezone), this abstract class can be extended to provide the functionality needed, and can then be passed to the appropriate `now()` method.

Instant

An `Instant` is a single, exact point in time (or **on the timeline**, you'll see the Javadoc say). This class offers arithmetic methods, much like `Period` and `Duration`. Parsing is also an option, with the string being an ISO-8601 instant format such as `1977-02-16T08:15:30Z`.

LocalDate

`LocalDate` is a date without a timezone. While the value of this class is a date (year, month, and day), there are accessor methods for other values, which are as follows:

- `getDayOfWeek()`: This returns the `DayOfWeek` enum for the day of the week represented by the date.
- `getDayOfYear()`: This returns the day of the year (1 to 365, or 366 for leap years) represented by the date. This is a 1-based counter from January 1 of the specified year.
- `getEra()`: This returns the ISO era for the given date.

Local dates can be parsed from a string, of course, but, this time, the format seems much more reasonable--`yyyy-mm-dd`. If you need a different format, the `parse()` method has been overridden to allow you to specify the `DateTimeFormatter` that can handle the format of the string.

LocalTime

`LocalTime` is the time-based equivalent of `LocalDate`. It stores `HH:MM:SS`, but does **not** store the timezone. Parsing times requires the format above, but, just like `LocalDate`, does allow you to specify a `DateTimeFormatter` for alternate string representations.

LocalDateTime

`LocalDateTime` is basically a combination of the last two classes. All of the arithmetic, factory, and extraction methods apply as expected. Parsing the text is also a combination of the two, except that `T` must separate the date and time portions of the string--`'2016-01-01T00:00:00'`. This class **does not** store or represent a timezone.

ZonedDateTime

If you need to represent a date/time **and** a timezone, then `ZonedDateTime` is the class you need. As you might expect, this class' interface is a combination of `LocalDate` and `LocalTime`, with extra methods added for handling the timezone.

As shown at length in the overview of duration's API (and hinted at, though not as clearly shown in the other classes), one of the strong points of this new API is the ability to manipulate and process various date and time artifacts mathematically. It is precisely this functionality that we will spend most of our time with in this project as we explore this new library.

Back to our code

The first part of the process we need to tackle is parsing the user-provided string into something we can use programmatically. If you were to search for a parser generator, you would find a myriad of options, with tools such as Antlr and JavaCC showing up near the top. It's tempting to turn to one of these tools, but our purposes here are pretty simple, and the grammar is not all that complex. Our functional requirements include:

- We want to be able to add/subtract time to/from a date or a time
- We want to be able to subtract one date or time from another to get the difference between the two
- We want to be able to convert a time from one timezone to another

For something as simple as this, a parser is far too expensive, both in terms of complexity and binary size. We can easily write a parser using tools built into the JDK, which is what we'll do.

To set the stage before we get into the code, the plan is this--we will define a number of **tokens** to represent logical parts of a date calculation expression. Using regular expressions, we will break down the given string, returning a list of these tokens, which will then be processed **left to right** to return the result.

That said, let's make a list of the types of token we'll need. We'll need one for a date, a time, the operator, any numeric amount, the unit of measure, and the timezone. Obviously, we won't need each of these for every expression, but that should cover all of our given use cases.

Let's start with a base class for our tokens. When defining a type hierarchy, it's always good to ask whether you want a base class or an interface. Using an interface gives the developer extra flexibility with regard to the class hierarchy should the need arise to extend a different class. A base class, however, allows us to provide default behavior at the cost of some rigidity in the hierarchy of the type. To make our `Token` implementations as simple as possible, we'd like to put as much in the base class as possible, so we'll use a base class as follows:

```
public abstract class Token<T> {
  protected T value;
  public interface Info {
    String getRegex();
    Token getToken(String text);
  }
  public T getValue() {
    return value;
```

```
      }
    }
```

Java 8 did introduce a means to provide default behavior from an interface, that being a **default methods**. A default method is a method on an interface that provides a concrete implementation, which is a significant departure from interfaces. Prior to this change, all interfaces could do was define the method signature and force the implementing class to define the body. This allows us to add methods to an interface and provide a default implementation so that existing implementations of the interface need not change. In our case, the behavior we're providing is the storing of a value (the instance variable `value`) and the accessor for it (`getValue()`), so an interface with a default method is not appropriate.

Note that we've also defined a nested interface, `Info`, which we will cover in more detail when we get to the parser.

With our base class defined, we can now create the tokens we will need as follows:

```
public class DateToken extends Token<LocalDate> {
  private static final String TODAY = "today";
  public static String REGEX =
    "\d{4}[-/][01]\d[-/][0123]\d|today";
```

To start the class, we define two constants. `TODAY` is a special string that we will allow the user to specify today's date. The second is the regular expression we'll use to identify a date string:

```
"\d{4}[-/][01]\d[-/][0123]\d|today"
```

It's no secret that regular expressions are ugly, and as these things go, this one's not too terribly complicated. We're matching 4 digits (`\d{4}`), either a - or / (`[-/]`), a 0 or 1 followed by any digit (`[01]\d`), another - or /, then a 0, 1, 2, or 3 followed by any digit. Finally, the last segment, `|today`, tells the system to match on the pattern that comes before, **or** the text `today`. All this regular expression can do is identify a string that **looks** like a date. In its current form, it can't actually ensure that it is valid. We can probably make a regex that can do exactly that, but the complexity that would introduce is just not worth it. What we can do though is let the JDK validate the string for us, which we'll do in the `of` method, as shown here:

```
public static DateToken of(String text) {
  try {
    return TODAY.equals(text.toLowerCase()) ?
      new DateToken(LocalDate.now()) :
      new DateToken(
```

```
                LocalDate.parse(text.replace("/", "-")));
        } catch (DateTimeParseException ex) {
            throw new DateCalcException(
              "Invalid date format: " + text);
          }
      }
  }
```

Here, we've defined a static method to handle the creation of the `DateToken` instance. If the user provides the string `today`, we provide the value `LocalDate.now()`, which does what you think it might. Otherwise, we pass the string to `LocalDate.parse()`, changing any forward slashes to dashes, as that's what the method expects. If the user provided an invalid date, but the regular expression still matched it, we'll get an error here. Since we have built-in support to validate the string, we can content ourselves with letting the system do the heavy lifting for us.

The other tokens look very similar. Rather than showing each class, much of which would be very familiar, we'll skip most of those classes and just look at the regular expressions, as some are quite complex. Take a look at the following code:

```
public class IntegerToken extends Token<Integer> {
    public static final String REGEX = "\d+";
```

Well, that one's not too bad, is it? One or more digits will match here:

```
public class OperatorToken extends Token<String> {
    public static final String REGEX = "\+|-|to";
```

Another relatively simple one, which will match a +, a -, or the `to` text:

```
public class TimeToken extends Token<LocalTime> {
    private static final String NOW = "now";
    public static final String REGEX =
      "(?:[01]?\d|2[0-3]):[0-5]\d *(?:[AaPp][Mm])?|now";
```

The regular expression breaks down like this:

- `(?:`: This is a non-capturing group. We need to group some rules together, but we don't want them to show up as separate groups when we process this in our Java code.
- `[01]?`: This is a zero or a one. The `?` indicates that this should occur once or not at all.
- `|2[0-3]`: We either want to match the first half, **or** this section, which will be a 2 followed by a 0, 1, 2, or 3.

- `)`: This ends the non-capturing group. This group will allow us to match 12 or 24-hour times.
- `::`: This position requires a colon. Its presence is not optional.
- `[0-5]\d`: Next, the pattern must match a digit of `0-5` followed by another digit. This is the minutes portion of the time.
- `' *'`: It's hard to see, so I've added quotes to help indicate it, but we want to match 0 or more (as indicated by the asterisk) spaces.
- `(?::`: This is another non-capturing group.
- `[AaPp][Mm]`: These are the A or P letters (of either case) followed by an M (also of either case).
- `)?`: We end the non-capturing group, but mark it with a `?` to indicate that it should occur once or not all. This group lets us capture any AM/PM designation.
- `|now`: Much like today above, we allow the user to specify this string to indicate the current time.

Again, this pattern may match an invalid time string, but we'll let `LocalTime.parse()` handle that for us in `TimeToken.of()`:

```
public static TimeToken of(final String text) {
  String time = text.toLowerCase();
  if (NOW.equals(time)) {
    return new TimeToken(LocalTime.now());
  } else {
      try {
        if (time.length() <5) {
            time = "0" + time;
        }
        if (time.contains("am") || time.contains("pm")) {
          final DateTimeFormatter formatter =
            new DateTimeFormatterBuilder()
            .parseCaseInsensitive()
            .appendPattern("hh:mma")
            .toFormatter();
          return new
          TimeToken(LocalTime.parse(
            time.replaceAll(" ", ""), formatter));
        } else {
            return new TimeToken(LocalTime.parse(time));
        }
      } catch (DateTimeParseException ex) {
          throw new DateCalcException(
          "Invalid time format: " + text);
      }
```

```
        }
     }
```

This is a bit more complex than others, primarily because of the default format expected by `LocalTime.parse()`, which is an ISO-8601 time format. Typically, time is specified in a 12-hour format with an am/pm designation. Unfortunately, that's not how the API works, so we have to make adjustments.

First, we pad the hour, if needed. Second, we look to see if the user specified `"am"` or `"pm"`. If so, we need to create a special formatter, which is done via `DateTimeFormatterBuilder`. We start by telling the builder to build a case-insensitve formatter. If we don't do that, `"AM"` will work, but `"am"` will not. Next, we append the pattern we want, which is hours, minutes, and am/pm, then build the formatter. Finally, we can parse our text, which we do by passing the string and the formatter to `LocalTime.parse()`. If all goes well, we'll get a `LocalTime` instance back. If not, we get an `Exception` instance, which we will handle. Note that we call `replaceAll()` on our string. We do that to strip any spaces out between the time and am/pm. Otherwise, the parse will fail.

Finally, we come to our `UnitOfMeasureToken`. This token isn't necessarily complex, but it's certainly not simple. For our units of measure, we want to support the words `year`, `month`, `day`, `week`, `hour`, `minute`, and `second`, all of which can be plural, and most of which can be abbreviated to their initial character. This makes the regular expression interesting:

```
public class UnitOfMeasureToken extends Token<ChronoUnit> {
    public static final String REGEX =
        "years|year|y|months|month|weeks|week|w|days|
        day|d|hours|hour|h|minutes|minute|m|seconds|second|s";
    private static final Map<String, ChronoUnit> VALID_UNITS =
    new HashMap<>();
```

That's not so much complex as ugly. We have a list of possible strings, separated by the logical OR operator, the vertical pipe. It is probably possible to write a regular expression that searches for each word, or parts of it, but such an expression will likely be very difficult to write correctly, and almost certainly hard to debug or change. Simple and clear is almost always better than clever and complex.

There's one last element here that needs discussion: VALID_UNITS. In a static initializer, we build a Map to allow looking up the correct ChronoUnit:

```
static {
  VALID_UNITS.put("year", ChronoUnit.YEARS);
  VALID_UNITS.put("years", ChronoUnit.YEARS);
  VALID_UNITS.put("months", ChronoUnit.MONTHS);
  VALID_UNITS.put("month", ChronoUnit.MONTHS);
```

And so on.

We're now ready to take a look at the parser, which is as follows:

```
public class DateCalcExpressionParser {
  private final List<InfoWrapper> infos = new ArrayList<>();

  public DateCalcExpressionParser() {
    addTokenInfo(new DateToken.Info());
    addTokenInfo(new TimeToken.Info());
    addTokenInfo(new IntegerToken.Info());
    addTokenInfo(new OperatorToken.Info());
    addTokenInfo(new UnitOfMeasureToken.Info());
  }
  private void addTokenInfo(Token.Info info) {
    infos.add(new InfoWrapper(info));
  }
```

When we build our parser, we register each of our Token classes in a List, but we see two new types: Token.Info and InfoWrapper. Token.Info is an interface nested inside the Token class:

```
public interface Info {
  String getRegex();
  Token getToken(String text);
}
```

We have added this interface to give us a convenient way to get the regular expression for a Token class, as well as the Token, without having to resort to reflection. DateToken.Info, for example, looks like this:

```
public static class Info implements Token.Info {
  @Override
  public String getRegex() {
    return REGEX;
  }

  @Override
```

```
public DateToken getToken(String text) {
  return of(text);
}
}
```

Since this is a nested class, we get easy access to members, including statics, of the enclosing class.

The next new type, `InfoWrapper`, looks like this:

```
private class InfoWrapper {
  Token.Info info;
  Pattern pattern;

  InfoWrapper(Token.Info info) {
    this.info = info;
    pattern = Pattern.compile("^(" + info.getRegex() + ")");
  }
}
```

This is a simple, private class, so some of the normal encapsulation rules can be set aside (although, should this class ever be made public, this would certainly need to be cleaned up). What we're doing, though, is storing a compiled version of the token's regular expression. Note that we're wrapping the regular expression with a couple of extra characters. The first, the caret (^), says that the match must be at the beginning of the text. We're also wrapping the regular expression in parentheses. However, this time this is a capturing group. We'll see why in the following parse method:

```
public List<Token> parse(String text) {
  final Queue<Token> tokens = new ArrayDeque<>();

  if (text != null) {
    text = text.trim();
    if (!text.isEmpty()) {
      boolean matchFound = false;
      for (InfoWrapper iw : infos) {
        final Matcher matcher = iw.pattern.matcher(text);
        if (matcher.find()) {
          matchFound = true;
          String match = matcher.group().trim();
          tokens.add(iw.info.getToken(match));
          tokens.addAll(
            parse(text.substring(match.length())));
          break;
        }
      }
      if (!matchFound) {
```

```
        throw new DateCalcException(
          "Could not parse the expression: " + text);
        }
      }
    }

    return tokens;
  }
```

We start by making sure that `text` is not null, then `trim()` it, then make sure it's not empty. With the sanity checks done, we loop through the `List` of info wrappers to find a match. Remember that the pattern compiled is a capturing group looking at the start of the text, so we loop through each `Pattern` until one matches. If we don't find a match, we throw an `Exception`.

Once we find a match, we extract the matching text from `Matcher`, then, using `Token.Info`, we call `getToken()` to get a `Token` instance for the matching `Pattern`. We store that in our list, then recursively call the `parse()` method, passing a substring of text starting after our match. That removes the matched text from the original, then repeats the process until the string is empty. Once the recursion ends and things unwind, we return a `Queue` of tokens that represent the string the user provided. We use a `Queue` instead of, say, a `List`, as that will make processing a bit easier. We now have a parser, but our work is only half done. Now we need to process those tokens.

In the spirit of Separation of Concerns, we've encapsulated the processing of these tokens-- the actual calculation of the expression--in a separate class, `DateCalculator`, which uses our parser. Consider the following code:

```
public class DateCalculator {
  public DateCalculatorResult calculate(String text) {
    final DateCalcExpressionParser parser =
      new DateCalcExpressionParser();
    final Queue<Token> tokens = parser.parse(text);

    if (tokens.size() > 0) {
      if (tokens.peek() instanceof DateToken) {
        return handleDateExpression(tokens);
      } else if (tokens.peek() instanceof TimeToken) {
        return handleTimeExpression(tokens);
      }
    }
    throw new DateCalcException("An invalid expression
      was given: " + text);
  }
}
```

Each time `calculate()` is called, we create a new instance of the parser. Also, note that, as we look at the rest of the code, we pass the `Queue` around. While that does make the method signatures a bit bigger, it also makes the class thread-safe, as there's no state held in the class itself.

After our `isEmpty()` check, we can see where the `Queue` API comes in handy. By calling `poll()`, we get a reference to the next element in the collection, but--and this is important--**we leave the element in the collection**. This lets us look at it without altering the state of the collection. Based on the type of the first element in the collection, we delegate to the appropriate method.

For handling dates, the expression syntax is `<date> <operator> <date | number unit_of_measure>`. We can start our processing, then, by extracting a `DateToken` and an `OperatorToken`, as follows:

```
private DateCalculatorResult handleDateExpression(
    final Queue<Token> tokens) {
    DateToken startDateToken = (DateToken) tokens.poll();
    validateToken(tokens.peek(), OperatorToken.class);
    OperatorToken operatorToken = (OperatorToken) tokens.poll();
    Token thirdToken = tokens.peek();

    if (thirdToken instanceof IntegerToken) {
      return performDateMath(startDateToken, operatorToken,
        tokens);
    } else if (thirdToken instanceof DateToken) {
        return getDateDiff(startDateToken, tokens.poll());
      } else {
        throw new DateCalcException("Invalid expression");
      }
}
```

To retrieve an element from a `Queue`, we use the `poll()` method, and we can safely cast that to `DateToken` since we checked that in the calling method. Next, we `peek()` at the next element and, via the `validateToken()` method, we verify that the element is not null and is of the type desired. If the token is valid, we can `poll()` and cast safely. Next, we `peek()` at the third token. Based on its type, we delegate to the correct method to finish the processing. If we find an unexpected `Token` type, we throw an `Exception`.

Before looking at those calculation methods, let's look at `validateToken()`:

```
private void validateToken(final Token token,
    final Class<? extends Token> expected) {
    if (token == null || !
      token.getClass().isAssignableFrom(expected)) {
```

```
                throw new DateCalcException(String.format(
                  "Invalid format: Expected %s, found %s",
                  expected, token != null ?
                  token.getClass().getSimpleName() : "null"));
            }
        }
```

There's nothing too terribly exciting here, but eagle-eyed readers might notice that we're returning the class name of our token, and, by doing so, we're leaking the name of a non-exported class to the end user. That's probably not ideal, but we'll leave fixing that as an exercise for the reader.

The method to perform date math looks like this:

```
        private DateCalculatorResult performDateMath(
          final DateToken startDateToken,
          final OperatorToken operatorToken,
          final Queue<Token> tokens) {
            LocalDate result = startDateToken.getValue();
            int negate = operatorToken.isAddition() ? 1 : -1;

            while (!tokens.isEmpty()) {
              validateToken(tokens.peek(), IntegerToken.class);
              int amount = ((IntegerToken) tokens.poll()).getValue() *
                negate;
              validateToken(tokens.peek(), UnitOfMeasureToken.class);
              result = result.plus(amount,
              ((UnitOfMeasureToken) tokens.poll()).getValue());
            }

            return new DateCalculatorResult(result);
        }
```

Since we already have our starting and operator tokens, we pass those in, as well as the `Queue` so that we can process the remaining tokens. Our first step is to determine if the operator is a plus or a minus, assigning a positive 1 or a –1 to `negate` as appropriate. We do this so we can use a single method, `LocalDate.plus()`. If the operator is a minus, we add a negative number and get the same result as subtracting the original number.

Finally, we loop through the remaining tokens, verifying each one before we process it. We get the `IntegerToken`; grab its value; multiply it by our negative modifier, `negate`; then add that value to the `LocalDate` using the `UnitOfMeasureToken` to tell what **kind** of value we're adding.

Calculating the difference between dates is pretty straightforward, as we see here:

```
private DateCalculatorResult getDateDiff(
  final DateToken startDateToken, final Token thirdToken) {
    LocalDate one = startDateToken.getValue();
    LocalDate two = ((DateToken) thirdToken).getValue();
    return (one.isBefore(two)) ? new
      DateCalculatorResult(Period.between(one, two)) : new
        DateCalculatorResult(Period.between(two, one));
}
```

We extract the `LocalDate` from our two `DateToken` variables, then call `Period.between()`, which returns a `Period` that indicates the elapsed amount of time between the two dates. We do check to see which date comes first so that we return a positive `Period` to the user as a convenience, since most people don't typically think in terms of negative periods.

The time-based methods are largely identical. The big difference is the time difference method:

```
private DateCalculatorResult getTimeDiff(
  final OperatorToken operatorToken,
  final TimeToken startTimeToken,
  final Token thirdToken) throws DateCalcException {
    LocalTime startTime = startTimeToken.getValue();
    LocalTime endTime = ((TimeToken) thirdToken).getValue();
    return new DateCalculatorResult(
      Duration.between(startTime, endTime).abs());
}
```

The notable difference here is the use of `Duration.between()`. It looks identical to `Period.between()`, but the `Duration` class offers a method that `Period` does not: `abs()`. This method lets us return the absolute value of `Period`, so we can pass our `LocalTime` variable to `between()` in any order we want.

One final note before we leave this--we are wrapping our results in a `DateCalculatorResult` instance. Since the various operations return several different, unrelated types, this allows us to return a single type from our `calculate()` method. It will be up to the calling code to extract the appropriate value. We'll do that in our command-line interface, which we'll look at in the next section.

A brief interlude on testing

Before we move on, we need to visit a topic we've not discussed yet, that being testing. Anyone who has been in the industry for a while has likely heard the term **Test-Driven Development** (or **TDD** for short). It's an approach to software development that posits that the first thing that should be written is a test, which will fail (since there's no code to run), then the code should be written that makes the test **green**, a reference to the green indicator given in IDEs and other tools to indicate that the test has passed. This process repeats as many times as necessary to build the final system, always making changes in small increments, and always starting with a test. A myriad of books have been written on the topic, which is both hotly debated and oftentimes heavily nuanced. The exact way the approach is implemented, if at all, almost always comes in flavors.

Clearly, in our work here, we haven't followed the TDD principle strictly, but that doesn't mean we haven't tested. While TDD purists are likely to quibble, my general approach tends to be a bit looser on the testing side until my API starts to solidify some. How long this takes depends on how familiar I am with the technologies being used. If I'm very familiar with them, I might sketch out a quick interface, then scaffold a test based on that as a means of testing the API itself, then iterate over that. For new libraries, I might write a very broad test to help drive the investigation of the new library, using the test framework as a means for bootstrapping a runtime environment in which I can experiment. Regardless, at the end of the development effort, the new system should be **fully** tested (with the exact definition of **fully** being another hotly debated concept), which is what I have striven for here. A full treatise on testing and test-driven development is beyond our scope here, though.

When it comes to testing in Java, you have a **lot** of options. However, the two most common ones are TestNG and JUnit, with JUnit probably being the most popular. Which one should you pick? That depends. If you are working with an existing code-base, you should probably use whatever is already in use, unless you have a good reason to do otherwise. For example, the library could be old and no longer supported, it could be demonstrably insufficient for your needs, or you've been given an express directive to update/replace the existing system. If any of those conditions, or others similar to these, are true, we circle back to the question--*Which should I choose?* Again, that depends. JUnit is extremely popular and common, so using it might make sense in order to lower the barrier of entry into a project. However, TestNG has what some feel to be a much better, cleaner API. For example, TestNG does not require the use of static methods for certain test setup methods. It also aims to be much more than just a unit testing framework, providing tools for unit, functional, end-to-end, and integration testing. For our tests here, we will be using TestNG.

To get started with TestNG, we need to add it to our project. To do that, we will add a test dependency to the Maven POM file as follows:

```
<properties>
  <testng.version>6.9.9</testng.version>
</properties>
<dependencies>
  <dependency>
    <groupId>org.testng</groupId>
    <artifactId>testng</artifactId>
    <version>${testng.version}</version>
    <scope>test</scope>
  </dependency>
</dependencies>
```

Writing the tests is very simple. With the defaults of the TestNG Maven plugin, the class simply needs to be in `src/test/java` and end with the `Test` string. Each test method needs to be annotated with `@Test`.

There are a number of tests in the library module, so let's start with some of the very basic ones that test the regular expressions used by the tokens to identify and extract the relevant parts of the expression. For example, consider the following piece of code:

```
public class RegexTest {
  @Test
  public void dateTokenRegex() {
    testPattern(DateToken.REGEX, "2016-01-01");
    testPattern(DateToken.REGEX, "today");
  }
  private void testPattern(String pattern, String text) {
    testPattern(pattern, text, false);
  }

  private void testPattern(String pattern, String text,
    boolean exact) {
      Pattern p = Pattern.compile("(" + pattern + ")");
      final Matcher matcher = p.matcher(text);

      Assert.assertTrue(matcher.find());
      if (exact) {
        Assert.assertEquals(matcher.group(), text);
      }
  }
}
```

This is a very basic test of the `DateToken` regular expression. The test delegates to the `testPattern()` method, passing the regular expression to test, and a string to test it with. Our functionality is tested by following these steps:

1. Compiling the `Pattern`.
2. Creating a `Matcher`.
3. Calling the `matcher.find()` method.

With that, the logic of the system under test is exercised. What remains is to verify that it worked as expected. We do that with our call to `Assert.assertTrue()`. We assert that `matcher.find()` returns `true`. If the regex is correct, we should get a `true` response. If the regex is not correct, we'll get a `false` response. In the latter case, `assertTrue()` will throw an `Exception` and the test will fail.

This test is certainly very basic. It could--should--be more robust. It should test a greater variety of strings. It should include some strings known to be bad to make sure we're not getting incorrect results in our tests. There are probably a myriad of other enhancements that could be made. The point here, though, is to show a simple test to demonstrate how to set up a TestNG-based environment. Before moving on, let's look at a couple more examples.

Here's a test to check for failure (a **negative test**):

```
@Test
public void invalidStringsShouldFail() {
  try {
    parser.parse("2016/12/25 this is nonsense");
    Assert.fail("A DateCalcException should have been
      thrown (Unable to identify token)");
  } catch (DateCalcException dce) {
  }
}
```

In this test, we expect the call to `parse()` to fail, with a `DateCalcException`. Should the call **not** fail, we have a call to `Assert.fail()` that will force the test to fail with the message provided. If the `Exception` is thrown, it's swallowed silently and the test finishes successfully.

Swallowing the `Exception` is one approach, but you can also tell TestNG to expect an `Exception` to be thrown, as we've done here via the `expectedExceptions` attribute:

```
@Test(expectedExceptions = {DateCalcException.class})
public void shouldRejectBadTimes() {
  parser.parse("22:89");
}
```

Again, we're passing a bad string to the parser. However, this time, we're telling TestNG to expect the exception via the annotation--`@Test(expectedExceptions = {DateCalcException.class})`.

Much more could be written on testing in general and TestNG in particular. A thorough treatment of both topics is beyond our scope, but if you are not familiar with either topic, you would be well served to find one of the many great resources available and study them thoroughly.

For now, let's turn our attention to the command-line interface.

Building the command-line interface

In the last chapter, we built a command-line tool using the Crest library from Tomitribe, and it worked out pretty well, so we will return to the library in building this command line as well.

To enable Crest in our project, we must do two things. First, we have to configure our POM file as follows:

```
<dependency>
  <groupId>org.tomitribe</groupId>
  <artifactId>tomitribe-crest</artifactId>
  <version>0.8</version>
</dependency>
```

We must also update our module definition in `src/main/java/module-info.java` as follows:

```
module datecalc.cli {
  requires datecalc.lib;
  requires tomitribe.crest;
  requires tomitribe.crest.api;
  exports com.steeplesoft.datecalc.cli;
}
```

We can now define our CLI class like this:

```
public class DateCalc {
  @Command
  public void dateCalc(String... args) {
    final String expression = String.join(" ", args);
    final DateCalculator dc = new DateCalculator();
    final DateCalculatorResult dcr = dc.calculate(expression);
```

Unlike in the last chapter, this command line will be extremely simple, as the only input we need is the expression to evaluate. With the preceding method signature, we tell Crest to pass all of the command-line arguments as the `args` value, which we then join back together via `String.join()` into `expression`. Next, we create our calculator and calculate the result.

We now need to interrogate our `DateCalcResult` to determine the nature of the expression. Consider the following piece of code as an example:

```
String result = "";
if (dcr.getDate().isPresent()) {
  result = dcr.getDate().get().toString();
} else if (dcr.getTime().isPresent()) {
  result = dcr.getTime().get().toString();
} else if (dcr.getDuration().isPresent()) {
  result = processDuration(dcr.getDuration().get());
} else if (dcr.getPeriod().isPresent()) {
  result = processPeriod(dcr.getPeriod().get());
}
System.out.println(String.format("'%s' equals '%s'",
  expression, result));
```

The `LocalDate` and `LocalTime` responses are pretty straightforward--we can simply call the `toString()` method on them, as the defaults are, for our purposes here, perfectly acceptable. Duration and periods are a bit more complicated. Both provide a number of methods to extract the details. We will hide those details in separate methods:

```
private String processDuration(Duration d) {
  long hours = d.toHoursPart();
  long minutes = d.toMinutesPart();
  long seconds = d.toSecondsPart();
  String result = "";
  if (hours > 0) {
    result += hours + " hours, ";
  }
  result += minutes + " minutes, ";
  if (seconds > 0) {
```

```
        result += seconds + " seconds";
    }

    return result;
}
```

The method itself is pretty simple--we extract the various parts from `Duration`, then build the string based on whether or not the part returns values.

The date-related method, `processPeriod()`, is similar:

```
private String processPeriod(Period p) {
    long years = p.getYears();
    long months = p.getMonths();
    long days = p.getDays();
    String result = "";

    if (years > 0) {
        result += years + " years, ";
    }
    if (months > 0) {
        result += months + " months, ";
    }
    if (days > 0) {
        result += days + " days";
    }
    return result;
}
```

Each of these methods returns the result as a string, which we then write to standard out. And that's it. It's not a terribly complicated command-line utility, but the purpose of the exercise here is found mostly in the library.

Summary

Our date calculator is now complete. The utility itself is not too terribly complex, although, it did serve as expected, which has to be a vehicle for experimenting with Java 8's Date/Time API. In addition to the new date/time API, we scratched the surface of regular expressions, a very powerful and complex tool to parse strings. We also revisited the command-line utility library from the last chapter, and dipped our toes in the waters of unit testing and test-driven development.

In the next chapter, we'll get a bit more ambitious and step into the world of social media, building an app to help us aggregate some of our favorite services into a single application.

21
Sunago - A Social Media Aggregator

For our next project, we'll try something a bit more ambitious; we'll build a desktop application that aggregates data from various social media networks and displays it in one seamless interaction. We're also going to try something new, and we're going to give this project a name, something that might be a bit more appealing than the dry, albeit accurate, `description-turned-name` that we've used to date. This application, then, we'll call Sunago, which is the phonetic spelling of the (Koine) Greek word συνάγω, which means **I gather together**, **collect**, **assemble**.

Building the app will cover several different topics, some familiar, some new. That list includes the following:

- JavaFX
- Internationalization and localization
- **Service Provider Interfaces (SPI)**
- REST API consumption
- `ClassLoader` manipulation
- Lambdas, lambdas, and more lambdas

As usual, those are the just the highlights with a number of interesting items sprinkled throughout.

Getting started

As with every application, before we get started, we need to think about what we want the application to do. That is, what are the functional requirements? At a high level, the description tells us what we want to achieve in broad terms, but, more specifically, we want the user to be able to do the following:

- Connect to several different social media networks
- Determine, on a network-by-network basis, which group of data (users, lists, and more) to retrieve
- See list of items from each network in a consolidated display
- Be able to determine from which network an item came
- Click on an item and have it loaded in the user's default browser

In addition to this list of things the application **should** do, the things it **shouldn't** do include the following:

- Respond/reply to items
- Comment on items
- Manage friends/following lists

These features would be great additions to the application, but they don't offer much that would be architecturally interesting beyond the basic application detailed previously, so, to keep things simple--and moving along--we'll limit the scope to the given basic set of requirements.

So where to start on the application? As in the previous chapters, we're going to make this a desktop application, so let's start there, with a JavaFX application. I'm going to tip my hand a little bit here to make things easier later on: this will be a multi-module project, so we first need to create the parent project. In NetBeans, click on **File** | **New Project...**, and select the `Maven` category, as seen in the following screenshot:

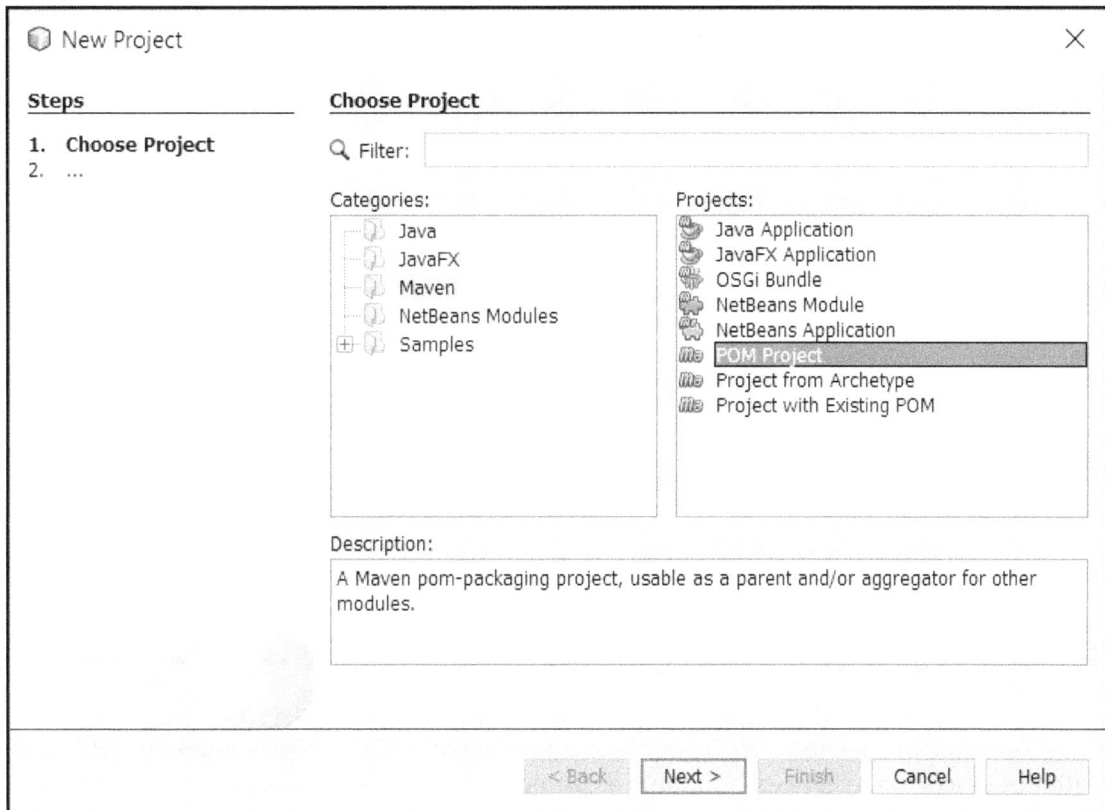

Click on the **Next** button, and fill in the project details, as shown next:

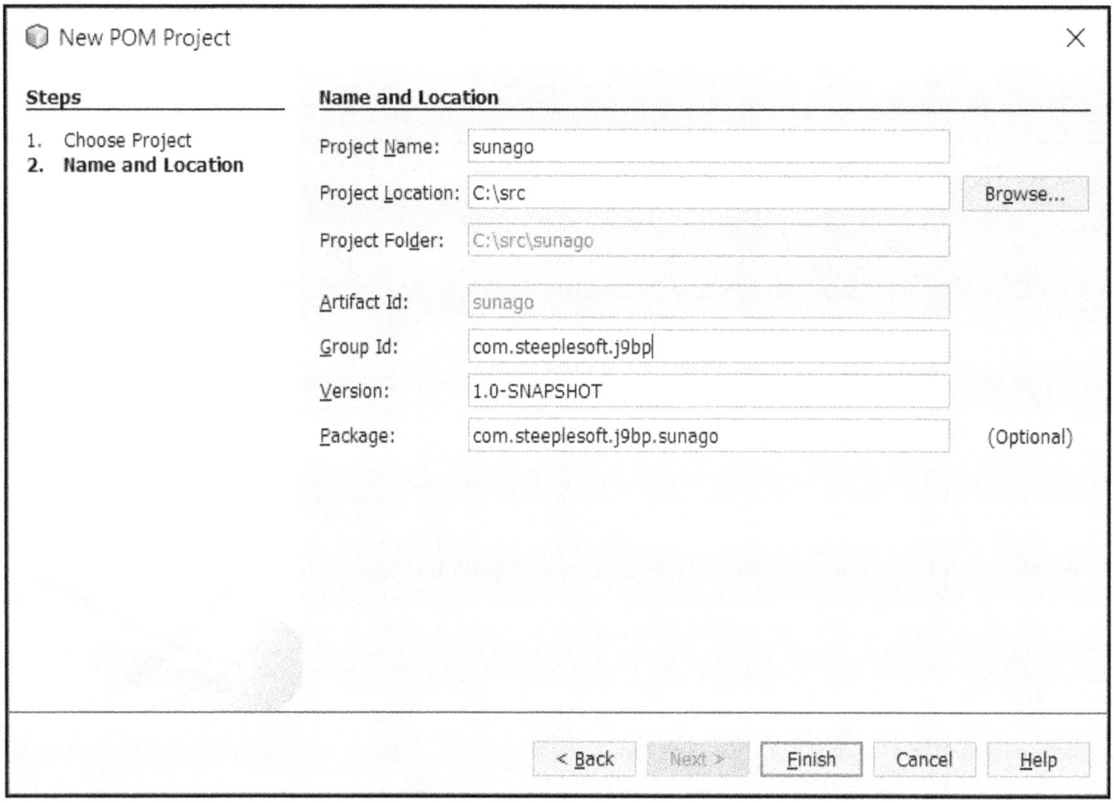

When you click on **Finish**, you will be presented with an empty project. Once we add modules to this project, differentiating them might become difficult, so something I do as a matter of practice is to give each module a distinct, "namespaced" name. That is to say, each module has its own name, of course, but I prefix that with the name of the project. For example, since this is the base POM of the project, I call it Master. To reflect that, I modify the generated POM to look something like this:

```xml
<?xml version="1.0" encoding="UTF-8"?>
<project xmlns="http://maven.apache.org/POM/4.0.0"
  xmlns:xsi="http://www.w3.org/2001/XMLSchema-instance"
  xsi:schemaLocation="http://maven.apache.org/POM/4.0.0
  http://maven.apache.org/xsd/maven-4.0.0.xsd">
  <modelVersion>4.0.0</modelVersion>
  <groupId>com.steeplesoft.sunago</groupId>
  <artifactId>master</artifactId>
  <version>1.0-SNAPSHOT</version>
```

```
    <name>Sunago - Master</name>
    <packaging>pom</packaging>
</project>
```

There's really not much to this yet. The advantage that a parent POM like this gives us is that we can build all the projects with one command if we so desire, and we can move any shared configuration to this shared parent POM to reduce duplication. What we need to add now, though, is a module, which NetBeans helps us do, as seen in this screenshot:

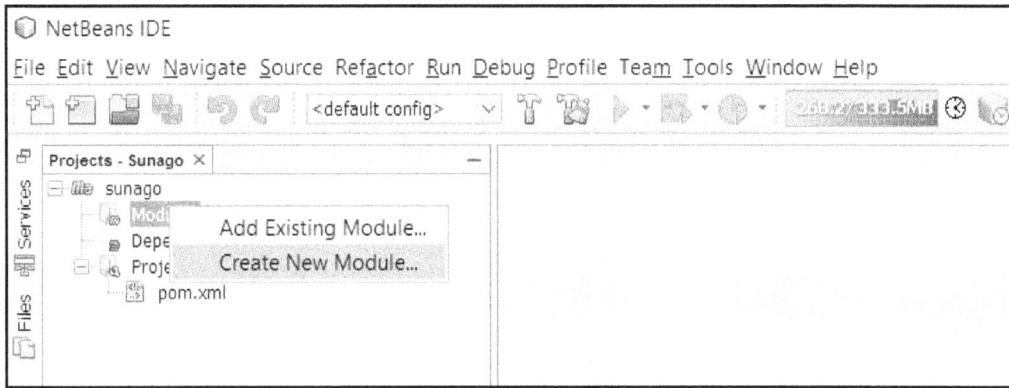

After clicking on **Create New Module...**, you will be presented with the familiar **New Project** window, from which you'll want to select **Maven | JavaFX Application**, and click on **Next**. In the **New Java Application** screen, enter app for the project name, and click on **Finish** (all of the other defaults are acceptable as-is).

Again, we want to give this module a meaningful name, so let's modify the generated pom.xml as follows:

```
<?xml version="1.0" encoding="UTF-8"?>
<project xmlns="http://maven.apache.org/POM/4.0.0"
  xmlns:xsi="http://www.w3.org/2001/XMLSchema-instance"
  xsi:schemaLocation="http://maven.apache.org/POM/4.0.0
  http://maven.apache.org/xsd/maven-4.0.0.xsd">
  <modelVersion>4.0.0</modelVersion>
  <parent>
    <groupId>com.steeplesoft.sunago</groupId>
    <artifactId>master</artifactId>
    <version>1.0-SNAPSHOT</version>
  </parent>
  <artifactId>sunago</artifactId>
  <name>Sunago - App</name>
  <packaging>jar</packaging>
</project>
```

When NetBeans creates the project, it will generate several artifacts for us--two classes, FXMLController and MainApp, as well as the resources, fxml/Scene.xml and styles/Styles.css. While this may be stating the obvious, artifacts should have names that clearly communicate their purpose, so let's rename these.

The class FxmlContoller should be renamed to SunagoController. Perhaps the quickest and easiest way to do this is to open the class by double-clicking on it in **Project View**, then, in the source editor, click on the name of the class in the class declaration, and press *Ctrl + R*. The **Rename Class** dialog should appear, in which you need to enter the new name, and press *Enter*. This will rename the class and the file for you. Now repeat that process for MainApp, renaming it to Sunago.

We also want to rename the generated FXML file, Scene.xml, to sunago.fxml. To do that, right-click on the file in **Project View** and select **Rename...** from the context menu. Enter the new name (without the extension) in the **Rename** dialog, and press *Enter*. While we're at it, let's also rename Styles.css to styles.css so that the case is consistent. It's a minor thing, but consistency in the code can help produce confidence in you in whoever might take over your code in the future.

Unfortunately, renaming these files doesn't adjust the references to them in the Java sources, so we need to edit Sunago.java to point to these new names, which is done as follows:

```
@Override
public void start(Stage stage) throws Exception {
  Parent root = fxmlLoader.load(
    getClass().getResource("/fxml/sunago.fxml"));

    Scene scene = new Scene(root);
    scene.getStylesheets().add("/styles/styles.css");

    stage.setTitle("Sunago, your social media aggregator");
    stage.setScene(scene);
    stage.show();
}
```

Note also that we changed the title to something more appropriate.

Setting up the user interface

If we wanted to, we could now run our application. It would be very boring, but it would run. Let's try to fix the boring part.

The default FXML created is just an **AnchorPane** with two children, a **Button** and a **Label**. We don't need any of those, so let's get rid of them. Our main user interface will be pretty simple--basically, just a vertical stack of components--so we can use a **VBox** as our root component. Perhaps, the easiest way to change the root component from the **AnchorPane** that's there to a **VBox** is to use Scene Builder to wrap that component in a **VBox**, and then delete the **AnchorPane**:

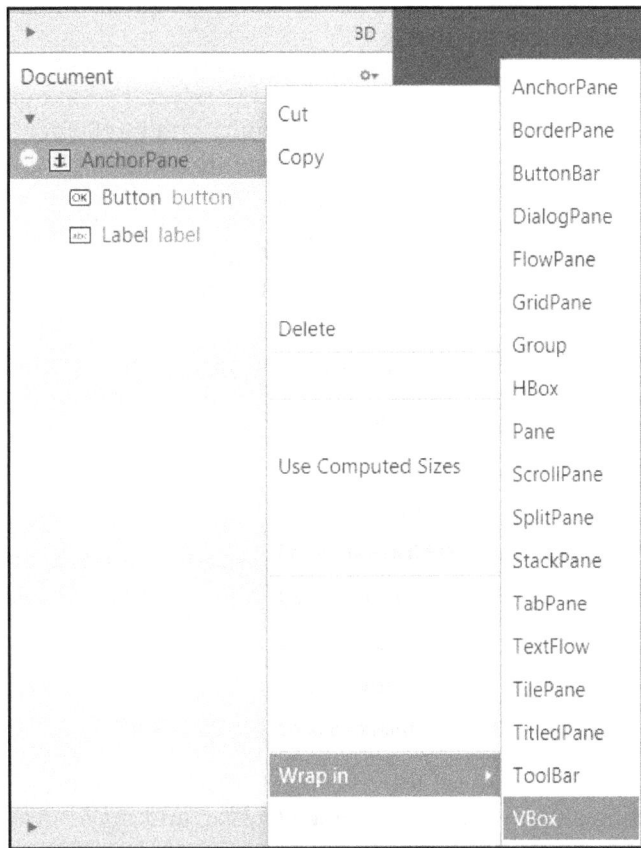

To do that, open the FXML file in Scene Builder by double-clicking on the file (assuming you've configured NetBeans correctly so that it knows where to find Scene Builder. If not, refer back to `Chapter 17`, *Introduction*). In Scene Builder, right-click on **AnchorPane** in the **Document** section of the accordion on the left, select **Wrap in**, and then **VBox**, as shown in the preceding screenshot. Scene Builder will then modify the FXML file, making **AnchorPane** a child of **VBox** as expected. Once that's done, you can right-click on **AnchorPane**, and click on **Delete** to remove it and its children. This leaves us with an empty user interface that's more boring than it was when we began. We can fix that now by adding a couple of controls--a **MenuBar** and a **ListView**. We do that by clicking on each component in the **Controls** section of the accordion and dragging them to **VBox**. If you drop the components on **VBox**, they will be appended to its list of children. Make sure that **MenuBar** comes before **ListView**, or you'll have a very strange user interface.

Let's configure these components a bit now before we return to the code. Selecting **VBox** from the **Document** section on the left, we then need to select the **Layout** section in the accordion on the right. For **Min Width** and **Min Height**, enter `640` and `480` respectively. This will make the window's default size larger and more user-friendly.

For **MenuBar**, we need to expand its entry under **Document**, then expand each of its **Menu** children, which should reveal one **MenuItem** per **Menu**. Click on the first **Menu**, then, on the right, set `Text` to `_File`, and check **Mnemonic Parsing**. This will allow the user to press *Alt + F* to activate (or show) this menu. Next, click on its `MenuItem` child, setting `Text` to `_Exit`, and check **Mnemonic Parsing.** (If the text for a `Menu`, `MenuItem`, `Button`, and more has an underscore in it, make sure that **Mnemonic Parsing** is checked. For brevity's sake, I won't flag this explicitly again.) Open the **Code** section, and set the **On Action** value to `closeApplication`.

The second `Menu` should have its **Text** value set to `_Edit`. Its `MenuItem` should be labeled `_Settings`, and have an **On Action** value of `showPreferences`. Finally, the third `Menu` should be labeled `_Help`, and its `MenuItem` labeled `About` with an **On Action** of `showAbout`.

Next, we want to give `ListView` an ID, so select that on the left, make sure the **Code** section is expanded on the right, and enter `entriesListView` for **fx:id**.

The last edit we need to make is to set the controller. We do that in the accordion on the left, in the **Controller** section at the very bottom. Expand that, and make sure that the **Controller class** value matches the Java class and package we just created in NetBeans, then save the file.

Setting up the controller

Back in NetBeans, we need to fix up our controller to reflect the changes we just made in our FXML. In `SunagoController`, we need to add the `entriesListView` property as follows:

```
@FXML
private ListView<SocialMediaItem> entriesListView;
```

Notice that the parameterized type is `SocialMediaItem`. That's a custom model we'll create in just a few moments. Before we tackle that, though, we need to finish wiring together our user interface. We defined three `onAction` handlers in the FXML. The corresponding code is as follows:

```
@FXML
public void closeApplication(ActionEvent event) {
   Platform.exit();
}
```

Closing the application is as simple as calling the `exit` method on the `Platform` class. Showing the "about" box is also fairly simple, as we see in the `showAbout` method:

```
@FXML
public void showAbout(ActionEvent event) {
   Alert alert = new Alert(Alert.AlertType.INFORMATION);
   alert.setTitle("About...");
   alert.setHeaderText("Sunago (συνάγω)");
   alert.setContentText("(c) Copyright 2016");
   alert.showAndWait();
}
```

Using the built-in `Alert` class, we construct an instance, and set the values appropriate for an About screen, then display it modally via `showAndWait()`.

The preferences window is a much more complicated piece of logic, so we wrap that up in a new controller class, and call its `showAndWait()` method.

```
@FXML
public void showPreferences(ActionEvent event) {
   PreferencesController.showAndWait();
}
```

Writing the model class

Before we look at that, though, there are a few more items in the main controller that we need to take care of. The first is the model class mentioned earlier, `SocialMediaItem`. As you can probably imagine, the structure of the data returned from a social network can be quite complex, and certainly, varied. The data requirements for a tweet, for example, are likely to be quite different from those for an Instagram post. What we'd like to be able to do, then, is to hide those complexities and differences behind a simple, reusable interface. In the real world, such a simple abstraction is not always possible, but, for our purposes here, we have such an interface in `SocialMediaItem`, as you can see in this piece of code:

```
public interface SocialMediaItem {
    String getProvider();
    String getTitle();
    String getBody();
    String getUrl();
    String getImage();
    Date getTimestamp();
}
```

One of the problems with abstractions is that, to make them reusable, you, occasionally, have to structure them in such a way that they expose properties that may not be used by every implementation. It's not obvious yet, but that is certainly the case here. It's a scenario that some consider to be unacceptable, and they may have a point, but it's really a question of trade-offs. Our options include a slightly bloated interface or a complex system in which each network support module (which we'll get to shortly) provides its own renderer, and the application has to interrogate each module, looking for the renderer that can handle each item while drawing `ListView`. There are likely others, of course, but faced with (at least) those two, for the sake of simplicity and performance, we'll take the first option. When faced with similar situations while designing your own systems, though, you'll need to evaluate the various requirements of your project, and make an appropriate choice. For our needs here, the simple approach is more than adequate.

At any rate, each social media network module will implement that interface to wrap its data. This will give a common interface for the application to consume without needing to know exactly where it came from. We do, though, now need to tell the `ListView` how to draw a cell containing a `SocialMediaItem`. We can do that with this line of code in the `initialize()` method of our controller, as follows:

```
entriesListView.setCellFactory(listView ->
    new SocialMediaItemViewCell());
```

Obviously, that's a lambda. For the curious, the pre-lambda version of the preceding method would look like this:

```
entriesListView.setCellFactory(
  new Callback<ListView<SocialMediaItem>,
  ListCell<SocialMediaItem>>() {
    @Override
    public ListCell<SocialMediaItem> call(
      ListView<SocialMediaItem> param) {
        return new SocialMediaItemViewCell();
    }
});
```

Finishing up the controller

Before we look at `SocialMediaItemViewCell`, there are two more controller items. The first is the list that holds the `ListView` data. Remember that `ListView` operates from an `ObservableList`. This lets us make changes to the data in the list, and have it automatically reflected in the user interface. To create that list, we'll use a JavaFX helper method when we define the class property as follows:

```
private final ObservableList<SocialMediaItem> entriesList =
  FXCollections.observableArrayList();
```

Then we need to connect that `List` to our `ListView`. Back in `intialize()`, we have the following:

```
entriesListView.setItems(entriesList);
```

To finish off the rendering of `SocialMediaItem` interfaces, let's define `SocialMediaItemViewCell` like this:

```
public class SocialMediaItemViewCell extends
  ListCell<SocialMediaItem> {
  @Override
  public void updateItem(SocialMediaItem item, boolean empty) {
    super.updateItem(item, empty);
    if (item != null) {
      setGraphic(buildItemCell(item));
      this.setOnMouseClicked(me -> SunagoUtil
        .openUrlInDefaultApplication(item.getUrl())));
    } else {
      setGraphic(null);
    }
  }
```

```
private Node buildItemCell(SocialMediaItem item) {
  HBox hbox = new HBox();
  InputStream resource = item.getClass()
    .getResourceAsStream("icon.png");
  if (resource != null) {
    ImageView sourceImage = new ImageView();
    sourceImage.setFitHeight(18);
    sourceImage.setPreserveRatio(true);
    sourceImage.setSmooth(true);
    sourceImage.setCache(true);
    sourceImage.setImage(new Image(resource));
    hbox.getChildren().add(sourceImage);
  }

  if (item.getImage() != null) {
    HBox picture = new HBox();
    picture.setPadding(new Insets(0,10,0,0));
    ImageView imageView = new ImageView(item.getImage());
    imageView.setPreserveRatio(true);
    imageView.setFitWidth(150);
    picture.getChildren().add(imageView);
    hbox.getChildren().add(picture);
  }

  Label label = new Label(item.getBody());
  label.setFont(Font.font(null, 20));
  label.setWrapText(true);
  hbox.getChildren().add(label);

  return hbox;
  }


}
```

There's a fair amount happening here, but updateItem() is our first point of interest. This is the method that is called every time the row is updated on the screen. Notice that we check to see if item is null. We do that because ListView calls this method not for every item in its List, but for every row in ListView that's visible, whether there's data for it or not. That means that, if List has five items but ListView is tall enough to show ten rows, this method will be called ten times, with the last five calls being made with a null item. In those cases, we call setGraphic(null) to clear out any item that may have been previously rendered.

If `item` is not null, though, we need to build the `Node` to display the item, which is done in `buildItemCell()`. For each item, we want to render three items--the social media network icon (so users can tell at a glance where the item is from), any image embedded in the item, and, finally, any text/caption from the item. To help arrange that, we start with an `HBox`.

Next, we try to find an icon for the network. If we had a formal contract written up, we would include language in it that would stipulate that the module include a file called `icon.png`, which is in the same package as the module's `SocialMediaItem` implementation. Using the `ClassLoader` for the implementation, then, we try to get an `InputStream` for the resource. We check for null, just to make sure the image was actually found; if so, we create an `ImageView`, set some properties, then wrap the resource in an `Image`, hand that to `ImageView`, then add `ImageView` to `HBox`.

Adding an image for the item

If the item has an image, we handle it in the same way that we did with the network icon image. This time, though, we actually wrap the `ImageView` in another `HBox` before adding it to the outer `HBox`. We do that so that we can add padding around the image (via `picture.setPadding(new Insets())`) to give this image some space between it and the network icon.

Finally, we create a `Label` to hold the item's body. We set the font size of the text to `20` points via `label.setFont(Font.font(null, 20))`, and add it to our `HBox`, which we then return to the caller, `updateItem()`.

> Any time you have a `ListView`, you are likely going to want a custom `ListCell` implementation like we have here. In some cases, calling `toString()` on the `List` contents might be appropriate, but that's not always the case, and you certainly can't have a complex `ListCell` structure like we have here without implementing `ListCell` yourself. If you're planning on doing much JavaFX development, you would be well advised to get comfortable with this technique.

Building the preferences user interface

We're finally **finished** with the main controller, and we can turn our attention to the next big piece, `PreferencesController`. Our preferences dialog will be, as is usually expected, a modal dialog. It will offer a tabbed interface with one tab for general settings, then a tab for each supported social network. We start that work by adding a new FXML file and controller to our project, and NetBeans has a great wizard for that. Right-click on the desired package, and click on **New | Other**. From the **Categories** list, select `JavaFX`, and then, from the **File Types** lists, select `Empty FXML` as shown in the following screenshot:

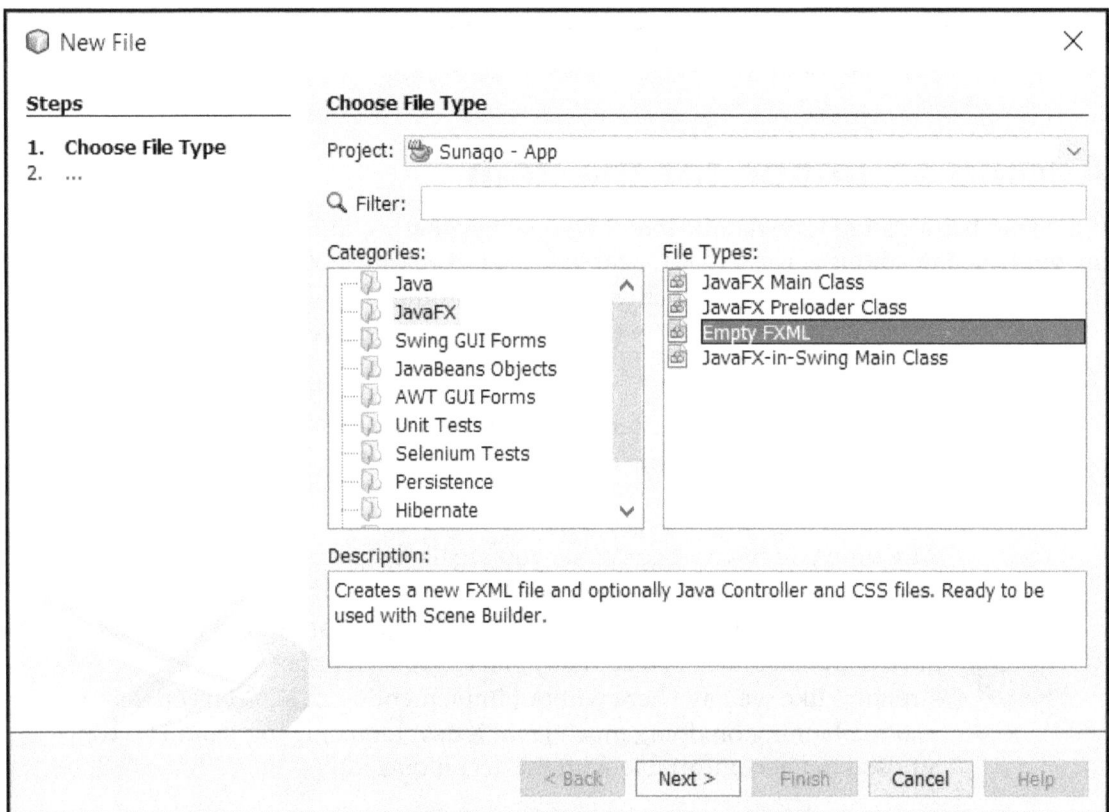

After clicking on **Next**, you should see the **FXML Name and Location** step. This will allow us to specify the name of our new file and the package in which it is created, as seen in this screenshot:

```
New Empty FXML                                                          ✕

Steps                          FXML File Name and Location
─────────────                  ────────────────────────────────────────
1.  Choose File Type           FXML Name:    prefs
2.  FXML Name and
    Location                   Project:      app
3.  Controller Class
4.  Cascading Style Sheet      Location:     Project Resources              ⌄

                              Package:      fxml                            ⌄

                              Created File:  C:\src\sunago\app\src\main\resources\fxml\prefs.fxml


                                      < Back      Next >     Finish     Cancel      Help
```

Clicking on **Next** brings us to the **Controller Class** step. Here we can either create a new controller class, or attach our file to an existing one. Since this is a new dialog/window for our app, we need to create a new controller as follows:

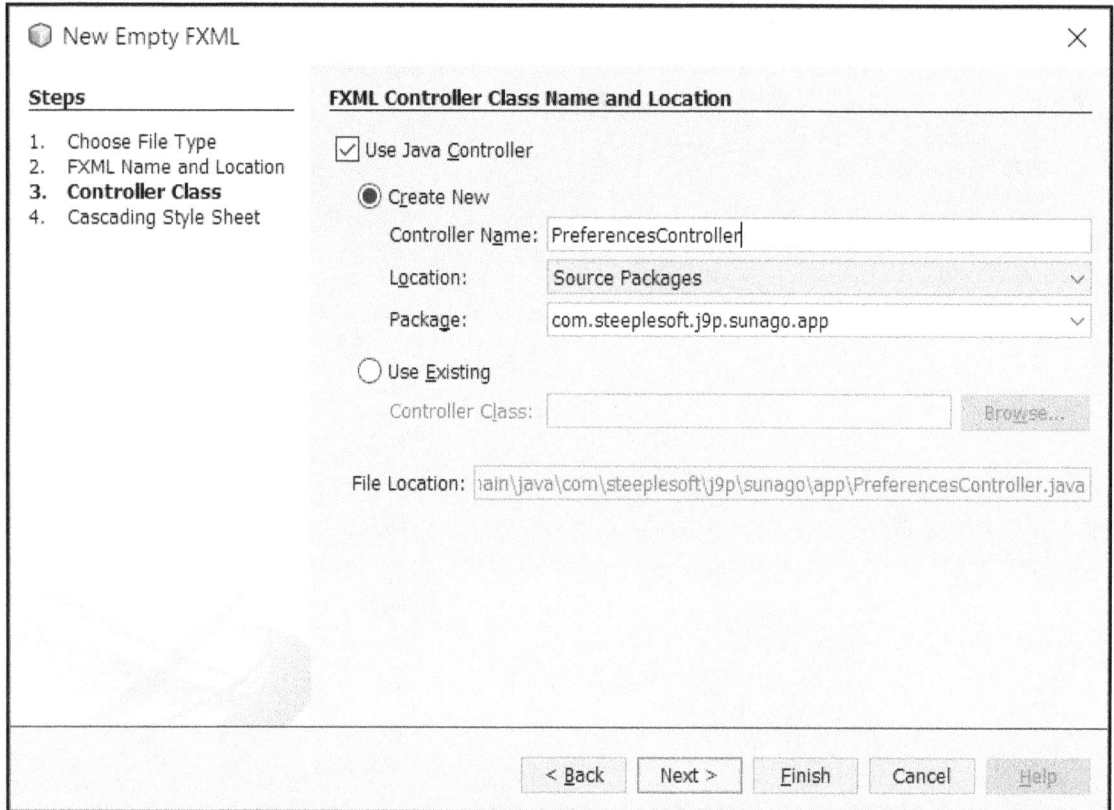

```
┌─────────────────────────────────────────────────────────────────────────────┐
│  ⬡ New Empty FXML                                                          ✕  │
│                                                                               │
│  Steps                          FXML Controller Class Name and Location       │
│  ─────────────                  ────────────────────────────────────────────│
│  1.  Choose File Type           ☑ Use Java Controller                         │
│  2.  FXML Name and Location                                                   │
│  3.  Controller Class             ◉ Create New                                │
│  4.  Cascading Style Sheet          Controller Name:  PreferencesController   │
│                                                                               │
│                                     Location:    Source Packages          ⌄  │
│                                                                               │
│                                     Package:     com.steeplesoft.j9p.sunago.app ⌄ │
│                                                                               │
│                                   ○ Use Existing                             │
│                                     Controller Class: [              ] Browse...│
│                                                                               │
│                                   File Location: ain\java\com\steeplesoft\j9p\sunago\app\PreferencesController.java │
│                                                                               │
│                                                                               │
│                                                                               │
│                         < Back    Next >    Finish    Cancel    Help          │
└─────────────────────────────────────────────────────────────────────────────┘
```

Check the **Use Java Controller** checkbox, enter `PreferencesController` for the name, and select the desired package. We could click on **Next**, which would take us to the **Cascading Style Sheet** step, but we're not interested in specifying that for this controller, so, we end the wizard by clicking on **Finish**, which will take us to the source of our newly created controller class.

Let's start by laying out the user interface. Double-click on the new `prefs.fxml` file to open it in Scene Builder. Like our last FXML file, the default root element is **AnchorPane**. For this window, we'd like to use a **BorderPane**, so we use the same technique that we did last time to replace **AnchorPane**--right-click on the component, and click on **Wrap in | BorderPane**. The **AnchorPane** is now nested in **BorderPane**, so we right-click on it again and select **Delete**.

To build the user interface, we now drag a **TabPane** control from the accordion on the left, and drop it in the **CENTER** area of **BorderPane**. This will add a **TabPane** with two tabs to our user interface. We only want one right now, so delete the second one. We want to give our tab a meaningful label. We can do that by double-clicking on the tab in the preview window (or selecting the **Text** property in the **Properties** section of the **Inspector**) and typing General. Finally, expand the Inspector's **Code** section, and enter tabPane for **fx:id**.

Now we need to provide a means by which the user can close the window, and either save or discard changes. We implement that by dragging a **ButtonBar** component to our border pane's **BOTTOM** area. That will add a **ButtonBar** with one button, but we need two, so we drag another button on to the **ButtonBar**. The nice thing about this control is that it will handle button placement and padding for us, so, when we drop the new button, it's automatically added in the proper place on the right. (This behavior can be overridden, but it works exactly how we want it to, so we can just accept the defaults.)

For each Button, we need to set three properties--text, fx:id, and onAction. The first property is in the **Properties** section of the inspector, and the last two in the **Code** section. The values for the first button are Save, savePrefs, and savePreferences. For the second button, the values are Cancel, cancel, and closeDialog. Select the **Layout** section for the ButtonBar in the inspector, and set the right padding to 10 to make sure Button is not pressed against the edge of the window.

Finally, we'll add our only preference at this point. We want to allow the user to specify the maximum number of items to retrieve from each social media network for a given request. We do that for those scenarios where the application hasn't been used in a while (or ever). In those cases, we don't want to try to download, for example, thousands of tweets. To add support for this, we add two controls, Label and TextField.

Getting the position of the **Label** control right is pretty simple, as it's the first component. Scene Builder will provide red guidelines to help you position the component exactly where you want it, as shown in this screenshot:

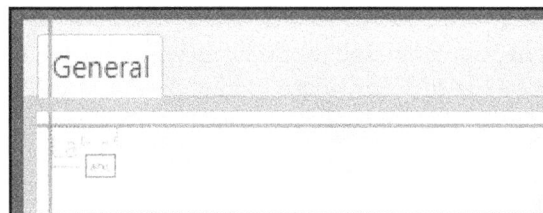

Making sure that `TextField` is lined up with the label can be trickier. By default, when you drop a component on **TabPane**, Scene Builder will add an **AnchorPane** to hold the new components. An **HBox** might be a better choice, but we'll go ahead and use **AnchorPane** to demonstrate this feature of Scene Builder. If you drag a **TextField** onto **TabPane** and try to position it, you should see more red lines show up. Positioned just right, you should see a red line running through the middle of the **Label** and the `TextField`, indicating that the two components are vertically aligned. This is what we want, so make sure there is a small space between `TextField` and the label and drop it.

We need to give **Label** some meaningful text, so double-click on it in the preview window, and enter `Number of items to retrieve`. We also need to give `TextField` an ID so that we can interact with it, so click on the component, expand the **Code** section in the Inspector, and set **fx:id** to `itemCount`.

Our user interface, while basic, is now as complete as we can make it here, so save the file, close Scene Builder, and return to NetBeans.

Saving user preferences

To allow our newly-defined user interface to be wired into our controller, we need to create instance variables to match the controls with the `fx:id` attributes set, so, we add these to `PreferencesController` as follows:

```
@FXML
protected Button savePrefs;
@FXML
protected Button cancel;
@FXML
protected TabPane tabPane;
```

In the `initialize()` method, we need to add support for loading the saved value for our `itemCount` field, so we need to talk a little bit about preferences.

Java, being the general-purpose language that it is, makes it possible to write any preference storing strategy that you can image. Fortunately, though, it also offers a couple of different standard APIs that allow you to do so in a more easily portable manner, those being `Preferences` and `Properties`.

The `java.util.Properties` class has been in the JDK since version 1.0, and while its basic, no-frills API might make that obvious, it's still a very useful abstraction. At its heart, `Properties` is a `Hashtable` implementation to which methods have been added for loading its data from input streams and readers, and writing its data to output streams and writers (in addition to a handful of other related methods). All the properties are treated as `String` values with `String` keys. Since `Properties` is a `Hashtable`, you can still use `put()` and `putAll()` to store non-string data, but that will result in `ClassCastException` should you call `store()`, so, it's probably best to avoid doing that.

The `java.util.prefs.Preferences` class was added in Java 1.4, and it's a much more modern API. Whereas with properties we have to handle persistence separately, preferences handle that for us opaquely--we don't need to worry about how or when it's written. In fact, the call to set a preference may return immediately, while the actual persistence may not occur for quite some time. The contract of the `Preferences` API guarantees that preferences will be persisted even if the JVM shuts down, assuming it's a normal, ordered shutdown (by definition, there's not much that can be done if the JVM process suddenly dies).

Additionally, the user also need not worry about how preferences are saved. The actual backing store is an implementation-specific detail. It could be a flat file, an OS-specific registry, a database or some sort of directory server. For the curious, the actual implementation is chosen by using the class name, if specified, in the `java.util.prefs.PreferencesFactory` system property. If that's not defined, the system will look for the file `META-INF/services/java.util.prefs.PreferencesFactory` (a mechanism known as SPI, which we will look at in depth later), and use the first class defined there. Finally, failing that, the implementation for the underlying platform is loaded and used.

So which to choose? Either will work as well as the other, but you have to decide if you want control of where the information is stored (`Properties`) or ease of implementation (`Preferences`). To a certain degree, portability might also be a concern. For example, if you have Java code running in some sort of a mobile or embedded device, you might not have permissions to write to the filesystem, and you might not have a filesystem at all. To show how similar the two implementations might be, though, we'll implement both.

To put my cards on the table a little bit, I would like for as much of this code as possible to be reusable in an Android environment. To help facilitate that, we'll create a very simple interface as follows:

```
public interface SunagoPreferences {
    String getPreference(String key);
    String getPreference(String key, String defaultValue);
    Integer getPreference(String key, Integer defaultValue);
    void putPreference(String key, String value);
    void putPreference(String key, Integer value);
}
```

We're only dealing with strings and integers, as the needs of the application are pretty basic. With the interface defined, how do we get a reference to an implementation? For that, we'll use a technique we've already seen mentioned briefly--the Service Provider Interface (SPI).

Plugins and extensions with the Service Provider Interface

We've already seen SPI mentioned before when we looked at the `Preferences` class, and how the implementation is selected and loaded, but what exactly is it? The Service Provider Interface is a somewhat generic term for an interface that a third party can implement (or a class, abstract or not, that can be extended) to provide extra functionality, replace existing components, and more.

In a nutshell, the author of the target system (for example, the JDK itself in our previous example) defines and publishes an interface. Ideally, this system would provide a default implementation, but that's not necessary in all cases. Any interested third party could then implement this interface, register it, and the target system could then load and use it. One of the advantages of this approach is that the target system can be extended easily, with no coupling to the third party. That is to say, while the third party knows about the target system via the interface, the target system has no knowledge at all of the third party. It's merely operating off the interface it defined.

How are these third-party plugins registered with the target system? The third-party developer would create a text file using a specific file in a specific directory. The file has the same name as the interface being implemented. For the `Preferences` class example, one would be implementing the `java.util.prefs.PreferencesFactory` interface, so that would be the name of the file, which would be in the `META-INF/services` directory in the root of the libraries classpath. In a Maven-based project, the file would be found in `src/main/resources/META-INF/services`. The file contains just the name of the class implementing the interface. It's also possible to have more than one class listed in the services file, each on a new line. It's up to the consuming system, though, as to whether or not each of those might be used.

So what does all of this look like for us? As noted earlier, we're going to take a rare opportunity to show multiple implementations for our `Preferences` support. Both classes are small enough that we can show the uses of both `Properties` and `Preferences`, and use SPI to pick one to use.

Let's start with the `Properties`-based implementation:

```
public class SunagoProperties implements SunagoPreferences {
  private Properties props = new Properties();
  private final String FILE = System.getProperty("user.home")
    + File.separator + ".sunago.properties";

  public SunagoProperties() {
    try (InputStream input = new FileInputStream(FILE)) {
      props.load(input);
    } catch (IOException ex) {
    }
  }
}
```

In the preceding code, we start by implementing our `SunagoPreferences` interface. We then create an instance of the `Properties` class, and we also define a constant for the file name and location, which we put--in a system-independent manner--in the user's home directory.

Resource handling with try-with-resources

The constructor shows something interesting that we haven't talked about--try-with-resources. Prior to Java 8, you might have written something like this:

```
public SunagoProperties(int a) {
  InputStream input = null;
  try {
```

```
        input = new FileInputStream(FILE);
        props.load(input);
    } catch  (IOException ex) {
    // do something
    } finally {
        if (input != null) {
          try {
              input.close();
          } catch (IOException ex1) {
              Logger.getLogger(SunagoProperties.class.getName())
                .log(Level.SEVERE, null, ex1);
          }
        }
      }
    }
```

This preceding, incredibly verbose code declares an `InputStream` outside the try block, then does some work with it in the `try` block. In the `finally` block, we try to close the `InputStream`, but we first have to check to see if it's null. If, say, the file doesn't exist (as it won't be the first time this class is created), an `Exception` will be thrown, and `input` will be null. If it's not null, we can call `close()` on it, but that might throw `IOException`, so we have to wrap that in a `try`/`catch` block as well.

Java 8 introduced the try-with-resources construct that makes this much smaller. If an object is an instance of `AutoCloseable`, then it can be defined **inside** the `try` declaration, and it will be closed automatically when the `try` block scope terminates regardless of whether or not an `Exception` was thrown. That allows us to take what would normally be fourteen lines of code, and express the exact same functionality in four with much less noise.

Aside from `AutoCloseable`, note that we load any existing values in the file into our `Properties` instance via `Properties.load(InputStream)`.

Moving on, what we see next are pretty straightforward getters and setters:

```
    @Override
    public String getPreference(String key) {
      return props.getProperty(key);
    }

    @Override
    public String getPreference(String key, String defaultValue) {
      String value = props.getProperty(key);
      return (value == null) ? defaultValue : value;
    }
```

```
@Override
public Integer getPreference(String key, Integer defaultValue) {
  String value = props.getProperty(key);
  return (value == null) ? defaultValue :
    Integer.parseInt(value);
}

@Override
public void putPreference(String key, String value) {
  props.put(key, value);
  store();
}

@Override
public void putPreference(String key, Integer value) {
  if (value != null) {
    putPreference(key, value.toString());
  }
}
```

The final method is the one that writes our preferences back out, which is as follows:

```
private void store() {
  try (OutputStream output = new FileOutputStream(FILE)) {
    props.store(output, null);
  } catch (IOException e) { }
}
```

This last method looks a lot like our constructor, but we create an OutputStream, and call Properties.store(OutputStream) to write our values out to a file. Note that we call this method from every put method to make sure, insofar as possible, that the user preferences are faithfully persisted to disk.

What would a Preferences-based implementation look like? Not much different.

```
public class SunagoPreferencesImpl implements SunagoPreferences {
  private final Preferences prefs = Preferences.userRoot()
    .node(SunagoPreferencesImpl.class.getPackage()
    .getName());
  @Override
  public String getPreference(String key) {
    return prefs.get(key, null);
  }
  @Override
  public String getPreference(String key, String defaultValue) {
    return prefs.get(key, defaultValue);
  }
```

```
@Override
public Integer getPreference(String key,Integer defaultValue){
  return prefs.getInt(key, defaultValue);
}
@Override
public void putPreference(String key,  String value) {
  prefs.put(key, value);
}
@Override
public void putPreference(String key,  Integer value) {
  prefs.putInt(key, value);
}
}
```

Two things to note. First, we don't need to handle persistence, as `Preferences` does that for us. Second, the instantiation of the `Preferences` instance needs some attention. Clearly, I think, we want these preferences to be scoped to the user, so we start with `Preferences.userRoot()` to get the root preference node. Then we ask for the node in which we want to store our preferences, which we have chosen to name after the package of our class.

Where does that put things? On Linux, the file might look something like `~/.java/.userPrefs/_!':!bw"t!#4!cw"0!'`!~@"w!'w!~@"z!'8!~g"0!#4!ag!5!')` `!c!!u!(:!d@"u!'%!~w"v!#4!}@"w!(!=/prefs.xml` (yes, that's a directory name). On Windows, those preferences are saved in the Windows Registry under the key `HKEY_CURRENT_USERSOFTWAREJavaSoftPrefscom.steeplesoft.sunago.app`. Unless you want to interact directly with these files, though, their exact location and format are merely implementation details. Sometimes, though, it's a good thing to know.

We have two implementations, so how do we pick which one to use? In the file (including the source root for clarity) `src/main/resources/META-INF/service/com.steeplesoft.sunago.api.SunagoPreferences`, we can put one of these two lines:

```
com.steeplesoft.sunago.app.SunagoPreferencesImpl
com.steeplesoft.sunago.app.SunagoProperties
```

You can list both, but only the first will be chosen, which we'll see now. To make things simple, we've wrapped this up in a utility method as follows:

```
private static SunagoPreferences preferences;
public static synchronized
    SunagoPreferences getSunagoPreferences() {
  if (preferences == null) {
    ServiceLoader<SunagoPreferences> spLoader =
```

```
        ServiceLoader.load(SunagoPreferences.class);
      Iterator<SunagoPreferences> iterator =
        spLoader.iterator();
      preferences = iterator.hasNext() ? iterator.next() : null;
    }
  return preferences;
}
```

In what may be a bit of an overkill for our purposes here, we've implemented a singleton by declaring the instance of the `SunagoPreferences` interface as a private static, and made it available via a synchronized method, which checks for `null`, and creates the instance if needed.

While that's interesting, don't let it distract you from the meat of the method. We use the `ServiceLoader.load()` method to ask the system for any implementations of the `SunagoPreferences` interface. It's worth noting again, just to be clear, that it won't pick up **any** implementation in the system, but **only** those listed in the services file we described earlier. Using the `ServiceLoader<SunagoPreferences>` instance, we grab an iterator, and if it has an entry (`iterator.hasNext()`), we return that instance (`iterator.next()`). If it does not, we return `null`. There is a chance here for a `NullPointerException` since we are returning `null`, but we're also providing an implementation, so we avoid that risk. However, in your own code, you need to either ensure you have an implementation as we've done here, or to make sure that the consuming code is `null`-ready.

Adding a network - Twitter

So far, we have a pretty basic application, which can save and load its preferences, but let's get down to what we're here for and start connecting to social networks. What we hope to develop is a framework that makes it easy to add support for different social networks. Technically, as we'll soon see, the **network** need not even be social as the only thing that will imply a specific type of source is the name of the classes and interfaces involved. However, we will, in fact, focus on social networks, and we'll use a couple of different ones to show some variety. To that end, we'll start with Twitter, the massively popular microblogging platform, and Instagram, the increasingly photo-focused network that is now part of Facebook.

Speaking of Facebook, why are we not demonstrating integration with that social network? Two reasons--One, it's not significantly different from Twitter, so there would not be much that was new to cover; two, most importantly, the permissions that Facebook offers make it virtually impossible to integrate with it in a way that would be of interest here. For example, the permission to read a user's home timeline (or wall) is only granted to applications targeted at those platforms where Facebook is not currently available, and not at all to desktop applications, which is our target here.

As noted previously, we'd like to expose a way to add more networks without having to change the core application, so we need to develop an API. What we'll cover here is that API in a more or less **finished** state (is any software every truly finished?). However, while you will see a reasonably complete API, a word of caution--attempts to create an abstraction that start with that abstraction--that is, writing the abstraction from scratch--rarely end well. It is usually best to write a specific implementation to get a better understanding of the details required, then extract an abstraction. What you will see here is the end result of that process, so that process will not be covered here in any depth.

Registering as a Twitter developer

To create an application that integrates with Twitter, we need to create a Twitter developer account, and then create a Twitter application. To create the account, we need to visit `https://dev.twitter.com`, and click on the **Join** button. Once you've created your developer account, you can click the **My Apps** link to go to `https://apps.twitter.com`. Here, we need to click on the **Create New App** button, which will get us a form that looks a bit like this:

Create an application

Application Details

Name *

<Your Unique Application Name>

Description *

<A description of the application>

Website *

<Your website>

Callback URL

<Not required or necessary for desktop app>

Developer Agreement

○ Yes. I have read and agree to the Twitter Developer Agreement.

Create your Twitter application

While the application we're developing is called *Sunago*, you won't be able to use that name, as it's already taken; you'll have to create a unique name of your own, assuming you're planning to run the application yourself. Once you've created the application, you'll be taken to the **Application Management** page for your new app. From this page, you can manage your app's permissions and keys, and, if needed, you can delete your app.

One thing to note on this page, as we'll need this soon, is where to find your application's **Consumer Key** and **Secret**. These are long, alphanumeric strings that your application will use to authenticate with Twitter's services. To interact with Twitter on behalf of a user--our ultimate goal--requires a different set of tokens, which we'll fetch shortly. Your **Consumer Key** and **Secret**--especially, **Consumer Secret**--should be kept, well, secret. If this combination is ever revealed publicly, other users will be able to masquerade as your app, potentially causing you serious headaches if they abuse the service. For that reason, you won't see the key/secret combination I generated anywhere in this book or the source code, which is why you will need to generate your own.

Armed now with our **Consumer Key** and **Secret**, we need to decide how to talk to Twitter. Twitter offers a public REST API, which they document on their site. If we were so inclined, we could pick an HTTP client of some sort, and start making calls. In the interests of simplicity and clarity, though, not to mention robustness, fault tolerance, and so on, we might be better served using a higher-level library of some sort. As luck would have it, there is a such a library, Twitter4J, which will make our integration much simpler and cleaner (for the curious, Twitter4J has over 200 Java classes. While we won't need all of the functionality represented there and exposed via the REST API, it should give you an idea of the scope of the effort required to write a reasonable wrapper for Twitter's REST interface).

As mentioned earlier, we want to be able to add networks to Sunago without having to change the core application, so we will write our Twitter integration in a separate Maven module. This will require that some of the code we've already written for Sunago be extracted into yet another module. Both our Twitter module and the main application module will then add a dependency on this new module. Since we'll have multiple modules at play here, we'll be sure to indicate to which module each class belongs. When we're finished, our project dependency graph will look like this:

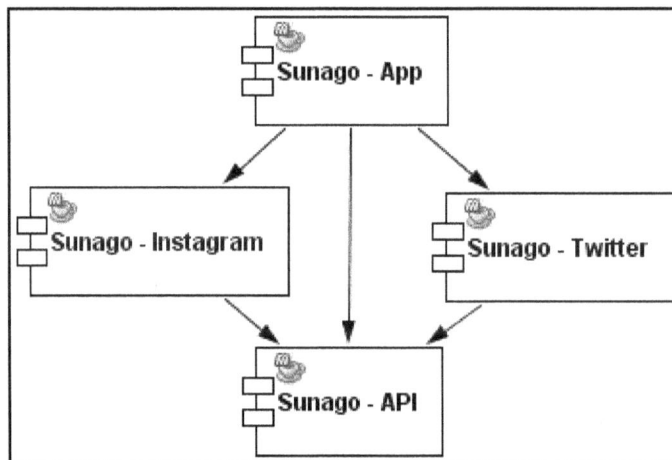

Technically, the only reason we show a dependency between the Application module and the Instagram and Twitter modules is because we're building them as part of the same project. A third-party developer, as we'll see, could easily develop an independent module, add it to the application's runtime classpath, and see the change in the application, all without this build-level dependency. Hopefully, though, this graph helps explain how the modules are related.

Adding Twitter preferences to Sunago

Let's start by adding Twitter to our preferences screen. Before we can do any integration, we need to be able to configure the application, or, more accurately, the Twitter module, so that it can connect as a specific user. To enable that, we'll add a new interface to the API module as follows:

```
public abstract class SocialMediaPreferencesController {
    public abstract Tab getTab();
    public abstract void savePreferences();
}
```

This interface will give Sunago two hooks into the module--one giving the module a chance to draw its own preferences user interface, and one to allow it to save those preferences. We can then implement that in our module. Before we do so, though, let's see how the application will find these implementations so that they can be used. For that, we will again turn to SPI. In Sunago's `PreferencesController` interface, we add this code:

```
private List<SocialMediaPreferencesController> smPrefs =
    new ArrayList<>();
@Override
public void initialize(URL url, ResourceBundle rb) {
    itemCount.setText(SunagoUtil.getSunagoPreferences()
      .getPreference(SunagoPrefsKeys.ITEM_COUNT.getKey(), "50"));
    final ServiceLoader<SocialMediaPreferencesController>
      smPrefsLoader = ServiceLoader.load(
        SocialMediaPreferencesController.class);
    smPrefsLoader.forEach(smp -> smPrefs.add(smp));
    smPrefs.forEach(smp -> tabPane.getTabs().add(smp.getTab()));
}
```

We have an instance variable to hold a list of any `SocialMediaPreferencesController` instances we find. Next, in `initialize()`, we call the now familiar `ServiceLoader.load()` method to find any implementations, which we then add to the `List` that we created previously. Once we have our list of controllers, we call `getTab()` on each of them, adding the returned `Tab` instance to the `PreferencesController` interface's `tabPane`.

With the loading part clarified, let's now take a look at the Twitter preferences user interface implementation. We start by implementing the controller that will back this part of the user interface as follows:

```
public class TwitterPreferencesController
    extends SocialMediaPreferencesController {
      private final TwitterClient twitter;
```

```
        private Tab tab;

        public TwitterPreferencesController() {
          twitter = new TwitterClient();
        }

        @Override
        public Tab getTab() {
          if (tab == null) {
            tab = new Tab("Twitter");
            tab.setContent(getNode());
          }

          return tab;
        }
```

We'll take a look at `TwitterClient` in a moment, but, first, a note on `getTab()`. Notice that we create the `Tab` instance, which we need to return, but we delegate the creation of its contents to the `getNode()` method. `Tab.setContent()` allows us to completely replace the contents of the tab with a single call, something we'll make use of next. The `getNode()` method looks like this:

```
        private Node getNode() {
          return twitter.isAuthenticated() ? buildConfigurationUI() :
            buildConnectUI();
        }
```

If the user has already authenticated, then we want to present some configuration options. If not, then we need to offer a means to connect to Twitter.

```
        private Node buildConnectUI() {
          HBox box = new HBox();
          box.setPadding(new Insets(10));
          Button button = new Button(MessageBundle.getInstance()
            .getString("connect"));
          button.setOnAction(event -> connectToTwitter());

          box.getChildren().add(button);

          return box;
        }
```

In this simple user interface, we create an HBox primarily so we can add some padding. Without the new Insets(10) instance we pass to setPadding(), our button would be pressed right up against the top and left edges of the window, which is not visually appealing. Next, we create the Button, and set the onAction handler (ignore that constructor parameter for now).

The interesting part is hidden away in connectToTwitter, as shown in this code:

```
private void connectToTwitter() {
  try {
    RequestToken requestToken =
      twitter.getOAuthRequestToken();
    LoginController.showAndWait(
      requestToken.getAuthorizationURL(),
      e -> ((String) e.executeScript(
        "document.documentElement.outerHTML"))
          .contains("You've granted access to"),
        e -> {
          final String html =
            "<kbd aria-labelledby="code-desc"><code>";
            String body = (String) e.executeScript(
              "document.documentElement.outerHTML");
            final int start = body.indexOf(html) +
             html.length();
            String code = body.substring(start, start+7);
            saveTwitterAuthentication(requestToken, code);
            showConfigurationUI();
        });
  } catch (TwitterException ex) {
    Logger.getLogger(getClass().getName())
      .log(Level.SEVERE, null, ex);
  }
}
```

OAuth and logging on to Twitter

We'll take a detour into `LoginController` in just a moment, but first, let's make sure we understand what's going on here. To log on to Twitter on behalf of a user, we need to generate an OAuth request token from which we get an authorization URL. The details of which are hidden nicely behind the Twitter4J API, but it is, basically, the OAuth authorization URL listed on the **Application Management** page with a request token passed as a query string. As we'll see, this URL is opened in a `WebView`, which prompts the user to authenticate against Twitter, and then authorize the application (or decline to):

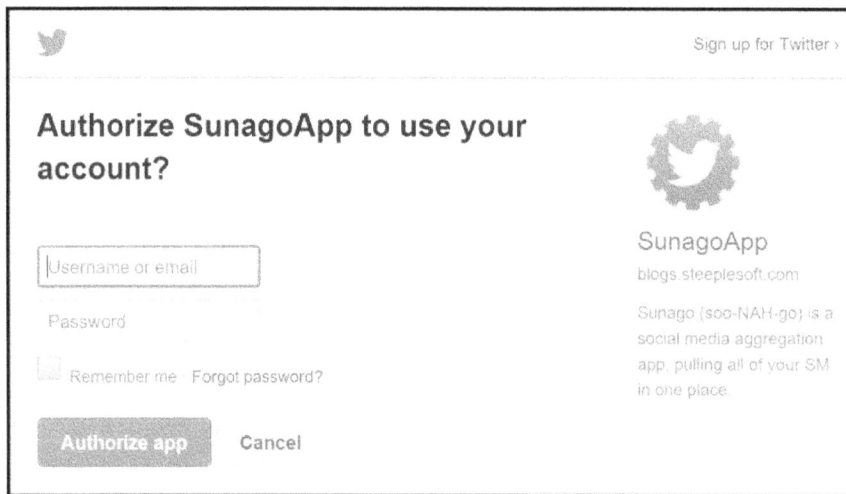

If the user successfully authenticates and authorizes the application, the `WebView` is redirected to a success page, which displays a numeric code that we need to capture to finish gathering the authentication/authorization credentials needed. The success page might look like this:

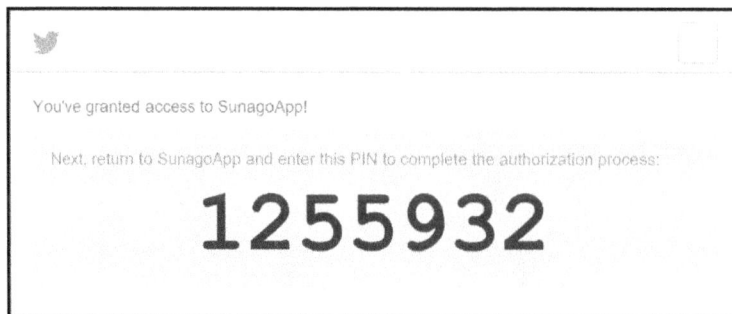

For those not familiar with OAuth, what this allows us to do is to authenticate as the user, now and at any arbitrary moment in the future, without needing to store the user's actual password. The end result of this handshake between our application and Twitter is a token and token secret, which we'll pass to Twitter for authentication. As long as this token is valid--the user can invalidate it at any time via Twitter's web interface--we can connect and act as that user. Should the key ever be compromised, the user can revoke the key, affecting only the intended app and anyone attempting to use the stolen key.

`LoginController`, which is part of the API module, handles all of the boilerplate code for us, as seen in this code:

```
public class LoginController implements Initializable {
  @FXML
  private WebView webView;
  private Predicate<WebEngine> loginSuccessTest;
  private Consumer<WebEngine> handler;

  public static void showAndWait(String url,
    Predicate<WebEngine> loginSuccessTest,
    Consumer<WebEngine> handler) {
      try {
        fxmlLoader loader = new fxmlLoader(LoginController
          .class.getResource("/fxml/login.fxml"));

        Stage stage = new Stage();
        stage.setScene(new Scene(loader.load()));
        LoginController controller =
            loader.<LoginController>getController();
        controller.setUrl(url);
        controller.setLoginSuccessTest(loginSuccessTest);
        controller.setHandler(handler);

        stage.setTitle("Login...");
        stage.initModality(Modality.APPLICATION_MODAL);

        stage.showAndWait();
      } catch (IOException ex) {
        throw new RuntimeException(ex);
      }
  }
}
```

This preceding code is a basic FXML-backed JavaFX controller, but we do have a static helper method to handle the details of creating, configuring, and showing an instance. We load the scene using FXML, get the controller (which is an instance of the enclosing class), set the `loginSuccessTest` and `handler` properties, and then show the dialog.

Do `loginSuccessTest` and `handler` look odd? They are instances of the Java 8 functional interfaces `Predicate<T>` and `Consumer<T>`. `Predicate` is a functional interface that takes a type, `WebEngine` in our case, and returns a `boolean`. It is designed to check for a certain condition given a variable of the specified type. In this instance, we call `WebEngine.executeScript().contains()` to extract a piece of the document, and see if it contains a certain piece of text indicating that we've been redirected to the login success page.

`Consumer<T>` is a functional interface (or, in our case, a lambda) that takes a single parameter of the specified type, and returns void. Our handler is a `Consumer`, which is called once our `Predicate` returns true. The lambda extracts the code from the HTML page, calls `saveTwitterAuthentication()` to finish authenticating the user, then `showConfigurationUI()` to change the user interface so that the user can configure Twitter-related settings.

The method `saveTwitterAuthentication()` is very straightforward, and is given as follows:

```
private void saveTwitterAuthentication(RequestToken requestToken,
  String code) {
    if (!code.isEmpty()) {
      try {
        AccessToken accessToken = twitter
          .getAcccessToken(requestToken, code);
        prefs.putPreference(TwitterPrefsKeys.TOKEN.getKey(),
          accessToken.getToken());
        prefs.putPreference(TwitterPrefsKeys.TOKEN_SECRET.getKey(),
          accessToken.getTokenSecret());
      } catch (TwitterException ex) {
        Logger.getLogger(TwitterPreferencesController
          .class.getName()).log(Level.SEVERE, null, ex);
      }
    }
}
```

The method `twitter.getAccessToken()` takes our request token and the code we extracted from the web page, and sends an HTTP POST to a Twitter REST endpoint, which generates the token secret we need. When that request returns, we store the token and token secret to our `Preferences` store (again, oblivious to where and how).

The method `showConfigurationUI()` and the related method should also be familiar.

```
private void showConfigurationUI() {
  getTab().setContent(buildConfigurationUI());
}
private Node buildConfigurationUI() {
  VBox box = new VBox();
  box.setPadding(new Insets(10));

  CheckBox cb = new CheckBox(MessageBundle.getInstance()
    .getString("homeTimelineCB"));
  cb.selectedProperty().addListener(
    (ObservableValue<? extends Boolean> ov,
      Boolean oldVal, Boolean newVal) -> {
        showHomeTimeline = newVal;
      });

  Label label = new Label(MessageBundle.getInstance()
    .getString("userListLabel") + ":");

  ListView<SelectableItem<UserList>> lv = new ListView<>();
  lv.setItems(itemList);
  lv.setCellFactory(CheckBoxListCell.forListView(
    item -> item.getSelected()));
  VBox.setVgrow(lv, Priority.ALWAYS);

  box.getChildren().addAll(cb, label, lv);
  showTwitterListSelection();

  return box;
}
```

One new item in this preceding method is the listener we add to the `selectedProperty` of the `CheckBox`. Any time the selected value changes, our listener is called, which sets the value of the `showHomeTimeline` boolean.

The `ListView` also needs special attention. Notice the parameterized type, `SelectableItem<UserList>`. What is that? That's an abstract class we've created to wrap items for use in `CheckBoxListCell`, which you can see in the call to `setCellFactory()`. That class looks like this:

```
public abstract class SelectableItem<T> {
  private final SimpleBooleanProperty selected =
    new SimpleBooleanProperty(false);
  private final T item;
  public SelectableItem(T item) {
    this.item = item;
  }
  public T getItem() {
    return item;
  }
  public SimpleBooleanProperty getSelected() {
    return selected;
  }
}
```

This class, which lives in the API module, is a simple wrapper around an arbitrary type that adds a `SimpleBooleanProperty`. We see how this property is manipulated when the cell factory is set up--`lv.setCellFactory(CheckBoxListCell .forListView(item -> item.getSelected()))`. We expose `SimpleBooleanProperty` via the `getSelected()` method, which the `CheckBoxListCell` uses to set and read the state of each line.

Our final user interface-related method is this:

```
private void showTwitterListSelection() {
  List<SelectableItem<UserList>> selectable =
    twitter.getLists().stream()
      .map(u -> new SelectableUserList(u))
      .collect(Collectors.toList());
  List<Long> selectedListIds = twitter.getSelectedLists(prefs);
  selectable.forEach(s -> s.getSelected()
    .set(selectedListIds.contains(s.getItem().getId())));
  itemList.clear();
  itemList.addAll(selectable);
}
```

Using the same `SelectableItem` class, we request from Twitter all of the lists the user might have created, which we wrap in `SelectableUserList`, a `SelectableItem` child that overrides the `toString()` method to provide user-friendly text in `ListView`. We load any checked lists from preferences, set their respective booleans/checkboxes, and update our `ObservableList` and, thus, the user interface.

The final method we need to implement to satisfy the `SocialMediaPreferencesController` contract is `savePreferences()`, which is as follows:

```
public void savePreferences() {
    prefs.putPreference(TwitterPrefsKeys.HOME_TIMELINE.getKey(),
      Boolean.toString(showHomeTimeline));
    List<String> selectedLists = itemList.stream()
      .filter(s -> s != null)
      .filter(s -> s.getSelected().get())
      .map(s -> Long.toString(s.getItem().getId()))
      .collect(Collectors.toList());
    prefs.putPreference(TwitterPrefsKeys.SELECTED_LISTS.getKey(),
      String.join(",", selectedLists));
}
```

This is a mostly straightforward saving of the user's options to preferences, but the list handling is worth pointing out. Rather than manually iterating over each item in the list, we can use a stream and apply a couple of `filter()` operations to strip out entries that are of no interest to us, `map()` each `SelectableUserList` that makes it through to `Long` (which is the list's ID), then collect them in a `List<String>`. We join that `List` using `String.join()`, and write it out to our preferences.

Adding a model for Twitter

There are still a couple of other interfaces that we need to implement to finish our Twitter support. The first, and simpler, one is `SocialMediaItem`:

```
public interface SocialMediaItem {
    String getProvider();
    String getTitle();
    String getBody();
    String getUrl();
    String getImage();
    Date getTimestamp();
}
```

This preceding interface provides us with a nice abstraction over the various types of data that a social network might return without being too heavily burdened with fields that aren't used by most (or many, at least) networks. The Twitter implementation of this `Tweet` class is as follows:

```
public class Tweet implements SocialMediaItem {
  private final Status status;
  private final String url;
  private final String body;

  public Tweet(Status status) {
    this.status = status;
    body = String.format("@%s: %s (%s)",
      status.getUser().getScreenName(),
      status.getText(), status.getCreatedAt().toString());
    url = String.format("https://twitter.com/%s/status/%d",
      status.getUser().getScreenName(), status.getId());
  }
```

Taking the Twitter4J class `Status`, we extract information of interest to us, and store it in instance variables (whose getters are not shown, as they're just simple getters). For the `getImage()` method, we make a reasonable effort to extract any image from the tweet, as follows:

```
public String getImage() {
  MediaEntity[] mediaEntities = status.getMediaEntities();
  if (mediaEntities.length > 0) {
    return mediaEntities[0].getMediaURLHttps();
  } else {
    Status retweetedStatus = status.getRetweetedStatus();
    if (retweetedStatus != null) {
      if (retweetedStatus.getMediaEntities().length > 0) {
        return retweetedStatus.getMediaEntities()[0]
          .getMediaURLHttps();
      }
    }
  }
  return null;
}
```

Implementing a Twitter client

The second interface is `SocialMediaClient`. This interface serves not only as an abstraction that Sunago can use to interact with an arbitrary social network integration, but also as a guideline for interested developers to show them the minimum requirements for the integration. It looks like this:

```
public interface SocialMediaClient {
  void authenticateUser(String token, String tokenSecret);
  String getAuthorizationUrl();
  List<? Extends SocialMediaItem> getItems();
  boolean isAuthenticated();
}
```

For Twitter support, this preceding interface is implemented by the class `TwitterClient`. Most of the class is pretty basic, so we won't reproduce that here (you can peruse it in the source repository if you'd like details), but one implementation detail might be worth spending some time over. That method is `processList()`, which is as follows:

```
private List<Tweet> processList(long listId) {
  List<Tweet> tweets = new ArrayList<>();

  try {
    final AtomicLong sinceId = new AtomicLong(
      getSinceId(listId));
    final Paging paging = new Paging(1,
      prefs.getPreference(SunagoPrefsKeys.
      ITEM_COUNT.getKey(), 50), sinceId.get());
    List<Status> statuses = (listId == HOMETIMELINE) ?
      twitter.getHomeTimeline(paging) :
       twitter.getUserListStatuses(listId, paging);
    statuses.forEach(s -> {
      if (s.getId() > sinceId.get()) {
        sinceId.set(s.getId());
      }
      tweets.add(new Tweet(s));
    });
    saveSinceId(listId, sinceId.get());
  } catch (TwitterException ex) {
      Logger.getLogger(TwitterClient.class.getName())
        .log(Level.SEVERE, null, ex);
  }
  return tweets;
}
```

There are several things going on in this last method. First, we want to limit how many tweets we actually retrieve. If this is the first time the app is used, or the first time that it's used in a long time, there could be a significant number of tweets. Retrieving all of them would be quite expensive in terms of network usage, memory and, perhaps, processing time. We implement that limit using the `Paging` object from Twitter4J.

We also don't want to retrieve tweets we already have, so, for each list, we keep a `sinceId`, which we can pass to the Twitter API. It will use this to find up to the specified number of tweets whose ID is greater than `sinceId`.

Wrapping all of this up in the `Paging` object, we call either `twitter.getHomeTimeline()` if the list ID is `-1` (an internal ID we've used to identify the home timeline) or `twitter.getUserListStatus()` for a user-defined list. For each `Status` returned, we update `sinceId` (which we've modeled using an `AtomicLong`, as any method variable used inside a lambda must be final or effectively final), and add the tweet to our `List`. Before exiting, we store `sinceId` for the list in our in-memory store, and then return the tweets for the Twitter list.

A brief look at internationalization and localization

While somewhat basic, our integration with Twitter is now complete, as it fulfills our functional requirements for the network. However, there is one more piece of code that we need to take a quick look at. Earlier, in some of the code samples, you might have noticed code that looks like this: `MessageBundle.getInstance().getString("homeTimelineCB")`. What is that, and what does it do?

The `MessageBundle` class is a small wrapper around the internationalization and localization facilities (also known as i18n and l10n, where the numbers represent the number of letters dropped from the words to make the abbreviation) provided by the JDK. The code for this class is as follows:

```
public class MessageBundle {
  ResourceBundle messages =
    ResourceBundle.getBundle("Messages", Locale.getDefault());

  private MessageBundle() {
  }

  public final String getString(String key) {
```

```
    return messages.getString(key);
  }
  private static class LazyHolder {
    private static final MessageBundle INSTANCE =
      new MessageBundle();
  }

  public static MessageBundle getInstance() {
    return LazyHolder.INSTANCE;
  }
}
```

There are two main items of interest here. We'll start at the end of the class with the `getInstance()` method. This is an example of what is known as the **initialize on demand holder** (**IODH**) pattern. There is a single, static instance of the class `MessageBundle` in the JVM. It is not initialized, however, until the `getInstance()` method is called. This is accomplished by taking advantage of how the JVM loads and initializes statics. As soon as a class is referenced in any way, it is loaded into `ClassLoader`, at which point any statics on the class will be initialized. The private static class `LazyHolder` is **not** initialized until the JVM is sure that something needs to access it. Once we call `getInstance()`, which references `LazyHolder.INSTANCE`, the class is initialized and the singleton instance created.

> It should be noted that are ways around the singleton nature we're trying to implement (for example, via reflection), but our use case here does not warrant any worries over such an attack.

The actual functionality is implemented in the first line of the class, which is as follows

```
ResourceBundle messages =
  ResourceBundle.getBundle("Messages", Locale.getDefault());
```

The `ResourceBundle` files, in the words of the Javadoc, *contain locale-specific objects.* Usually, this means Strings, as it does in our case. The `getBundle()` method will attempt to find and load a bundle with the name given for the specified locale. In our case, we're looking for a bundle named `Messages`. Technically, we're looking for a bundle in a family of bundles with the shared base name `Messages`. The system will use the `Locale` specified to find the correct file. This resolution will follow the same lookup logic that `Locale` uses, so the `getBundle()` method will return the bundle with the most specific matching name available.

Let's say we're running this application on my computer. I live in the United States, so my system's default locale is en_US. Following the rules of the `Locale` lookup, then, `getBundle()` will try to locate files in this order:

1. `Messages_en_US.properties`.
2. `Messages_en.properties`.
3. `Messages.properties`.

The system will go from the most specific file to the least until it finds the key requested. If it's not found in any file, `MissingResourceException` is thrown. Each file consists of key/value pairs. Our `Messages.properties` file looks like this:

```
homeTimelineCB=Include the home timeline
userListLabel=User lists to include
connect=Connect
twitter=Twitter
```

It is just a simple mapping of keys to localized text. We could have `Messages_es.properties` with this line:

```
userListLabel=Listas de usuarios para incluir
```

If that were the only entry in the file, that one label in the file would be in Spanish, with everything else being in the default from `Message.properties`, which, in our case, is English.

Making our JAR file fat

With that, our implementation is now complete. Before this can be used in the way we intend, though, we need to make a build change. If you recall the discussion of the requirements at the beginning of the chapter, we want to build a system that easily allows third-party developers to write modules that will add support for arbitrary social networks without the need to modify the core application. To deliver that functionality, these developers would need to offer a JAR that Sunago users could drop in a folder. When the application is started, the new functionality is now available.

That leaves us, then, with the task of bundling all of the required code. As the project stands now, a single JAR is created, which holds just our classes. That's not entirely sufficient, though, as we depend on the Twitter4J jar. Other modules could have even more dependencies. Requiring users to drop in, say, half a dozen or more jars is probably asking a bit much. Fortunately, Maven has a mechanism that will allow us to avoid that problem altogether: the shade plugin.

By configuring this plugin in our build, we can generate a single jar that holds our classes and resources, plus those of every dependency declared in the project. This is often called a **fat jar**, and is as follows:

```
<build>
  <plugins>
    <plugin>
      <artifactId>maven-shade-plugin</artifactId>
        <version>${plugin.shade}</version>
          <executions>
            <execution>
              <phase>package</phase>
                <goals>
                  <goal>shade</goal>
                </goals>
            </execution>
          </executions>
    </plugin>
  </plugins>
</build>
```

This is an official Maven plugin, so we can omit `groupId`, and we've defined a property, `plugin.shade`, somewhere up the POM's inheritance tree. When the package phase is run, the shade goal of this plugin will execute and build our fat jar.

```
$ ll target/*.jar
  total 348
  -rwx------+ 1 jason None  19803 Nov 20 19:22 original-twitter-1.0-
  SNAPSHOT.jar
  -rwx------+ 1 jason None 325249 Nov 20 19:22 twitter-1.0-
  SNAPSHOT.jar
```

The original jar, which is considerably smaller, is renamed to `original-twitter-1.0-SNAPSHOT.jar`, and the fat jar receives the configured final name. It is this fat jar that is installed in the local maven repository, or deployed to an artifact manager, such as Artifactory.

There is a small bug, though. Our twitter module depends on the API module so that it can see the interfaces and classes exposed by the application. Currently, even those are included in the fat jar, which we don't want, as that can cause some `ClassLoader` issues down the road in some situations. To prevent that, we mark that dependency as `provided`, as shown next:

```
<dependency>
  <groupId>${project.groupId}</groupId>
  <artifactId>api</artifactId>
  <version>${project.version}</version>
  <scope>provided</scope>
</dependency>
```

If we issue a `mvn clean install` now, we'll have a nice fat jar with only the classes we need to bundle, and one that's ready for distribution.

To make things as simple as possible, we're just going to declare a dependency on this jar in Sunago's app module, as follows:

```
<dependencies>
  <dependency>
    <groupId>${project.groupId}</groupId>
    <artifactId>api</artifactId>
    <version>${project.version}</version>
  </dependency>
  <dependency>
    <groupId>${project.groupId}</groupId>
    <artifactId>twitter</artifactId>
    <version>${project.version}</version>
  </dependency>
</dependencies>
```

If we run Sunago now, we'll see Twitter added to our settings screen, and, once connected and configured, we'll see tweets showing up on the main screen. We'll also notice that the main screen is a little plain, and, more importantly, doesn't provide any way of refreshing the contents, so let's fix that.

Adding a refresh button

In the **Projects** window, find `sunago.fxml`, right-click on it, and select `Edit`. We'll make this user interface change by hand, only for the sake of experience. Scroll down until you find the closing `Menubar` tag (`</Menubar>`). On the line right after that, insert these lines:

```
<ToolBar >
  <items>
    <Button fx:id="refreshButton" />
    <Button fx:id="settingsButton" />
  </items>
</ToolBar>
```

In `SunagoController`, we need to add the instance variables as follows:

```
@FXML
private Button refreshButton;
@FXML
private Button settingsButton;
```

Then, in `initialize()`, we need to set them up like this:

```
refreshButton.setGraphic(getButtonImage("/images/reload.png"));
refreshButton.setOnAction(ae -> loadItemsFromNetworks());
refreshButton.setTooltip(new Tooltip("Refresh"));

settingsButton.setGraphic(getButtonImage("/images/settings.png"));
settingsButton.setOnAction(ae -> showPreferences(ae));
settingsButton.setTooltip(new Tooltip("Settings"));
```

Notice that we're doing a bit more than setting up an action handler. The first thing we do is call `setGraphic()`. Remember from our discussion of the Twitter preference tab, calling `setGraphic()` will replace the child nodes with the `Node` that you specify. In these two cases, that `Node` is an `ImageView`, and comes from the `getButtonImage()` method.

```
private ImageView getButtonImage(String path) {
  ImageView imageView = new ImageView(
    new Image(getClass().getResourceAsStream(path)));
  imageView.setFitHeight(32);
  imageView.setPreserveRatio(true);
  return imageView;
}
```

After we set the action handler, we also set a tooltip. This will give our graphical buttons a textual description when the user hovers over the button with the mouse, as seen in this screenshot:

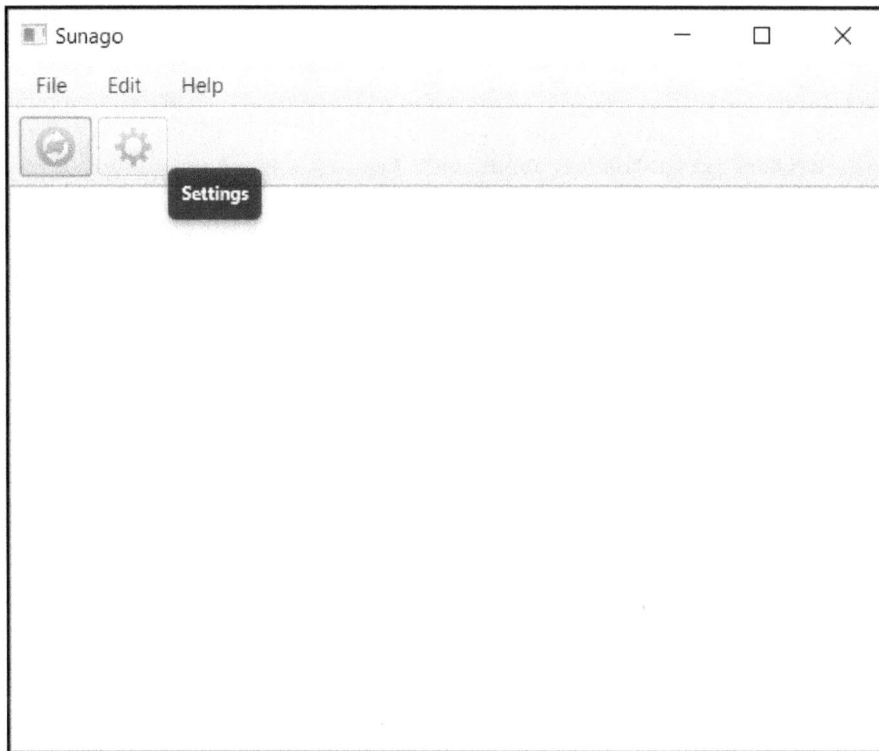

The action handler for the refresh button is worth looking at, and is given as follows:

```
private void loadItemsFromNetworks() {
  List<SocialMediaItem> items = new ArrayList<>();
  clientLoader.forEach(smc -> {
    if (smc.isAuthenticated()) {
        items.addAll(smc.getItems());
    }
  });

  items.sort((o1, o2) ->
    o2.getTimestamp().compareTo(o1.getTimestamp()));
  entriesList.addAll(0, items);
}
```

This is the same method that we call from `initialize()`. Using the Service Provider Interface that we discussed earlier, we iterate over each `SocialMediaClient` available in the system. If the client has authenticated against its network, we call the `getItems()` method, and add whatever it may return to a local variable, `items`. Once we've queried all of the networks configured in the system, we then sort our list. This will cause the entries of the various networks to be intermingled, as they're sorted by their timestamps in descending chronological order. This sorted list is then added to our `ObservableList` at the head, or the zeroth element, to cause them to appear at the top of the list in the user interface.

Adding another network - Instagram

So that we can see another type of integration, as well as to demonstrate how the interfaces we've defined make adding new networks relatively quick and easy, let's add one more network to Sunago--Instagram. While Instagram is owned by Facebook, at the time of this writing, its APIs are much more permissive than the social-media giant's, so we'll be able to add an interesting integration relatively easily.

Much like with Twitter, we have a choice to make about how our interactions with the Instragram API will be handled. Just like Twitter, Instagram offers a public REST API that is secured using OAuth. Also, just like Twitter, though, manually implementing a client to consume those APIs is not an attractive proposition due to the level of effort required. Again, unless there's a compelling reason to write your own client library, I would suggest that using some sort of client wrapper should be the preferred route if one is available. Fortunately, there is--jInstagram.

Registering as an Instagram developer

Before starting to write our client, we need to register a new Instagram client with the service. We do that by first creating, if needed, an Instagram developer account at `https://www.instagram.com/developer`. Once we have an account, we need to register our application either by clicking the **Register Your Application** button on the page, or by visiting `https://www.instagram.com/developer/clients/manage/` directly. From here, we need to click on **Register a New Client**, which will present this form:

Register new Client ID

Details   Security

Application Name:

Do not use **Instagram, IG, insta** or **gram** in your app name. Make sure to adhere to the API Terms of Use and Brand Guidelines.

Description:

Company Name:

Website URL:

Valid redirect URIs:

Press Enter to confirm.

The redirect_uri specifies where we redirect users after they have chosen whether or not to authenticate your application.

Privacy Policy URL:

Contact email:

An email that Instagram can use to get in touch with you. Please specify a valid email address to be notified of important information about your app.

Register   Cancel

Once you've registered your new client, you can click on the **Manage** button on the resulting web page to get your client ID and secret. Hold on to those, as you'll need them in a moment.

Next, we'll start the actual client by creating a new module just like we did for the Twitter module. This one, though, we'll call `Sunago - Instagram` and the `artifactId` `instagram`. We'll also go ahead and add the jInstagram dependency as follows:

```
<artifactId>instagram</artifactId>
<name>Sunago - Instagram</name>
<packaging>jar</packaging>
<dependencies>
  <dependency>
    <groupId>${project.groupId}</groupId>
    <artifactId>api</artifactId>
    <version>${project.version}</version>
    <scope>provided</scope>
  </dependency>
  <dependency>
    <groupId>com.sachinhandiekar</groupId>
    <artifactId>jInstagram</artifactId>
    <version>1.1.8</version>
  </dependency>
</dependencies>
```

Note that we have the Sunago `api` dependency added as well already, scoped as provided. We also need to add the Shade plugin configuration, which looks just like it does in the Twitter module, so it's not shown here.

Implementing the Instagram client

With our new module created, we need to create three specific items to fulfill the contract provided by the Sunago API module. We need `SocialMediaPreferencesController`, `SocialMediaClient`, and `SocialMediaItem`.

Our `SocialMediaPreferencesController` instance is `InstagramPreferencesController`. It has the same `getTab()` method required by the interface, which is as follows:

```
public Tab getTab() {
  if (tab == null) {
    tab = new Tab();
    tab.setText("Instagram");
```

```
      tab.setContent(getNode());
   }

   return tab;
}

private Node getNode() {
   Node node = instagram.isAuthenticated()
     ? buildConfigurationUI() : buildConnectUI();
   return node;
}
```

To save time and space, for this example, we've left the Instagram implementation much more basic than the one we created for Twitter, so the user interface definition does not hold much of interest. However, the authentication handling is interesting, as, while it has the same OAuth flow that Twitter uses, the data is returned in a manner that is much more easily consumed. The connect button calls this method:

```
private static final String CODE_QUERY_PARAM = "code=";
private void showConnectWindow() {
   LoginController.showAndWait(instagram.getAuthorizationUrl(),
     e -> e.getLocation().contains(CODE_QUERY_PARAM),
     e -> {
       saveInstagramToken(e.getLocation());
       showInstagramConfig();
     });
}
```

This uses the `LoginController` that we saw with Twitter, but our `Predicate` and `Consumer` are much more concise. The page to which the user is redirected has the code in the URL as a query parameter, so there's no need to scrape the HTML. We can just pull it straight from the URL as follows:

```
private void saveInstagramToken(String location) {
   int index = location.indexOf(CODE_QUERY_PARAM);
   String code = location.substring(index +
     CODE_QUERY_PARAM.length());
   Token accessToken = instagram.
     verifyCodeAndGetAccessToken(code);
   instagram.authenticateUser(accessToken.getToken(),
     accessToken.getSecret());
}
```

Once we have the code, we use an API on our `instagram` object to get the access token, which we then use to authenticate the user. So what does the `instagram` object look like? Like `TwitterClient`, `InstagramClient` is a `SocialMediaClient` that wraps the jInstagram API.

```
public final class InstagramClient implements
SocialMediaClient {

    private final InstagramService service;
    private Instagram instagram;
```

The jInstagram API has two objects that we need to use. `InstagramService` encapsulates the OAuth logic. We get an instance of it using a builder as follows:

```
service = new InstagramAuthService()
 .apiKey(apiKey)
 .apiSecret(apiSecret)
 .callback("http://blogs.steeplesoft.com")
 .scope("basic public_content relationships follower_list")
 .build();
```

As discussed earlier, to run the application locally, you'll need to provide your own API key and secret pair. The only use we have for the callback URL is to provide Instagram with a place to redirect our client to. Once it does that, we pull the code from the query parameters as we saw previously. Finally, we have to provide a list of scopes, which is what Instagram calls permissions, roughly. This list will allow us to get a list of the accounts that the authenticated user follows, which we'll use to get images:

```
@Override
public List<? extends SocialMediaItem> getItems() {
  List<Photo> items = new ArrayList<>();
  try {
    UserFeed follows = instagram.getUserFollowList("self");
    follows.getUserList().forEach(u ->
      items.addAll(processMediaForUser(u)));
  } catch (InstagramException ex) {
    Logger.getLogger(InstagramClient.class.getName())
      .log(Level.SEVERE, null, ex);
  }

  return items;
}
```

If you read the jInstagram documentation, you'll be tempted to use the method `instagram.getUserFeeds()`, and if you do, you'll get what I got--a `404` error page. Instagram has done some work on their API that jInstagram has not yet reflected. What we need to do, then, is implement our own wrapper for that, which jInstagram makes fairly simple. Here, we get a list of the people that the user follows. For each user, we call `processMediaForUser()` to fetch and store any pending images.

```
private List<Photo> processMediaForUser(UserFeedData u) {
  List<Photo> userMedia = new ArrayList<>();
  try {
    final String id = u.getId();
    instagram.getRecentMediaFeed(id,
      prefs.getPreference(SunagoPrefsKeys.ITEM_COUNT
        .getKey(), 50),
      getSinceForUser(id), null, null, null).getData()
        .forEach(m -> userMedia.add(new Photo(m)));
    if (!userMedia.isEmpty()) {
      setSinceForUser(id, userMedia.get(0).getId());
    }
  } catch (InstagramException ex) {
    Logger.getLogger(InstagramClient.class.getName())
      .log(Level.SEVERE, null, ex);
  }
  return userMedia;
}
```

Using the same **since ID** and max count approach we used for the Twitter client, we request any recent media for the user. Each returned item is wrapped (via the lambda) in a `Photo` instance, which is our `SocialMediaItem` child for Instagram. Once we have our list, if it is not empty, we grab the first `Photo`, which we know is the oldest, because that's how the Instagram API returns its data, and we get the ID, which we store as the since ID for the next time this method is called. Finally, we return the `List` so that it can be added to the main `Photo` list given earlier.

Loading our plugins in Sunago

With that, our new integration is done. To see it in action, we add the dependency to Sunago's POM as follows:

```
<dependency>
  <groupId>${project.groupId}</groupId>
  <artifactId>instagram</artifactId>
  <version>${project.version}</version>
</dependency>
```

We then run the application.

Clearly, adding a dependency for each new integration is not an ideal solution, if for no other reason than that the user won't be running the application from an IDE or with Maven. What we need, then, is a way for the application to find any modules (or plugins, if you prefer that term) at runtime on the user's machine. The simplest solution would be to launch the application via a shell script like this:

```
#!/bin/bash
JARS=sunago-1.0-SNAPSHOT.jar
SEP=:
for JAR in `ls ~/.sunago/*.jar` ; do
  JARS="$JARS$SEP$JAR"
done

java -cp $JARS com.steeplesoft.sunago.app.Sunago
```

This preceding shell script creates a classpath using the main Sunago jar, plus any JARs found in ~/.sunago, and then runs the application. This is simple and effective, but does require per-operating system versions. Fortunately, that just means this shell script for Mac and Linux, plus a batch file for Windows. That's not hard to do or difficult to maintain, but it does require that you have access to those operating systems to test and verify your scripts.

Another option is to make use of classloaders. As simple as it may seem to say it out loud, a ClassLoader is simply an object that is responsible for loading classes (and other resources). There are several classloaders at work in any given JVM, all arranged in a hierarchical fashion, starting with the bootstrap ClassLoader, then the platform ClassLoader, and, finally, the system--or application--ClassLoader. It is possible that a given application or runtime environment, such as a **Java Enterprise Edition** (**Java EE**) application server, might add one or more ClassLoader instances as children of the application ClassLoader. These added ClassLoader instances may themselves be hierarchical or they may be **siblings**. Either way, they are almost certainly children of the application ClassLoader.

A full treatment of classloaders and all that they entail is well beyond the scope of this book, but suffice it to say that we can create a new ClassLoader to allow the application to find the classes and resources in our **plugin** jars. To do this, we need to add a few methods-- three to be exact--to our application class, Sunago. We'll start with the constructor:

```
public Sunago() throws Exception {
  super();
  updateClassLoader();
}
```

Typically (though not always), when a JavaFX application starts, the `public static void main` method is run, which calls the `launch()` static method on the `Application` class, which we subclass. According to the Javadoc for `javafx.application.Application`, the JavaFX runtime performs the following steps when starting an application:

1. Constructs an instance of the specified `Application` class.
2. Calls the `init()` method.
3. Calls the `start(javafx.stage.Stage)` method.
4. Waits for the application to finish, which happens when any of the following occur:
    1. The application calls `Platform.exit()`.
    2. The last window has been closed, and the `implicitExit` attribute on platform is true.
5. Calls the `stop()` method.

We want to perform our `ClassLoader` work at step 1, in the constructor of our `Application`, to make sure that everything that follows has an up-to-date `ClassLoader`. That work is done in the second method that we need to add, which is this:

```
private void updateClassLoader() {
  final File[] jars = getFiles();
  if (jars != null) {
    URL[] urls = new URL[jars.length];
    int index = 0;
    for (File jar : jars) {
      try {
        urls[index] = jar.toURI().toURL();
        index++;
      } catch (MalformedURLException ex) {
          Logger.getLogger(Sunago.class.getName())
            .log(Level.SEVERE, null, ex);
      }
    }
    Thread.currentThread().setContextClassLoader(
      URLClassLoader.newInstance(urls));
  }
}
```

We start by getting a list of the jar files (we'll see that code in a moment), then, if the array is non-null, we need to build an array of URLs, so, we iterate over the File array, and call .toURI().toURL() to do so. Once we have our URL array we create a new ClassLoader (URLClassLoader.newInstance(urls)), then set the ClassLoader for the current Thread via Thread.currentThread().setContextClassLoader().

This is our final additional method getFiles():

```
private File[] getFiles() {
    String pluginDir = System.getProperty("user.home")
    + "/.sunago";
    return new File(pluginDir).listFiles(file -> file.isFile() &&
    file.getName().toLowerCase().endsWith(".jar"));
}
```

This last method simply scans the files in $HOME/.sunago, looking for a file that ends with .jar. A list of zero or more jar files is returned to our calling code for inclusion in the new ClassLoader, and our work is done.

So there you have two ways of adding plugin jars to the runtime dynamically. Each has its strengths and weaknesses. The first requires multi-platform development and maintenance, while the second is a bit riskier, as classloaders can be tricky. I have tested the second approach on Windows and Linux and Java 8 and 9 with no errors detected. Which approach you use will, of course, depend on your unique environment and requirements, but you have at least two options with which to start your evaluation.

Summary

With all of that said, our application is complete. Of course, hardly any software is truly complete, and there's much more that could be done to Sunago. Twitter support could be expanded to include direct messages. The Instagram module needs some configuration options added. While the capabilities exposed via the Facebook API are limiting, some sort of meaningful Facebook integration could be added. Sunago itself could be modified to, say, add support for in-application viewing of social media content (as opposed to shelling out to the host operating system's default browser). There are a handful of minor user experience bugs that could be addressed. And the list can go on and on. What we do have, though, is a moderately complex, networked application, that demonstrates a number of features and capabilities of the Java platform. We've built an extensible, internationalized JavaFX application that demonstrates the use of the Service Provider Interface and `ClassLoader` magic, and offers many more examples of lambdas, stream operations, and functional interfaces.

In the next chapter, we're going to build on the ideas presented here, and build an Android port of Sunago so that we can take our social media aggregation on-the-go with us.

Sunago - An Android Port
22

In the last chapter, we built Sunago, a social media aggregation application. In that chapter, we learned that Sunago is a JavaFX-based application that can pull posts, tweets, photos, and so on from a variety of social media networks and display them in one place. The application certainly provided a number of interesting architectural and technical examples, but the application itself could be more practical--we tend to interact with social networks from mobile devices such as phones and tablets, so a mobile version would be much more useful. In this chapter, then, we'll write an Android port, reusing as much of the code as possible.

Android applications, while built in Java, look quite a bit different than, say, a desktop application. While we can't cover every aspect of Android development, we'll cover enough in this chapter to get you started, including the following:

- Setting up an Android development environment
- Gradle builds
- Android views
- Android state management
- Android services
- Application packaging and deployment

Like the other chapters, there will be too many small items to call out each of them, but we'll do our best to highlight the new ones as they're introduced.

Getting started

The first step is to get the Android development environment set up. As with *regular* Java development, an IDE isn't strictly necessary, but it sure helps, so we'll install Android Studio, which is an IDE based on IntelliJ IDEA. If you already have IDEA installed, you can just install the Android plugin and have everything you need. For our purposes here, though, we'll assume you don't have either installed.

1. To download Android Studio, go to
   `https://developer.android.com/studio/index.html`, and download the
   package appropriate for your operating system. When you start **Android Studio**
   for the first time, you should see following screen:

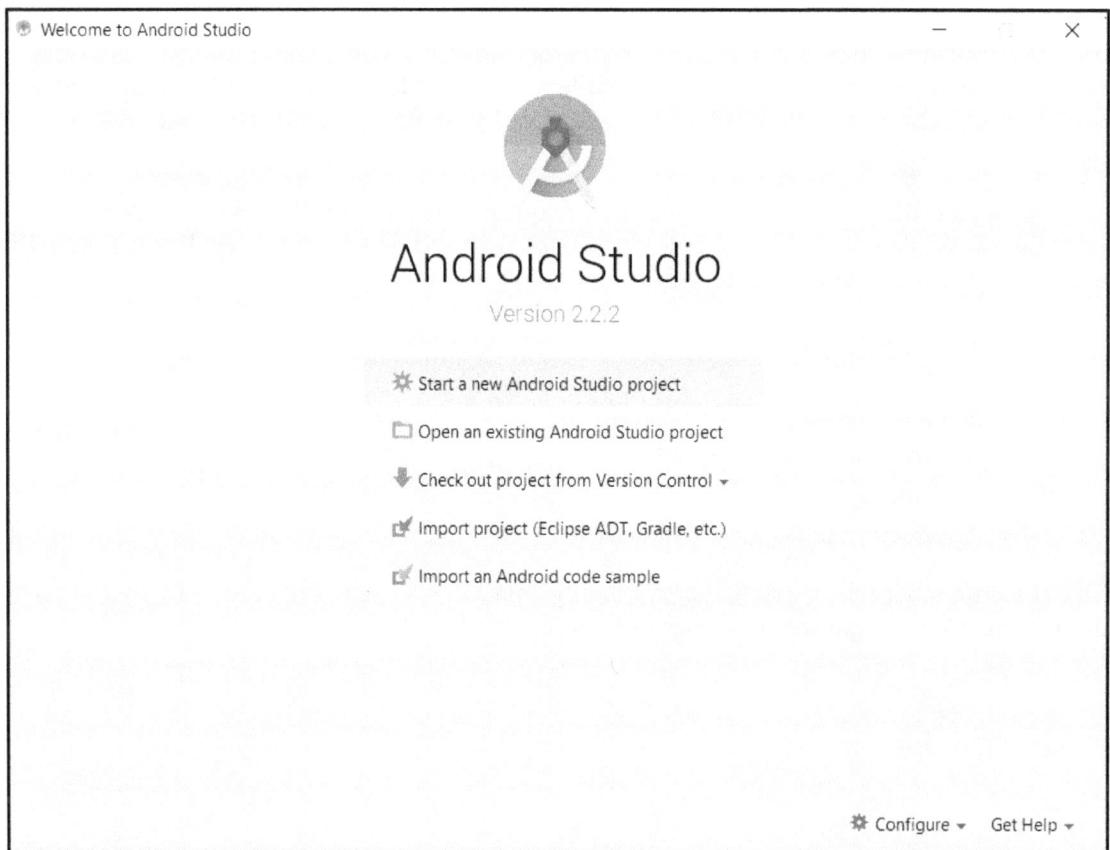

2. Before we start a new project, let's configure the Android SDKs that are available. Click on the **Configure** menu in the bottom-right corner, then click on **SDK Manager** to get this screen:

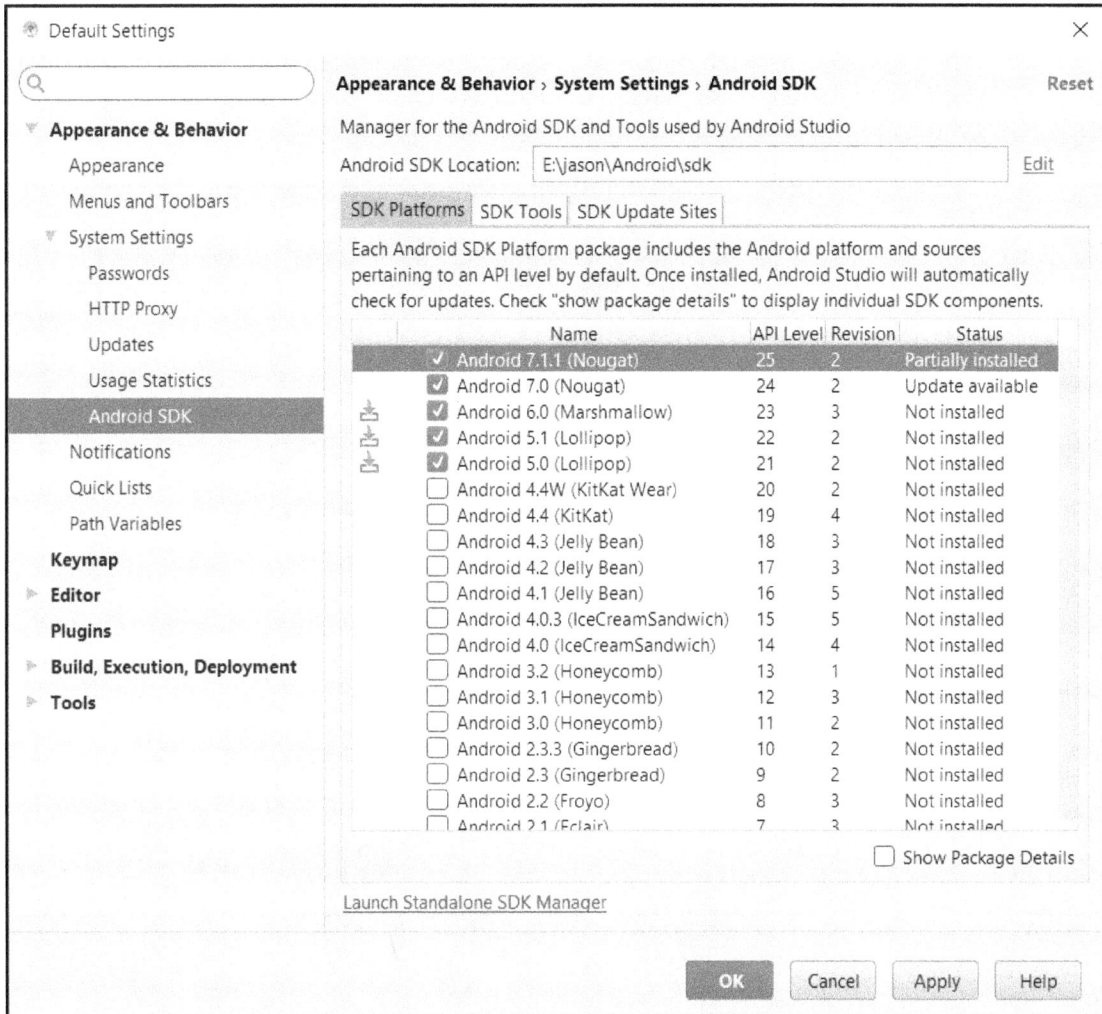

Which SDKs you select will vary depending on your needs. You may need to support older devices as far back as, say, Android 5.0, or maybe you just want to support the very latest with Android 7.0 or 7.1.1.

3. Once you know what need, select the appropriate SDKs (or do as I've done in the preceding screenshot and select everything from 5.0 and forward), then click on **OK**. You will need to read and accept the license before continuing.

4. Once you've done that, Android Studio will begin downloading the selected SDKs and any dependencies. This process can take a while, so be patient.

5. When the SDK installation completes, click on the **Finish** button, which will take you take to the Welcome screen. Click on **Start a new Android Studio** project to get the following screen:

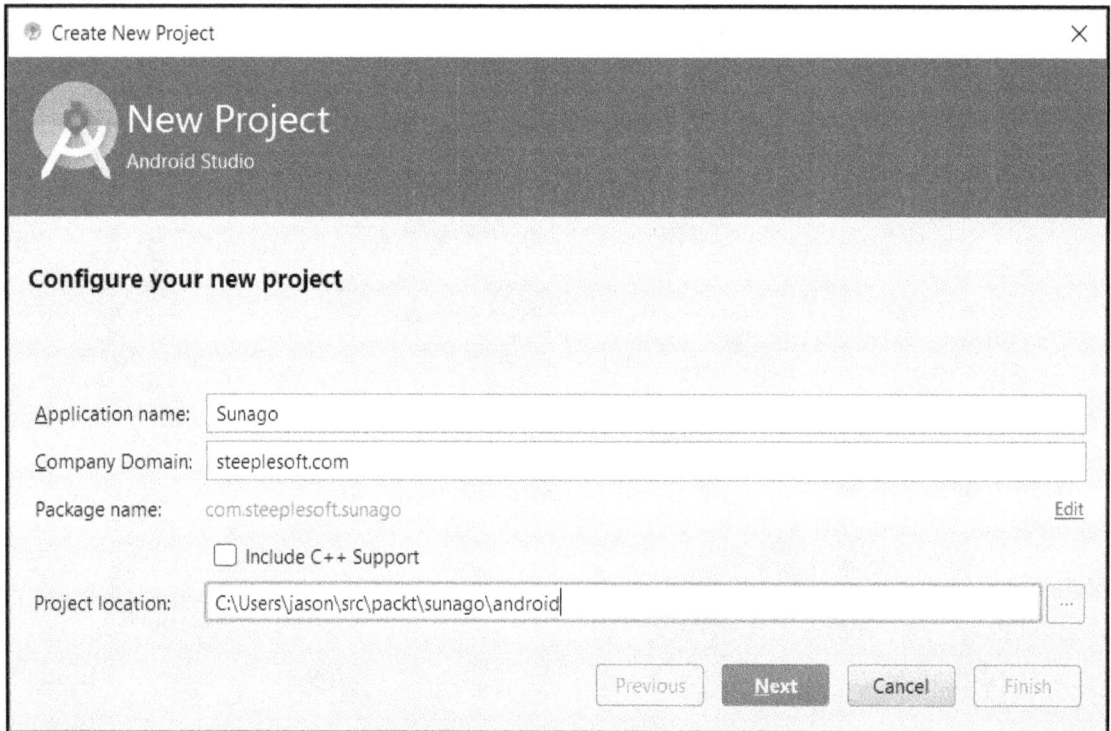

6. Nothing exciting here--we need to specify the **Application name**, **Company domain**, and **Project location** of our app:

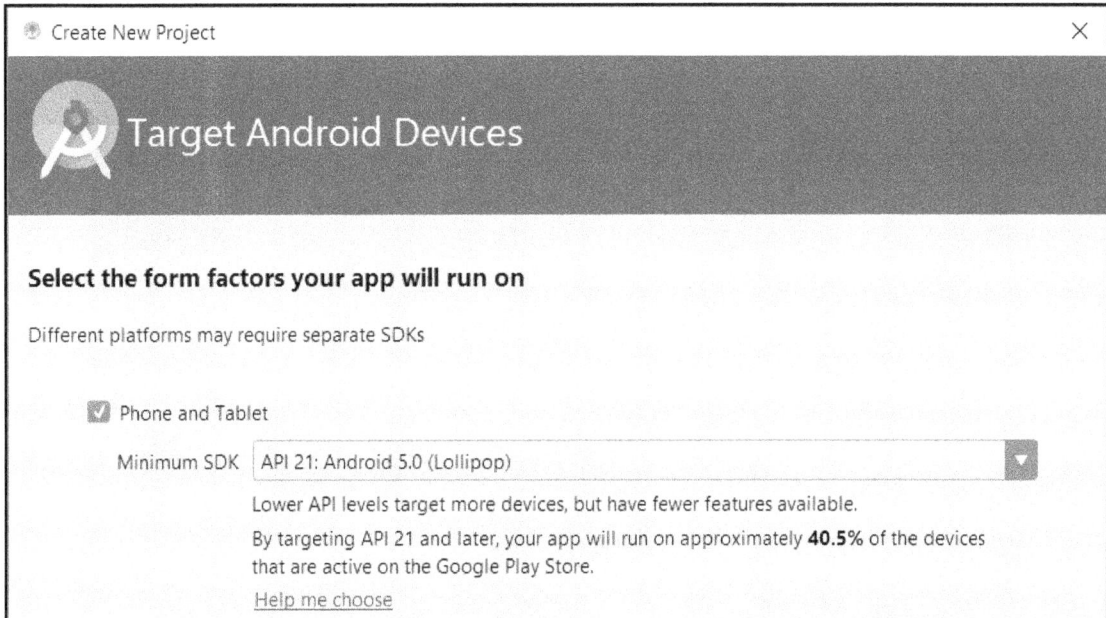

7. Next, though, we need to specify the form factor for our app. Our options are Phone and Tablet, Wear, TV, Android Auto, and Glass. As seen in this preceding screenshot, all we're interested in for this application is **Phone and Tablet**.

8. On the next window, we need to select a type for the main `Activity` for the application. In an Android application, what we might refer to as a *screen* (or maybe *page*, if you're coming from a web application background) is known as an `Activity`. Not every `Activity` is a screen, though.

   From the Android developer documentation (`https://developer.android.com/reference/android/app/Activity.html`), we learn the following:

   > *[a]n activity is a single, focused thing that the user can do. Almost all activities interact with the user, so the Activity class takes care of creating a window for you...*

For our purposes, it's probably acceptable to equate the two, but do so loosely, and always with this caveat in mind. The wizard gives us many options, as seen in this screenshot:

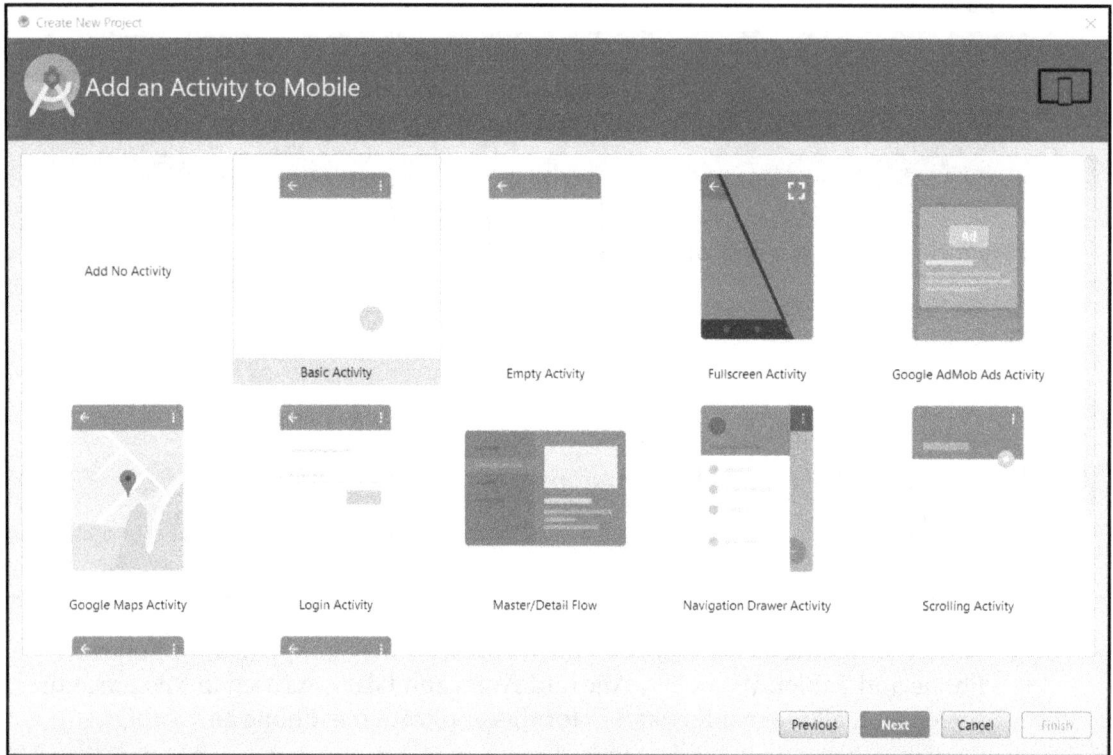

9. As you can see, there are several options: **Basic, Empty, Fullscreen, Google AdMobs Ads, Google Maps, Login**, and so on. Which to choose depends, again, on what your requirements are for the application. Our bare minimum requirements, in terms of user interface, are that it tells the user the name of the app, shows the list of social media items, and provides a menu for changing the application settings. From the preceding list, then, the **Basic Activity** is the closest match, so we select that, and click on **Next**:

10. The defaults in the preceding screen are mostly acceptable (notice that **Activity Name** was changed), but before we click on **Finish**, there are a few final words. When building an Android application of any size, you are going to have a lot of layouts, menus, activities, and so on. I have found it helpful to name these artifacts as you see here--the layout for an `Activity` is named `activity_` plus the `Activity` name; menus are `menu_` plus the activity name, or, for shared menus, a meaningful summary of its contents. Each artifact type is prefixed by its type. This general pattern will help you quickly navigate to the source file as the number of files grows, as the arrangement of these files is very flat and shallow.

11. Finally, notice the **Use a Fragment** checkbox. *A Fragment is a piece of an application's user interface or behavior that can be placed in an Activity.* It is, effectively, a way for you, as the developer, to decompose the user interface definition into multiple pieces (or Fragments, thus, the name) that can be composed into a whole in an Activity in different ways depending on the current context of the application. For example, a Fragment-based user interface might have two screens for certain operations on a phone, but might combine those into one Activity for the larger screen on a tablet. It's a bit more complicated than that, of course, but I include that brief and incomplete description simply to give some explanation of the checkbox. We will not be using Fragments in our application, so we leave that unchecked, and click on **Finish**.

After processing for some time, Android Studio now creates a basic application for us. Before we start coding the application, let's run it to see what that process looks like. We can run the app in a few ways--we can click on **Run** | **Run 'app'**; click on the green play button in the middle of the toolbar, or press *Shift + F10*. All three will bring up the same **Select Deployment Target** window, as follows:

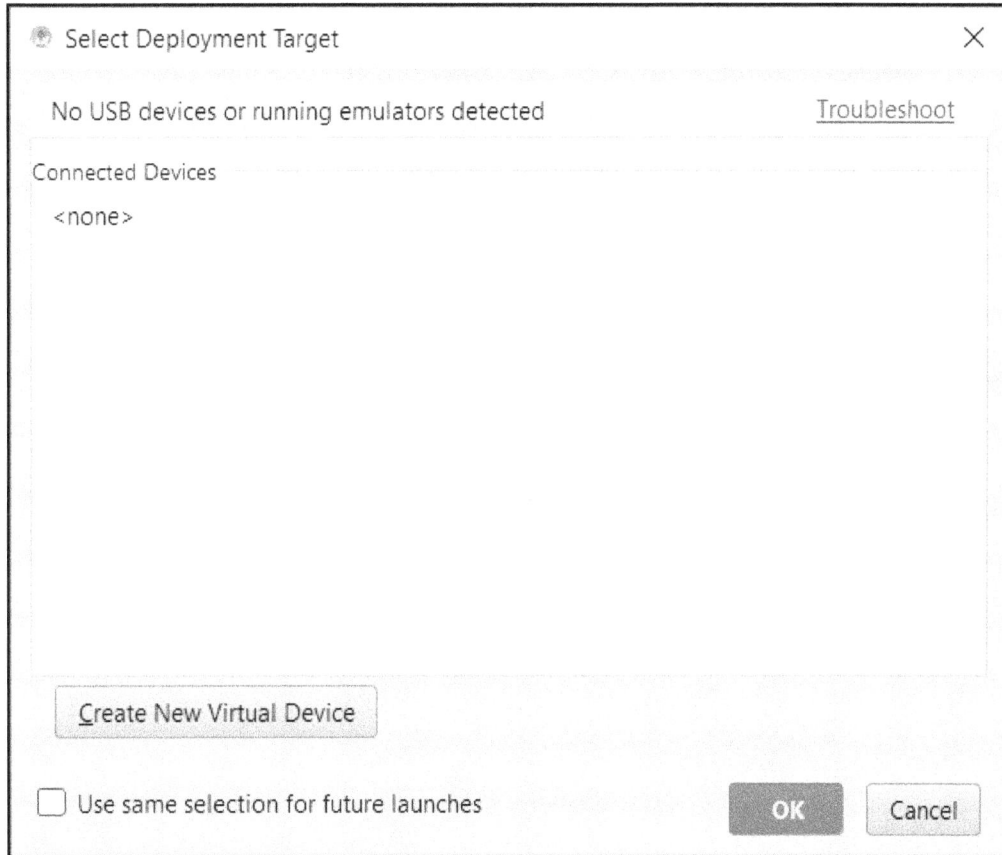

```
Select Deployment Target                                    ✕

   No USB devices or running emulators detected      Troubleshoot

Connected Devices
  <none>










     Create New Virtual Device

  ☐ Use same selection for future launches      OK      Cancel
```

Since we just installed Android Studio, we don't have any emulators created, so we need to do that now. To create the emulators, follow these steps:

1. Clicking on the **Create New Virtual Device** button gets us this screen:

2. Let's start with a reasonably modern Android phone--select the **Nexus 6** profile, and click on **Next**:

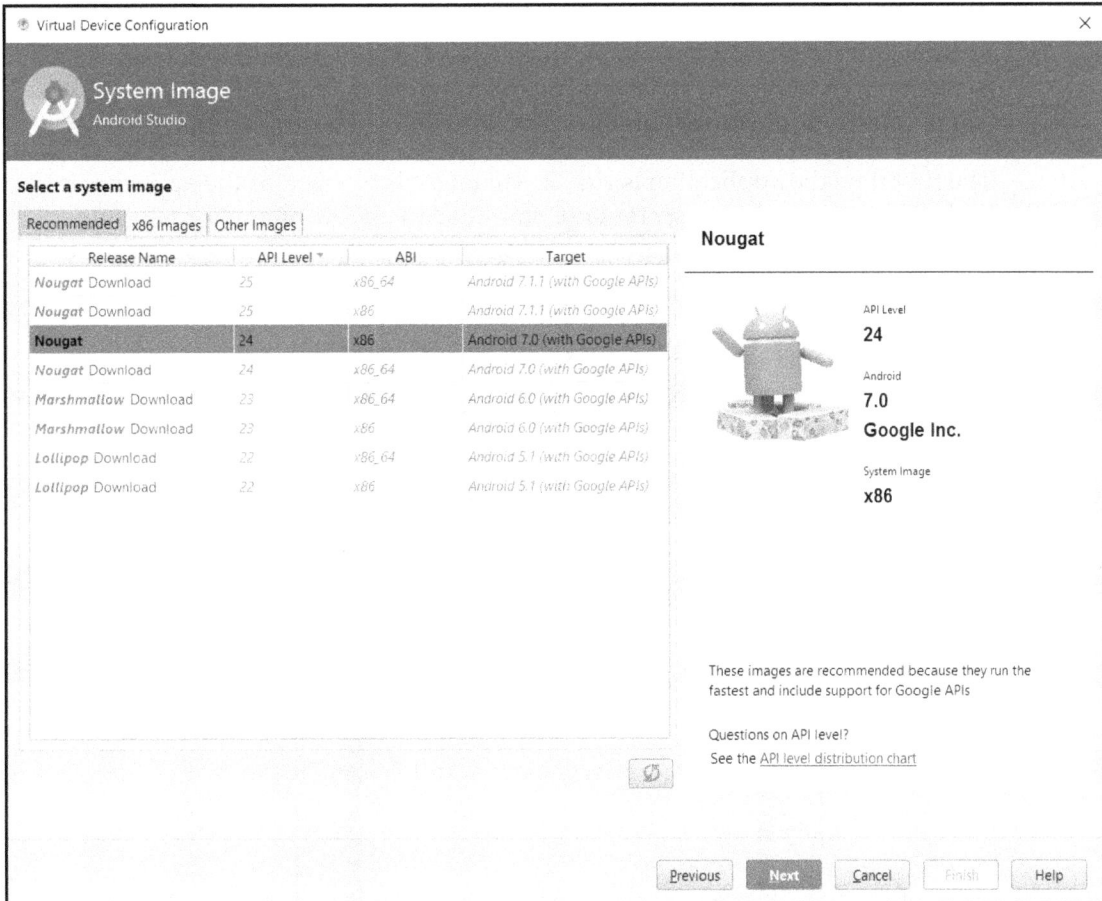

In the preceding screen, your options will vary based on which SDKs you've installed. Which SDK you choose, again, depends on your target audience, application needs, and so on. As enjoyable as it always is to use the latest and greatest, we don't strictly need any APIs from, say, **Nougat**. Choosing Android 7.x would restrict the availability of Sunago to those on very new phones, and do so for no good reason. We will, then, target **Lollipop** (**Android 5.0**), which strikes a good balance between supporting as many users as possible and providing access to newer Android features.

3. Click the **Download** link if necessary for the **x86_64** ABI, select that release, click on **Next**, and then click on **Finish** on the **Verify Configuration** screen.

4. With an emulator created, we can now select it in the **Select Deployment Target** screen, and run the application by clicking on **OK**. If you want to skip the selection screen the next time you run the application, you can check the **Use same selection for future launches** checkbox before clicking on **OK**.

The first time the application is run, it will take a bit longer, as the application is built and packaged and the emulator started. After a few moments, you should see the following screen:

It's nothing special, but it shows that everything is working as expected. Now, we're ready to start the real work in porting Sunago.

Building the user interface

Put simply, Android user interfaces are based on Activities, which use layout files to describe the structure of the user interface. There's more to it, of course, but this simple definition should be sufficient for our work on Sunago. Let's start, then, by looking at our `Activity`, `MainActivity`, which is as follows:

```
public class MainActivity extends AppCompatActivity {
  @Override
  protected void onCreate(Bundle savedInstanceState) {
    super.onCreate(savedInstanceState);
    setContentView(R.layout.activity_main);
    Toolbar toolbar = (Toolbar) findViewById(R.id.toolbar);
    setSupportActionBar(toolbar);

    FloatingActionButton fab =
        (FloatingActionButton) findViewById(R.id.fab);
    fab.setOnClickListener(new View.OnClickListener() {
      @Override
      public void onClick(View view) {
        Snackbar.make(view,
              "Replace with your own action",
              Snackbar.LENGTH_LONG)
          .setAction("Action", null).show();
      }
    });
  }

  @Override
  public boolean onCreateOptionsMenu(Menu menu) {
    getMenuInflater().inflate(R.menu.menu_main, menu);
    return true;
  }
  @Override
  public boolean onOptionsItemSelected(MenuItem item) {
    int id = item.getItemId();

    if (id == R.id.action_settings) {
      return true;
    }

    return super.onOptionsItemSelected(item);
  }
}
```

This last bit of code is the class exactly as it was generated by Android Studio. It's very basic, but it has most of what you need to create an `Activity`. Note that the class extends `AppCompatActivity`. While Google has been very active in pushing the Android platform, they have also worked tirelessly to make sure that older devices aren't left behind any sooner than they have to be. To achieve that, Google has backported many new features in "compat" (or compatibility) packages, which means many of the newer APIs will actually run on older versions of Android. The changes, though, since they are in separate packages, won't break any existing functionality--they must be explicitly opted for, which is what we're doing here. While we're not planning on supporting older versions of Android, such as KitKat, it is still suggested that your `Activity` classes extend the compatibility classes, like this one, as there is a significant number of features built in to these classes that we would otherwise have to implement ourselves. Let's walk through this class to get a sense of what all is going on in the following steps:

1. The first method is `onCreate()`, which is an `Activity` life cycle method (we'll talk more about Activity life cycle in a moment). When the system creates the `Activity` class, this method is called. It is here that we initialize the user interface, setting values, connection controls to data sources, and so on. Note that the method takes a **Bundle**. This is how Android passes in the Activity state so that it may be restored.

    In the `setContentView(R.layout.activity_main)` method, we tell the system what layout we want to use for this `Activity`. Once we've set the content `View` for `Activity`, we can then start acquiring references to various elements. Notice that we first look for the `Toolbar` defined in the view, `findViewById(R.id.toolbar)`, then we tell Android to use that as our action bar via `setSupportActionBar()`. This is an example of a functionality that is implemented for us via the `compat` class. If we extended, say, `Activity` directly, we would be required to do much more work to make the action bar work. As it is, we call one setter and we're done.

2. Next, we look up another user interface element, the `FloatingActionButton`. In the preceding screenshot, this is the button in the lower-right corner with the email icon. We will actually be removing this, but, since Android Studio generated it, we can learn what we can from it before it is removed. Once we have a reference to it, we can attach listeners. In this case, we're adding an `on Click` listener by creating an anonymous inner class of type `View.OnClickListener`. This works, but we've just spent the last five chapters getting rid of those.

3. The Android build system now natively supports using Java 8, so we can modify the `onClick` listener registration to look like this:

```
fab.setOnClickListener(view -> Snackbar.make(view,
    "Replace with your own action",
        Snackbar.LENGTH_LONG)
    .setAction("Action", null).show());
```

When the user taps the button, the Snackbar appears. According to the Google documentation, *Snackbars provide brief feedback about an operation through a message at the bottom of the screen.* And that's exactly what we get--a message telling us to replace the `onClick` result with our own action. As stated earlier, though, we don't need the floating button, so we'll remove this method and, later, the view definition from the layout.

4. The next method in the class is `onCreateOptionsMenu()`. This method is called when the options menu is first opened to populate the list of items. We use `MenuInflater` to inflate the menu definition file, and add what it defined there to `Menu` that the system passes in. This method is called only once, though, so if you need a menu that changes, you should override `onPrepareOptionsMenu(Menu)`.

5. The final method, `onOptionsItemSelected()`, is called when the user taps an options menu item. The specific `MenuItem` selected is passed in. We get its ID, and call the method appropriate for the menu item.

That's a basic `Activity`, but what does a layout look like? Here are the contents of `activity_main.xml`:

```
<?xml version="1.0" encoding="utf-8"?>
<android.support.design.widget.CoordinatorLayout
  xmlns:android="http://schemas.android.com/apk/res/android"
  xmlns:app="http://schemas.android.com/apk/res-auto"
  xmlns:tools="http://schemas.android.com/tools"
  android:layout_width="match_parent"
  android:layout_height="match_parent"
  android:fitsSystemWindows="true"
  tools:context="com.steeplesoft.sunago.MainActivity">

  <android.support.design.widget.AppBarLayout
    android:layout_width="match_parent"
    android:layout_height="wrap_content"
    android:theme="@style/AppTheme.AppBarOverlay">

    <android.support.v7.widget.Toolbar
```

```
        android:id="@+id/toolbar"
        android:layout_width="match_parent"
        android:layout_height="?attr/actionBarSize"
        android:background="?attr/colorPrimary"
        app:popupTheme="@style/AppTheme.PopupOverlay" />

    </android.support.design.widget.AppBarLayout>

    <include layout="@layout/content_main" />

    <android.support.design.widget.FloatingActionButton
        android:id="@+id/fab"
        android:layout_width="wrap_content"
        android:layout_height="wrap_content"
        android:layout_gravity="bottom|end"
        android:layout_margin="@dimen/fab_margin"
        app:srcCompat="@android:drawable/ic_dialog_email" />

</android.support.design.widget.CoordinatorLayout>
```

That's a fair bit of XML, so let's walk through the major items of interest quickly, as follows:

1. The root element is `CoordinatorLayout`. Its Java document describes it as a super-powered `FrameLayout`. One of its intended purposes is as *a top-level application decor or chrome layout*, which is exactly what we're using it for here. Layouts such as `CoordinatorLayout` are roughly analogous to JavaFX's containers. Different layouts (or `ViewGroup`) provide a variety of capabilities such as laying out elements with exact X/Y coordinates (`AbsoluteLayout`), in a grid (`GridLayout`), relative to each other (`RelativeLayout`), and so on.

2. In addition to providing our top-level container, the element defines a number of required XML namespaces. It also sets the height and width for the control. There are three possible values for this field--`match_parent` (in earlier versions of the SDK, this was called `fill_parent` should you ever come across that), which means that the control should match the value of its parent, `wrap_content`, which means the control should be just big enough for its contents; or an exact number.

3. The next element is `AppBarLayout`, which is a `ViewGroup` that implements a number of the material designs app bar concepts. **Material design** is the latest **visual language** being developed and supported by Google. It provides a modern, consistent look and feel across Android apps. Its usage is encouraged by Google, and fortunately, the new `Activity` wizard has set us up to use it out of the box. The layout's width is set to `match_parent` so that it fills the screen, and the width is set to `wrap_content` so that's it's just big enough to show its content, which is a single `Toolbar`.

4. Skipping the `include` element for a moment, the last element in the view is `FloatingActionButton`. Our only interest here is noting that the widget exists, should the need for one arise in other projects. As we did in the `Activity` class though, we need to remove this widget.

5. Finally, there's the `include` element. This does what you would think it should-- the specified file is included in the layout definition as if its contents were hard coded into the file. This allows us to keep our layout files small, reuse user interface element definitions (which is especially helpful for complex scenarios), and so on.

The included file, `content_main.xml`, looks like this:

```
<RelativeLayout
  xmlns:android="http://schemas.android.com/apk/res/android"
  xmlns:app="http://schemas.android.com/apk/res-auto"
  xmlns:tools="http://schemas.android.com/tools"
  android:id="@+id/content_main"
  android:layout_width="match_parent"
  android:layout_height="match_parent"
  android:paddingBottom="@dimen/activity_vertical_margin"
  android:paddingLeft="@dimen/activity_horizontal_margin"
  android:paddingRight="@dimen/activity_horizontal_margin"
  android:paddingTop="@dimen/activity_vertical_margin"
  app:layout_behavior="@string/appbar_scrolling_view_behavior"
  tools:context="com.steeplesoft.sunago.MainActivity"
  tools:showIn="@layout/activity_main">

  <TextView
    android:layout_width="wrap_content"
    android:layout_height="wrap_content"
    android:text="Hello World!" />
</RelativeLayout>
```

This preceding view uses `RelativeLayout` to wrap its only child, a `TextView`. Note that we can set the padding of a control. This controls how much space is *inside* the control around its children. Think of it like packing a box--inside the box, you may have a fragile ceramic antique, so you pad the box to protect it. You can also set the margin of a control, which is the space *outside* the control, akin to the personal space around us we are so often fond of.

The `TextView`, though, isn't helpful, so we'll remove that, and add what we really need, which is a `ListView`, as follows:

```
<ListView
  android:id="@+id/listView"
  android:layout_width="match_parent"
  android:layout_height="match_parent"
  android:layout_alignParentTop="true"
  android:layout_alignParentStart="true"/>
```

`ListView` is a control that shows items in a vertically scrolling list. In terms of user experience, this works pretty much like the `ListView` we looked at in JavaFX. How it works, though, is quite different. To see how, we need to make some adjustments to activity's `onCreate()` method as follows:

```
protected void onCreate(Bundle savedInstanceState) {
    super.onCreate(savedInstanceState);
    setContentView(R.layout.activity_main);

    if (!isNetworkAvailable()) {
        showErrorDialog(
            "A valid internet connection can't be established");
    } else {
        Toolbar toolbar = (Toolbar) findViewById(R.id.toolbar);
        setSupportActionBar(toolbar);
        findPlugins();

        adapter = new SunagoCursorAdapter(this, null, 0);
        final ListView listView = (ListView)
            findViewById(R.id.listView);
        listView.setAdapter(adapter);
        listView.setOnItemClickListener(
                new AdapterView.OnItemClickListener() {
            @Override
            public void onItemClick(AdapterView<?> adapterView,
                    View view, int position, long id) {
                Cursor c = (Cursor)
                    adapterView.getItemAtPosition(position);
                String url = c.getString(c.getColumnIndex(
```

```
                    SunagoContentProvider.URL));
            Intent intent = new Intent(Intent.ACTION_VIEW,
                Uri.parse(url));
            startActivity(intent);
        }
    });

    getLoaderManager().initLoader(0, null, this);
    }
}
```

There are several things going on here, which sets us up nicely for discussing data access in Android. Before we get to that in detail, though, a quick overview is in order:

1. We check to make sure that the device has a working network connection via `isNetworkAvailable()`, which we'll look at later in this chapter.

2. If the connection is available, we configure the user interface, starting with setting the toolbar.

3. Next, we create an instance of `SunagoCursorAdapter`, which we'll discuss in detail later. For now, though, just note that an `Adapter` is how the `ListView` is connected to the data source, and they can be backed by things as varied as an SQL datasource or an `Array`.

4. We pass the adapter to `ListView`, thus completing this connection via `ListView.setAdapter()`. Much like JavaFX's `Observable` model property, we'll be able to use this to update the user interface without direct interaction any time the data changes.

5. Next, we set up an `onClick` listener for the items in the list. We'll use this to display the item the user taps (or clicks) on in an external browser. In a nutshell, given the `position` parameter, we get the item at that position, a `Cursor`, extract the URL of the item, then display the page at that URL using the device's default browser via an `Intent` (which we'll discuss in detail later).

6. Finally, completing our data binding, we initialize the `LoaderManager` that will handle loading and updating the `Adapter` in an asynchronous manner.

One last bit of code to look at before diving into data access--`isNetworkAvailable()`-- is as follows:

```
        public boolean isNetworkAvailable() {
          boolean connected = false;
          ConnectivityManager cm = (ConnectivityManager)
            getSystemService(Context.CONNECTIVITY_SERVICE);
          for (Network network : cm.getAllNetworks()) {
            NetworkInfo networkInfo = cm.getNetworkInfo(network);
```

```
        if (networkInfo.isConnected() == true) {
            connected = true;
            break;
        }
      }
    return connected;
  }

  private void showErrorDialog(String message) {
    AlertDialog alertDialog = new AlertDialog.Builder(this)
      .create();
    alertDialog.setTitle("Error!");
    alertDialog.setMessage(message);
    alertDialog.setIcon(android.R.drawable.alert_dark_frame);
    alertDialog.setButton(DialogInterface.BUTTON_POSITIVE,
    "OK", new DialogInterface.OnClickListener() {
      @Override
      public void onClick(DialogInterface dialog, int which) {
        MainActivity.this.finish();
      }
    });

    alertDialog.show();
  }
```

In the preceding code, we start by getting a reference to the system service, `ConnectivityManager`, then we loop through each `Network` known to the system. For each `Network`, we get a reference to its `NetworkInfo` and call `isConnected()`. If we find one connected network, we return true, otherwise, we return false. In the calling code, if our return value is `false`, we show an error dialog, the method for which is shown here as well. This is a standard Android dialog. We have, however, added an `onClick` listener to the **OK** button, which closes the application. Using this, we tell the user that a network connection is needed, then close the app when the user taps on **OK**. It is debatable, of course, if this behavior is desirable, but the process for determining a device's network state is interesting enough, so I've included it here.

Let's turn our attention now to how data access is often done in Android apps-- `CursorAdapters`.

Android data access

With any platform, there are multiple ways to access data, from built-in facilities to homegrown APIs. Android is no different, so while you can write your own way to load data from some arbitrary data source, unless you have very particular requirements, there is often no need, as Android has a system built in--the `ContentProvider`.

The Android documentation will tell you that a *content provider manages access to a central repository of data*, and that it offers a consistent, *standard interface to data that also handles inter-process communication and secure data access*. If you intend to expose your application's data to external sources (either for read or write), `ContentProvider` is a great way to go. However, if you don't intend to expose your data, you are more than welcome to write the needed CRUD methods yourself, manually issuing various SQL statements. In our case, we'll use a `ContentProvider`, as we have an interest in allowing third-party developers access to the data.

To create a `ContentProvider`, we need to create a new class that extends `ContentProvider` as follows:

```
public class SunagoContentProvider extends ContentProvider {
```

We also need to register the provider in `AndroidManfest.xml`, which we'll do like this:

```
<provider android:name=".data.SunagoContentProvider
  android:authorities="com.steeplesoft.sunago.SunagoProvider" />
```

Interaction with `ContentProvider` is never done directly. The client code will specify the URL of the data to be manipulated, and the Android system will direct the request to the appropriate provider. To make sure our `ContentProvider` functions as expected, then, we need to register the provider's authority, which we've already seen in the previous XML. In our provider, we'll create some static fields to help us manage the parts of our authority and the related URLs in a DRY manner.

```
private static final String PROVIDER_NAME =
  "com.steeplesoft.sunago.SunagoProvider";
private static final String CONTENT_URL =
  "content://" + PROVIDER_NAME + "/items";
public static final Uri CONTENT_URI = Uri.parse(CONTENT_URL);
```

The first two fields in the preceding bit of code are private, as they're not needed outside the class. We define them as separate fields here, though, for clarity's sake. The third field, `CONTENT_URI`, is public, as we'll be referencing that field elsewhere in our app. Third-party consumers won't have access to the field, obviously, but will need to know its value, `content://com.steeplesoft.sunago.SunagoProvider/items`, which we would document somewhere for add-on developers. The first part of the URL, the protocol field, tells Android that we're looking for a `ContentProvider`. The next section is the authority, which uniquely identifies a particular `ContentProvider`, and the final field specifies the type of data, or model, that we're interested in. For Sunago, we have a single data type, `items`.

Next, we need to specify the URIs we want to support. We only have two--one for the items collection, and one for a particular item. Please, refer to following code snippet:

```
private static final UriMatcher URI_MATCHER =
  new UriMatcher(UriMatcher.NO_MATCH);
private static final int ITEM = 1;
private static final int ITEM_ID = 2;
static {
  URI_MATCHER.addURI(PROVIDER_NAME, "items", ITEM);
  URI_MATCHER.addURI(PROVIDER_NAME, "items/#", ITEM_ID);
}
```

In the last code, we start by creating a `UriMatcher`. Note that we pass `UriMatcher.NO_MATCH` to the constructor. It's not immediately clear what this value is for, but this is the value that will be returned if the user passes in a URI that doesn't match any of those registered. Finally, we register each URI with a unique `int` identifier.

Next, like many Android classes, we need specify an `onCreate` lifecycle hook as follows:

```
public boolean onCreate() {
  openHelper = new SunagoOpenHelper(getContext(), DBNAME,
    null, 1);
  return true;
}
```

`SunagoOpenHelper` is a child of `SQLiteOpenHelper`, which manages the creation and/or update of the underlying SQLite database. The class itself is pretty simple, and is given as follows:

```
public class SunagoOpenHelper extends SQLiteOpenHelper {
  public SunagoOpenHelper(Context context, String name,
      SQLiteDatabase.CursorFactory factory, int version) {
    super(context, name, factory, version);
  }
```

```
@Override
public void onCreate(SQLiteDatabase db) {
  db.execSQL(SQL_CREATE_MAIN);
}

@Override
public void onUpgrade(SQLiteDatabase db, int oldVersion,
  int newVersion) {
}
}
```

I've not shown the table creation DDL, as it's a pretty simple table creation, but this class is all you need to create and maintain your database. If you have multiple tables, you would issue multiple creates in `onCreate`. When the application updates, `onUpgrade()` is called to allow you to modify the schema if needed.

Back in our `ContentProvider`, we need to implement two methods, one to read data, and one to insert (given the nature of the app, we're not interested in deletes or updates right now). For reading data, we override `query()` as follows:

```
public Cursor query(Uri uri, String[] projection,
  String selection, String[] selectionArgs,
  String sortOrder) {
    switch (URI_MATCHER.match(uri)) {
      case 2:
        selection = selection + "_ID = " +
          uri.getLastPathSegment();
        break;
    }
    SQLiteDatabase db = openHelper.getReadableDatabase();
    Cursor cursor = db.query("items", projection, selection,
      selectionArgs, null, null, sortOrder);
    cursor.setNotificationUri(
      getContext().getContentResolver(), uri);
    return cursor;
}
```

This last code is where our URIs and their `int` identifiers come in. Using `UriMatcher`, we check the `Uri` passed in by the caller. Given that our provider is simple, the only one we need to do anything special for is #2, which is the query for a specific item. In that case, we extract the ID passed in as the last path segment, and add it to the selection criteria specified by the caller.

Once we have the query configured as requested, we get a readable `SQLiteDatabase` from our `openHelper`, and query it using the values passed by the caller. This is one of the areas where the `ContentProvider` contract comes in handy--we don't need to write any `SELECT` statements manually.

Before returning the cursor, we need to do something to it, as follows:

```
cursor.setNotificationUri(getContext().getContentResolver(), uri);
```

With this preceding call, we tell the system that we want the cursor notified when the data is updated. Since we're using a `Loader`, this will allow us to update the user interface automatically when data is inserted.

For inserting data, we override `insert()` as follows:

```
public Uri insert(Uri uri, ContentValues values) {
    SQLiteDatabase db = openHelper.getWritableDatabase();
    long rowID = db.insert("items", "", values);

    if (rowID > 0) {
        Uri newUri = ContentUris.withAppendedId(CONTENT_URI,
            rowID);
        getContext().getContentResolver().notifyChange(newUri,
            null);
        return newUri;
    }

    throw new SQLException("Failed to add a record into " + uri);
}
```

Using `openHelper`, this time, we get a writable instance of the database, on which we call `insert()`. The insert method returns the ID of the row just inserted. If we get a non-zero ID, we generate a URI for the row, which we'll eventually return. Before we do so, however, we notify the content resolver of the change in the data, which triggers our auto-reload in the user interface.

We have one more step to finish our data loading code, though. If you look back on `MainActivity.onCreate()`, you'll see this line:

```
getLoaderManager().initLoader(0, null, this);
```

This last line tells the system that we want to initialize a `Loader` and that the `Loader` is `this` or `MainActivity`. In our definition of `MainActivity`, we've specified that it implements the `LoaderManager.LoaderCallbacks<Cursor>` interface. This requires us to implement a few methods as follows:

```
public Loader<Cursor> onCreateLoader(int i, Bundle bundle) {
   CursorLoader cl = new CursorLoader(this,
     SunagoContentProvider.CONTENT_URI,
     ITEM_PROJECTION, null, null,
       SunagoContentProvider.TIMESTAMP + " DESC");
   return cl;
}

public void onLoadFinished(Loader<Cursor> loader, Cursor cursor) {
   adapter.swapCursor(cursor);
}

public void onLoaderReset(Loader<Cursor> loader) {
   adapter.swapCursor(null);
}
```

In `onCreateLoader()`, we specify both what to load and where to load it. We pass in the URI of the `ContentProvider` we just created, we specify the fields we're interested in via the `ITEM_PROJECTION` variable (which is a `String[]`, and not shown here), and, finally, the sort order (which we've specified as the timestamp of the items in descending order so that we get the newest items on top). The method `onLoadFinished()` is where the auto-reload happens. Once a new `Cursor` is created for the updated data, we swap it in for the `Cursor` that `Adapter` is currently using. While you can write your own persistence code, this highlights why using the platform facilities, whenever possible, can be a wise choice.

There is one large item left to look at with regard to data handling--`SunagoCursorAdapter`. Looking again at the Android Javadocs, we learn that *an* `Adapter` *object acts as a bridge between an* `AdapterView` *and the underlying data for that view*, and that `CursorAdapter` *exposes data from a* `Cursor` *to a* `ListView` *widget.* Often--if not in the majority of cases--a particular `ListView` will require a custom `CursorAdapter` to allow the underlying data to be rendered correctly. Sunago is no exception. To create our `Adapter`, then, we create a new class as follows:

```
public class SunagoCursorAdapter extends CursorAdapter {
   public SunagoCursorAdapter(Context context, Cursor c,
   int flags) {
     super(context, c, flags);
}
```

This is pretty standard fare. The truly interesting parts come in the view creation, which is one of the reasons for being for a `CursorAdapter`. When the `Adapter` needs to create a new view to hold the data pointed to by the cursor, it calls the following method. This is where we specify what the view should look like with the call to `LayoutInflater.inflate()`:

```
public View newView(Context context, Cursor cursor,
    ViewGroup viewGroup) {
  View view = LayoutInflater.from(context).inflate(
  R.layout.social_media_item, viewGroup, false);
  ViewHolder viewHolder = new ViewHolder();
  viewHolder.text = (TextView)
  view.findViewById(R.id.textView);
  viewHolder.image = (ImageView) view.findViewById(
  R.id.imageView);

  WindowManager wm = (WindowManager) Sunago.getAppContext()
    .getSystemService(Context.WINDOW_SERVICE);
  Point size = new Point();
  wm.getDefaultDisplay().getSize(size);
  viewHolder.image.getLayoutParams().width =
    (int) Math.round(size.x * 0.33);

  view.setTag(viewHolder);
  return view;
}
```

We'll look at our layout definition in a moment, but first, let's take a look at `ViewHolder`:

```
private static class ViewHolder {
  public TextView text;
  public ImageView image;
}
```

Finding views by ID can be an expensive operation, so a very common pattern is this `ViewHolder` approach. After the view is inflated, we immediately look up the fields we're interested in, and store those references in a `ViewHolder` instance, which is then stored as the tag on the `View`. Since views are recycled by the `ListView` class (meaning, they're reused as needed as you scroll through the data), this expensive `findViewById()` is called once and cached per `View` rather than once per item in the underlying data. For large datasets (and complex views), this can be a substantial performance boost.

In this method, we also set the size of the `ImageView` class. Android doesn't support setting the width of a view to a percentage via the XML markup (given next), so we do that manually here as we create the `View`. We get the `WindowManager` system service from which we get the default display's size. We multiply the display's width by 0.33, which will restrict the image, if any, to 1/3 of the display's width, and set the `ImageView`'s width to that.

So, what does the view look like for each row?

```
<LinearLayout
  xmlns:android="http://schemas.android.com/apk/res/android"
  xmlns:app="http://schemas.android.com/apk/res-auto"
  xmlns:tools="http://schemas.android.com/tools"
  android:layout_width="match_parent"
  android:layout_height="match_parent"
  android:orientation="horizontal">

  <ImageView
    android:id="@+id/imageView"
    android:layout_width="wrap_content"
    android:layout_height="wrap_content"
    android:layout_marginEnd="5dip"
    android:layout_gravity="top"
    android:adjustViewBounds="true"/>

  <TextView
    android:layout_width="match_parent"
    android:layout_height="wrap_content"
    android:id="@+id/textView"
    android:scrollHorizontally="false"
    android:textSize="18sp" />
</LinearLayout>
```

As the `ViewHolder` hinted, our view consists of an `ImageView` and a `TextView`, presented horizontally, thanks to the enclosing `LinearLayout`.

While `CursorAdapter` calls `newView()` to create a `View`, it calls `bindView()` to--if you can imagine--bind the `View` to a specific row in the `Cursor`. This is where `View` recycling comes into play. The `Adapter` has a number of `View` instances cached, and passes one to this method as needed. Our method looks like this:

```
public void bindView(View view, Context context, Cursor cursor) {
  final ViewHolder viewHolder = (ViewHolder) view.getTag();
  String image = cursor.getString(INDEX_IMAGE);
  if (image != null) {
    new DownloadImageTask(viewHolder.image).execute(image);
```

```
    } else {
      viewHolder.image.setImageBitmap(null);
      viewHolder.image.setVisibility(View.GONE);
    }
    viewHolder.body.setText(cursor.getString(INDEX_BODY));
  }
```

We start by getting the `ViewHolder` instance. As discussed previously, we'll use the widget references stored here to update the user interface. Next, we pull the image URL from the cursor. It's up to each `SocialMediaItem` to decide how this field is populated, but it might be a tweeted image or a photo in an Instagram post. If the item has one, we need to download it so that it can be displayed. Since this requires a network operation, and we're running on the user interface thread, we hand that work off to `DownloadImageTask`. If there is no image for this item, we need to set the bitmap for the image to `null` (otherwise, the image that was there the last time this view instance was used would be displayed again). That frees up some memory, which is always good, but we also set the `ImageView` class' visibility to `GONE`, which hides it from the user interface. You might be tempted to use `INVISIBLE`, but that only makes it invisible **while preserving its space in the user interface**. The end result of that would be a big blank square, which is not what we want. Finally, we set the text of the `TextView` body to the text specified for the item.

The image downloading is handled off-thread by an `AsyncTask`, which is as follows:

```
private static class DownloadImageTask extends
    AsyncTask<String, Void, Bitmap> {
  private ImageView imageView;

  public DownloadImageTask(ImageView imageView) {
    this.imageView = imageView;
  }
```

Android will create a background `Thread` on which to run this task. The main entry point for our logic is `doInBackground()`. Please refer the following snippet:

```
protected Bitmap doInBackground(String... urls) {
  Bitmap image = null;
  try (InputStream in = new URL(urls[0]).openStream()) {
    image = BitmapFactory.decodeStream(in);
  } catch (java.io.IOException e) {
    Log.e("Error", e.getMessage());
  }
  return image;
}
```

This is not the most robust download code imaginable (for example, redirect status codes are happily ignored), but it's certainly usable. Using Java 7's `try-with-resources`, we create a `URL` instance on which we call `openStream()`. Assuming no `Exception` is thrown in either of those operations, we call `BitmapFactory.decodeStream()` to convert the incoming bytes into a `Bitmap`, which is what the method is expected to return.

So, what happens to the `Bitmap` once we return it? We process that in `onPostExecute()` like this:

```
protected void onPostExecute(Bitmap result) {
  imageView.setImageBitmap(result);
  imageView.setVisibility(View.VISIBLE);
  imageView.getParent().requestLayout();
}
```

In this last method, we update `ImageView` with our now downloaded `Bitmap`, makes it `VISIBLE`, then request that the view update itself on the screen.

So far, we've built an app that's capable of displaying `SocialMediaItem` instances, but we have nothing for it to show. We'll fix that now with a look at Android Services.

Android services

For the desktop version of Sunago, we defined an API that would allow third-party developers (or ourselves) to add support for an arbitrary social network to Sunago. That was a great goal for the desktop, and it's a great goal for mobile. Fortunately, Android provides us with a mechanism that can be used to do just that: Services. *A Service is an application component representing either an application's desire to perform a longer-running operation while not interacting with the user or to supply functionality for other applications to use.* While services were designed for more than extensibility, we can leverage this facility to that end.

While there are a number of ways to implement and interact with services, we are going to bind the services to our `Activity` so that their life cycle is tied to that of our `Activity`, and we'll send messages to them asynchronously. We'll start by defining our class as follows:

```
public class TwitterService extends IntentService {
  public TwitterService() {
    super("TwitterService");
  }

 @Override
  protected void onHandleIntent(Intent intent) {
}
```

Technically, these are the only methods required to create a service. Clearly, it doesn't do much, but we'll fix that in just a moment. Before we do that, we need to declare our new `Service` to Android which is done in `AndroidManifest.xml`, as follows:

```
<service android:name=".twitter.TwitterService"
 android:exported="false">
  <intent-filter>
    <action
      android:name="com.steeplesoft.sunago.intent.plugin" />
    <category
      android:name="android.intent.category.DEFAULT" />
  </intent-filter>
</service>
```

Notice that, in addition to the service declaration, we also specify an `IntentFilter` via the `intent-filter` element. We'll use that in `MainActivity` later to find and bind our services. While we're looking at our service, though, let's look at this side of the binding process. We'll need to implement these two lifecycle methods:

```
public IBinder onBind(Intent intent) {
  receiver = new TwitterServiceReceiver();
  registerReceiver(receiver,
    new IntentFilter("sunago.service"));
  return null;
 }

public boolean onUnbind(Intent intent) {
  unregisterReceiver(receiver);
  return super.onUnbind(intent);
}
```

These preceding methods are called when the service is bound and unbound, which give us an opportunity to register our receiver, which may lead to the question: What's that? Android provides an **Interprocess Communication (IPC)**, but it is somewhat limited in that the payload size can not exceed 1 MB. Though our payload is only text, we can (and certainly will, based on my testing) exceed that. Our approach, then, will be to use asynchronous communication, via a receiver, and have the service persist the data via our `ContentProvider`.

To create a receiver, we extend `android.content.BroadcastReceiver` as follows:

```
private class TwitterServiceReceiver extends BroadcastReceiver {
  @Override
  public void onReceive(Context context, Intent intent) {
    if ("REFRESH".equals(intent.getStringExtra("message"))) {
      if (SunagoUtil.getPreferences().getBoolean(
          getString(R.string.twitter_authd), false)) {
        new TwitterUpdatesAsyncTask().execute();
      }
    }
  }
}
```

Our message scheme is very simple--Sunago sends the message `REFRESH`, and the service performs its work, which we have wrapped up in `TwitterUpdatesAsyncTask`. In `onBind()`, we register the receiver with a specific `IntentFilter` that specifies the `Intent` broadcasts that we're interested in. In `onUnbind()`, we unregister our receiver as the service is released.

The rest of our service is in our `AsyncTask`, which is given as follows:

```
private class TwitterUpdatesAsyncTask extends
AsyncTask<Void, Void, List<ContentValues>> {
  @Override
  protected List<ContentValues> doInBackground(Void... voids) {
    List<ContentValues> values = new ArrayList<>();
    for (SocialMediaItem item :
         TwitterClient.instance().getItems()) {
      ContentValues cv = new ContentValues();
      cv.put(SunagoContentProvider.BODY, item.getBody());
      cv.put(SunagoContentProvider.URL, item.getUrl());
      cv.put(SunagoContentProvider.IMAGE, item.getImage());
      cv.put(SunagoContentProvider.PROVIDER,
          item.getProvider());
      cv.put(SunagoContentProvider.TITLE, item.getTitle());
      cv.put(SunagoContentProvider.TIMESTAMP,
          item.getTimestamp().getTime());
```

```
        values.add(cv);
    }
    return values;
}

@Override
protected void onPostExecute(List<ContentValues> values) {
  Log.i(MainActivity.LOG_TAG, "Inserting " + values.size() +
    " tweets.");
  getContentResolver()
    .bulkInsert(SunagoContentProvider.CONTENT_URI,
      values.toArray(new ContentValues[0]));
  }
}
```

We need to make sure that the network operation isn't performed on the user interface thread, so we perform the work in `AsyncTask`. We don't need any parameters passed into the task, so we set the `Params` and `Progress` types to `Void`. We are, though, interested in the `Result` type, which is `List<ContentValue>`, which we see reflected in both the type declaration and the return type of `execute()`. In `onPostExecute()`, we then issue a bulk insert on `ContentProvider` to save the data. In this way, we can make the newly-retrieved data available to the application without running afoul the 1 MB limit with `IBinder`.

With our service defined, we need now to look at how to find and bind the services. Looking back at `MainActivity`, we'll finally look at a method we've already seen mentioned, `findPlugins()`:

```
private void findPlugins() {
 Intent baseIntent = new Intent(PLUGIN_ACTION);
 baseIntent.setFlags(Intent.FLAG_DEBUG_LOG_RESOLUTION);
 List<ResolveInfo> list = getPackageManager()
        .queryIntentServices(baseIntent,
        PackageManager.GET_RESOLVED_FILTER);
 for (ResolveInfo rinfo : list) {
    ServiceInfo sinfo = rinfo.serviceInfo;
    if (sinfo != null) {
        plugins.add(new
            ComponentName(sinfo.packageName, sinfo.name));
    }
  }
}
```

To find the plugins we're interested in, we create an `Intent` with a specific action. In this case, that action is `com.steeplesoft.sunago.intent.plugin`, which we've already seen in the service definition in `AndroidManifest.xml`. Using this `Intent`, we query `PackageManager` for all `IntentServices` matching Intent. Next, we iterate over the list of `ResolveInfo` instances, getting the `ServiceInfo` instances, and create and store a `ComponentName` representing the plugin.

The actual binding of the services is done in the following `bindPlugins()` method, which we call from the `onStart()` method to make sure the binding occurs at the appropriate time in activity's lifecycle:

```
private void bindPluginServices() {
    for (ComponentName plugin : plugins) {
        Intent intent = new Intent();
        intent.setComponent(plugin);
        PluginServiceConnection conn =
            new PluginServiceConnection();
        pluginServiceConnections.add(conn);
        bindService(intent, conn, Context.BIND_AUTO_CREATE);
    }
}
```

For each plugin found, we create an `Intent` using the `ComponentName` we created earlier. Each service binding will need a `ServiceConnection` object. For that, we created `PluginServiceConnection`, which implements the interface. Its methods are empty, so we'll not look at that class here. With our `ServiceConnection` instance, we can now bind the service with a call to `bindService()`.

Finally, to clean up as the application is closing, we need to unbind our services. From `onStop()`, we call this method:

```
private void releasePluginServices() {
    for (PluginServiceConnection conn :
            pluginServiceConnections) {
        unbindService(conn);
    }
    pluginServiceConnections.clear();
}
```

Here, we simply loop through our `ServiceConnection` plugins, passing each to `unbindService()`, which will allow Android to garbage collect any services we may have started.

So far, we've defined a service, looked it up, and bound it. But how do we interact with it? We'll go the simple route, and add an option menu item. To do that, we modify `res/menu/main_menu.xml` as follows:

```xml
<menu xmlns:android="http://schemas.android.com/apk/res/android"
  xmlns:app="http://schemas.android.com/apk/res-auto"
  xmlns:tools="http://schemas.android.com/tools">
  <item android:id="@+id/action_settings"
    android:orderInCategory="100"
    android:
    app:showAsAction="never" />
 <item android:id="@+id/action_refresh"
    android:orderInCategory="100"
    android:
    app:showAsAction="never" />
</menu>
```

To respond to the menu item being selected, we need to revisit `onOptionsItemSelected()` here:

```java
@Override
public boolean onOptionsItemSelected(MenuItem item) {
  switch (item.getItemId()) {
    case R.id.action_settings:
        showPreferencesActivity();
        return true;
    case R.id.action_refresh:
        sendRefreshMessage();
        break;
  }

  return super.onOptionsItemSelected(item);
}
```

In the `switch` block of the preceding code, we add a `case` label for `R.id.action_refresh`, which matches the ID of our newly added menu item in which we call the method `sendRefreshMessage()`:

```java
private void sendRefreshMessage() {
  sendMessage("REFRESH");
}

private void sendMessage(String message) {
  Intent intent = new Intent("sunago.service");
  intent.putExtra("message", message);
  sendBroadcast(intent);
}
```

The first method is pretty straightforward. In fact, it might not even be necessary, given its simplicity, but it does add semantic clarity to the consuming code, so I think it's a good method to add.

The interesting part, however, is the method `sendMessage()`. We start by creating an `Intent` that specifies our action, `sunago.service`. This is an arbitrary string that we define, and then document for any third-party consumers. This will help our services filter out messages that are of no interest, which is exactly what we did in `TwitterService.onBind()` with the call to `registerReceiver(receiver, new IntentFilter("sunago.service"))`. We then add the message that our app wants to send (`REFRESH`, in this case) as an extra on `Intent`, which we then broadcast via `sendBroadcast()`. From here, Android will handle delivering the message to our service, which is already running (since we've bound it to our `Activity`) and listening (as we registered a `BroadcastReceiver`).

Android tabs and fragments

We've looked at quite a bit, but there is still a fair bit we haven't seen, such as the implementation for `TwitterClient`, as well as any details on the integration of networks, such as Instagram, which we saw in the last chapter. For the most part, `TwitterClient` is identical to what we saw in Chapter 21, *Sunago - A Social Media Aggregator*. The only major difference is in the use of the stream APIs. Some APIs are only available in certain Android versions, specifically, version 24, also known as Nougat. Since we're targeting Lollipop (SDK version 21), we are unable to use them. That aside, the internal logic and API usage are identical. You can see the details in the source repository. Before we finish, though, we need to take a look at the Twitter preferences screen, as there are some interesting items there.

We'll start with a tab layout activity, as follows:

```
public class PreferencesActivity extends AppCompatActivity {
  private SectionsPagerAdapter sectionsPagerAdapter;
  private ViewPager viewPager;

  @Override
  protected void onCreate(Bundle savedInstanceState) {
    super.onCreate(savedInstanceState);
    setContentView(R.layout.activity_preferences);

    setSupportActionBar((Toolbar) findViewById(R.id.toolbar));
    sectionsPagerAdapter =
    new SectionsPagerAdapter(getSupportFragmentManager());
```

```
viewPager = (ViewPager) findViewById(R.id.container);
viewPager.setAdapter(sectionsPagerAdapter);

TabLayout tabLayout = (TabLayout) findViewById(R.id.tabs);
tabLayout.setupWithViewPager(viewPager);
}
```

For making a tabbed interface, we need two things--`FragmentPagerAdapter` and `ViewPager`. The `ViewPager` is a user-interface element that actually shows the tabs. Think of it as `ListView` for tabs. The `FragmentPagerAdapter`, then, is like `CursorAdapter` for the tabs. Instead of an SQL-backed data source, though, `FragmentPagerAdapter` is an adapter that represents pages as Fragments. In this method, we create an instance of our `SectionsPagerAdapter`, and set it as the adapter on our `ViewPager`. We also associate the `ViewPager` element with the `TabLayout`.

`SectionsPagerAdapter` is a simple class, and is written as follows:

```
public class SectionsPagerAdapter extends FragmentPagerAdapter {
  public SectionsPagerAdapter(FragmentManager fm) {
  super(fm);
}

@Override
public Fragment getItem(int position) {
    switch (position) {
        case 0 :
            return new TwitterPreferencesFragment();
        case 1 :
            return new InstagramPreferencesFragment();
        default:
            throw new RuntimeException("Invalid position");
    }
}

@Override
public int getCount() {
    return 2;
}

@Override
public CharSequence getPageTitle(int position) {
    switch (position) {
        case 0:
            return "Twitter";
        case 1:
            return "Instagram";
```

```
    }
     return null;
  }
 }
```

The method `getCount()` tells the system how many tabs we support, the title for each tab that is returned by `getPageTitle()`, and the `Fragment` representing the selected tab is returned from `getItem()`. In this example, we create a `Fragment` instance as needed. Note, we hint at Instagram support here, but its implementation looks strikingly similar to the Twitter implementation, so we won't go into detail on that here.

`TwitterPreferencesFragment` looks as follows:

```
public class TwitterPreferencesFragment extends Fragment {
  @Override
   public View onCreateView(LayoutInflater inflater,
   ViewGroup container, Bundle savedInstanceState) {
   return inflater.inflate(
    R.layout.fragment_twitter_preferences,
    container, false);
 }

 @Override
 public void onStart() {
   super.onStart();
   updateUI();
 }
```

Fragments have a slightly different lifecycle than an `Activity`. Here, we inflate the view in `onCreateView()`, then we update the user interface with the current state from `onStart()`. What does the view look like? That's determined by `R.layout.fragment_twitter_preferences`.

```
<LinearLayout
  xmlns:android="http://schemas.android.com/apk/res/android"
  xmlns:tools="http://schemas.android.com/tools"
  android:layout_width="match_parent"
  android:layout_height="match_parent"
  android:paddingBottom="@dimen/activity_vertical_margin"
  android:paddingLeft="@dimen/activity_horizontal_margin"
  android:paddingRight="@dimen/activity_horizontal_margin"
  android:paddingTop="@dimen/activity_vertical_margin"
  android:orientation="vertical">

 <Button
   android:text="Login"
```

```
    android:layout_width="wrap_content"
    android:layout_height="wrap_content"
    android:id="@+id/connectButton" />

<LinearLayout
  android:orientation="vertical"
  android:layout_width="match_parent"
  android:layout_height="match_parent"
  android:id="@+id/twitterPrefsLayout">

<CheckBox
  android:text="Include the home timeline"
  android:layout_width="match_parent"
  android:layout_height="wrap_content"
  android:id="@+id/showHomeTimeline" />

<TextView
  android:text="User lists to include"
  android:layout_width="match_parent"
  android:layout_height="wrap_content"
  android:id="@+id/textView2" />

<ListView
  android:layout_width="match_parent"
  android:layout_height="match_parent"
  android:id="@+id/userListsListView" />
</LinearLayout>
</LinearLayout>
```

In a nutshell, as you can see in the preceding code, we have a button for logging in and out, and a `ListView` for allowing the user to select which Twitter lists from which to load data.

Given the frequent use of the network for interacting with Twitter plus Android's aversion to network access on the user interface thread, the code here gets a little complicated. We can see the start of that in `updateUI()`, as follows:

```
private void updateUI() {
  getActivity().runOnUiThread(new Runnable() {
    @Override
    public void run() {
      final Button button = (Button)
      getView().findViewById(R.id.connectButton);
      final View prefsLayout =
      getView().findViewById(R.id.twitterPrefsLayout);
      if (!SunagoUtil.getPreferences().getBoolean(
      getString(R.string.twitter_authd), false)) {
        prefsLayout.setVisibility(View.GONE);
```

```
button.setOnClickListener(
  new View.OnClickListener() {
@Override
public void onClick(View view) {
 new TwitterAuthenticateTask().execute();
}
});
} else {
  button.setText(getString(R.string.logout));
  button.setOnClickListener(
  new View.OnClickListener() {
    @Override
    public void onClick(View view) {
      final SharedPreferences.Editor editor =
      SunagoUtil.getPreferences().edit();
      editor.remove(getString(
      R.string.twitter_oauth_token));
      editor.remove(getString(
      R.string.twitter_oauth_secret));
      editor.putBoolean(getString(
      R.string.twitter_authd), false);
      editor.commit();
      button.setText(getString(R.string.login));
      button.setOnClickListener(
      new LoginClickListener());
    }
  });

  prefsLayout.setVisibility(View.VISIBLE);
  populateUserList();
}
}
});
}
```

The first thing that should stand out in the last code is that first line. Since we're updating the user interface, we have to make sure this code runs on the user interface thread. To make that happen, we wrap our logic in a Runnable, and pass that to the method runOnUiThread(). In Runnable, we check to see if the user is logged in or not. If not, we set the prefsLayout section's visibility to GONE, set the Button's text to Login, and set its onClick listener to a View.OnClickListener method that executes TwitterAuthenticateTask.

If the user is not logged in, we do the opposite--make `prefsLayout` visible, set the `Button` text to Logout, set the `onClick` to an anonymous `View.OnClickListener` class that removes the authentication-related preferences, and recursively call `updateUI()` to make sure the interface is updated to reflect the logout.

`TwitterAuthenticateTask` is another `AsyncTask` that handles authenticating with Twitter. To authenticate, we have to get a Twitter request token, which requires network access, so this must be done off of the user interface thread, thus, `AsyncTask`. Please refer to the following code snippet:

```
private class TwitterAuthenticateTask extends
    AsyncTask<String, String, RequestToken> {
  @Override
  protected void onPostExecute(RequestToken requestToken) {
    super.onPostExecute(requestToken);

    Intent intent = new Intent(getContext(),
      WebLoginActivity.class);
    intent.putExtra("url",
      requestToken.getAuthenticationURL());
    intent.putExtra("queryParam", "oauth_verifier");
    startActivityForResult(intent, LOGIN_REQUEST);
  }

  @Override
  protected RequestToken doInBackground(String... strings) {
    try {
      return TwitterClient.instance().getRequestToken();
    } catch (TwitterException e) {
      throw new RuntimeException(e);
    }
  }
}
```

Once we have the `RequestToken`, we show the `WebLoginActivity` from which the user will enter the credentials for the service. We'll look at that in the next code.

When that activity returns, we need to check the results and respond appropriately.

```
public void onActivityResult(int requestCode, int resultCode,
Intent data) {
  super.onActivityResult(requestCode, resultCode, data);
  if (requestCode == LOGIN_REQUEST) {
    if (resultCode == Activity.RESULT_OK) {
      new TwitterLoginAsyncTask()
        .execute(data.getStringExtra("oauth_verifier"));
```

```
        }
      }
    }
```

When we started `WebLoginActivity`, we specified that we wanted to get a result, and we specified an identifier, `LOGIN_REQUEST`, which is set to 1, to uniquely identify which `Activity` was returning the result. If `requestCode` is `LOGIN_REQUEST`, and the result code is `Activity.RESULT_OK` (see `WebLoginActivity` given next), then we have a successful response, and we need to finish the login process, for which we'll use another `AsyncTask`.

```
private class TwitterLoginAsyncTask
extends AsyncTask<String, String, AccessToken> {
  @Override
  protected AccessToken doInBackground(String... codes) {
    AccessToken accessToken = null;
    if (codes != null && codes.length > 0) {
        String code = codes[0];
        TwitterClient twitterClient =
          TwitterClient.instance();
        try {
          accessToken = twitterClient.getAcccessToken(
            twitterClient.getRequestToken(), code);
        } catch (TwitterException e) {
          e.printStackTrace();
        }
        twitterClient.authenticateUser(accessToken.getToken(),
          accessToken.getTokenSecret());
    }

   return accessToken;
  }

  @Override
  protected void onPostExecute(AccessToken accessToken) {
    if (accessToken != null) {
      SharedPreferences.Editor preferences =
        SunagoUtil.getPreferences().edit();
      preferences.putString(getString(
          R.string.twitter_oauth_token),
        accessToken.getToken());
      preferences.putString(getString(
          R.string.twitter_oauth_secret),
        accessToken.getTokenSecret());
      preferences.putBoolean(getString(
          R.string.twitter_authd), true);
      preferences.commit();
    updateUI();
```

```
      }
    }
  }
```

In `doInBackground()`, we perform the network operation. When we have a result, the `AccessToken`, we use that to authenticate our `TwitterClient` instance, then we return the token. In `onPostExecute()`, we save the `AccessToken` details to `SharedPreferences`. Technically, all of this could have been done in `doInBackground()`, but I find it helpful, especially when learning something new, not to cut corners. Once you're comfortable with how all of this works, you are, of course, free to cut corners when and where you feel comfortable doing so.

We have one last piece to look over, `WebLoginActivity`. Functionally, it is identical to `LoginActivity`--it presents a web view which displays the login page for the given network. When the login succeeds, the needed information is returned to the calling code. This being Android rather than JavaFX, the mechanics are, of course, a little different.

```java
public class WebLoginActivity extends AppCompatActivity {
  @Override
  protected void onCreate(Bundle savedInstanceState) {
    super.onCreate(savedInstanceState);
    setContentView(R.layout.activity_web_view);
    setTitle("Login");
    Toolbar toolbar = (Toolbar) findViewById(R.id.toolbar);
    setSupportActionBar(toolbar);
    Intent intent = getIntent();
    final String url = intent.getStringExtra("url");
    final String queryParam =
        intent.getStringExtra("queryParam");
    WebView webView = (WebView)findViewById(R.id.webView);
    final WebViewClient client =
        new LoginWebViewClient(queryParam);
    webView.setWebViewClient(client);
    webView.loadUrl(url);
  }
```

Most of this preceding code looks very much like the other `Activity` classes we've written. We do some basic user interface set up, then, getting a reference to the `Intent`, we extract the two parameters of interest--the URL of the login page, and the query parameter that indicates a successful login.

To participate in the page loading life cycle, we extend `WebViewClient` (which we then attach to `WebView` in `Activity`, as seen previously). This is done as follows:

```
private class LoginWebViewClient extends WebViewClient {
  private String queryParam;

  public LoginWebViewClient(String queryParam) {
    this.queryParam = queryParam;
  }

  @Override
  public void onPageStarted(WebView view, String url,
        Bitmap favicon) {
    final Uri uri = Uri.parse(url);
    final String value = uri.getQueryParameter(queryParam);
    if (value != null) {
        Intent resultIntent = new Intent();
        for (String name : uri.getQueryParameterNames()) {
            resultIntent.putExtra(name,
                uri.getQueryParameter(name));
        }
        setResult(Activity.RESULT_OK, resultIntent);
        finish();
    }
    super.onPageStarted(view, url, favicon);
  }
}
```

While `WebViewClient` offers a myriad of life cycle events, we're only concerned with one right now, `onPageStarted()`, which is fired, as expected, when the page starts to load. By hooking in here, we can look at the URL before the related network activity begins. We can examine the desired URL to see if the query parameter of interest is present. If it is, we create a new `Intent` to pass data back to the caller, copy all of the query parameters to it, set the `Activity` result to `RESULT_OK`, and finish the `Activity`. If you look back at `onActivityResult()`, you should see now from where `resultCode` comes.

Summary

With that, our application is complete. It's not a perfect application, but it is a complete Android application, which demonstrates a number of features you might need in your own app including `Activities`, services, database creation, content providers, messaging, and asynchronous processing. Clearly, there are parts of the application where the error handling could be more robust, or the design generalized a bit more to be more readily reusable. Doing so in this context, however, would obscure the basics of the application too much. Making these changes, then, will make a great exercise for the reader.

In the next chapter, we'll take a look at a completely different type of application. We'll build a small utility to handle what can be a serious problem--too much email. This application will allow us to describe a set of rules that will delete or move emails. It's a simple concept, but it will allow us to work with JSON APIs and the `JavaMail` package. You'll learn a bit and end up with a useful little utility as well.

23
Email and Spam Management with MailFilter

In computer science, we have a number of **laws**, the most famous of which is, perhaps, Moore's Law, which addresses the rate at which the computer processing power increases. Another law, although not as well known, and certainly not as serious, is one known as **Zawinski's Law**. Jamie Zawinski, best known for his role at Netscape and Mozilla, once noted that "Every program attempts to expand until it can read mail. Those programs which cannot so expand are replaced by ones which can." While Zawinski's Law hasn't been quite as accurate as Moore's Law, there does seem to be a ring of truth to it, doesn't there?

In the spirit of Zawinski's Law, even if not quite the letter, we will turn our attention to email in this chapter and see if we can address something that plagues us all: email clutter. Ranging from spam to mailing list postings, those messages just keep coming, and they keep piling up.

I have several email accounts. As the head--and head geek--of my household, I'm often tasked with managing, whether they realize it or not, our digital assets, and while one little piece of spam might seem like nothing, over time, it can become a real problem. At a certain point, it almost seems too daunting to handle.

In this chapter, we'll take this very real, if perhaps somewhat overstated problem, and try to address it. That will give us the perfect excuse to use the standard Java email API, appropriately called JavaMail.

In this chapter, we'll cover the following topics:

- The JavaMail API
- Email protocols

- Some more JavaFX work (of course)
- Creating job schedules in Java with Quartz
- Installing OS-specific services written in Java

It may be that you have your email inboxes well under control, in which case, congratulations! However, despite how tidy or overwhelming your mail client may be, we should have fun in this chapter while exploring the small but capable JavaMail API and the wonderful world of electronic mail.

Getting started

Before we get too far into the application, let's stop and take a quick look at what is involved in email. For being such a ubiquitous tool, it seems that it's a fairly opaque topic for most people, even the technically minded who might be inclined to read a book such as this. If we're going to work with it, it will be extremely helpful to understand it, even if just a bit. If you are not interested in the details of the protocols themselves, then feel free to skip ahead to the next section.

A brief look at the history of email protocols

Like many great computing concepts, **email--electronic mail**--was first introduced in the 1960s, though it looked much different then. A thorough history of email, while certainly a great technical curiosity, is beyond the scope of our purposes here, but I think it would be helpful to take a look at a few of the email protocols still relevant today, those being SMTP for sending mail, and POP3 and IMAP for (from your email client's perspective) receiving mail. (Technically, the email is received by the server via SMTP as that is the on-the-wire protocol used by **Mail Transfer Agents** (**MTAs**), to transfer mail from one server to another. We non-MTA authors never think of it in those terms, so we need not be overly concerned by that distinction).

We'll start with sending an email, as our focus in this chapter will be more on folder management. **SMTP** (**Simple Mail Transport Protocol**), created in 1982 and last updated in 1998, is the dominant protocol to send an email. Typically, in the days of SSL and TLS-secured connections, clients connected to the SMTP server via port 587. The conversation between the server and a client, often referred to as a dialog, may look like this (as taken from the SMTP RFC at `https://tools.ietf.org/html/rfc5321`):

```
S: 220 foo.com Simple Mail Transfer Service Ready
C: EHLO bar.com
```

```
S: 250-foo.com greets bar.com
S: 250-8BITMIME
S: 250-SIZE
S: 250-DSN
S: 250 HELP
C: MAIL FROM:<Smith@bar.com>
S: 250 OK
C: RCPT TO:<Jones@foo.com>
S: 250 OK
C: RCPT TO:<Green@foo.com>
S: 550 No such user here
C: RCPT TO:<Brown@foo.com>
S: 250 OK
C: DATA
S: 354 Start mail input; end with <CRLF>.<CRLF>
C: Blah blah blah...
C: ...etc. etc. etc.
C: .
S: 250 OK
C: QUIT
S: 221 foo.com Service closing transmission channel
```

In this simple example, the client shakes hands with the server, then says who the email is from and who it's going to. Note that the email addresses are listed twice, but it is only these first instances (MAIL FROM and RCPT TO, the latter of which is repeated for each recipient) that matter. The second set is simply for the formatting and display of the email. That peculiarity noted, the actual email comes after the DATA line, which should be fairly self-explanatory. The lone period on a line marks the end of the message, at which point, the server confirms receipt of the message, and we sign off by saying QUIT. This example looks very simple, and it is, but things get much more complicated when the message has an attachment, such as an image or office document, or if the email is formatted in HTML.

While SMTP is used to send mail, the POP3 protocol is used to retrieve it. POP, or Post Office Protocol, was first introduced in 1984. The bulk of the current standard, POP3, was introduced in 1988 with an update released in 1996. POP3 servers are meant to receive or download mail by a client such as Mozilla Thunderbird. If the server allows, the client can make an unsecured connection on port 110, with secure connections typically being made on port 995.

POP3 at one point was the dominant protocol by which users downloaded their mail. It was quick and efficient, and, for a while, our only option. Folder management was something that had to be done on the client side, as POP3 sees the mailbox as one big store, with no notion of folders (POP4 was intended to add some notion of folders, among other things, but there has not been any progress on the proposed RFC for several years). The POP3 (RC 1939, found at `https://tools.ietf.org/html/rfc1939`) gives this example dialog:

```
S:   <wait for connection on TCP port 110>
C:   <open connection>
S:      +OK POP3 server ready <1896.697170952@dbc.mtview.ca.us>
C:      APOP mrose c4c9334bac560ecc979e58001b3e22fb
S:      +OK mrose's maildrop has 2 messages (320 octets)
C:      STAT
S:      +OK 2 320
C:      LIST
S:      +OK 2 messages (320 octets)
S:      1 120
S:      2 200
S:      .
C:      RETR 1
S:      +OK 120 octets
S:      <the POP3 server sends message 1>
S:      .
C:      DELE 1
S:      +OK message 1 deleted
C:      RETR 2
S:      +OK 200 octets
S:      <the POP3 server sends message 2>
S:      .
C:      DELE 2
S:      +OK message 2 deleted
C:      QUIT
S:      +OK dewey POP3 server signing off (maildrop empty)
C:   <close connection>
S:   <wait for next connection>
```

Note that the client sends a RETR command to retrieve the message, followed by a DELE command to remove it from the server. This seems to be the standard/default configuration for most POP3 clients.

Although, many clients can be configured to leave the mail on the server either for a certain number of days, or forever, possibly deleting the message from the server when it is deleted locally. If you've ever managed your mail this way, you've seen firsthand how this can complicate email management.

For example, back in the days before laptops, imagine you have one desktop computer at the office and one at the house. You'd like to be able to read your email in both locations, so you set up your POP3 client on both machines. You spend your work day reading, deleting, and maybe sorting email. When you get home, those, say, 40 messages you managed at work are now sitting in your inbox, in big bold letters to indicate an unread message. You now have to repeat your email management tasks at home if you have any hope of keeping the two clients in similar states. It was tedious and error prone, and that led us to the creation of IMAP.

IMAP or **Internet Access Message Protocol**, was created in 1986, with one of its design goals being permitting the complete management of a mailbox, folders, and all, by multiple clients. It has seen several revisions over the years, with IMAP 4 revision 1 being the current standard. Clients connect to an IMAP server on port 143 for unsecured connections, and 993 for SSL to TLS-based connections.

IMAP, since it offers much more robust functionality than POP, is a more complicated protocol. From the RFC (`https://tools.ietf.org/html/rfc3501`), we can look at the following sample dialog:

```
S:   * OK IMAP4rev1 Service Ready
C:   a001 login mrc secret
S:   a001 OK LOGIN completed
C:   a002 select inbox
S:   * 18 EXISTS
S:   * FLAGS (Answered Flagged Deleted Seen Draft)
S:   * 2 RECENT
S:   * OK [UNSEEN 17] Message 17 is the first unseen message
S:   * OK [UIDVALIDITY 3857529045] UIDs valid
S:   a002 OK [READ-WRITE] SELECT completed
C:   a003 fetch 12 full
S:   * 12 FETCH (FLAGS (Seen) INTERNALDATE
     "17-Jul-1996 02:44:25 -0700"
   RFC822.SIZE 4286 ENVELOPE ("Wed,
       17 Jul 1996 02:23:25 -0700 (PDT)"
   "IMAP4rev1 WG mtg summary and minutes"
   (("Terry Gray" NIL "gray" "cac.washington.edu"))
   (("Terry Gray" NIL "gray" "cac.washington.edu"))
   (("Terry Gray" NIL "gray" "cac.washington.edu"))
   ((NIL NIL "imap" "cac.washington.edu"))
   ((NIL NIL "minutes" "CNRI.Reston.VA.US")
   ("John Klensin" NIL "KLENSIN" "MIT.EDU")) NIL NIL
   "<B27397-0100000@cac.washington.edu>")
     BODY ("TEXT" "PLAIN" ("CHARSET" "US-ASCII") NIL NIL "7BIT" 3028
     92))
S:    a003 OK FETCH completed
```

```
C:      a004 fetch 12 body[header]
S:      * 12 FETCH (BODY[HEADER] {342}
S:      Date: Wed, 17 Jul 1996 02:23:25 -0700 (PDT)
S:      From: Terry Gray <gray@cac.washington.edu>
S:      Subject: IMAP4rev1 WG mtg summary and minutes
S:      To: imap@cac.washington.edu
S:      cc: minutes@CNRI.Reston.VA.US, John Klensin <KLENSIN@MIT.EDU>
S:      Message-Id: <B27397-0100000@cac.washington.edu>
S:      MIME-Version: 1.0
S:      Content-Type: TEXT/PLAIN; CHARSET=US-ASCII
S:
S:      )
S:      a004 OK FETCH completed
C:      a005 store 12 +flags deleted
S:      * 12 FETCH (FLAGS (Seen Deleted))
S:      a005 OK +FLAGS completed
C:      a006 logout
S:      * BYE IMAP4rev1 server terminating connection
S:      a006 OK LOGOUT completed
```

As you can see, there's much more detail there than in our example POP3 dialog. This should also highlight why we're using an API like JavaMail rather than opening a socket and talking directly to the server ourselves. Speaking of JavaMail, let's turn our attention to this standard API and see what it can do for us.

JavaMail, the Standard Java API for Email

The JavaMail API is a set of abstractions that provide a protocol and platform-independent way of working with email. While it is a required part of **Java Enterprise Edition (Java EE)**, it is an add-on library for Java SE, meaning you'll have to download it separately, which we'll handle via our POM file.

Our primary interest with this chapter's application is message management, but we'll take a bit of time to look at sending email using the API, so you'll have something to work with should you ever find yourself needing to do so.

To start sending mails, we need to get a JavaMail `Session`. To do that, we'll need to set up some properties as follows:

```
Properties props = new Properties();
props.put("mail.smtps.host", "smtp.gmail.com");
props.put("mail.smtps.auth", "true");
props.put("mail.smtps.port", "465");
props.put("mail.smtps.ssl.trust", "*");
```

We'll send email through Gmail's server, and we'll use SMTP over SSL. With this `Properties` instance, we can create our `Session` instance as follows:

```
Session session = Session.getInstance(props,
  new javax.mail.Authenticator() {
  @Override
  protected PasswordAuthentication getPasswordAuthentication() {
    return new PasswordAuthentication(userName, password);
  }
});
```

To log in to the server, we need to specify credentials, which we do via the anonymous `PasswordAuthentication` instance. Once we have our `Session` instance, we need to create a `Transport` as follows:

```
transport = session.getTransport("smtps");
  transport.connect();
```

Note that for the protocol parameter, we specify `smtps`, which tells the JavaMail implementation that we want SMTP over SSL/TLS. We're now ready to build our message using the following block of code:

```
MimeMessage message = new MimeMessage(session);
message.setFrom("jason@steeplesoft.com");
message.setRecipients(Message.RecipientType.TO,
  "jason@steeplesoft.com");
message.setSubject("JavaMail Example");
```

An email message is modeled using the `MimeMessage` class, so we create an instance of that using our `Session` instance. We set the from and to addresses, as well as the subject. To make things more interesting, we'll attach a file using a `MimeBodyPart`, as we see here:

```
MimeBodyPart text = new MimeBodyPart();
text.setText("This is some sample text");

MimeBodyPart attachment = new MimeBodyPart();
attachment.attachFile("src/test/resources/rules.json");

Multipart multipart = new MimeMultipart();
multipart.addBodyPart(text);
multipart.addBodyPart(attachment);
message.setContent(multipart);
```

Our message will have two parts, modeled using `MimeBodyPart`, one is the body of the message, which is simple text, and the other is an attachment. In this case, we're simply attaching a data file from our tests, which we'll see later. Once we've defined the parts, we combine them using `MimeMultipart`, then set it as the content on our message, which we can now using the `transport.sendMessage()` method:

```
transport.sendMessage(message, new Address[] {
  new InternetAddress("jason@steeplesoft.com") });
  if (transport != null) {
    transport.close();
  }
```

Within just a few seconds, you should see the following email show up in your inbox:

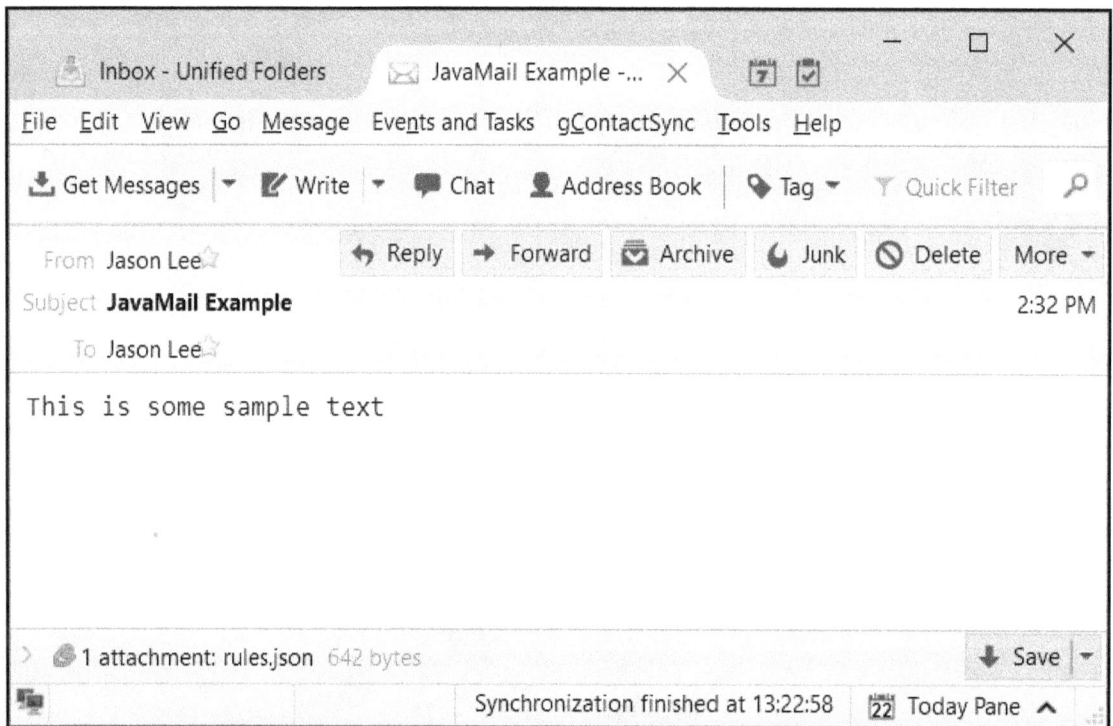

If you want to send an HTML email with a text alternative, you can do this using the following code:

```
MimeBodyPart text = new MimeBodyPart();
text.setContent("This is some sample text", "text/plain");
MimeBodyPart html = new MimeBodyPart();
```

```
html.setContent("<strong>This</strong> is some <em>sample</em>
    <span style="color: red">text</span>", "text/html");
Multipart multipart = new MimeMultipart("alternative");
multipart.addBodyPart(text);
multipart.addBodyPart(html);
message.setContent(multipart);
transport.sendMessage(message, new Address[]{
    new InternetAddress("jason@example.com")});
```

Note that we set the content on each `MimeBodyPart`, specifying the mime type, and when we create the `Multipart`, we pass alternative as the `subtype` parameter. Failure to do so will result in an email that shows both parts, one after the other, which is certainly not what we want. If we've written our application correctly, we should see something like the following in our email client:

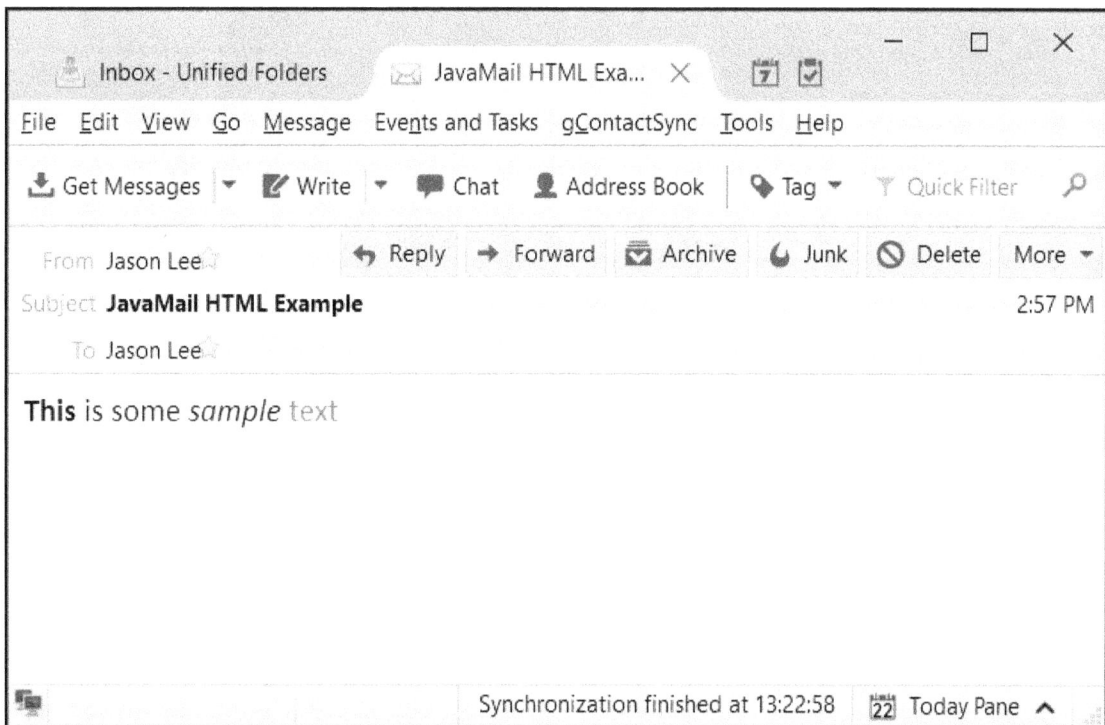

You can't see the red text, of course, in black and white print, but you can see the bold and italicized text, which means the HTML version was shown, rather than the text version. Mission accomplished!

Sending emails is pretty fun, but we're here to learn about folder and message management, so let's turn our attention to that, and we'll start by setting up our project.

Building the CLI

This project, like the others, will be a multi-module Maven project. We'll have one module for all of the core code, and we'll have another for the GUI we'll write to help manage the rules.

To create the project, we'll do something a little different this time. Rather than creating the project using NetBeans, we'll create it from the command line using Maven archetypes, which can be thought of roughly as project templates, so you can see how it's done that way:

```
$ mvn archetype:generate  -DarchetypeGroupId=
  org.codehaus.mojo.archetypes  -DarchetypeArtifactId=pom-root -
  DarchetypeVersion=RELEASE
  ...
Define value for property 'groupId': com.steeplesoft.mailfilter
Define value for property 'artifactId': mailfilter-master
Define value for property 'version':  1.0-SNAPSHOT
Define value for property 'package':  com.steeplesoft.mailfilter
```

Once Maven has finished processing, change directory into the new project's directory, `mailfilter-master`. From here, we can create the first of our projects, the CLI:

```
$ mvn archetype:generate  -DarchetypeGroupId=
  org.apache.maven.archetypes  -DarchetypeArtifactId=
  maven-archetype-quickstart  -DarchetypeVersion=RELEASE
Define value for property 'groupId': com.steeplesoft.mailfilter
Define value for property 'artifactId': mailfilter-cli
Define value for property 'version':  1.0-SNAPSHOT
Define value for property 'package':  com.steeplesoft.mailfilter
```

This will create a new project under `mailfilter-master` called `mailfilter-cli`. We can now open `mailfilter-cli` in NetBeans and get to work.

The first thing we need to do is spec out how we want this tool to work. At a high level, we want to be able to specify an arbitrary number of rules for an account. These rules will allow us to move or delete emails based on certain criteria, such as the sender or the email's age. To keep things simple, we'll scope all of the rules to a specific account, and limit the operations to move and delete.

Let's start by taking a look at what the account may look like:

```
public class Account {
  @NotBlank(message="A value must be specified for serverName")
  private String serverName;
  @NotNull(message = "A value must be specified for serverPort")
  @Min(value = 0L, message = "The value must be positive")
  private Integer serverPort = 0;
  private boolean useSsl = true;
  @NotBlank(message = "A value must be specified for userName")
  private String userName;
  @NotBlank(message = "A value must be specified for password")
  private String password;
  private List<Rule> rules;
```

This is basically a very simple **POJO (Plain Old Java Object)** with six properties: serverName, serverPort, useSsl, userName, password, and rules. What are those annotations, though? Those come from a library called Bean Validation that provides some annotations and supporting code that allows us to express, declaratively, constraints on the values , which the variable can hold. Here are the annotations we're using, and what they mean:

- @NotBlank: This tells the system that the value can't be null, nor can it be an empty string (effectively, string != null && !string.trim() .equals(""))
- @NotNull: This tells the system that the value can't be null
- @Min: This describes a minimum valid value

There are, of course, many, many others, and the system defines a means for you to define your own, so it's a very simple, yet very powerful framework to validate input, which brings up an important point: these constraints are only validated when the Bean Validation framework is asked to do so. We could easily build up a large collection of these Account instances with every field holding invalid data, and the JVM would be perfectly happy with that. The only way to apply the Bean Validation constraints is to ask it to check the instances we provide it with. In a nutshell, it's the API and not the JVM that enforces these constraints. That may seem obvious, but, sometimes, it pays to be explicit.

Before we go any further, we need to add Bean Validation to our project. We'll use the reference implementation: Hibernate Validator. We'll also need the Expression Language API and an implementation in our project. We get all of those by adding the following dependencies to pom.xml:

```
<dependency>
  <groupId>org.hibernate</groupId>
```

```
        <artifactId>hibernate-validator</artifactId>
        <version>5.3.4.Final</version>
    </dependency>
    <dependency>
        <groupId>javax.el</groupId>
        <artifactId>javax.el-api</artifactId>
        <version>2.2.4</version>
    </dependency>
    <dependency>
        <groupId>org.glassfish.web</groupId>
        <artifactId>javax.el</artifactId>
        <version>2.2.4</version>
    </dependency>
```

Getting back to our model, there are some getters and setters, of course, but those are not very interesting. What is interesting, though, is the implementation of `equals()` and `hashCode()`. Josh Bloch, in his seminal work, Effective Java, says this:

> *Always override* `hashCode` *when you override* `equals`.

The main point of his assertion is that failure to do so violates the `equals()` contract, which states that equals objects must have equals hashes, which can result in incorrect and/or unpredictable behavior if your class is used in any hash-based collection, such as `HashMap`. Bloch then lists some rules to create a good `hashCode` implementation, as well as a good `equals` implementation, but here's my advice: let the IDE do the work for you, which is what we've done in the following code block for `equals()`:

```
    public boolean equals(Object obj) {
        if (this == obj) {
            return true;
        }
        if (obj == null) {
            return false;
        }
        if (getClass() != obj.getClass()) {
            return false;
        }
        final Account other = (Account) obj;
        if (this.useSsl != other.useSsl) {
            return false;
        }
        if (!Objects.equals(this.serverName, other.serverName)) {
            return false;
        }
        if (!Objects.equals(this.userName, other.userName)) {
            return false;
```

```
      }
      if (!Objects.equals(this.password, other.password)) {
        return false;
      }
      if (!Objects.equals(this.serverPort, other.serverPort)) {
        return false;
      }
      if (!Objects.equals(this.rules, other.rules)) {
          return false;
      }
      return true;
    }
```

We have done the same for `hashCode()` here:

```
    public int hashCode() {
      int hash = 5;
      hash = 59 * hash + Objects.hashCode(this.serverName);
      hash = 59 * hash + Objects.hashCode(this.serverPort);
      hash = 59 * hash + (this.useSsl ? 1 : 0);
      hash = 59 * hash + Objects.hashCode(this.userName);
      hash = 59 * hash + Objects.hashCode(this.password);
      hash = 59 * hash + Objects.hashCode(this.rules);
      return hash;
    }
```

Note that every method tested in `equals()` is also used in `hashCode()`. It's absolutely vital that your implementations follow this rule, or you'll end up with methods that don't really work as they should. It's possible that your IDE can help with this as you are generating the methods, but you must make sure that you are indeed using the same list of fields, and certainly, should you ever modify one of the methods, the other method must be updated accordingly.

We now have `Account`, so what does `Rule` look like? Let's take a look at the following piece of code:

```
    @ValidRule
    public class Rule {
      @NotNull
      private RuleType type = RuleType.MOVE;
      @NotBlank(message = "Rules must specify a source folder.")
      private String sourceFolder = "INBOX";
      private String destFolder;
      private Set<String> fields = new HashSet<>();
      private String matchingText;
      @Min(value = 1L, message = "The age must be greater than 0.")
      private Integer olderThan;
```

The validation on this class is two-fold. First, we can see the same field-level constraints we saw on `Account`: `type` cannot be null, `sourceFolder` cannot be blank, and `olderThan` must be at least 1. While you may not recognize it for what it is, we also have a class-level constraint in `@ValidRule`.

Field-level constraints can see only the field to which they have been applied. This means that if the valid values for a field are dependent on the value of some other field, these types of constraints are not appropriate. Class-level rules, though, allow us to look at the whole object when doing validation, so we can look to see what the value of one field is when validating another. This also means a bit more code for us, so we'll start with the following annotation:

```
@Target({ElementType.TYPE, ElementType.ANNOTATION_TYPE})
@Retention(RetentionPolicy.RUNTIME)
@Constraint(validatedBy = ValidRuleValidator.class)
@Documented
public @interface ValidRule {
  String message() default "Validation errors";
  Class<?>[] groups() default {};
  Class<? extends Payload>[] payload() default {};
}
```

In case you've never seen the source for an annotation before, this is a fairly typical example. Rather than declaring the type of the object to be `class` or `interface`, we used `@interface`, a subtle but important difference. The fields of the annotation are also a bit different, as there are no visibility modifiers, and the types cannot be primitives. Note the use of the `default` keyword.

The annotation itself also has annotations, which are as follows:

- `@Target`: This restricts the types of elements this annotation can be applied to; in this case, types and other annotations.
- `@Retention`: This instructs the compiler whether or not it should write the annotation to the class file, and making it available at runtime.
- `@Constraint`: This is a Bean Validation annotation that identifies our annotation as a new constraint type. The value of this annotation tells the system what `ConstraintValidator` processes the validation logic for this constraint.
- `@Documented`: This indicates that the presence of this annotation on any type should be considered a part of that type's public API.

Our `ConstraintValidator` implementation to handle this new constraint is a bit more complicated. We declared the class like this:

```
public class ValidRuleValidator implements
    ConstraintValidator<ValidRule, Object> {
```

Bean Validation provides a parameterized interface for constraint validation that takes the type of the constraint and the object type to which the logic in the validator applies. This allows you to write different validators of a given constraint for different object types. In our case, we could specify `Rule` rather than `Object`. If we were to do that, any time something other than `Rule` is annotated with `@ValidRule` and the instance is validated, the calling code will see an exception thrown. What we've done instead, as you will see, is validate the annotated type, specifically adding a constraint violation if needed.

The interface requires that we implement this method as well, but we have no work to be done here, so it has an empty method body, as shown here:

```
@Override
public void initialize(ValidRule constraintAnnotation) {
}
```

The interesting method is called `isValid()`. It's a bit long, so let's step through it piece by piece:

```
public boolean isValid(Object value,
    ConstraintValidatorContext ctx) {
      if (value == null) {
        return true;
      }
```

The first step is to make sure `value` is not null. We have two choices: return `true` if it's null, indicating there's no problem, or return `false`, indicating that there is a problem. Our choice depends on how we want the application to behave. Reasonable arguments can be made for either approach, but it seems that it would make sense for a null `Rule` to be considered invalid, so let's change the body of that for it to look like this:

```
ctx.disableDefaultConstraintViolation();
ctx.buildConstraintViolationWithTemplate(
  "Null values are not considered valid Rules")
  .addConstraintViolation();
return false;
```

We build `ConstraintViolation` using the specified message, add that to `ConstraintValidatorContext`, `ctx`, and return false to indicate a failure.

Next, we want to make sure we're dealing with an instance of `Rule`:

```
if (!(value instanceof Rule)) {
  ctx.disableDefaultConstraintViolation();
  ctx.buildConstraintViolationWithTemplate(
    "Constraint valid only on instances of Rule.")
  .addConstraintViolation();
  return false;
}
```

Once we're sure we have a non-null instance of `Rule`, we can get to the heart of our validation logic:

```
boolean valid = true;
Rule rule = (Rule) value;
if (rule.getType() == RuleType.MOVE) {
  valid &= validateNotBlank(ctx, rule, rule.getDestFolder(),
  "A destination folder must be specified.");
}
```

We'd like to be able to gather all of the violations, so we create a `boolean` variable to hold the current state, then we cast the value as `Rule` to make dealing with the instance a bit more natural. In our first test, we make sure that, if the type of `Rule` is `RuleType. MOVE`, it has a destination folder specified. We do so using this private method:

```
private boolean validateNotBlank(ConstraintValidatorContext ctx,
  String value, String message) {
  if (isBlank(value)) {
    ctx.disableDefaultConstraintViolation();
    ctx.buildConstraintViolationWithTemplate(message)
    .addConstraintViolation();
    return false;
  }
  return true;
}
```

If `value` is blank, we add `ConstraintViolation`, as we've already seen, using the specified message, and return `false`. If it is not blank, we return `true`. This value is then ANDed with `valid` to update the current state of the `Rule` validation.

The `isBlank()` method is very simple:

```
private boolean isBlank(String value) {
  return (value == null || (value.trim().isEmpty()));
}
```

This is a very common check, and is actually logically identical to the validator behind Bean Validation's `@NotBlank`.

Our next two tests are related. The logic is this: the rule must specify either text to match, or a maximum age in days. The test for that looks like this:

```
if (!isBlank(rule.getMatchingText())) {
  valid &= validateFields(ctx, rule);
} else if (rule.getOlderThan() == null) {
  ctx.disableDefaultConstraintViolation();
  ctx.buildConstraintViolationWithTemplate(
    "Either matchingText or olderThan must be specified.")
  .addConstraintViolation();
  valid = false;
}
```

If `Rule` specifies `matchingText`, then we validate that `fields` has been set properly. If neither `matchingText` nor `olderThan` were set, then we add `ConstraintViolation` with a message to that effect and set `valid` to false. Our `fields` validation looks like this:

```
  private boolean validateFields(ConstraintValidatorContext ctx, Rule
rule) {
    if (rule.getFields() == null || rule.getFields().isEmpty()) {
      ctx.disableDefaultConstraintViolation();
      ctx.buildConstraintViolationWithTemplate(
        "Rules which specify a matching text must specify the field(s)
          to match on.")
        .addConstraintViolation();
      return false;
    }
    return true;
  }
```

We make sure that `fields` is neither null nor empty. We do not do any validation here on the actual contents of the field `Set`, though we certainly could.

We have now written, possibly, our very first custom validation. Your reaction is likely something like, "Wow! That's a lot of code for a 'simple' validation", and you're right. Before you throw the baby out with the bath water, think about this: the value of Bean Validation is that you can take potentially complex validation logic and hide it behind a very small annotation. You can then reuse this logic wherever you want simply by placing your constraint annotation in the appropriate places. The logic is expressed in one place, maintained in one place, but used in many, all very neatly and concisely.

So, yes, that's a good deal of code, but you only have to write it once, and the consumers of the constraints never need to see it. There's not really much extra work over and above what you'd normally write, but it's up to you to decide if this extra bit of work is worth the time.

Now that we've taken a quick look at custom Bean Validation constraints, let's return to our data model. The final piece to show is the `RuleType` enum:

```
public enum RuleType {
  DELETE, MOVE;
  public static RuleType getRuleType(String type) {
    switch(type.toLowerCase()) {
      case "delete" : return DELETE;
      case "move" : return MOVE;
      default : throw new IllegalArgumentException(
        "Invalid rule type specified: " + type);
    }
  }
}
```

This is a basic Java `enum` with two possible values, `DELETE` and `MOVE`, but we've also added a helper method to return the appropriate `RuleType` instance for a given String representation. This will help us when we're unmarshaling a `Rule` from JSON, for example.

With our data model defined, we're ready to start writing the code for the utility itself. While the Maven module is called `mailfilter-cli`, we will not concern ourselves here with a robust command-line interface, like we saw in previous chapters. Instead, we'll provide a very basic interaction with the command line, leaving an OS service, which we'll look at later, as the preferred means of usage.

It is at this point that we will begin using the JavaMail API, so we need to make sure we have our project set up correctly, so we add the following lines of code to `pom.xml`:

```
<dependency>
  <groupId>com.sun.mail</groupId>
  <artifactId>javax.mail</artifactId>
  <version>1.5.6</version>
</dependency>
```

In our IDE, we create a new class, `MailFilter`, and create the familiar `public static void main` method as follows:

```
public static void main(String... args) {
  try {
    final MailFilter mailFilter =
```

```
      new MailFilter(args.length > 0 ? args[1] : null);
    mailFilter.run();
    System.out.println("tDeleted count: "
      + mailFilter.getDeleted());
    System.out.println("tMove count:    "
      + mailFilter.getMoved());
  } catch (Exception e) {
    System.err.println(e.getLocalizedMessage());
  }
}
```

> **TIP**
>
> NetBeans supports a number of code templates. The template of interest here is psvm, which will create a public static void main method. To use it, make sure you are on an empty line inside the class definition (to avoid odd formatting issues), then type psvm and press tab. NetBeans creates the method for you and places the cursor on the first line of the empty method, ready for you to start coding. You can find dozens of other helpful code templates by navigating to **Tools | Options | Editor | Code Templates**. You can even define your own.

In our main() method, we create an instance of MainFilter, passing in any rule definition file that may have been specified on the command line, and calling run():

```
public void run() {
  try {
    AccountService service = new AccountService(fileName);

    for (Account account : service.getAccounts()) {
      AccountProcessor processor =
        new AccountProcessor(account);
      processor.process();
      deleted += processor.getDeleteCount();
      moved += processor.getMoveCount();
    }
  } catch (MessagingException ex) {
    Logger.getLogger(MailFilter.class.getName())
    .log(Level.SEVERE, null, ex);
  }
}
```

We start by creating an instance of AccountService, which wraps up the details of reading and writing the Rules file. For each account in the specified file, we create AccountProcessor, which encapsulates the rule processing logic.

The `AccountService` instance may not sound very exciting, but there are some pretty interesting technical bits hidden away behind that public interface. We see where the Bean Validation constraints are actually checked, and we also see the use of the Jackson JSON library to read and write the `Rules` file. Before we can start using Jackson, we need to add it to our project, which we do by adding this `pom.xml`:

```xml
<dependency>
  <groupId>com.fasterxml.jackson.core</groupId>
  <artifactId>jackson-databind</artifactId>
  <version>2.8.5</version>
</dependency>
```

You should, as always, make sure that you are on the latest version of the library.

This is not a big class to start with, but only three methods are of any interest here. We'll start with the most basic one, which is as follows:

```java
private File getRulesFile(final String fileName) {
    final File file = new File(fileName != null ? fileName
      : System.getProperty("user.home") + File.separatorChar
      + ".mailfilter" + File.separatorChar + "rules.json");
    if (!file.exists()) {
      throw new IllegalArgumentException(
        "The rules file does not exist: " + rulesFile);
    }
    return file;
}
```

The only reason I include this here is that reading a file from the user's home directory is something I find myself doing fairly frequently, and you might too. This example shows you how to do just that, attempting to find the rule file at `~/.mailfilter/rules.json` if the user does not specify a file explicitly. Generated or specified, if the rule file can't be found, we throw an exception.

Perhaps the most interesting method is the `getAccounts()` method. We'll step through this one slowly:

```java
public List<Account> getAccounts() {
    final Validator validator = Validation
      .buildDefaultValidatorFactory().getValidator();
    final ObjectMapper mapper = new ObjectMapper()
      .configure(DeserializationFeature.
      ACCEPT_SINGLE_VALUE_AS_ARRAY, true);
    List<Account> accounts = null;
```

These three statements are setting up some objects required to process the accounts. The first is `Validator`, which is the Bean Validation class that is our entry point to apply and check the constraints we've described on our data models. The next, `ObjectMapper`, is a Jackson class that will map a JSON data structure onto our Java data model. We need to specify `ACCEPT_SINGLE_VALUE_AS_ARRAY` to make sure that Jackson properly handles any lists in our model. Finally, we create `List` to hold our `Account` instances.

Reading the rules file into memory and getting that as instances of our data model is extremely easy with Jackson:

```
accounts = mapper.readValue(rulesFile,
    new TypeReference<List<Account>>() {});
```

Since the property names in our Java classes match the keys used in our JSON file, `ObjectMapper` can easily read the data from the JSON file and build our in-memory model with just this one line. Note the `TypeReference` instance. We want Jackson to return a `List<Account>` instance, but due to some design decisions in the JVM, direct access to parameterized types at runtime is not possible. The `TypeReference` class, however, helps capture this information, which Jackson then uses in creating the data model. If we passed `List.class`, we would get a type cast failure at runtime.

Now that we have our `Account` instances, we're ready to start validation:

```
accounts.forEach((account) -> {
    final Set<ConstraintViolation<Account>> violations =
        validator.validate(account);
    if (violations.size() > 0) {
        System.out.println(
            "The rule file has validation errors:");
        violations.forEach(a -> System.out.println("   " + a));
        throw new RuntimeException("Rule validation errors");
    }
    account.getRules().sort((o1, o2) ->
        o1.getType().compareTo(o2.getType()));
});
```

Using `List.forEach()`, we iterate over each account in `List` (the null check was not shown here). For each `Account`, we call `validator.validate()`, which is when the constraints are actually validated. Up to this point, they were just annotations stored in the class, with the JVM happily carrying them along, but not doing anything else with them. Bean Validation, as we discussed earlier, is the enforcer of the constraints described by the annotations, and here we see that manual API call.

When the call to the `validator` returns, we need to see if there were any `ConstraintViolations`. If there were, we fairly naively print a message to standard out detailing each of the failures. If the rule has multiple violations, thanks to how we wrote our validator, we'll see them all at once, so the user can fix them without having to attempt to process the rules multiple times. Printing these to the console is not necessarily the best approach, as we can't process them programmatically, but it is sufficient for our needs at the moment.

> **TIP**
>
> Where Bean Validation really shines is in frameworks that integrate it on your behalf. For example, JAX-RS, the standard Java API to build REST resources, offers this type of integration. We see a usage of the functionality in this sample REST resource method:
> ```
> @GET
> public Response getSomething (
> @QueryParam("foo") @NotNull Integer bar) {
> ```
> When a request is routed to this method, JAX-RS ensures that the query parameter `foo` is converted, if possible, to an `Integer`, and that it is not `null`, so in your code, you can assume that you have a valid `Integer` reference.

The final method we want to look at in this class is `saveAccounts()`, which, as crazy as it may sound, saves the `Account` instances to the rules file specified:

```
public void saveAccounts(List<Account> accounts) {
  try {
    final ObjectMapper mapper =
      new ObjectMapper().configure(DeserializationFeature.
      ACCEPT_SINGLE_VALUE_AS_ARRAY, true);
    mapper.writeValue(rulesFile, accounts);
  } catch (IOException ex) {
    // ...
  }
}
```

Much like reading the file, writing to it is extremely simple, so long as your Java classes and your JSON structures match. If you do have differing names (for example, the Java class may have the `accountName` property, while the JSON file uses `account_name`), Jackson offers some annotations that can be applied to the POJO to explain how to map the fields correctly. You can find complete details for those on Jackson's website (`https://github.com/FasterXML/jackson`).

With our `Account` instances loaded into memory and validated for correctness, we now need to process them. The entry point is the `process()` method:

```
public void process() throws MessagingException {
  try {
    getImapSession();

    for (Map.Entry<String, List<Rule>> entry :
      getRulesByFolder(account.getRules()).entrySet()) {
      processFolder(entry.getKey(), entry.getValue());
    }
  } catch (Exception e) {
    throw new RuntimeException(e);
  } finally {
    closeFolders();
    if (store != null) {
      store.close();
    }
  }
}
```

The three lines to pay attention to are the calls to `getImapSession()`, `getRulesByFolder()`, and `processFolder()`, which we'll look at in detail now:

```
private void getImapSession()
  throws MessagingException, NoSuchProviderException {
  Properties props = new Properties();
  props.put("mail.imap.ssl.trust", "*");
  props.put("mail.imaps.ssl.trust", "*");
  props.setProperty("mail.imap.starttls.enable",
    Boolean.toString(account.isUseSsl()));
  Session session = Session.getInstance(props, null);
  store = session.getStore(account.isUseSsl() ?
    "imaps" : "imap");
  store.connect(account.getServerName(), account.getUserName(),
    account.getPassword());
}
```

To get an IMAP `Session`, as we saw earlier in this chapter, we create a `Properties` instance and set a few important properties. We get a `Store` reference using the protocol specified by the user in the rule file: `imap` for non-SSL-based connections and `imaps` for SSL-based connections.

Once we have our session, we then iterate over our rules, grouping them by source folder:

```
private Map<String, List<Rule>> getRulesByFolder(List<Rule> rules) {
  return rules.stream().collect(
    Collectors.groupingBy(r -> r.getSourceFolder(),
    Collectors.toList()));
}
```

We can now process the folder as follows:

```
private void processFolder(String folder, List<Rule> rules)
  throws MessagingException {
  Arrays.stream(getFolder(folder, Folder.READ_WRITE)
    .getMessages()).forEach(message ->
    rules.stream().filter(rule ->
    rule.getSearchTerm().match(message))
    .forEach(rule -> {
      switch (rule.getType()) {
        case MOVE:
          moveMessage(message, getFolder(
            rule.getDestFolder(),
            Folder.READ_WRITE));
        break;
        case DELETE:
          deleteMessage(message);
        break;
      }
  }));
}
```

Using `Stream`, we iterate over each message in the source folder, filtering for only those that match `SearchTerm`, but what is that, and where did it come from?

There are a couple of extra items on the `Rule` class that we haven't looked at yet:

```
private SearchTerm term;
@JsonIgnore
public SearchTerm getSearchTerm() {
  if (term == null) {
    if (matchingText != null) {
      List<SearchTerm> terms = fields.stream()
      .map(f -> createFieldSearchTerm(f))
      .collect(Collectors.toList());
      term = new OrTerm(terms.toArray(new SearchTerm[0]));
    } else if (olderThan != null) {
      LocalDateTime day = LocalDateTime.now()
      .minusDays(olderThan);
      term = new SentDateTerm(ComparisonTerm.LE,
```

```
          Date.from(day.toLocalDate().atStartOfDay()
          .atZone(ZoneId.systemDefault()).toInstant()));
      }
    }
    return term;
  }
```

We add a private field to cache `SearchTerm` so we don't have to create it more than once. It's a minor optimization, but we want to avoid unnecessary performance hits from recreating `SearchTerm` for every message on a large folder. If the rule has a `matchingText` set, we create a `List<SearchTerm>` based on the fields specified. Once we have that list, we wrap it in `OrTerm`, which will instruct JavaMail to match the message if *any* of the specified fields match the text.

If `olderThan` is set, then we create `SentDateTerm` to match any messages that were sent at least `olderThan` days ago. We save the `SearchTerm` reference in our private instance variable then return it.

Notice that the method has the `@JsonIgnore` annotation. We use this to make sure that Jackson doesn't try to marshall the value returned by this getter to the JSON file.

For the curious, `createFieldSearchTerm()` looks like this:

```
    private SearchTerm createFieldSearchTerm(String f) {
      switch (f.toLowerCase()) {
        case "from":
          return new FromStringTerm(matchingText);
        case "cc":
          return new RecipientStringTerm(
            Message.RecipientType.CC, matchingText);
        case "to":
          return new RecipientStringTerm(
            Message.RecipientType.TO, matchingText);
        case "body":
          return new BodyTerm(matchingText);
        case "subject":
          return new SubjectTerm(matchingText);
        default:
            return null;
      }
    }
```

So, how are the messages actually moved or deleted? There is, of course, a JavaMail API for that, whose usage might look something like this:

```
private static final Flags FLAGS_DELETED =
   new Flags(Flags.Flag.DELETED);
private void deleteMessage(Message toDelete) {
  if (toDelete != null) {
    try {
      final Folder source = toDelete.getFolder();
      source.setFlags(new Message[]{toDelete},
        FLAGS_DELETED, true);
      deleteCount++;
    } catch (MessagingException ex) {
      throw new RuntimeException(ex);
    }
  }
}
```

We do a quick null check, then we get a reference to the messages `Folder`. With that, we instruct JavaMail to set a flag, `FLAGS_DELETED`, on the messages in the folder. The JavaMail API more often than not works on arrays of `Message` (`Message[]`), so we need to wrap `Message` in an array as we pass it to `setFlags()`. As we finish up, we increment our deleted message counter so we can print our report when we're finished.

Moving a `Message` is very similar:

```
private void moveMessage(Message toMove, Folder dest) {
  if (toMove != null) {
    try {
      final Folder source = toMove.getFolder();
      final Message[] messages = new Message[]{toMove};
      source.setFlags(messages, FLAGS_DELETED, true);
      source.copyMessages(messages, dest);
      moveCount++;
    } catch (MessagingException ex) {
      throw new RuntimeException(ex);
    }
  }
}
```

The bulk of this method looks just like `deleteMessage()`, but there is a subtle difference. JavaMail doesn't have a `moveMessages()` API. What we have to do instead is call `copyMessages()` to create a copy of the message in the destination folder, then delete the message from the source folder. We increment the moved counter and return.

The final two methods of interest deal with folders. First, we need to get the folder, which we do here:

```
final private Map<String, Folder> folders = new HashMap<>();
private Folder getFolder(String folderName, int mode) {
  Folder source = null;
  try {
    if (folders.containsKey(folderName)) {
      source = folders.get(folderName);
    } else {
      source = store.getFolder(folderName);
      if (source == null || !source.exists()) {
        throw new IllegalArgumentException(
          "Invalid folder: " + folderName);
      }
      folders.put(folderName, source);
    }
    if (!source.isOpen()) {
      source.open(mode);
    }
  } catch (MessagingException ex) {
    //...
  }
  return source;
}
```

For performance reasons, we cache each `Folder` instance in `Map`, keyed by the folder name. If we find `Folder` in `Map`, we use that. If we do not, then we ask the IMAP `Store` for a reference to the desired `Folder`, and cache it in `Map`. Finally, we make sure `Folder` is open, or our move and delete commands will throw `Exception`.

We also need to make sure we close the `Folder` when we're finished:

```
private void closeFolders() {
  folders.values().stream()
  .filter(f -> f.isOpen())
  .forEachOrdered(f -> {
    try {
      f.close(true);
    } catch (MessagingException e) {
    }
  });
}
```

We filter our stream of `Folder` for only those that are open, then call `folder.close()`, swallowing any failure that might occur. At this point in the processing, there's not much that can be done.

Our mail filter is now technically complete, but it's not as usable as it could be. We need some way to run this on a schedule, and being able to view and edit the rules in a GUI would be really nice, so we'll build both of those. Since it doesn't make sense to schedule something if we have nothing to run, we'll start with the GUI.

Building the GUI

Since we want to make this as easy to use as possible, we'll now build a GUI to help manage these rules. To create the project, we'll use the same Maven archetype we used in creating the CLI:

```
$ mvn archetype:generate  -DarchetypeGroupId=org.apache.maven.archetypes  -
DarchetypeArtifactId=maven-archetype-quickstart  -DarchetypeVersion=RELEASE
Define value for property 'groupId': com.steeplesoft.mailfilter
Define value for property 'artifactId': mailfilter-gui
Define value for property 'version':  1.0-SNAPSHOT
Define value for property 'package':  com.steeplesoft.mailfilter.gui
```

Once the POM has been created, we need to edit it a bit. We need to set the parent by adding this element to `pom.xml`:

```
<parent>
  <groupId>com.steeplesoft.j9bp.mailfilter</groupId>
  <artifactId>mailfilter-master</artifactId>
  <version>1.0-SNAPSHOT</version>
</parent>
```

We will also add a dependency on the CLI module as follows:

```
<dependencies>
  <dependency>
    <groupId>${project.groupId}</groupId>
    <artifactId>mailfilter-cli</artifactId>
    <version>${project.version}</version>
  </dependency>
</dependencies>
```

Since we're not depending on NetBeans to generate the JavaFX project for us, we'll also need to create a few basic artifacts by hand. Let's start with the application's entry point:

```
public class MailFilter extends Application {
  @Override
  public void start(Stage stage) throws Exception {
    Parent root = FXMLLoader.load(getClass()
    .getResource("/fxml/mailfilter.fxml"));
    Scene scene = new Scene(root);
    stage.setTitle("MailFilter");
    stage.setScene(scene);
    stage.show();
  }

  public static void main(String[] args) {
    launch(args);
  }
}
```

This is a very typical JavaFX main class, so we'll skip right to the FXML file. For now, we'll just create a stub using the following piece of code:

```
<?xml version="1.0" encoding="UTF-8"?>
<?import java.lang.*?>
<?import java.util.*?>
<?import javafx.scene.*?>
<?import javafx.scene.control.*?>
<?import javafx.scene.layout.*?>

<AnchorPane id="AnchorPane" prefHeight="200" prefWidth="320"
  xmlns:fx="http://javafx.com/fxml"
  fx:controller=
    "com.steeplesoft.mailfilter.gui.Controller">
  <children>
    <Button layoutX="126" layoutY="90" text="Click Me!"
      fx:id="button" />
    <Label layoutX="126" layoutY="120" minHeight="16"
      minWidth="69" fx:id="label" />
  </children>
</AnchorPane>
```

And finally, we create the controller:

```
public class Controller implements Initializable {
  @Override
  public void initialize(URL url, ResourceBundle rb) {
  }
}
```

This gives us a working JavaFX application that starts and runs, but doesn't do much else. In previous chapters, we've walked through building a JavaFX application in painstaking detail, so we won't do that again here, but there are some interesting challenges in this one that are worth taking a look at.

To give you a sense of what we're working toward, here's a screenshot of the final user interface:

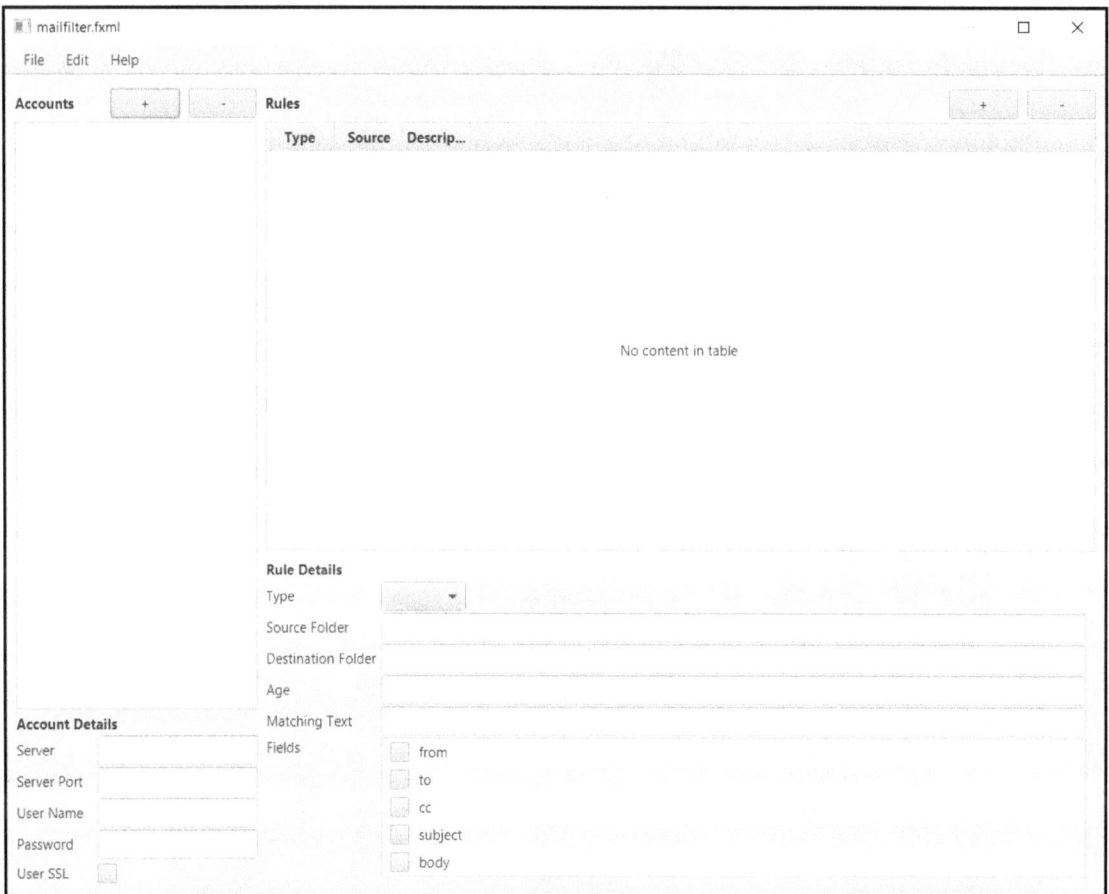

On the left, we have ListView to display the Account configured in our rules file. Below ListView, we have a few controls to edit the currently selected Account. On the right, we have TableView to display the Rule, and a similar area below it for editing a Rule.

When the user clicks on `Account` or `Rule`, we want the form area below to be populated with the relevant information. As the user modifies the data, `Account/Rule` as well as `ListView/TableView` should be updated.

Ordinarily, this is one of the areas in which JavaFX really shines, that of property binding. We've already seen a small part of that with `ObservableList`: we can add an item to `List`, and it is automatically added to the UI component to which it has been bound. The situation we find ourselves in now is a little different though, in that our model is a POJO, one that doesn't use any JavaFX APIs, so we don't get that functionality quite so easily. Let's look at what it will take to wire these things together.

First, let's look at the `Account` list. We have `ObservableList`:

```
private final ObservableList<Account> accounts =
    FXCollections.observableArrayList();
```

We add our accounts to this `ObservableList` as follows:

```
private void configureAccountsListView() {
    accountService = new AccountService();
    accounts.addAll(accountService.getAccounts());
```

Then, we bind `List` and `ListView`, as follows:

```
accountsListView.setItems(accounts);
```

Here is where things change a little bit. To encapsulate our POJO binding setup, we'll create a new class called `AccountProperty`, which we'll look at shortly. Although, let's first add the following code snippet to handle the `ListView` clicks:

```
accountProperty = new AccountProperty();
accountsListView.setOnMouseClicked(e -> {
    final Account account = accountsListView.getSelectionModel()
    .getSelectedItem();
    if (account != null) {
        accountProperty.set(account);
    }
});
```

When the user clicks on `ListView`, we set `Account` on the `AccountProperty` instance. Before we leave this method and look at `AccountProperty`, we need to set up one last item:

```
final ChangeListener<String> accountChangeListener =
  (observable, oldValue, newValue) ->
  accountsListView.refresh();
serverName.textProperty().addListener(accountChangeListener);
userName.textProperty().addListener(accountChangeListener);
```

We define `ChangeListener`, which simply calls `accountsListView.refresh()`, which instructs `ListView` to redraw itself. We'll want it to do this when the model itself is updated, a change that `ObservableList` doesn't bubble up to `ListView`. The next two lines add `Listener` to `serverName` and `userNameTextField`. These two controls edit the properties by the same name on `Account`, and are the only two used to generate the display String for `ListView`, which we don't show here.

`AccountProperty` is a custom JavaFX property, so we extend `ObjectPropertyBase` as follows:

```
private class AccountProperty extends ObjectPropertyBase<Account> {
```

This offers part of the binding solution, but the heavy lifting is handled by a class from the excellent JFXtras project, `BeanPathAdapter`:

```
private final BeanPathAdapter<Account> pathAdapter;
```

> The JFXtras library is not, as of the writing of this book, Java 9 compatible. All we need from the library is this one class, so I have copied the source of class from the JFXtras repository into this project for the time being. Once JFXtras runs under Java 9, we can remove this copy.

The documentation describes this class as an "adapter that takes a POJO bean and internally and recursively binds/unbinds its fields to other `Property` components". This is an extremely powerful class that we can't cover in its entirety here, so we'll just jump to our particular usage, which is as follows:

```
public AccountProperty() {
    pathAdapter = new BeanPathAdapter<>(new Account());
    pathAdapter.bindBidirectional("serverName",
        serverName.textProperty());
    pathAdapter.bindBidirectional("serverPort",
        serverPort.textProperty());
    pathAdapter.bindBidirectional("useSsl",
        useSsl.selectedProperty(), Boolean.class);
```

```
pathAdapter.bindBidirectional("userName",
    userName.textProperty());
pathAdapter.bindBidirectional("password",
    password.textProperty());
addListener((observable, oldValue, newValue) -> {
    rules.setAll(newValue.getRules());
});
}
```

`BeanPathAdapter` allows us to bind a JavaFX `Property` to a property on a POJO, which could be nested to an arbitrary depth and referenced using a dot-separated path notation. In our case, the properties are top-level properties on the `Account` object, so the path is short and simple. After we've bound our controls to the properties, we add a `Listener` to update the `ObservableList` rules with `Rule` for the current account.

The `set()` method that is called in the preceding code when the `Account` selection changes in `ListView` is very straightforward:

```
@Override
public void set(Account newValue) {
    pathAdapter.setBean(newValue);
    super.set(newValue);
}
```

With these pieces in place, the `Account` object is updated as we type in the various controls, and the `ListView` label is updated as the `serverName` and/or `userName` fields are edited.

Now we need to do the same for the `TableView` that will display each `Rule` the user has configured. The setup is almost identical:

```
private void configureRuleFields() {
    ruleProperty = new RuleProperty();
    fields.getCheckModel().getCheckedItems().addListener(
      new RuleFieldChangeListener());
    final ChangeListener<Object> ruleChangeListener =
        (observable, oldValue, newValue) ->
            rulesTableView.refresh();
    sourceFolder.textProperty()
      .addListener(ruleChangeListener);
    destFolder.textProperty().addListener(ruleChangeListener);
    matchingText.textProperty()
        .addListener(ruleChangeListener);
    age.textProperty().addListener(ruleChangeListener);
    type.getSelectionModel().selectedIndexProperty()
        .addListener(ruleChangeListener);
}
```

Here, we see the same basic structure: instantiate `RuleProperty`, create `ChangeListener` to request that `TableView` refresh itself, and add that listener to the relevant form fields.

`RuleProperty` is also similar to `AccountProperty`:

```
private class RuleProperty extends ObjectPropertyBase<Rule> {
  private final BeanPathAdapter<Rule> pathAdapter;

  public RuleProperty() {
    pathAdapter = new BeanPathAdapter<>(new Rule());
    pathAdapter.bindBidirectional("sourceFolder",
      sourceFolder.textProperty());
    pathAdapter.bindBidirectional("destFolder",
      destFolder.textProperty());
    pathAdapter.bindBidirectional("olderThan",
      age.textProperty());
    pathAdapter.bindBidirectional("matchingText",
      matchingText.textProperty());
    pathAdapter.bindBidirectional("type",
      type.valueProperty(), String.class);
    addListener((observable, oldValue, newValue) -> {
      isSelectingNewRule = true;
      type.getSelectionModel().select(type.getItems()
      .indexOf(newValue.getType().name()));

      IndexedCheckModel checkModel = fields.getCheckModel();
      checkModel.clearChecks();
      newValue.getFields().forEach((field) -> {
        checkModel.check(checkModel.getItemIndex(field));
      });
      isSelectingNewRule = false;
    });
  }
```

The biggest difference here is `Listener` that is created. Given the use of `CheckListView`, a custom control from the great ControlsFX project, it's worth noting the logic: we get `IndexedCheckModel`, which we clear, then we iterate over each field, finding its index in `CheckModel` and checking it.

We control updating the value of the fields set on `Rule` via `RuleFieldChangeListener`:

```
private class RuleFieldChangeListener implements ListChangeListener {
  @Override
  public void onChanged(ListChangeListener.Change c) {
    if (!isSelectingNewRule && c.next()) {
      final Rule bean = ruleProperty.getBean();
      bean.getFields().removeAll(c.getRemoved());
```

```
        bean.getFields().addAll(c.getAddedSubList());
      }
    }
  }
```

`ListChangeListener` tells us what was removed and what was added, so we processed those accordingly.

There are several other moving parts to the GUI, but we've seen them in one for another in previous chapters, so we'll not cover them here. If you're curious about these details, you can find them in this book's source code repository. Let's turn our attention to the final part of our project: the OS-specific service.

Building the service

One of the stated goals of this project is to be able to define rules to manage and filter email, and to have it run more or less all the time, not just when the email client is running. (There is, of course, not much we can do about the machine running this being turned off, so we can't promise constant coverage). To fulfill this part of the promise, we'll need a few extra parts. We already have the part of the system that does the actual work, but we also need a way to run that part on a schedule, and we also need a part that will start the scheduled job.

For the scheduling aspect, we have many options, but we'll use a library called Quartz. The Quartz Job Scheduling Library is an open source library that can be used in Java SE as well as Java EE applications. It provides a clean and simple API that is perfect for use here. To add Quartz to our project, we need to do this to `pom.xml`:

```
<dependency>
  <groupId>org.quartz-scheduler</groupId>
  <artifactId>quartz</artifactId>
  <version>2.2.3</version>
</dependency>
```

How simple is the API? Here's our `Job` definition:

```
public class MailFilterJob implements Job {
  @Override
  public void execute(JobExecutionContext jec)
    throws JobExecutionException {
    MailFilter filter = new MailFilter();
    filter.run();
  }
}
```

We extend `org.quartz.Job` overriding `execute()`, in which we simply instantiate `MailFilter` and call `run()`. That's really all there is to it. With our job defined, we just need to schedule it, which we'll do in `MailFilterService`:

```
public class MailFilterService {
  public static void main(String[] args) {
    try {
      final Scheduler scheduler =
        StdSchedulerFactory.getDefaultScheduler();
      scheduler.start();

      final JobDetail job =
        JobBuilder.newJob(MailFilterJob.class).build();
      final Trigger trigger = TriggerBuilder.newTrigger()
      .startNow()
      .withSchedule(
        SimpleScheduleBuilder.simpleSchedule()
        .withIntervalInMinutes(15)
        .repeatForever())
      .build();
      scheduler.scheduleJob(job, trigger);
    } catch (SchedulerException ex) {
      Logger.getLogger(MailFilterService.class.getName())
      .log(Level.SEVERE, null, ex);
    }
  }
}
```

We begin by getting a reference to the default `Scheduler` and starting it. Next, we create a new job using `JobBuilder`, then build `Trigger` using `TriggerBuilder`. We tell `Trigger` to start executing now, but note that it won't start until it is actually built and assigned to `Scheduler`. Once that happens, `Job` will execute immediately. Finally, we define `Schedule` for `Trigger` using the `SimpleScheduleBuilder` helper class, specifying a fifteen minute interval, which will run forever. We want this to run until the computer is shut down or the service is stopped.

If we run/debug `MailFilterService` now, we can watch `MailFilter` run. If you do this, and you're not extremely patient, I would suggest that you lower the interval to something more reasonable.

This leaves us with one final piece: the OS integration. In a nutshell, what we want to be able to do is run `MailFilterService` when the operating system boots up. Ideally, we'd prefer not to have ad hoc scripts cobble together to make this happen. Fortunately, we are again presented with a number of options.

We will be using the excellent Java Service Wrapper library from Tanuki Software (details of which can be found at `https://wrapper.tanukisoftware.com`). While we can manually build the service artifacts, we'd much rather let our build do the work for us, and, of course, there's a Maven plugin, called `appassembler-maven-plugin`, to do just that. To integrate them both into our project, we need to modify the `build` section of our POM by adding the following code snippet:

```
<build>
  <plugins>
    <plugin>
      <groupId>org.codehaus.mojo</groupId>
      <artifactId>appassembler-maven-plugin</artifactId>
      <version>2.0.0</version>
```

The transitive dependencies of this plugin will pull in everything we need for the Java Service Wrapper, so all we need to do is configure our usage .We start by adding an execution, telling Maven to run the `generate-daemons` goal when packaging the project:

```
<executions>
  <execution>
    <id>generate-jsw-scripts</id>
    <phase>package</phase>
    <goals>
      <goal>generate-daemons</goal>
    </goals>
```

Next we need to configure the plugin, which we do with the `configuration` element:

```
<configuration>
  <repositoryLayout>flat</repositoryLayout>
```

The `repositoryLayout` option tells the plugin to build a **lib** style repository, as opposed to the Maven 2 style layout, which is a number of nested directories. This is largely a style concern, at least for our purposes here, but I find it helpful to be able to scan the generated directory and see what is included at a glance.

Next, we need to define the **daemons** (another term for OS service that comes from the Unix world and which stands for **Disk And Execution Monitor**) as follows:

```
<daemons>
  <daemon>
    <id>mailfilter-service</id>
    <wrapperMainClass>
      org.tanukisoftware.wrapper.WrapperSimpleApp
    </wrapperMainClass>
    <mainClass>
```

```
      com.steeplesoft.mailfilter.service.MailFilterService
    </mainClass>
    <commandLineArguments>
      <commandLineArgument>start</commandLineArgument>
    </commandLineArguments>
```

The Java Service Wrapper is a very flexible system, providing a number of ways to wrap your Java project. Our needs are simple, so we instruct it to use `WrapperSimpleApp` and point it to the main class, `MailFilterService`.

The plugin supports a couple of other service wrapper methods, but we're interested in the Java Service Wrapper, so we specify that here, with the `platform` element:

```
    <platforms>
      <platform>jsw</platform>
    </platforms>
```

Finally, we need to configure the generator, telling it which OS to support:

```
    <generatorConfigurations>
      <generatorConfiguration>
        <generator>jsw</generator>
        <includes>
          <include>linux-x86-64</include>
          <include>macosx-universal-64</include>
          <include>windows-x86-64</include>
        </includes>
      </generatorConfiguration>
    </generatorConfigurations>
  </daemon>
</daemons>
```

Each of those OS definitions offers a 32-bit option that you can add if needed, but, for the sake of brevity, I've omitted them here.

When we build the app now, either via `mvn package` or `mvn install`, this plugin will generate a wrapper for our service, complete with binaries appropriate for the configured operating systems. The nice thing is that it will build wrappers for each OS, regardless of what OS the build is actually run under. For example, here's the output of building this on a Windows machine (note the Linux and Mac binaries):

	Name ^	Type	Size
∨ 　mailfilter ^	☐ mailfilter-service	File	16 KB
> 　cli	☐ mailfilter-service.bat	Windows Batch File	4 KB
∨ 　gui	☐ wrapper-linux-x86-64	File	109 KB
> 　　src	☐ wrapper-macosx-universal-64	File	248 KB
∨ 　　target	⬤ wrapper-windows-x86-64.exe	Application	216 KB
> 　　　classes			
∨ 　　　generated-resources			
∨ 　　　　appassembler			
∨ 　　　　　jsw			
∨ 　　　　　　mailfilter-service			
bin			
etc			
lib			

The wrapper is capable of much, much more, so if you're interested, you can read all the details on Tanuki Software's website.

Summary

Just like that, once again, our application is **finished**. We've covered quite a bit in this chapter. We started by learning a little bit about the history and technical details of several email protocols (SMTP, POP3, and IMAP4), then learned how to interact with services based on those using the JavaMail API. In the process of doing so, we discovered the Jackson JSON Parser and used it to marshal and unmarshal POJOs to and from the disk. We used the ControlsFX class, `BeanPathAdapter`, to bind non-JavaFX-aware POJOs to JavaFX controls, and the Quartz Job Scheduling Library to execute code on a schedule. Finally, we wrapped up our application using the Java Service Wrapper to create installation artifacts.

We're left with what I hope is an application that is both interesting and helpful. There are several ways to improve on it, of course, if you feel so motivated. The account/rule data structure could be extended to allow defining global rules that are shared across accounts. The GUI could support viewing email in the folders on the account and generating rules based on live data. The build could be extended to create an installer for the application. You can probably think of many more. Always feel free to check out the code and hack away. If you come up with something interesting, be sure to share it, as I'd love to see what you've done.

With another project wrapped up (no pun intended), we're ready to turn our attention to another. In the next chapter, we'll spend our entire time in a GUI and build a photo management system. This will give us the opportunity to look at some of JDK's imaging handling capabilities, including the newly added TIFF support, a feature that should make image aficionados quite happy. Turn the page and let's get started!

24
Photo Management with PhotoBeans

So far, we've written libraries. We've written command-line utilities. We've also written GUIs using JavaFX. In this chapter, we're going to try something completely different. We're going to build a photo management system, which, of course, needs to be a graphical application, but we're going to take a different approach. Rather than using pure JavaFX and building everything from the ground up, we'll use an existing application framework. That framework is the NetBeans **Rich Client Platform** (**RCP**), a mature, stable, and powerful framework, that powers not just the NetBeans IDE we've been using, but countless applications in a myriad of industries from oil and gas to air and space.

In this chapter, we'll cover the following topics:

- How to bootstrap a NetBeans RCP project
- How to integrate JavaFX with the NetBeans RCP
- The fundamentals of an RCP application such as Nodes, Actions, Lookups, Services, and TopComponents

Without further ado then, let's jump right in.

Getting started

Probably the question at or near the top of your list is, **Why would I want to use NetBeans RCP?**. Before we get into the details of the application, let's address this very fair question, and try to understand why we're building it the way we are.

One of the first things you'll notice when you start looking into the NetBeans platform is the strong notion of modularity. With the Java Module System being such a prominent feature of Java 9, this may seem like a minor detail, but NetBeans exposes this concept to us at the application level, making plugins incredibly simple, as well as allowing us to update the application on a piecemeal basis.

The RCP also provides a robust, well-tested framework for handling windows, menus, actions, nodes, services, and so on. If we were to build this application from scratch, as we've done in the previous chapters using **plain** JavaFX, we would have to manually define areas on the screen, then handle window placement by hand. With the RCP, we have a rich windowing specification already defined, which we can easily use. It offers features such as maximizing/minimizing windows, sliding, detaching, and docking windows, and so on.

The RCP also provides a strong notion of **nodes**, an encapsulation of domain-specific data in a user interface concept, which is most often seen as entries in a tree view on the left side of an application, as well as actions that can be associated with these nodes (or menu items) to act on the data they represent. Again, all of this can be done in JavaFX (or Swing), but you would have to code all of these features yourself. In fact, there are a number of open source frameworks that offer to do just that, such as Canoo's Dolphin Platform (`http://www.dolphin-platform.io`), though none have had the years of production hardening and testing that the NetBeans RCP has had, so we'll keep our focus here.

Bootstrapping the project

How you create a NetBeans RCP project will have a very fundamental impact on how the rest of the project will be approached. By default, NetBeans uses Ant as the build system for all RCP apps. Almost all of the online documentation from the NetBeans project, and blog entries from the NetBeans evangelists, often reflect this preference as well. We've been using Maven for every other project, and we're not going to change that here. Fortunately, NetBeans does allow us to create an RCP project with Maven, which is what we'll do.

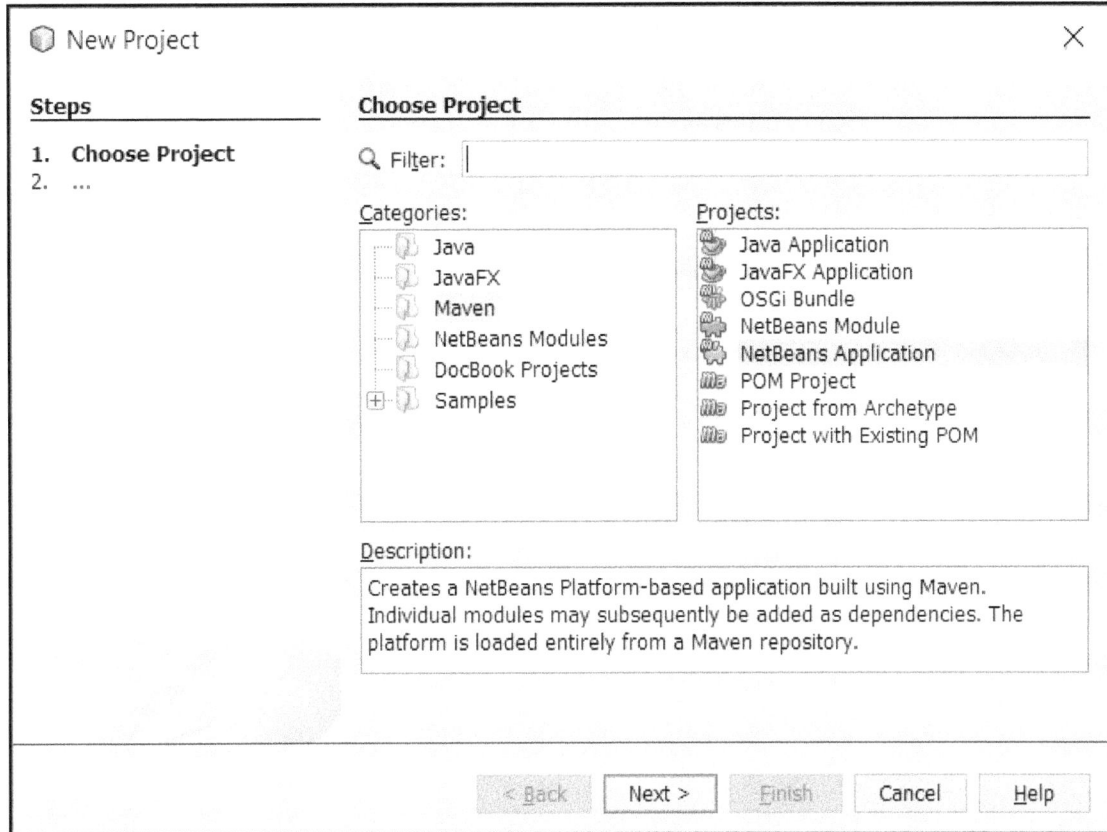

In the **New Project** window, we select **Maven**, then **NetBeans Application**. On the next screen, we configure the project as usual, specifying the project name, photobeans, project location, package, and so on.

When we click on **Next**, we'll be presented with the **Module Options** step of the **New Project** wizard. In this step, we configure some basic aspects of the RCP application. Specifically, we need to specify the version of the NetBeans APIs we'll use, and whether or not we want to use OSGi bundles as dependencies, as seen in the following screenshot:

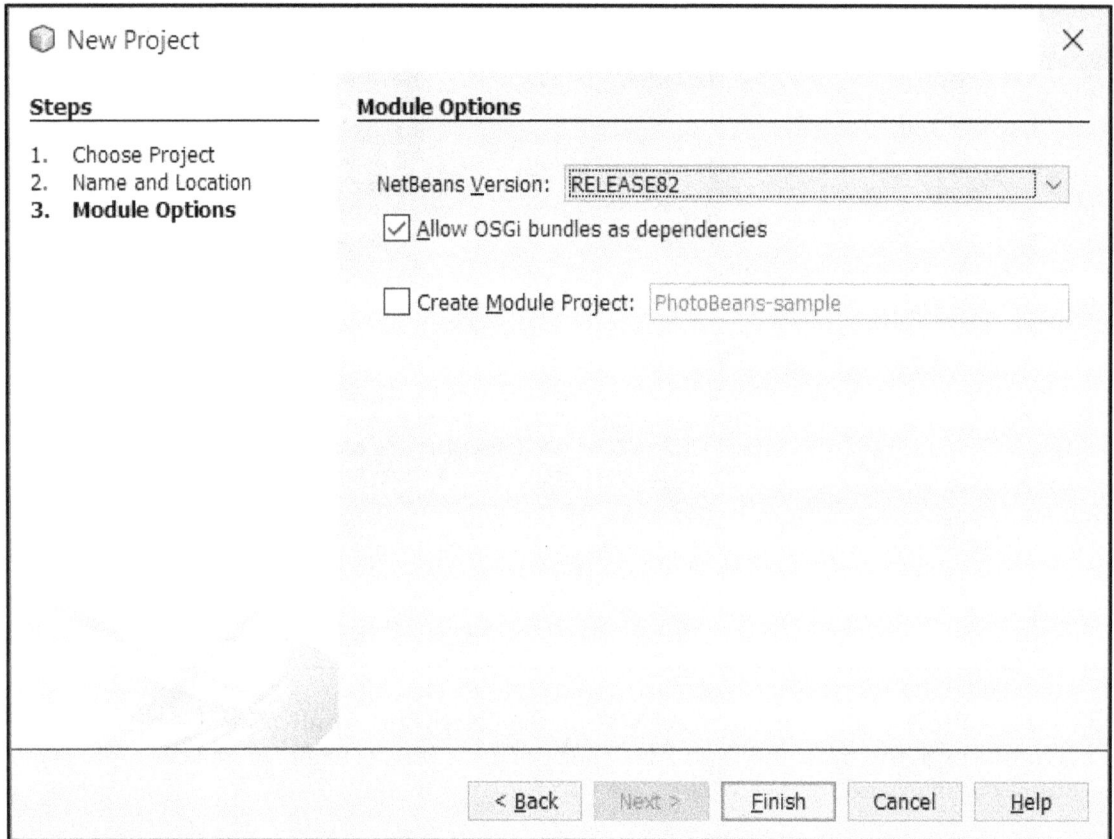

At the time of writing, the latest platform version is **RELEASE82**. By the time Java 9 ships, it is reasonable to expect that NetBeans 9.0, and, therefore **RELEASE90**, will be available. We want the latest version available, but note that, depending on the release schedule of the NetBeans project, it may very well *not* be 9.0. For the **Allow OSGi bundles as dependencies** option we can safely accept the default, though changing it won't cause us any issues, and we can easily change the value later should the need arise.

Once the project is created, we should see three new entries in the projects window: `PhotoBeans-parent`, `PhotoBeans-app`, and `PhotoBeans-branding`. The `-parent` project has no real deliverables. Like the `master` projects from other chapters, this serves merely to organize related modules, coordinate dependencies, and so on.

Branding your application

The `-branding` module is where we can define, as you may have already guessed, the details of the application's branding. You can access these branding properties by right-clicking on the branding module, and selecting `Branding...` near the bottom of the content menu. Upon doing so, you will be prompted with a screen like this one:

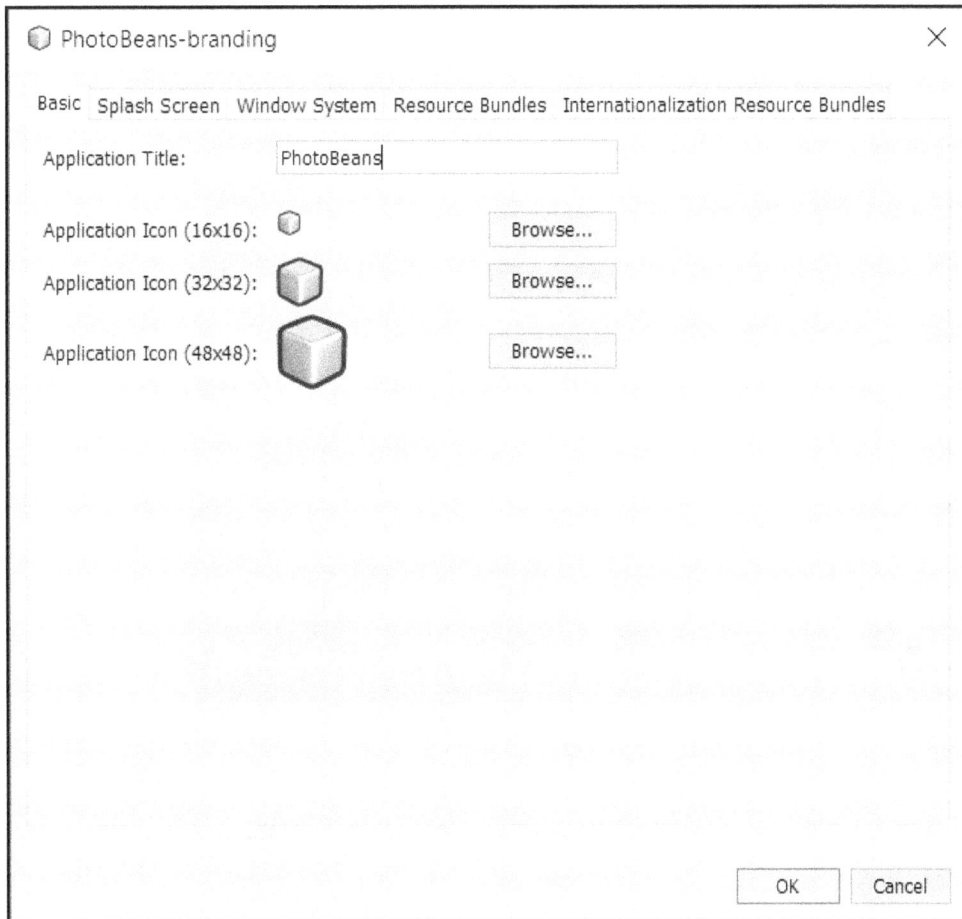

In this preceding tab, you can set or change the name of the application, as well as specify the application icon.

In the **Splash Screen** tab, you can configure, most importantly, the image that is displayed on the splash screen as the application loads. You can also enable or disable the progress bar, and set the colors, font sizes, and positions of the progress bar and startup messages:

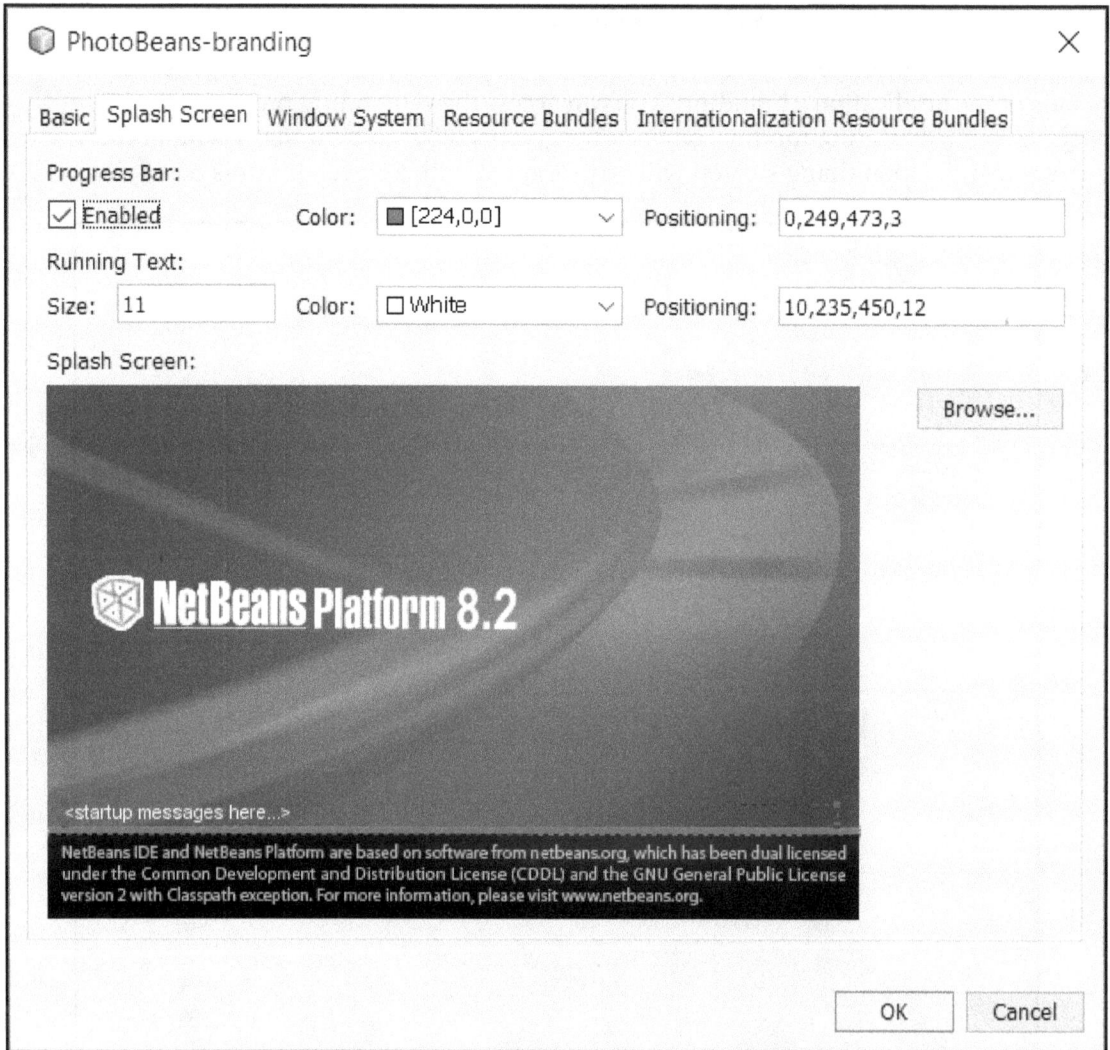

The only other tab that is of interest to us at the moment is the **Window System** tab. In this tab, we can configure a number of features such as window drag and drop, window sliding, closing, and so on:

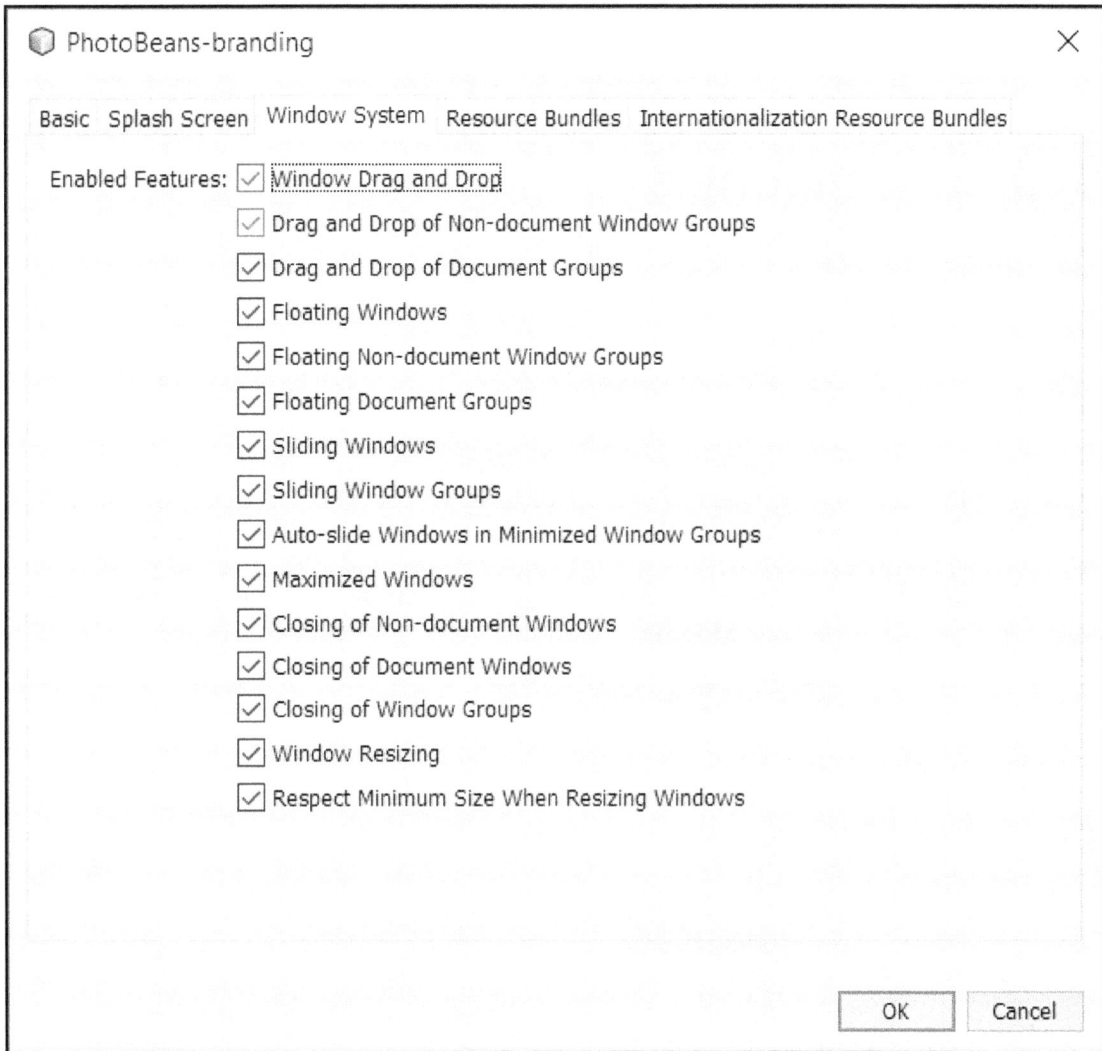

More likely than not, the defaults are acceptable for our purposes here. However, in your own NetBeans RCP application, this screen may be much more important.

Our main interest is the `-app` module. This module is the one that will define all of the application's dependencies, and will be its entry point. Unlike the JavaFX applications we've seen in previous chapters, though, we don't need to define a `public static void main` method, as NetBeans handles that for us. In fact, the `-app` module doesn't have any Java classes in it at all, yet the app can run right out-of-the-box, though it doesn't do much. We'll fix that now.

NetBeans modules

One of the strengths of the NetBeans platform is its modularity. If you've ever used the NetBeans IDE itself (before, say, reading this book), you've seen this modularity in action when working with plugins: every NetBeans plugin is made up of one or more modules. In fact, NetBeans itself is composed of numerous modules. That's how RCP applications are designed to work. It promotes decoupling, and makes extending and upgrading the application much simpler.

The generally accepted pattern is to, say, put the API classes in one module and the implementations in another. This makes the API classes reusable by other implementers, can help enforce low coupling by hiding private classes, and so on. To keep things simple as we learn the platform, though, we are going to create just one module that will provide all of the core functionality. To do that, we right-click on the **Modules** node under the parent project, and select **Create New Module...**: as shown in the following screenshot:

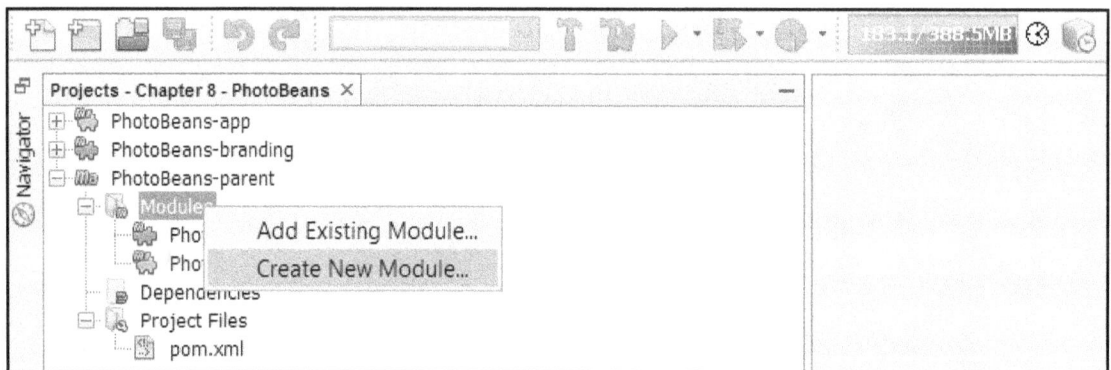

Once selected, you will be shown the **New Project** window. Here, you will need to select the **Maven** category, and the **NetBeans Module** project type, as follows:

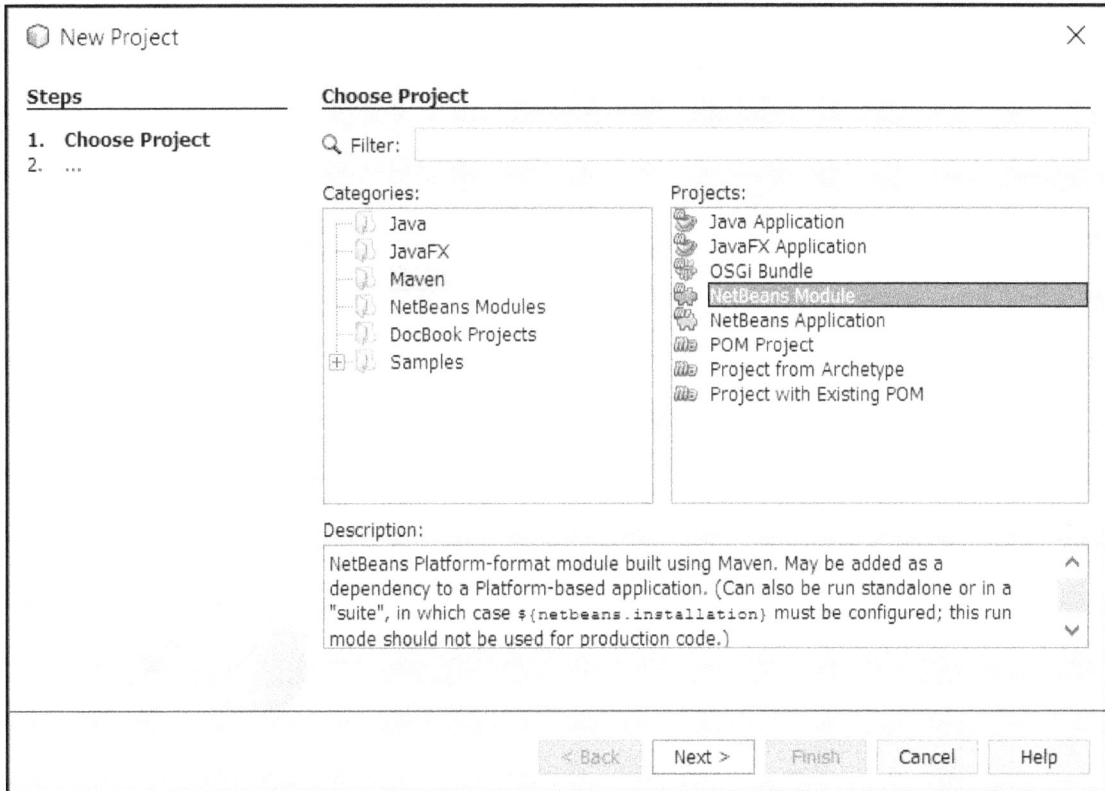

Clicking on **Next** will get you the **Name** and **Location** step we've seen several times already in this book. On this pane, we'll name the module `main`, set the package to `com.steeplesoft.photobeans.main`, and accept the defaults for the other fields. On the next pane, **Module Options**, we will make sure that the **NetBeans Version** is the same as was selected earlier, and click on **Finish**.

TopComponent - the class for tabs and windows

We now have a module that is mostly empty. NetBeans created a few artifacts for us, but we need not concern ourselves with those, as the build will manage those for us. What we do need to do, though, is create our first GUI element, which will be something that NetBeans calls a TopComponent. From the NetBeans Javadoc, found at `http://bits.netbeans.org/8.2/javadoc/`, we find this definition:

> *Embeddable visual component to be displayed in NetBeans. This is the basic unit of display--windows should not be created directly, but rather use this class. A top component may correspond to a single window, but may also be a tab (e.g.) in a window. It may be docked or undocked, have selected nodes, supply actions, etc.*

As we'll see, this class is the main component of a NetBeans RCP application. It will hold and control various related user interface elements. It is, to put it another way, at the top of a component hierarchy in the user interface. To create TopComponent, we can use the NetBeans wizard by right-clicking on our now empty package in the **Project Explorer** tree, and selecting **New | Window**. If **Window** is not an option, select **Other | Module Development | Window**.

You should now see the following **Basic Settings** window:

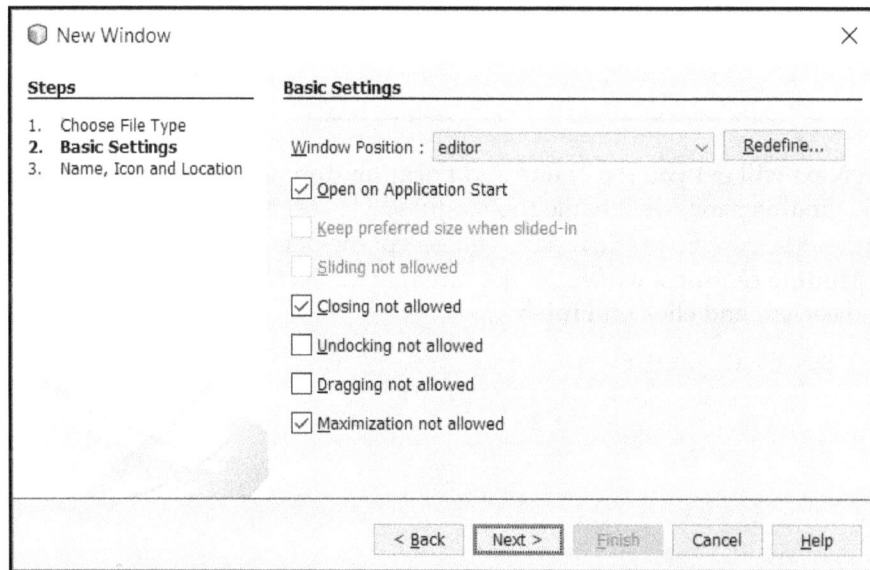

We have a number of options in the preceding window. What we're creating is a window that will show a list of photos, so some reasonable settings would be to select the following:

- **Open on Application Start**
- **Closing not allowed**
- **Maximization not allowed**

These options seem pretty straightforward, but what is **Window Position**? Another of the benefits of using the NetBeans RCP as opposed to writing everything from scratch is that the platform provides a number of predefined concepts and facilities so that we don't need to worry about them. One such concern is window positioning and placement. The NetBeans user interface specification (which can be found on the NetBeans site at `https://ui.netbeans.org/docs/ui/ws/ws_spec-netbeans_ide.html`) defines the following areas:

- **Explorer:** This is used for all windows that provide access to user objects, usually in tree browsers
- **Output:** This is used for the Output window and VCS Output window by default
- **Debugger:** This is used for all the debugger windows and other supporting windows that require a horizontal layout
- **Palette:** This is used for the component palette window
- **Inspector:** This is used for the component inspector window
- **Properties:** This is used for the properties window
- **Documents:** This is used for all the document windows

The documentation also provides this helpful illustration:

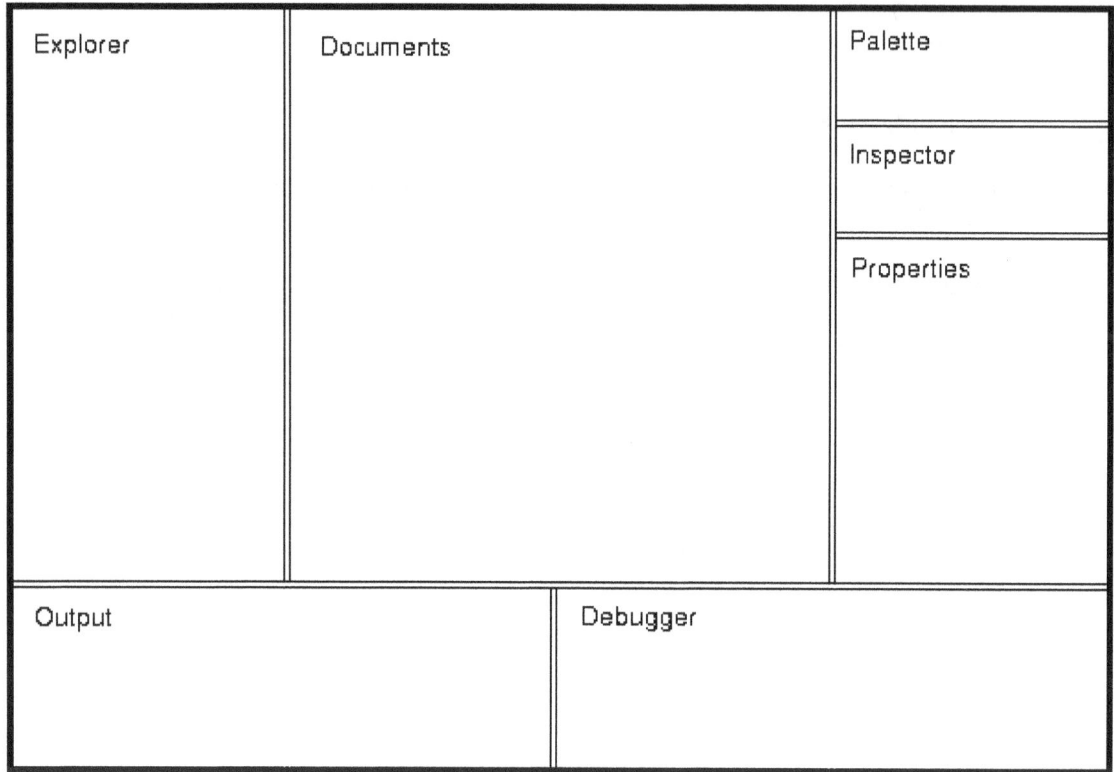

Explorer	Documents		Palette
			Inspector
			Properties
Output		Debugger	

The specification page has a great deal of additional information, but this should be enough for now to get you going. We would like our photo list to be on the left side of the application window, so we select editor for the window position. Clicking on **Next**, we configure the name and icon for the component. Strictly speaking, we don't need to specify an icon for TopComponent, so we can just enter `PhotoList` for **Class Name Prefix:**, and click on **Finish**:

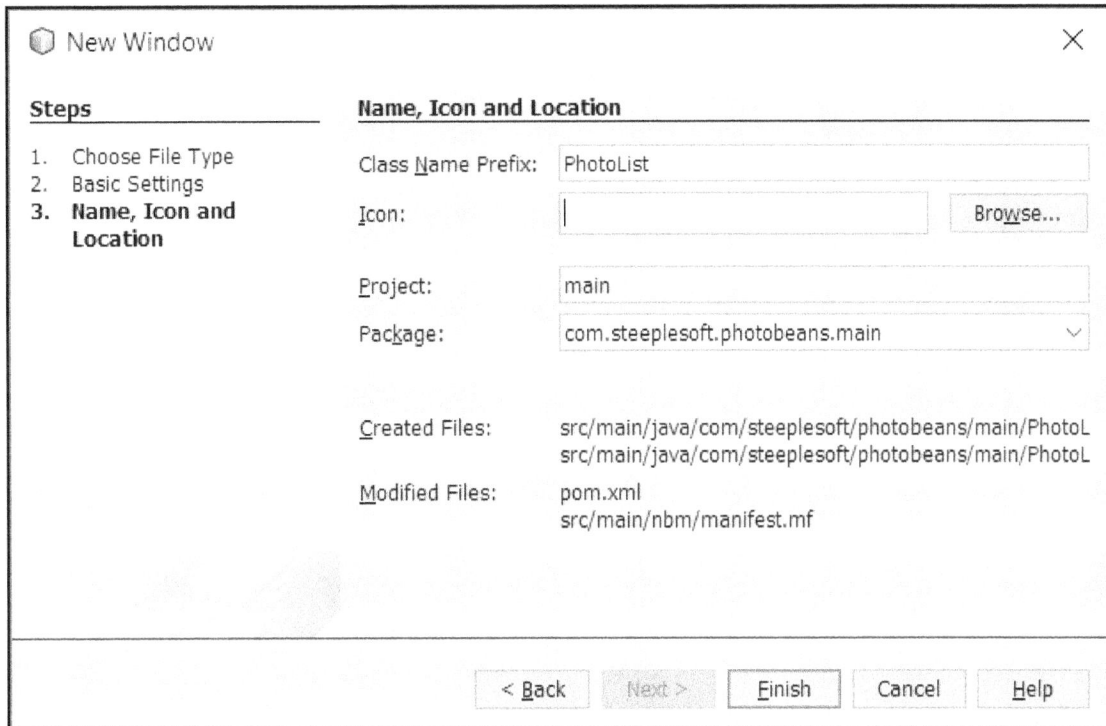

When you click on **Finish** here, NetBeans will create a couple of files for you, though only one will show up in the **Project Explorer** tree, that being `PhotoListTopComponent.java`. There is also a file called `PhotoListTopComponent.form` that you need to know about, though you will never edit it directly. NetBeans provides a very nice **WYSIWYG** (**what you see is what you get**) editor for building your user interface. The user interface definition is stored in the `.form` file, which is simply an XML file. As you make changes, NetBeans modifies this file for you, and generates the equivalent Java code in a method called `initComponents()`. You'll also notice that NetBeans will not allow you to modify the method. You can, of course, use another editor to do so, but any changes you make that way will be lost if you make changes in the GUI editor, so it's best just to leave the method alone. What does the rest of TopComponent look like?

```
@ConvertAsProperties(
    dtd = "-//com.steeplesoft.photobeans.main//PhotoList//EN",
    autostore = false
)
@TopComponent.Description(
    preferredID = "PhotoListTopComponent",
    //iconBase="SET/PATH/TO/ICON/HERE",
```

```
    persistenceType = TopComponent.PERSISTENCE_ALWAYS
)
@TopComponent.Registration(mode = "editor",
 openAtStartup = true)
@ActionID(category = "Window", id =
   "com.steeplesoft.photobeans.main.PhotoListTopComponent")
@ActionReference(path = "Menu/Window" /*, position = 333 */)
@TopComponent.OpenActionRegistration(
   displayName = "#CTL_PhotoListAction",
   preferredID = "PhotoListTopComponent"
)
@Messages({
   "CTL_PhotoListAction=PhotoList",
   "CTL_PhotoListTopComponent=PhotoList Window",
   "HINT_PhotoListTopComponent=This is a PhotoList window"
})
public final class PhotoListTopComponent
 extends TopComponent {
```

That's a lot of annotations, but is also a good reminder of how much the NetBeans platform is doing for you. During the build process, these annotations are processed to create the metadata that the platform will use at runtime to configure and wire together your application.

Some of the highlights are as follows:

```
@TopComponent.Registration(mode = "editor",
   openAtStartup = true)
```

This registers our `TopComponent`, and reflects our choices of where to put it and when to open it.

We also have some internationalization and localization work being done for us, as shown next:

```
@ActionID(category = "Window", id =
   "com.steeplesoft.photobeans.main.PhotoListTopComponent")
@ActionReference(path = "Menu/Window" /*, position = 333 */)
@TopComponent.OpenActionRegistration(
   displayName = "#CTL_PhotoListAction",
   preferredID = "PhotoListTopComponent"
)
@Messages({
   "CTL_PhotoListAction=PhotoList",
   "CTL_PhotoListTopComponent=PhotoList Window",
   "HINT_PhotoListTopComponent=This is a PhotoList window"
})
```

Without getting too far into the details and risking confusing things, the first three annotations register an open Action, and expose an item in the `Window` menu of our application. The last annotation, `@Messages`, is used to define the localization keys and strings. When this class is compiled, a class called `Bundle` is created in the same package, which defines methods using the specified keys to return the localized string. For example, for `CTL_PhotoListAction`, we get the following:

```
static String CTL_PhotoListAction() {
  return org.openide.util.NbBundle.getMessage(Bundle.class,
    "CTL_PhotoListAction");
}
```

This preceding code looks up the key in the standard Java `.properties` file for a localized message. These key/value pairs are merged with any entries found in the `Bundle.properties` file that the NetBeans wizard generated for us.

The following constructor of our `TopComponent` is also of interest:

```
public PhotoListTopComponent() {
  initComponents();
  setName(Bundle.CTL_PhotoListTopComponent());
  setToolTipText(Bundle.HINT_PhotoListTopComponent());
  putClientProperty(TopComponent.PROP_CLOSING_DISABLED,
    Boolean.TRUE);
  putClientProperty(TopComponent.PROP_MAXIMIZATION_DISABLED,
    Boolean.TRUE);
}
```

In the preceding constructor, we can see how the component's name and tool tip are set, as well as where our window-related options are set.

If we run our application now, we won't see any changes. What we need to do, then, is add a dependency on the main module to the application. We do that by right-clicking on the **Dependencies** node of the app module, as shown in this screenshot:

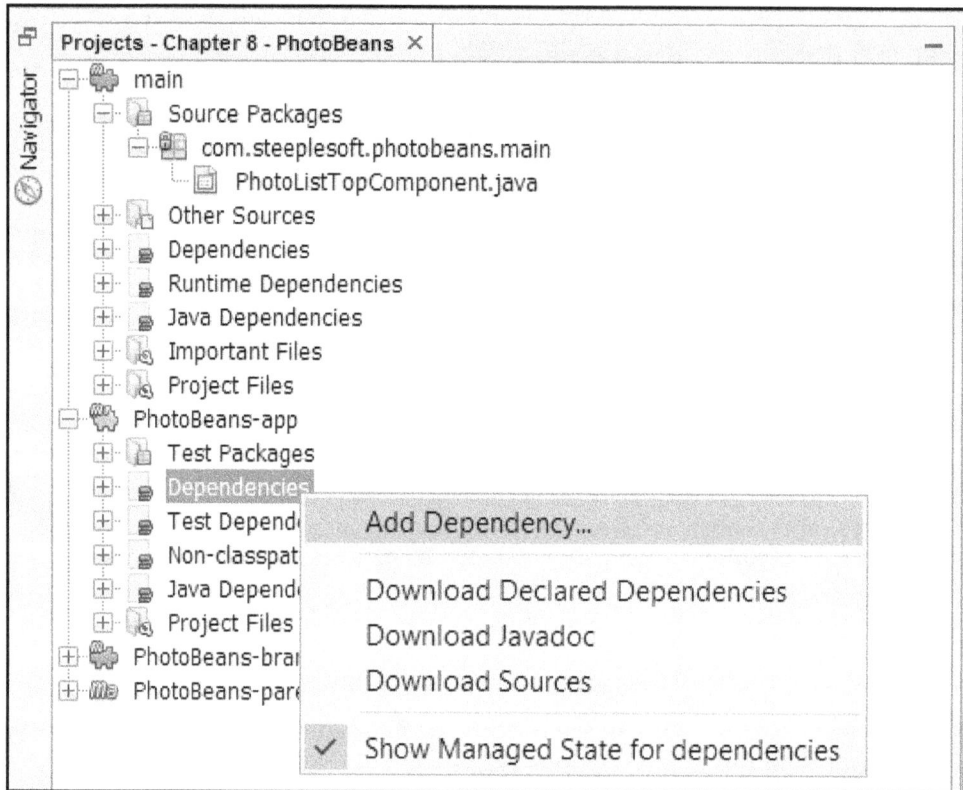

You should now see the **Add Dependency** window. Select the **Open Projects** tab, then select main as shown in this screenshot:

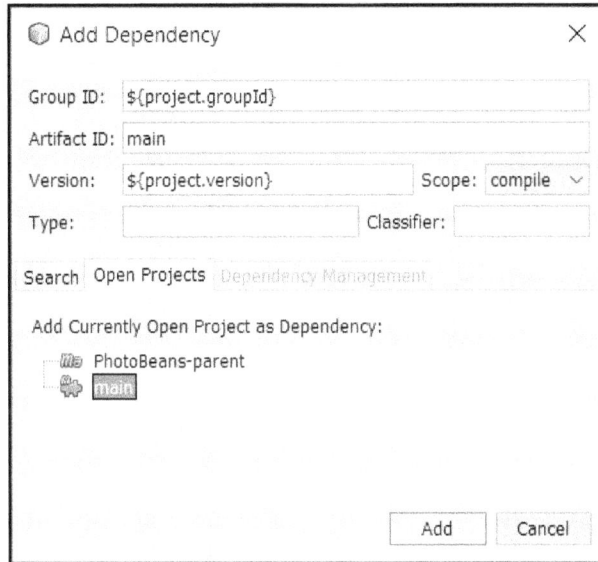

Once we've added the dependency, we need to build both modules, first `main` and then `app`, and then we'll be ready to run PhotoBeans for the first time:

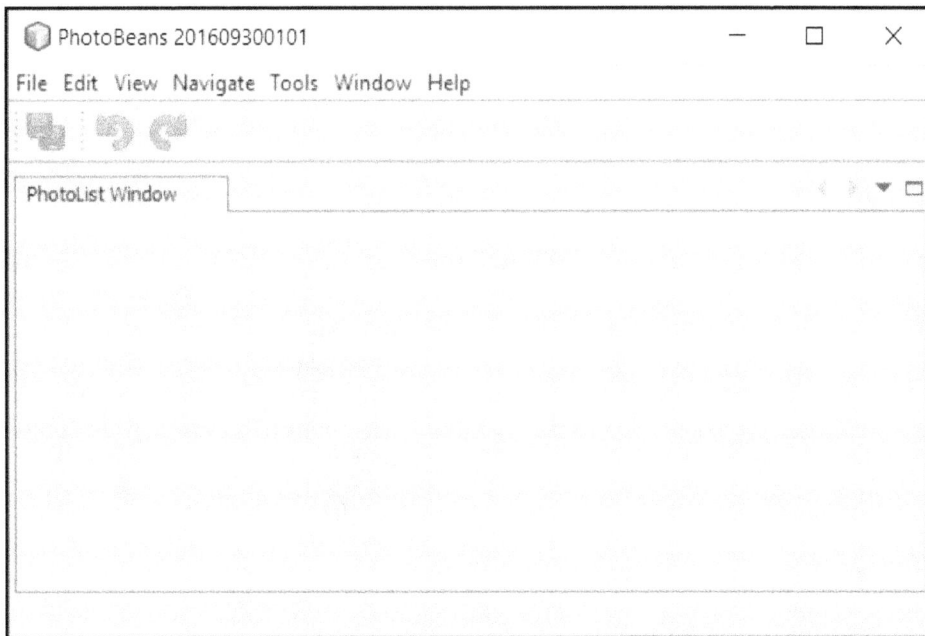

Notice the odd date in the window title in the preceding screen? That's the build date of the NetBeans platform, and it's not very pretty in our app, so, let's fix that. We have two options. The first is to use the Branding user interface we looked at earlier. The other is to edit the file directly. To keep things interesting, and to help understand where things are on the disk, we'll use this second approach.

In the branding module, under **Other Sources** | **nbm-branding**, you should find the `modules/org-netbeans-core-windows.jar/org/netbeans/core/windows/view/ui/Bundle.properties` file. In this file, you should see these lines:

```
CTL_MainWindow_Title=PhotoBeans {0}
CTL_MainWindow_Title_No_Project=PhotoBeans {0}
```

All we need to do is remove the `{0}` portions, rebuild this module and the app, and our title bar is much prettier. While that looks better, what about our TopComponent? To fix that, we need to learn a few new concepts.

Nodes, a NetBeans presentation object

You've already heard the term Node. I've used it several times to describe what and where to click. Officially, a Node represents one element in a hierarchy of objects (beans). It provides all the methods that are needed for communication between an explorer view and the bean. In the explorer section of our application, we want to represent a list of photos to the user. We'll represent each photo, as well as the year and month in which it was taken, as a Node. To display these Nodes, we'll use a NetBeans class called the `BeanTreeView`, which will display this node hierarchy as a tree. There are a few more concepts to learn, but let's start with what we have first.

We'll begin by defining our Nodes, which will serve as a sort of wrapper or bridge between our application's business domain model and the NetBeans APIs. We have not, of course, defined such a model, so we need to settle on that now. Our basic data item is a photograph, a file on disk that holds an image. In the application, we're going to display these photos in a nested tree structure, grouping the photos by year, then month. If you expand a year node, you'll see a list of month Nodes, and if you expand a month Node, you'll see a list of photo Nodes. It's a very basic, somewhat naive data model, but it's both, effective enough to demonstrate the concepts, and simple enough that we don't obscure the concepts.

As with all hierarchies, we need a root node, so we'll start with that:

```
public class RootNode extends AbstractNode
```

The base class of all nodes is, technically, Node, but extending that class puts much more of a burden on us, so we use the NetBeans-provided `AbstractNode`, which implements a fair amount of the basic behavior of the node for us with reasonable defaults.

Next, we define some constructors as follows:

```
public RootNode() {
  this(new InstanceContent());
}

protected RootNode(InstanceContent ic) {
  super(Children.create(new YearChildFactory(), true),
   new AbstractLookup(ic));
  setDisplayName(Bundle.LBL_RootNode());
  setShortDescription(Bundle.HINT_RootNode());

  instanceContent = ic;
}
```

Note that we have two constructors, one `public` and one `protected`. The reason for that is that we want to create and capture an instance of `InstanceContent`, which can be used by us, the creators of this class' Lookup, to control what is actually in the lookup. Since we need to pass `Lookup` to our class' parent constructor, we have this two-step approach to object instantiation.

Lookup, a NetBeans fundamental

What's a Lookup? It is a **general registry permitting clients to find instances of services (implementation of a given interface)**. To put it another way, it is a mechanism by which we can publish various artifacts, and other parts of the system can look up these artifacts by a key (either a `Class` or a `Lookup.Template`, which we'll not discuss here), with no coupling between the modules.

This is often used, as we'll see, to look up the implementations of a service interface. Do you recall earlier when I mentioned that often we see APIs defined in one module and implementations in another? This is where that comes in especially handy. Suppose you're developing an API to retrieve photos from an online service (which would be a great feature for this application!). You plan to deliver an implementation for one service, say Google Photos, but want to enable a third-party developer to provide an implementation for, say, Flickr. If you put the required API interfaces, classes, and so on in one module, and your Google Photos implementation in another, the third-party developer can depend on your API module alone, and avoid the weight of your implementation module. The Flickr module would declare an implementation of the photo service API, and we could load both that and our own Google Photos implementation via a request to the Lookup. In a nutshell, the system allows for decoupling the API definition, implementation, and instance acquisition in a very clean, simple API.

That's Lookup, but what is `InstanceContent`? The Lookup API only exposes methods for getting items. There is no mechanism for adding items to the Lookup, which makes sense as the Lookup instance is used by unknown third parties, and we don't want them changing the contents of our Lookup randomly. We, however, may actually want to change those contents, and we do that via `InstanceContent`, which exposes the methods we need to add or remove items. We'll see a demonstration of this concept later in the application.

Writing our own nodes

The preceding section covered those two classes, but what is `YearChildFactory`? The class `RootNode` defines for the system the root node of what will become our tree. Each node, though, if it has children, is responsible for loading and building those child Nodes, which is done through this `ChildFactory` class. Our instance looks like this:

```java
public class YearChildFactory extends ChildFactory<String> {
  private final PhotoManager photoManager;
  private static final Logger LOGGER =
    Logger.getLogger(YearChildFactory.class.getName());
  public YearChildFactory() {
    this.photoManager =
      Lookup.getDefault().lookup(PhotoManager.class);
    if (photoManager == null) {
      LOGGER.log(Level.SEVERE,
      "Cannot get PhotoManager object");
      LifecycleManager.getDefault().exit();
    }
  }
}
```

```
@Override
protected boolean createKeys(List<String> list) {
  list.addAll(photoManager.getYears());
  return true;
}

@Override
protected Node createNodeForKey(String key) {
  return new YearNode(Integer.parseInt(key));
}
}
```

We are creating a `ChildFactory` interface that will return nodes that operate on Strings. If you have a more complex data model, one that uses, for example, POJOs, you would specify that class as the parameterized type.

In our constructor, we see an example of finding a service implementation via the Lookup, which is this:

```
this.photoManager=Lookup.getDefault().lookup(
  PhotoManager.class);
```

We'll look at defining services later, but, for now, all you need to understand is that we're asking the global Lookup (which is, unlike the Lookup we created previously, not tied to a particular class) for an instance of the `PhotoManager` interface. Perhaps naively, we assume there is only one instance of this interface, but since we're not exporting the interface, we are safe in our assumption. We do, though, check to make sure there is at least one, exiting the application if there is not.

The next two methods are how the factory is used to create the child Nodes. The first method, `createKeys(List<String> list)`, is called by the system to generate a list of keys for the child nodes. In our implementation, we ask the `PhotoManager` interface for a list of years (which, as we'll see, is a simple query of the database to get a list of the years for which we have photos in the system). The platform then takes these keys, and passes them, one at a time, to `createNodeForKey(String key)` to create the actual node. Here, we create an instance of `YearNode` to represent the year.

`YearNode`, like `RootNode`, extends `AbstractNode`.

```
public class YearNode extends AbstractNode {
  public YearNode(int year) {
    super(Children.create(new MonthNodeFactory(year), true),
     Lookups.singleton(year));
    setName("" + year);
    setDisplayName("" + year);
  }
}
```

The preceding is clearly a simpler node, but the basics are the same--we create `ChildFactory` to create our children, and we create a Lookup, which, in this case, holds a single value, the year that the Node represents.

`MonthNodeFactory` looks almost exactly like `YearNodeFactory` with the exception that it loads months for the given year, so we'll not show the source here. It also creates `MonthNode` instances for each month in the list. Like `YearNode`, `MonthNode` is pretty simple, as you can see in the following code snippet:

```
public class MonthNode extends AbstractNode {
  public MonthNode(int year, int month) {
    super(Children.create(
      new PhotoNodeFactory(year, month), true),
     Lookups.singleton(month));
    String display = month + " - " +
     Month.values()[month-1].getDisplayName(
       TextStyle.FULL, Locale.getDefault());
    setName(display);
    setDisplayName(display);
  }
}
```

We do a bit more work to give the Node a meaningful name and display name, but it's pretty much the same. Note also that we have yet another `ChildFactory` that will generate, as the name implies, the PhotoNodes we'll need as children. The factory itself has nothing new of interest, but `PhotoNode` does, so let's take a look at that:

```
public class PhotoNode extends AbstractNode {
  public PhotoNode(String photo) {
    this(photo, new InstanceContent());
  }

  private PhotoNode(String photo, InstanceContent ic) {
    super(Children.LEAF, new AbstractLookup(ic));
    final String name = new File(photo).getName();
```

```
    setName(name);
    setDisplayName(name);

    ic.add((OpenCookie) () -> {
      TopComponent tc = findTopComponent(photo);
      if (tc == null) {
        tc = new PhotoViewerTopComponent(photo);
        tc.open();
      }
      tc.requestActive();
    });
  }
```

Here we again see the dual constructor approach, though, in this case, we do make use of `InstanceContent`. Note that the first parameter to `super()` is `Children.LEAF`, indicating that this Node does not have any children. We also pass the now familiar `new AbstractLookup(ic)`.

After setting the name and display name, we add a lambda to our `InstanceContent` object. The non-lambda version of this would look like this:

```
    ic.add(new OpenCookie() {
      @Override
      public void open() {
      }
    });
```

What is `OpenCookie`? It's a child of the marker interface `Node.Cookie`, and a cookie is **a design pattern used to add behaviors to existing data objects and nodes, or to separate implementation from the main object**. Using this cookie, we can neatly abstract away the signaling that something can be opened as well as how to open it.

In this case, when the system tries to open the photo represented by the node, it will call our definition of `OpenCookie.open()`, which will attempt to find an open instance of the photo. Whether it finds an existing one or needs to create a new one, it instructs the system to make it active (or give it focus).

Note that the open photo is represented by another TopComponent. To find it, we have this method:

```
    private TopComponent findTopComponent(String photo) {
      Set<TopComponent> openTopComponents =
        WindowManager.getDefault().getRegistry().getOpened();
      for (TopComponent tc : openTopComponents) {
        if (photo.equals(tc.getLookup().lookup(String.class))) {
          return tc;
```

```
      }
    }
    return null;
  }
```

We ask the Lookup of `WindowManager` for all the opened TopComponents, then iterate through each, comparing `String photo`, which is the full path of the image, with any `String` stored in the Lookup of TopComponent. If there's a match, we return that TopComponent. This lookup by `String` is somewhat naive though, and could, in more complex applications, result in unexpected matches. We're likely safe enough in this application, but you'll need to make sure in your own application that the matching criteria are strict and unique enough to avoid false hits.

Performing Actions

We'll look at `PhotoViewerTopComponent` in a moment, but there are a few more items we need to look at before moving on to that.

`PhotoNode` overrides two additional methods, which are as follows:

```
@Override
public Action[] getActions(boolean context) {
  return new Action[]{SystemAction.get(OpenAction.class)};
}

@Override
public Action getPreferredAction() {
  return SystemAction.get(OpenAction.class);
}
```

Unsurprisingly, the `getActions()` method returns an array of Actions for this Node. Actions are an abstraction (from Swing, not NetBeans) that allow us to add items to menus, and provide a means for a user to interact with the system. Each entry you see in the main menu or a context menu is backed by an Action. In our case, we're associating the NetBeans-defined `OpenAction` with our node, which will, when clicked, look for an `OpenCookie` instance in the Node's lookup and call `OpenCookie.open()`, which we defined previously.

We also override `getPreferredAction()`, which lets us define the behavior for when a Node is double-clicked. The combination of these two methods makes it possible for the user to right-click a Node and select `Open`, or double-click a Node, with the end result being that the TopComponent for that Node is opened.

Services - exposing decoupled functionality

Before looking at the definition of our `TopComponent`, let's look at `PhotoManager`, and learn a bit about its services. The `PhotoManager` interface itself is pretty simple:

```
public interface PhotoManager extends Lookup.Provider {
  void scanSourceDirs();
  List<String> getYears();
  List<String> getMonths(int year);
  List<String> getPhotos(int year, int month);
}
```

There is little of interest in the preceding code beyond the `extends Lookup.Provider` portion. Adding this here, we can force implementations to implement the lone method on that interface, as we'll need that later. The interesting part comes from the implementation, which is as follows:

```
@ServiceProvider(service = PhotoManager.class)
public class PhotoManagerImpl implements PhotoManager {
```

That is all it takes to register a service with the platform. The annotation specifies the metadata needed, and the build takes care of the rest. Let's take a look at the rest of the implementation:

```
public PhotoManagerImpl() throws ClassNotFoundException {
  setupDatabase();

  Preferences prefs =
    NbPreferences.forModule(PhotoManager.class);
  setSourceDirs(prefs.get("sourceDirs", ""));
  prefs.addPreferenceChangeListener(evt -> {
    if (evt.getKey().equals("sourceDirs")) {
      setSourceDirs(evt.getNewValue());
      scanSourceDirs();
    }
  });

  instanceContent = new InstanceContent();
  lookup = new AbstractLookup(instanceContent);
  scanSourceDirs();
}
```

In this preceding, very simple, implementation, we're going to use SQLite to store information about the photos we find. The service will provide the code to scan the configured source directories, store information about the photos found, and expose methods for retrieving those pieces of that information that vary in specificity.

To start with, we need to make sure that the database is properly set up if this is the first time the application is run. We could include a prebuilt database, but creating it on the user's machine adds a bit of resilience for those situations where the database is accidentally deleted.

```java
private void setupDatabase() {
  try {
   connection = DriverManager.getConnection(JDBC_URL);
   if (!doesTableExist()) {
     createTable();
   }
  } catch (SQLException ex) {
    Exceptions.printStackTrace(ex);
  }
}

private boolean doesTableExist() {
   try (Statement stmt = connection.createStatement()) {
     ResultSet rs = stmt.executeQuery("select 1 from images");
     rs.close();
     return true;
   } catch (SQLException e) {
     return false;
   }
}

private void createTable() {
   try (Statement stmt = connection.createStatement()) {
     stmt.execute(
       "CREATE TABLE images (imageSource VARCHAR2(4096), "
       + " year int, month int, image VARCHAR2(4096));");
       stmt.execute(
         "CREATE UNIQUE INDEX uniq_img ON images(image);");
   } catch (SQLException e) {
     Exceptions.printStackTrace(e);
   }
}
```

Next, we ask for a reference to the NetBeans preferences for the module `PhotoManager`. We'll look at managing preferences later in the chapter where we'll delve into this API in more detail, but, for now, we'll say only that we are going to ask the system for the `sourceDirs` preference, which we'll then use to configure our scanning code.

We also create `PreferenceChangeListener` to capture when the user changes the preferences. In this listener, we verify that the preference we care about, `sourceDirs`, was changed, and, if it was, we store the new value in our `PhotoManager` instance, and initiate a directory scan.

Finally, we create `InstanceContent`, create and store a Lookup, and start a directory scan to make sure the application is up-to-date with the state of the photos on disk.

The `getYears()`, `getMonths()`, and `getPhotos()` methods are largely the same, differing only, of course, in the type of data they're working with, so we'll let `getYears()` serve as an explanation of all three:

```
@Override
public List<String> getYears() {
  List<String> years = new ArrayList<>();
  try (Statement yearStmt = connection.createStatement();
  ResultSet rs = yearStmt.executeQuery(
    "SELECT DISTINCT year FROM images ORDER BY year")) {
      while (rs.next()) {
        years.add(rs.getString(1));
      }
    } catch (SQLException ex) {
      Exceptions.printStackTrace(ex);
    }
  return years;
}
```

If you are familiar with JDBC, this should not be surprising. We use Java 7's `try-with-resources` syntax to declare and instantiate both our `Statement` and our `ResultSet` objects. For those not familiar with this construct, it allows us to declare certain types of resource, and not have to worry about closing them as the system automatically closes them for us once the scope of the `try` terminates. The major restriction to be aware of with this, however, is that the class must implement `AutoCloseable`; a `Closeable` will not work. The other two `get*` methods are logically similar, so they are not shown here.

The last major piece of functionality here is the scanning of source directories, which is coordinated by the `scanSourceDirs()` method, given as follows:

```
private final ExecutorService executorService =
  Executors.newFixedThreadPool(5);
public final void scanSourceDirs() {
  RequestProcessor.getDefault().execute(() -> {
    List<Future<List<Photo>>> futures = new ArrayList<>();
    sourceDirs.stream()
      .map(d -> new SourceDirScanner(d))
```

```
        .forEach(sds ->
        futures.add((Future<List<Photo>>)
        executorService.submit(sds)));
      futures.forEach(f -> {
        try {
          final List<Photo> list = f.get();
          processPhotos(list);
        } catch (InterruptedException|ExecutionException ex) {
          Exceptions.printStackTrace(ex);
        }
      });
      instanceContent.add(new ReloadCookie());
    });
}
```

To speed the process up a bit, we create Future for each configured source directory, which we pass to our ExecutorService. We have it configured at a maximum of five threads in the pool, which is largely arbitrary. A more sophisticated approach might make this configurable, or perhaps, auto-tuned, but this should be sufficient for our purposes here.

Once the Futures are created, we iterate over the list, requesting each result. If the number of source directories exceeds the size of our thread pool, the excess Futures will wait until a Thread becomes available, at which point the ExecutorService will pick one to run. Once they're all done, the calls to .get() will no longer block, and the application can continue. Note that we're not blocking the user interface to allow this to work, as we pass the bulk of this method as a lambda to RequestProcessor.getDefault().execute() to request that this run off the user interface thread.

When the list of photos has been built and returned, we process those photos with this method:

```
        private void processPhotos(List<Photo> photos) {
          photos.stream()
            .filter(p -> !isImageRecorded(p))
            .forEach(p -> insertImage(p));
        }
```

The isImageRecorded() method checks to see if the image path is already in the database, returning true if it is. We filter() the stream based on the result of this test, so forEach() only operates on previously unknown images, which are then inserted into the database via insertImage(). Those two methods look like this:

```
        private boolean isImageRecorded(Photo photo) {
          boolean there = false;
          try (PreparedStatement imageExistStatement =
```

```
        connection.prepareStatement(
          "SELECT 1 FROM images WHERE image = ?")) {
            imageExistStatement.setString(1, photo.getImage());
            final ResultSet rs = imageExistStatement.executeQuery();
            there = rs.next();
            close(rs);
        } catch (SQLException ex) {
            Exceptions.printStackTrace(ex);
        }
    return there;
}

private void insertImage(Photo photo) {
    try (PreparedStatement insertStatement =
     connection.prepareStatement(
       "INSERT INTO images (imageSource, year, month, image)
       VALUES (?, ?, ?, ?);")) {
            insertStatement.setString(1, photo.getSourceDir());
            insertStatement.setInt(2, photo.getYear());
            insertStatement.setInt(3, photo.getMonth());
            insertStatement.setString(4, photo.getImage());
            insertStatement.executeUpdate();
        } catch (SQLException ex) {
          Exceptions.printStackTrace(ex);
        }
    }
}
```

We are using `PreparedStatement`, as it is, generally, unwise to create SQL statements via concatenation, which can, and often does, lead to SQL injection attacks, so we can't use `try-with-resources` fully in the first method, requiring us to close the `ResultSet` manually.

PhotoViewerTopComponent

We can now find images, but we still can't tell the system where to look. Before turning our attention to handling preferences with the NetBeans platform, though, we have one more TopComponent to look at--`PhotoViewerTopComponent`.

If you think back to our discussion of the areas provided by the NetBeans window system, when we view an image, we want the image to be loaded in the `Editor` area. To create a TopComponent for that, we instruct NetBeans to create a new `Window` by right-clicking on the desired package, and selecting **New** | **Window**:

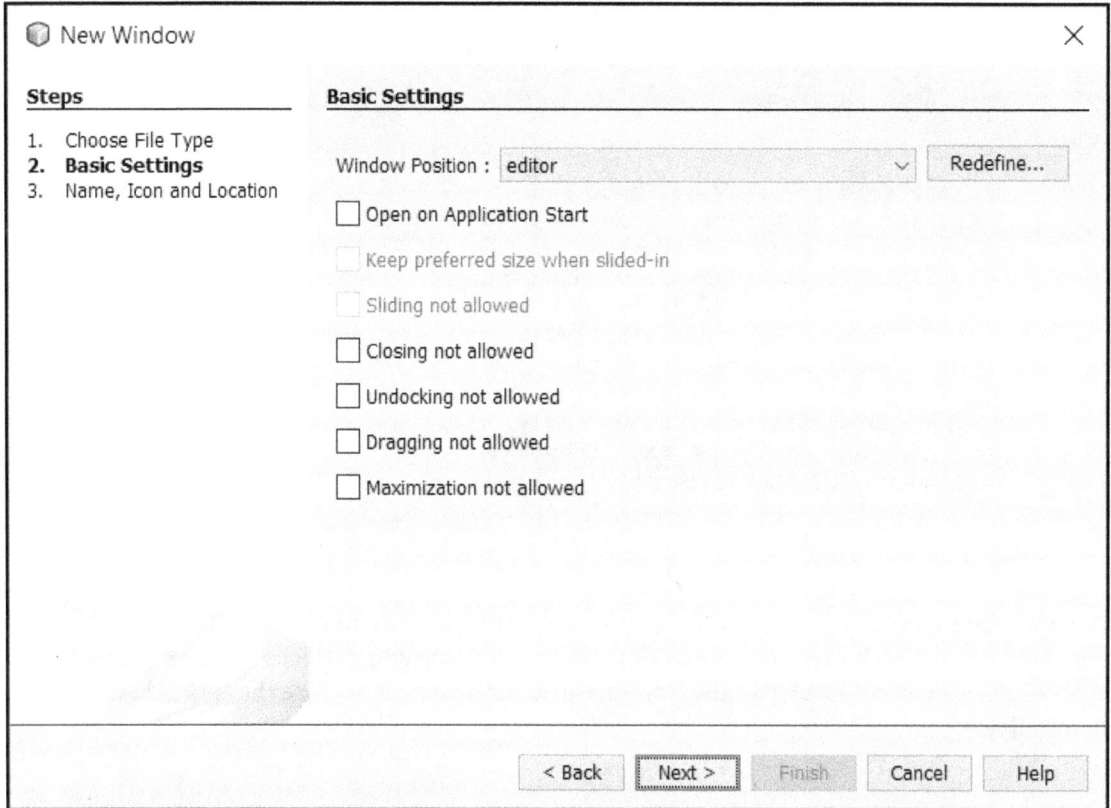

```
New Window                                                            X

Steps                         Basic Settings

1. Choose File Type
2. Basic Settings             Window Position :  editor            ▽    Redefine...
3. Name, Icon and Location
                              ☐ Open on Application Start
                              ☐ Keep preferred size when slided-in
                              ☐ Sliding not allowed
                              ☐ Closing not allowed
                              ☐ Undocking not allowed
                              ☐ Dragging not allowed
                              ☐ Maximization not allowed


                                    < Back    Next >    Finish    Cancel    Help
```

In the next pane, we specify a class name prefix for our new TopComponent--`PhotoViewer` as seen in the following screenshot:

New Window   ✕

Steps   **Name, Icon and Location**

1. Choose File Type   Class <u>N</u>ame Prefix: PhotoViewer|
2. Basic Settings
3. **Name, Icon and**   <u>I</u>con: Bro<u>w</u>se...
   Location

                            <u>P</u>roject: main

                            Pac<u>k</u>age: com.steeplesoft.photobeans.main   ⌄

                            <u>C</u>reated Files: src/main/java/com/steeplesoft/photobeans/main/PhotoViewerTop
                                                          src/main/java/com/steeplesoft/photobeans/main/PhotoViewerTop

                            <u>M</u>odified Files: pom.xml
                                                          src/main/nbm/manifest.mf

                                            < <u>B</u>ack   Next >   <u>F</u>inish   Cancel   <u>H</u>elp

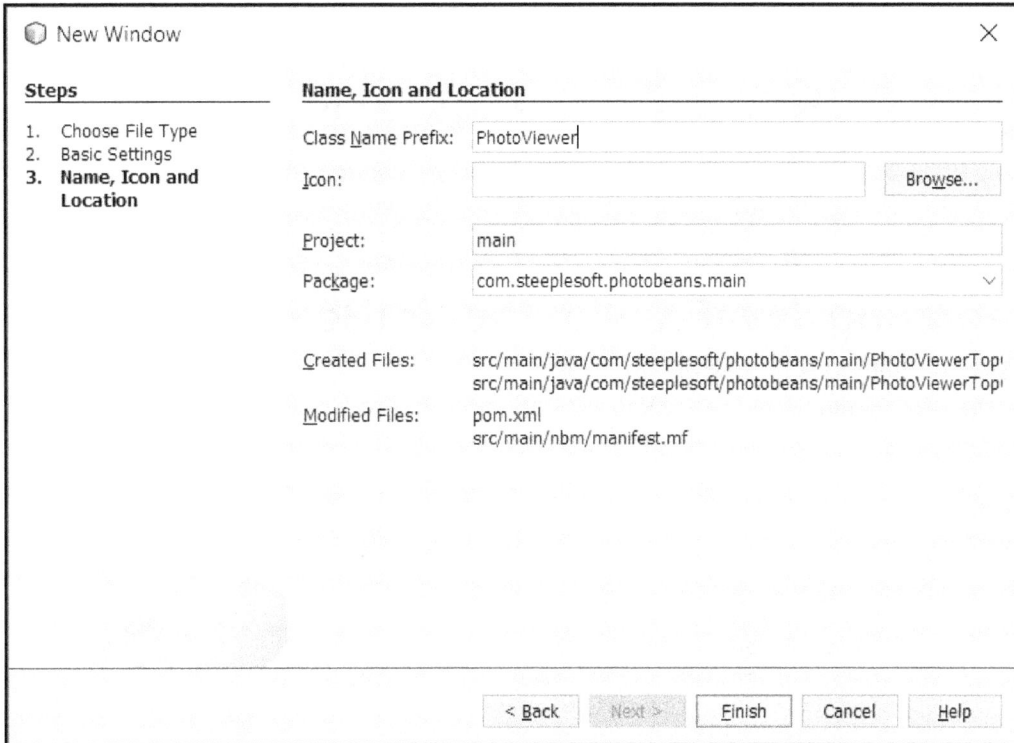

NetBeans will now create the files `PhotoViewerTopComponent.java` and
`PhotoViewerTopComponent.form` just as was discussed earlier. For this TopComponent,
though, we need to make a couple of changes. When we open the `Window`, we need to
specify an image for it to load, so we need to provide a constructor that takes the path to the
image. However, TopComponents must have a no-argument constructor, so we leave it but
have it call our new constructor with an empty image path.

```
public PhotoViewerTopComponent() {
  this("");
}

public PhotoViewerTopComponent(String photo) {
  initComponents();
  this.photo = photo;
  File file = new File(photo);
  setName(file.getName());
  setToolTipText(photo);
  associateLookup(Lookups.singleton(photo));
  setLayout(new BorderLayout());
```

```
        init();
    }
```

While it may seem like a lot, the steps here are simple: we save the photo path in an instance variable, we create a `File` instance from it to get the file name more easily, add the photo path to TopComponent's Lookup (which is how we find the TopComponent for a given photo), change the layout, and then initialize the window.

Integrating JavaFX with the NetBeans RCP

The `init()` method is interesting, though, in that we're going to do something slightly different; we're going to use JavaFX to view the image. There's no reason we couldn't use Swing like we are in our other TopComponent, but this gives us a good opportunity to demonstrate both how to integrate JavaFX and Swing, as well as JavaFX and the NetBeans platform.

```java
private JFXPanel fxPanel;
private void init() {
  fxPanel = new JFXPanel();
  add(fxPanel, BorderLayout.CENTER);
  Platform.setImplicitExit(false);
  Platform.runLater(this::createScene);
}
```

`JFXPanel` is a Swing component that is used to embed JavaFX into Swing. Our Window's layout is `BorderLayout`, so we add our `JFXPanel` to it in the `CENTER` area, and let it expand to fill the `Window`. Any complex layout of the JavaFX components will be handled by yet another container inside our `JFXPanel`. Our user interface, though, is fairly simple. As with our earlier JavaFX systems, we define our user interface via FXML as follows:

```xml
<BorderPane fx:id="borderPane" prefHeight="480.0"
  prefWidth="600.0"
  xmlns="http://javafx.com/javafx/8.0.111"
  xmlns:fx="http://javafx.com/fxml/1"
  fx:controller=
    "com.steeplesoft.photobeans.main.PhotoViewerController">
  <center>
    <ScrollPane fx:id="scrollPane">
      <content>
        <Group>
          <children>
            <ImageView fx:id="imageView"
              preserveRatio="true" />
          </children>
```

```
        </Group>
      </content>
    </ScrollPane>
  </center>
</BorderPane>
```

Since FXML needs a root element, we specify a `BorderLayout`, which, as discussed, gives us a `BorderLayout` in a `JFXPanel` in a `BorderLayout`. That may sound really odd, but that's how embedding JavaFX works. Note also that we still specify a controller. In that controller, our `initialize()` method looks like this:

```
@FXML
private BorderPane borderPane;
@FXML
private ScrollPane scrollPane;
public void initialize(URL location,
 ResourceBundle resources) {
    imageView.fitWidthProperty()
    .bind(borderPane.widthProperty());
    imageView.fitHeightProperty()
    .bind(borderPane.heightProperty());
}
```

In this last method, all we're doing is binding the width and height properties to those of the border pane. We've also set `preserveRatio` to `True` in the FXML, so the image won't be distorted. This will be important as we rotate the image next.

We haven't seen the code for rotation, so let's look at that now. We'll start by adding a button as follows:

```
<top>
  <ButtonBar prefHeight="40.0" prefWidth="200.0"
     BorderPane.alignment="CENTER">
     <buttons>
       <SplitMenuButton mnemonicParsing="false"
         text="Rotate">
         <items>
           <MenuItem onAction="#rotateLeft"
             text="Left 90°" />
           <MenuItem onAction="#rotateRight"
             text="Right 90°" />
         </items>
       </SplitMenuButton>
     </buttons>
  </ButtonBar>
</top>
```

To the `top` section of `BorderPane`, we add `ButtonBar`, to which we add a single `SplitMenuButton`. That gives us a button like the one to the right. In its non-focused state, it looks like a normal button. When the user clicks on the arrow, the menu, as seen here, is presented to the user, offering the ability to rotate the image in the directions listed:

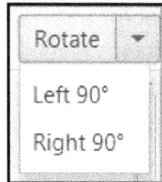

We've tied those MenuItems to the appropriate methods in the controller in our FXML definition:

```
@FXML
public void rotateLeft(ActionEvent event) {
   imageView.setRotate(imageView.getRotate() - 90);
}
@FXML
public void rotateRight(ActionEvent event) {
   imageView.setRotate(imageView.getRotate() + 90);
}
```

Using the APIs provided by the JavaFX `ImageView`, we set the image rotation.

We can find images, view them, and rotate them, but we still can't tell the system where to look for those images. It's time to fix that.

NetBeans preferences and the Options panel

The key to managing preferences is two-fold: `NbPreferences` and the **Options** panel. `NbPreferences` is the means by which preferences are stored and loaded, and the options panel is the means by which the user is presented with a user interface for editing those preferences. We'll start by looking at how to add an **Options** panel, which will lead naturally to the `NbPreferences` discussion. Next is the NetBeans Options window:

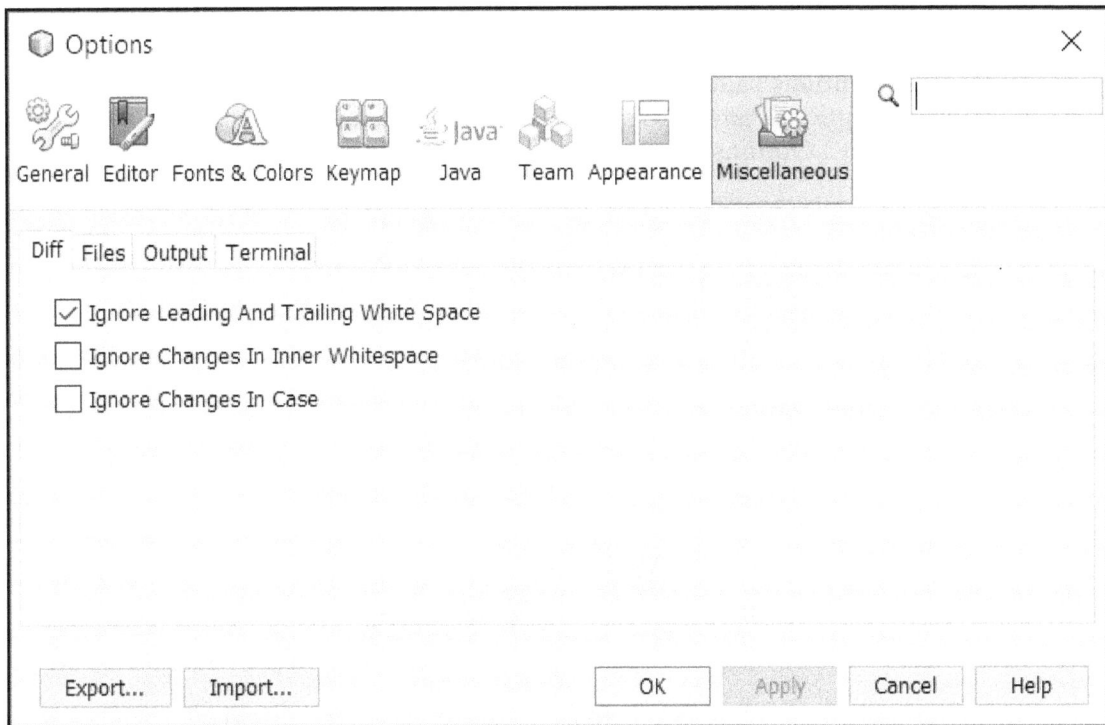

In the preceding window, we can see the two types of **Options** panel--primary and secondary. A primary **Options** panel is represented by icons across the top: **General**, **Editor**, **Fonts & Colors**, and so on. A secondary **Options** panel is a tab like we see in the middle section: **Diff**, **Files**, **Output**, and **Terminal**. When adding an **Options** panel, you must choose either primary or secondary. We'd like to add a new primary panel, as it will separate our preferences from the rest of the panels visually as well as giving us an opportunity to create both types of panel.

Adding a primary panel

To create a primary **Options** panel, right-click on the desired package or the project node, and click on **New** | **Options Panel**. If **Options Panel** is not visible, select **New** | **Other** | **Module Development** | **Options Panel**. Next, select **Create Primary Panel**:

We must specify a label, which is the text we'll see under the icon. We must also select an icon. The system will let you select something other than a 32x32 image, but if it's not the right size, it will look strange in the user interface; so, choose carefully. The system will also require you to enter keywords, which will be used if the user applies a filter to the Options window. Finally, select **Allow Secondary Panels**. The primary panel doesn't have any real content and serves only to display secondary panels, which we'll create shortly.

When you click on **Next**, you will be asked for the class prefix and package:

When you click on **Finish**, NetBeans will create this single file, `package-info.java`:

```
@OptionsPanelController.ContainerRegistration(id = "PhotoBeans",
  categoryName = "#OptionsCategory_Name_PhotoBeans",
  iconBase = "com/steeplesoft/photobeans/main/options/
  camera-icon-32x32.png",
  keywords = "#OptionsCategory_Keywords_PhotoBeans",
  keywordsCategory = "PhotoBeans")
@NbBundle.Messages(value = {
  "OptionsCategory_Name_PhotoBeans=PhotoBeans",
  "OptionsCategory_Keywords_PhotoBeans=photo"})
package com.steeplesoft.photobeans.main.options;

import org.netbeans.spi.options.OptionsPanelController;
import org.openide.util.NbBundle;
```

Adding a secondary panel

With the primary panel defined, we're ready to create the secondary panel, which will do our work. We right-click on the package again, and select **New | Options Panel**, this time selecting **Create Secondary Panel**:

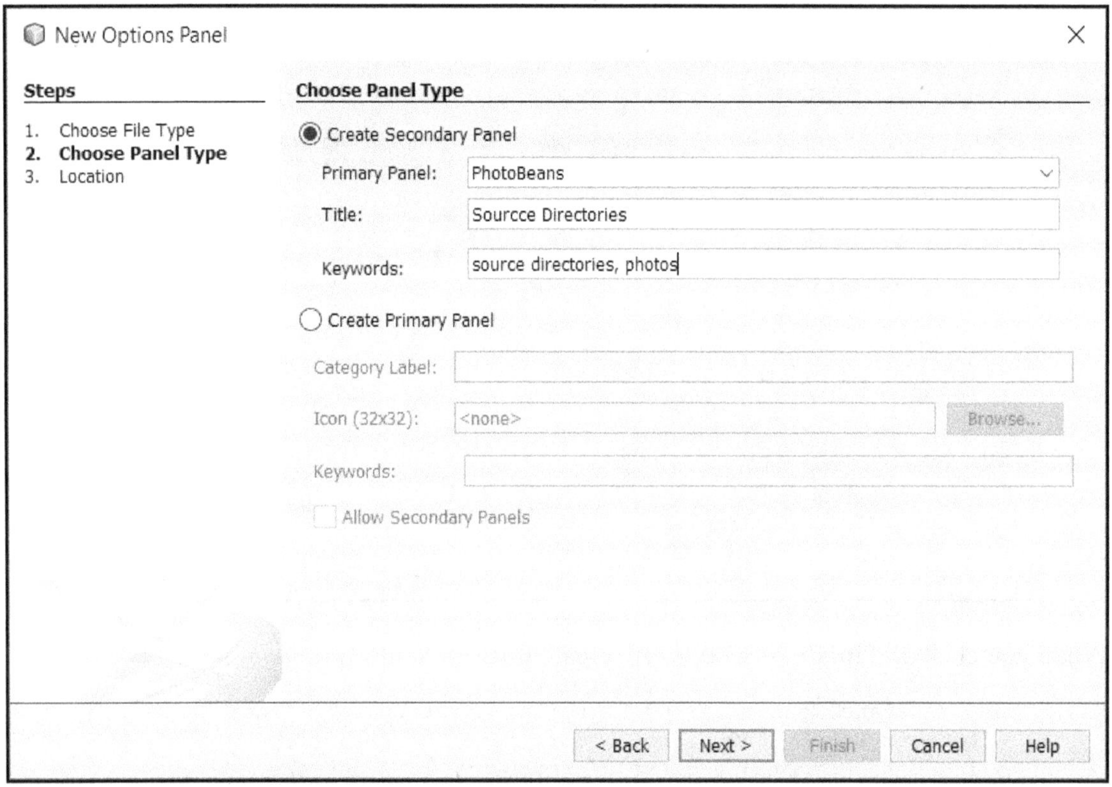

Since we've defined our own primary panel, we can select that as our parent, and we set the title and keywords as we did before. Click on **Next**, select and/or verify the class prefix and package, then click on **Finish**. This will create three artifacts--
`SourceDirectoriesOptionPanelController.java`, `SourceDirectoriesPanel.java`, and `SourceDirectoriesPanel.form`, and NetBeans will present you with the GUI editor for your panel.

We want to add four elements to our panel--a label, a list view, and two buttons. We add those by dragging them from the palette on the right, and arranging them in the form as shown next:

To make working with these user interface elements more meaningful, we need to set the variable names. We also need to set the text of the user interface so that each element is meaningful for the user. We can do both by right-clicking on each element, as shown in this screenshot:

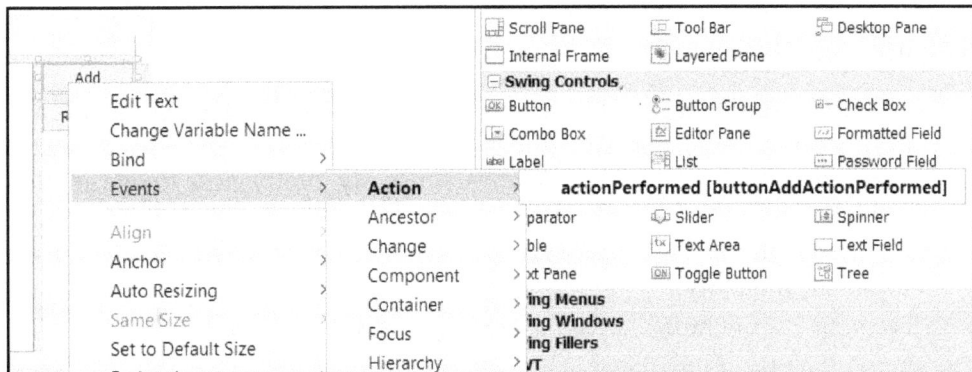

In the preceding screen, we can see the three items of interest--**Edit Text**, **Change Variable Name...**, and **Events | Action | actionPeformed [buttonAddActionPerformed]**. For our buttons, we need to use all three, so we set the text to `Add` (or `Remove`), change the variable name to `buttonAdd`/`buttonRemove`, and select `actionPerformed`. Back in our Java source, we see a method created for us, which we need to fill out:

```
private void buttonAddActionPerformed(ActionEvent evt) {
  String lastDir = NbPreferences
   .forModule(PhotoManager.class).get("lastDir", null);
  JFileChooser chooser = new JFileChooser();
```

```
if (lastDir != null) {
  chooser.setCurrentDirectory(
    new java.io.File(lastDir));
}
chooser.setDialogTitle("Add Source Directory");
chooser.setFileSelectionMode(
  JFileChooser.DIRECTORIES_ONLY);
chooser.setAcceptAllFileFilterUsed(false);
if (chooser.showOpenDialog(null) ==
  JFileChooser.APPROVE_OPTION) {
    try {
      String dir = chooser.getSelectedFile()
      .getCanonicalPath();
      ensureModel().addElement(dir);
      NbPreferences.forModule(PhotoManager.class)
      .put("lastDir", dir);
    } catch (IOException ex) {
        Exceptions.printStackTrace(ex);
      }
  } else {
      System.out.println("No Selection ");
    }
}
```

We have quite a bit going on here:

1. We start by retrieving the `lastDir` preference value. If set, we'll use this as the starting point for selecting the directories to add. Typically, at least in my experience, the directories of interest are, usually, pretty close to one another in the filesystem, so we use this preference to save the user some clicks.

2. Next we create `JFileChooser`, which is the Swing class that will allow us to choose the directory.

3. If `lastDir` is not null, we pass it to `setCurrentDirectory()`.

4. We set the title of the dialog to something meaningful.

5. We specify that the dialog should only let us choose directories.

6. Finally, we disable the **Select All file filter** option.

7. We call `chooser.showOpenDialog()` to present the dialog to the user, and wait for it close.

8. If the return code from the dialog is `APPROVE_OPTION`, we need to add the chosen directory to our model.

9. We get the canonical path for the selected file.

10. We call `ensureModel()`, which we'll look at in a moment, to get the model for our `ListView`, then add this new path to it.

11. Finally, we store the chosen path as `lastDir` in our preferences to set the starting directory as discussed earlier.

12. The action for the **Remove** button is much simpler, and is as follows:

```
private void buttonRemoveActionPerformed(ActionEvent evt) {
  List<Integer> indexes = IntStream.of(
    sourceList.getSelectedIndices())
    .boxed().collect(Collectors.toList());
  Collections.sort(indexes);
  Collections.reverse(indexes);
  indexes.forEach(i -> ensureModel().remove(i));
}
```

When we are removing items from the model, we remove them by the item index. However, when we remove an item, the index numbers for anything after that change. What we do here, then, is create a List of the selected indices, sort it to make sure it's in the right order (which is possibly excessive here, but it's a relatively inexpensive operation, and makes the next operation safer), then we reverse the order of the List. With our indices now in descending order, we can iterate over the List, removing each index from our model.

We've used `ensureModel()` a couple of times now, so let's see what that looks like:

```
private DefaultListModel<String> ensureModel() {
  if (model == null) {
    model = new DefaultListModel<>();
    sourceList.setModel(model);
  }
  return model;
}
```

It's important that we treat the model as `DefaultListModel` rather than the `ListModel` type that `ListView` expects, as the latter does not expose any methods for mutating the contents of the model, whereas the former does. By dealing with `DefaultListModel`, we can add and remove items as needed, as we've done here.

Loading and saving preferences

There are two more methods we need to look at in this class, the ones that load and store the options represented in the panel. We'll start with `load()`, which is as follows:

```
protected void load() {
  String dirs = NbPreferences
    .forModule(PhotoManager.class).get("sourceDirs", "");
  if (dirs != null && !dirs.isEmpty()) {
    ensureModel();
    model.clear();
    Set<String> set = new HashSet<>(
      Arrays.asList(dirs.split(";")));
    set.forEach(i -> model.addElement(i));
  }
}
```

`NbPreferences` does not support storing a list of strings, so, as we'll see below, we store the list of source directories as a semicolon-delimited list of strings. Here, we load the value of `sourceDirs`, and, if not null, we split on the semicolon, and add each entry to our `DefaultListModel`.

Saving the source directories is also fairly straightforward:

```
protected void store() {
  Set<String> dirs = new HashSet<>();
  ensureModel();
  for (int i = 0; i < model.getSize(); i++) {
    final String dir = model.getElementAt(i);
    if (dir != null && !dir.isEmpty()) {
      dirs.add(dir);
    }
  }
  if (!dirs.isEmpty()) {
    NbPreferences.forModule(PhotoManager.class)
    .put("sourceDirs", String.join(";", dirs));
  } else {
    NbPreferences.forModule(PhotoManager.class)
      .remove("sourceDirs");
  }
}
```

We iterate over `ListModel`, adding each directory to a local `HashSet` instance, which helps us remove any duplicate directories. If `Set` is not empty, we use `String.join()` to create our delimited list, and `put()` it into our preferences store. If it is empty, we remove the preference entry from the store to clear out any old data that may have been persisted earlier.

Reacting to changes in preferences

Now that we can persist changes, we need to make the application react to the changes. Fortunately, the NetBeans RCP provides a neat, decoupled way to handle that. We need not explicitly call a method from our code here. We can attach a listener at the point in the system where we're interested in the change. We've already seen this code back in `PhotoManagerImpl`:

```
prefs.addPreferenceChangeListener(evt -> {
  if (evt.getKey().equals("sourceDirs")) {
    setSourceDirs(evt.getNewValue());
    scanSourceDirs();
  }
});
```

When we save any preference for the `PhotoManager` module, this listener is called. We simply check to make sure it's for a key that we're interested in, and act accordingly, which, as we've seen, involves restarting the source directory scanning process.

Once new data has been loaded, how do we make the user interface reflect that change? Do we have to update the user interface manually? Again, thanks to the RCP, the answer is no. We've seen the first half at the end of `scanSourceDirs()`, which is this:

```
instanceContent.add(new ReloadCookie());
```

NetBeans has a number of cookie classes for indicating that certain actions should take place. While we don't share the class hierarchy (due to the unfortunate dependency on the Nodes API), we do share the same nomenclature with the hope of stealing, so to speak, a bit of the familiarity. So what does `ReloadCookie` look like? There's not much to it; it is given like this:

```
public class ReloadCookie {
}
```

In our case, we just have an empty class. We don't intend for this to be used elsewhere, so we don't need to encode any functionality in the class. We will just be using this as an indicator, as we see in the constructor of RootNode, which is as follows:

```
reloadResult = photoManager.getLookup().lookup(
    new Lookup.Template(ReloadCookie.class));
reloadResult.addLookupListener(event -> setChildren(
    Children.create(new YearChildFactory(), true)));
```

Lookup.Template is used to define the pattern by which the system can filter our Lookup requests. Using our template, we create a Lookup.Result object, reloadResult, and add a listener to it via a lambda. The lambda creates a new set of children using Children.create() and the YearChildFactory we looked at earlier, and passes those to setChildren() to update the user interface.

That may seem like a fair bit of code just to update the user interface when a preference is changed, but the decoupling is certainly worth it. Imagine a more complicated application or a dependent module tree. Using this listener approach, we need not expose methods, or even classes, to the outside world, allowing our internal code to be modified without breaking client code. That is, in short, one of the primary reasons for decoupled code.

Summary

Once again, we've come to the end of another application. You learned how to bootstrap a Maven-based NetBeans Rich Client Platform application. You learned about RCP modules, and how to include those modules in our application build. You also learned the basics of the NetBeans RCP Node API, how to create our own nodes, and how to nest child nodes. We explained how to use the NetBeans Preferences API, including creating new Options panels for editing preferences, how to load and store them, and how to react to changes in preferences.

One final word on the NetBeans RCP--While we have built a respectable application here, we have in no way pushed the limits of the RCP. I have attempted to cover just enough of the platform to get you going, but you will almost certainly need to learn more if you are to continue using the platform. While the official documentation is helpful, the go-to source for comprehensive coverage is *NetBeans Platform for Beginners* by Jason Wexbridge and Walter Nyland (`https://leanpub.com/nbp4beginners`). It's a great book, and I highly recommend it.

In the next chapter, we're going to dip our toes into the waters of client/server programming, and implement our own note-taking application. It won't be as robust and full-featured as the competitors already in the market, but we'll make good headway in that direction and, hopefully, learn a lot along the way.

25
Taking Notes with Monumentum

For our eighth project, we will again do something new--we'll build a web app. Whereas all of our other projects have been command lines, GUIs, or some combination thereof, this project will be a single module consisting of a REST API and a JavaScript frontend, all built with an eye toward the current microservice trend.

To build the application, you'll learn about the following topics:

- Some of the Java options to build microservice applications
- Payara Micro and `microprofile.io`
- Java API for RESTful Web Services
- Document data stores and MongoDB
- OAuth authentication (against Google, specifically)
- **JSON Web Tokens (JWT)**

As you can see, this will be, in many ways, a much different type of project than what we've looked at to this point.

Getting started

Most of us have likely used some sort of note-taking application such as EverNote, OneNote, or Google Keep. They're an extremely handy way of jotting down notes and thoughts, and having them available from just about every environment imaginable-- desktop, mobile, and web. In this chapter, we'll build a fairly basic clone of these industry giants in order to exercise a number of concepts. We will call this app Monumentum, which is Latin for a reminder or memorial, an apt name for this type of application.

Before we get into those, let's take some time to list the requirements for our application:

- Be able to create notes
- Be able to list notes
- Be able to edit notes
- Be able to delete notes
- Note bodies must be capable of storing/displaying rich text
- Be able to create a user account
- Must be able to log into the application using OAuth2 credentials against an existing system

Our non-functional requirements are fairly modest:

- Must have a RESTful API
- Must have an HTML 5/JavaScript frontend
- Must have a flexible, scalable data store
- Must be easily deployable on resource-constrained systems

Of course, this list of non-functional requirements was chosen in part because they reflect real-world requirements, but they also set us up very nicely to discuss some of the technologies I'd like to cover in this chapter. To cut to the chase, we'll create a web application that provides both a REST-based API and a JavaScript client. It will be backed by a document data store, and built using one of the many microservice libraries/frameworks available to the JVM.

So what does this stack look like? Let's take a quick survey of our options before we settle on a particular choice. Let's start with a look at the microservice frameworks.

Microservice frameworks on the JVM

While I am reluctant to spend a great deal of time on what a microservice is given that most people are familiar with the topic at this point, I think it would be a remiss not to give at least a brief description in case you are not familiar with the idea. With that said, here is a nice, concise definition of microservice from SmartBear, a provider of software quality tools perhaps best known for their stewardship of the Swagger API and related libraries:

> *Essentially, microservice architecture is a method of developing software applications as a suite of independently deployable, small, modular services in which each service runs a unique process and communicates through a well-defined, lightweight mechanism to serve a business goal.*

To put it another way, rather than the older, more established approach of bundling several related systems in one web application and deploying it to a large application server, such as GlassFish/Payara Server, Wildfly, WebLogic Server, or WebSphere, each of these systems would instead be run separately in their own JVM process. The benefits of this approach include easier, piecemeal upgrades, increased stability through process isolation, smaller resource requirements, greater machine utilization, and so on. The concept itself is not necessarily new, but it has certainly gained popularity in recent years, and continues to grow at a rapid pace.

So what do our options look like on the JVM? We have several, including, in no particular order, the following:

- **Eclipse Vert.x**: This is officially *a tool-kit for building reactive applications on the JVM*. It provides an event-driven application framework that lends itself well to writing microservices. Vert.x can be used in a number of languages, including Java, Javascript, Kotlin, Ceylon, Scala, Groovy, and Ruby. More information can be found at `http://vertx.io/`.
- **Spring Boot**: This is a library to build stand alone Spring applications. Spring Boot applications have full access to the entire Spring ecosystem, and can be run using a single fat/uber JAR. Spring Boot lives at `https://projects.spring.io/spring-boot/`.
- **Java EE MicroProfile**: This is a community and vendor-led effort to create a new profile for Java EE, specifically tailored to microservices. At the time of writing, the profile includes **Java API for RESTful Web Services** (**JAX-RS**), CDI, and JSON-P, and is sponsored by several companies including Tomitribe, Payara, Red Hat, Hazelcast, IBM, and Fujitsu, and user groups such as London Java Community and SouJava. The MicroProfile home page is `http://microprofile.io/`.

- **Lagom**: This fairly new framework is a reactive microservices framework from Lightbend, the company behind Scala. It is described as an opinionated microservice framework, and is built using two of Lightbend's more famous libraries--Akka and Play. Lagom applications can be written either in Java or Scala. More details can be found at
  `https://www.lightbend.com/platform/development/lagom-framework`.
- **Dropwizard**: This is a Java framework to develop ops-friendly, high-performance, RESTful web services. It is a framework that offers Jetty for HTTP, Jersey for REST services, and Jackson for JSON. It also provides support for other libraries such as Guava, Hibernate Validator, Freemarker, and others. You can find Dropwizard at `http://www.dropwizard.io/`.

There are a few other options, but it should be clear that, as JVM developers, we have a myriad of choices, which is almost always good. Since we can only build using one, I have chosen to use the MicroProfile. Specifically, we'll base our application on Payara Micro, Payara's implementation, which is based on the GlassFish sources (plus Payara's bug fixes, enhancements, and so on).

By choosing the MicroProfile and Payara Micro, we choose, implicitly, JAX-RS as the basis for our REST services. We are free, of course, to use whatever we want, but deviating from what the framework offers lessens the value of the framework itself.

That leaves us with our choice of data store. One option we've already seen is the relational database. It is a tried and true choice that powers a wide swath of the industry. They are, however, not without their limitations and problems. While databases themselves can be complicated in terms of classifications and functionality, perhaps the most popular alternatives to relational databases are NoSQL databases. While these have existed for half a century, the idea had not gained any significant market traction until sometime in the last decade or so with the advent of **Web 2.0**.

While the term **NoSQL** is very broad, most examples of this type of database tend to be key-value, document, or graph data stores, each offering distinct performance and behavior characteristics. A full treatment of each type of NoSQL database and its various implementations is beyond the scope of this book, so, in the interest of time and space, we'll just get straight to our selection--MongoDB. Its scalability and flexibility, especially in regard to document schemas, meshes well with our target use case.

Finally, on the client side, we have a myriad of options again. Among the most popular are ReactJS from Facebook and Angular from Google. There is a variety of other frameworks, including older options such as Knockout and Backbone, as well as newer ones such as Vue.js. It is this latter option that we'll use. Not only is it a very powerful and flexible option, it also presents the least amount of friction getting started. Since this book is focused on Java, I felt it prudent to select an option that will require the least amount of setup while meeting our needs.

Creating the application

To use Payara Micro, we create a Java web application like we normally would. In NetBeans, we will select **File** | **New Project** | **Maven** | **Web Application** and click on **Next**. For the project name, enter `monumentum`, select the appropriate **Project Location**, and fix up the **Group ID** and **Package** as desired:

The next window will ask us to choose a server, which we can leave blank, and a Java EE version, which we want to set to **Java EE 7 Web**:

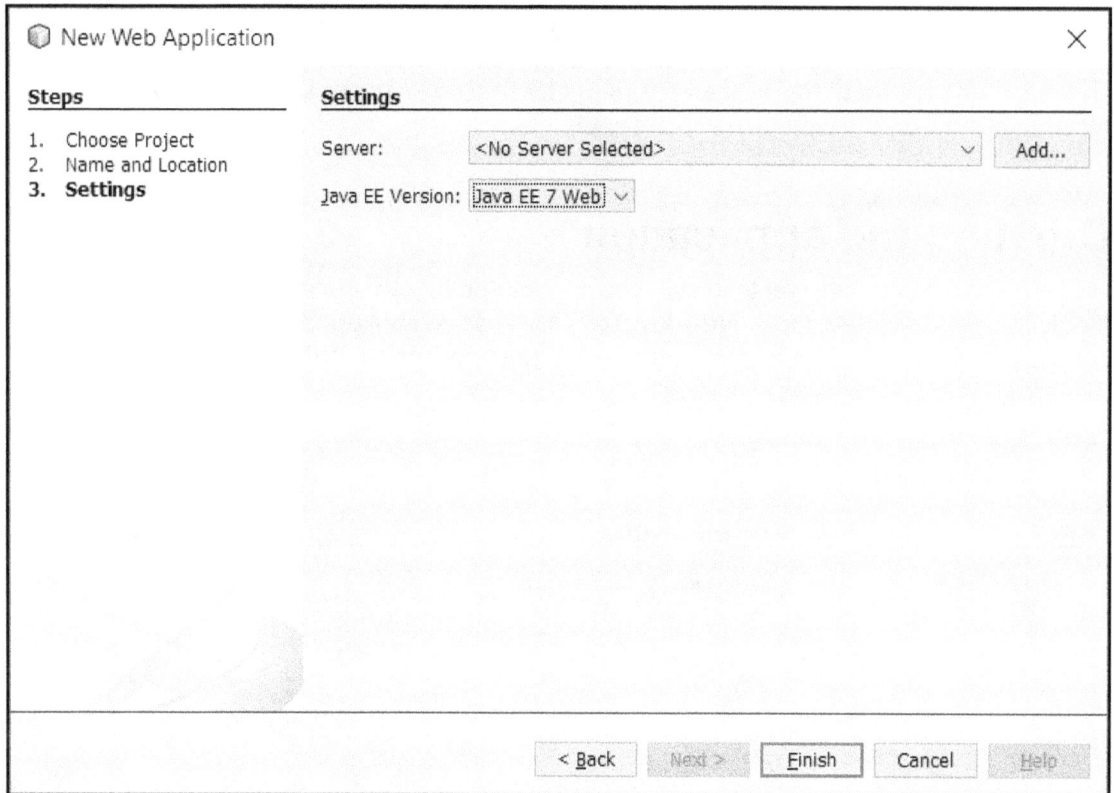

```
New Web Application                                                    ✕

Steps                      Settings

1.  Choose Project         Server:          <No Server Selected>           ∨    Add...
2.  Name and Location
3.  Settings               Java EE Version:  Java EE 7 Web  ∨




                                        < Back    Next >    Finish    Cancel    Help
```

After a few moments, we should have our project created and ready to go. Since we created a Java EE 7 web application, NetBeans has already added the Java EE API dependency to the project. Before we jump into coding, let's add Payara Micro to the build to get that part ready. To do that, we need to add a plugin to the build. That will look something like this (though we've only shown the highlights here):

```
<plugin>
  <groupId>org.codehaus.mojo</groupId>
  <artifactId>exec-maven-plugin</artifactId>
  <version>1.5.0</version>
  <dependencies>
    <dependency>
      <groupId>fish.payara.extras</groupId>
      <artifactId>payara-microprofile</artifactId>
      <version>1.0</version>
```

```
      </dependency>
    </dependencies>
```

This sets up the Maven exec plugin, which is used to execute either an external application or, as we'll do here, a Java application:

```
<executions>
  <execution>
    <id>payara-uber-jar</id>
    <phase>package</phase>
    <goals>
      <goal>java</goal>
    </goals>
```

Here, we're associating the execution of this plugin with Maven's package phase. This means that when we run Maven to build our project, the plugin's java goal will be run as Maven starts to package the project, allowing us to alter exactly what gets packaged in the JAR:

```
<configuration>
  <mainClass>
    fish.payara.micro.PayaraMicro
  </mainClass>
  <arguments>
    <argument>--deploy</argument>
    <argument>
      ${basedir}/target/${warfile.name}.war
    </argument>
    <argument>--outputUberJar</argument>
    <argument>
      ${basedir}/target/${project.artifactId}.jar
    </argument>
  </arguments>
</configuration>
```

This last section configures the plugin. It will run the `PayaraMicro` class, passing the `--deploy <path> --outputUberJar ...` command. Effectively, we're telling Payara Micro how to run our application, but, rather than executing the package right now, we want it to create an uber JAR that will run the application later.

Typically, when you build your project, you get a jar file that contains only the classes and resources that are directly included in your project. Any external dependencies are left as something that the execution environment has to provide. With an uber JAR, all of the dependencies are included in our project's jar as well, which is then configured in such a way that the execution environment can find them as needed.

The problem with the setup is that, left as is, when we build, we'll get an uber JAR, but we won't have any easy way to run the application from NetBeans. To fix that, we need a slightly different plugin configuration. Specifically, it needs these lines:

```
<argument>--deploy</argument>
<argument>
  ${basedir}/target/${project.artifactId}-${project.version}
</argument>
```

These replace the preceding `deploy` and `outputUberJar` options. To help speed up our builds, we also don't want the uber JAR created until we ask for it, so we can separate these two plugin configurations into two separate profiles, as follows:

```
<profiles>
  <profile>
    <id>exploded-war</id>
    <!-- ... -->
  </profile>
  <profile>
    <id>uber</id>
    <!-- ... -->
  </profile>
</profiles>
```

When we're ready to build the deployment artifact, we activate the uber profile when we execute Maven, and we'll get our executable jar:

```
$ mvn -Puber install
```

The `exploded-war` profile is the configuration that we'll use from the IDE, which runs Payara Micro, pointing it at the exploded war in our build directory. To instruct NetBeans to use that, we need to modify a couple of action configurations. To do that, right-click on the project in NetBeans and select **Properties** from the bottom of the context menu. Under **Actions**, find **Run Project** and select it, then enter `exploded-war` under **Activate Profiles**:

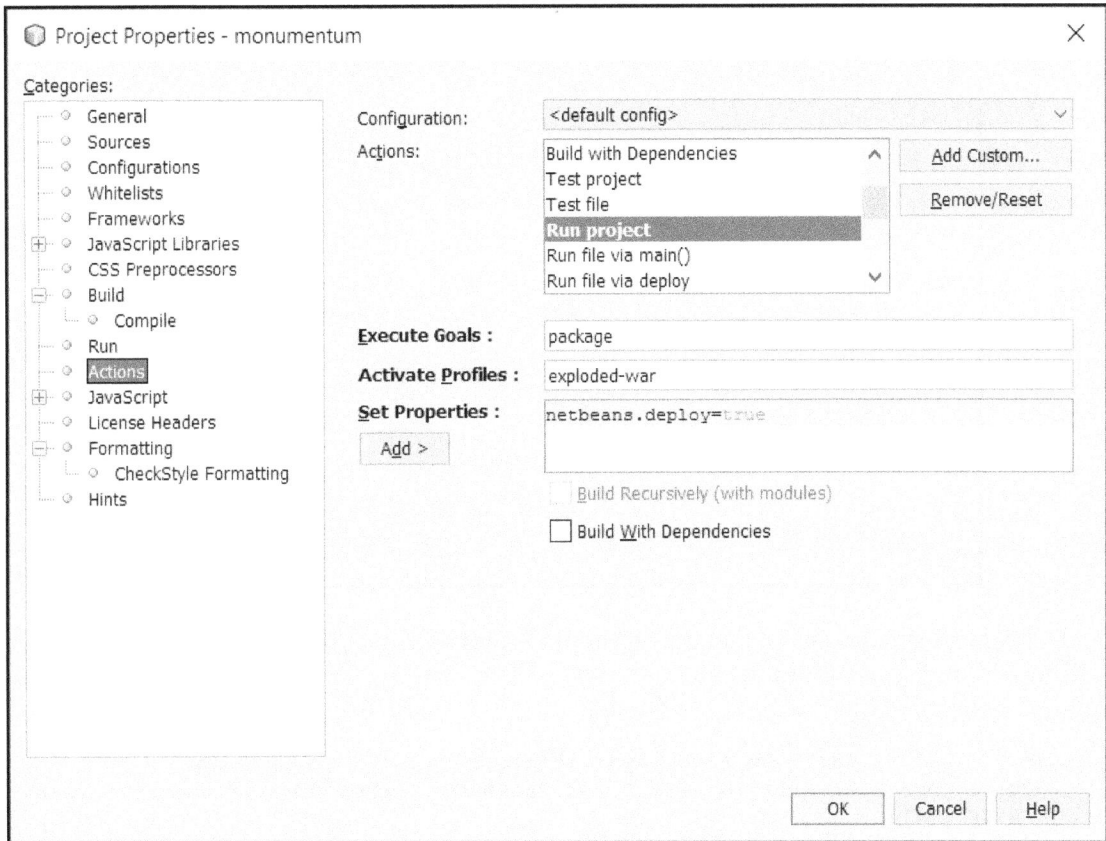

If we run the application now, NetBeans will complain because we haven't selected a server. While this is a web application and those have typically needed a server, we're using Payara Micro, so we don't need an application server defined. Fortunately, NetBeans will let us tell it that, as demonstrated in the following screenshot:

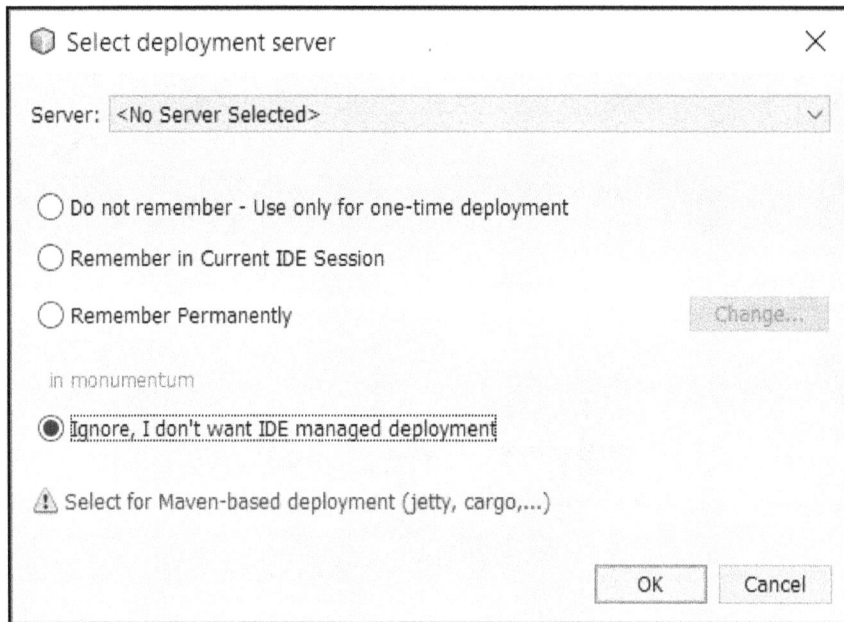

Select **Ignore, I don't want IDE managed deployment** and click on **OK**, then watch the output window. You should see a fair amount of text scroll by, and after a few seconds, you should see text like this:

```
Apr 05, 2017 1:18:59 AM fish.payara.micro.PayaraMicro bootStrap
INFO: Payara MicroProfile  4.1.1.164-SNAPSHOT (build ${build.number}) ready
in 9496 (ms)
```

Once you see that, we're ready to test our application, such as it is at this point. In your browser, open `http://localhost:8080/monumentum-1.0-SNAPSHOT/index.html` and you should see a large and exciting *Hello World!* message on the page. If you see this, you have successfully bootstrapped a Payara Micro project. Take a moment to congratulate yourself, and then we'll make the application do something useful.

Creating REST Services

This being basically a Java EE application, albeit one that it is packaged and deployed a bit differently, everything you may have learned about writing Java EE applications most likely still applies. Of course, you may not have ever written such an application, so we'll walk through the steps.

REST applications in Java EE are written using JAX-RS, and our starting point for JAX-RS is an `Application`. The `Application` is a deployment-agnostic means for declaring root-level resources to the runtime. How the runtime finds the `Application` is, of course, dependent on the runtime itself. For a MicroProfile application like ours, we'll be running in a Servlet 3.0 environment, so we need not do anything special, as Servlet 3.0 supports a descriptor-less deployment option. The runtime will scan for a class of type `Application` that is annotated with `@ApplicationPath` and uses that to configure the JAX-RS application, as shown here:

```
@ApplicationPath("/api")
  public class Monumentum extends javax.ws.rs.core.Application {
  @Override
  public Set<Class<?>> getClasses() {
    Set<Class<?>> s = new HashSet<>();
    return s;
  }
}
```

With the `@ApplicationPath` annotation, we specify the root URL of our application's REST endpoints, which is, of course, relative to the web application's root context itself. `Application` has three methods we can override, but we're only interested in the one listed here: `getClasses()`. We'll provide more details on this method shortly, but, for now, keep in mind that this is how we will describe to JAX-RS what our top-level resources are.

Monumentum will have a very simple API, with the primary endpoint being that to interact with notes. To create that endpoint, we create a simple Java class and mark it up with the appropriate JAX-RS annotations:

```
@Path("/notes")
@RequestScoped
@Produces(MediaType.APPLICATION_JSON)
public class NoteResource {
}
```

With this class, we're describing an endpoint that will live at /api/notes and will produce JSON results. JAX-RS supports, for example, XML, but most REST developers are accustomed to JSON and are expecting nothing else, so we need not support anything other than JSON. The needs of your application may vary, of course, so you can adjust the list of supported media types as needed.

While this will compile and run, and JAX-RS will attempt to handle requests to our endpoint, we haven't actually defined it yet. To do that, we need to add some methods to our endpoint that will define the inputs and outputs of the endpoint, as well as the HTTP verb/method we'll use. Let's start with the notes collection endpoint:

```
@GET
public Response getAll() {
  List<Note> notes = new ArrayList<>();
  return Response.ok(
    new GenericEntity<List<Note>>(notes) {}).build();
}
```

We now have an endpoint that answers GET requests at /api/notes and returns a List of Note instances. There is some debate among REST developers on the proper return from methods like these. There are some who prefer to return the actual type the client will see, for example List<Note> in our case, as it makes it clear to developers reading the source, or documentation generated from it. Others prefer, as we've done here, to return a JAX-RS Response object, as that gives greater control over the response, including HTTP headers, status code, and more. I tend to prefer this second approach as we've done here. You, of course, are free to use either approach.

One last thing to note here is the way in which we build the response body:

```
new GenericEntity<List<Note>>(notes) {}
```

Typically, at runtime, the parameterized type of the List is lost due to type erasure. Using a GenericEntity like this allows us to capture the parameterized type, allowing the runtime to marshal the data. Using this allows us to avoid writing our own MessageBodyWriter. Less code is almost always a good thing.

If we run our application now, we'll get the following response, albeit a very boring one:

```
$ curl http://localhost:8080/monumentum-1.0-SNAPSHOT/api/notes/
[]
```

That's both satisfying, and it's not, but it does demonstrate that we're on the right track. Clearly, we want that endpoint to return data, but we have no way of adding a note, so let's fix that now.

Creating a new entity via REST is accomplished by POSTing a new entity to its collection. That method looks like this:

```
@POST
public Response createNote(Note note) {
  Document doc = note.toDocument();
  collection.insertOne(doc);
  final String id = doc.get("_id",
    ObjectId.class).toHexString();

  return Response.created(uriInfo.getRequestUriBuilder()
    .path(id).build())
  .build();
}
```

The @POST annotation indicates the use of the HTTP POST verb. The method takes a Note instance, and returns a Response as we saw in the preceding code. Notice that we don't deal with JSON directly. By specifying a Note in the method signature, we can take advantage of one of JAX-RS's great features--POJO mapping. We've already seen a hint of it in the previous code with GenericEntity. JAX-RS will attempt to unmarshal--that is, convert from a serialized form to a model object--the JSON request body. If the client sends a JSON object in the correct format, we get a usable Note instance. If the client sends an improperly built object, it gets a response. This feature allows us to deal solely with our domain objects and not worry about JSON encoding and decoding, which can save considerable time and energy.

Adding MongoDB

In the body of the method, we get our first glimpse of the integration with MongoDB. To make this compile, we need to add a dependency on the MongoDB Java Driver:

```
<dependency>
  <groupId>org.mongodb</groupId>
  <artifactId>mongodb-driver</artifactId>
  <version>3.4.2</version>
</dependency>
```

MongoDB deals with documents, so we need to convert our domain model to a Document, which we accomplish via a method on our model class. We haven't looked at the details of the Note class, so let's do that now:

```
public class Note {
  private String id;
  private String userId;
```

```
            private String title;
            private String body;
            private LocalDateTime created = LocalDateTime.now();
            private LocalDateTime modified = null;

            // Getters, setters and some constructors not shown

            public Note(final Document doc) {
              final LocalDateTimeAdapter adapter =
                new LocalDateTimeAdapter();
              userId = doc.getString("user_id");
              id = doc.get("_id", ObjectId.class).toHexString();
              title = doc.getString("title");
              body = doc.getString("body");
              created = adapter.unmarshal(doc.getString("created"));
              modified = adapter.unmarshal(doc.getString("modified"));
            }

            public Document toDocument() {
              final LocalDateTimeAdapter adapter =
                 new LocalDateTimeAdapter();
              Document doc = new Document();
              if (id != null) {
                 doc.append("_id", new ObjectId(getId()));
              }
              doc.append("user_id", getUserId())
               .append("title", getTitle())
               .append("body", getBody())
               .append("created",
                 adapter.marshal(getCreated() != null
                 ? getCreated() : LocalDateTime.now()))
               .append("modified",
                 adapter.marshal(getModified()));
              return doc;
            }
          }
```

This is mostly just a normal POJO. We have added a constructor and an instance method to handle converting to and from MongoDB's Document type.

There are a couple of things to call out here. The first is how the ID of the MongoDB Document is handled. Every document stored in a MongoDB database gets _id assigned to it. In the Java API, this _id is represented as ObjectId. We don't want that detail exposed in our domain model, so we convert it to a String and back again.

We also need to do some special handling for our date fields. We've chosen to represent the `created` and `modified` properties as `LocalDateTime` instances since the new date/time API is superior to the old `java.util.Date`. Unfortunately, the MongoDB Java Driver does not yet support Java 8, so we need to handle the conversion ourselves. We'll store these dates as strings and convert them as needed. That conversion is handled via the `LocalDateTimeAdapter` class:

```
public class LocalDateTimeAdapter
    extends XmlAdapter<String, LocalDateTime> {
    private static final Pattern JS_DATE = Pattern.compile
        ("\d{4}-\d{2}-\d{2}T\d{2}:\d{2}:\d{2}\.\d+Z");
    private static final DateTimeFormatter DEFAULT_FORMAT =
        DateTimeFormatter.ISO_LOCAL_DATE_TIME;
    private static final DateTimeFormatter JS_FORMAT =
        DateTimeFormatter.ofPattern
        ("yyyy-MM-dd'T'HH:mm:ss.SSS'Z'");

    @Override
    public LocalDateTime unmarshal(String date) {
        if (date == null) {
            return null;
        }
        return LocalDateTime.parse(date,
            (JS_DATE.matcher(date).matches())
            ? JS_FORMAT : DEFAULT_FORMAT);
    }

    @Override
    public String marshal(LocalDateTime date) {
        return date != null ? DEFAULT_FORMAT.format(date) : null;
    }
}
```

This is probably a bit more complicated than you might expect, and that's because it's doing more than we've discussed so far. The usage we're looking at now, that from our model class, is not this class' primary purpose, but we'll get to that in a moment. That aside, the class' behavior is pretty straightforward--take a `String`, determine which of the two supported formats it represents, and convert it to a `LocalDateTime`. It also goes the other way.

This class' primary purpose is for JAX-RS' use. When we pass `Note` instances across the wire, `LocalDateTime` needs to be unmarshalled as well, and we can tell JAX-RS how to do this via an `XmlAdapter`.

With the class defined, we need to tell JAX-RS about it. We can do that in a couple of different ways. We could use an annotation on each property in our model like this:

```
@XmlJavaTypeAdapter(value = LocalDateTimeAdapter.class)
private LocalDateTime created = LocalDateTime.now();
```

While this works, it's a fairly large annotation, as far as these kinds of things go, and you have to put this on every `LocalDateTime` property. If you have several models with fields of this type, you will have to touch each property. Fortunately, there's a way to associate the type with the adapter once. We can do that in a special Java file called `package-info.java`. Most people have never heard of this file, and even fewer use it, but it is simply a place for package-level documentation and annotations. It is this latter use case that interests us. In the package for our model class, create `package-info.java` and put this in it:

```
@XmlJavaTypeAdapters({
  @XmlJavaTypeAdapter(type = LocalDateTime.class,
    value = LocalDateTimeAdapter.class)
})
package com.steeplesoft.monumentum.model;
```

We have the same annotation we saw in the preceding code, but it's wrapped in `@XmlJavaTypeAdapters`. The JVM allows only annotation of a given type on an element, so this wrapper allows us to work around that limitation. We also need to specify the type parameter on the `@XmlJavaTypeAdapter` annotation since it is no longer on the target property. With this in place, every `LocalDateTime` property will be handled correctly without any additional work.

That's quite a bit of setup, but we're still not quite ready. We have everything set up on the REST side. We now need to get the MongoDB classes in place. To connect to a MongoDB instance, we start with a `MongoClient`. From the `MongoClient`, we then acquire a reference to a `MongoDatabase` from which we get a `MongoCollection`:

```
private MongoCollection<Document> collection;
private MongoClient mongoClient;
private MongoDatabase database;

@PostConstruct
public void postConstruct() {
  String host = System.getProperty("mongo.host", "localhost");
  String port = System.getProperty("mongo.port", "27017");
  mongoClient = new MongoClient(host, Integer.parseInt(port));
  database = mongoClient.getDatabase("monumentum");
  collection = database.getCollection("note");
}
```

The @PostConstruct method runs on the bean after the constructor has run. In this method, we initialize our various MongoDB classes and store them in instance variables. With these classes ready, we can revisit, for example, getAll():

```
@GET
public Response getAll() {
  List<Note> notes = new ArrayList<>();
  try (MongoCursor<Document> cursor = collection.find()
  .iterator()) {
    while (cursor.hasNext()) {
      notes.add(new Note(cursor.next()));
    }
  }

  return Response.ok(
    new GenericEntity<List<Note>>(notes) {})
  .build();
}
```

We can now query the database for our notes, and with the implementation of createNote() shown in the preceding code, we can create the following notes:

```
$ curl -v -H "Content-Type: application/json" -X POST -d '{"title":"Command
line note", "body":"A note from the command line"}'
http://localhost:8080/monumentum-1.0-SNAPSHOT/api/notes/
*   Trying ::1...
* TCP_NODELAY set
* Connected to localhost (::1) port 8080 (#0)
> POST /monumentum-1.0-SNAPSHOT/api/notes/ HTTP/1.1
...
< HTTP/1.1 201 Created
...
$ curl http://localhost:8080/monumentum-1.0-SNAPSHOT/api/notes/ | jq .
[
  {
    "id": "58e5d0d79ccd032344f66c37",
    "userId": null,
    "title": "Command line note",
    "body": "A note from the command line",
    "created": "2017-04-06T00:23:34.87",
    "modified": null
  }
]
```

> For this to work on your machine, you'll need an instance of MongoDB running. You can download an installer appropriate for your operating system as well as find installation instructions on the MongoDB website (`https://docs.mongodb.com/manual/installation/`).

Before we move on to the other resource methods, let's take one last look at our MongoDB API instances. While instantiating the instances like we have works, it also puts a fair amount of work on the resource itself. Ideally, we should be able to move those concerns elsewhere and inject the instances. Hopefully, this sounds familiar to you, as this is exactly the type of concern that **dependency injection** (**DI**) or **inversion of control** (**IoC**) frameworks were created to solve.

Dependency injection with CDI

Java EE provides a framework such as CDI. With CDI, we can inject any container-controlled object into another with compile-time type safety. The problem, though, is the objects in question need to be container controlled, which our MongoDB API objects are not. Fortunately, CDI provides a means by which the container can create these instances, a facility known as producer methods. What might this look like? Let's start with the injection point, as that is the simplest piece:

```
@Inject
@Collection("notes")
private MongoCollection<Document> collection;
```

When the CDI container sees `@Inject`, it inspects the element the annotation is on to determine the type. It will then attempt to look up an instance that will satisfy the injection request. If there is more than one, the injection would typically fail. Although, we have used a qualifier annotation to help CDI determine what to inject. That annotation is defined like this:

```
@Qualifier
@Retention(RetentionPolicy.RUNTIME)
@Target({ElementType.METHOD, ElementType.FIELD,
  ElementType.PARAMETER, ElementType.TYPE})
public @interface Collection {
  @Nonbinding String value() default "unknown";
}
```

With this annotation, we can pass hints to the container that will help it select an instance for injection. As we've mentioned, `MongoCollection` is not container-managed, so we need to fix that, which we do via the following producer method:

```
@RequestScoped
public class Producers {
  @Produces
  @Collection
  public MongoCollection<Document>
    getCollection(InjectionPoint injectionPoint) {
      Collection mc = injectionPoint.getAnnotated()
      .getAnnotation(Collection.class);
      return getDatabase().getCollection(mc.value());
  }
}
```

The `@Produces` method tells CDI that this method will produce instances needed by the container. CDI determines the type of the injectable instance from the method signature. We also place the qualifier annotation on the method as an additional hint to the runtime as it tries to resolve our injection request.

In the method itself, we add `InjectionPoint` to the method signature. When CDI calls this method, it will provide an instance of this class, from which we can get information about each particular injection point as they are processed. From `InjectionPoint`, we get the `Collection` instance from which we can get the name of the MongoDB collection we're interested in. We are now ready to get the `MongoCollection` instance we saw earlier. The `MongoClient` and `MongoDatabase` instantiation is handled internally in the class and is not changed significantly from our earlier usage.

There is one small setup step for CDI. In order to avoid potentially expensive classpath scanning by the CDI container, we need to tell the system that we want the CDI turned on, so to speak. To do that, we need a `beans.xml` file, which can either be full of CDI configuration elements, or completely empty, which is what we'll do. For Java EE web applications, `beans.xml` needs to be in the `WEB-INF` directory, so we create the file in `src/main/webapp/WEB-INF`.

> **TIP** Make sure that the file is truly empty. If there's even a blank line, Weld, Payara's CDI implementation, will attempt to parse the file, giving you an XML parsing error.

Finish the notes resource

Before we can move on from the `Note` resource, we need to finish up a few operations, namely, read, update, and delete. Reading a single note is very straightforward:

```
@GET
@Path("{id}")
public Response getNote(@PathParam("id") String id) {
  Document doc = collection.find(buildQueryById(id)).first();
  if (doc == null) {
    return Response.status(Response.Status.NOT_FOUND).build();
  } else {
    return Response.ok(new Note(doc)).build();
  }
}
```

We've specified the use of the HTTP verb `GET` as we've already seen, but we have an additional annotation on this method, `@Path`. Using this annotation, we tell JAX-RS that this endpoint has additional path segments that the request needs to be matched against. In this case, we specify one additional segment, but we've wrapped it in curly braces. Without those braces, the match would be a literal match, that is to say, "Does this URL have the string 'id' on the end?" With the braces, though, we're telling JAX-RS that we want to match the additional segment, but its contents can be anything, and we want to capture that value and give it the name `id`. In our method signature, we instruct JAX-RS to inject the value via the `@PathParam` annotation, giving us access to the user-specified `Note` ID in our method.

To retrieve the note from MongoDB, we get our first real glimpse of how one queries MongoDB:

```
Document doc = collection.find(buildQueryById(id)).first();
```

In a nutshell, pass `BasicDBObject` to the `find()` method on `collection`, which returns a `FindIterable<?>` object, on which we call `first()` to get what should be the only element returned (assuming there is one, of course). The interesting bits here are hidden in `buildQueryById()`:

```
private BasicDBObject buildQueryById(String id) {
  BasicDBObject query =
    new BasicDBObject("_id", new ObjectId(id));
  return query;
}
```

Our query filter is defined using this `BasicDBObject`, which we initialize with a key and value. In this case, we want to filter by the `_id` field in the document, so we use that as a key, but note that we pass `ObjectId` as the value, and not just `String`. If we want to filter by more fields, we would append more key/value pairs to the `BasicDBObject` variable, which we will see later.

Once we've queried the collection and gotten the document the user requested, we convert it from `Document` to `Note` using the helper method on `Note`, and return it with a status code of 200 or `OK`.

Updating a document in the database is a bit more complicated, but not excessively so, as you can see here:

```
@PUT
@Path("{id}")
public Response updateNote(Note note) {
  note.setModified(LocalDateTime.now());
  UpdateResult result =
    collection.updateOne(buildQueryById(note.getId()),
    new Document("$set", note.toDocument()));
  if (result.getModifiedCount() == 0) {
    return Response.status(Response.Status.NOT_FOUND).build();
  } else {
    return Response.ok().build();
  }
}
```

The first thing to notice is the HTTP method--PUT. There is some debate on what verb to use for updates. Some, such as Dropbox and Facebook, say POST, while others, such as Google (depending on which API you look at), say PUT. I would contend that the choice is largely up to you. Just be consistent in your choice. We will be completely replacing the entity on the server with what the client passes in, so the operation is idempotent. By choosing PUT, we can signal this fact to the client, making the API a bit more self-describing for clients.

Inside the method, we start by setting the modified date to reflect the operation. Next, we call `Collection.updateOne()` to modify the document. The syntax is a little odd, but here's what's happening--we're querying the collection for the note we want to modify, then telling MongoDB to replace the loaded document with the new one we're providing. Finally, we query `UpdateResult` to see how many documents were updated. If none were, then the requested document doesn't exist, so we return `NOT_FOUND` (404). If it's non-zero, we return `OK` (200).

Finally, our delete method looks like this:

```
@DELETE
@Path("{id}")
public Response deleteNote(@PathParam("id") String id) {
    collection.deleteOne(buildQueryById(id));
    return Response.ok().build();
}
```

We tell MongoDB to filter the collection using the same query filter we've seen before, then delete one document, which should be all it finds, of course, given our filter, but `deleteOne()` is a sensible safeguard. We could do a check like we did above in `updateNote()` to see if something was actually deleted, but there's little point--whether the document was there at the start of the request or not, it's not there at the end and that's our goal, so there's little to be gained from returning an error response.

We can now create, read, update, and delete notes, but the eagle-eyed among you may have noticed that anyone can read every note in the system. For a multi-user system, that's not a good thing, so let's fix that.

Adding authentication

Authentication systems can easily get extremely complex. From homegrown systems, complete with custom user management screens, to sophisticated single sign-on solutions, we have a lot of options. One of the more popular options is OAuth2, and there are a number of options. For Monumentum, we'll implement sign in using Google. To do that, we need to create an application in Google's Developer Console, which can be found at `https://console.developers.google.com`.

Once you've logged in, click on the project dropdown at the top of page and click on **Create Project**, which should present this screen to you:

New Project

Project name

My Project

Your project ID will be cohesive-pad-164004   Edit

Please email me updates regarding feature announcements, performance suggestions, feedback surveys and special offers.

    Yes   No

I agree that my use of any services and related APIs is subject to my compliance with the applicable Terms of Service.

    Yes   ● No

CANCEL   CREATE

Provide **Project Name**, make your choices for the next two questions, then click on **CREATE**. Once the project has been created, you should be redirected to the Library page. Click on the **Credentials** link on the left, then click on **Create credentials** and select **OAuth Client ID**. If needed, fill out the **OAuth Consent** screen as directed. Select **Web Application** for **Application Type**, enter **Name**, and provide **Authorized redirect URIs** as shown in this screenshot:

Client ID for Web application

Client ID

Client secret

Creation date   Mar 30, 2017, 10:58:46 PM

Name

Monumentum Web UI

Restrictions
Enter JavaScript origins, redirect URIs, or both

Authorized JavaScript origins
For use with requests from a browser. This is the origin URI of the client application. It can't contain a wildcard (http://*.example.com) or a path (http://example.com/subdir). If you're using a nonstandard port, you must include it in the origin URI.

http://localhost:8080   ✕

http://www.example.com

Authorized redirect URIs
For use with requests from a web server. This is the path in your application that users are redirected to after they have authenticated with Google. The path will be appended with the authorization code for access. Must have a protocol. Cannot contain URL fragments or relative paths. Cannot be a public IP address.

http://localhost:8080/monumentum-1.0-SNAPSHOT/api/auth/callback   ✕

http://www.example.com/oauth2callback

Save   Cancel

Before this is moved to production, we will need to add a production URI to this screen, but this configuration will work in development just fine. When you click on **Save**, you will be shown your new client ID and client secret. Make note of these:

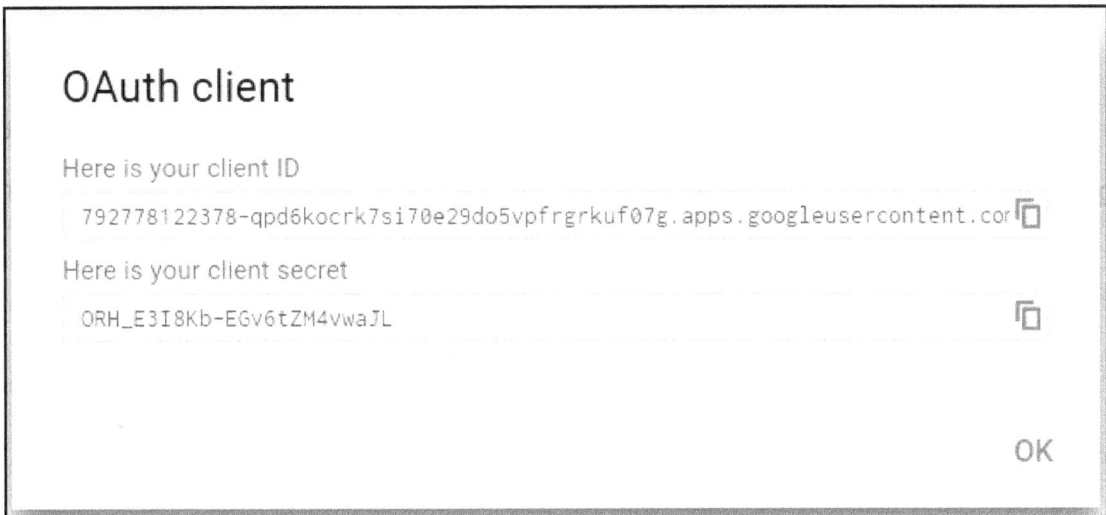

OAuth client

Here is your client ID

792778122378-qpd6kocrk7si70e29do5vpfrgrkuf07g.apps.googleusercontent.cor

Here is your client secret

ORH_E3I8Kb-EGv6tZM4vwaJL

OK

With this data (note that these are not my actual ID and secret, so you'll have to generate your own), we are ready to start working on our authentication resource. We'll start by defining the resource as follows:

```
@Path("auth")
public class AuthenticationResource {
```

We need to register this in our `Application`, as follows:

```
@ApplicationPath("/api")
public class Monumentum extends javax.ws.rs.core.Application {
  @Override
  public Set<Class<?>> getClasses() {
    Set<Class<?>> s = new HashSet<>();
    s.add(NoteResource.class);
    s.add(AuthenticationResource.class);
    return s;
  }
}
```

To work with the Google OAuth provider, we'll need to declare a few instance variables and instantiate a few Google API classes:

```
private final String clientId;
private final String clientSecret;
private final GoogleAuthorizationCodeFlow flow;
private final HttpTransport HTTP_TRANSPORT =
  new NetHttpTransport();
private static final String USER_INFO_URL =
  "https://www.googleapis.com/oauth2/v1/userinfo";
private static final List<String> SCOPES = Arrays.asList(
  "https://www.googleapis.com/auth/userinfo.profile",
  "https://www.googleapis.com/auth/userinfo.email");
```

The variables `clientId` and `clientSecret` will hold the values that Google just gave us. The other two classes are necessary for the process we're about to walk through, and `SCOPES` holds the permissions we want from Google, which is just access to the user's profile and email. The class constructor finishes the setup of these items:

```
public AuthenticationResource() {
  clientId = System.getProperty("client_id");
  clientSecret = System.getProperty("client_secret");
  flow = new GoogleAuthorizationCodeFlow.Builder(HTTP_TRANSPORT,
    new JacksonFactory(), clientId, clientSecret,
    SCOPES).build();
}
```

The first part of the authentication flow is to create an authentication URL, which is done like this:

```
@Context
private UriInfo uriInfo;
@GET
@Path("url")
public String getAuthorizationUrl() {
  return flow.newAuthorizationUrl()
  .setRedirectUri(getCallbackUri()).build();
}
private String getCallbackUri()
  throws UriBuilderException, IllegalArgumentException {
  return uriInfo.getBaseUriBuilder().path("auth")
    .path("callback").build()
    .toASCIIString();
}
```

Using the JAX-RS class, `UriInfo`, we create a `URI` that points to another endpoint in our application, `/api/auth/callback`. We then pass that to `GoogleAuthorizationCodeFlow` to finish building our login URL. When the user clicks on the link, the browser will be directed to a login dialog from Google. Upon successful authentication, the user will be redirected to our callback URL, which is handled by this method:

```
@GET
@Path("callback")
public Response handleCallback(@QueryParam("code")
@NotNull String code) throws IOException {
  User user = getUserInfoJson(code);
  saveUserInformation(user);
  final String jwt = createToken(user.getEmail());
  return Response.seeOther(
    uriInfo.getBaseUriBuilder()
    .path("../loginsuccess.html")
    .queryParam("Bearer", jwt)
    .build())
  .build();
}
```

When Google redirects to our `callback` endpoint, it will provide a code that we can use to finish the authentication. We do that in the `getUserInfoJson()` method:

```
private User getUserInfoJson(final String authCode)
throws IOException {
  try {
    final GoogleTokenResponse response =
      flow.newTokenRequest(authCode)
      .setRedirectUri(getCallbackUri())
      .execute();
    final Credential credential =
      flow.createAndStoreCredential(response, null);
    final HttpRequest request =
      HTTP_TRANSPORT.createRequestFactory(credential)
      .buildGetRequest(new GenericUrl(USER_INFO_URL));
    request.getHeaders().setContentType("application/json");
    final JSONObject identity =
      new JSONObject(request.execute().parseAsString());
    return new User(
      identity.getString("id"),
      identity.getString("email"),
      identity.getString("name"),
      identity.getString("picture"));
  } catch (JSONException ex) {
```

```
        Logger.getLogger(AuthenticationResource.class.getName())
        .log(Level.SEVERE, null, ex);
        return null;
    }
}
```

Using the authentication code we just got from Google, we send another request to Google, this time to get the user information. When the request returns, we take the JSON object in the response body and use it to build a `User` object, which we return.

Back in our REST endpoint method, we call this method to save the user to the database, if needed:

```
private void saveUserInformation(User user) {
  Document doc = collection.find(
    new BasicDBObject("email", user.getEmail())).first();
  if (doc == null) {
    collection.insertOne(user.toDocument());
  }
}
```

Once we've gotten the user's information from Google, we no longer need the code as we do not need to interact with any other Google resources, so we do not persist it anywhere.

Finally, we want to return something to the client --some kind of token -- which can be used to prove the client's identity. To do that, we'll use a technology called a JSON Web Token, or JWT for short. JWT is *a JSON-based open standard (RFC 7519) for creating access tokens that assert some number of claims*. We'll create a JWT using the user's email address. We'll sign it with a key only the server uses, so we can safely pass it to the client, which will pass it back with each request. Since it must be encrypted/signed with the server key, untrustworthy clients will not be able to alter or forge the token successfully.

To create JWTs, we need to add the library to our project as follows:

```
<dependency>
  <groupId>io.jsonwebtoken</groupId>
  <artifactId>jjwt</artifactId>
  <version>0.7.0</version>
</dependency>
```

We can then write this method:

```
@Inject
private KeyGenerator keyGenerator;
private String createToken(String login) {
  String jwtToken = Jwts.builder()
```

```
.setSubject(login)
.setIssuer(uriInfo.getAbsolutePath().toString())
.setIssuedAt(new Date())
.setExpiration(Date.from(
  LocalDateTime.now().plusHours(12L)
.atZone(ZoneId.systemDefault()).toInstant()))
.signWith(SignatureAlgorithm.HS512,
  keyGenerator.getKey())
.compact();
return jwtToken;
}
```

The subject of the token is the email address, our API's base address is the issuer, the expiration date and time is 12 hours in the future, and the token is signed by a key we generate with a new class, `KeyGenerator`. When we call `compact()`, a URL-safe String is generated, which we return to the caller. We can use the JWT debugger at `http://jwt.io` to look inside the token:

Clearly, the claims in the token are readable, so don't store anything sensitive in them. What makes this secure is the use of a secret key when signing the token, making it impossible, in theory, to change its contents without detection.

The `KeyGenerator` class used to give us our signing key looks like this:

```
@Singleton
public class KeyGenerator {
  private Key key;
  public Key getKey() {
    if (key == null) {
      String keyString = System.getProperty("signing.key",
        "replace for production");
      key = new SecretKeySpec(keyString.getBytes(), 0,
        keyString.getBytes().length, "DES");
    }
    return key;
  }
}
```

The class is annotated with `@Singleton`, so the container guarantees that one and only one instance of this bean will exist in the system. The `getKey()` method will use the system property `signing.key` as the key, allowing the user to specify a unique secret when starting the system. Of course, completely random keys are safer, but that adds some complexity should we ever try to scale this system out horizontally. We would need all instances to use the same signing key so that JWTs can be validated regardless of what server the client is directed to. A data grid solution, such as Hazelcast, would be an appropriate tool for those situations. As it is now, this is sufficient for our needs here.

Our authentication resource is now complete, but our system has not actually been secured yet. To do that, we need to tell JAX-RS how to authenticate requests, and we'll do that with a new annotation and `ContainerRequestFilter`.

If we were to install a request filter with no additional information, it would apply to every resource, including our authentication resource. That would mean we'd have to authenticate in order to authenticate. Clearly that doesn't make sense, so we need a way to discriminate between requests so that only requests for certain resources have this filter applied, and that means a new annotation:

```
@NameBinding
@Retention(RetentionPolicy.RUNTIME)
@Target({ElementType.TYPE, ElementType.METHOD})
public @interface Secure {
}
```

We've defined an annotation that is semantically meaningful. The `@NameBinding` annotation tells JAX-RS to apply the annotation only to certain resources, which are bound by name (as opposed to dynamically bound at runtime). With the annotation defined, we need to define the other side of things, the request filter:

```
@Provider
@Secure
@Priority(Priorities.AUTHENTICATION)
public class SecureFilter implements ContainerRequestFilter {
  @Inject
  private KeyGenerator keyGenerator;

  @Override
  public void filter(ContainerRequestContext requestContext)
   throws IOException {
    try {
      String authorizationHeader = requestContext
      .getHeaderString(HttpHeaders.AUTHORIZATION);
      String token = authorizationHeader
      .substring("Bearer".length()).trim();
      Jwts.parser()
      .setSigningKey(keyGenerator.getKey())
      .parseClaimsJws(token);
    } catch (Exception e) {
      requestContext.abortWith(Response.status
      (Response.Status.UNAUTHORIZED).build());
    }
  }
}
```

We start by defining a class that implements the `ContainerRequestFilter` interface. We have to annotate it with `@Provider` so that JAX-RS will recognize and load the class. We apply the `@Secure` annotation to associate the filter with the annotation. We'll apply this to the resource in a moment. Finally, we apply the `@Priority` annotation to instruct the system that this filter should be applied earlier in the request cycle.

Inside the filter, we inject the same `KeyGenerator` we looked at earlier. Since this is a singleton, we are guaranteed that the key used here and in the authentication method are the same. The only method on the interface is `filter()`, and in this method, we get the Authorization header from the request, extract the Bearer token, which is the JWT, and validate it using the JWT API. If we can decode and validate the token, then we know the user has successfully authenticated against the system. To tell the system about this new filter, we need to modify our JAX-RS `Application` as follows:

```
@ApplicationPath("/api")
```

```
public class Monumentum extends javax.ws.rs.core.Application {
  @Override
  public Set<Class<?>> getClasses() {
    Set<Class<?>> s = new HashSet<>();
    s.add(NoteResource.class);
    s.add(AuthenticationResource.class);
    s.add(SecureFilter.class);
    return s;
  }
}
```

The system knows about the filter now, but before it will do anything, we need to apply it to the resources that we want to secure. We do that by applying the @Secure annotation to the appropriate resources. It can either be applied at class level, which means that every endpoint in the class will be secured, or at the resource method level, which means that only those particular endpoints will be secured. In our case, we want every Note endpoint secured, so put the following annotation on the class:

```
@Path("/notes")
@RequestScoped
@Produces(MediaType.APPLICATION_JSON)
@Secure
public class NoteResource {
```

Just a few more steps, and our application will be secured. We need to make some modifications to NoteResource so that it knows who is logged in, and so that notes are associated with the authenticated user. We will start by injecting User:

```
@Inject
private User user;
```

This is obviously not a container-managed class, so we need to write another Producer method. There's a small bit of work to do there, so we'll wrap that in its own class:

```
@RequestScoped
public class UserProducer {
  @Inject
  private KeyGenerator keyGenerator;
  @Inject
  HttpServletRequest req;
  @Inject
  @Collection("users")
  private MongoCollection<Document> users;
```

We define this as a request-scoped CDI bean, and inject our `KeyGenerator,` the `HttpServletRequest,` and our users collection. The actual work is done in the `Producer` method:

```
@Produces
public User getUser() {
  String authHeader = req.getHeader(HttpHeaders.AUTHORIZATION);
  if (authHeader != null && authHeader.contains("Bearer")) {
    String token = authHeader
    .substring("Bearer".length()).trim();
    Jws<Claims> parseClaimsJws = Jwts.parser()
    .setSigningKey(keyGenerator.getKey())
    .parseClaimsJws(token);
    return getUser(parseClaimsJws.getBody().getSubject());
  } else {
    return null;
  }
}
```

Using the Servlet request, we retrieve the `AUTHORIZATION` header. If it's present and contains the `Bearer` string, we can process the token. If that condition is not true, we return null. To process the token, we extract the token value from the header, and then have `Jwts` parse the claims for us, which returns an object of type `Jws<Claims>`. We build the user in the `getUser()` method as follows:

```
private User getUser(String email) {
  Document doc = users.find(
    new BasicDBObject("email", email)).first();
  if (doc != null) {
    return new User(doc);
  } else {
    return null;
  }
}
```

With the claims parsed, we can extract the subject and use it to query our `Users` collection, returning either the `User` if it is found, or `null` if not.

Back in our `NoteResource`, we need to modify our resource methods to be `User-aware`:

```
public Response getAll() {
  List<Note> notes = new ArrayList<>();
  try (MongoCursor<Document> cursor =
    collection.find(new BasicDBObject("user_id",
    user.getId())).iterator()) {
    // ...
```

```
@POST
public Response createNote(Note note) {
  Document doc = note.toDocument();
  doc.append("user_id", user.getId());
  // ...
@PUT
@Path("{id}")
public Response updateNote(Note note) {
  note.setModified(LocalDateTime.now());
  note.setUser(user.getId());
  // ...
private BasicDBObject buildQueryById(String id) {
  BasicDBObject query =
  new BasicDBObject("_id", new ObjectId(id))
   .append("user_id", user.getId());
  return query;
}
```

We now have a complete and secured REST API. Other than a command-line tool like curl, we don't have any nice way to use it, so let's build a user interface.

Building the user interface

For a UI, we have a number of options. We've already looked at JavaFX and the NetBeans RCP in this book. While those are great options, we'll do something a little different for this app and build a web-based interface. Even here, we have many, many options: JSF, Spring MVC, Google Web Toolkit, Vaadin, and more. Oftentimes, in real-world applications, while we may have a Java backend, we may have a JavaScript frontend, so that's what we'll do here, and that's where your choices can get really dizzying.

The two biggest players in that market at the time of the writing of this book are React from Facebook and Angular from Google. There are several smaller contenders, such as React API-compatible Preact, VueJS, Backbone, Ember, and so on. Which you choose will have a significant impact on the application, everything from architecture to the more mundane things such as building the project itself, or you could let architecture drive the framework if there's a compelling need for a specific architecture. As always, your particular environment will vary and should drive that decision more than what you read in a book or online.

Since this is a Java book, and I'd like to avoid getting too far into the intimate details of JavaScript build systems and alternate **JavaScript VM** languages, transpiling, and so on, I've chosen to use Vue, as it is a fast, modern, and popular framework that meets our needs, yet still allows us to build a simple system without requiring complicated build configurations. If you have experience with, or a preference for, another framework, it should be fairly simple for you to build a comparable system using the framework of your choice.

> Note that I am *not* a JavaScript developer. The application we'll build in this part of the chapter should not be construed to be an example of best practices. It is merely an attempt to build a usable, albeit plain, JavaScript frontend to demonstrate a full stack application. Please consult the documentation for Vue or your framework of choice for details on how to build idiomatic applications with the tool.

Let's start with the index page. In the project explorer window in NetBeans, expand the **Other Sources** node, right-click on the **webapp** node, and select **New** | **Empty File**, giving it the name `index.html`. The bare minimum we need in the file at this point is the following:

```html
<!DOCTYPE html>
  <html>
    <head>
      <title>Monumentum</title>
      <meta charset="UTF-8">
      <link rel="stylesheet" href="monumentum.css">
      <script src="https://unpkg.com/vue"></script>
    </head>
    <body>
      <div id="app">
        {{ message }}
      </div>
      <script type="text/javascript" src="index.js"></script>
    </body>
  </html>
```

This will display a blank page at the moment, but it does import the source for Vue, as well as the JavaScript for our client app, `index.js`, which we need to create:

```javascript
var vm = new Vue({
  el: '#app',
  data: {
    message : 'Hello, World!'
  }
});
```

If we deploy those changes (HINT: If the app is already running, just press *F11* to tell NetBeans to build; that won't make any Java changes take effect, but it will copy these static resources to the output directory) and refresh the page in the browser, we should now see *Hello, World!* on the page.

Roughly put, what's happening is that we're creating a new `Vue` object, anchoring to the (`el`) element with the `app` ID. We're also defining some state for this component (`data`), which includes the single property, `message`. On the page, anywhere inside the element `app`, we can access the component's state using the Mustache syntax we see in the index page--`{{ message }}`. Let's expand our component a bit:

```
var vm = new Vue({
  el: '#app',
  store,
  computed: {
    isLoggedIn() {
      return this.$store.state.loggedIn;
    }
  },
  created: function () {
    NotesActions.fetchNotes();
  }
});
```

We've added three items here:

- We've introduced a global data store, aptly called `store`
- We've added a new property called `isLoggedIn`, which gets its value from a method call
- We've added a lifecycle method, `created`, which will load `Note` from the server when the component is created on the page

Our data store is based on Vuex, a state-management pattern + library for `Vue.js` applications. It serves as a centralized store for all the components in an application, with rules ensuring that the state can only be mutated in a predictable fashion. (`https://vuex.vuejs.org`). To add it to our application, we need to add the following line of code to our page:

```
<script src="https://unpkg.com/vuex"></script>
```

We then add a field called `store` to our component, which you can see in the preceding code. Most of the work so far takes place in the `NotesActions` object:

```
var NotesActions = {
  buildAuthHeader: function () {
    return new Headers({
      'Content-Type': 'application/json',
      'Authorization': 'Bearer ' +
      NotesActions.getCookie('Bearer')
    });
  },
  fetchNotes: function () {
    fetch('api/notes', {
      headers: this.buildAuthHeader()
    })
    .then(function (response) {
      store.state.loggedIn = response.status === 200;
      if (response.ok) {
        return response.json();
      }
    })
    .then(function (notes) {
      store.commit('setNotes', notes);
    });
  }
}
```

When the page loads, the application will immediately send a request to the backend for Notes, sending the bearer token, if there is one, in the `Authorization` header. When the response returns, we update the state of the `isLoggedIn` property in the store, and, if the request was successful, we update the list of `Notes` on the page. Note that we're using `fetch()`. That is the new, experimental API for sending XHR, or Ajax, requests in browsers. As of the writing of this book, it is supported in every major browser except Internet Explorer, so be careful using this in production apps if you can't dictate the client's browser.

We've seen the store used a few times, so let's take a look at it:

```
const store = new Vuex.Store({
  state: {
    notes: [],
    loggedIn: false,
    currentIndex: -1,
    currentNote: NotesActions.newNote()
  }
};
```

The store is of type `Vuex.Store`, and we specify the various state fields in its `state` property. Handled properly, any Vue component bound to one of these state fields is automatically updated for you. You don't need to track and manage state, manually reflecting changes on the page as the application state changes. Vue and Vuex handle that for you. Mostly. There are some situations, such as array mutation (or replacement), that require some special handling. Vuex offers **mutations** to help with that. For example, `NotesAction.fetchNotes()`, upon a successful request, we will make this call:

```
store.commit('setNotes', notes);
```

The preceding code tells the store to `commit` a mutation called `setNotes`, with `notes` as the payload. We define mutations like this:

```
mutations: {
  setNotes(state, notes) {
    state.notes = [];
    if (notes) {
      notes.forEach(i => {
        state.notes.push({
          id: i.id,
          title: i.title,
          body: i.body,
          created: new Date(i.created),
          modified: new Date(i.modified)
        });
      });
    }
  }
}
```

What we are passing into this mutation (you can probably think of this as a function or a method with a peculiar invocation syntax if that helps) is a JSON array (hopefully, we show no type checking here), so we start by clearing out the current list of notes, then iterating over this array, creating and storing new objects, and reformatting some of the data as we do so. Strictly using only this mutation to replace the set of notes, we can guarantee that the user interface is kept in sync with the changing state of the application, all for free.

So how are these notes displayed? To do that, we define a new Vue component and add it to the page, as follows:

```
<div id="app">
  <note-list v-bind:notes="notes" v-if="isLoggedIn"></note-list>
</div>
```

Here, we've referenced a new component called `note-list`. We've bound the template variable `notes` to the application variable of the same name, and specified that the component is only displayed if the user is logged. The actual component definition happens in JavaScript. Back in `index.js`, we have this:

```
Vue.component('note-list', {
  template: '#note-list-template',
  store,
  computed: {
    notes() {
      return this.$store.state.notes;
    },
    isLoggedIn() {
      return this.$store.state.loggedIn;
    }
  },
  methods: {
    loadNote: function (index) {
      this.$store.commit('noteClicked', index);
    },
    deleteNote: function (index) {
      if (confirm
        ("Are you sure want to delete this note?")) {
          NotesActions.deleteNote(index);
        }
    }
  }
});
```

This component is named `note-list`; its template is found in an element with the `note-list-template` ID; it has two computed values: `notes` and `isLoggedIn`; and it provides two methods. In a typical Vue application, we would have a number of files, all ultimately compiled together using something like Grunt or Gulp, and one of these files would be our component's template. Since we are trying to make this as simple as possible by avoiding the JS build processes, we have everything declared right on our page. In `index.html`, we can find the template for our component:

```
<script type="text/x-template" id="note-list-template">
  <div class="note-list">
    <h2>Notes:</h2>
    <ul>
      <div class="note-list"
        v-for="(note,index) in notes" :key="note.id">
      <span :
        v-on:click="loadNote(index,note);">
        {{ note.title }}
```

```
      </span>
        <a v-on:click="deleteNote(index, note);">
          <img src="images/x-225x225.png" height="20"
            width="20" alt="delete">
        </a>
      </div>
    </ul>
    <hr>
  </div>
</script>
```

Using a `script` tag with with the `text/x-template` type, we can add the template to the DOM without it rendering on the page. Inside this template, the interesting part is the `div` tag with the `note-list` class. We have the `v-` attribute on it, which means the Vue template processor will iterate over the `notes` list using this `div` as a template for displaying each `note` in the array.

Each note will be rendered using the `span` tag. Using the template markup `:title`, we are able to create a value for the title tag using our application state (we can't say because string interpolation was deprecated in Vue 2.0). The sole child of the `span` tag is the `{{ note.title }}` expression, which renders the title of the `note` list as a string. When the user clicks on the note title on the page, we want to react to that, so we bind the `onClick` handler to the DOM element via `v-on:click`. The function referenced here is the `loadNote()` function that we defined in the `methods` block of our component definition.

The `loadNote()` function calls a mutation we haven't looked at yet:

```
noteClicked(state, index) {
  state.currentIndex = index;
  state.currentNote = state.notes[index];
  bus.$emit('note-clicked', state.currentNote);
}
```

This mutation modifies the state to reflect the note that the user clicked on, then fires (or emits) an event called `note-clicked`. The event system is really quite simple. It is set up like this:

```
var bus = new Vue();
```

That's literally it. This is just a bare bones, globally scoped Vue component. We fire events by calling `bus.$emit()` method, and register event listeners by calling the `bus.$on()` method. We'll see what that looks like in the note form.

We will add the note form component to the page like we did the `note-list` component:

```
<div id="app">
  <note-list v-bind:notes="notes" v-if="isLoggedIn"></note-list>
  <note-form v-if="isLoggedIn"></note-form>
</div>
```

And, again, the component is defined in `index.js` as follows:

```
Vue.component('note-form', {
  template: '#note-form-template',
  store,
  data: function () {
    return {
      note: NotesActions.newNote()
    };
  },
  mounted: function () {
    var self = this;
    bus.$on('add-clicked', function () {
      self.$store.currentNote = NotesActions.newNote();
      self.clearForm();
    });
    bus.$on('note-clicked', function (note) {
      self.updateForm(note);
    });
    CKEDITOR.replace('notebody');
  }
});
```

The template is also in `index.html`, as shown here:

```
<script type="text/x-template" id="note-form-template">
  <div class="note-form">
    <h2>{{ note.title }}</h2>
    <form>
      <input id="noteid" type="hidden"
        v-model="note.id"></input>
      <input id="notedate" type="hidden"
        v-model="note.created"></input>
      <input id="notetitle" type="text" size="50"
        v-model="note.title"></input>
      <br/>
      <textarea id="notebody"
        style="width: 100%; height: 100%"
        v-model="note.body"></textarea>
      <br>
      <button type="button" v-on:click="save">Save</button>
```

```
      </form>
    </div>
  </script>
```

This is mostly normal HTML form. The interesting bit is the v-model that ties the form element to the component's property. Changes made on the form are automatically reflected in the component, and changes made in the component (for example, via an event handler) are automatically reflected in the UI. We also attach an `onClick` handler via the now familiar `v-on:click` attribute.

Did you notice the reference to CKEDITOR in our component definition? We'll use the rich text editor CKEditor to provide a better experience. We could go to CKEditor and download the distribution bundle, but we have a better way--WebJars. The WebJars project takes popular client-side web libraries and packages them as JARs. This makes adding supported libraries to the project very simple:

```
<dependency>
   <groupId>org.webjars</groupId>
   <artifactId>ckeditor</artifactId>
   <version>4.6.2</version>
</dependency>
```

When we package the application, this binary jar is added to the web archive. However, if it's still archived, how do we access the resources? There are a number of options depending on the type of application you are building. We'll make use of Servlet 3's static resource handling (anything under `META-INF/resources` that's packaged in the web application's `lib` directory are automatically exposed). In `index.html`, we add CKEditor to the page with this simple line:

```
<script type="text/javascript"
   src="webjars/ckeditor/4.6.2/standard/ckeditor.js"></script>
```

CKEditor is now ready to use.

One last major piece on the frontend is enabling the user to log in. To do that, we'll create another component as follows:

```
<div id="app">
  <navbar></navbar>
  <note-list v-bind:notes="notes" v-if="isLoggedIn"></note-list>
  <note-form v-if="isLoggedIn"></note-form>
</div>
```

Then, we will add the following component definition:

```
Vue.component('navbar', {
  template: '#navbar-template',
  store,
  data: function () {
    return {
      authUrl: "#"
    };
  },
  methods: {
    getAuthUrl: function () {
      var self = this;
      fetch('api/auth/url')
      .then(function (response) {
        return response.text();
      })
      .then(function (url) {
        self.authUrl = url;
      });
    }
  },
  mounted: function () {
    this.getAuthUrl();
  }
});
```

And, finally, we will add the template as follows:

```
<script type="text/x-template" id="navbar-template">
  <div id="nav" style="grid-column: 1/span 2; grid-row: 1 / 1;">
    <a v-on:click="add" style="padding-right: 10px;">
      <img src="images/plus-225x225.png" height="20"
        width="20" alt="add">
    </a>
    <a v-on:click="logout" v-if="isLoggedIn">Logout</a>
    <a v-if="!isLoggedIn" :href="authUrl"
      style="text-decoration: none">Login</a>
  </div>
</script>
```

When this component is **mounted** (or attached to the element in the DOM), we call the
getAuthUrl() function that sends an Ajax request to the server for our Google login URL.
Once that's fetched, the login anchor tag is updated to refer to the URL.

There are a few more details in the JavaScript file we've not covered here explicitly, but interested parties can check out the source code in the repository and read through it for the remaining details. We do have a working JavaScript frontend for our note-taking app that supports listing, creating, updating, and deleting notes, as well as supporting multiple users. It's not a pretty application, but it works. Not bad for a Java guy!

Summary

Now we're back to the familiar refrain--our application is **finished**. What have we covered in the chapter? We've created a REST API using JAX-RS that doesn't require direct JSON manipulation. We've learned how to apply request filters to JAX-RS endpoints to restrict access to authenticated users, which we authenticate against their Google accounts using Google's OAuth2 workflow. We've packaged the application using Payara Micro, a great option to develop microservices, and we've integrated MongoDB into our application using the MongoDB Java API. Finally, we built a very basic JavaScript client using Vue.js to access our application.

There are a lot of new concepts and technologies interacting in this application, which makes it interesting from a technical perspective, but there's still more that could be done. The application could use a great deal of styling, and support for embedded images and videos would be nice, as would a mobile client. There is lots of room for improvements and enhancements with the app, but interested parties have a solid foundation to start from. Although, for us, it's time to turn to the next chapter and a new project, where we'll jump into the world of cloud computing with Functions as a Service.

26
Serverless Java

In recent years, the concept of microservices, which we've already looked at, has swept across the industry, quickly displacing the battle-tested application server with something smaller and leaner. Right on the heels of microservices comes a new concept--Functions as a Service, more commonly called **serverless**. In this chapter, you'll learn more about this new deployment model and build an application to demonstrate how to use it.

The application will be a simple notification system using the following technologies:

- Amazon Web Services
    - Amazon Lambda
    - Amazon **Identity and Access Management** (**IAM**)
    - Amazon **Simple Notification System** (**SNS**)
    - Amazon **Simple Email System** (**SES**)
    - Amazon DynamoDB
- JavaFX
- The options offered by cloud providers can be quite vast, and Amazon Web Services is no exception. In this chapter, we will attempt to use just enough of what AWS has to offer to help us build a compelling application as we wade into cloud-native application development.

Getting started

Before we get to our application, we should spend some time getting a better understanding of the term **Function as a Service (FaaS)**. The term itself is a continuation of the **blank** as a service trend we've seen for a few years now. There is a host of such terms and offerings, but the big three are **Infrastructure as a Service (IaaS)**, **Platform as a Service (PaaS)**, and **Software as a Service (SaaS)**. Oftentimes, these three build on each other as seen in the following diagram:

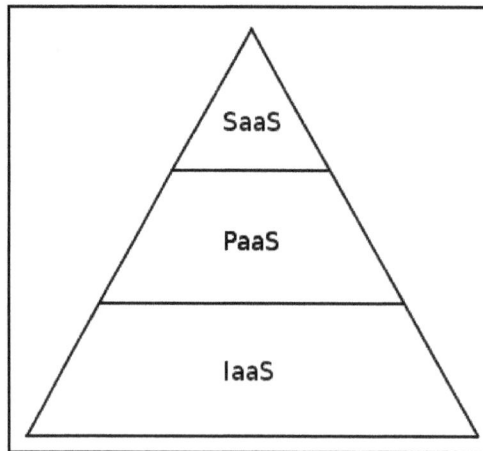

The lowest level of the cloud computing offerings, Infrastructure as a Service providers, offers infrastructure-related assets **in the cloud**. Typically, this can be as simple as file storage, but usually means virtual machines. By using an Infrastructure as a Service provider, clients need not worry about buying, maintaining, or replacing hardware, as that is handled by the provider. Clients are billed, instead, only on resources used.

Moving up the stack, Platform as a Service providers offer cloud-hosted application execution environments. This may include things such as an application server, a database server, a web server, and so on. The details of the physical environment are abstracted away, with customers specifying storage and RAM requirements. Some providers also allow the customer to choose the operating system, as this can have implications on the application stack, support tools, and more.

Software as a Service is a higher-level abstraction that doesn't focus on the hardware at all but, instead, offers hosted software that customers subscribe to, typically per user, and typically on a monthly or yearly basis. This is often seen in complicated business software, such as financial systems or human resource applications, but it is also seen with simpler systems, such as blogging software. The user simply subscribes and uses the software, leaving the installation and maintenance, including upgrades, to the provider. While this can reduce flexibility for the user (for example, it is often not possible to customize the software), it also reduces operational costs by pushing maintenance costs to the provider as well as guaranteeing, in most cases, access to the latest version of the software.

There are several other variations on this type of service, such as **Mobile Backend as a Service** (**MBaas**) and **Database as a Service** (**DBaaS**). As the market continues to gain confidence in cloud computing, and as the internet speeds up while the prices go down, we are likely to see more and more of these types of systems developed, which brings us to our topic in this chapter.

Function as a Service, or **serverless** computing, is the deployment of a small piece of code, very literally a function, that can be called from other applications, usually via some sort of trigger. Use cases include things such as image conversion, log analysis, and, as we will build in this chapter, notification systems.

Despite what the name **serverless** implies, there is actually a server involved, which only stands to reason; however, you, as an application developer, need not think about the server too deeply. In fact, as we'll see in this chapter, the only thing we need to worry about is how much memory our function will need. Everything else about the server is completely handled by the Function as a Service provider--the operating system, storage, networking, even starting and stopping the virtual machine are all handled for us by the provider.

With that basic understanding of serverless, we need to pick a provider. As can be expected, there are a number of options--Amazon, Oracle, IBM, Red Hat, and more. Unfortunately, currently, there is no standardized means by which we can write a serverless system and deploy it to an arbitrary provider, so that means our solution will be necessarily tied to a specific provider, which will be **Amazon Web Services** (**AWS**), the dominant provider of cloud computing services. As mentioned in the introduction to this chapter, we use a number of AWS offerings, but the centerpiece will be AWS Lambda, Amazon's serverless computing offering.

Let's jump in.

Planning the application

The application we will build is a very simple **cloud notification** service. In a nutshell, our function will **listen** for messages, then forward those messages to email addresses and phone numbers registered in the system. While our system will be somewhat contrived and certainly very simple, hopefully the more practical use cases are clear:

- Our system reminds students and/or parents about upcoming events
- Parents are notified when children enter or leave certain geographic boundaries
- Systems administrators are notified of certain events as they occur

The possibilities are quite vast. For our purposes here, we'll develop not only the cloud-based system, but also a simple desktop application to simulate these types of scenarios. We'll start where the fun is: in the cloud.

Building your first function

The heart of Functions as a Service is, of course, the function. In Amazon Web Services, these are deployed using the service AWS Lambda. That's not the only AWS feature we'll use, as we've already mentioned. Once we have a function, we need a way to execute it. This is done via one or more triggers, and the function itself has tasks it needs to perform, so we'll demonstrate more service usage via API calls when we finally write the function.

It might be helpful at this point, given that our application is structured significantly differently than anything else we've looked at, to look at a system diagram:

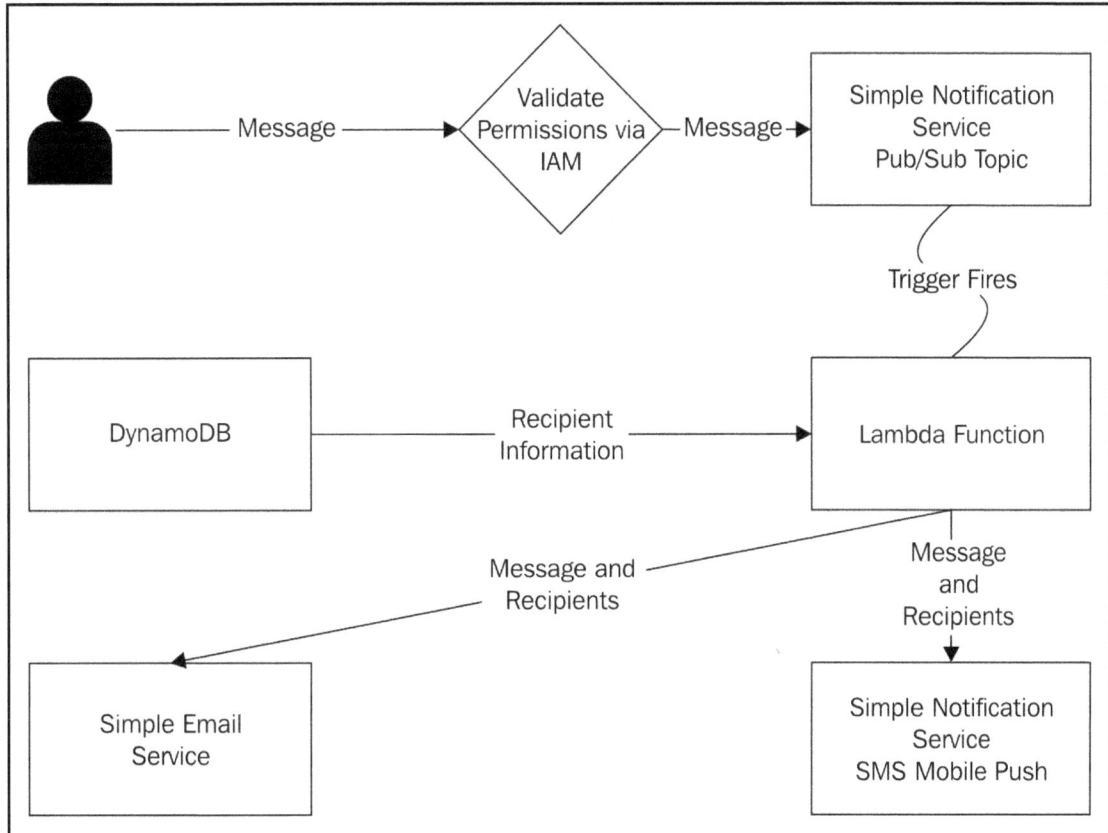

Here's the rough flow:

- A message is published to a topic in the Simple Notification System
- Once the permissions of the caller have been verified, the message is delivered
- Upon message delivery, a trigger is fired, delivering the message from the topic to our function
- Inside the function, we'll query Amazon's **DynamoDB** to get the list of recipients that have signed up, providing either an email address, cell phone number, or both
- All of the cell phone numbers will be sent a text message via **Simple Notification System**
- All the email addresses will be sent an email via **Simple Email Service**

To start building the function, we need to create a Java project. Like many of our other projects, this will be a multi-module Maven project. In NetBeans, click on **File** | **New Project** | **Maven** | **POM Project**. We'll call the CloudNotice project.

The project will have three modules--one for the function, one for a test/demo client, and one for a shared API. To create the function module, right-click on the Modules node in the project explorer and select **Create new module**. In the window, select **Maven** | **Java Application**, click on **Next**, and set the project name to function. Repeat those steps and create a module called api.

Before we go any further, we have to address the fact that, at the time of writing, AWS does not support Java 9. We must, therefore, target Java 8 (or earlier) for anything we will ship to Lambda. To do that, we need to modify our pom.xml file like this:

```
<properties>
  <maven.compiler.source>1.8</maven.compiler.source>
  <maven.compiler.target>1.8</maven.compiler.target>
</properties>
```

Modify the POM for both api and function. Hopefully, AWS will support Java 9 as quickly as possible after its release. Until then, we'll just have to target JDK 8.

With our project configured, we're ready to write our function. AWS Lambdas are implemented as RequestHandler instances:

```
public class SnsEventHandler
  implements RequestHandler<SNSEvent, Object> {
    @Override
    public Object handleRequest
      (SNSEvent request, Context context) {
        LambdaLogger logger = context.getLogger();
        final String message = request.getRecords().get(0)
          .getSNS().getMessage();
        logger.log("Handle message '" + message + "'");
        return null;
    }
}
```

Ultimately, we want our function to be triggered when a message is delivered to an SNS topic, so we specify SNSEvent as the input type. We also specify Context. There are several things we can get from the Context, such as the request ID, memory limit, and others, but all we're interested in is getting a LambdaLogger instance. We could just write to standard out and standard error, and those messages would be saved in Amazon CloudWatch, but LambdaLogger allows us to respect system permissions and the container configuration.

To make this compile, we need to add some dependencies to our application, so we add the following lines to `pom.xml`:

```
<properties>
  <aws.java.sdk.version>[1.11, 2.0.0)</aws.java.sdk.version>
</properties>
<dependencies>
  <dependency>
    <groupId>com.amazonaws</groupId>
    <artifactId>aws-java-sdk-sns</artifactId>
    <version>${aws.java.sdk.version}</version>
  </dependency>
  <dependency>
    <groupId>com.amazonaws</groupId>
    <artifactId>aws-lambda-java-core</artifactId>
    <version>1.1.0</version>
  </dependency>
  <dependency>
    <groupId>com.amazonaws</groupId>
    <artifactId>aws-lambda-java-events</artifactId>
    <version>1.3.0</version>
  </dependency>
</dependencies>
```

We can now start implementing the method as follows:

```
final List<Recipient> recipients =  new CloudNoticeDAO(false)
  .getRecipients();
final List<String> emailAddresses = recipients.stream()
  .filter(r -> "email".equalsIgnoreCase(r.getType()))
  .map(r -> r.getAddress())
  .collect(Collectors.toList());
final List<String> phoneNumbers = recipients.stream()
  .filter(r -> "sms".equalsIgnoreCase(r.getType()))
  .map(r -> r.getAddress())
  .collect(Collectors.toList());
```

We have a couple of new classes to look at, but to recap this code first, we will get a list of `Recipient` instances, which represents the numbers and email addresses that have been subscribed to our service. We then create a stream from the list, filtering for each recipient type, `SMS` or `Email`, extracting the value via `map()`, then collecting them in a `List`.

We will get to `CloudNoticeDAO` and `Recipient` in a moment, but let's finish up with our function first. Once we have our lists, we can then send the messages as follows:

```
final SesClient sesClient = new SesClient();
final SnsClient snsClient = new SnsClient();

sesClient.sendEmails(emailAddresses, "j9bp@steeplesoft.com",
 "Cloud Notification", message);
snsClient.sendTextMessages(phoneNumbers, message);
sesClient.shutdown();
snsClient.shutdown();
```

We have encapsulated two more AWS APIs behind our own client classes, `SesClient` and `SnsClient`. This may seem a bit excessive, but these types of things tend to grow, and this approach puts us in a good position to manage that.

That leaves us with three APIs to look at: DynamoDB, Simple Email Service, and Simple Notification Service. We'll take them in order.

DynamoDB

Amazon DynamoDB is a NoSQL database, very much like MongoDB, which we looked at in `Chapter 25`, *Taking Notes with Monumentum*, though DynamDB supports both document and key-value store models. A thorough comparison of the two, as well as a recommendation as to which to choose, is well outside the scope of our work here. We chose DynamoDB here, since it is already provisioned in the Amazon Web Service, and, thus, easily configured for our application.

To get started with the DynamoDB API, we need to add some dependencies to our application. In the `api` module, add this to the `pom.xml` file:

```
<properties>
  <sqlite4java.version>1.0.392</sqlite4java.version>
</properties>
<dependency>
  <groupId>com.amazonaws</groupId>
  <artifactId>aws-java-sdk-dynamodb</artifactId>
  <version>${aws.java.sdk.version}</version>
</dependency>
<dependency>
  <groupId>com.amazonaws</groupId>
  <artifactId>DynamoDBLocal</artifactId>
  <version>${aws.java.sdk.version}</version>
  <optional>true</optional>
```

```
    </dependency>
    <dependency>
      <groupId>com.almworks.sqlite4java</groupId>
      <artifactId>sqlite4java</artifactId>
      <version>${sqlite4java.version}</version>
      <optional>true</optional>
    </dependency>
```

Before we start writing our DAO class, let's define our simple model. The DynamoDB API provides an object-relational mapping facility, much like the Java Persistence API or Hibernate, which will require a POJO and just a few annotations as we see here:

```
    public class Recipient {
      private String id;
      private String type = "SMS";
      private String address = "";

      // Constructors...

      @DynamoDBHashKey(attributeName = "_id")
      public String getId() {
        return id;
      }
      @DynamoDBAttribute(attributeName = "type")
      public String getType() {
        return type;
      }

      @DynamoDBAttribute(attributeName="address")
      public String getAddress() {
        return address;
      }
      // Setters omitted to save space
    }
```

In our POJO, we declared three properties, id, type, and address, then annotated the getters with @DyanoDBAttribute to help the library understand how to map the object.

> Note that, while most of the property names match the field names in the table, you can override the property-to-field name mapping as we did with id.

Before we can do anything with our data, we need to declare our table. Remember that DynamoDB is a NoSQL database, and we will use it as a document store just as we did with MongoDB. However, before we can store any data, we have to define **where** to put it. In MongoDB, we would create a collection. DynamoDB, though, still refers to this as a table, and, while it is technically schemaless, we do need to define a primary key, which is made up of a partition key and an optional sort key.

We create the table through the console. Once you've logged on to the AWS DynamoDB console, you will click on the **Create Table** button, which will bring you to a screen like this:

We will name our table `recipients`, and specify `_id` as the partition key. Click on the **Create Table** button and give AWS time to create the table.

We are now ready to start writing our DAO. In the API module, create a class called `CloudNoticeDAO`, to which we'll add this constructor:

```
protected final AmazonDynamoDB ddb;
protected final DynamoDBMapper mapper;
public CloudNoticeDAO(boolean local) {
  ddb = local ? DynamoDBEmbedded.create().amazonDynamoDB()
    : AmazonDynamoDBClientBuilder.defaultClient();
```

```
      verifyTables();
      mapper = new DynamoDBMapper(ddb);
    }
```

The local property is used to determine whether or not to use a local DynamoDB instance. This is here to support testing (as is the call to `verifyTables`), which we will explore in a moment. In production, our code will call `AmazonDynamoDBClientBuilder.defaultClient()` to acquire an instance of `AmazonDynamoDB`, which talks to the Amazon-hosted instance. Finally, we create an instance of `DynamoDBMapper`, which we'll use for our object mapping.

To facilitate creating a new `Recipient`, we will add this method:

```
      public void saveRecipient(Recipient recip) {
        if (recip.getId() == null) {
          recip.setId(UUID.randomUUID().toString());
        }
        mapper.save(recip);
      }
```

This method will either create a new entry in the database, or update an existing one if the primary key already exists. In some scenarios, it might make sense to have separate save and update methods, but our use case is so simple that we don't need to worry about that. All we need to do is create the key value if it's missing. We do so by creating a random UUID, which helps us avoid key collisions should there be more than one process or application writing to the database.

Deleting a `Recipient` instance or getting a list of all of the `Recipient` instances in the database is just as simple:

```
      public List<Recipient> getRecipients() {
        return mapper.scan(Recipient.class,
         new DynamoDBScanExpression());
      }

      public void deleteRecipient(Recipient recip) {
        mapper.delete(recip);
      }
```

Before we leave our DAO, let's take a quick look at how we can test it. Earlier, we noted the `local` parameter and the `verifyTables()` method, which exist for testing.

Generally speaking, most people will frown, and rightfully so, on adding methods to production classes just for testing. There's a difference between writing a class that is testable, and adding test methods to a class. I would agree that adding methods to a class just for testing is something that should be avoided, but I am violating that principle a little here for the sake of simplicity and brevity.

The `verifyTables()` method checks to see if the table exists; if the table doesn't, we call another method that will create it for us. While we manually created the production table using the preceding console, we could also let this method create that table for us. What approach you use is completely up to you. Be aware that there will be performance and permissions issues that will need to be addressed. That said, that method looks something like this:

```java
private void verifyTables() {
  try {
    ddb.describeTable(TABLE_NAME);
  } catch (ResourceNotFoundException rnfe) {
    createRecipientTable();
  }
}

private void createRecipientTable() {
  CreateTableRequest request = new CreateTableRequest()
   .withTableName(TABLE_NAME)
   .withAttributeDefinitions(
     new AttributeDefinition("_id", ScalarAttributeType.S))
   .withKeySchema(
     new KeySchemaElement("_id", KeyType.HASH))
   .withProvisionedThroughput(new
     ProvisionedThroughput(10L, 10L));

  ddb.createTable(request);
  try {
    TableUtils.waitUntilActive(ddb, TABLE_NAME);
  } catch (InterruptedException  e) {
    throw new RuntimeException(e);
  }
}
```

With the call to the `describeTable()` method, we can check to see if the table exists. In our test, this will fail every time, which will cause the table to be created. In production, should you use this method to create the table, this call will fail only on the first invocation. In `createRecipientTable()`, we can see how a table is created programmatically. We also wait until the table is active to make sure our reads and writes won't fail while the table is being created.

Our tests, then, are very simple. For example, consider the following code snippet:

```
private final CloudNoticeDAO dao = new CloudNoticeDAO(true);
@Test
public void addRecipient() {
  Recipient recip = new Recipient("SMS", "test@example.com");
  dao.saveRecipient(recip);
  List<Recipient> recipients = dao.getRecipients();
  Assert.assertEquals(1, recipients.size());
}
```

This test helps us verify that our model mapping is correct, and that our DAO methods function as expected. You can see additional testing in the `CloudNoticeDaoTest` class, in the source bundle.

Simple Email Service

To send emails, we will use the Amazon Simple Email Service, or SES, which we will wrap in the `SesClient` class in the `api` module.

IMPORTANT: Before you can send an email, you have to verify either your sending/from address or domain. The verification process is fairly simple, but how to do that is probably best left to Amazon's documentation, which you can read here: http://docs.aws.amazon.com/ses/latest/DeveloperGuide/verify-email-addresses.html.

The Simple Email Service API is quite simple. We need to create a `Destination`, which tells the system to whom to send the emails; a `Message` that describes the message itself, including subject, body, and recipients; and a `SendEmailRequest` that ties everything together:

```
private final AmazonSimpleEmailService client =
  AmazonSimpleEmailServiceClientBuilder.defaultClient();
public void sendEmails(List<String> emailAddresses,
  String from,
```

```
        String subject,
        String emailBody) {
      Message message = new Message()
        .withSubject(new Content().withData(subject))
        .withBody(new Body().withText(
          new Content().withData(emailBody)));
      getChunkedEmailList(emailAddresses)
        .forEach(group ->
          client.sendEmail(new SendEmailRequest()
            .withSource(from)
            .withDestination(
              new Destination().withBccAddresses(group))
              .withMessage(message)));
      shutdown();
    }

    public void shutdown() {
      client.shutdown();
    }
```

There is an important caveat though, which is in the preceding bolded code. SES limits the
number of recipients per message to 50, so we need to take our list of email addresses and
process them 50 at a time. We will do that using the getChunkedEmailList() method:

```
    private List<List<String>> getChunkedEmailList(
      List<String> emailAddresses) {
        final int numGroups = (int) Math.round(emailAddresses.size() /
          (MAX_GROUP_SIZE * 1.0) + 0.5);
        return IntStream.range(0, numGroups)
          .mapToObj(group ->
            emailAddresses.subList(MAX_GROUP_SIZE * group,
            Math.min(MAX_GROUP_SIZE * group + MAX_GROUP_SIZE,
            emailAddresses.size()))))
            .collect(Collectors.toList());
    }
```

To find the number of groups, we divide the number of addresses by 50 and round up (for
example, 254 addresses would get us 6 groups--5 of 50 and 1 of 4). Then, using an
IntStream to count from 0 to the number of groups (exclusive), we extract sublists from
the original list. Each of these lists is then collected into yet another List, giving us the
nested Collection instances we see in the method signature.

Design note: Many developers will avoid using nested `Collection` instances like this, as it can quickly become difficult to understand what exactly the variable represents. It is considered by many to be a best practice in situations like this to create a new type to hold the nested data. For example, if we were to follow that advice here, we could create, perhaps, a new `Group` class that had a `List<String>` property to hold the group's email addresses. We have not done so for the sake of brevity, but that would definitely be a good enhancement to this code.

Once we've **chunked** our list, we can send the same `Message` to each group, and thus fulfill the API contract.

Simple Notification Service

We've already seen the Simple Notification System at work, at least in theory, as that is what delivers the outbound message to our function: a client of some sort publishes a message in a specific SNS topic. We have a subscription to that topic (I'll show you how to create that later) that calls our method with the message for us to deliver. We will use the SNS API now to send text (or SMS) messages to the users who have subscribed a phone number to the system.

With SNS, to send a message to more than one phone number you must do so through a topic to which each number is subscribed. What we'll do then is follow these steps:

1. Create a topic.
2. Subscribe all of the phone numbers.
3. Publish the message to the topic.
4. Delete the topic.

If we use a persistent topic, we will likely get unpredictable results if we have more than one instance of the function running simultaneously. The method that orchestrates all of this work looks like this:

```
public void sendTextMessages(List<String> phoneNumbers,
  String message) {
    String arn = createTopic(UUID.randomUUID().toString());
    phoneNumbers.forEach(phoneNumber ->
      subscribeToTopic(arn, "sms", phoneNumber));
    sendMessage(arn, message);
    deleteTopic(arn);
}
```

To create a topic, we have the following method:

```
private String createTopic(String arn) {
  return snsClient.createTopic(
    new CreateTopicRequest(arn)).getTopicArn();
}
```

To subscribe the numbers to the topic, we have this method:

```
private SubscribeResult subscribeToTopic(String arn,
  String protocol, String endpoint) {
    return snsClient.subscribe(
      new SubscribeRequest(arn, protocol, endpoint));
}
```

Publishing a message is equally simple, as we see here:

```
public void sendMessage(String topic, String message) {
  snsClient.publish(topic, message);
}
```

And finally, you can delete the topic with this simple method:

```
private DeleteTopicResult deleteTopic(String arn) {
  return snsClient.deleteTopic(arn);
}
```

All of these methods are clearly very simple, so the calls to the SNS API could be made directly inline in the calling code, but this wrapper does provide us with a way to hide the details of the API from our business code. This is more important, for example, in `createTopic()`, where extra classes are needed, but, to be consistent, we'll encapsulate everything behind our own facade.

Deploying the function

We have now completed our function and we're almost ready to deploy it. To do that, we need to package it. AWS allows us to upload either a ZIP or a JAR file. We'll use the latter. However, we have some external dependencies, so we'll use the **Maven Shade** plugin to build a fat jar with our function and all of its dependencies. In the `function` module, add the following piece of code to the `pom.xml` file:

```
<plugin>
  <groupId>org.apache.maven.plugins</groupId>
  <artifactId>maven-shade-plugin</artifactId>
  <version>3.0.0</version>
```

```
        <executions>
          <execution>
              <phase>package</phase>
              <goals>
                  <goal>shade</goal>
              </goals>
              <configuration>
                  <finalName>
                      cloudnotice-function-${project.version}
                  </finalName>
              </configuration>
          </execution>
        </executions>
      </plugin>
```

Now, when we build the project, we'll get a large file (about 9MB) in the target directory. It is this file that we will upload.

Creating a role

Before we can upload the function, we need to prepare our AWS environment by creating the appropriate role. Log on to AWS and navigate to the **Identity and Access Management Console** (https://console.aws.amazon.com/iam). In the navigation pane on the left, click on **Roles**, then click on **Create new role**:

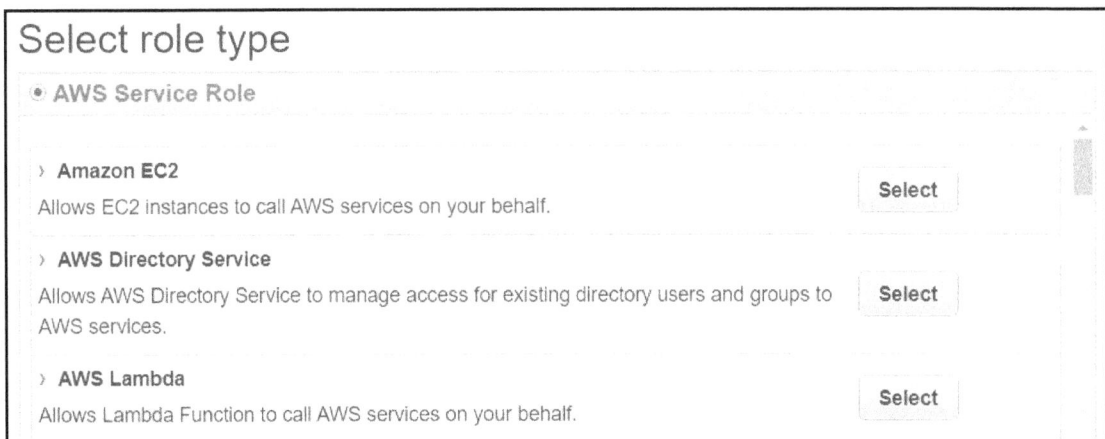

When prompted to select a role, we want to select AWS Lambda. On the next page, we will attach the policies:

Attach Policy

Select one or more policies to attach. Each role can have up to 10 policies attached.

Filter: Policy Type ▾ | Filter — Showing 262 results

		Policy Name ⇕	Attached Entities ⇕	Creation Time ⇕	Edited Time ⇕
☑		AmazonSNSFullAcc...	3	2015-02-06 12:41 CDT	2015-02-06 12:4...
☐		AmazonS3FullAccess	2	2015-02-06 12:40 CDT	2015-02-06 12:4...
☑		AWSLambdaFullAc...	2	2015-02-06 12:40 CDT	2017-05-25 14:0...
☐		AmazonAPIGatewa...	1	2015-07-09 12:34 CDT	2015-07-09 12:3...
☐		AmazonAPIGatewa...	1	2015-07-09 12:36 CDT	2015-07-09 12:3...
☑		AmazonSESFullAcc...	1	2015-02-06 12:41 CDT	2015-02-06 12:4...

Click on **Next**, set the name to `j9bp`, and click on **Create role**.

Creating a topic

To make creating the function and the associated trigger simpler, we will create our topic first. Navigate to the SNS console. Given that not all AWS functionality is always available in every region, we need to choose a specific region. We can do that in the upper-left corner of the web page. If the region does not say N. Virginia, select it--**US East (N. Virginia)**-- from the drop-down menu before continuing.

Once the region is set correctly, click on **Topics** in the left navigation bar, then click on **Create new topic** and specify the name as `cloud-notice`:

Create new topic

A topic name will be used to create a permanent unique identifier called an Amazon Resource Name (ARN).

Topic name   cloud-notice   ❶

Display name   Enter topic display name. Required for topics with SMS subscriptions.   ❶

Cancel   **Create topic**

Deploying the function

We can now navigate to the Lambda console and deploy our function. We will start by clicking on the **Create a lambda** function button. We'll be asked to select a blueprint. The only option suitable for a Java-based function is **Blank Function**. Once we click on that option, we are presented with the **Configure Triggers** screen. When you click on the empty square, you will be presented with a drop-down menu, as seen in this screenshot from the AWS console:

Configure triggers

You can choose to add a trigger that will invoke your function.

▷   Lambda

SNS

SNS

You can either scroll down to find **SNS**, or enter SNS in the filter box as in the preceding screenshot. Either way, when you click on **SNS** in the list, you will be asked to select the topic to which you want to subscribe:

Click on **Next**. We now need to specify the details of our function:

Scrolling down the page, we also need to specify the Lambda function handler and role. The **Handler** is the fully-qualified class name, followed by two colons, and the method name:

Lambda function handler and role		
Handler*	com.steeplesoft.cloudnotice.function.SnsEv	ⓘ
Role*	Choose an existing role ▼	ⓘ
Existing role*	j9bp ▼	ⓘ

We now need to select the function archive by clicking on the upload button and selecting the jar file created by our Maven build. Click on **Next**, verify the details of the function, and then click on **Create function**.

We now have a usable AWS Lambda function. We can test it using the Lambda Console, but instead we'll build a small JavaFX application to do that, which will simultaneously test all of the service integrations, as well as demonstrate how a production application would interact with the function.

Testing the function

To help test and demonstrate the system, we'll create a new module, called `manager`, in the `CloudNotice` project. To do that, click on the **modules** node in the NetBeans project explorer, then click on **Create New Module... | Maven | JavaFX Application**. Call the project `Manager` and click on **Finish**.

> 💡 **TIP**
>
> I have renamed `MainApp` to `CloudNoticeManager`, `FXMLController` to `CloudNoticeManagerController`, and `Scene.fxml` to `manager.fxml`.

Our `Application` class will look a little different than in previous JavaFX applications. Some of the AWS client APIs require that they be shut down explicitly when you are finished with them. Failure to do so means that our application won't fully quit, leaving behind **zombie** processes that must be killed. To make sure we properly shut down our AWS clients, we need to add a cleanup method to our controller, which we'll call from the `stop()` method in our application:

```
private FXMLLoader fxmlLoader;
@Override
public void start(final Stage stage) throws Exception {
  fxmlLoader = new FXMLLoader(getClass()
   .getResource("/fxml/manager.fxml"));
  Parent root = fxmlLoader.load();
  // ...
}

@Override
public void stop() throws Exception {
  CloudNoticeManagerController controller =
    (CloudNoticeManagerController) fxmlLoader.getController();
  controller.cleanup();
  super.stop();
}
```

Now, regardless of whether the user clicks on **File** | **Exit** or clicks on the **Close** button on the window, our AWS clients can be cleaned up correctly.

In terms of layout, there's nothing new to discuss, so we'll not dwell on that aspect here. This is what our manager app will look like:

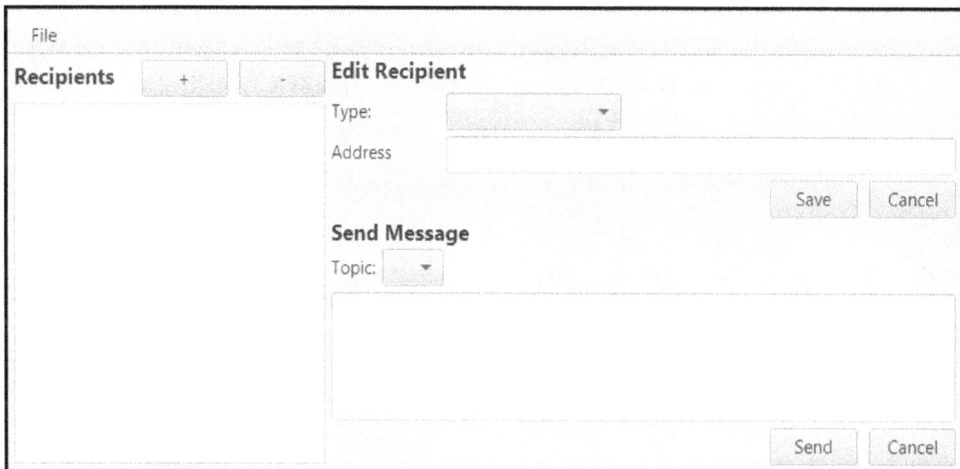

We have a list of the subscribed recipients on the left, an area for adding and editing a recipient at the top right, and an area for sending a test message at the bottom right. We do have some interesting bindings, so let's take a look at this.

First, in `CloudNoticeManagerController`, we need to declare some containers for our data, so we declare a number of `ObservableList` instances:

```
private final ObservableList<Recipient> recips =
  FXCollections.observableArrayList();
private final ObservableList<String> types =
  FXCollections.observableArrayList("SMS", "Email");
private final ObservableList<String> topics =
  FXCollections.observableArrayList();
```

These three `ObservableList` instances will back the UI controls matching their names. We will populate two of those lists (`type` is hardcoded) in `initalize()` as follows:

```
public void initialize(URL url, ResourceBundle rb) {
  recips.setAll(dao.getRecipients());
  topics.setAll(sns.getTopics());

  type.setItems(types);
  recipList.setItems(recips);
  topicCombo.setItems(topics);
```

Using our DAO and SES client, we fetch any already subscribed recipients, as well as any topics configured in the account. This will get *every* topic, so if you have a lot, this may be a problem, but this is just a demonstration application, so that should be fine here. Once we have these two lists, we add them to the `ObservableList` instances we created earlier, then associate the `List` with the appropriate UI controls.

To make sure the `Recipient` list displays correctly, we need to create a `CellFactory` as follows:

```
recipList.setCellFactory(p -> new ListCell<Recipient>() {
  @Override
  public void updateItem(Recipient recip, boolean empty) {
    super.updateItem(recip, empty);
    if (!empty) {
      setText(String.format("%s - %s", recip.getType(),
        recip.getAddress()));
    } else {
        setText(null);
    }
  }
});
```

Remember that, if the cell is empty, we need to set the text to null to clear out any previous value. Failure to do that will result, at some point, in a `ListView` with **phantom** entries.

Next, we need to update the edit controls when the user clicks on a `Recipient` in the list. We do this by adding a listener to the `selectedItemProperty`, which is run every time the selected item changes:

```
recipList.getSelectionModel().selectedItemProperty()
        .addListener((obs, oldRecipient, newRecipient) -> {
    type.valueProperty().setValue(newRecipient != null ?
        newRecipient.getType() : "");
    address.setText(newRecipient != null ?
        newRecipient.getAddress() : "");
});
```

If `newRecipient` is not null, we set the value of the controls to the appropriate value. Otherwise, we clear the values.

We now need to add handlers for the various buttons--the **Add** and **Remove** buttons above the `Recipient` list, and the `Save` and `Cancel` buttons in the two **form** areas on the right.

The UI control's `onAction` property can be bound to the method in the class by editing the FXML directly, as shown here:

```
<Button mnemonicParsing="false"
  onAction="#addRecipient" text="+" />
<Button mnemonicParsing="false"
  onAction="#removeRecipient" text="-" />
```

It can also be bound to the method by editing the property in Scene Builder, as shown in the following screenshot:

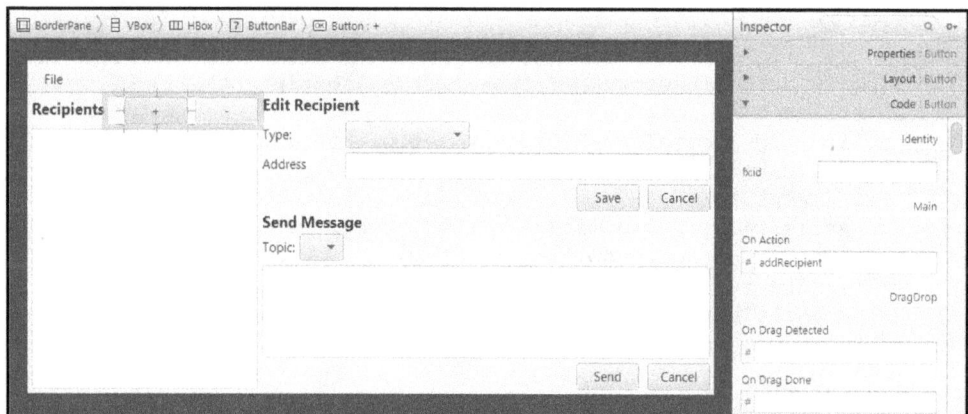

Either way, the method will look like this:

```
@FXML
public void addRecipient(ActionEvent event) {
  final Recipient recipient = new Recipient();
  recips.add(recipient);
  recipList.getSelectionModel().select(recipient);
  type.requestFocus();
}
```

We're adding a `Recipient`, so we create a new one, add it to our `ObservableList`, then tell the `ListView` to select this entry. Finally, we ask the `type` control to request focus so the user can easily change the value with the keyboard, if so desired. The new Recipient isn't saved to DynamoDB until the user clicks on Save, which we will look at in a moment.

When we delete a `Recipient`, we need to remove it from the UI as well as from DynamoDB:

```
@FXML
public void removeRecipient(ActionEvent event) {
  final Recipient recipient = recipList.getSelectionModel()
    .getSelectedItem();
  dao.deleteRecipient(recipient);
  recips.remove(recipient);
}
```

Saving is a bit more complicated, but not much:

```
@FXML
public void saveChanges(ActionEvent event) {
  final Recipient recipient =
    recipList.getSelectionModel().getSelectedItem();
  recipient.setType(type.getValue());
  recipient.setAddress(address.getText());
  dao.saveRecipient(recipient);
  recipList.refresh();
}
```

Since we're not binding the values of the edit controls to the selected item in the list, we need to get the reference to the item, then copy the values from the controls to the model. Once that's done, we save it to the database via our DAO, then ask `ListView` to refresh itself so that any model changes are reflected in the list.

We aren't binding the controls to the item in the list as that leads to a slightly confusing user experience. If we did bind, as the user made changes to the model `ListView` would reflect those changes. It is conceivable that the user would then assume that the changes are being saved to the database when, in fact, they are not. That doesn't happen until the user clicks on **Save**. To avoid this confusion, and the loss of data, we have *not* bound the controls and manage the data manually.

To cancel the change, all we need to do is get a reference to the unchanged model from `ListView`, and copy its values over those in the edit controls:

```
@FXML
public void cancelChanges(ActionEvent event) {
  final Recipient recipient = recipList.getSelectionModel()
    .getSelectedItem();
  type.setValue(recipient.getType());
  address.setText(recipient.getAddress());
}
```

That leaves us with the **send a message** section of the UI. Thanks to our SNS wrapper API, these methods are very simple:

```
@FXML
public void sendMessage(ActionEvent event) {
  sns.sendMessage(topicCombo.getSelectionModel()
    .getSelectedItem(), messageText.getText());
  messageText.clear();
}

@FXML
public void cancelMessage(ActionEvent event) {
  messageText.clear();
}
```

From our desktop application, we can now add, edit, and remove recipients, as well as send test messages.

Configuring your AWS credentials

Those paying very close attention may be asking a very important question--How do the AWS client libraries know how to log on to our account? Clearly, we need to tell them, and we have a few options.

The AWS SDK, when run locally, will check three places for the credentials--environment variables (`AWS_ACCESS_KEY_ID` and `AWS_SECRET_ACCESS_KEY`), system properties (`aws.accessKeyId` and `aws.secretKey`), and the default credentials profiles file (`$HOME/.aws/credentials`). What credentials you use is up to you, but I will show you here how to configure the profiles file.

Just like a Unix or Windows system, your AWS account has a `root` user that has complete access to your system. It would be extremely imprudent to run any client code connected as this user. To avoid that, we need to create a user, which we can do on the **Identity and Access Management** console (`https://console.aws.amazon.com/iam`).

Once you've logged on, click on **Users** on the left, then **Add user** at the top, the result of which is shown in the following screenshot:

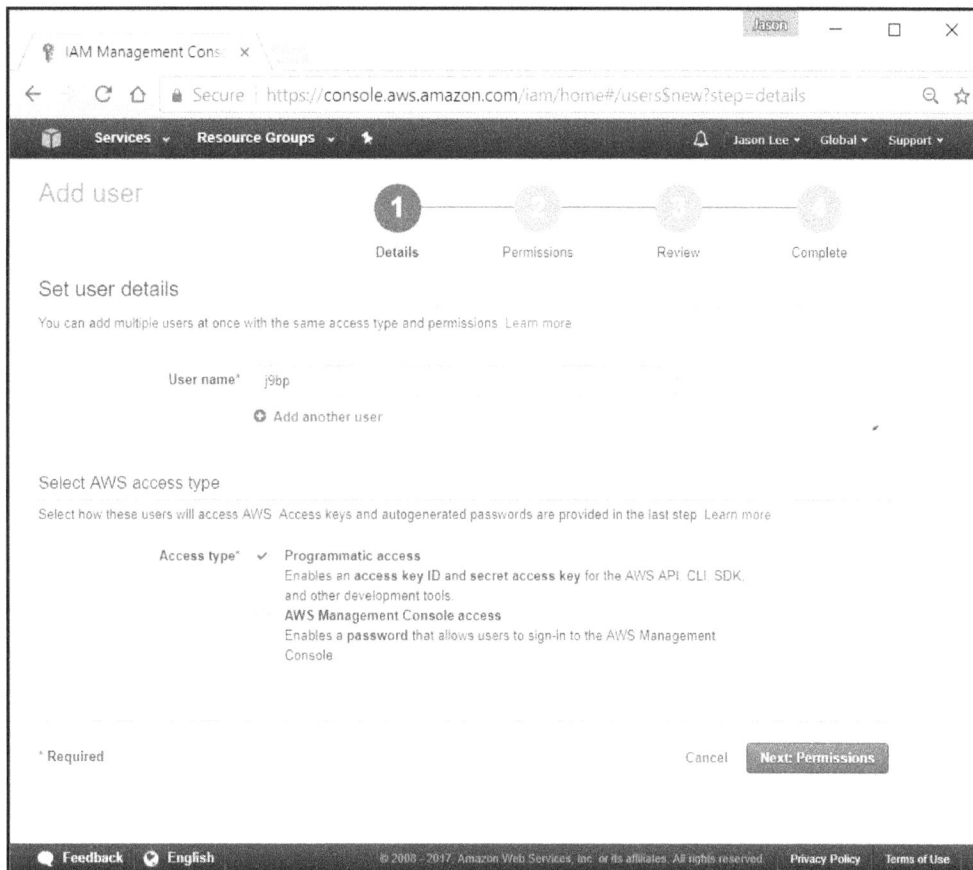

Click on **Next: Permissions** and check the entry in the **Group** list for our role, j9bp. Click on **Next: Review**, then **Create User**. This will take you to the **Add user** screen, which should have a success message box. The important part is the user information listed toward the bottom of the screen. On the right side of this table, you should see the columns **Access key ID** and **Secret access key**. Click on **Show** on the access key to reveal the value. Make a note of both of these, as there is no way to retrieve the access key once you leave this page. If you lose it, you will have to generate a new set of keys, which will break any other application using the old credentials.

	User	Access key ID	Secret access key
▸ ⊘	j9bp	AKIAISQVOILE6KCNQ7EQ	Npe9UiHJfFewasdi0KVVFWqD+KjZXat69W HnWbZT Hide

In a text editor, we need to create the ~/.aws/credentials file. On a Unix system, that may be /home/jdlee/.aws, and on a Windows machine that will be something like C:Usersjdleeaws. The credentials file should look something like this:

```
[default]
aws_access_key_id = AKIAISQVOILE6KCNQ7EQ
aws_secret_access_key = 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
```

In the same directory, we need to create another file called config. We'll use this file to tell the SDK which region we want to work in:

```
[default]
region = us-east-1
```

When the AWS clients start up now, they will default to connecting as the j9bp user in the us-east-1 region. Should you need to override that, you can either edit this file or set the environment variables or system properties noted above in the section, *Configuring your AWS Credentials*.

Summary

We've done it! We've created, many of us, our very first AWS Lambda function, and it really wasn't all that difficult. It is a simple application, of course, but I hope you can see how this type of application could be very useful. Using this as a starting point, you can write systems, with the help of a mobile application, to help keep track of your family's location. Using embedded devices such as Raspberry PI, for example, you can build devices to track inventory as it is shipped across the country, reporting location, speed, environmental conditions, sudden drops or impacts, and so on. A piece of software running on a server could constantly report various metrics about the system, such as CPU temperature, free disk space, memory allocated, system load, and so on. Your options are limited only by your imagination.

To wrap up, let's take a quick look back at what we've learned. We learned about some of the various **... as a service** systems that are being offered today, and what **serverless** really means and why it may appeal to us as application developers. We learned how to configure various Amazon Web Services offerings, including Identity and Access Management, Simple Notification System, Simple Email Service, and, of course Lambda, and we learned how to write an AWS Lambda function in Java and how to deploy it to the service. And finally, we learned how to configure triggers that would tie an SNS publish/subscribe topic to our Lambda function.

There's no denying that our application is somewhat simple, and there's no way in the space of a single chapter to make you an expert in all that Amazon Web Services or any other cloud provider has to offer. Hopefully, you have enough to get you going--and get you excited--about writing cloud-based applications using Java. For those wanting to go deeper, there are a number of great books, web pages, and so on to help you delve deeper into this rapidly changing and expanding area. In our next chapter, we'll return from the cloud and turn our attention to another great space for Java developers--your mobile phone.

27
DeskDroid - A Desktop Client for Your Android Phone

We've come at long last to our final project. To close our time together here, we're going to build a very practical application, one that lets us send and receive SMS messages from the comfort of our desktop. There are a number of products on the market that let you do this now, but they typically require a third-party service, meaning your message travels through someone else's servers. For the privacy-minded, that can be a real problem. We'll build a system that is 100% local.

Building the app will cover several different topics, some familiar, some new. That list includes the following:

- Android applications
- Android services
- REST servers
- Server-sent events for event/data streaming
- Data access using Content Providers

There will also be a host of other, smaller tidbits along the way as we finish out our time together on a strong, high note.

Getting started

This project will have two parts:

- The Android application/server (not to be confused with application server, of course)
- The desktop/JavaFX application

The desktop piece is somewhat useless without the **server** piece, so we'll start by building the Android side first.

Creating the Android project

While we have been using NetBeans for most of our work so far, we will again use Android Studio for this piece of the project. While there is some semblance of Android support for NetBeans, as of this writing, the project seems to have stalled. Android Studio, on the other hand, is very actively developed by Google and is, in fact, the official IDE for Android development. I will leave it as an exercise for the reader, if needed, to install the IDE and the SDK.

To create a new project, we click on **File | New Project**, and specify **Application name**, **Company domain**, and **Project location**, as shown in the following screenshot:

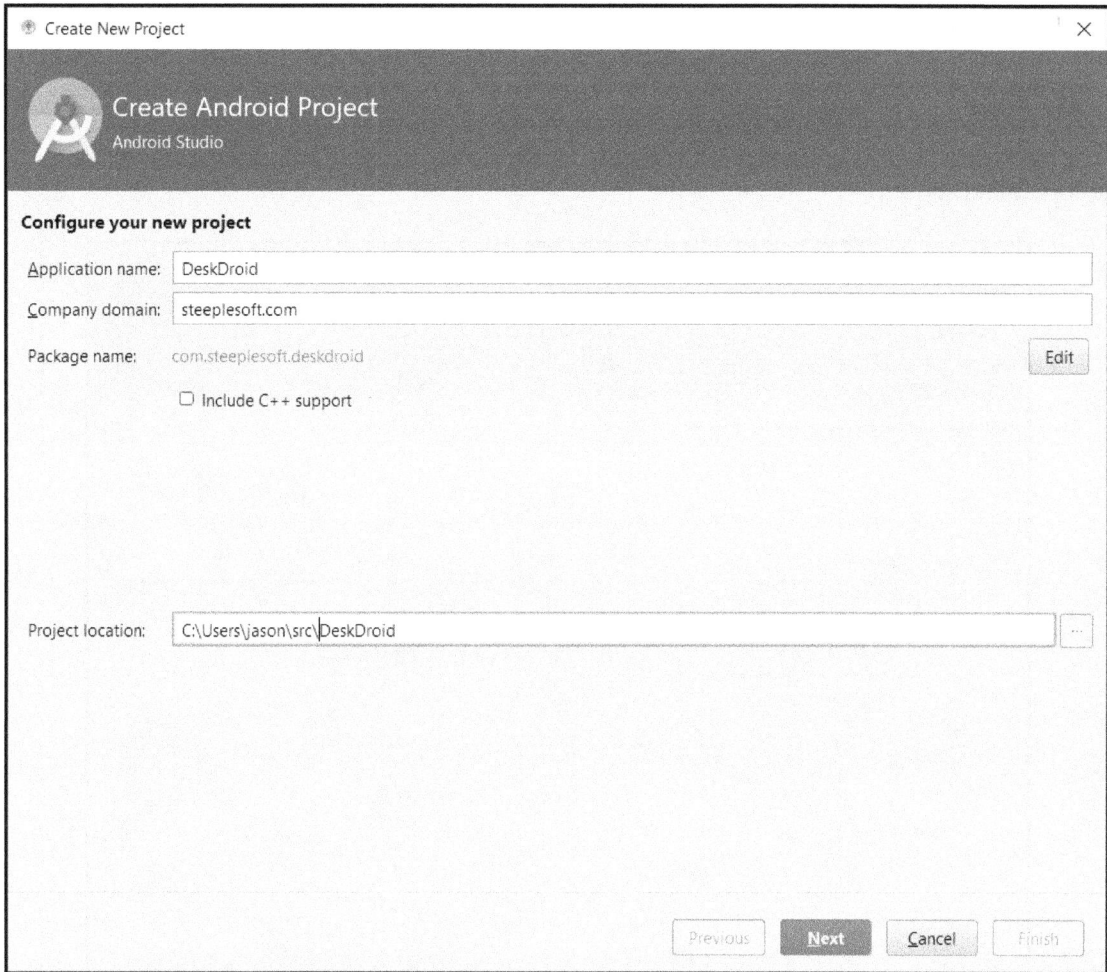

Next, we need to specify the API version we want to target. This can be a tricky choice. On the one hand, we'd like to be on the cutting edge and have all of the great new features that Android offers available to us, but on the other hand, we don't want to target such a new API level that we make the application unusable (read uninstallable) for a larger number of Android users than is necessary. In this case, Android 6.0, or Marshmallow, seems like an acceptable trade-off:

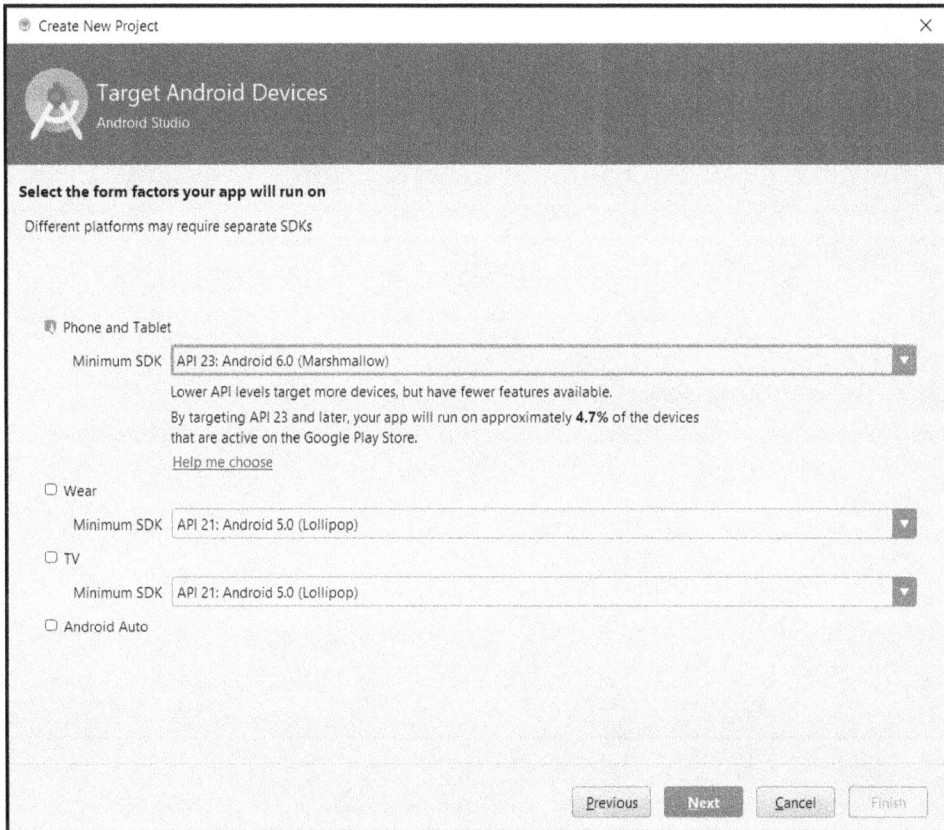

Click on **Next**, select **Blank Activity**, **Next**, and **Finish**, and our project is ready for development.

On the Android side, we are not going to do much in the way of user interface. Once we have finished the project, you will likely have all sorts of ideas of what could be done, which is great, but we won't spend the time here doing any of those. That said, the first thing we really need to do is ask the user for permission to access the text messages on their phone.

Requesting permissions

In earlier versions of Android, permissions were an all or nothing proposition. Starting with Android 6, though, the user is prompted for each permission that the application requests, allowing for the possibility of a user to grant some permissions while denying others. We will need to request some permissions--we need to be able to read and write SMS messages, and we'll need access to the contacts (so we can try to figure out who sent us a given message). Android provides an API for requesting those permissions very easily, which we'll put in our `onCreate()` method, as follows:

```
public static final int PERMISSION_REQUEST_CODE = 42;
@Override
protected void onCreate(Bundle savedInstanceState) {
  super.onCreate(savedInstanceState);
  // ...
 ActivityCompat.requestPermissions(this,
        new String[]{
                Manifest.permission.SEND_SMS,
                Manifest.permission.RECEIVE_SMS,
                Manifest.permission.READ_CONTACTS
        },
        PERMISSION_REQUEST_CODE);
}
```

When this preceding code runs, Android will prompt the user to grant or deny the requested permissions. This is done asynchronously, so, in your applications, you need to make sure you don't attempt any operation that requires any permission that you request until the user has had a chance to grant the permission (and, should the user deny the permission, the application should degrade, or fail, gracefully).

To allow the application to respond to permission grants, Android provides a callback. In our callback, we want to make sure the user grants us both permissions:

```
@Override
public void onRequestPermissionsResult(int requestCode,
  String permissions[], int[] grantResults) {
    switch (requestCode) {
      case PERMISSION_REQUEST_CODE: {
        if (grantResults.length != 3
          || grantResults[0] !=
              PackageManager.PERMISSION_GRANTED
          || grantResults[1] !=
              PackageManager.PERMISSION_GRANTED
          || grantResults[2] !=
              PackageManager.PERMISSION_GRANTED) {
                AlertDialog.Builder dialog =
```

```
      new AlertDialog.Builder(this);
   dialog.setCancelable(false);
   dialog.setTitle("Error");
   dialog.setMessage("This app requires access
    to text messages and contacts. Click OK
    to close.");
   dialog.setPositiveButton("OK",
    new DialogInterface.OnClickListener() {
      @Override
      public void onClick(DialogInterface dialog,
       int id) {
         finish();
      }
   });

   final AlertDialog alert = dialog.create();
   alert.show();
  }
 }
 }
 }
```

When Android calls back in to our application, we need to make sure that the
`requestCode` is what we specified-- `PERMISSION_REQUEST_CODE`--to make sure that we
only respond to our own requests.

Once we've identified an appropriate response, we make sure that `grantResults` is the
correct length, and that each entry is `PERMISSION_GRANTED`. If the array is too short, or if
either array element is not the correct type, we display a dialog informing the user that both
permissions are required, and then exit the application.

In our example, we are requesting both permissions simultaneously, so we respond to both
simultaneously. If you have a complex set of permissions, for example, if your application
can work with only some of the requested permissions, you can make multiple calls to
`ActivityCompat.requestPermissions`, providing a distinct `requestCode` for each. You
would then need to expand your switch block in `onRequestPermissionsResult()` to
cover each new `requestCode`.

One final word on permissions. Typically, you should always check to make sure that you have the permission needed to perform a given task. You can do that with a method as follows:

```
protected boolean checkPermission(Permissions permission) {
    return ContextCompat.checkSelfPermission(this,
        permission.permission) ==
        PackageManager.PERMISSION_GRANTED;
}
```

In our case, we just don't allow the application to run if we aren't granted the required permissions, so we need not worry about additional permission checks.

Creating the service

The heart of the Android portion of the project is our REST endpoints. We would like these endpoints to be available whenever the phone is on, so we can't use an `Activity` to host them. What we want is a `Service`. The Android documentation defines a `Service` as *an application component that can perform long-running operations in the background, and it does not provide a user interface*. There are three types of Services--`scheduled` (which runs on a schedule), `started` (which can be started explicitly by another application component), and `bound` (which is bound to an application component via the `bindService()` call, and runs until all the bound components are destroyed). Since we want this to be available all the time, we want a started service.

To create the service, click on **File** | **New** | **Service** | **Service**. Enter `DeskDroidService` for the service, uncheck **Exported**, and click on **Finish**. That will get you the following stubbed code:

```
public class DeskDroidService extends Service {
    public DeskDroidService() {
    }

    @Override
    public IBinder onBind(Intent intent) {
        throw new UnsupportedOperationException(
            "Not yet implemented");
    }
}
```

The wizard also updates `AndroidManifest.xml` as follows:

```
<service
  android:name=".DeskDroidService"
  android:enabled="true"
  android:exported="false" />
```

The method `onBind()` is abstract, so it must be implemented. We are not creating a bound service, so we can leave this unimplemented, although we will change it so that it returns `null` rather than throwing an `Exception`. We are, though, interested in when the service is started and stopped, so we need to override these two relevant lifecycle methods:

```
public int onStartCommand(Intent intent, int flags, int startId) {
  super.onStartCommand(intent, flags, startId);
}
public void onDestroy() {
}
```

It's in these methods that we'll place our REST service code. We will once again use Jersey, the JAX-RS reference implementation, which provides a nice way of bootstrapping a server in a Java SE environment, such as what we find ourselves in here in our Android application. We'll encapsulate that logic in a new method called `startServer()` as follows:

```
protected static Server server;
protected void startServer() {
  WifiManager WifiMgr = (WifiManager) getApplicationContext()
    .getSystemService(Service.Wifi_SERVICE);
  if (WifiMgr.isWifiEnabled()) {
    String ipAddress = Formatter.
     formatIpAddress(WifiMgr.getConnectionInfo()
       .getIpAddress());
    URI baseUri = UriBuilder.fromUri("http://" + ipAddress)
     .port(49152)
     .build();
    ResourceConfig config =
      new ResourceConfig(SseFeature.class)
        .register(JacksonFeature.class);
    server = JettyHttpContainerFactory.createServer(baseUri,
     config);
  }
}
```

The first thing we do is check to make sure that we're on Wi-Fi. This isn't strictly necessary, but it seemed to be a prudent precaution to prevent the application from listening for connections, regardless of the network state. If the phone is not on Wi-Fi, there's a good chance the intended laptop is not either. There may be legitimate use cases for allowing the endpoints to listen even on a cellular network, however. Making this restriction configurable is a great candidate for a preferences-driven option.

For this code to work, we need to add this new permission to the manifest:

```
<uses-permission android:name=
    "android.permission.ACCESS_WIFI_STATE" />
```

Once we're sure that we're on Wi-Fi, we look up our IP address, and bootstrap a Jetty-based Jersey server. With a nod to the Venerable Commodore 64, for those of us old enough to remember that computing pioneer, we listen on port `49152` on the Wi-Fi network interface.

Next, we create a `ResourceConfig` instance, providing two feature references that we're interested in--`SseFeature` and `JacksonFeature`. We've already seen `JacksonFeature`; that's what lets us work with POJOs, leaving the JSON concerns to Jersey. What is `SseFeature`, though?

Server-sent events

SSE, or server-sent events, is a means by which we can stream data from the server to the client. Typically, a REST request is very short-lived--make a connection, send the request, get a response, close the connection. Sometimes, though, the REST server may not have all of the data that the client wants at the time of the request (for example, reading data from another data source such as a log file or network socket). So, it would be nice to be able to push that data to the client as it becomes available. That's exactly what SSE allows us to do. We'll look into that in more detail later.

Finally, we start the server instance with a call to `JettyHttpContainerFactory.createServer()`. Since we need to be able to stop the server later, we capture the server instance, and store it in an instance variable. We call `startServer()` from `onStartCommand()` as follows:

```
private static final Object lock = new Object();
public int onStartCommand(Intent intent, int flags, int startId) {
    super.onStartCommand(intent, flags, startId);
    synchronized (lock) {
        if (server == null) {
            startServer();
```

```
        messageReceiver = new BroadcastReceiver() {
          @Override
          public void onReceive(Context context,
            Intent intent) {
              String code = intent.getStringExtra("code");
              DeskDroidService.this.code = code;
              Log.d("receiver", "Got code: " + code);
          }
        };
        LocalBroadcastManager.getInstance(this).
         registerReceiver(
           messageReceiver,
            new IntentFilter(CODE_GENERATED));
      }
    }
    return Service.START_STICKY;
  }
```

Notice that we've wrapped our call to `startServer()` in a `synchronized` block. For those that might be unaware, `synchronized` is one of the more basic approaches to concurrent code available to Java developers. The net effect of this keyword is that multiple threads that try to execute this block of code must do so synchronously, or one a time. We do this here so that if we have two different processes attempting to start the server, we can guarantee that at most one is running. Without this block, the first thread could start the server and store the instance in the variable, while a second thread could do the same thing, but its server instance, which gets stored in the variable, fails to start. We would now have a running server with no valid reference to it, so we would be unable to stop it.

We have also registered a `BroadcastReceiver` that listens for CODE_GENERATED. We'll come back and explain this later in the chapter, so don't worry about this for now.

Controlling the service state

If we run the application now, our service won't run, so we need to make it such that it will run. We'll do that in a couple of different ways. The first way will be from our application. We want to make sure the service is running when we open the application, especially after it is just installed. To do that, we need to add one line to `MainActivity.onCreate()` as follows:

```
startService(new Intent(this, DeskDroidService.class));
```

When the application is started now, it will guarantee that the service is running. We don't, though, want to require that the user open the application to run the service. Fortunately, we have a way to start the application when the phone starts. We can do that by installing a `BroadcastReceiver` that listens for boot events, as shown here:

```
public class BootReceiver extends BroadcastReceiver {
  @Override
  public void onReceive(Context context, Intent intent) {
    context.startService(new Intent(context,
      DeskDroidService.class));
  }
}
```

The body of the preceding method is identical to our recent addition to `MainActivity`. We do, though, need to register the service, and ask for permission. In `AndroidManifest.xml`, we need to add this:

```
<uses-permission android:name=
  "android.permission.RECEIVE_BOOT_COMPLETED" />
<receiver android:name=".BootReceiver" android:enabled="true">
  <intent-filter>
    <action android:name=
    "android.intent.action.BOOT_COMPLETED" />
  </intent-filter>
</receiver>
```

We now have a service that starts either at device boot or application startup. It does not, however, do anything of interest, so we need to add some endpoints to our server.

Adding endpoints to the server

As covered in `Chapter 25`, *Taking Notes with Monumentum*, a JAX-RS resource lives in a POJO with certain annotations. To stub out our endpoint class, we can start with this:

```
@Path("/")
@Produces(MediaType.APPLICATION_JSON)
protected class DeskDroidResource {
}
```

We will also need to register this class with JAX-RS, which we do with this line in `startServer()`:

```
config.registerInstances(new DeskDroidResource());
```

Ordinarily, we would pass, say, `DeskDroidResource.class`, to the `ResourceConfig` constructor, like we did with `JacksonFeature.class`. We will be accessing Android resources, and to do that, we're going to need the `Service`'s `Context` instance. There are a number of resources on the internet that will suggest creating a custom `Application` class and storing it in a `public static`. While that does seem to work, it will also leak memory, so, Android Studio, for example, will complain if you try that. We can, however, avoid that by using nested classes. That approach can get a bit unwieldy, but our classes should be small enough that it remains manageable.

Getting conversations

Let's start by adding an endpoint to get all of the conversations on the phone, as follows:

```
@GET
@Path("conversations")
public Response getConversations() {
  List<Conversation> conversations = new ArrayList<>();
  Cursor cur = getApplication().getContentResolver()
  .query(Telephony.Sms.Conversations.CONTENT_URI,
  null, null, null, null);
  while (cur.moveToNext()) {
    conversations.add(buildConversation(cur));
  }

  Collections.sort(conversations, new ConversationComparator());

  return Response.ok(new GenericEntity<List<Conversation>>(
  conversations) {}).build();
}
```

Here is where we see the Android artifacts start to show up--we are going to use a `ContentProvider` to access the SMS data. A `ContentProvider` is a way for an application, or, in this case, an Android subsystem, to expose data to outside consumers in a portable, storage-agnostic manner. We don't care how the data is stored. We simply specify what fields we want, what filters or restrictions we want placed on that data, and `ContentProvider` does the rest.

Using ContentProviders, we specify the type of data not by a table name, like we would with SQL, but with a Uri. In this case, we specify Telephony.Sms.Conversations.CONTENT_URI. We pass several null values to query() as well. These represent the projection (or field list), the selection (or filter), the selection arguments, and the sort order. Since these are all null, we want every field and every row in the natural sort order for the provider. That gets us a Cursor object, which we then iterate over, creating Conversation objects, and add them to our List.

We create the Conversation instances with this method:

```
private Conversation buildConversation(Cursor cur) {
    Conversation conv = new Conversation();
    final int threadId =
      cur.getInt(cur.getColumnIndex("thread_id"));
    conv.setThreadId(threadId);
    conv.setMessageCount(
      cur.getInt(cur.getColumnIndex("msg_count")));
    conv.setSnippet(cur.getString(cur.getColumnIndex("snippet")));
    final List<Message> messages =
      getSmsMessages(conv.getThreadId());
    Set<String> participants = new HashSet<>();
    for (Message message : messages) {
      if (!message.isMine()) {
        participants.add(message.getAddress());
      }
    }
    conv.setParticipants(participants);
    conv.setMessages(messages);
    return conv;
}
```

Each conversation is just a thread ID, message count, and snippet, which is the last message received. To get the actual messages, we call getSmsMessages() as follows:

```
private List<Message> getSmsMessages(int threadId) {
    List<Message> messages = new ArrayList<>();
    Cursor cur = null;
    try {
      cur = getApplicationContext().getContentResolver()
        .query(Telephony.Sms.CONTENT_URI,
        null, "thread_id = ?", new String[]
        {Integer.toString(threadId)},
        "date DESC");

      while (cur.moveToNext()) {
        Message message = new Message();
```

```
      message.setId(cur.getInt(cur.getColumnIndex("_id")));
      message.setThreadId(cur.getInt(
        cur.getColumnIndex("thread_id")));
      message.setAddress(cur.getString(
        cur.getColumnIndex("address")));
      message.setBody(cur.getString(
        cur.getColumnIndexOrThrow("body")));
      message.setDate(new Date(cur.getLong(
        cur.getColumnIndexOrThrow("date"))));
      message.setMine(cur.getInt(
        cur.getColumnIndex("type")) ==
          Telephony.Sms.MESSAGE_TYPE_SENT);
      messages.add(message);
    }
  } catch (Exception e) {
      e.printStackTrace();
  } finally {
      if (cur != null) {
        cur.close();
      }
  }
  return messages;
}
```

This method, and the processing logic, is mostly identical to that for conversations. The `Uri` for the `ContentProvider`, `Telephony.Sms.CONTENT_URI`, is different, of course, and we specify a filter for the query as follows:

```
cur = getApplicationContext().getContentResolver().query(
  Telephony.Sms.CONTENT_URI,
   null, "thread_id = ?", new String[]
   {Integer.toString(threadId)},
   "date DESC");
```

We do have a slight bit of data analysis here. We need to know which of the messages are the ones we sent and which are the ones we received so that we can display the thread more meaningfully. On the device, the messages we've sent have the type `Telephony.Sms.MESSAGE_TYPE_SENT`. The values for this field translate roughly to folders (sent, received, draft, and so on). Rather than leaking part of the Android API into ours by sharing the value of the constant, we have a `boolean` field, `isMine`, which is true if the message is of type `MESSAGE_TYPE_SENT`. It is, admittedly, a slightly clumsy alternative, but it works and should be clear enough.

Once we return the list of messages, we iterate over the list, getting a list of the unique participants (which should be only one, since we are dealing with SMS messages).

Finally, we return this `List<Conversation>` to the client using Jersey's POJO-mapping feature as follows:

```
return Response.ok(new GenericEntity<List<Conversation>>(
    conversations) {}).build();
```

If we click either the run or debug buttons (the large triangle or the triangle-over-a-bug icons in the tool bar), you'll be asked for the deployment target, as seen in this screenshot:

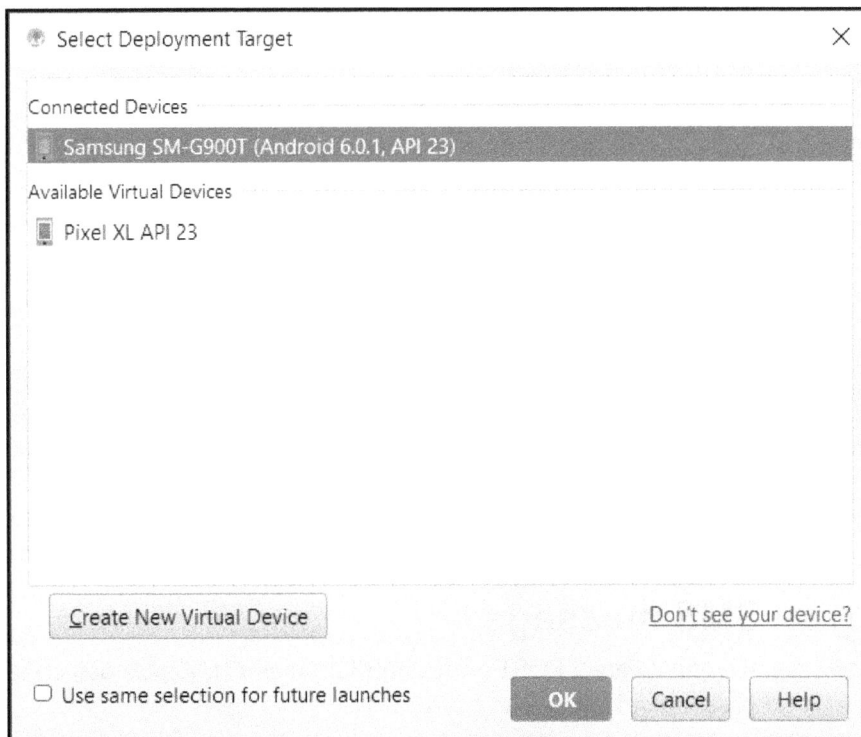

Since we require Wi-Fi, I select my physical device. If you want to configure an emulator with Wi-Fi, that would work as well. Click on **OK**, and after a few moments, the application should start on the device you have selected, and we can make our first REST request as follows:

```
$ curl http://192.168.0.2:49152/conversations | jq .
[
{
  "messageCount": 2,
  "messages": [
    {
      "address": "5551234567",
      "body": "Demo message",
      "date": 1493269498618,
      "id": 301,
      "mine": true,
      "threadId": 89
    },
    {
      "address": "+15551234567",
      "body": "Demo message",
      "date": 1493269498727,
      "id": 302,
      "mine": false,
      "threadId": 89
    }
  ],
  "participants": [ "+15551234567" ],
  "snippet": "Demo message",
  "threadId": 89
}
]
```

This preceding sample code shows a conversation I'm having with myself. Too many late nights, perhaps, but you can see where the first message, the oldest message, is marked as mine, which is the one I sent to myself, and the second is where I received it back. Pretty cool, but how do you send a message? It turns out that that's actually quite simple.

Sending an SMS message

To send a message, we will create a POST endpoint that takes a `Message` object, which we'll then pull apart and pass to Android's telephony APIs.

```
@POST
@Path("conversations")
```

```
public Response sendMessage(Message message)
throws InterruptedException {
    final SmsManager sms = SmsManager.getDefault();
    final ArrayList<String> parts =
    sms.divideMessage(message.getBody());
    final CountDownLatch sentLatch =
    new CountDownLatch(parts.size());
    final AtomicInteger statusCode = new AtomicInteger(
    Response.Status.CREATED.getStatusCode());
    final BroadcastReceiver receiver = new BroadcastReceiver() {
    @Override
    public void onReceive(Context context, Intent intent) {
        if (getResultCode() != Activity.RESULT_OK) {
                statusCode.set(
                    Response.Status.INTERNAL_SERVER_ERROR
                        .getStatusCode());
        }
         sentLatch.countDown();
      }
    };
    registerReceiver(receiver,
    new IntentFilter("com.steeplesoft.deskdroid.SMS_SENT"));
    ArrayList<PendingIntent> sentPIs = new ArrayList<>();
    for (int i = 0; i < parts.size(); i++) {
       sentPIs.add(PendingIntent.getBroadcast(
          getApplicationContext(), 0,
          new Intent("com.steeplesoft.deskdroid.SMS_SENT"), 0));
    }
    sms.sendMultipartTextMessage(message.getAddress(), null,
    parts, sentPIs, null);

    sentLatch.await(5, TimeUnit.SECONDS);
    unregisterReceiver(receiver);
    return Response.status(statusCode.get()).build();
}
```

There's a lot going on this method. Here is the breakdown:

1. We get a reference to the `SmsManager` class. This class will do all of the work for us.
2. We ask `SmsManager` to divide the message for us. Text messages are, typically, limited to 160 characters, so this will split the message as needed.
3. We create a `CountDownLatch` with a count that matches the number of parts in the message.

4. We create an `AtomicInteger` to store the status code. As we'll see in a moment, we need to change the value of this variable from inside an anonymous class. However, for an anonymous class to access variables from its enclosing scope, those variables must be `final`, which means that we can not have a `final int`, as then we would not be able to change the value. With `AtomicInteger`, though, we can call `set()` to change the value while leaving the instance reference, which is what the variable will hold, unchanged.

5. We create a new `BroadcastReceiver`, which will handle `Intents` broadcast (as we'll see further) when the message is sent. In `onReceive()`, if the result code is not `ACTIVITY.RESULT_OK`, we call `AtomicInteger.set()` to reflect the failure. We then call `sentLatch.countDown()` to indicate that this message part has been processed.

6. With the call to `registerReceiver()`, we let the operating system know about our new receiver. We provide an `IntentFilter` to restrict which `Intents` our receiver has to process.

7. We then create a new `PendingIntent` for each part our message has been split into. This will allow us to react to each part's send attempt individually.

8. We call `sendMultipartTextMessage()` to send the message part(s). Android handles the details of a multipart message for us, so there's no extra effort required.

9. We need to wait for all of the message parts to be sent, so we call `sentLatch.await()` to give the system time to send the message. We don't want to wait forever, though, so we give it a timeout of five seconds, which should be long enough. It is conceivable that some networks may be very slow about sending text messages, so this value may need to be adjusted.

10. Once we pass the latch, we `unregister` our receiver, and return the status code.

Using curl again, we can now test sending a message (be sure to click on `Run` or `Debug` again to deploy your updated code):

```
$ curl -v -X POST -H 'Content-type: application/json'
http://192.168.0.2:49152/conversations -d
'{"address":"++15551234567", "body":"Lorem ipsum dolor sit
 amet..."}'
> POST /conversations HTTP/1.1
> Content-type: application/json
> Content-Length: 482
< HTTP/1.1 201 Created
```

In the preceding `curl` we send some `lorem ipsum` text to our recipient, which gives us a nice, long message (482 total characters for the request payload), which is correctly chunked up and sent to the destination phone number, as indicated by the `201 Created` response status.

We now have a working REST service on the phone, which lets us read the existing messages and send new ones. Interacting with the service with `curl` has worked well enough, but it's time to build our desktop client, and put a nice face on this project.

Creating the desktop application

To build our application, we'll return to NetBeans and JavaFX. As in the previous chapters, we'll create a new Maven-based JavaFX application by clicking on **File** | **New Project**:

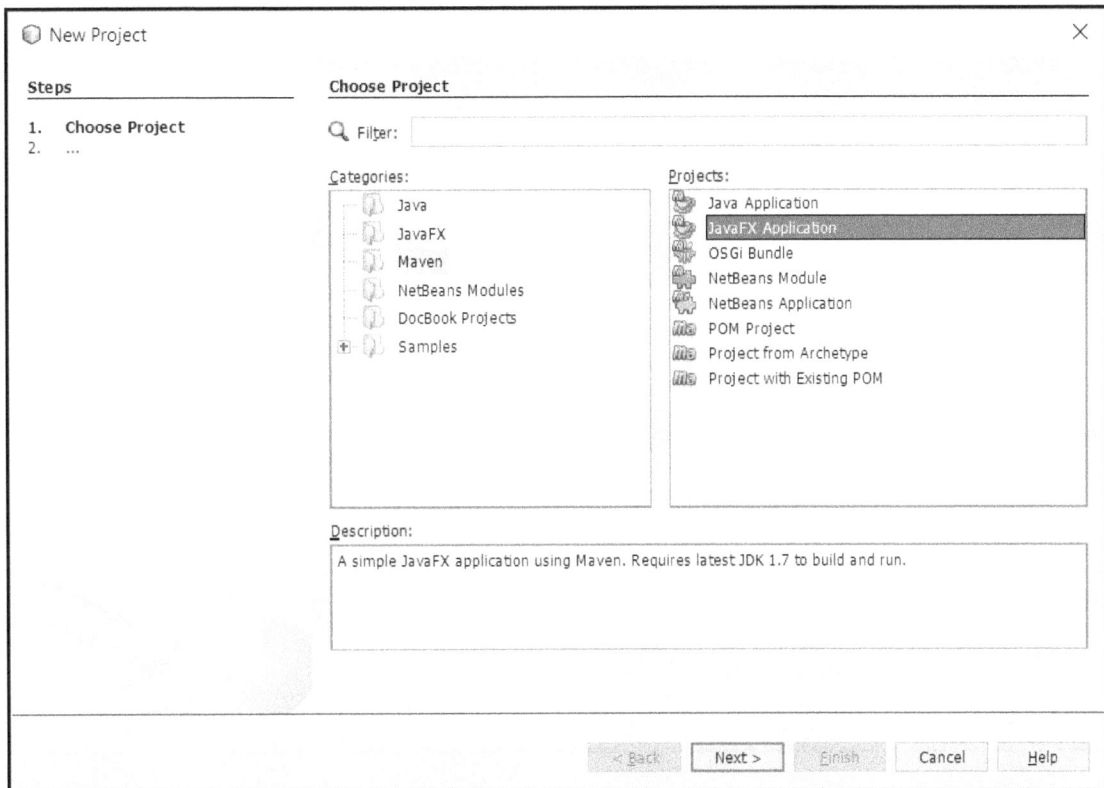

In the next step, call the project `deskdroid-desktop`, verify the package name, and click on **Finish**. While not strictly necessary, let's clean up the naming a bit, changing the controller to `DeskDroidController`, and the FXML file to `deskdroid.fxml`. We'll also need to modify the references to the FXML and the CSS in the controller, and the reference to the controller in the FXML. Click on **Run | Run Project** to make sure everything is wired up correctly. Once the app starts, we can immediately close it so we can start making changes.

Defining the user interface

Let's start by building up the user interface. Here's what the application will look like:

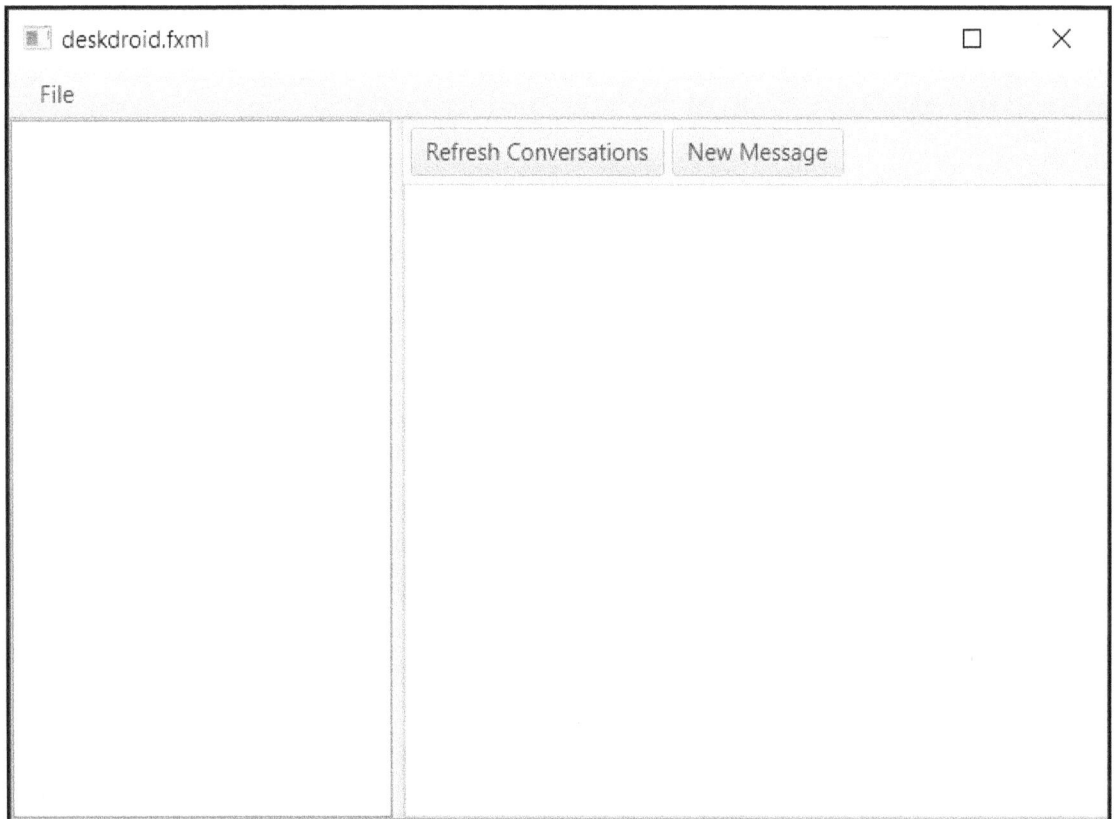

In the preceding screen, we'll have our list of conversations on the left, and we will display the selected conversation on the right. We will add a mechanism for auto-refreshing, but the **Refresh Conversations** will allow for a manual refresh, if needed. **New Message** should be self-explanatory.

We can use Gluon's Scene Builder to build the user interface, of course, but let's take a look at the FXML. We'll start, as usual, with a `BorderPane`, as follows:

```
<BorderPane fx:id="borderPane" minWidth="1024" prefHeight="768"
xmlns="http://javafx.com/javafx/8.0.111"
xmlns:fx="http://javafx.com/fxml/1"
fx:controller="com.steeplesoft.deskdroid.
desktop.DeskDroidController">
```

For the `top` section, we're going to add a menu bar as follows:

```
<MenuBar BorderPane.alignment="CENTER">
  <menus>
    <Menu text="_File">
        <items>
            <MenuItem onAction="#connectToPhone"
                text="_Connect to Phone" />
            <MenuItem onAction="#disconnectFromPhone"
                text="_Disconnect from Phone" />
            <MenuItem onAction="#closeApplication"
                text="E_xit">
                <accelerator>
                    <KeyCodeCombination alt="ANY" code="F4"
                        control="UP" meta="UP" shift="UP"
                        shortcut="UP" />
                </accelerator>
            </MenuItem>
        </items>
    </Menu>
  </menus>
</MenuBar>
```

We'll have three `MenuItems` in the `FileMenu`: `connectToPhone`, `disconnectFromPhone`, and `Exit`. Each menu item will have a mnemonic, as indicated by the underscores. The `ExitMenuItem` has an accelerator key, `ALT-F4`.

We'll put the bulk of the user interface in the `center` section. The vertical split allows us to resize the two sides of the user interface. For that, we use a `SplitPane` as follows:

```
<center>
  <SplitPane dividerPositions="0.25"
    BorderPane.alignment="CENTER">
  <items>
```

With `dividerPositions`, we set the default split at the 25% mark along the horizontal rule. The `SplitPane` has a nested `items` element to hold its children to which we add the left element, `ListView`:

```
<VBox>
  <children>
    <ListView fx:id="convList" VBox.vgrow="ALWAYS" />
  </children>
</VBox>
```

We wrap `ListView` in a `VBox` to make the `ListView` grow and shrink, as needed, more easily.

Finally, let's build the right side of the user interface:

```
<VBox fx:id="convContainer">
  <children>
  <HBox>
      <children>
        <Button mnemonicParsing="false"
                onAction="#refreshConversations"
                text="Refresh Conversations">
          <HBox.margin>
            <Insets right="5.0" />
          </HBox.margin>
        </Button>
        <Button fx:id="newMessageBtn"
            text="New Message" />
      </children>
      <padding>
        <Insets bottom="5.0" left="5.0"
            right="5.0" top="5.0" />
      </padding>
    </HBox>
    <ListView fx:id="messageList" VBox.vgrow="ALWAYS" />
  </children>
</VBox>
```

On the right side, we also have a VBox, which we use to arrange our two user interface elements. The first is HBox, which holds two buttons: **Refresh Conversation** and **New Message**. The second is our ListView for displaying the selected conversation.

Defining user interface behavior

While we can define the structure of the user interface in FXML in all but the most trivial applications, the user interface still requires some Java code to finish defining its behavior. We'll do that now in DeskDroidController.initialize(). We'll start with the left side of the user interface, the conversation list, as follows:

```
@FXML
private ListView<Conversation> convList;
private final ObservableList<Conversation> conversations =
FXCollections.observableArrayList();
private final SimpleObjectProperty<Conversation> conversation =
new SimpleObjectProperty<>();
@Override
public void initialize(URL url, ResourceBundle rb) {
  convList.setCellFactory(list ->
  new ConversationCell(convList));
  convList.setItems(conversations);
   convList.getSelectionModel().selectedItemProperty()
      .addListener((observable, oldValue, newValue) -> {
          conversation.set(newValue);
          messages.setAll(newValue.getMessages());
          messageList.scrollTo(messages.size() - 1);
  });
```

We declare an injectable variable to hold a reference to our ListView. JavaFX will set that value for us, thanks to the annotation @FXML. ListView will need a model to display, which we declare as conversations, and we declare conversation to hold the currently selected conversation.

In the initialize() method, we wire everything together. Since ListView will be displaying our domain object, we need to declare a CellFactory for it, which we do with the lambda passed to setCellFactory(). We'll look at ListCell in a moment.

Next, we associate ListView with its model, conversations, and define what is, in effect, an onClick listener. We achieve that, though, by adding a listener to SelectionModel on ListView. In that listener, we update the currently selected conversation, update the messages ListView to display the conversation, and scroll that ListView to the very bottom so that we see the most recent message.

Initializing the message `ListView` is much simpler. We need these instance variables:

```
@FXML
private ListView<Message> messageList;
private final ObservableList<Message> messages =
FXCollections.observableArrayList();
```

We also need these lines in `initialize()`:

```
messageList.setCellFactory(list -> new MessageCell(messageList));
messageList.setItems(messages);
```

And the **New Message** button needs a handler:

```
newMessageBtn.setOnAction(event -> sendNewMessage());
```

`ConversationCell` tells JavaFX how to display a `Conversation` instance. To do that, we create a new `ListCell` child as follows:

```
public class ConversationCell extends ListCell<Conversation> {
```

Then we override `updateItem()`:

```
@Override
protected void updateItem(Conversation conversation,
boolean empty) {
super.updateItem(conversation, empty);
if (conversation != null) {
    setWrapText(true);
    final Participant participant =
        ConversationService.getInstance()
            .getParticipant(conversation
                .getParticipant());
    HBox hbox = createWrapper(participant);

    hbox.getChildren().add(
        createConversationSnippet(participant,
            conversation.getSnippet()));
    setGraphic(hbox);
} else {
    setGraphic(null);
}
}
}
```

If the cell is given a `Conversation`, we process it. If not, we set the cell's graphic to null. If we fail to do that, we'll have unpredictable results when scrolling through the lists.

To build the cell contents, we start by getting the `Participant` and creating the wrapper component as follows:

```
protected HBox createWrapper(final Participant participant) {
  HBox hbox = new HBox();
  hbox.setManaged(true);
  ImageView thumbNail = new ImageView();
  thumbNail.prefWidth(65);
  thumbNail.setPreserveRatio(true);
  thumbNail.setFitHeight(65);
  thumbNail.setImage(new Image(
    ConversationService.getInstance()
      .getParticipantThumbnail(
        participant.getPhoneNumber())));
  hbox.getChildren().add(thumbNail);
  return hbox;
}
```

This is pretty standard JavaFX fare--create an `HBox`, and add to it an `ImageView`. We are, though, using a class we haven't looked at yet--`ConversationService`. We'll look at this later, but for now, it's enough to know that we will encapsulate our REST calls in this class. Here, we're calling an endpoint (that we haven't seen yet) to get the contact information for the phone number at the other end of this conversation.

We also need to create the conversation snippet as follows:

```
protected VBox createConversationSnippet(
  final Participant participant, String snippet) {
  VBox vbox = new VBox();
  vbox.setPadding(new Insets(0, 0, 0, 5));
  Label sender = new Label(participant.getName());
  sender.setWrapText(true);
  Label phoneNumber = new Label(participant.getPhoneNumber());
  phoneNumber.setWrapText(true);
  Label label = new Label(snippet);
  label.setWrapText(true);
  vbox.getChildren().addAll(sender, phoneNumber, label);
  return vbox;
}
```

Using `VBox` to ensure vertical alignment, we create two labels, one with the participants' information, and the other with the snippet of the conversation.

While that finishes the cell definition, if we were to run the application the way it is now, the `ListCell`'s contents would likely be cropped by the edge of `ListView` itself. For example, see the difference between the top list and the bottom list in the following screenshot:

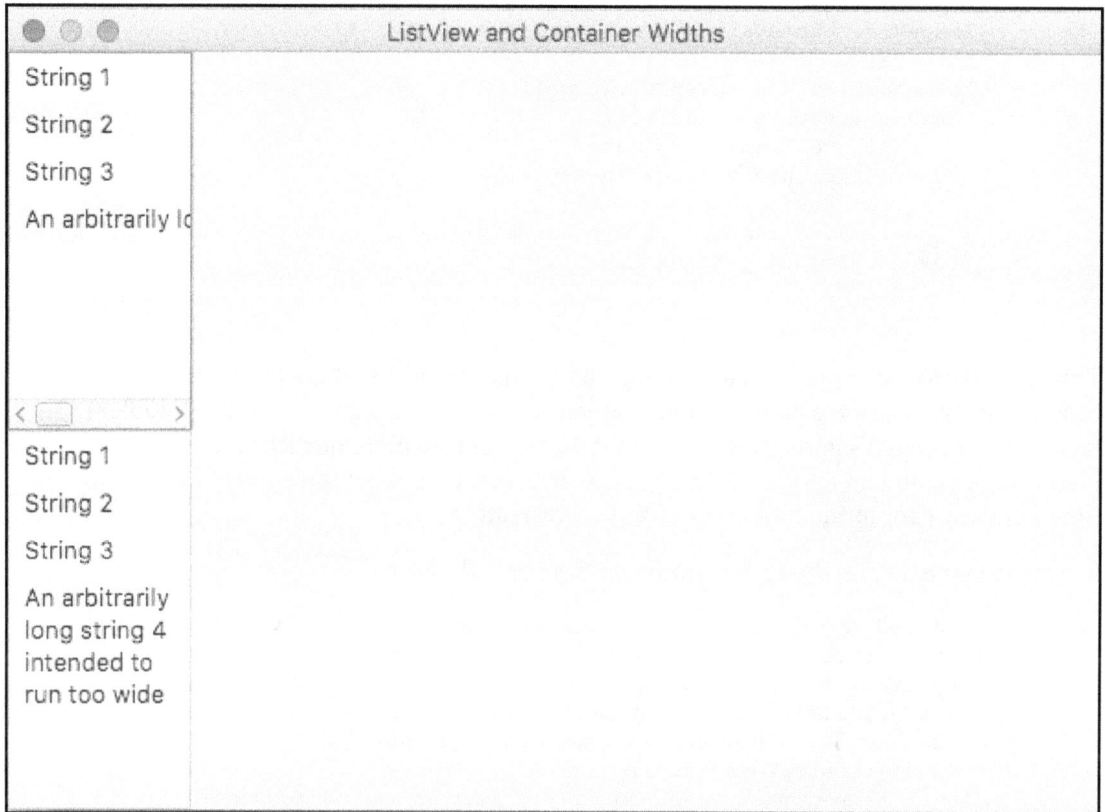

To make our `ListCell` behave as we see at the bottom of the last screen, we need to make one more change to our code, which is as follows:

```
public ConversationCell(ListView list) {
    super();
    prefWidthProperty().bind(list.widthProperty().subtract(2));
    setMaxWidth(Control.USE_PREF_SIZE);
}
```

In our preceding `CellFactory`, we pass in the reference to the enclosing `ListView`.

```
convList.setCellFactory(list -> new ConversationCell(convList));
```

In the constructor, we then bind the preferred width of our cell to the actual width of the list (and subtract a small amount to adjust for the control borders). When rendered now, our cell will wrap just as we expected.

The `MessageCell` definition is similar, and goes as follows:

```
public class MessageCell extends ListCell<Message> {
  public MessageCell(ListView list) {
      prefWidthProperty()
        .bind(list.widthProperty().subtract(20));
      setMaxWidth(Control.USE_PREF_SIZE);
  }

  @Override
  public void updateItem(Message message, boolean empty) {
      super.updateItem(message, empty);
      if (message != null && !empty) {
          if (message.isMine()) {
              wrapMyMessage(message);
          } else {
              wrapTheirMessage(message);
          }
      } else {
          setGraphic(null);
      }
  }
}
```

For *my* message, we create the contents this way:

```
private static final SimpleDateFormat DATE_FORMAT =
 new SimpleDateFormat("EEE, MM/dd/yyyy hh:mm aa");
private void wrapMyMessage(Message message) {
 HBox hbox = new HBox();
 hbox.setAlignment(Pos.TOP_RIGHT);
 createMessageBox(message, hbox, Pos.TOP_RIGHT);
 setGraphic(hbox);
}
private void createMessageBox(Message message, Pane parent,
 Pos alignment) {
   VBox vbox = new VBox();
   vbox.setAlignment(alignment);
   vbox.setPadding(new Insets(0,0,0,5));
   Label body = new Label();
```

```
        body.setWrapText(true);
        body.setText(message.getBody());

        Label date = new Label();
        date.setText(DATE_FORMAT.format(message.getDate()));

        vbox.getChildren().addAll(body, date);
        parent.getChildren().add(vbox);
    }
```

The **message box** is much like the previous conversation snippet--a vertical display of the message, followed by its date and time. This format will be used by *my* messages and *their* messages, so we use `javafx.geometry.Pos` to align the controls to the right or left, respectively.

The *their* message is created this way:

```
        private void wrapTheirMessage(Message message) {
           HBox hbox = new HBox();
           ImageView thumbNail = new ImageView();
           thumbNail.prefWidth(65);
           thumbNail.setPreserveRatio(true);
           thumbNail.setFitHeight(65);
           thumbNail.setImage(new Image(
                ConversationService.getInstance()
                    .getParticipantThumbnail(
                        message.getAddress())));
           hbox.getChildren().add(thumbNail);
           createMessageBox(message, hbox, Pos.TOP_LEFT);
           setGraphic(hbox);
        }
```

This is similar to the *my* message, with the exception that we display the sender's profile picture, if there is one associated with the contact on the phone, which we retrieve from the phone via the `ConversationService` class.

We have a bit more work to do, but this is what the application will look like with data:

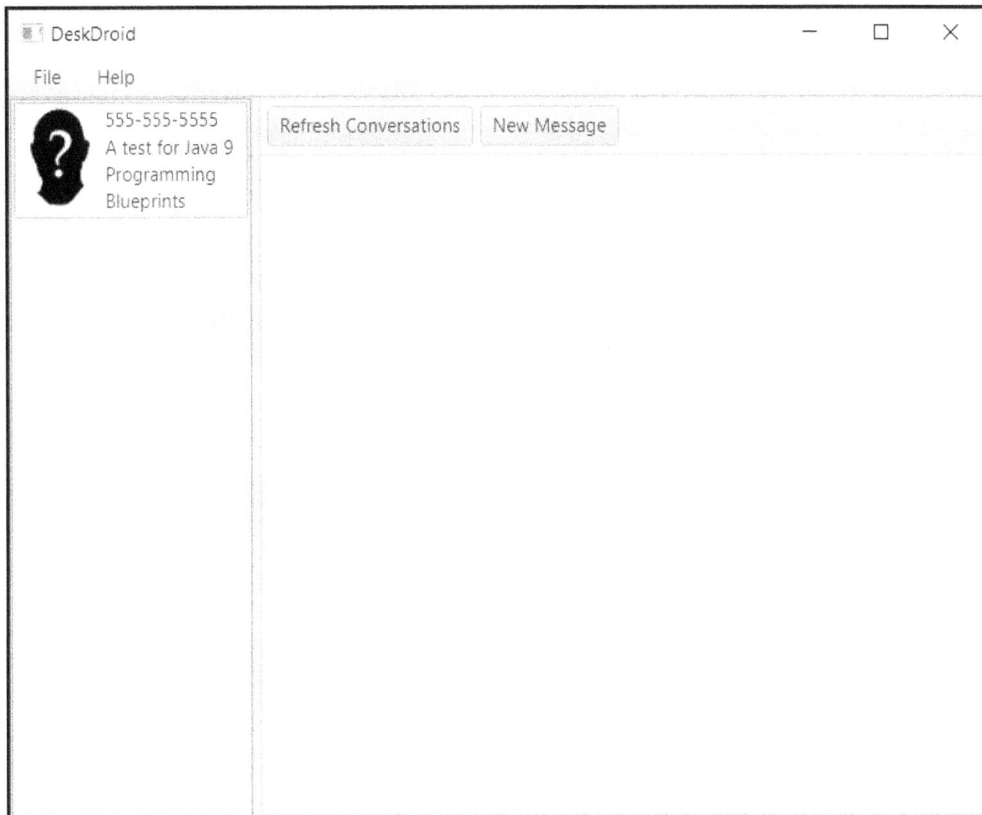

To get the data, we need a REST client, and that is found in `ConversationService`:

```
public class ConversationService {
  public static class LazyHolder {
    public static final ConversationService INSTANCE =
        new ConversationService();
  }
  public static ConversationService getInstance() {
    return LazyHolder.INSTANCE;
  }
  private ConversationService() {
    Configuration configuration = new ResourceConfig()
            .register(JacksonFeature.class)
            .register(SseFeature.class);
    client = ClientBuilder.newClient(configuration);
  }
```

Using the so-called *Initialize-on-Demand Holder* idiom, we create a sort of a poor man's singleton. Since the constructor is private, it can't be called from outside this class. The nested static class, `LazyHolder`, is initialized only when it is finally referenced, which happens on the first call to `getInstance()`. Once that method is called, `LazyHolder` is loaded and initialized, at which point, the constructor is run. The instance created is stored in the static variable, and lives as long as the JVM runs. Every subsequent call will return the same instance. This is important for us, as we have some objects that are expensive to create as well as some simple caching in the class:

```
protected final Client client;
protected final Map<String, Participant> participants =
  new HashMap<>();
```

In the preceding code, we initialize our client instance, registering the `JacksonFeature`, which gets us the POJO mapping we've already discussed. We also register `SseFeature`, a more advanced feature of Jersey that we'll discuss in detail later.

We've already seen the conversation list. That is generated using data from this method:

```
public List<Conversation> getConversations() {
  List<Conversation> list;
  try {
   list = getWebTarget().path("conversations")
             .request(MediaType.APPLICATION_JSON)
             .header(HttpHeaders.AUTHORIZATION,
                getAuthorizationHeader())
             .get(new GenericType<List<Conversation>>() {});
  } catch (Exception ce) {
    list = new ArrayList<>();
  }
  return list;
}
public WebTarget getWebTarget() {
return client.target("http://"
        + preferences.getPhoneAddress() + ":49152/");
}
```

`WebTarget` is a JAX-RS class that represents the *resource target identified by the resource URI*. We're pulling the address for the phone from preferences, which we'll discuss later. Once we have our `WebTarget`, we complete building the URI by appending `conversations`, specify the request mime type, and issue the `GET` request. Note that our request here is somewhat optimistic, as we don't do any status code checking. Should an `Exception` be thrown, we simply return an empty `List`.

The other method we've seen is `getParticipant()`, which is as follows:

```
public Participant getParticipant(String number) {
  Participant p = participants.get(number);
  if (p == null) {
    Response response = getWebTarget()
            .path("participants")
            .path(number)
            .request(MediaType.APPLICATION_JSON)
            .header(HttpHeaders.AUTHORIZATION,
                getAuthorizationHeader())
            .get(Response.class);
    if (response.getStatus() == 200) {
        p = response.readEntity(Participant.class);
        participants.put(number, p);
        if (p.getThumbnail() != null) {
            File thumb = new File(number + ".png");
            try (OutputStream stream =
                    new FileOutputStream(thumb)) {
                byte[] data = DatatypeConverter
                    .parseBase64Binary(p.getThumbnail());
                stream.write(data);
            } catch (IOException e) {
                e.printStackTrace();
            }
        }
    }
  }
  return p;
}
```

In the last method, we see our cache come into play. When a `Participant` is requested, we look to see if this information has already been fetched. If so, we return the cached information. If not, we can make a request for it.

Much like `getConversations()`, we build a request for the appropriate endpoint, and send the `GET` request. This time, though, we do check for the status code. Only if the status is `200` (`OK`) do we continue processing the response. In this case, we ask JAX-RS for the `Participant` instance returned, which `JacksonFeature` happily builds for us from the JSON response body, and which we immediately add to our cache.

If the server found a thumbnail for the contact, we need to process that. The server piece, which we will look at immediately after we finish discussing this method, sends the thumbnail as a base 64-encoded string in the body of the JSON object, so we convert it back to the binary representation, and save that to a file. Notice that we are using try-with-resources, so we need not worry about cleaning up after ourselves.

```
try (OutputStream stream = new FileOutputStream(thumb))
```

We haven't seen the server side of this operation, so let's look at that now. In our Android application in Android Studio, we have this method on `DeskDroidResource`:

```
@GET
@Path("participants/{address}")
public Response getParticipant(@PathParam("address")
String address) {
  Participant p = null;
  try {
    p = getContactsDetails(address);
    } catch (IOException e) {
    return Response.serverError().build();
  }
  if (p == null) {
    return Response.status(Response.Status.NOT_FOUND).build();
    } else {
    return Response.ok(p).build();
  }
}
```

We attempt to build the `Participant` instance. If an Exception is thrown, we return a 500 (Server Error). If `null` is returned, we return a 404 (Not Found). If a participant is found, we return 200 (OK) and the participant.

To build the participant, we need to query the phone contacts. This works in much the same way as the SMS queries:

```
protected Participant getContactsDetails(String address) throws
  IOException {
  Uri contactUri = Uri.withAppendedPath(
    ContactsContract.PhoneLookup.CONTENT_FILTER_URI,
    Uri.encode(address));
  Cursor phones = deskDroidService.getApplicationContext()
  .getContentResolver().query(contactUri,
  new String[]{
    ContactsContract.CommonDataKinds.Phone.DISPLAY_NAME,
    "number",
    ContactsContract.CommonDataKinds.Phone
```

```
        .PHOTO_THUMBNAIL_URI},
        null, null, null);
    Participant participant = new Participant();
    if (phones.moveToNext()) {
      participant.setName(phones.getString(phones
      .getColumnIndex(
      ContactsContract.CommonDataKinds.Phone
      .DISPLAY_NAME)));
      participant.setPhoneNumber(phones.getString(
        phones.getColumnIndex("number")));
      String image_uri = phones.getString(
        phones.getColumnIndex(
          ContactsContract.CommonDataKinds.Phone
          .PHOTO_THUMBNAIL_URI));
      if (image_uri != null) {
        try (InputStream input = deskDroidService
          .getApplicationContext().getContentResolver()
          .openInputStream(Uri.parse(image_uri));
        ByteArrayOutputStream buffer =
          new ByteArrayOutputStream()) {
            int nRead;
            byte[] data = new byte[16384];

            while ((nRead = input.read(data, 0,
                data.length)) != -1) {
              buffer.write(data, 0, nRead);
            }

            buffer.flush();
            participant.setThumbnail(Base64
                .encodeToString(buffer.toByteArray(),
                  Base64.DEFAULT));
        } catch (IOException e) {
            e.printStackTrace();
          }
        }
    }
    phones.close();
    return participant;
  }
```

The preceding is the same type of query and cursor management that we saw earlier with conversations, but there is one exception. If the contact has a thumbnail, the query returns a `Uri` to that image. We can use `ContentResolver` to open an `InputStream` using that `Uri` to read the contents, which we load into `ByteArrayOutputStream`. Using Android's `Base64` class, we encode this binary image into a `String`, and add that to our `Participant` model. We saw the decoding half of this operation previously.

Sending messages

Now that we can see the conversations that we've been having, we need to add the ability to take part in those conversations--to send new text messages. We'll start on the client. We've actually already seen the handler for the `New Message` button assigned. It is as follows:

```
newMessageBtn.setOnAction(event -> sendNewMessage());
```

What we need to do now is to look at this `sendNewMessage()` method itself:

```
private void sendNewMessage() {
  Optional<String> result = SendMessageDialogController
    .showAndWait(conversation.get());
  if (result.isPresent()) {
    Conversation conv = conversation.get();
    Message message = new Message();
    message.setThreadId(conv.getThreadId());
    message.setAddress(conv.getParticipant());
    message.setBody(result.get());
    message.setMine(true);
    if (cs.sendMessage(message)) {
      conv.getMessages().add(message);
      messages.add(message);
    } else {
      Alert alert = new Alert(AlertType.ERROR);
      alert.setTitle("Error");
      alert.setHeaderText(
          "An error occured while sending the message.");
      alert.showAndWait();
    }
  }
}
```

The actual dialog is displayed in another window, so we have a separate FXML file, `message_dialog.fxml`, and controller, `SendMessageDialogController`. When the dialog closes, we check the return `Optional` to see if the user entered a message. If so, process the message as follows:

1. Get a reference to the selected `Conversation`.
2. Create a new message, setting the conversation ID, recipient, and body.
3. Using `ConversationService`, we attempt to send the message:
   1. If successful, we update the user interface with the new message.
   2. If unsuccessful, we display an error message.

`SendMessageController` works just like the other controllers we've looked at. The most interesting is the method `showAndWait()`. We'll use that method to show the dialog, wait for it to close, and return any user response to the caller. The dialog looks as follows:

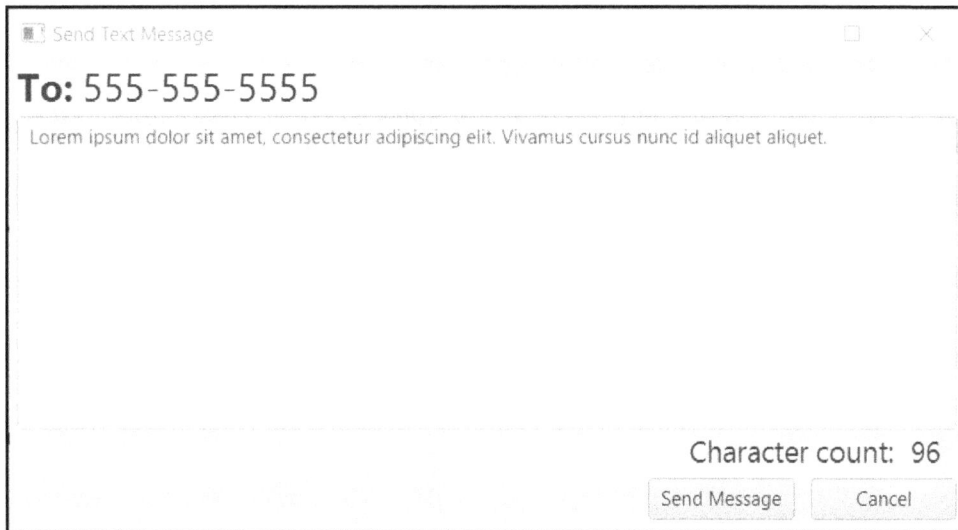

The method looks as follows:

```
public static Optional<String> showAndWait(
  Conversation conversation) {
  try {
    FXMLLoader loader =
        new FXMLLoader(SendMessageDialogController.class
            .getResource("/fxml/message_dialog.fxml"));
    Stage stage = new Stage();
    stage.setScene(new Scene(loader.load()));
```

```
        stage.setTitle("Send Text Message");
        stage.initModality(Modality.APPLICATION_MODAL);
        final SendMessageDialogController controller =
            (SendMessageDialogController) loader.getController();
        controller.setConversation(conversation);
        stage.showAndWait();
        return controller.getMessage();
    } catch (IOException ex) {
        throw new RuntimeException(ex);
    }
}
```

The first few lines in the preceding method are what we've normally seen, which is creating the loader and the `Stage`. Before showing the `Stage`, we set the modality, and pass in the current `Conversation`. Finally, we call `showAndWait()`, at which point the method blocks until the user closes the dialog, and then we return the entered message:

```
public Optional<String> getMessage() {
    return Optional.ofNullable(message);
}
```

A Java `Optional` is a *container object which may or may not contain a non-null value*. The value of `message` may or may not be set depending on which button is clicked in the dialog. Using the `Optional`, we can return a, possibly, null value, and handle it more safely in the caller--if (result.isPresent()).

The sending of the message is a simple POST operation in the `ConversationService`, which is as follows:

```
public boolean sendMessage(Message message) {
    Response r = getWebTarget().path("conversations")
        .request()
        .header(HttpHeaders.AUTHORIZATION,
          getAuthorizationHeader())
        .post(Entity.json(message));
    return r.getStatus() == Response.Status.CREATED
        .getStatusCode();
}
```

The client side is simple, but what about the server side? Unsurprisingly, that's where the complexity lies:

```
@POST
@Path("conversations")
public Response sendMessage(Message message) throws
InterruptedException {
```

```
final SmsManager sms = SmsManager.getDefault();
final ArrayList<String> parts =
  sms.divideMessage(message.getBody());
```

To add the endpoint, we define a new method with the correct annotations. This method will listen on the path `conversations` for `POST` requests, and expect a `Message` as its payload. The actual work of sending a message is handled by `SmsManager`, so we acquire a reference to the default manager. The next step calls `divideMessage()`, but what's that all about?

Text messages are technically limited to 160 characters. Twitter users are probably somewhat familiar with that already. Twitter limits tweets to 140 characters, leaving 20 characters for the sender's name. While Twitter has stuck hard to that limit, regular SMS users have a better experience. If the message is longer than 160 characters, most modern phones will chunk the message into 153 character segments when sending (with 7 characters for segmentation information used to piece the segments back together), which are merged back into one message on the receiving end if the phone supports it. The `SmsManager` API handles this complexity for us with `divideMessage()`.

Once the message is *chunked*, though, our job gets a little more difficult. We would like to be able to return a status code indicating whether or not the message was sent successfully. To do that, we need to check the status of each chunk of the message, be it one or ten. Sending a text message with `SmsManager`, Android broadcasts an `Intent` with the results. To react to that, we need to register a receiver. Put that all together, and we get this code:

```
final CountDownLatch sentLatch = new CountDownLatch(parts.size());
final AtomicInteger statusCode =
  new AtomicInteger(
    Response.Status.CREATED.getStatusCode());
final BroadcastReceiver receiver = new BroadcastReceiver() {
  @Override
  public void onReceive(Context context, Intent intent) {
    if (getResultCode() != Activity.RESULT_OK) {
      statusCode.set(Response.Status.
        INTERNAL_SERVER_ERROR.getStatusCode());
    }
    sentLatch.countDown();
  }
};
deskDroidService.registerReceiver(receiver,
  new IntentFilter("com.steeplesoft.deskdroid.SMS_SENT"));
ArrayList<PendingIntent> sentPIs = new ArrayList<>();
for (int i = 0; i < parts.size(); i++) {
  sentPIs.add(PendingIntent.getBroadcast(
    deskDroidService.getApplicationContext(), 0,
```

```
        new Intent("com.steeplesoft.deskdroid.SMS_SENT"), 0));
    }
    sms.sendMultipartTextMessage(message.getAddress(), null,
    parts, sentPIs, null);
    sentLatch.await(5, TimeUnit.SECONDS);
    deskDroidService.unregisterReceiver(receiver);
    return Response.status(statusCode.get()).build();
```

To make sure that we've received the `Intent` for each message chunk, we start by creating a `CountDownLatch` with a count matching the number of chunks in the message. We also create an `AtomicInteger` to hold the status code. The reason we do this is that we need a final variable which we can access from our `BroadcastReceiver`, but we also need to be able to change the value. `AtomicInteger` allows us to do that.

We create and register a `BroadcastReceiver`, which analyzes the result code on `Intent`. If it's not `Activity.RESULT_OK`, we set `statusCode` to `INTERNAL_SERVER_ERROR`. Either way, we count down the latch.

With our receiver ready, we create a `List` of `PendingIntent`s, one for each chunk, then we pass that, with our list of message chunks, to `SmsManager.sendMultipartTextMessage()`. Message sending is asynchronous, so we call `sentLatch.await()` to wait for the results to be returned. We limit the wait to five seconds so that we don't wait forever. Once the wait time expires or the latch is cleared, we unregister our receiver and return the status code.

Getting updates

So far, we can see all of the conversations, view individual messages in a conversation, and send new messages. What we can't do yet is get updates when new messages arrive on the device, so let's implement that now, starting with the server piece this time.

To get a constant stream of events, we'll use a feature called Server-Sent Events, a W3C specification for receiving push notifications from the server. We enabled this feature in Jersey by registering the `SseFeature` in both the client and server setup steps. To create an SSE endpoint, we specify that the method returns the media type `SERVER_SENT_EVENTS`, and we return an `EventOutput` as the payload:

```
@GET
@Path("status")
@Produces(SseFeature.SERVER_SENT_EVENTS)
@Secure
public EventOutput streamStatus() {
```

```
    final EventOutput eventOutput = new EventOutput();
    // ...
    return eventOutput;
}
```

From the Jersey documentation, we learn this:

> *After the eventOutput is returned from the method, the Jersey runtime recognizes that this is a ChunkedOutput extension and does not close the client connection immediately. Instead, it writes the HTTP headers to the response stream and waits for more chunks (SSE events) to be sent. At this point the client can read headers and starts listening for individual events.*

The server, then, keeps the socket to the client open, and pushes data down it. But where does the data come from? The Server-sent Event endpoints create a Thread that writes data to the EventOutput instance we created earlier. When the Thread is finished, it calls eventOutput.close(), which signals to the runtime that it is appropriate to close the client connection. To stream updates, our Thread looks as follows:

```
final Thread thread = new Thread() {
  @Override
  public void run() {
    final LinkedBlockingQueue<SmsMessage> queue =
      new LinkedBlockingQueue<>();
    BroadcastReceiver receiver = null;
    try {
      receiver = new BroadcastReceiver() {
        @Override
        public void onReceive(Context context,
          Intent intent) {
          Bundle intentExtras = intent.getExtras();
          if (intentExtras != null) {
            Object[] sms = (Object[])
              intentExtras.get("pdus");
            for (int i = 0; i < sms.length; ++i) {
              SmsMessage smsMessage =
                SmsMessage.createFromPdu(
                  (byte[]) sms[i]);
                  queue.add(smsMessage);
            }
          }
        }
      };
      deskDroidService.registerReceiver(receiver,
       new IntentFilter(
         "android.provider.Telephony.SMS_RECEIVED"));
```

```
          while (!eventOutput.isClosed()) {
            SmsMessage message = queue.poll(5,
              TimeUnit.SECONDS);
            while (message != null) {
              JSONObject json = new JSONObject()
               .put("participant", message.
               getDisplayOriginatingAddress())
               .put("body", message.
               getDisplayMessageBody());
              eventOutput.write(new OutboundEvent.Builder()
               .name("new-message")
               .data(json.toString())
               .build()
              );
              message = queue.poll();
            }
          }
        } catch (JSONException | InterruptedException |
          IOException e) {
        } finally {
            try {
              if (receiver != null) {
                deskDroidService.unregisterReceiver(receiver);
              }
              eventOutput.close();
            } catch (IOException ioClose) {
              // ...
            }
        }
    }
};
thread.setDaemon(true);
thread.start();
```

As we've seen before, we set up a `BroadcastReceiver`, which we register here and unregister before the `Thread` ends, but this time, we're listening for broadcasts that an SMS message has been received. To make sure our `Thread` isn't in a small, tight, fast loop, which would quickly kill the battery on the device, we use `LinkedBlockingQueue`. When a message is received, we pull the `SmsMessage`(s) from `Intent`, and add them to `queue`. In our while loop, we attempt to `take()` an item from `queue`. If we find one, we process it and any more that might either already be in the queue or be added while we are processing. Once `queue` is empty, we go back to waiting. We have a timeout on `take()` to make sure that the thread can respond to the exit criteria, most notably, the client disconnecting. This will run as long as the client remains connected. Let's look, then, at the client.

We encapsulated the details in
`ConversationService.subscribeToNewMessageEvents()` as follows:

```
public void subscribeToNewMessageEvents(
  Consumer<Message> callback) {
    Thread thread = new Thread() {
      @Override
      public void run() {
        stopListening = false;
        EventInput eventInput = getWebTarget().path("status")
         .request()
         .header(HttpHeaders.AUTHORIZATION,
          getAuthorizationHeader())
           .get(EventInput.class);
        while (!eventInput.isClosed() && !stopListening) {
          final InboundEvent inboundEvent =
            eventInput.read();
          if (inboundEvent == null) {
            // connection has been closed
            break;
          }
          if ("new-message".equals(inboundEvent.getName())){
            Message message =
              inboundEvent.readData(Message.class);
            if (message != null) {
              callback.accept(message);
            }
          }
        }
      }
    };
    thread.setDaemon(true);
    thread.start();
}
```

In the preceding code, we create a `Thread`, in which we make the call to the SSE endpoint.
The return type on the client is `EventInput`. We loop to process each incoming event,
which we get as an `InboundEvent`. If it is null, then the connection has been closed, so we
break out of our processing loop. If it is not null, we make sure that the event name matches
what we're waiting for--`new-message`. If found, we extract the event payload, a `Message`,
and call our callback, which we pass in as `Consumer<Message>`.

From the application proper, we subscribe to the status stream this way:

```
cs.subscribeToNewMessageEvents(this::handleMessageReceived);
```

`handleMessageReceived()` looks like this:

```
protected void handleMessageReceived(final Message message) {
  Platform.runLater(() -> {
    Optional<Conversation> optional = conversations.stream()
      .filter(c -> Objects.equal(c.getParticipant(),
       message.getAddress()))
      .findFirst();
    if (optional.isPresent()) {
      Conversation c = optional.get();
      c.getMessages().add(message);
      c.setSnippet(message.getBody());
      convList.refresh();
      if (c == conversation.get()) {
        messages.setAll(c.getMessages());
        messageList.scrollTo(messages.size() - 1);
      }
    } else {
        Conversation newConv = new Conversation();
        newConv.setParticipant(message.getAddress());
        newConv.setSnippet(message.getBody());
        newConv.setMessages(Arrays.asList(message));
        conversations.add(0, newConv);
    }
    final Taskbar taskbar = Taskbar.getTaskbar();
    if (taskbar.isSupported(Taskbar.Feature.USER_ATTENTION)) {
      taskbar.requestUserAttention(true, false);
    }
    Toolkit.getDefaultToolkit().beep();
  });
}
```

The first step in handling this new message is very important--we pass a `Runnable` to `Platform.runLater()`. If we don't do this, any attempts to modify the user interface will fail. You have been warned. In our `Runnable`, we create a `Stream` of `Conversations`, `filter()` it, looking for a `Conversation` whose participant matches the `Message` sender, then grab the first (and only) match.

If we find the `Conversation` in the list, we add this new `Message` to its list, and update the snippet (which is just the `Conversation`'s last message body). We also ask the `Conversation` list to `refresh()` itself to make sure the user interface reflects these changes. Finally, if the `Conversation` is the currently selected one, we update the message list and scroll to the bottom to make sure the new message shows.

If we don't find the `Conversation` in the list, we create a new one, and add it to the `ConversationObservable`, which results in the `List` automatically updating on the screen.

Finally, we attempt a couple of desktop integration tasks. If `Taskbar` supports the `USER_ATTENTION` feature, we request user attention. From the Javadocs we learn that, *depending on the platform, this may be visually indicated by a bouncing or flashing icon in the task area*. Regardless, we issue a beep to get the user's attention.

Security

There's one last major piece that we haven't discussed, and that's security. Currently, anybody with the desktop application can, in theory, connect to your phone, see your messages, send others, and so on. Let's fix that now.

Securing the endpoints

To secure the REST server, we will use a filter just like we used in Chapter 25, *Taking Notes with Monumentum*. We'll start by defining the annotation that will specify which endpoints need to be secured, as follows:

```
@NameBinding
@Retention(RetentionPolicy.RUNTIME)
@Target({ElementType.TYPE, ElementType.METHOD})
public @interface Secure {}
```

We will apply this preceding annotation to each secured endpoint (annotations condensed to one line for brevity):

```
@GET @Path("conversations") @Secure
public Response getConversations() {
    ...
    @POST @Path("conversations") @Secure
    public Response sendMessage(Message message)
     throws InterruptedException {
        ...
```

```
@GET @Path("status") @Produces(SseFeature.SERVER_SENT_EVENTS)
@Secure
public EventOutput streamStatus() {
  ...
  @GET @Path("participants/{address}") @Secure
  public Response getParticipant(
    @PathParam("address") String address) {
      ...
```

We will also need a filter to enforce security, which we add as follows:

```
@Provider
@Secure
@Priority(Priorities.AUTHENTICATION)
public class SecureFilter implements ContainerRequestFilter {
  private DeskDroidService deskDroidService;

  public SecureFilter(DeskDroidService deskDroidService) {
    this.deskDroidService = deskDroidService;
  }

  @Override
  public void filter(ContainerRequestContext requestContext)
    throws IOException {
      try {
        String authorizationHeader = requestContext.
         getHeaderString(HttpHeaders.AUTHORIZATION);
        String token = authorizationHeader.
         substring("Bearer".length()).trim();
        final Key key = KeyGenerator.
         getKey(deskDroidService.getApplicationContext());
        final JwtParser jwtParser =
          Jwts.parser().setSigningKey(key);
        jwtParser.parseClaimsJws(token);
      } catch (Exception e) {
         requestContext.abortWith(Response.status(
           Response.Status.UNAUTHORIZED).build());
      }
  }
}
```

Much like in Chapter 25, *Taking Notes with Monumentum*, we'll be using **JSON Web Tokens** **(JWT)** to help authenticate and authorize clients. In this filter, we extract the JWT from the request headers and validate it through these steps:

1. Get the signing key from KeyGenerator.
2. Create the JwtParser using the signing key.
3. Parse the claims in the JWT. For our purposes here, this is, basically, just a validation of the token itself.
4. Abort the request with UNAUTHORIZED (401) should the token be invalid.

The KeyGenerator itself looks a bit like what we saw in Chapter 25, *Taking Notes with Monumentum*, but has been modified to use Android APIs in this manner:

```
public class KeyGenerator {
  private static Key key;
  private static final Object lock = new Object();

  public static Key getKey(Context context) {
    synchronized (lock) {
      if (key == null) {
        SharedPreferences sharedPref =
          context.getSharedPreferences(
            context.getString(
              R.string.preference_deskdroid),
             Context.MODE_PRIVATE);
            String signingKey = sharedPref.getString(
              context.getString(
                R.string.preference_signing_key), null);
            if (signingKey == null) {
              signingKey = UUID.randomUUID().toString();
              final SharedPreferences.Editor edit =
                sharedPref.edit();
              edit.putString(context.getString(
                R.string.preference_signing_key),
                 signingKey);
              edit.commit();
            }
            key = new SecretKeySpec(signingKey.getBytes(),
             0, signingKey.getBytes().length, "DES");
      }
    }

    return key;
  }
}
```

Since we might possibly receive requests from multiple clients at a time, we need to be careful about how the key is generated. To make sure it's done once and only once, we'll use the same type of synchronization/locking we saw in the server startup.

Once we've acquired the lock, we perform a null check to see if the process has already generated (or read) the key. If not, we then read the signing key from `SharedPreferences`. If it's null, we create a random string (here, just a UUID), and save it to `SharedPreferences` for reuse next time. Note that to save to Android preferences, we have to get an instance of `SharedPreferences.Editor`, write the string, then `commit()`. Once we have the signing key, we create the actual `SecretKeySpec` that we'll use to sign and verify our JWTs.

Handling authorization requests

With our endpoints now secured, we need a way for the clients to request authorization. To do that, we'll expose a new endpoint, unsecured, of course, as follows:

```
@POST
@Path("authorize")
@Consumes(MediaType.TEXT_PLAIN)
public Response getAuthorization(String clientCode) {
  if (clientCode != null &&
    clientCode.equals(deskDroidService.code)) {
      String jwt = Jwts.builder()
       .setSubject("DeskDroid")
       .signWith(SignatureAlgorithm.HS512,
        KeyGenerator.getKey(
          deskDroidService.getApplicationContext()))
           .compact();
      LocalBroadcastManager.getInstance(
        deskDroidService.getApplicationContext())
       .sendBroadcast(new Intent(
          DeskDroidService.CODE_ACCEPTED));
    return Response.ok(jwt).build();
  }
  return Response.status(Response.Status.UNAUTHORIZED).build();
}
```

Rather than require a more complicated authorization system that might require a username and password or an OAuth2 provider, what we'll implement is a simple system that requires only a random number:

1. On the phone, the user requests that a new client be added, and is presented with a random number.
2. In the desktop application, the user enters the number, which the desktop application then POSTs to the server.
3. If the numbers match, the client is given a JWT, which it will send with every request.

3. The JWT is verified each time to make sure the client is authorized to access the target resource.

In this method, we get the number POSTed by the client (which we let JAX-RS extract from the request body), then compare it to the number generated on the phone. If they match, we create the JWT, and return it to the client. Before doing so, we broadcast an intent with the action CODE_ACCEPTED.

Where does the number come from, and why are we broadcasting this intent? We haven't looked at this in detail yet, but in the main layout, activity_main.xml, there is a FloatingActionButton. To this, we attach an onClick listener as follows:

```
FloatingActionButton fab =
  (FloatingActionButton) findViewById(R.id.fab);
fab.setOnClickListener(new View.OnClickListener() {
  @Override
  public void onClick(View view) {
    startActivityForResult(new Intent(
      getApplicationContext(),
      AuthorizeClientActivity.class), 1);
  }
});
```

When the user taps on the button, the following screen will be shown:

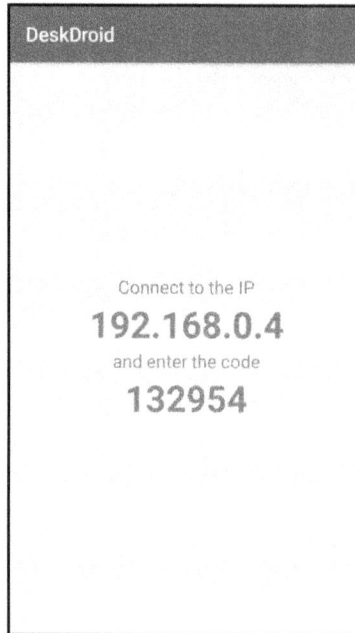

The client will use this information to connect and gain authorization. The `Activity` itself is fairly basic. It needs to present the IP address and code, and then respond to a client connecting. All of this is done in `onCreate()` in our new `AuthorizeClientActivity` class. We get the IP from `WifiManager`:

```
WifiManager wifiMgr = (WifiManager) getApplicationContext().
  getSystemService(WIFI_SERVICE);
String ipAddress = Formatter.formatIpAddress(wifiMgr.
  getConnectionInfo().getIpAddress());
```

Remember that we require that the client be on a Wi-Fi network. The code is just a random, 6-digit number:

```
String code = Integer.toString(100000 +
  new Random().nextInt(900000));
```

To listen for the `Intent` we saw earlier, which indicates that a client has been authenticated (which, presumably, will happen shortly after this `Activity` has been displayed), we register another receiver as follows:

```
messageReceiver = new BroadcastReceiver() {
  @Override
  public void onReceive(Context context, Intent intent) {
    clientAuthenticated();
  }
};
LocalBroadcastManager.getInstance(this).registerReceiver(
  messageReceiver, new IntentFilter(
    DeskDroidService.CODE_ACCEPTED));
```

We also need to tell the `Service` what this new code is so that it can verify it. To do that, we broadcast an `Intent` as follows:

```
Intent intent = new Intent(DeskDroidService.CODE_GENERATED);
intent.putExtra("code", code);
LocalBroadcastManager.getInstance(this).sendBroadcast(intent);
```

We've already seen the other half of this broadcast in `DeskDroidService.onStartCommand()` earlier, where the code is retrieved from the `Intent`, and stored in the service for use by `DeskDroidResource.getAuthorization()`.

Finally, this method, which handles the authentication notice, simply cleans up the receiver and closes the `Activity`:

```
protected void clientAuthenticated() {
  LocalBroadcastManager.getInstance(this).
    unregisterReceiver(messageReceiver);
  setResult(2, new Intent());
  finish();
}
```

With this, when a client connects and successfully authenticates, the `Activity` closes, and the user is returned to the main `Activity`.

Authorizing the client

Up until this point, everything has assumed that the desktop is already connected to the phone. We have enough pieces in place now that we can talk about that in a meaningful manner.

In the application's main `Menu`, we have two `MenuItems`: `Connect to Phone` and `Disconnect from Phone`. The `Connect to Phone` handler looks as follows:

```
@FXML
protected void connectToPhone(ActionEvent event) {
  ConnectToPhoneController.showAndWait();
  if (!preferences.getToken().isEmpty()) {
    refreshAndListen();
  }
}
```

We're going to use the now-familiar `showAndWait()` pattern to display a modal dialog, and to get the response using the new `ConnectToPhoneController`. The user interface is very simple, and is shown in this screenshot:

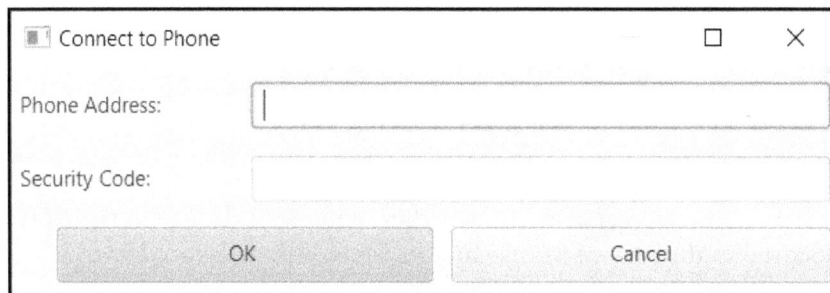

When the user clicks on **OK**, we save the address and the code in the application's preferences, then attempt to authorize against the server, as follows:

```
@FXML
public void connectToPhone(ActionEvent event) {
  String address = phoneAddress.getText();
  String code = securityCode.getText();
  preferences.setPhoneAddress(address);
  final ConversationService conversationService =
    ConversationService.getInstance();

  conversationService.setPhoneAddress(address);
  Optional<String> token = conversationService
    .getAuthorization(code);
  if (token.isPresent()) {
    preferences.setToken(token.get());
    closeDialog(event);
  }
}
```

Notice the use of `Optional<String>` as the return type for `ConversationService.getAuthorization()`. Using `Optional`, as we've discussed before, makes working with potentially `null` values much safer. In this case, if `Optional` has a value present, then we've successfully authenticated. So, we save the token to preferences, and close the dialog.

The actual authentication is handled by `ConversationService`:

```
public Optional<String> getAuthorization(String code) {
  Response response = getWebTarget().path("authorize")
    .request(MediaType.APPLICATION_JSON)
    .post(Entity.text(code));
  Optional<String> result;
  if(response.getStatus()==Response.Status.OK.getStatusCode()) {
    token = response.readEntity(String.class);
    result = Optional.of(token);
  } else {
      result = Optional.empty();
  }
  return result;
}
```

This last method sends the code to the server via a `POST`, and if the status code is `200`, we create an `Optional` with the returned token. Otherwise, we return an empty `Optional`.

Summary

In this chapter, we built a different kind of project. We've had applications that run on Android, and some that run on the desktop. This one, though, runs on both platforms simultaneously. One is no good without the other. That requires that we build things a bit differently to make sure the two are synchronized. While there are a variety of ways to go about this, we chose to use a REST server on the phone, with the desktop acting as a REST client.

By the end of the chapter, we built an Android application that provides not only a user interface, but a background process (called `Service`), and embedded our REST server in the Android application using Jersey and its Java SE deployment option. You also learned how to interact with text (SMS) messages on Android using the system-provided Content Providers and platform APIs, and streaming those messages to the client using Server-Sent Events. We demonstrated how to send messages between processes/threads in Android using `Intents`, broadcasts, and `BroadcastReceivers`. Finally, on the desktop side, we built a JavaFX client to display and send text messages, which connects to the REST server on the phone via the Jersey REST client, and we consumed the Server-sent Event stream, updating the user interface as appropriate.

With all of the moving parts, this was probably the most complex of our projects. It was certainly a great way to round out our list of projects. In the next chapter, we'll take a look at what's next for Java, as well as some other technologies that might be good to have on your radar.

28
What is Next?

At last, we have come to our final chapter together. We've built a number of different types of application, attempting to highlight and demonstrate different parts of the Java platform, especially those new to Java 9. As we've discussed, it's impossible to write something with **only** new-in-Java-9 technologies and APIs, so we also saw a variety of interesting items from Java 7 and 8. As Java 9 is finally shipping, it makes sense to look ahead to see what Java's future might hold for us, but it's also wise to look around and see what other languages are offering so that we can decide if our next Java will actually **be** Java. In this chapter, we'll do just that.

We will cover the following topics in this chapter:

- Recapping topics we previously covered
- What we can expect in the future

Looking back

Before looking forward to Java 10 and beyond, let's quickly recap some of the things we've covered in this book:

- The Java Platform Module System, perhaps the largest, most anticipated addition to the platform in this release. We saw how to create a module and discussed its implications on the runtime system.
- We walked through the new process management APIs in Java 9 and learned how to view processes, and even kill them, if needed.
- We looked at some of the major functional interfaces introduced in Java 8, discussing how they could be used, and showing how code might look with and without the lambdas that these interfaces support.

- We discussed Java 8's `Optional<T>` at length, showing how to create instances of the class, the various methods it exposes, and how one might use it.
- We spent a good deal of time building JavaFX-based applications, demonstrating various tips and tricks, working around several **gotchas**, and so on.
- Using the Java NIO File and Path APIs, we walked the filesystem, looking for duplicate files.
- We implemented data persistence using the Java Persistence API, demonstrating how to use the API in a Java SE environment, how to define entities, and so on.
- We built a calculator using the Java 8 Date/Time APIs, exposing the functionality as both a library and a command-line utility.
- As part of that effort, we briefly compared a few command-line utility frameworks (specifically focusing on Crest and Airline), before settling on Crest and demonstrating how to create and consume command-line options.
- While we didn't focus on it in every chapter, we did take a break to discuss and demonstrate unit testing.
- We learned about **Service Provider Interfaces (SPIs)** as a means to provide multiple alternate implementations for an interface that can be loaded dynamically at runtime.
- We implemented a couple of REST services, demonstrating not only the basic functionality of JAX-RS, how to deploy it in a Java SE environment, and POJO mapping, but also some more advanced features including server-sent events and securing endpoints using `Filter`.
- We built a couple of Android applications and discussed and demonstrated activities, fragments, services, content providers, asynchronous messaging, and background tasks.
- We saw OAuth2 authentication flows in action, including how to set up credentials using the Google OAuth provider and the Java code necessary to drive the process.
- We discovered JSON Web Tokens, a cryptographically secure way to pass data back and forth between, for example, a client and a server, and saw their very basic use as part of an authentication system.
- We toured the JavaMail API, learning a bit of the history and workings of common email protocols, such as POP3 and SMTP.
- We learned about job scheduling using the Quartz scheduler library.
- We saw how to specify constraints for our data in a declarative manner, then how to validate data in the light of those constraints using the Bean Validation API.

- Changing gears completely, we built a moderately sophisticated application using the feature-rich NetBeans Rich Client Platform.
- We looked briefly at world document databases with MongoDB.
- And we learned about dependency injection and how to use it with the CDI specification.

That's quite a list, and that doesn't cover all of it. One of the stated purposes of the book is to discuss and demonstrate the new features of Java 9. There are almost 100 **Java Enhancement Proposals** (**JEPs**) shipping with the release, making some of them difficult, at best, to demonstrate, but we've done our best.

Looking forward

With Java 9 done, then, the natural question is, **What is next?** As you might expect, the engineers at companies such as Oracle, Red Hat, IBM, Azul Systems, and others have been thinking about this question even while Java 9 was being planned and developed. While it is next to impossible to say what Java 10 will hold with any certainty (remember it took three major releases to get the module system done), we do have several items that are currently being discussed and designed, with the hope of shipping them in the next release. Over the next few pages, we'll explore some of these to get an early look at what our life as Java developers might be like in a couple of years.

Project Valhalla

Project Valhalla is an *incubation grounds for advanced language-VM co-development projects*. It is being led by Oracle engineer, Brian Goetz. As of this writing, there are three planned features for Valhalla. They are value types, generic specialization, and reified generics.

Value types

The goal of this effort is to update the Java Virtual Machine, and, if possible, the Java language, to support small, immutable, **identity-less** value types. Currently, if you instantiate a new `Object`, it is given an identifier by the JVM, which allows the **variable** instance to be referenced.

For example, if you create a new integer, `new Integer(42)`, a variable with the identity of `java.lang.Integer@68f29546`, but the value of `42`, the value of this variable will never change, and that's all we, as developers, typically care about. However, the JVM doesn't really know that, so it has to maintain the identity of the variable, with all of the overhead that entails. According to Goetz, that means every instance of this object will require up to 24 additional bytes to store the instance. If you have a large array of these, for example, that can be a significant amount of memory to manage and, eventually, to garbage-collect.

What the JVM engineers hope to achieve, then, is a way to **gently extend** the Java Virtual Machine byte code and the Java language itself to support the notion of a small, immutable aggregate type (think of a class with 0 or more properties) that lacks identity, which will result, it is hoped, in "memory-and locality-efficient programming idioms without sacrificing encapsulation". Their hope is that Java developers will be able to create these new types and treat them as just another primitive. If they do their jobs correctly, Goetz says, the feature can be summarized as **Codes like a class, works like an int!**

The current proposal, as of April 2017 (`http://cr.openjdk.java.net/~jrose/values/shady-values.html`), offers the following code snippet as an example of how one might define a value type:

```
@jvm.internal.value.DeriveValueType
public final class DoubleComplex {
  public final double re, im;
  private DoubleComplex(double re, double im) {
    this.re = re; this.im = im;
  }
  ... // toString/equals/hashCode, accessors,
    math functions, etc.
}
```

When instantiated, instances of this type could be created on the stack, rather than the heap, and use much less memory. This is a very low-level and technical discussion, which is far beyond the scope of this book, but if you are interested in more details, I would suggest reading the page linked earlier, or the effort's initial announcement at `http://cr.openjdk.java.net/~jrose/values/values-0.html`.

Generic specialization

Generic specialization is, perhaps, a bit easier to understand. Currently, generic type variables can hold only reference types. For example, you can create a `List<Integer>`, but not a `List<int>`. There are some pretty complex reasons why this is so, but being able to use primitives, and value types, would make collections more efficient in terms of memory and computation. You can read more about this feature in this document from, again, Brian Goetz--`http://cr.openjdk.java.net/~briangoetz/valhalla/specialization.html`. Jesper de Jong also has a good write-up about the complexities of primitives in generic type variables here:

`http://www.jesperdj.com/2015/10/12/project-valhalla-generic-specialization/`

Reified generics

The term **reified generics** is one that, more often than not, it seems, causes very vocal, animated reactions. Currently, if you declare a variable to be of type `List<Integer>`, the byte code generated has no real notion of the parameterized type, so it's not discoverable at runtime. If you were to examine the variable at runtime, you would see no mention of `Integer`. You could, of course, look at the types of each element, but, even then, you can't be sure of the type of the `List`, as there is nothing enforcing that **only** the `Integer` can be added to the `List`.

Java developers have been clamoring for reified generics, or, put simply, generics that retain their type information at runtime since generics were introduced in Java 5. As you might guess, making Java's generics reified is no trivial task, but, finally, we have a formal effort to see if it can be done and, if it can be done, to find a backwards-compatible way that doesn't have, for example, negative performance characteristics.

Project Panama

While not yet targeted for any particular Java release, Project Panama offers some hope for those who use, or hope to use, third-party, native libraries. Currently, the primary way of exposing native libraries (that is, OS-specific libraries written in, say, C or C++) to the JVM is via the **Java Native Interface** (**JNI**). The problem with JNI, or at least one of them, is that it requires that every Java programmer who wants to expose a native library to the JVM also become a C programmer, which means not only the C language itself, but also the related build tools for each supported platform.

Project Panama hopes to ameliorate that issue by offering the Java developer a new means of exposing native libraries without needing a deep understanding of the library language's ecosystem, or the JVM's. The JEP for Project Panama (`http://openjdk.java.net/jeps/191`) lists these design goals:

- A metadata system to describe native library calls (call protocol, argument list structure, argument types, return type) and the native memory structure (size, layout, typing, life cycle).

- Mechanisms to discover and load native libraries. These capabilities may be provided by the current `System.loadLibrary` or may include additional enhancements for locating platform or version-specific binaries appropriate to the host system.

- Mechanisms for binding, based on metadata, a given library/function coordinate to a Java endpoint, likely via a user-defined interface backed by plumbing to make the native downcall.

- Mechanisms for binding, based on metadata, a specific memory structure (layout, endianness, logical types) to a Java endpoint, either via a user-defined interface or a user-defined class, in both cases backed by plumbing to manage a real block of native memory.

- Appropriate support code to marshal Java data types to native data types and vice-versa. This will, in some cases, require the creation of FFI-specific types to support bit widths and numeric signs that Java can't represent.

JNI has been available for quite some time, and it's finally getting some long overdue attention.

Project Amber

Project Amber's goal is to **explore and incubate smaller, productivity-oriented Java language features**. The current list includes local-variable type inference, enhanced enums, and lambda leftovers.

Local-Variable Type Inference

As we have seen countless times in this book alone, when you declare a variable in Java, you have to declare the type twice, once on the left-hand and once on the right-hand side, plus a variable name:

```
AtomicInteger atomicInt = new AtomicInteger(42);
```

The problem here is that this code is verbose and repetitive. The Local-Variable Type Inference effort hopes to fix that, enabling something like this:

```
var atomicInt = new AtomicInteger(42);
```

This code is more concise, making it more readable. Notice the addition of the `val` keyword. Typically, the compiler knows that a line of code, for example, is a variable declaration when it sees `<type> <name> = ....`. Since the effort would remove the need for a type on the left-hand side of the declaration, we need a cue for the compiler, which the authors of this JEP propose as `var`.

There is also some discussion around simplifying the declaration of immutable, or `final`, variables. Among the proposals are `final var` as well as `val`, as seen in other languages such as Scala. At the time of writing, no decision that has been made on which proposal will make the final cut.

Enhanced enums

Enhanced enums will augment *the expressiveness of the enum construct in the Java Language by allowing type-variables in enums (generic enums), and performing sharper type-checking for enum constants.* (`http://openjdk.java.net/jeps/301`). What this means is that enums will finally support a parameterized type, allowing something like this (taken from the JEP at the link mentioned previously):

```
enum Primitive<X> {
  INT<Integer>(Integer.class, 0) {
    int mod(int x, int y) { return x % y; }
    int add(int x, int y) { return x + y; }
  },
  FLOAT<Float>(Float.class, 0f)  {
    long add(long x, long y) { return x + y; }
  }, ... ;

  final Class<X> boxClass;
  final X defaultValue;

  Primitive(Class<X> boxClass, X defaultValue) {
    this.boxClass = boxClass;
    this.defaultValue = defaultValue;
  }
}
```

Note that, in addition to specifying a generic type for each `enum` value, we can also define type-specific methods for each `enum` type. This will make it much easier to define a set of predefined constants, but also to define type-safe and type-aware methods for each of the constants.

Lambda leftovers

There are currently two items labeled as `leftovers` from the lambda work in Java 8. The first is the use of the underscore for unused parameters in lambda declarations. For example, in this very contrived example, all we care about are the `Map` values:

```
Map<String, Integer> numbers = new HashMap<>();
numbers.forEach((k, v) -> System.out.println(v*2));
```

That results in things like this in the IDE:

```
Map<String, Integer> numbers = new HashMap<>();
// ...
                  Parameter k is not used
numbers.forEach((k, v) -> System.out.println(v * 2));
```

Once the use of the underscore is allowed, this code will look like this:

```
numbers.forEach((_, v) -> System.out.println(v*2));
```

This allows better static checking of unused variables, allowing tools (and developers) to more easily identify such parameters and either correct or mark them.

The other leftover is allowing lambda parameters to shadow variables from the enclosing scope. If you were to try that now, you would get the same error if you tried to redefine a variable inside a statement block--**variable is already defined**:

```
Map<String, Integer> numbers = new HashMap<>();
String key = someMethod();
numbers.forEach((key, value) ->
  System.out.println(value*2)); // error
```

With this change, the preceding code would compile and run just fine.

Looking around

The JVM has supported alternative languages for years. Some of the better known ones include Groovy and Scala. Both of these languages have influenced Java in one way or another over the years, but, like any language, they are not without their problems. Many feel that Groovy doesn't perform as well as Java (though the `invokedynamic` bytecode instruction is supposed to have addressed that), and many find Groovy's more dynamic nature less appealing. Scala, on the other hand, suffers (fairly or not, depending on who you ask) from the perception that it's too complex. Compilation time is also a common complaint. Also, many organizations are quite happily using both, so they are definitely worth considering to see if they will work in your environment and for your needs.

While those may be great languages, we are taking some time here to see what's next, and there are at least two languages that seem to stand out from the crowd--Ceylon and Kotlin. We can't give each of these languages an exhaustive treatment, but, over the next few pages, we'll take a quick look at the languages to see what they offer JVM developers now, and, perhaps, see how they might influence future changes to the Java language.

Ceylon

Ceylon, a language sponsored by Red Hat, first appeared around 2011. Led by Gavin King of the Hibernate and Seam Framework fame, the team set out to solve, at a language and library level, some of the pain points they had experienced over the years in developing their own frameworks and libraries. While they confess to being **unapologetic fans** of the Java language, they also readily acknowledge that the language is not perfect, especially with regard to some of the standard libraries, and aim to fix those flaws in Ceylon. The goals of the language include readability, predictability, toolability, modularity, and metaprogrammability (`https://ceylon-lang.org/blog/2012/01/10/goals`).

One of the biggest differences you are likely to notice when getting started with Ceylon is that the idea of modules is already baked into the language. In many ways, it looks very similar to Java 9's module declaration, which is as follows:

```
module com.example.foo "1.0" {
  import com.example.bar "2.1";
}
```

There is, however, a very obvious difference--Ceylon modules **do** have version information, which allows various modules to depend on different versions of a module that may already be in the system.

There is at least one more rather significant difference between Ceylon and, say, Java--Ceylon has a build tool built in. While there is, for example, a Maven plugin, the preferred approach is to use Ceylon's native tooling to build and run the project:

```
$ ceylonb new hello-world
Enter project folder name [helloworld]: ceylon-helloworld
Enter module name [com.example.helloworld]:
Enter module version [1.0.0]:
Would you like to generate Eclipse project files? (y/n) [y]: n
Would you like to generate an ant build.xml? (y/n) [y]: n
$ cd ceylon-helloworld
$ ceylonb compile
Note: Created module com.example.helloworld/1.0.0
$ ceylonb run com.example.helloworld/1.0.0
Hello, World!
```

Other than the module system, what might Ceylon offer a Java developer? One of the more immediately useful and practical features is improved null-handling support. Just as we have to do in Java, we still have to check for null in Ceylon, but the language offers a much nicer approach, and it all starts with the type system.

One of the complaints about Scala (whether its truly warranted or not) is that the type system is too complicated. Regardless of whether or not you agree, it seems clear that there's certainly room for improvement over what Java offers (even the Java language architects agree as evidenced by, for example, the proposed local variable type inference proposal). Ceylon offers a very powerful addition to the type system--union types and intersection types.

Union types allow a variable to have more than one type, but only one at a time. Where this comes into play in discussing nulls is that `String? foo = ...`, which declares a variable of type `String` that is nullable, is actually the same as `String|Null foo = ....`

This declares a variable, foo, whose type is either `String` or `Null`, but not both. The `?` syntax is just syntactic sugar over the union type declaration (`A | B` or A or B). If we have a method, then that takes this union type; we know that the variable is nullable, so we need to check it using the following code snippet:

```
void bar (String? Foo) {
  if (exists foo) {
    print (foo);
  }
}
```

Since this is a union type, we can also do this:

```
void bar (String? Foo) {
  if (is String foo) {
    print (foo);
  }
}
```

Note that, once we've tested with `exists` or `is`, we can assume that the variable is not null and is a `String`. The compiler won't complain, and we won't have an unexpected `NullPointerException` at runtime (they actually don't exist in Ceylon as the compiler requires that you be very explicit in your handling of nullable variables). This type of compiler awareness of null and type checks is called **flow-sensitive** typing. Once you've verified the type of something, the compiler knows and remembers, so to speak, the results of that check for that remainder of that scope so you can write cleaner, more concise code.

While union types are either A or B, intersection types are A **and** B. For a completely arbitrary example, let's say you have a method whose parameter must be, say, `Serializable` **and** `Closeable`. In Java, you'd have to check manually by writing the following lines of code:

```
public void someMethod (Object object) {
  if (!(object instanceof Serializable) ||
    !(object instanceof Closeable)) {
    // throw Exception
  }
}
```

With intersection types, Ceylon would let us write this:

```
void someMethod(Serializable&Closeable object) {
  // ...
}
```

If we try to call that method with something that doesn't implement **both** interfaces, or, say, extends one class and implements the other interfaces, then we get an error at **compile time**. That's very powerful.

Before adopting a new language, or even a library, in an enterprise, one often looks to see who else is using it. Are there notable adoption stories? Are there other companies confident enough in the technology to build a production system using it? Unfortunately, the Ceylon website (at the time of writing) is very thin on the details of adoption outside Red Hat, so it's hard to answer that question. However, Red Hat is spending a good deal of money designing the language and building tooling and a community around it, so it should be a safe bet. It is, of course, a decision your enterprise will have to make after careful consideration. You can find out more about Ceylon at `https://ceylon-lang.org`.

Kotlin

Another up-and-coming language is Kotlin. It is a statically-typed language from JetBrains, the makers of IntelliJ IDEA, that targets both the JVM and Javascript. It even has nascent support to compile directly to machine code via LLVM for those environments, such as iOS, embedded systems, and so on, where a virtual machine is not desired or allowed.

Kotlin was started in 2010, and open sourced in 2012, as a means to address some common issues JetBrains was facing in large-scale Java development. Having surveyed the then-current language landscape, their engineers felt that none of those languages adequately addressed their concerns. Scala, considered for years now by many to be the **next Java**, was, for example, deemed to be too slow in compiling, despite having an acceptable feature set, so JetBrains began designing their own, eventually releasing 1.0 in February of 2016.

The design goals of the Kotlin team include expressiveness, scalability, and interoperability. They aim to allow developers to write less code that does more in a clearer fashion via language and library features, and in a language that is 100% interoperable with Java. They have added features such as coroutines to enable Kotlin-based systems to scale quickly and easily.

With all of that said, what does Kotlin look like and why should we, as Java developers, be interested? Let's start with variables.

As you'll recall, Java has both primitive (`int`, `double`, `float`, `char`, and so on) and reference, or **wrapper** types (`Integer`, `Double`, `Float`, `String`, and so on). As we've discussed in this chapter, the JVM engineers are working on ways to ameliorate some of the behavioral and capability differences this dichotomy brings. Kotlin avoids this altogether, as every value is an object, so there's no concern over `List<int>` versus `List<Integer>`.

Furthermore, Kotlin already supports local variable type inference, as well as immutablity. For example, consider the following Java code as an example:

```
Integer a = new Integer(1);
final String s = "This is a string literal";
```

The preceding lines of code could be written like this in Kotlin:

```
var a = 1;
val s = "This is a string literal";
```

Notice the use of the `var` and `val` keywords. As discussed earlier with regard to future Java language changes, these keywords allow us to declare mutable and immutable variables (respectively). Also notice that we need not declare the type of the variable, as the compiler handles that for us. In certain situations, we may need to explicitly declare the type, for example, in situations where the compiler might guess incorrectly or when it just does not have enough information to make a guess, at which point, it will stop compiling and present an error message. In those situations, we can declare the type this way:

```
var a: Int  = 1;
val s: String = "This is a string literal";
```

With Java 8, as we've seen, we have `Optional<T>` to help deal with null values. Kotlin has null support as well, but it's built into the language. By default, all variables in Kotlin are **not** nullable. That is to say, if the compiler can tell that you are attempting to assign a null value to a variable, or if it can't determine whether or not a value might be null (for example, a return value from a Java API), you'll get a compiler error. To indicate that a value is null-capable, you add a `?` to the variable declaration as follows:

```
var var1 : String = null; // error
var var2 : String? = null; // ok
```

Kotlin also offers improved null-handling support in method calls. Suppose, for example, you want to get a user's city. In Java, you may do something like this:

```
String city = null;
User user = getUser();
if (user != null) {
  Address address = user.getAddress();
  if (address != null) {
    city address.getCity();
  }
}
```

In Kotlin, that can be expressed in a single line, as follows:

```
var city : String? = getUser()?.getAddress()?.getCity();
```

If, at any point, one of the methods returns null, the method call chain ends, and null is assigned to the variable city. Kotlin doesn't stop there with null handling. It provides, for an example, the `let` function that can serve as a shortcut for if-not-null checks. For example, consider the following lines of code:

```
if (city != null) {
   System.out.println(city.toUpperCase());
}
```

The preceding lines of code become this in Kotlin:

```
city?.let {
   println(city.toUpperCase())
}
```

This could, of course, be written as `city?.toUpperCase()`. What this should demonstrate, though, is the ability to safely use a nullable variable in an arbitrarily large, complex block of code. It's also worth noting that, inside the `let` block, the compiler knows that `city` is not null so no further null checks are necessary.

Hidden, perhaps, in the preceding example is Kotlin's support for lambdas, without which, it seems, no modern language is worth considering. Kotlin does, indeed, have full support for lambdas, higher order functions, underscores as lambda parameter names, and so on. Its support and syntax are very similar to Java's, so Java developers should be very comfortable with Kotlin's lambdas.

The big question is, of course, **Is Kotlin ready for prime time?** JetBrains definitely thinks so, as they have it in use in many of their applications, both internal and external. Other notable users include Pinterest, Gradle, Evernote, Uber, Pivotal, Atlassian, and Basecamp. Kotlin is even officially supported by Google (in Android Studio) for Android development, so it's definitely a production-grade language.

There's much, much more to this great new language, of course, and space won't allow us to discuss all of it, but you can browse through `https://kotlinlang.org` to learn more and see if Kotlin is a good fit for your organization.

Summary

There is much more that can be discussed of course, about Java 10 and these two languages, and the myriad of other projects happening in and around the Java Virtual Machine. After over 20 years of development, Java--the language **and** the environment--is still going strong. In the pages of this book, I've tried to demonstrate some of these great advancements in the language, giving you a variety of starting points for your own projects, sample code to study and reuse, and explanations of various libraries, APIs, and technologies that may be helpful in your day-to-day work. I hope you've enjoyed the examples and explanations as much as I've enjoyed preparing them, and, more importantly, I hope they help you build the Next Big Thing.

Good luck!

Bibliography

This Learning Path combines some of the best that Packt has to offer in one complete, curated package. It includes content from the following Packt products:

- *Mastering Java 9*, Dr. Edward Lavieri and Peter Verhas
- *Java 9 Programming Blueprints*, Jason Lee

Index

@

@Deprecated annotation 306
@SafeVarargs annotation
  using 53

A

Abstract Syntax Trees (ASTs) 260
Abstract Windows Toolkit (AWT) 422
Access Management Console
  reference 789
access-control boundary violations
  about 82
  runtime 82
Acorn RISC Machine (ARM) 393
actions
  performing 706
additional concurrency updates
  about 317
  CompletableFuture API enhancements 323
  Java concurrency 317
ALPN (Application Layer Protocol Negotiation) 347
Amazon Web Services (AWS) 775
Android developer
  documentation link 603
Android development environment
  setting up 600, 603, 608, 609
Android project
  creating 804, 806
  permissions, requesting 807, 809
  service, creating 809, 811
  starting with 804
Android services
  interacting with 627, 629, 632, 633
Android Studio
  reference 600
Android user interfaces

building 611, 614, 617
Android
  data access 619, 621, 624, 626
  tabs and fragments 633, 638, 640
AnnotatedConstruct interface 265
ANTLR parser 423
application module path 81
assets
  listing 150
Atomic Toolkit
  working with 49
Authenticated Encryption with Associated Data
    (AEAD) 337
Authority Info Access (AIA) 356
authorization requests
  authorization request, handling 851
  client, authorizing 851, 853

B

BeanInfo annotations [JEP-256]
  about 287
  BeanProperty 288
  JavaBean 287
  SwingContainer 289
BeanInfo classes
  about 289
  benefits 289
BeanProperty
  about 288
  optional elements 288
benchmarking options
  about 205
  modes 206
  time units 207
Berkeley Packet Filters (BPF) 414
best practices, Java 9

Common Locale Data Repository (CLDR) 396
Linux/AArch64 port 393
multi-resolution images 394
support for UTF-8 377
Unicode 7.0.0 390

C

C header files 76
camel case search 274
Cascading Style Sheets (CSS) 27
CDI
　dependency injection, using 746
CDS archives [JEP 250]
　interned strings, storing 26
Ceylon
　about 863, 866
　URL 863, 866
Class Data Sharing (CDS) 26
classes
　accessing 244
　updated, in Java 9 36
CLI
　building 652, 657, 660, 663, 666, 670
clock
　about 524
　Instant 524
　LocalDate 525
　LocalDateTime 525
　LocalTime 525
　ZonedDateTime 525
cloud notification 776
CMS garbage collection 176
collection literals
　benefits 298
　reference link 298
collections [JEP-269]
　factory methods, used for 298
　new collection literals, using 301
　using, before Java 9 298, 299
command line flags
　compiler control [JEP 165] 365
　diagnostic commands [JEP 228] 368
　heap profiling agent [JEP 240] 370
　JHAT [JEP 241], removing 371
　JVM command-line flag argument validation [JEP

245] 372
　older platform versions [JEP 247], compiling for
　373
　unified JVM logging [JEP 158] 359
command-line interface
　building 493, 496, 499, 502, 503, 540, 542
Common Locale Data Repository (CLDR) 396
communication protocol 332
compact strings [JEP 254]
　about 30
　Java 9, updates 31
　pre-Java 9 status 31
compare-and-swap (CAS) 416
compilation module path 81
compile time 865
compiler control [JEP 165]
　about 365
　C1 compilation mode 366
　C2 compilation mode 366
　compilation modes 365
　compiler control, in Java 9 367
　tiered compilation 366
compiler tree API
　enums 261
　interfaces 262
CompletableFuture API enhancements 323
CompleteableFuture*T* class
　about 324
　enhancements 328
concurrent Java
　using, with Future interface 479, 482, 486
concurrent mark sweep (CMS) 160, 164, 402
constant folding
　about 209
　eliminating 209
contended locking [JEP 143]
　about 16
　goals, improving 17
ControlDaemon class 228, 231
CPU instructions
　leveraging, for GHASH 351
　leveraging, for RSA 351
critical sections [JEP 270]
　stack areas, reserved 36
CSS APIs

preparing, for modularization [JEP 253] 27
current process
  PID, obtaining 215

D

data streams 310
Database as a Service (DBaaS) 775
datagram 332
Datagram Transport Layer Security (DTLS)
  about 332
  security, considerations 337
  supporting, in Java 9 337
date calculator
  creating 520
dead-code
  about 209
  eliminating 209
decoupled functionality
  exposing 707, 709
  NetBeans preferences 716
  Options panel 716
  PhotoViewerTopComponent 711, 714
default methods 527
dependency injection (DI)
  about 746
  with CDI 746
depreciation warnings
  suppressing, on import statements [JEP 211] 52
desktop application
  creating 821
  messages, sending 836, 839
  security 845
  updates, obtaining 840, 845
  user interface behavior, defining 825, 830, 834
  user interface, defining 822, 825
Deterministic Random Bit Generator (DRBG)
  about 356
  reference link 357
development tools
  about 72
  deployment tool 72
  internationalization tool 72
  monitoring tool 73
  RMI tools 73
  security tool 73

troubleshooting tool 73
  web services tool 74
diagnostic commands [JEP 228] 369
diamond operator
  about 56
  using 56
Disk And Execution Monitor (daemons) 679
Distributed Services level 403
Doclet API [JEP-221]
  pre-Java 9 Doclet API 256
  simplifying 256
Doclet API, Java 9
  about 260
  compiler tree API 260, 261
  language model API 264
Doclet API
  pre-existing, issues 260
Doclint warning [JEP 212]
  reference link 20
  resolving 20
Document Object Model (DOM) 32
documented set 256
Dolphin Platform
  reference 684
DPI-aware application 34
DPI-unaware application 34
DRBG-Based SecureRandom Implementations 357
DRY (Don't Repeat Yourself) 476
DTLS protocol version 1.0 332
DTLS protocol version 1.2 334, 336
dynamic linking
  of language-defined object models [JEP 276] 38
dynamic randomly accessed memory (DRAM) 210
DynamoDB 780, 782, 785

E

eavesdropping 332
Eclipse
  reference link 111
  URL, for downloading 193
electronic mail 644
Elliptic Curve Diffie-Hellman (ECDH) 337
email and spam management
  starting with 644

email protocols
  history 644
EMCAScript 280
endpoints, adding to server
  conversations, obtaining 814, 817
  SMS message, sending 818, 821
enhanced deprecation [JEP-277]
  @Deprecated annotation 306
  about 305, 306
enhanced enums 861
enhanced method handles [JEP-274]
  about 302, 303
  additional combinations 304, 305
  lookup functions 303
  MethodHandle argument, handling 304
  need for 303
Executable Linkable Files (ELFs) 414
external processes
  controlling 11

F

factory methods
  used, for collections [JEP-269] 298
features, Java 8
  about 430
  default methods 434
  java.time package 434
  lambdas 430, 432
features, Java 9
  about 436
  concurrency changes 438
  Java Platform Module System/Project Jigsaw
   436
  process handling API 437
  REPL (Read-Eval-Print-Loop) 438
feedback modes
  about 143, 147
  custom feedback mode, creating 148
finalize() method 170, 171
Flow API
  about 313
  Flow.Processor interface 315
  Flow.Publisher interface 314
  Flow.Subscriber interface 314
  Flow.Subscription interface 314

  sample implementation 315
flow-sensitive typing 865
Foreign Function Interfaces (FFI) 406
forgery 332
Forward Secrecy (FS) 337
Function as a Service (FaaS) 774
function deployment
  about 788
  role, creating 789
  topic, creating 790
future changes, Java Compiler
  pluggable static analyzers 411
  policy for retiring javac -source and -target
   options 410
future changes, JavaX
  about 419
  GTK3 Look and Feel Implementation,
   modernizing 420
  JMX specific annotations, for registration of
   managed resources 419
future changes, JDK
  JDK changes targeted for Java 10 400
  JDK-related drafted proposals 404
  JDK-related submitted proposals 402
future changes, JVM
  JVM-related drafted proposals 414
  JVM-related submitted proposals 411
future developments, Java platform
  Java Compiler 410
  JavaX 419
  JDK 400

G

G1 [JEP 278]
  humongous objects, tests 39
G1 garbage collection
  about 161
  options 167
Galois HASH (GHASH)
  about 352
  CPU instructions, leveraging 351
garbage collection algorithms
  about 160
  concurrent mark sweep (CMS) algorithm 160
  G1 garbage collection 161

mark and sweep 160
    parallel garbage collection 161
    serial garbage collection 161
garbage collection logging
    considerations 185
    gc tag 184
    macros 184
    options 182
garbage collection, issues
    about 186
    object eligibility 186, 188
garbage collection
    about 157, 158, 191
    combination Flag 178
    combinations, depreciating 177
    configuration Flag 178
    default garbage collection 175
    finalize() method 170, 171
    Java methods 167
    object, life cycle 158
    options 162
    System.gc() method 168, 169
    upgrading, in Java 8 173
    visualizing 172
    with new Java platform 175
Garbage-first (G1)
    about 8, 123
    performance, enhancing 11
generic specialization
    about 859
    references 859
GIMP toolbox 43
Graal VM 13
graphical user interface (GUI)
    building 504, 505, 507, 509, 511, 512, 514,
      517, 670, 673, 676
Graphical User Interfaces (GUI) 43
GStreamer 33
GStreamer [JEP 257]
    JavaFX/Media, updating to new version of 33
GTK 3
    AWT 44
    enabling, on Linux [JEP 283] 43
    JavaFX 44
    Swing 44

H

HarfBuzz font-layout engine [JEP 258] 33
HartBuzz 33
hashing 352
Heap Profiling (HPROF) 370
heap profiling agent [JEP 240] 370
HiDPI graphics
    about 34
    for Linux [JEP 263] 34
    for Windows [JEP 263] 34
HotSpot 43
HotSpot build system [JEP 284] 45
HotSpot C++ unit-test framework [JEP 281] 43
    enhancement, goals 43
HTML5 Javadoc [JEP-224] 268, 270, 272
HTTP 2.0
    starting with 12
HTTP client [JEP-110]
    about 250
    benefits 253
    creating, for Java 9 253
    Java 9 250
    new API, limitations 254
humongous objects
    tests, in G1 [JEP 278] 39
Hypertext Transfer Protocol (HTTP) 250

I

Identity and Access Management (IAM)
    about 773
    reference 799
identity-less value types 857
import statements [JEP 211]
    depreciation warnings, suppressing 52
import statements [JEP 216]
    processing, correctly 60, 62
information
    obtaining, about process 216
Infrastructure as a Service (IaaS) 774
infrastructure framework, Oracle
    reference link 45
initialize on demand holder (IODH) pattern 583
Instagram client
    implementing 591, 594

Instagram developer
  registering as 590
Instagram
  adding, to Sunago 589
  reference 590
instance, StackWalker
  enum constants 244
  obtaining 240
  RETAIN_CLASS_REFERENCE 240
  SHOW_HIDDEN_FRAMES 241, 244
  SHOW_REFLECT_FRAMES 241
Integrated Development Environment (IDE) 27,
    111, 193
IntelliJ
  URL 111
internal APIs [JEP-260]
  encapsulating 91
internal catalog resolver 297
internationalization 582
interned strings
  issues 26
  solutions 27
  storing, in CDS archives [JEP 250] 26
Internet Access Message Protocol (IMAP) 647
Internet Engineering Task Force (IETF) 334
Internet of Things (IoT) 424
Internet Protocol version 6 (IPv6) 407
inversion of control (IoC) 746

J

J-link tool 455
JAR file
  size, increasing 584
Java 8
  garbage collection, upgrading 173
Java 9
  about 7
  best practices 377
  changes 390
  DTLS, supporting 337
  HTTP client [JEP-110] 250
  HTTP client [JEP-110], creating 253
  implications 29
  updates 31, 37
  URL 128

Java APIs for XML Processing (JAXP) 31, 32
Java Archive (JAR) 65
Java Community Process (JCP)
  about 8, 68
  URL 68
Java Compiler
  future changes 410
  Java Virtual Machine 411
Java concurrency
  about 317
  concurrency 317
  concurrency improvements 322
  Java threads 319
  system configurations 318
Java DB
  references 77
Java Development Kit (JDK) 429
  about 65
  future changes 400
Java ecosystem 444
Java Enhancement Plan (JEP) 175
Java Enhancement Program #271 (JEP-271) 178
Java Enhancement Program (JEP) 136
Java Enhancement Program 214 (JEP 214) 178
Java Enhancement Proposal (JEP) 451
Java Enhancement Proposal 237 (JEP 237) 393
Java Enhancement Proposals (JEPs) 249, 309
Java Enterprise Edition (Java EE) 595, 648
Java environment (jEnv)
  about 129
  URL 129
Java Heap Analysis Tool (JHAT) 371, 377
Java Keystore (JKS)
  about 338, 343
  builder class 339
  CallbackHandlerProtection class 340
  PasswordProtection class 340
  PrivateKeyEntry class 341
  SecretKeyEntry class 341
  TrustedCertificateEntry class 342
Java linker 93
Java Linker (JLink) 84, 85, 89
Java Linker [JEP-282] 89
Java Management Extension (JMX) 403, 416
Java memory model 405

Java Microbenchmark Harness (JMH)
  about 8, 191, 213
  Eclipse, installing 193
  experiments 196, 198
  Java 9, installing 193
  performance, measuring 11
  using 193
Java module systems
  about 9
  benefits 10
Java Native Access (JNA) 406
Java Native Interface (JNI) 76, 406, 859
Java Native Runtime (JNR) 406
Java Network Launch Protocol (JNLP)
  about 109, 124
  reference link 126
Java Packager
  about 84
  options 85
Java Persistence API (JPA)
  about 475, 481
  used, for accessing modern database 486, 490,
    493
Java Platform Module System (JPMS)
  about 66
  reviewing 66, 70
Java runtime environment (JRE) 65, 74
Java Shell (JShell)
  about 8, 10, 135, 136, 157
  advanced editing commands 153
  advanced scripting 155
  assets, listing 150
  basic navigation 152
  command functionality 138
  editing in 151
  feedback modes 143, 145
  historical navigation 152
  practical uses 142
  starting 136, 141, 142
  text, modifying 151
Java Specification Request (JSR 310) 519
Java Stack
  overview 233
Java Virtual Machine (JVM)
  about 74, 191

future changes 411
  sizing options 162
Java Virtual Machine Debug Interface (JVMDI) 369
Java Virtual Machine Profiling Interface (JVMPI)
  369
Java Virtual Machine Tool Interface (JVMTI) 76,
  369, 415, 416
Java Web Start 74, 124
Java-level JVM compiler interface [JEP-243] 286
java.net.ssl package extension 350
java.Security.CodeSource package 345
java.util.logging package
  about 293
  ConsoleHandler class 293
  ErrorManager class 293
  FileHandler class 293
  Formatter class 294
  Handler class 294
  Level class 294
  LogManager class 294
  LogRecord class 294
  MemoryHandler class 294
  SimpleFormatter class 294
  SocketHandler class 294
  StreamHandler class 294
  XMLFormatter class 294
Java
  base module 97
  encapsulation 99
  future developments 399
  modules 96
  reliable configuration 98
JavaBean 287
javac 19
javac [JEP 215]
  tiered attribution 20
javac [JEP 235]
  test class-file attributes, generated 24
javac wrapper tool
  reference link 19
Javadoc search [JEP-225]
  about 273
  camel case search 274
Javadoc tool
  reference link 273

JavaFX 27
JavaFX tools 74
JavaFX UI controls
  preparing, for modularization [JEP 253] 27
JavaFX-based application
  bootstrapping 455
JavaFX/Media
  about 33
  updating, to GStreamer [JEP 257] new version 33
JavaMail 648, 651
JavaScript Object Notation (JSON) 367
JavaScript VM language 763
javax.net.ssl package 348
JavaX
  future changes 419
JAXP [JEP 255]
  selected Xerces 2.11.0 updates, merging into 31
JAXP processors
  about 297
  interfaces 297
JDK 9
  features 12
  generics, over primitive types 12
  reified generics 13
  URL 193
  URL, for downloading 8
JDK Bug System
  reference link 20
JDK changes, targeted for Java 10
  about 400
  Native-header tool removal 401
  repository consolidation 400
JDK classes
  de-privileging 80
JDK Enhancement Proposal (JEP)
  about 15
  reference link 15
JDK Enhancement Proposal 199
  code compilation, improving 19
JDK source code [JEP-201]
  about 74
  C header files 76
  database 77
  deployment tools 72

JavaFX tools 74
JDK source code reorganized 77
JRE 74
libraries 75
modularizing 70
pre-Java 9 JDK source code organization 71
JDK-related drafted proposals
  IPv6 support, improving 407
  about 404
  efficient array comparison intrinsics 410
  enhanced MandelblotSet demo, value types used 409
  finalization promptness 404
  Foreign Function Interfaces (FFI) 406
  isolated methods 406
  Java memory model 405
  metaspace waste, reducing 406
  unboxed argument lists, for method handles 408
JDK-related submitted proposals
  about 402
  Full GC Phase, parallelizing in CMS 402
  REST APIs, for JMX 402
  support heap allocation 404
JEP 223
  versioning schema 23
JHAT [JEP 241]
  removing 371
JPAQL (Java Persistence API Query Language) 489
JSON Web Tokens (JWT) 729, 847
jstat 73
JVM command-line flag argument validation [JEP 245] 372
JVM Compiler Interface (JVMCI) 286
JVM process status tool (jps) 73
JVM-related drafted proposals
  about 414
  Concurrent Monitor Deflation 415
  Diagnostic Command Framework 416
  Enhanced Class Redefinition 417
  JVM Access Checks, aligning 419
  Low-Overhead way of sampling Java Heap Allocations, providing 416
  NUMA mode, enabling by default 417
  USDT probe points, providing on JVM compiled

methods 414
Value objects 418
JVM-related submitted proposals
about 411
Container aware Java 412
Epsilon GC 413
Java methods execution, enabling on GPU 413
JVM
Eclipse Vert.x 731
Java EE MicroProfile 731
microservice framework 731
Spring Boot 731

K

keystore primer 338
keystores
benefits 338
Kotlin
about 866, 868
URL 868

L

LALR parser 423
Lambda console
AWS credentials, configuring 798
function, deploying 791
function, testing 793, 798
language model API
about 264
AnnotatedConstruct interface 265
SourceVersion enum 265, 266, 267
UnknownEntityException exception 267
language-defined object models [JEP 276]
dynamic linking 38
last-in-first-out (LIFO) 233
launch-time JRE version selection [JEP-231]
selecting 274, 275
library
building 477, 520
timely interlude 522
link time 93
Lint warning
about 19
reference link 19

Linux [JEP 263]
HiDPI graphics 34
Linux [JEP 283]
GTK 3, enabling 43
Linux/AArch64 port 393
Local-Variable Type Inference 861
localization 582
logging API [JEP-264]
about 292
in Java 9 295
java.util.logging package 293
logging service [JEP-264]
about 292
in java 9 295
java.util.logging package 293
Lookup 701
lookup functions 303

M

Mail Transfer Agents (MTAs) 644
main class 225
marker annotation 21
Marlin graphics renderer [JEP 265] 35
Maven
about 130
M2Eclipse IDE, obtaining 131
microbenchmarking 198, 205
reference 444
references 130, 133, 199
MavMaven Shade plugin 788
MBean 403, 419
Mebibyte (MiB) 167
memory leak 159
menus
adding 467, 469
MethodHandle agrument
handling 304
microbenchmarking
about 192
Analysis phase 192
avoiding, techniques 207
cache capacity 210
constant folding, eliminating 209
dead-code, eliminating 209
Design phase 192

Enhancement phase 192
Execution phase 192
Implement phase 192
JMH, using 193
OS schedulers 208
power management 208
run-to-run variance 210
time-sharing 208
with Maven 198, 205
migration, issues
  extension mechanism 107
  internal APIs, accessing 104
  internal JARs, accessing 105
  JAR URL, depreciation 106
  JRE 104
  JSK modularization 108
migration
  Java application, testing 100
  planning 100
  potential issues 103
mJRE (Multiple JRE) 274
Mobile Backend as a Service (MBaas) 775
modes 206
modular 64
Modular Java application [JEP-275]
  Java Linker 85
  packaging 84
modular primer 64
modular runtime images [JEP-220]
  about 77
  common operations, supporting 80
  existing behaviors, preserving 80
  JDK classes, de-privileging 80
  restructuring 78
  runtime format, adopting 78
modularization [JEP 253]
  CSS APIs, preparing 27
  Java 9, implications 29
  JavaFX UI controls, preparing 27
modularizing
  JDK source code [JEP-201] 70
module paths
  about 81
  application module path 81
  compilation module path 81

system modules 81
upgrade module path 81
module system [JEP-261]
  about 80
  access-control boundary violations 82
  module paths 81
modules
  in Java 96
MongoDB
  reference 746
Monumentum
  authentication, adding 751, 754, 757, 759, 762
  creating 730, 733, 738
  MongoDB, adding 741, 743, 746
  notes resources, finishing 748, 750
  REST Services, creating 739, 740
  user interface, building 762, 764, 767, 772
multi-release JAR files [JEP-238]
  about 283
  identifying 284
  JDK changes 285
multi-resolution images 394
mutations 766

N

Nashorn [JEP-236]
  EMCAScript 280
  parser API 275, 281, 282, 283
nashorn identifier 279
Nashorn
  about 39, 275
  using, as command-line tool 276, 277, 278, 279
  using, as embedded interpreter 279, 280
National Institute of Standards and Technology
  (NIST) 337
NetBeans Javadoc
  reference 692
NetBeans RCP project
  application, branding 687, 690
  bootstrapping 684, 687
  JavaFX, integrating with 714
NetBeans
  modules 690, 691
  reference 444, 693
  URL 111

network packet 332
new API
  limitations 255
new collection literals
  using 301
Nodes
  about 684, 700
  writing 702, 705
Non-Uniform Memory Access (NUMA) 417
notification system
  building 774, 775
  first function, building 776, 779
  planning 776

O

OASIS XML Catalog standard
  about 296
  reference link 296
object-relational mapping (ORM) 487
object
  creating 158
  destruction 159
  life cycle 158
  storing 159
Online Certificate Status Protocol (OCSP) stapling
    for TLS 353
  Java 9 platform, changes 355
  process 354
Operand Stack 234
Options panel
  about 716
  preferences changes, reacting to 725
  preferences, loading 724
  preferences, saving 724
  primary panel, adding 718
  secondary panel, adding 720, 723
Oracle
  --add-exports option 118
  --add-opens option 118
  --permit-illegal-access option 119
  -target options 113, 114
  about 109
  application, compiling 111
  deployment 124
  encapsulation, breaking 117

excluded features 122
FX XML extension 125
garbage collection, updating 123
Java 9 -source 114
Java version schema 119
jdeps, executing 114
JDK 9 early access build, obtaining 110
JDK layout 120
JNLP file syntax 127
JNLP, updating 125
JRE layout 120
JRE version selection 124
nested resources 125
numeric version, comparison 128
pre-Java 9 -source 113
preparatory steps 110
program, executing 110
runtime image, modifications 119
serialized applets 124
third-party libraries and tools, updating 110
OS schedulers 208

P

package checking algorithm 346
parallel garbage collection 161, 176
parameters class 227
ParamsAndHandle class 227
parser API 281, 282, 283
Path Maximum Transition Unit (PMTU) 333
Perfect Forward Secrecy (PFS) 337
Pipeline 2.0 [JEP 217]
  annotations 21
PKCS12 keystores
  creating 338
  default keystore 343
  Java Keystore (JKS) 338
  keystore primer 338
plain JavaFX 684
Plain Old Java Object (POJO) 487, 653
Platform as a Service (PaaS) 774
platform-specific desktop features [JEP-272] 301,
  302
plugin jars 595
power management 208
pre-Java 9 Doclet API

about 256
classes 258
enums 258
interfaces 259
pre-Java 9 garbage collection
about 171
games, written with Java case study 174
private interface methods
using 58
process controller application
about 224
ControlDaemon class 225, 228, 231
main class 225
parameters class 225, 226
ParamsAndHandle class 225, 227
process identifier (PID)
about 213
obtaining, of current process 215
process list
updating 471, 473
processes
about 214
allProcess() 220
children, listing 218
descendants, listing 219
information, obtaining 216
listing 218, 220
terminating 222, 224
waiting for 221
ProcessHandle interface
about 215
references 223
Project Amber
about 860
enhanced enums 861
Lambda leftovers 862
Local-Variable Type Inference 860
Project Coin [JEP 213]
@SafeVarargs annotation, using 53
about 53
changes 53
diamond operator, using 56
private interface methods, using 58
reference link 53
try-with-resource statement 54

underscore, discontinuing 57
Project Jigsaw
about 9
classpath 94
monolithic nature 95
reviewing 94
Project Panama
about 859
URL 860
Project Valhalla
about 857
generic specialization 859
reified generics 859
value types 857
projects
about 439
Android desktop synchronization client 443
client/server note application 442
creating 452
Date Calculator 440
Duplicate File Finder 439
email filter 441
JavaFX photo management 442
Process Viewer/Manager 439
serverless Java 443
Social Media Aggregator 440
starting with 444, 449
public javafx.css package
classes 30
public javafx.scene.control.skin package
classes, moved from internal packages 29
Public Key Cryptography Standards (PKCS) 343
Public Key Infrastructure (PKI) 355

Q

quarantined 475

R

reactive programming
about 12, 310
standardization 311
Reactive Streams 311
refresh button
adding 587, 589

reified generics 859
Remote Method Invocation (RMI) 73
Representational State Transfer (REST) 402
ResourceBundle class
  about 378
  fields and constructors 383
  methods 384
  nested class 379
retina display 34
Rich Client Platform (RCP) 683
Rich Internet Applications (RIAs) 125
RISC (Reduced Instruction Set Computing) 393
Rivest-Shamir-Adleman (RSA)
  about 337, 352
  CPU instructions, leveraging 351
run-time compiler tests [JEP 233]
  generating, automatically 23
run-to-run variance 210
runtime format
  adopting 78

S

Scene Builder 27
  reference 456
scripts
  loading 154
  saving 154
  startup scripts 153
  working with 153
security application
  java.Security.CodeSource package 345
  package checking algorithm 346
  performance, improving 343
  permission, evaluating 345
  security policy, enforcing 344
security policy
  classes, used 345
  enforcing 344
security, desktop application
  authorization requests, handling 848
  endpoints, securing 845, 848
segmented code cache JEP (197)
  about 17
  memory allocation 18
selected Xerces 2.11.0 updates

merging, into JAXP [JEP 255] 31
semantic versioning 23
serial garbage collection 161, 176
server stalls 174
server-sent events (SSE)
  about 811
  endpoints, adding to server 813
  service state, controlling 812
serverless 773
serverless computing 775
Service Provider Interface (SPI) 396
Service Provider Interfaces (SPIs) 543, 856
service
  building 677, 681
siblings 595
Simple Email Service (SES) 785, 787
Simple Notification Service (SNS) 787, 788
smart Java compilation (sjavac) 19
SMTP (Simple Mail Transport Protocol) 644
SMTP RCF
  reference 644
Software as a Service (SaaS) 774
SourceVersion enum
  about 265, 266, 267
  method 267
  methods 266
special projects
  about 420
  Annotations pipeline 2.0 422
  Audio Synthesis Engine 422
  Caciocavallo 422
  Common VM Interface 422
  Compiler Grammar 423
  Da Vinci Machine 423
  Device I/O 423
  Graal 423
  HarfBuzz Integration 424
  Kona 424
  OpenJFX 424
  Panama 424
  Shenandoah 425
speculative attribution 20
spin-wait
  about 329
  hint 329

SSL / TLS protocol 333
stack areas
  in pre-Java 9 situation 36
  Java 9, updates 37
  reserved, for critical sections [JEP 270] 36
stack information
  about 235
  callers, restricting example 236, 238
  importance 234
  logger, obtaining for caller example 239
StackFrame
  about 247
  getByteCodeIndex() 247
  getClassName() 247
  getDeclaringClass() 247
  getFileName() 247
  getLineNumber() 247
  getMethodName() 247
  isNativeMethod() 247
StackWalker
  classes, accessing 244
  instance, obtaining 240
  performance 248
  walking methods 245, 246
  working with 240
Standard Edition (SE) 481
startup scripts 153
string concatenation [JEP 280] 42
string space 27
sun.misc.Unsafe class
  using 51
Sunago
  controller, finishing up 553
  controller, setting up 551
  image, adding for item 555
  Instagram, adding 589
  model class, writing 552
  network, adding 567
  plugins and extensions, using with Service
    Provider Interface 562
  plugins, loading 594, 597
  preferences user interface, building 556, 559
  resource, handling with try-with-resources 563,
    567
  setting up 550

  starting with 544, 546, 548
  Twitter preferences, adding 571
  user interface, setting up 549
  user preferences, saving 560
SwingContainer
  about 289
  optional elements 289
system modules 81
System.gc() method 168

T

tampering 332
tenuring threshold 163
test class-file attributes
  generated, by javac [JEP 235] 24
  unused, by JVM 26
Test-Driven Development (TDD) 537
test-failure troubleshooting [JEP 279]
  environmental information 41
  improving 41
  Java process, information 42
testing interlude 537
throughput (thrpt) 206
tiered attribution
  for javac [JEP 215] 20
TIFF image input/output [JEP-262]
  about 290
  static methods 290
  static methods, returning Booleans 291
time units 207
time-based unit of time 522
time-sharing 208
timely interlude
  clock 524
  code 526, 535
  duration 522
  period 523
TLAB (Thread Local Allocation Blocks) 163
TLS ALPN extension 348
TLS protocol 332
Tool Interface (TI) 370
tools
  about 128
  jEnv 129
  Maven 130

TopComponent 692, 695, 698
Transport Layer 333
Transport Layer Security (TLS)
  about 332, 347, 353
  OCSP stapling 353
try-with-resource statement 54
Twitter client
  implementing 581, 582
Twitter developer
  registering as 568, 570
Twitter
  adding, to Sunago 567
  logging on 574, 579
  model, adding 579
  OAuth authorization 574, 579

U

underscore character
  discontinuing 57
Unicode 7.0.0
  about 390
  additional significance 392
  java.lang package 391
  java.text package 392
Unicode 8.0 [JEP 267]
  about 35
  Java 9, updated classes 36
  new features 35
Unicode Transformation Format-8 (UTF-8)
  about 377
  ResourceBundle class 378
unified garbage collection logging
  about 178
  JEP-271 181
  unified JVM logging (JEP-158) 179
unified JVM logging [JEP 158]
  about 179, 359
  command-line options 181, 360
  decorations 180, 363
  levels 180, 364
  output 181, 364
  tags 179, 365
Uniform Resource Identifier (URI) 78
UnknownEntityException exception 267
upgrade module path 81

URL (Uniform Resource Locator) 78
user interface
  defining 456, 458
  initializing 459, 461, 463, 466
User-level Statistically Defined Tracing (USDT)
  414
UTF-8 property resource bundle 378

V

value types
  about 857
  references 858
variable 857
variable handlers [JEP 193]
  Atomic Toolkit, working 49
  components 49
  sun.misc.Unsafe class, using 51
  working with 48

W

walking methods 245, 246
Windows [JEP 263]
  HiDPI graphics 34
work stealing 480
Wrapper library
  reference 679
wrapper types 866
WYSIWYG 695

X

Xerces 31
XML (eXtensible Markup Language) 296
XML Catalogs [JEP-268]
  about 296
  Java 9 platform, updates 297
  JAXP processors 297
  OASIS XML Catalog standard 296
  prior to Java 9 297

Y

young garbage collection
  options 163

Z

www.ingramcontent.com/pod-product-compliance
Lightning Source LLC
Chambersburg PA
CBHW081207220326
41598CB00037B/6695